A Companion to
Poe Studies

A COMPANION TO POE STUDIES

Edited by
Eric W. Carlson

GREENWOOD PRESS
Westport, Connecticut • London

Library of Congress Cataloging-in-Publication Data

A companion to Poe studies / edited by Eric W. Carlson.
    p. cm.
    Includes bibliographical references (p.   ) and index.
    ISBN 0–313–26506–2 (alk. paper)
    1. Poe, Edgar Allan, 1809–1849. 2. Detective and mystery stories,
American—History and criticism. 3. Fantastic literature, American—
History and criticism. 4. Horror tales, American—History and
criticism. 5. Authors, American—19th century—Biography.
    I. Carlson, Eric W.
    PS2631.C66   1996
    818'.309—dc20   95–40034

British Library Cataloguing in Publication Data is available.

Library of Congress Catalog Card Number: 95–40034
ISBN: 0–313–26506–2

First published in 1996

Greenwood Press, 88 Post Road West, Westport, CT 06881
An imprint of Greenwood Publishing Group, Inc.

Printed in the United States of America

The paper used in this book complies with the
Permanent Paper Standard issued by the National
Information Standards Organization (Z39.48–1984).

10 9 8 7 6 5 4 3 2 1

Contents

Acknowledgments

In acknowledgment of its always reliable support, I wish to thank the Research Foundation at the University of Connecticut for funding the cost of copying materials and the services of graduate student James Andersen as my very competent library assistant. My special thanks to Marilyn Brownstein and George Butler, editors at Greenwood Publishing Group, to my old friends and Poe coworkers for their encouragement and advice: Professors Richard P. Benton, James W. Gargano, and John E. Reilly, and to my son, Neal, for lending his creative skills in helping me computerize the index.

Abbreviations

AL	*American Literature* (quarterly)
ALS	*American Literary Scholarship*
AQ	Arthur H. Quinn, *Poe: A Critical Biography* (1941)
ATQ	*American Transcendental Quarterly*
BJ	*Broadway Journal*
CE	*Critical Essays on Poe*, ed. E. W. Carlson
ESQ	*Emerson Society Quarterly*
H	Harrison edition of *The Complete Works*
M 1, 2, or 3	Mabbott edition of *The Collected Works:* vol. 1, *The Poems*; vols. 2 and 3, *The Tales and Sketches*
Marg. (with no.)	''Marginalia'' in *P* 2
O 1 or 2	Ostrom, *The Letters,* vols. 1, 2
PoeL	Poe Log, ed. Thomas and Jackson
PoeS	*Poe Studies*
PQ	Patrick Quinn, ed. *Edgar Allan Poe: Poems and Tales* (Library of America)
P 1, 2, 3, or 4	Volumes in Pollin's edition of the *Collected Writings*
Pym	*The Narrative of Arthur Gordon Pym*
REAP	*Recognition of Edgar Allan Poe*, ed. Carlson
SLM	*Southern Literary Messenger*

T	G. R. Thompson, ed., *Edgar Allan Poe: Essays and Reviews* (New York: Library of America, 1984)
TPoe	Thompson's *Poe's Fiction*
UMSE	*University of Mississippi Studies in English*

A Companion to
Poe Studies

Introduction

ERIC W. CARLSON

This reference guide is intended for the student and the common reader as well as the scholar in the study of Poe biography, criticism, aesthetics, philosophy, and influence. It draws on some of our outstanding Poe scholars for their knowledge and insight. To review, research, and represent the published criticism on any major aspect of Poe's career is a demanding and challenging assignment. By and large, each contributor has attempted to report not only the known facts but also some of the major critical approaches and interpretations, old and new, and to do so in an objective, balanced way. The Modern Language Association (MLA) system of documentation has generally been used: in-text source references to Works Cited at the end of each chapter and a Bibliography for more general or frequent sources at the end of the volume. Some sources cited in the text will be found only in the Bibliography where the more frequently used reference sources are listed.

Research and publication on Poe for the past half century rivals, if it does not exceed, the "renaissance" that has occurred in Emerson, Melville, and Henry James studies—eloquent testimony to Poe's continuing influence and role today. Since 1845, when his work, first recognized in France by Baudelaire, began to spread throughout Europe, his status has had its ups and downs—up during anniversary celebrations in 1874, 1909, 1924, and 1949. More significantly, Poe societies have sprung up in support of Poe interests by sponsoring lectures, symposia, and performances of his work in Baltimore, Richmond, Philadelphia, the Bronx, and Hyderabad, India, and occasional performances by individual actors before college and community audiences. The Poe Studies Association (PSA) was formed in 1972 as an affiliate of the Modern Language Association and, since 1973, with subsidies from various colleges, has published a semiannual *PSA Newsletter*. The journal *Poe Studies/Dark Romanticism* initially appeared in 1968 and is published semiannually by Washington State University Press. The PSA organizes Poe sessions held at the MLA conventions, the regional MLA meetings, and, recently, the American Literature Association. In addition, radio and television programs, dramatic readings, plays and operas on stage and screen, the visual arts (especially illustrations of Poe's works), and musical compositions based on the poems and tales continue to reflect both popular and academic interest in Poe's life and writings, as described in Chapter 23 by Burton R. Pollin. The same may be said for the popularity of Poe as a subject in poetry, fiction, drama, and especially film, as reported in Chapter 22 by John E. Reilly.

The chapters in Part II are textual, dealing with primary works by Poe. In Parts III and IV, the chapters are topical and tend to be more theoretical. On some of the major works, there are commentaries in both topical and textual chapters, traceable through the Index. The chapters vary somewhat in length according to the demands of the subject. Reports on critical approaches are necessarily selective, but over the span of the volume as a whole, there are examples of biographical, historical, phenomenological, New Critical, reader-response, postmodern, stylistic, perspectivist, philosophical, Freudian, cultural, deconstructionist, Romantic-ironist, feminist, and aesthetic critiques. Such divergence of methodology is in keeping with the pluralistic nature of this guide.

The overall organization is evident from the table of contents, which moves from the two opening biographical chapters of Part I through Poe's works, thought, aesthetics, and influence. Part II is chronological within the chapters on the poems, the tales and sketches, and the nonfiction prose, allowing for the developmental study of each genre as such. As the poems, tales, colloquies, essays, and reviews were not all prepared for book publication by Poe, they are presented chronologically within genre groupings. In Parts III and IV on Poe's thought and art, Poe scholars will find challenging views of Poe's metaphysics, aesthetics, feminism, and postmodernism. The chapters on Poe in the fine arts (Pollin) and the popular arts (Reilly) and the concluding chapters on Poe's influence as a world author (Vines), especially in "the world of books" (Hatvary), are the work of the most professional authorities in those areas. Lois Vines's *Poe Abroad: Influences and Affinities* is forthcoming from the University of Iowa Press.

A GUIDE TO THE INDIVIDUAL CHAPTERS

Most readers will prefer to begin with the two biographical chapters, which might be followed profitably by the chapters on Poe's thought, art, and *Eureka* for an understanding, at the outset, of Poe's outlook on life and art. In that context, the chapters on the writings will make more sense, as will the variety of critical interpretations.

Chapters 1 and 2 on Poe the man necessarily begin with the Poe "legend" that was partly self-created but mostly the result of Griswold's infamous obituary and memoir, the damaging effects of which lingered to the end of the century. Ian Walker's detailed account of how this legend developed ends with the first full-scale, objective "life" by A. H. Quinn in 1941, also the starting point for Hammond's Chapter 2. Alexander Hammond, standing by his firm belief in objective biography, does not fully accept the biographer's role as one of finding the right relationship between the subject's creative self and his or her social personality. But in the biographies by Silverman and Meyers, it becomes evident that, as neither author is very familiar with the symbolic nature of Poe's literary writings, they have been read mainly on the literal, biographical level for the "mournful and never-ending remembrance" of lost relatives and friends. In passing, Silverman identifies the recurrent theme of the "dead-alive" without seeming to sense its relationship to the transcendental idea of "death as metamorphosis," although he does clarify Poe's transcendentalism to a degree (Silverman, 265).

In her Chapter 3 on the early poems, Elizabeth Phillips presents Poe as a very young aspirant to poetic fame working his way to increased sensibility and artistic discipline from 1824 to 1835. In Chapter 4, Dwayne Thorpe then carries the story through the middle and later years of Poe's poetic career, pointing up the basic issues and values inherent in Poe's quest for Ideal love and beauty, sometimes realized, but more often denied by the "trap of time" and ironically by the romantic Ideal itself as an impossible dream.

The six chapters on the tales begin with Richard Benton's cogent and pointed exposition of the social and political undercurrents of meaning, especially the flashes of comic satire in the first group of five tales in 1832 to the *Eleven Tales of the Arabesque* (later called *The Tales of the Folio Club)* and, in 1835, "Berenice" and "Morella," among others. In the next chapter, the Levines, Stuart and Susan, continue the report on the comic satires and grotesques in a light, informal tone and manner of criticism that has proved itself in the classroom. William Goldhurst's chapter deals deftly with the philosophical implications of Poe's most existentialist short fiction—the "Tales of the Human Condition."

The two chapters by Eric Carlson report on selected critiques of some distinction, major or minor, from D. H. Lawrence's in 1919–1923 to those of the late 1980s and early 1990s. Each of the five tales of psychal conflict has its own reason for being, but because of the greater subtleties of style and suggestion in "Ligeia" and "Usher," those tales receive more attention, though none too much. In some of these tales we find the earliest evidence of the "dynamic organicism" toward which Poe was moving (Jacobs, *Poe,* viii).

Joswick's "Moods of Mind" deals not only with the detective stories but also with "The Black Cat," "The Tell-Tale Heart," "The Pit," "The Cask," and other tales of violence and vengeance. Readings reported here illustrate how Poe probed the irrational moods and motives beneath stark surfaces, revealing hidden compulsions to confess, rationalizations of guilt and other soul-destroying devices for evading the inner truth. To Joswick, detective and madman alike are subject to similar "moods of mind." In "The Man of the Crowd," the narrator discovers in himself an unconscious drive like that of the stranger. This doubling of motive and theme is then applied to the tales of detection as well.

In Grace Farrell's chapter on *The Narrative of Arthur Gordon Pym* and *The Journal of Julius Rodman*, these journeys to unexplored places are presented as "Dream Texts," hinting of imaginary events and actors and primitive or primal wilderness. Beginning with a careful account of sources, publication, and reception and then the genesis, structure, unity, and genre of *Pym*, Farrell delves into critical approaches by surveying *Pym* criticism from early studies through Davidson (1957), followed by the 1960s (Lynen), the 1970s (Halliburton and Thompson), to "Visionary Journeys" (O'Donnell, Hoffman, Farrell, Wilbur, Hussey, Hernandez, Ljungquist, St. Armand), into the 1980s (Fukuchi, Kopley)—ranging from the mythic to biographical criticism. "Darker Visions" adds to the earlier, affirmative readings a "shadow side" (Helen Lee, Porte, Pollin, Moldenhauer, Peden, Carringer, Beaver). The postmodern critics rejected all previous concerns over unity of meaning and structure on the ground that, to them, in Farrell's words, "meaning cannot be determined, and the more indeterminate the text, the better" (32). Several French critics of this school are introduced briefly, along with some American deconstructionists (Rowe, Kennedy, Thompson, Irwin) who claim *Pym* to be the central or crucial text in understanding Poe because it is really about writing as a way of displacing death and avoiding the abyss. In a concluding section on cultural studies (Levin, Kaplan, Fiedler, Mottram, Nelson, Rowe), special attention is paid to John Limon's use of the nature-philosophic tradition (*Naturphilosophie*) of Hegel, Schelling, and Oken and to *Eureka* as an intellectual context for the ending of the novel.

In their chapter on Poe's science fiction and landscape sketches, David Sloane and Michael Pettengell first examine the balloon hoaxes for the journey motif, comic satire, and occasional suggestions of higher consciousness, especially in "Hans Pfaall." "Mesmeric Revelation" provides a point of departure for analyzing "Valdemar" and "Ragged Mountains." With the exception of "Wissahiccon," the landscape sketches occupy a "special place in the Poe canon" in reflecting "an idealistic reaching for a more perfect spiritual state." Although Zanger and Dayan are among critics cited, their commentaries run counter to Poe's own appreciation of the transcendental theme of supernal "spiritual beauty" in "The Domain of Arnheim."

The next two chapters are complementary. Chapter 13 is a penetrating survey of the essays and "Marginalia" for Poe's theory of poetry and the tale. Beverly Voloshin reports on the studies of Alterton, Jacobs, and Richard, then the French responses of Baudelaire, Mallarmé, and Valéry (Patrick Quinn, Edmund Wilson) and the recent New Theorists (Derrida, Lacan, et al.). A few of Poe's major essays are examined one by one for his critical principles: the early "Letter to B—," the review of Euripides' plays, in which Poe borrowed from Schlegel the concept of ideality, the Drake–Halleck review for more on ideality and faculty psychology. Other reviews are tapped as sources of the concept of the "mystic or undercurrent of meaning." The theory of the tale is analyzed by Voloshin at length for Poe's use of the terms *arabesque* and *grotesque,* for the organic unity of plot, and for scientific analogies in *Eureka.* The reviews of Hawthorne's tales are mined for an extended discussion of originality, simulation, and the simulacrum. A long section on Poe's late theory of poetry carries over the concept of simulacrum into an original analysis of "The Philosophy of Composition."

Chapter 14, "The Reviews: Evolution of a Critic" by James M. Hutchisson, meticulously traces Poe's career as a reviewing critic from 1835 at the *Southern Literary Messenger* through his positions at *Burton's, Graham's,* and the *Broadway Journal* (1845–1849). In that time, Poe wrote almost 1,000 reviews, essays, articles, columns, and critical notices. From the reviews, Hutchisson has selected the most valuable as sources of understanding both the literature reviewed and the critical principles evolving into what Edmund Wilson called "the most remarkable body of criticism ever produced in the United States." Hutchisson also identifies the best editions and studies of the reviews and then offers his own description and evaluation of each selected review, highlighting the ones on Drake-Halleck, Bird's *Sheppard Lee,* Bryant's poetry, allegory, Longfellow's poetry, the "Longfellow War," and Hawthorne's tales, among others. In a longer discussion of the controversial Drayton–Paulding review, to which he has contributed new data, Hutchisson has laid the groundwork for a reconsideration of the alleged Poe authorship of this review as evidence of his racism.

Barbara Cantalupo's Chapter 15 on *Eureka* describes the original lecture version with Preface, Poe's summaries for two correspondents, and the essay version with new ending that aroused objections from orthodox readers. Criticism is represented by overviews and analyses from the 1890s to the present, the modern period beginning with Richard Benton's *Poe as Literary Cosmologer* (1975) and Roland Nelson's "Apparatus for a Definitive Edition" (1978). Cantalupo's section on Poe's Methodology includes concise and clear definitions of "infinity," "limited space," "intuition," Poe's semantics, use of analogy, and involution. The section on the Science of *Eureka* reports what scientists have had to say about *Eureka* during the past fifty years, including new commentary not before published. Literary critics also have their say, Holman and Limon in particular. In *Eureka* as a Poetic Vision, Richard Wilbur, Joan Dayan, and Halliburton are heard from. *Eureka* as Organic Pantheism sums up views from Poe's time as well as ours and concludes with Poe's own words on the subject.

In Part III, "Poe's Thought," a fitting sequel to the previous chapter is Kenneth Alan Hovey's original and fascinating account of how Poe developed his "Materialist Metaphysics of Man." That the most important "materialism" for Poe was Epicurean is fully documented here. Hovey shows that Poe's references to Epicurus are serious, not ironic, even in the four early comic satires. The materiality of the soul was first suggested comically in "Bon-Bon" and confirmed by the works of the Reverend Townshend and by the Reverend George Bush, who described it as "*matter* . . . [in] its more refined and subtle forms" akin to the "active energies" with which "all nature is pervaded" (quoted 18). In Epicurean ethics, the most moral man is the man of finest taste. The implications of phrenology for individual freedom of will and discipline appear in "Ligeia" and "Arnheim." The Epicurean Poe chose "the pursuit of happiness" over public duty and social progress. His was "a kind of materialistic idealism" (Feidelson) that transcended rational mechanism and avoided sensuality, celebrating a beauty that survives in the immortally material soul.

In " 'Strange Alchemy of Brain': Poe and Alchemy," Randall Clack looks to the hermetic tradition to demonstrate how, throughout Poe's work, chemical analogies and imagery suggest or symbolize the theme of spiritual renewal in an extraordinary state of "vision." This study benefits from the earlier scholarship of Barton Levi St. Armand, Karl E. Oelke on the poems, and Burton Pollin. Emerson, Hawthorne, and Margaret Fuller also "found in the idea of alchemical transmutation a powerful metaphor for the transformation of both the individual and society" (Clack). After explaining the nature of alchemy, Clack reports what critics have done with "Von Kempelen" and the early poems and, notably, in longer critiques by St. Armand of "The Gold-Bug" and "Usher." Clack offers his own analysis of "The Assignation," probably an early attempt by Poe "to use the alchemical metaphors of Hermeticism as a paradigm for his readers versed in esoteric lore" (24). "Ligeia," rich with hermetic images and allusions, is interpreted as a final prime example.

In "Feminist 'Re-Visioning' of the Tales of Women," feminist criticism is less allied to the New Theory than to the women's liberation and human potential movements of the past twenty-five years. In fact, feminists reject postmodernism, their goal being a radical reconstruction of society, not a nihilistic denial of it. But from Paula Kot's survey of the most recent publications by literary feminist critics—Judith Fetterley, Cynthia S. Jordan, Joan Dayan, Leland S. Person, Jr., J. Gerald Kennedy, Monika Elbert, Jacqueline Doyle, and Elisabeth Bronfen—it is clear that they have made appreciable inroads into mainstream Poe criticism. Yet, it would seem that, until the present extreme antipatriarchalism is outgrown, feminists will not attain the balanced androgynous perspective called for recently by Jordan and Person and in 1972 by social feminist Wilma Scott Heide (see Carlson 1972). Another serious weakness of feminist critiques of Poe is the failure to allow for his use of Gothic symbolism; literal readings have long since been superseded by metaphorical and symbolic interpretations based on a knowledge of the Gothic tradition and of Poe's symbology and philosophic perspective (see Clark Griffith, "Poe and the Gothic"). An example of the fallacy of literal readings is the chapter called "Poe's Most Poetic Subject" in Bassein's *Women and Death*. Despite her long litany of victimized women in Poe's works, Bassein concludes with this admission: "However, given the abundance of Gothic romances written by women . . . , and given the number of female readers of those Gothic tales, it can be said that repulsion from the stereotypes that the Gothic tale perpetuates is not as strong as one would wish it to be" (55). Bassein fails to ask herself whether it was because those readers did not take Gothic romances literally any more than television viewers today take violent programs literally.

"Poe and Postmodernism," David Hirsch's historical-critical survey, begins with the attack by postmodernists on the humanist tradition represented by Matthiessen's *American Renaissance* (especially as Poe was there relegated to a footnote, though Matthiessen later made amends with his long essay on Poe in the *Literary History of the United States*) and by Killis Campbell, Brownell, and Davidson. With the famous seminar on "The Purloined Letter" (Derrida and Lacan), Poe again became internationally prominent between 1966 and 1990 or so. In recent years, postmodernists have shifted their attention to *Pym* as a central work in the Poe canon. To them, it represents writing not as content or meaning but as writing or language for its own sake (Rowe and Irwin), as an example of indeterminacy (Robinson, Kennedy), and as an American arabesque (Thompson). In writing *The Deconstruction of Literature: Criticism after Auschwitz* (1991), Hirsch felt that Paul de Man used deconstructionist theory about literature and society to cover up his pro-Nazi past. To resolve a controversy, Joseph Ridgely examined closely the Paulding–Drayton review and concluded that Poe's authorship is doubtful. John Limon also disagreed with Rowe's and Dayan's views of Poe as racist. Like Kenneth Hovey, Limon anchors Poe's work in the philosophy that regards nature as matter spiritualized organically from within.

In "Poe's Aesthetics," David Halliburton focuses on the role of experience, for "the *experiential* intensities" produce a sense of "what it would be like to live" the events in the story. "In experience, all of Poe's favorite themes and motifs may be seen to intersect." After a treatment of "the offices and provinces of criticism," four sections deal with the experience of the audience, the histrionic experience, experiencing "the true poetical effect," and the merger of the experiential with the experimental ("a venerable nexus in Western thought since the Renaissance"). A section on the aesthetics of revolution centers on the passage in *Eureka* suggesting that "only by a rapid whirling on his heel could he hope to comprehend the panorama in the sublimity of its oneness" (*H* 16: 186), in other words, a revolution of experiencing "the earthly-cosmic design of things" (Halliburton, 28), which is supported by Poe's own words: " 'the cycle within cycle without end—yet all revolving around one far-distant center . . . life within life . . . all within the Spirit Divine' " (*M* 2: 601). The revolutionary impulse in Poe's life and writings included his opposition to the Eastern literary establishment and his proposals for new, radical standards for literature and criticism as a cultural institution.

In "The Language and Style of the Prose," Donald Barlow Stauffer takes another approach to Poe's art. Although long recognized as one of the great stylists of the nineteenth century, Poe has baffled most critics by the absence of any one distinctive style. Stauffer finds the solution in Poe's theory of language, noting his search, as a "Platonic transcendentalist," for the "ultimately unsayable." Although far from systematic, Poe's views on style, especially word choice, syntax, and grammar, become the basis for his preference for brevity, precision, terseness, simplicity, and lucidity. In larger measure, Stauffer distinguishes Poe's so-called three ratiocinative, neoclassical styles and the two intuitive styles. The section on Poe's diction includes coined compounds and virtuoso displays of vocabulary, his use of archaisms, foreign terms from eight languages, technical language, unusual words, dialect. Summing up, Stauffer emphasizes that the tales survive largely because of the "transformative power of their language."

In Part V, "Poe's Influence," John Reilly's "Poe in Literature and Popular Culture" as represented in poetry, fiction, film, and drama confirms Poe's desire for both popularity with the "mass of mankind" and fame with cultivated readers. His popularity is mostly based on the core of poems and the tales frequently reprinted or filmed, reinforced by the "legend" of Poe as a strange, haunted genius, an image that remains dominant today, made more fascinating as Poe's detractors, from Griswold on, demonized his character. Hundreds of poems, dozens of plays, novels, and short stories contributed to this distorted view, as have film, radio, and television productions, dramatic readings, comic books, and so on—a "subversive" literature increasingly being recognized as worthy of serious study. Poetry especially has recorded the impact of the image of Poe from his own lifetime to the present, as in poems by friends attempting to encourage the suffering genius and, after his death, portrayals of Poe as a devil and/or an angel. Reilly follows the trail through the time of spiritualist "contacts" with Poe in the 1950s and 1960s, the partisan Poe cult beginning in 1875 with the dedication of a monument in Baltimore, Mallarmé's famous sonnet in 1877, the Zolnay bust in 1899, culminating in the 1909 centennial. Since then, prominent poets have continued to celebrate Poe—Vachel Lindsay, Hart Crane, Dave Smith, Allen Ginsberg, among others. Ginsberg's poem "Haunting Poe's Baltimore" outdoes Poe in its necrophilia.

The section on Poe in fiction consists of fictional biographies, short-story fantasies, and fantasy novels. Except for *Plumes in the Dust,* attempts at dramatization lost touch with the facts of Poe's life. Here as elsewhere, Reilly's analyses of filmed Poe biographies and the Argento opera are definitively precise. Solo performances by an actor costumed as Poe have been very popular in recent years despite the failure to distance the man Poe from his creations.

Burton R. Pollin, "Poe in Art, Music, Opera, and Dance," states that the influence of Poe on the fine arts around the world matches that of his influence on creative writers. Over twenty years, Professor Pollin has collected thousands of illustrations—paintings, drawings, book plates, engravings, and others—of the more popular poems and tales from 1844 to 1955. Illustrations by Cropsey, Darley, Manet, Redon, Doré, Ensor, Gauguin, Beardsley, Whistler, and Kubin are most noteworthy. In his vast knowledge of this field and his eye for concrete detail, Pollin offers an interesting, encyclopedic, and evaluative survey as he moves around the world from country to country. In this limited space, it is impossible to do justice to the qualitative and quantitative aspects of this chapter.

That is also true of Part II in this chapter, "Poe Set to Music," which is another worldwide, historical survey of musical interpretations based on selected poems and tonal or mood passages in the sketches and tales. In the latter, moods or tones vary from humor and light satire to the grotesque or morbid, as in "Usher" or "Masque." Of three full-length operas, the most ambitious is Dominick Argento's "Bicentenary" *Voyage of Edgar Allan Poe* (1976).

In Part III, "Poe and the Dance," significant references to, or uses of, dancing are noted in Poe's poems and tales, for example, in "Usher," leading to the use of the whole tale as a scenario for a ballet. "Typically," Pollin writes, "Poe associates immorality or sensuality with the dance." Given the masquerade dance in "The Masque of the Red Death," that tale has most frequently been turned into ballets. *Seafall* (1969), one of the finest dances based on "Annabel Lee," has been shown on American television.

Lois Vines, "A Writer for the World," states that most common readers and many academics are grossly ignorant of Poe's influence as a "world author," though he is often so labeled. A specialist in French literature, especially Valéry and Poe, Vines recounts how, from the middle 1840s, several translations and essays appeared in France, notably by Baudelaire, who introduced to French readers for the first time Poe's life and the unique qualities of his writings. Then the "Poe legend" gathered momentum after Griswold's infamous Poe obituary and memoir were published and distributed throughout Europe and the United States. In the controversy that followed, Sarah Helen Whitman's defense of Poe's character and work was one of the best, as was Willa Cather's 1895 college essay thirty-five years later.[1] Other famous admirers included Mallarmé, Thomas Mann, Joseph Conrad, Robert Frost, William Carlos Williams. The British response was long poisoned by the Griswold effect until John Ingram's Poe biography in 1880 and the enthusiasm of Tennyson, Kipling, H. G. Wells, and D. H. Lawrence somewhat offset Griswold. Painters inspired by Poe included Manet, Whistler, Magritte; the Symbolists, the Decadents, Valéry, Dostoyevski, and Konstantin Balmont (the Russian Baudelaire) responded in different ways. Vines continues with similar reports of the influence on Scandinavian writers, notably Ola Hansson. The documentation includes writers in Serbo-Croatian, Hungarian, Romanian, Czech, Italian, Hispanic (including Latin American, e.g., Ruben Dario), and Portuguese literatures—the list of countries and writers goes on and on, to Luis Borges, Julio Cortazar, Carlos Fuentes, then Japan, China, and India. This interesting, readable chapter of "Poe abroad" ranks him as "the most influential of American authors" a century and a half after the first translation in France.

In "Poe and the World of Books," George Egon Hatvary draws on his knowledge of Poe in the wide context of New York libraries, book auctions, and bookstores. In "Poe's Use of Books," he refers to the list of esoteric books in "Usher" as the best indication of "Poe's use of books primarily for the sake of his own art." Though Poe owned few books, he had access to excellent libraries of friends and university and private libraries in New York, Richmond,

Baltimore, Philadelphia, West Point, and the University of Virginia, as well as review copies from publishers. Although he read extensively, he read not as a scholar but as a magazine editor and as a creative writer. ''Poe's Relations with Publishers and Editors'' describes his difficulties in getting his early poems and tales published in volume format, in contrast to easy magazine publication (for a pittance). ''The Reception of Poe's Works'' was favorable in reviews, poor in sales. ''The Collecting and Recording'' of his works is a complex, interesting story as rare numbers of small printings have become collectors' items of ever higher value, *Tamerlane* selling for $165,000 in 1990, *Prose Romances* for $60,500, and *Tales of the Grotesque and Arabesque* for $130,000 at the same auction. Poe manuscripts have always fetched high prices. Some of the major checklists by dealers and collectors are here identified, followed by early bibliographies in book form, especially the evolution of the Heartman–Rede from 1932 to the Heartman–Canny in 1940 and its controversial reception and revised edition in 1943, which Mabbott called ''invaluable for the student of the works of Poe.'' Also important is the seventh volume (including Poe) in 1983 of the ''meticulous and unbiased'' Jacob Blanck's *Bibliography of American Literature*. The section on ''Posthumous Editions'' begins with Griswold, then Ingram (1874–1875), Claude Richard (1974), Harrison (1902), Campbell, Stovall, Quinn and O'Neill, Mabbott (1969–1978), Pollin (1981–1988), with extended evaluations of the last two and of the standards applied in editing primary works by the MLA Center for Scholarly Editions. In a paragraph on each, ''Secondary Studies'' identifies major works of scholarship, biography, and criticism. Following his chapter bibliography, Hatvary lists ''Works by Poe in Collected Sets'' (nine) and in ''Composite Volumes'' (sixteen, mostly selections of poems, tales, or criticism).

FRAMES OF REFERENCE FOR POE CRITICISM

The problem for Poe studies posed by deconstruction has been its rejection of the mainstream of Poe criticism, resulting in an appreciable loss of humanist values in literature and a deplorable ignorance of the history of Poe criticism— of its major achievements for the past 150 years, including the modern period, whether dated from D. H. Lawrence or Valéry or Edmund Wilson or Tate or Wilbur. In the words of one Poe scholar:

There is a tendency not to independently research the critical history, but just to build upon the paraphrasing of critics who fail to cite their sources, thus disrupting the dialogue of criticism. The whole enterprise of scholarly studies presupposes the importance of individual voices in dialogue over the course of time. Acknowledging one's predecessors has been an appropriate formality in the profession. Of course, if we want to kill the past by ignoring it or failing to understand it, then we become pseudo-scholars at best.

Another prominent Poe critic, after characterizing *Pym* as ''perhaps the most important of Edgar Allan Poe's work'' (despite Poe's reference to it as a ''very silly book'') and after failing in several attempts to make sense of this ''novel,'' concluded that the work is an ambiguous and indeterminate ''abyss of interpretation.'' If it is that bad, why not accept Poe's own dismissal of *Pym* as a serious interpretive work? The great majority of Poe critics realize that deconstruction and its predecessor, the New Criticism, overlooked or ignored the fundamental fact that a work of art can neither be created nor be understood in a vacuum— without reference to its context or contexts: the life and/or mind of its creator, the zeitgeist (the spirit of his time), his or her ''philosophic perspective'' (Tate) and ''artistic perspective,'' and so on.

Brooks and Warren (1950): The New Criticism in Wider Perspective

This realization came to light in a landmark event in the history of American literary criticism. In 1950, a revised, complete edition of Cleanth Brooks and Robert Penn Warren's widely used text *Understanding Poetry* appeared. The major addition consisted of Section X, ''THE POEM VIEWED IN WIDER PERSPECTIVE'' (611–82). As a rationale for this and other revisions, a postscript added to their original ''Letter to the Teacher'' (1938) stated that, in the twelve-year interval, ''our personal tastes have changed a little . . . at the same time . . . our fundamental approach to poetry remains the same.'' Whereas, a decade earlier, ''the chief need was for a sharp focus on the poem itself,'' now (1950) it was no longer safe ''to leave to implication the relation of the poem to its historical background, to its place in the context of the poet's work, and to biographical and historical study generally.'' Some teachers had pointed out that these relationships were ''not simple but intricate and rich. In this revised edition, therefore, . . . we have tried to relate criticism to other literary studies,'' specifically, to the ''historical situation'' of the poem and ''to the body of the poet's work'' in such a way as to show that ''history, literary and general, may be related to poetic meaning.'' To illustrate the relation of the single poem to the whole body of the poet's work, Section X consisted of an extended essay suggesting the unity of style and theme in Wordsworth (631–45) and the continuity of the poet's work in treatments of Eliot (645–67) and Marvell (667–82). In short, ''even in a poet of great variety and complication, there is some central concern, some fundamental attitude, from which the richness exfoliates. Once we understand this, we find that one poem serves as a gloss upon the next.'' With such an understanding of the poet's philosophic perspective, the reader should realize that ''the creative process is deep and complicated . . . and that it is primarily a process of search for meanings and explorations of meanings . . . that, in the full sense, the poem is not a vehicle for its idea, but *is* its idea, its meaning.'' This ''intrinsic poetic value . . . can never exist in isolation.'' That poetic value is inseparable from the other values in ''the kind of *being* the poem has'' and the reader's ''total experience of the poem'' (xxii–xxv). In adding Section X and parts of other sections, Brooks and Warren, qualifying their earlier focus on "the poem as a poem," took a giant step toward an organic, creative conception of poetry in the "wider perspective" of human "values," as distinguished from the purely technical theory of art implicit in "the poem as such." But the "wider perspective" of Brooks and Warren's revision came too late to be accepted as a new, broader, more viable form of the New Criticism.

During the past forty-five years since Allen Tate's "The Angelic Imagination," perspectivist studies have been made of Poe works as related to *Eureka,* the colloquies, the essays, the *Marginalia,* the reviews, and other "frames of reference." One need only examine the Poe criticism of Richard Wilbur, Moldenhauer, Lynen, Jacobs, Finholt, Beebe, Benton, Ketterer, Halliburton, Hovey, Patrick Quinn, Davidson, St. Armand, to cite a few exemplary critics (see the preceding "Guide to Individual Chapters").

The New Critics' narrow doctrine that literary criticism should concern itself only with "literature as such" led to its demise. Deconstruction, its successor, is now said to be "dead," at least in the American academy.[2] The *New York Times* of September 4, 1994, for instance, reported: "Recent years have seen books called 'In the Wake of Theory,' 'After Poststructuralism,' and 'Beyond Deconstruction.' . . . Patricia Meyer Spacks, current president of the M.L.A., says 'Contrary to the general view in the press that the profession is dominated by it, deconstruction is pretty much dead—except for one or two people at Yale' " (E6).

Ever since Jacques Lacan's 1966 seminar on "The Purloined Letter" and Jacques Derrida's response to it, Poe's story has been at the center of the deconstructionist controversy, thus drawing some, but not the majority, of Poe specialists into the debate. With only the "text" as all-important to most deconstructionists—in theory, at least—the traditional idea that the "mind" or the "life" of the author should be studied as the creative source of any art form was ruled out of order. All interpretations became "misreadings," there being no right or best reading. Ironically, to say the least, Nealon reminds us that Derrida, the fountainhead of deconstruction, stresses the central importance of philosophic perspective in literary criticism: "Each time that a rhetoric defines a metaphor, not only is *a* philosophy implied, but also a conceptual network in which philosophy *itself* has been constituted" (quoted by Nealon, 1274). Undecidability is not solely concerned with, or brought about by, the equivocality or ambivalence of some metaphor or figure of speech but is "symptomatic rather of the structure of the signifying field itself" (Nealon 1274).

What, then, is the structure of Poe's signifying field (philosophic perspective)? The single most determinative clue to Poe's idea of psychal conflict/integrity is undoubtedly the passage on "the world of mind" in "The Poetic Principle":

Dividing the world of mind into its three most immediately obvious distinctions, we have the Pure Intellect, Taste, and the Moral Sense. I place Taste in the middle, because it is just this position which, in the mind, it occupies. It holds intimate relations with either extreme; but from the Moral Sense is separated by so faint a difference that Aristotle has not hesitated to place some of its operations among the virtues themselves. Nevertheless, we find the *offices* of the trio marked with a sufficient distinction. Just as the Intellect concerns itself with Truth, so Taste informs us of the Beautiful while the Moral Sense is regardful of Duty. (*T, 76*)

In the next paragraph, Poe speaks of "a sense of the Beautiful" as "an immortal instinct, deep within the spirit of man"—a sense of both the "Beauty before us" and "the Beauty above." The supernal Beauty we make a "wild effort to reach" despite "our inability to grasp *now,* wholly, here on earth, at once and for ever, those divine and rapturous joys, of which *through* the poem, or *through* the music, we attain to but brief and indeterminate glimpses." The higher Poetic Sentiment is a "pleasurable elevation, or excitement, *of the soul.*" Two years earlier in "Marginalia" entry 150 for March 1846, Poe described these "visions" as "ecstasies" or "psychal fancies":

They seem to me rather psychal than intellectual. They arise in the soul (alas, how rarely!) only at its epochs of most intense tranquility—when the bodily and mental health are in perfection—and at those mere points of time where the confines of the waking world blend with those of the world of dreams. . . . These "fancies" have in them a pleasurable ecstasy. . . . I regard the visions, even as they arise, with an awe which, in some measure, moderates or tranquilizes the ecstasy—I so regard them, through a conviction (which seems a portion of the ecstasy itself) that this ecstasy, in itself, is of a character supernal to the Human Nature—it is a glimpse of the spirit's outer world. . . . It is as if the five senses were supplanted by five myriad others alien to mortality. . . . I am not to be understood as supposing that the fancies, or psychal impressions, to which I allude, are confined to my individual self—are not, in a word, common to all mankind—for on this point it is quite impossible that I should form an opinion. (*P 2, 257–59; T, 1382–85*)

Here we have the best clues to the meaning of certain key terms in Poe's criticism: *psychal, soul, ecstasy, supernal, vision.* From these passages, Richard Wilbur derived his allegory of "the hypnagogic state," and from them also I coined the term *psychal transcendentalism* for my lectures of 1969 and 1972. These passages have been quoted or referred to in all of Wilbur's major essays on Poe. Silverman also in his recent biography mentions these ideas but praises them only for the "assurance, clarity, and coherence" of their expression as a poetic credo ("The Poetic Principle," 348).

Another key document is "Mesmeric Revelation" (1844), which Poe regarded as "a somewhat detailed" statement of his "faith." Death is seen as a "metamorphosis" from the "ordinary life" into the "ultimate life" of "nearly unlimited perception" and "unlimited comprehension." In this earthly "life," this trancelike condition may be produced by drugs, illness, faintness, music, near-madness, and sleep-waking (not sleepwalking). In *Eureka,* Poe called it "identity with God" or with "Divine Will" or "Heart Divine" or "that identity which at death is or is not lost forever." In "Ligeia," the narrator, through willed insight, is reunited with the Ligeia depths in himself (or "born again" into the God that is "every where," as Poe said on another occasion).

Although in "Shadow," "Silence," and the sea tales the Universe seems indifferent and God, if not dead, "silent," this existentialist phase of Poe's mind and career is only that—a phase. As the previous excerpts clearly indicate, it is not his central, major outlook on life. Even when confronted by the maelstrom abyss, Poe's hero feels a strong "wish to explore the depths . . . an unconquerable desire—to *know*," which Poe equated with "the sense of the beautiful, of the sublime, and of the mystical" (Drake-Halleck review). The longest and most forceful statement of his transcendentalism appears in the climactic paragraphs of *Eureka*, concluding with his distinction between "a proper identity" and "secondly and by faint indeterminate glimpses, of an identity with the Divine Being of whom we speak—of an identity with God." Ultimately, "when the bright stars become blended into One. . . . the individual identity will be gradually merged in the general conciousness. . . . In the meantime bear in mind that all is Life—Life—Life within Life—the less within the greater, and all within the *Spirit Divine*."

My "Frames of Reference for Poe's Symbolic Language" sets forth this perspectivist contxt, which, years earlier, Allen Tate had expounded in "The Angelic Imagination" (1951). In this approach, *Eureka*, the colloquies, the essays, the "Marginalia," and the reviews have been increasingly recognized as the keys to a functional Poe aesthetic and criticism, just as every astronomer measuring the distance to a star must first establish a baseline from which to make a triangulation. This method of *parallax* is similar to the postmodernist's *intertextuality* but more focused and disciplined. (For a more detailed analysis of this critical method, see my essay in *Critical Essays on Edgar Allan Poe*.)

A "New American Literary History"?

In 1995, with much fanfare, *American Literature* quarterly announced a series, past and forthcoming, of Special Issues/Sections on "what's happening in American literary studies." From them, seventeen essays were reprinted in *Subjects and Citizens: Nation, Race, and Gender,* edited by Michael Moon and Cathy N. Davidson, and three original essays added. In defining "the New American literary history" the editors held that

these essays show how issues of race and gender challenge nationalist paradigms and realign the borders of both the nation and the field of American literary history. . . . The volume is united by three interrelated questions: where does "American literature" begin? (the question of origin); what does "*American* literature" mean? (the question of nation); and what does American literature include and exclude and how? (the question of race and gender). (1–2)

And all this through a variety of theoretical perspectives and methodologies. The only essay on Poe is Joan Dayan's already reprinted article on

"Amorous Bondage: Poe, Ladies, and Slaves" (see Chapters 10, 14, 19 in this book).

Another compilation from the same perspective, though limited to Poe's work, is the very recent *The American Face of Edgar Allan Poe,* edited by Shawn Rosenheim and Stephen Rachman. Of the thirteen essays, at least six are reprints (including the twice reprinted Dayan piece on "Amorous Bondage"). The editors are motivated by the earlier omission of Poe from "synthetic interpretations of American literary culture," as in "the critical dismissal of Poe" by Matthiessen in *American Renaissance* (see Chapter 10 in this volume for the facts); by the recent rise of interest in Poe's writing; and by the need "to expose and to make sense of the apparent jumble of Poe's cultural physiognomy" (x), especially the "growing impulse to resist Poe's wholesale assimilation" to psychoanalytical and psycholinguistic criticism. Even the French New Theorists, otherwise highly praised for their "critical fertility," failed to sense how "Poe's most extravagant literary maneuvers were usually based in the specific cultural and political climate of antebellum America" (x–xi). As the old "illusory myths" of American culture (the "American Adam," etc.) have receded, they have been replaced by competing models, "sociologically inclined stories" based on "extensive social analyses of antebellum culture" (xi).

Poe's American face is seen as four-sided: the literary relations of language in philosophy, poetry, and plagiarism; generic logic; gender (feminist), class, the "body"; and culture (nationalism, identity, etc.). Through the "mutual amplification" of these aspects, the essays are said to offer insights into the relations of literary issues and democratic culture, with the result that Poe's contradictions are less a problem than a vast influence: "The cultural vexations that animate his texts have become the full-blown preoccupations of our culture and our writing.... Because he was always both in and out of his time, Poe can now stand, Janus-faced, in—and out—of ours as well" (xx). As an example of Poe's attunement to the Romanticism of his day, the editors cite his fixation on the ethereal, the other-worldly, and the timeless, accepting this transcendentalism as another sociological detail in his milieu, not as a major element of Poe's metaphysics and symbology. Thus social history is mistaken for literary criticism. In short, the four faces of *this* American Poe are not the faces of Poe the artist—the poet, the fiction writer, and the literary critic. These two new studies offer a wealth of historical information on Poe's *social* perspective (cf. Marchand), but leave essentially unchanged Poe's *philosophic* perspective as defined earlier in this Introduction.

NOTES

1. *The World and the Parish: Willa Cather's Articles and Reviews 1893–1902,* ed. William M. Curtin (Lincoln: U of Nebraska P, 1970), 157–63.

2. See especially "The Discipline of Deconstruction" by Jeffrey T. Nealon in *PMLA* 107, no. 3 (Oct. 1992) 1266–79, which begins: "Deconstruction, it seems, is dead in

[American] literature departments today . . . its heyday has apparently passed'' (1266). Nealon distinguishes Paul de Man's ''undecidability'' as a general doctrine from Derrida's idea of ''unreadability'' and a second stage, the search for textual decidability. Interesting responses to this article appeared in *PMLA* for May and October 1993. Other references to postmodernism and deconstruction are included in the Bibliography: works by Abrams, Bloom, R. Barth, Culler, de Man, Ellis, Graff, Kennedy, Mitchell, Muller (*Purloined Letter*), Rowe, Thompson (1989).

Part I

POE'S LIFE AND TIMES

1

The Poe Legend

IAN WALKER

The earliest biographical sketches of Poe were published during his lifetime. Although these articles were either written by Poe himself or assembled from information supplied by him, they do not conform to Peter Pendulum's dictum in "The Business Man": "In biography the truth is everything, and in auto-biography it is especially so" (*M* 3, 483). These curious documents (which were to mislead Poe's biographers for years to come) were never intended to provide reliable biographical information but, rather, were intended to contribute toward the creation of a fanciful romantic persona.

The first of these (auto)biographies appeared in 1842 in Rufus Griswold's popular and widely reviewed anthology *The Poets and Poetry of America*. Poe met his future biographer, editor, and literary executor in Philadelphia in the spring of 1841; Griswold was newly arrived in the city with a contract to com-pile what promised to be the most extensive and authoritative anthology of its kind, and, although Poe was scarcely known as a poet at this time, he hoped to be represented. He followed up the meeting with a letter offering Griswold "such poems as I think my best" (*O* 1, 161), together with an autobiographical "Memorandum" riddled with distortions and inaccuracies, from the first words, "Born January 1811" (in reality, 1809), to his final mysterious confession: "Lately have written articles continuously for two British journals whose names I am not permitted to mention" (*H* 1, 344–46). Almost every aspect of Poe's life was altered or fabricated in order to mask his real origins and circumstances and to project an image of himself in keeping with his literary ambitions. The contours of this largely fictional biography become clearer in its extended form in the *Philadelphia Saturday Museum*.

Early in 1843, Poe reached agreement with Thomas C. Clarke, a Philadelphia newspaper publisher, to issue his long-planned literary monthly, which was by this time to be called the *Stylus*. In order to publicize his project, he arranged to have a full-page biography of himself printed in Clarke's "mammoth" paper, the *Saturday Museum*; the article appeared on the front page on February 25 and again on March 4 and aroused enough interest to justify edited versions in papers in Baltimore and Boston. Poe had originally asked his friend F. W. Thomas to prepare the biography from "notes" supplied by him, but Thomas declined the task, pleading "partiality of friendship." Although in letters Poe identified his associate, Henry B. Hirst, as the "biographer," it is evident from the style and contents that Poe himself was the real authority behind the sketch (Pollin 1993, 147–50).

The *Museum* narrative is a mixture of transformed realities and Byronic fantasies. It begins by emphasizing Poe's illustrious family heritage: he is "descended from one of the oldest and most respectable families in Baltimore . . . the family claim connexion with many of the noblest in England," while through his marriage he became "closely connected with many of the Best families in Maryland." His paternal grandfather, "General" Poe, is elevated into a leading Revolutionary patriot, "one of the most intimate friends of La Fayette"; he spent the vast sum of $40,000 on military supplies but, because of some technicality, "received no portion of the sum." Poe's early life was one of privilege: his wealthy foster father "adopted" him, took him to Britain, where they "made the tour," and made it clear that he intended "to make him his sole heir." But Poe's financial security was again blighted, this time by his father's "[g]ross nature"—he married a "lady young enough to be his grand-daughter" and died leaving his promised heir nothing.

Deprived of his inheritance, Poe turned to literature for a living. Hearing of his singular triumphs in the *Saturday Visiter* competition, Thomas White invited him to take control of the *SLM,* where he was an outstanding commercial and critical success—Poe assembled more than thirty extracts from newspaper notices and private letters to testify to his "unequalled" skills and virtuosity as a story writer, critic, and cryptographer. He is also depicted as an amazingly precocious poet who "wrote verses as soon as he could write at all," and his first collection, which appeared "before he had completed his fifteenth year," rivaled Keats and Shelley. "To Helen" was written even earlier and was even more remarkable: "These lines by a boy of fourteen, will compare favorably with any written, at any age, *by any poet whatsoever.*" In addition, he claimed that he was the author of a two-volume novel written under a nom de plume "never acknowledged," papers on American topics for Parisian journals, and anonymous articles in British periodicals. (No evidence of these writings has ever been found, and it is unlikely that they ever existed apart from wishful thinking.) Another fiction promoted by the *Museum* (auto)biography was that of Poe's youthful history as a scholar adventurer. At the University of Virginia, he fell in with the "exceedingly dissolute" student lifestyle; nevertheless, he "took the first honors of the college, without any difficulty" (in reality, he was withdrawn after one session), before embarking "with scarcely a dollar" to join the Greek struggle for independence. However, for some unexplained reason, he became stranded in St. Petersburg, where he "became involved in serious difficulties" from which he was extricated by the American consul. Later, at West Point, the young hero planned to fight for Polish freedom: "All our cadet's former chivalric ardor had now returned, and with tenfold vigor. He burned to be a participant in the affray." Unfortunately, Warsaw capitulated before Poe could arrange his discharge—so he "repaired to Baltimore" instead (Pollin 1993, 163–65).

The *Museum* text concludes with tales of Poe's youthful athletic feats. These stories may seem superfluous to a literary biography; but they support the overall design of the narrative, which was to create a myth of Poe as a gifted romantic hero—an American Byron—though with no hint of the British poet's sexual irregularities. The comparison with Byron is specifically made in the story of Poe's "Herculean" swim in the James River: "Byron's paddle across the Hellespont was mere child's play in comparison and, indeed, would never have been thought worthy of mention, by any true swimmer, or by any other than a lord and dandy" (Pollin 1993, 171).

CONTRASTING CONTEMPORARY VIEWS

The image of Poe projected by the *Saturday Museum* is one of glamor and success (even his portrait, which accompanies the text, exudes confidence), but the reality was quite different. For much of his adult life, Poe was handicapped by poverty and a temperamental instability that found expression in periodic bouts of drinking. For many of his contemporaries, Poe was an ambiguous figure whose work and personality aroused conflicting responses. From the 1830s onward, he was widely recognized as a daring and innovative critic and story writer and, after the success of "The Raven," as a powerful and ingenious poet. In his biographical/critical essay "Edgar Allan Poe," written for *Graham's Magazine* in 1845, James Russell Lowell described Poe as a literary genius: "Mr. Poe has that indescribable something which men have agreed to call *genius*," and Lowell went on to anticipate great achievements from him: "When we say that Mr. Poe has genius, we do not mean to say that he has produced evidence of the highest. But to say that he possesses it at all is to say that he needs only zeal, industry, and a reverence for the trust reposed in him, to achieve the proudest triumphs and the greenest laurels" (*REAP*, 11; Walker, 162). By the time he came to write *A Fable for Critics* (1848), however, Lowell was rather more uncertain of Poe's literary standing:

> There comes Poe, with his raven, like Barnaby Rudge,
> Three fifths of him genius and two fifths sheer fudge,
> Who talks like a book of iambs and pentameters,
> In a way to make people of common sense damn metres,
> Who has written some things quite the best of their kind,

But the heart somehow seems all squeezed out by the mind
(Lowell 1848, 59)

The feeling that Poe's writings lacked "heart" was commonplace at the time;
it was developed, for example, by Philip Pendleton Cooke in his updating of
Lowell's essay for the *SLM* in 1848, where he expressed the hope that Poe
would write a "cheerful book . . . a book full of homely doings, of successful
toils . . . a book healthy and happy throughout" (Walker, 274). Lowell also
toned down his earlier enthusiasm for Poe in the revised version of "Edgar
Allan Poe" published by Griswold in 1850. He praised Poe's skillful exploitation of themes of mystery and terror but proclaimed, "The loftiest muse has
ever a household and fireside charm about her" and concluded by defining Poe's
limitations as a critic and presumably as a person: "As a critic, Mr. Poe was
aesthetically deficient. . . . he seemed wanting in the faculty of perceiving the
profounder ethics of art" (*REAP*, 16; Walker, 167).

A series of unfortunate events during the last three years of Poe's life dam-
aged his reputation both publicly and privately. His romantic friendship with
Mrs. Osgood during Virginia's illness inevitably led to gossip and hostility from
some of the New York literary set. His unwillingness to compose a new poem
for the prestigious Boston Lyceum reading and his subsequent mockery of his
audience did not enhance his professional standing. His series of articles on
Longfellow's "plagiarisms" also caused controversy, as did his "Literati" papers, notably, his personal attack on his former associate, Thomas Dunn English,
which provoked an equally personal and angry response. Poe's subsequent libel
suit against Hiram Fuller and the *New York Mirror* was successful, but comment
in the New York press was harmful to him. During the period of crisis leading
up to, and following, the death of Virginia in 1847, Poe seems to have had little
control over his drinking, and he was vilified in print by his enemies as a
drunken wretch. For example, in 1846, Thomas Dunn English wrote a savage
caricature of Poe in a novel entitled *1844; or, The Power of the "S.F.,"* printed
in the *New York Mirror:* He is recognizable as Marmaduke Hammerhead, a
pretentious and pedantic critic who is constantly abusive and drunk and who
ends up in an insane asylum raving about Thomas Carlyle. Again, in 1847, in
C. F. Briggs's newspaper novel, *The Trippings of Tom Pepper,* Poe appears as
Austin Wicks, a drunken, bragging critic who abuses women and reduces his
family "into a starving condition by his irregularities" (Moss, 194–202). Hiram
Fuller in the *New York Mirror* (July 20, 1846) was more pityingly explicit in
his description of Poe and Mrs. Clemm in New York City—"A Sad Sight":

A poor creature of this description [drunk], called at our office the other day, in a
condition of sad, wretched imbecility, bearing in his feeble body the evidences of evil
living, and betraying by his talk, such radical obliquity of sense, that every spark of
harsh feeling towards him was extinguished, and we could not even entertain a feeling
of contempt for one who was evidently committing a suicide upon his body, as he had

already done upon his character. Unhappy man! He was accompanied by an aged female relative, who was going a weary round in the hot streets, following his steps to prevent him indulging in a love of drink; but he had eluded her watchful eye by some means, and was already far gone in a state of inebriation. After listening awhile with painful feelings to his profane ribaldry, he left the office, accompanied by his good genius, to whom he owed the duties which she was discharging for him, and we muttered involuntarily, *"remote, unfriended, solitary alone."* (Moss, 70)

Grotesque distortions such as these appealed to popular temperance sentiment; they undoubtedly influenced public opinion and later filtered into Griswold's "Ludwig" notice and "Memoir," where they were given wide and apparently authoritative circulation.

REPORTS OF POE'S DEATH

Poe died in the Washington College Hospital, Baltimore, on October 7, 1849, from what news reports variously described as "congestion of the brain," "a melancholy attack," or "mania a potu." The precise circumstances of his death were not then, and are not now, readily determined. His cousin, Neilson Poe, who attended the funeral, wrote to Mrs. Clemm on October 11, saying that he could discover few particulars: "At what time he arrived in this city, where he spent the time he was here, or under what circumstances, I have been unable to ascertain" (*AQ*, 642). Nevertheless, various stories later appeared full of sensational details about Poe's unhappy end.

Joseph E. Snodgrass

In 1856, Dr. Joseph E. Snodgrass wrote a harrowing account of how he had been called on to rescue Poe from a disreputable bar; the poet, who was "utterly stupefied with liquor," had been apparently robbed of his clothing and was now dressed in a coarse and unseemly manner; he was too drunk to speak, "mere mutterings were all that were heard," and he had to be carried out "as if a corpse" (*PoeL*, 845). But Snodgrass was a strong advocate of temperance; his story first appeared in a temperance paper and was evidently designed as an awful warning against the dangers of drink. In a second account, written eighteen years after the event, Snodgrass remarkably recalled details of Poe's wretched footwear and his "muttering some scarcely intelligible oaths, and other forms of imprecation upon those who were trying to rescue him from destitution and disgrace" (*H* 1, 333).

Dr. John Moran

Another unreliable witness to Poe's end was Dr. John Moran, the resident physician at Washington College Hospital who treated Poe and was potentially a source of deathbed information. Moran wrote to Mrs. Clemm on October 15, telling what he knew of Poe's last hours: the poet was admitted in a state of delirium; when he briefly returned to consciousness, Moran questioned him— "But his answers were incoherent & unsatisfactory"; then he he called for someone named "Reynolds" throughout the night (*PoeL,* 846). The name "Reynolds" stirred the interest of later Poe biographers (Allen 2, 846; *AQ,* 640), though he may have been a figment of Moran's imagination (Bandy 1987, 31). By 1885, however, Dr. Moran remembered these events quite differently and wrote at some length to say so. He claimed that Poe was not admitted to the hospital under the influence of drink; moreover, "In the latter part of his life, four years previous to his death, he was perfectly temperate" (Moran, 30). Moran then went on to invent an elaborate deathbed drama in which Poe rather gloomily affirmed his belief in the afterlife and upheld the temperance ideal— Moran offered the poet a medicinal glass of toddy: "He opened wide his eyes, and fixed them so steadily upon me, and with anguish in them that I had to look from him to the wall beyond the bed. He then said, 'Sir, if I thought its potency would transport me to the Elysian bowers of the undiscovered spirit world, I would not take it' " (Moran, 65).

John R. Thompson

Another fanciful story concerning Poe's death claimed that he was a victim of political violence, probably because he was found at Gunner's Hall, a Baltimore tavern, which was also used as a polling station. T. O. Mabbott traced this legend back to John R. Thompson's lecture on "The Genius and Character of Edgar Allan Poe," in which he said that Poe was "seized by lawless agents of a political club, imprisoned in a cellar . . . and next day in a state bordering on frenzy made to vote in eleven different wards" (*M* 1, 569). In 1874, W. Hand Browne sent John Ingram a version of the same story (Miller 1977, 68–69). Mabbott dismissed the whole episode as "twaddle"; but it was circulated in Poe biographies for many years (Ingram, 427; Gill, 237–38; Didier, 74; Allen 1926, 672). The attraction of this story for Poe's apologists is that it transfers responsibility for his wretched end to an external source and establishes him as a victim rather than a culprit.

OBITUARY AND RELATED NOTICES

The Temperance Press

Poe's contemporary reputation was influenced by his lifestyle, and this was reflected in obituary notices. His death was immediately seized upon by a press sensitive to the pervasive influence of the temperance movement as a prime example of a life and career ruined by drink and self-indulgence. This was the message behind the brief notice in the *Boston Evening Transcript* of October 9:

"He had talents, with which he might have done great things, had he united to them stable principles, earnest purposes and self-denying habits" (Pollin 1986, 157), and the notice in the *Baltimore Patriot* said much the same: "It is deeply to be deplored that his great powers, which might have enabled him to soar so high and to have acquired for himself so much of fame and popularity, were obscured and crippled by the frailties and weaknesses which have too often attended eminent genius in all ages" (Walker, 305). In papers formally identified with the temperance movement, the moral of Poe's death was driven home. The *Journal of the American Temperance Union,* for instance, declared: "Edgar A. Poe, author of the 'Raven' and other poetical writings, recently died of a melancholy attack in a hospital in Baltimore—alas! for brandy and poetry," while readers of the *New York Organ* were offered an awful warning: "Think of Poe's miserable end, and then resolve to touch not, taste not the cup that poisoned him. When tempted to break your pledge, point to that grave and answer, No, never!" (Pollin 1986, 158).

Rufus Griswold's "Ludwig"

Most influential in defining Poe's character and significance at the time of his death was the notice written by Rufus Griswold under the pseudonym "Ludwig" for the *New York Daily Tribune* of October 9. It began by starkly declaring that while Poe's death might be a loss to literature, on a personal level few would miss him: "Edgar Allan Poe is dead. He died in Baltimore the day before yesterday. This announcement will startle many, *but few will be grieved by it.* The poet was well known personally or by reputation, in all this country; he had readers in England, and in several of the states of Continental Europe; *but he had few or no friends* (*REAP*, 28; Walker, 294). It depicted Poe as a wild, alienated figure, a "dreamer—dwelling in ideal realms—in heaven or hell," a lost soul who "walked the streets, in madness or melancholy, with lips moving in indistinct curses," whose "harsh experience had deprived him of all faith in man or woman" (*REAP*, 32–33; Walker, 299–300). Griswold completed his caricature by likening Poe to Francis Vivian, the cynical reprobate in Bulwer-Lytton's novel *The Caxtons.* Although the "Ludwig" article is cruel and melodramatic, it does represent an important strand of contemporary opinion, and Griswold did not consider that he had been unfair. In his subsequent "Memoir," he defended his "very kind article," and, in reply to a mild rebuke from Sarah Helen Whitman ("I cannot doubt the justice of your remarks, although my personal experience would lead me to think his disposition more gentle and more gracious than you esteem it to be"), he declared: "I was not his friend, nor was he mine, as I remember to have told you; but I endeavoured always to do him justice; and though the sketch has been deemed harsh, I did not mean that it should be so" (Bayless, 173).

Henry B. Hirst, George Lippard, Lambert Wilmer

Griswold's attack on Poe and his assertion that he died friendless did not go unchallenged, especially by writers whom Poe had known and worked with in Philadelphia. Henry Hirst, who claimed to have known Poe "perhaps better than any other man living, and loved him, despite his infirmities," declared him "a man of great and original genius" brought low by poverty and literary neglect (Walker, 313–17). George Lippard also strongly defended Poe's character: "[H]e was a man of genius—a man of high honor—a man of good heart. He was not an intemperate man" (Walker, 317–19); while Lambert Wilmer denounced Griswold's notice in unequivocal terms: "Some circumstances mentioned by the slanderous hypocrite we *know* to be false, and we have no doubt in the world that nearly all of his statements intended to throw odium and discredit on the character of the deceased are scandalous inventions"; but Wilmer had no hard facts, and he later admitted: "I do not know that this *vindication* was copied by a single paper; whereas the whole press of the country seemed desirous of giving circulation and authenticity to the slanders" (Wilmer, 25–26).

N. P. Willis, Frances Osgood

Effective responses to Griswold also came from N. P. Willis and Frances Osgood, both of whom attempted to create alternative and more socially agreeable images of Poe. Writing from personal experience and offering letters to support his case, Willis presented Poe as an exemplary figure—"quiet, patient, industrious, and most gentlemanly person, commanding the utmost respect and good feeling by his unvarying deportment and ability." As for Poe's "lamentable irregularities," Willis knew from "hearsay" that these were the result of a "sad infirmity of physical constitution," which caused him to become "palpably insane," a "reversed character," after a "*single glass* of wine." Clearly, Poe should then be seen as the victim of an unfortunate constitution, rather than as a confirmed inebriate. Willis also appealed to the sentimental appetites of the readers of the *Home Journal* when he described the devotion to Poe of the "beautiful and saintly" Mrs. Clemm, "one of those angels upon earth that women in adversity can be." Willis then went on to ask, "[W]hat does not a devotion like this—pure, disinterested, and holy as the watch of an invisible spirit—say for him who inspired it?" (Walker, 307–12). Frances Osgood, who was close to both Poe and Griswold, also described Poe's domestic harmony at Fordham and recalled him as a charming gentleman: "I have never *seen* him otherwise than gentle, generous, well-bred and fastidiously refined. To a sensitive and delicately nurtured woman, there was a peculiar, an irresistible charm in the chivalric, graceful and almost tender reverence with which he invariably approached all women who won his respect" (Pollin 1990, 31). Curiously, Griswold later incorporated Mrs. Osgood's recollections into his own "Memoir," though he concealed the original publication and pretended they had been written especially for him.

John Daniel

Despite the "Ludwig" article, Griswold was invited by Mrs. Clemm to superintend the publication of a collected edition of Poe's writings—he was a successful editor and had many contacts in the publishing world. Griswold persuaded his friend J. S. Redfield to take on the project, and the first two volumes were ready by January 1850. Many of the reviewers, however, seemed more concerned with Poe's personality than with his writings, and old enmities and loyalties reemerged. For example, John Daniel fueled the controversy in Richmond about Poe's status and character. He pronounced Poe a genius: "These half told tales and broken poems are the only records of a wild, hard life; and all that is left of a real genius,—genius in the true sense of the word, unmistakable and original. No other American has half a chance of a remembrance in the history of literature" (Walker, 357); but he also stressed Poe's social and moral defects, his "Ishmaelite" behavior, and his dreadful drinking habits (quite different from Willis's one glass): "Whenever he tasted alcohol he seldom stopped drinking it as long as he was able. He did drink most barbarously" (Walker, 364).

John Neal and George Graham

Reviews by John Neal and George Graham caused Griswold particular irritation, because they not only repudiated his characterization of Poe but also questioned his integrity as an editor. Writing in the *Portland Advertiser* (April 1850), Neal claimed that Poe had been "greatly misunderstood, and greatly misrepresented, for many years before he vanished from our midst" (Walker, 385) and that Griswold, "a Radamanthus," was entirely unfitted to be his literary executor. George Graham, who claimed to have known Poe better than Griswold had (he had employed them both), rejected Griswold's characterization as a lie, "a fancy sketch of a perverted, jaundiced vision" (Walker, 377), and recalled Poe "in his better days," much as Willis had done, as a figure of integrity and domestic virtue:

For three or four years I knew him intimately, and for eighteen months saw him almost daily, much of the time writing or conversing at the same desk, knowing all his hopes, his fears, and little annoyances of life, as well as his high-hearted struggle with adverse fate; yet he was always the same polished gentleman, the quiet unobtrusive, thoughtful scholar, the devoted husband, frugal in his personal expenses, punctual and unwearied in his industry, *and the soul of honor* in all his transactions. (Walker, 379)

GRISWOLD'S "MEMOIR"

The third volume of Poe's *Works* appeared in September 1850, containing "Marginalia" and the "Literati" papers, together with Griswold's new "Memoir" of the dead writer. Griswold admitted to Mrs. Whitman that he had not been on friendly terms with Poe; his dislike probably went back to Poe's hostile notices of *The Poets and Poetry of America,* but there may also have been more private reasons for their estrangement (Benton, 15). Griswold was clearly angry that his "kind" obituary notice had been publicly branded as malicious by Neal and Graham, so he now produced "evidence" to support his claim that Poe was a reprobate. The "Memoir" reads like a temperance tract, which, in a way, it is, being the story of a life ruined by drink, and Griswold cleverly exploited the feelings of an audience deeply imbued with temperance sympathies. He littered his text with stories, often either fabricated or distorted, of opportunities lost through dissipation—for example, his largely invented account of how Poe lost his post on the *SLM:* "On receiving a month's salary he gave himself up to habits which only necessity had restrained at Baltimore. For a week he was in a condition of brutish drunkenness, and Mr. White dismissed him" (Griswold, xxx). Griswold also fabricated a story of Poe behaving disgracefully on the eve of his announced marriage to "one of the most brilliant women of New England": "He left town the same evening, and the next day was reeling through the streets of the city which was the lady's home, and in the evening—that should have been the evening before the bridal—in his drunkenness he committed at her house such outrages as made necessary a summons of the police" (Griswold, xlvi). Griswold again highlighted this fictional episode in an unsigned review of his own edition in the *Westminster Review* (January 1852); but, on this occasion, W. J. Pabodie, Mrs. Whitman's friend and adviser, wrote a letter to the *New York Tribune* (June 2, 1852) completely denying Griswold's allegations (Gill, 219–21; *AQ,* 679–80)—though it is likely that a letter to a paper would be overlooked or soon forgotten, while Griswold's travesty seemed to possess authority.

Griswold's "Memoir" also made it clear that Poe's "melancholy history" was self-inflicted, the result largely of "voluntary faults in conduct"; accordingly, it was the responsibility of the biographer to draw out the moral lesson of his life story: "His career is full of instruction and warning, and it has always been made a portion of the penalty of wrong that its anatomy should be displayed for the common study and advantage" (Griswold, xlvii). Griswold argued, moreover, that Poe's moral deficiencies were reflected in his morally empty writings: "Poe exhibits scarcely any virtue in either his life or his writings. Probably there is not another instance in the literature of our language in which so much has been accomplished without a recognition or a manifestation of conscience" (Griswold, xlvii). This argument—that Poe's life and hence his writings lacked moral direction—would be restated many times and widely circulated in America and Britain during the next half century. According to Griswold, one of the proofs of Poe's lack of moral standards was his tendency to plagiarism: "Indeed some of his plagiarisms are scarcely paralleled for their audacity in all literary history" (Griswold, xlviii). It is ironic that, while Griswold was accusing Poe of plagiarism and tampering with documents, he himself was engaged in the same occupation: he certainly altered and probably forged letters and papers to his advantage and to Poe's discredit. (*AQ*, 669–70).

There was little public dissent from Griswold's caricature of Poe; he had been appointed Poe's literary executor, and doubtless many thought that he was in possession of the facts. Also, some friends and associates had already written in Poe's defense when the "Ludwig" article appeared, while others, particularly his women friends, may well have been wary of involving themselves in potentially controversial debate. Mrs. Whitman, for instance, knew from Pabodie that Griswold could be vicious and unscrupulous when contradicted. In October 1850, George Graham promised readers of his magazine a series of articles "from the leading writers of the country, upon the life and character of Edgar A. Poe . . . for the purpose of putting before the country these generous tributes to the dead poet and critic." By December, however, he had scrapped the plan: "The wounds made by his criticisms are too fresh—the conflicting interests too many, to hope now to do that justice which time and sober second thought of educated minds will accord to his memory" (Bayless, 188–89).

George Gilfillan

Griswold belatedly completed his edition of Poe in 1856; thereafter, the "Memoir" was reprinted almost every year until 1871. In Britain, too, Griswold's caricature attracted a good deal of interest. The "Memoir" was first pirated by Vizetelly in 1852; but also a number of biographical sketches and essays by British commentators during the 1850s helped to confirm and circulate Griswold's story. For example, the influential Scottish critic George Gilfillan denounced Poe in 1854 as "no more a gentleman than he was a saint. His heart was as rotten as his conduct was infamous. He knew not what the terms honour and honourable meant. He had absolutely no virtue or good quality." He was, Gilfillan claimed, "as licentious as he was intemperate" and had broken his wife's heart and constitution, "hurrying her to a premature grave, that he might write 'Annabel Lee' and 'The Raven.' " That Gilfillan was a Presbyterian minister is reflected in his notion that Poe had submitted to diabolical possession ("the bound victim of infernal influence") and in his excited description of Poe's unhallowed end: "He died, as he had lived, a raving, cursing, self-condemned, conscious cross between the fiend and the genius, believing nothing, hoping nothing, loving nothing, fearing nothing" (Gilfillan, 153–57).

DEFENSES OF POE

Sarah Helen Whitman

In the "Preface" to *Edgar Poe and His Critics* (1860), Sarah Helen Whitman summarized Poe's standing in the decade following his death: "Dr. Griswold's memoir of Edgar Poe has been extensively read and circulated; its perverted facts and baseless assumptions have been adopted into every subsequent memoir and notice of the poet, and have been translated into many languages. For ten years this great wrong to the dead has passed unchallenged and unrebuked." Mrs. Whitman waited until after Griswold's death in 1857 to venture publicly in Poe's defense, and then she wrote about his life only in general terms. She criticized Griswold for his "remorseless violations of the trust confided to him" and denounced his narrative as "notoriously deficient in the great essentials of candor and authenticity" (Whitman, 14). Her own recollections of Poe dwelt on his "habitual courtesy and good-nature," his domestic happiness and his spirituality, "may we not say his *unearthliness* of nature" (Whitman 25, 44). More important at this time, when Poe's work was not generally held in high esteem in America, Mrs. Whitman asserted Poe's greatness as a writer; she recognized the importance of loss and remembrance in his work and affirmed his centrality to the literature of his time:

Then, sadder, and lonelier, and more unbelieving than any of these [English Romantic poets], Edgar Poe came to sound the very depths of the abyss. The unrest and faithlessness of the age culminated in him. Nothing so solitary, nothing so hopeless, nothing so desolate as his spirit in its darker moods has been instanced in the literary history of the nineteenth century. (Whitman, 65)

Charles Baudelaire

The 1850s in France saw the beginnings of a quite different Poe legend. When, in 1846 or 1847, Charles Baudelaire first encountered fragments of Poe's work, he felt, he later recalled, "une commotion singulière. . . . Et alors je trouvais, . . . des poèmes et des nouvelles dont j'avais eu la pensée, mais vague et confuse, mal ordonnée, et que Poe avait su combiner et mener à la perfection" (Bandy 1973, xvi). Baudelaire became obsessed with Poe, whom he thought he resembled both in his tragic life and in his views on art and society. He eagerly sought editions of his tales and poems and learned what he could about his life. Remarkably, he discovered in Paris files of the *SLM* 1849–1850 containing articles on Poe by J. R. Thompson and John Daniel. His first long essay on "Edgar Allan Poe: sa vie et ses ouvrages" appeared in the *Revue de Paris* in 1852; it was then revised to introduce his translations of Poe's tales, *Histoires Extraordinaires* (1856). Baudelaire's third essay, "Notes nouvelles sur Edgar Poe," served as the preface to his second volume of translations entitled *Nouvelles Histoires Extraordinaires* (1857). Although Baudelaire had no new facts about Poe (he relied largely for his information on Daniel and Thompson), his interpretation of Poe's character and significance was quite different from theirs and Griswold's. He refused to accept the characterization of the "pedagogue-vampire" by Griswold; instead, he presented Poe to French readers as a victim and martyr:

All the documents that I have read lead to the conviction that for Poe the United States was nothing more than a vast prison which he traversed with the feverish agitation of a being made to breathe a sweeter air,—nothing more than a great gas-lighted nightmare,—and that his inner, spiritual life, as a poet or even as a drunkard, was nothing but a perpetual effort to escape the influence of this unfriendly atmosphere. (Baudelaire, 1856; Hyslop, 91)

Even Poe's drinking habits were accounted for in a positive, creative manner: "I believe that often, . . . Poe's drunkenness was a mnemonic means, a method of work, drastic and fatal, but adapted to his passionate nature. The poet had learned to drink, just as a careful writer takes pains to keep notes" (Baudelaire, 1856; Hyslop, 114). For Baudelaire, Poe had faced up to and articulated key nineteenth-century insights into human nature: "But more important than anything else: we shall see that this author, product of a century infatuated with itself, child of a nation more infatuated with itself than all others, has clearly seen, has imperturbably affirmed the natural wickedness of man" (Baudelaire, 1857; Hyslop, 125).

For sixteen years, Baudelaire strove to make Poe a great writer in France, and he succeeded in his endeavors. His image of Poe as the alienated artist struggling in an uncaring, utilitarian environment attracted Mallarmé and the Symboliste writers; and his translations inspired French scholars such as Lauvrière, Mauclair, and Marie Bonaparte to undertake wide-ranging and exacting studies of Poe's work, while his writings were still relatively neglected in America.

J. H. INGRAM AND HIS RIVALS

A significant contribution to the development of Poe biography was made by John Henry Ingram, an English civil servant working in London. Ingram read an account of Poe in *Chambers's Journal* in 1853 when he was twenty-one; thereafter, he claimed that he "adored him" and "longed to write his life" (Miller 1979, 11). Ingram, like Baudelaire, became obsessed with Poe (he even changed his year of birth from 1842 to 1849 to coincide with Poe's death) and, in the early 1870s, began his lifelong mission to establish the facts of Poe's life and rescue his reputation from "Griswold's filthy lies" (Miller 1977, 2). He conducted an extensive and intense correspondence with those who had known Poe intimately—notably, Sarah Helen Whitman, Annie Richmond, and Marie Louise Shew Houghton—in a quest for information that would help to clear Poe's name. From the ensuing flow of letters, documents, clippings, and photographs, Ingram constructed his defense of Poe; his "Memoir" prefaced his edition of Poe's *Works* (1874–1875), and it was expanded into a two-volume *Life, Letters and Opinions* in 1880. In his biography, Ingram printed a good deal of new Poe correspondence and was able to expose some of Griswold's distortions concerning Poe's life at university, his time at West Point, the circumstances of the *Saturday Visiter* competition, and his engagement to Sarah Helen Whitman. Ingram also made a comprehensive survey of Poe's literary productions and was sensitive to the private implications of some of the texts. In his discussion of "Berenice," for instance, he writes: "We find, as in so many of his youthful works, constant allusions to hereditary traits and visions of ancestral glories; but these boyish dreams are not, as generally supposed, referable to paternal but to maternal bygone splendors: to Arnheim—to the *hold* or *home* of the Arns (i.e., the Arnolds)" (Ingram 1880, 1: 116). But Ingram was not an altogether reliable biographer; he was passionately involved with his materials, and his intention was to defend Poe's character rather than to create an impartial account of his life and work. Consequently, he glossed over Poe's "frailties" and other shortcomings, repressed material that did not suit his purposes, and generally cast his subject in a romantic and idealistic light. His description of Poe's school days in Richmond illustrates his tone:

Admired by his fellow students for his superior educational attainments, his daring athletic feats, and for a certain magnetic rather than sympathetic influence which he exercised over them, it is not surprising to learn that he was introduced into, and mingled with, the best society of the Old Dominion. In the coteries into which he was received was a little maiden but a year or two younger than himself, who speedily became fascinated by the charms of his presence. (Ingram 1880, 1: 39)

Eugene Didier, William F. Gill

Ingram was highly proprietary about his materials and contacts and deeply resentful of what he saw as the intrusions of American competitors (William Gill, Eugene Didier, and R. H. Stoddard) into his private domain. Mrs. Whitman not only corresponded voluminously with Ingram but also wrote and sent materials to Gill and Didier, much to Ingram's annoyance, and, when their biographies appeared in 1877, he reviewed them with hostility and contempt. In reality, however, Ingram had little to fear from his American rivals, who were careless with facts and amateurish in approach: Didier claimed that Poe's parents had died in the fire that destroyed Richmond Theatre and gave undue credence to the recollections of figures like Joseph H. Clarke, Poe's Richmond schoolteacher, who claimed in old age to remember in detail his twelve-year-old pupil's mastery of Greek and Latin. In his "Preface," Gill declared: "It has been the aim of the writer to give an unpartisan transcript of the life and character of Edgar Allan Poe" (Gill, iv), but his plan was not successful. Although his biography does contain some new material, notably from Thomas C. Clarke of the Philadelphia *Saturday Museum,* Gill was primarily interested in vindicating Poe's memory, and, like Ingram and Didier, he was reluctant to confront the darker side of Poe's character and relationships.

Richard Henry Stoddard

Stoddard, however, had little good to say of Poe, whom he had encountered in the office of the *Broadway Journal* in 1845, and, thirty years later in his "Memoir," he recalled what he considered Poe's erratic and inconsiderate treatment of his youthful poetic efforts. Stoddard had been friendly with Griswold, and he continued his negative and hostile characterization of Poe. He lost no opportunity to point out Poe's weaknesses of character and sometimes described situations he could not possibly have known anything about, as when he writes about Poe's childhood relations with his foster parents: "[Poe] quickly detected the weak points of his adopted parents, and took advantage of them, so much so that dissimulation and evasion became habitual with him" (Stoddard, 27).

GRISWOLD'S LEGACY

Henry James

It was widely accepted in later nineteenth-century America that Poe's writings reflected his personality and that he lacked the essential moral seriousness required for the creation of great literature. Henry James expressed something of this view in his 1876 review of Baudelaire:

For American readers, furthermore, Baudelaire is compromised by his having made himself the apostle of our own Edgar Poe. He translated, very carefully and exactly, all of Poe's prose writings, and, we believe, some of his very valueless verses. With all due respect to the very original genius of the author of the "Tales of Mystery," it seems to us that to take him with more than a certain degree of seriousness is to lack seriousness one's self. An enthusiasm for Poe is the mark of a decidedly primitive stage of reflection. (Carlson 1966, 65–66)

Later in his career, however, James seems to have found more to value in Poe's writings: in the first chapter of *The Golden Bowl* (1904), Prince Amerigo "remembered to have read, as a boy, a wonderful tale by Allan Poe . . . which was a thing to show, by the way, what imagination Americans *could* have—the story of the shipwrecked Gordon Pym" (Pollin 1986, 199; *REAP*, 65).

Walt Whitman

For the ceremonies to commemorate the dedication of the Poe Monument in Baltimore in 1875, Stéphane Mallarmé contributed his sonnet on "Le Tombeau d'Edgar Poe" (*REAP*, 64–65); from England came a version of Ingram's new and sympathetic Poe biography and an enthusiastic letter of support from Charles Swinburne; but Poe's eminent contemporaries, the "household" poets, Bryant, Whittier, Longfellow, and Holmes, sent only brief, noncommittal notes

(Rice, 65–92). The only writer of lasting significance to attend the ceremony was Walt Whitman, and he declined to participate. Writing in *Specimen Days* (1880), Whitman recalled the occasion and his feelings about Poe's work: "For a long while, and until lately, I had a distaste for Poe's writings. I wanted, and still want for poetry, the clear sun shining, and the fresh air blowing—the strength and power of health, not of delirium, even amid the stormiest passions—with always the background of the eternal moralities" (Carlson 1966, 75). Many of Whitman's American readers would probably have agreed with these sentiments. In 1893, the *New York Critic* conducted a poll of the "best" American texts; Emerson's essays headed the list, followed by *The Scarlet Letter*; Poe's name did not appear in the top ten, which the English critic Edmund Gosse thought "extraordinary and sinister." Whitman's friend John Burroughs defended the American readers' choice in terms similar to those employed by Lowell in 1848: compared with Longfellow or Whittier, "[Poe] had less heart, less soul, less sympathy,—in fact, was far less a man, a human being. . . . But back of his literary and artistic talent what is there? Hardly any normal, healthful human throb; hardly one valuable idea" (Burroughs, 214).

NEW SCHOLARSHIP

George E. Woodberry

The first scholarly biography of Poe was written by George E. Woodberry in 1885 for the "American Men of Letters" series. Woodberry had been trained in historical scholarship at Harvard (Henry Adams and Charles Eliot Norton were among his teachers), and he claimed to have approached his subject with an open mind: "My attention had never been drawn to Poe, nor my interest specially excited by his works" (Woodberry 1909, 1: v). Woodberry planned to write an objective study: "[T]he author has made this, so far as was possible, a documentary biography, has verified all facts positively stated at first hand" (Woodberry 1885, vi). He avoided gossip and unsupported recollections, consulted a wider range of published and unpublished sources than his predecessors, and presented his findings in a scrupulously professional manner. Woodberry also unearthed new information about Poe's military experience: Ingram had maintained on information supplied by Mrs. Houghton that Poe had spent the period 1827–1828 on a romantic expedition to Europe; Gill cast doubt on this story, and Woodberry revealed that Poe had, in fact, enlisted in the army as "Edgar A. Perry." However, although Woodberry was scholarly in his methods, he sometimes had difficulty in appreciating Poe's artistry and was critical of some of his achievements: he declared that *Eureka* "affords one of the most striking instances in literature of a naturally strong intellect tempted by overweening pride to an Icarian flight and betrayed, notwithstanding its merely specious knowledge, into an ignoble exposure of its own presumption and ignorance" (Woodberry 1885, 300). Moreover, as his narrative progressed,

Woodberry's distaste for Poe's personality grew stronger, and, in his final chapter, he summed up Poe's life in a manner reminiscent of Griswold (whose "Ludwig" article he admired as "a piece of writing that has the power of genius"):

[Poe] repeatedly forfeited prosperity and even the homely honor of an honest man. He ate opium and drank liquor; whatever was the cause, these were instruments of his ruin, and before half his years were run they had done their work with terrible thoroughness— he was a broken man. He died under circumstances of exceptional ugliness, misery, and pity, but not accidentally, for the end and the manner of it were clearly near and inevitable. (Woodberry 1885, 348)

In 1909, the Poe centenary year, Woodberry revised and extended his biography into two volumes entitled *The Life of Edgar Allan Poe, Personal and Literary*. Much new information concerning Poe's literary career and milieu had come to light since 1885, notably from the papers of Chivers, Lowell, Griswold, and Snodgrass, and this material was now carefully edited and incorporated into the new biography. Woodberry again adopted a documentary approach and claimed that "this biography seems the work really of many hands rather than of my own, and my part mainly that of investigation and arrangement" (Woodberry 1909, 1: vii). Woodberry's attitude to Poe's personality mellowed over the years; he now omitted his harsh assessment of 1885 and, instead, concluded his biography with positive and generous tributes to Poe's gentlemanly character by those who had known him well, including J. P. Kennedy, George Graham, N. P. Willis, and Frances Osgood. Because of its scholarship, independence, and critical discrimination, Woodberry's *Life* still remains one of the most reliable of Poe biographies.

James A. Harrison

James A. Harrison, the distingushed philologist and editor of Poe's writings, contributed a biography to the Virginia edition of 1902. Harrison was content, however, to follow in the general direction of Ingram, Didier, and Gill; he evidently saw his task as "placing fairly before the people the bright side of the character of the poet Poe" (*H* 1, 320); consequently, he avoided unsavory episodes that could discredit Poe's character, preferring to concentrate on sentimental scenes, especially of his life in Virginia: "Little Edgar's childhood and youth were passed in an atmosphere of sociability, open-air sports, oratory, and elocution" (*H* 1, 13). Harrison was surprisingly uncritical of his sources and relied heavily on friendly, though often unverifiable, recollections of Poe by elderly people looking backward, in some cases, over seventy years. His critical sense was not strong, as is evidenced by his comments on the relationship between Poe's army experience and his literary style: "Perhaps the precision of the army routine had something to do with the growing precision of Poe's style, a precision which grew on him while he lived and which is sometimes in his more faultless prose almost painful'' (*H* 1, 72).

POPULAR BIOGRAPHIES

Mary E. Phillips

Mary Phillips's *Edgar Allan Poe—The Man* was one of three new Poe biographies published in 1926. It is very long (1,685 pages) and heavily weighed down by an excess of secondary materials from which she quoted extensively and indiscriminately. It is also poorly organized, strangely written, and lacking in scholarly method; Ms. Phillips apparently believed almost any legend about Poe, provided it was to his credit. She was also entirely uncritical of Poe's personality and employed current psychological theories, probably derived from Robertson's psychoanalytical biography of 1923, to support her claim that his behavior patterns were the result of a nervous disorder: ''Hypersensitive nerve heritage marked Poe as abnormally sensitive to *all* stimulants; and stranded in such shallows by the effects of mental shocks on his *physique* from the age of fifteen, this nervous malady grew with years into spells of depression. . . . Consequences on this score should absolve such victims from responsibility in breaking all the Ten Commandments'' (Phillips, 2, 1600). However, despite its faults, *Edgar Allan Poe—The Man* is an interesting compendium of opinion on Poe by those who remembered him (or thought they did) and a valuable pictorial record of his life.

Hervey Allen

Hervey Allen's *Israfel: The Life and Times of Edgar Allan Poe* also appeared in 1926 in two substantial volumes (it was revised and issued in one volume in 1934, with an offending wine glass excised from the portrait of Longfellow). Allen was a professional author, and his work is better organized and better written than that of Phillips. He consulted some primary sources, including the Ellis and Allan papers, for information on Poe's childhood and youth and took advantage of recent scholarship, such as T. O. Mabbott's work on Poe's relations with his elder brother. Allen also examined with care the intellectual and physical environment in which Poe worked and gathered together useful information on his relations with his literary contemporaries, such as George Graham, Henry B. Hirst, John Neal, and F. W. Thomas. He had a relatively nonjudgmental attitude toward Poe's drinking; but he did raise questions about his marriage and sexuality resulting from a supposed addiction to opium. Allen's approach to his subject, however, was essentially romantic and dramatic, as his chapter headings indicate—''The Two Orphans,'' ''Lady Bountiful Claims Israfel,'' ''Israfel Salutes the Marquis,'' ''Elmira and the Enchanted Garden,'' ''A Handkerchief Soaked in Ether,'' ''Lenore and the Edge of the World,'' and so on.

He also adopted fictional techniques to heighten the dramatic effect, for example, his description of the Clemm household in 1829:

Grandma Poe would be drawn up close to the small coal fire, and they would discuss the last depressing letter from ''Pa'' in Richmond, while Virginia chattered, or did her sums with ''Cousin Eddie'' to help. Then bed-time . . . Henry complaining, and coughing himself into a restless slumber, while Edgar, as long as the candle lasted, bent over his papers, driving the pen on and on toward that far-off shining goal. He was arrested at last by the midnight ghosts of ''Helen'' and Elmira, or his dear ''Ma'' with the agate lamp in her hand in the old house on Tobacco Alley. (Allen 1934, 205–6)

PSYCHOANALYTICAL VIEWS

Emile Lauvrière, John W. Robertson

From the early years of the century, Poe attracted detailed psychoanalytical criticism. In 1904, Emile Lauvrière published a long-winded thesis entitled *Edgar Poe: sa vie et son oeuvre. Étude de psychologie pathologique,* which claimed (unsuccessfully) to show that Poe was insane; his readings of the French alienists convinced him that Poe was a victim of brain degeneration brought about by inherited tendencies to alcohol and opiate abuse. He naively identified Poe with characters in his stories, such as the deranged Egeus in ''Berenice'' and William Wilson, and unwisely relied on Griswold as his primary source of biographical information.

John W. Robertson in *Poe: A Psychopathic Study* (1923) disagreed with Lauvrière's analysis; instead, he argued that Poe revealed the classic symptoms of dypsomania, but his evidence was far from being conclusive: ''It must be remembered that in the life history of those who suffer from dypsomania, in addition to the craving for alcohol there are periods of both elation and depression. Often visionary schemes are undertaken without corresponding capacity to understand their real difficulties or impracticabilities'' (Robertson, 93).

Joseph Wood Krutch

Joseph Wood Krutch in *Edgar Allan Poe: A Study in Genius* (1926) also explained Poe as a victim of psychological degeneration. He argued that ''no more completely personal writer than Poe ever existed'' (Krutch, 17) and that his writings betray his obsessions and disappointments. Krutch speculated that Poe suffered from a sexual disorder connected to the traumatic loss of his mother: ''Poe could not love in the normal fashion and the reason lay, or at least seemed to him to lie, in the death of some woman upon whom his desire had irrecoverably fixed itself'' (Krutch, 62). This is not far removed from D. H. Lawrence's critique of Poe's abnormal love in *Studies in Classic American Literature* (1923): ''Doomed he was. He died wanting more love, and love killed him. A ghastly disease love'' (Carlson 1966, 126). Krutch also claimed that Poe felt a deep sense of social insecurity stemming from his expulsion from the Allan family home and fortune and that his literary ambitions were closely linked with attempts to regain what he thought of as his rightful status as an aristocrat.

Marie Bonaparte

The most exhaustive and influential psychoanalytical study of Poe is Marie Bonaparte's *Life and Works of Edgar Allan Poe,* published in Paris in 1933 and translated into English by John Rodker in 1949. Along with Krutch, she argued that Poe's life and writings were determined by infantile traumas related to the sickness and death of his mother: "Ever since he was three, in fact, Poe had been doomed by fate to live in constant mourning. A fixation on a dead mother was to bar him forever from earthly love, and make him shun health and vitality in his loved ones" (Bonaparte 1949, 83). This view of Poe's psychology has been adopted by Kenneth Silverman in his 1992 biography, aptly subtitled *Mournful and Never-Ending Remembrance.* Bonaparte believed that Poe's childhood trauma not only twisted his life—he was impotent and fearful of "sexual commerce"—but also completely invaded his imaginative writings, which she reads as compulsive elaborations of the same theme, as her section headings suggest: "The Life-in-Death Mother," "The Mother as Landscape," "The Confession of Impotence," and "Tales of the Murdered Mother." Bonaparte's arguments are ingenious, and they sometimes provide startling insights into Poe's treatment of women in his fiction, but, as Patrick F. Quinn and Roger Forclaz have pointed out, they blur the distinction between hypothesis and fact, and "to read Poe's stories and poems, as Mme Bonaparte does, as if they essentially were transcripts of dreams, is to do violence to psychoanalysis as well as to Poe" (*PQ,* 21).

ARTHUR HOBSON QUINN

Arthur Hobson Quinn brought high standards of academic scholarship to *Edgar Allan Poe, A Critical Biography* (1941). He incorporated into his work the scholarship that had accumulated since Woodberry's time, including his own researches into Poe's family background and his life in Philadelphia. Quinn went back to original letters and documents whenever possible and printed them fully and correctly, sometimes for the first time in the case of the correspondence Griswold tampered with or the letters to Annie Richmond, which Ingram had cut for reasons of delicacy. Quinn realized that Poe's letters were crucial for understanding his personality: "Poe's own letters are so interesting and reveal his nature so clearly that it seems to me impertinent to paraphrase them, or to present mere abstracts" (*AQ,* viii). He also studied Poe in his cultural context and clarified his relations "with the critics, editors and publishers who determined the conditions under which a creative artist of that time must live" (*AQ,* vii). Quinn's historical research and his scrupulous handling of documentary evidence are admirable, as is his determination to be fair to Poe and to eliminate the rumors and legends associated with him. Quinn had great respect for Poe, not only as a writer of genius but also as a figure of moral courage and honor. After surveying Poe's literary achievement arising out of a life of acute emotional and financial stress, he concluded:

When his weaknesses have been catalogued, however, there rises above them the real Edgar Poe, the industrious, honourable gentleman whom Graham and Willis knew, the warm friend and courteous host whom Hirst, Mayne Reed and many others remembered. There was the brilliant thinker—whose charm came from that inner radiance that shone upon Helen Whitman and Susan Talley. Those who knew him best, loved him best. His wife and mother adored the self-sacrificing, devoted husband and son. His friendships with Frances Osgood, Helen Whitman, Annie Richmond, Louise Shew, and Elmira Shelton, met the supreme test of separation under high emotional tension or even the embittered tongues of slander. Yet every one of them treasured the memory of his utter refinement and unfailing chivalry to her. (*AQ,* 694)

Quinn was unfailingly generous to Poe and consequently sometimes exaggerated his refinement and underestimated the more negative aspects of his character, such as his dependent and, at times, manipulative relationships with women or his drinking bouts, from which he even emerges with dignity: "The testimony of unimpeachable quality has been given already to show that for long periods Poe was absolutely sober. His hard fight against a temptation, stronger to him than to normal people, and his remorse when he yielded, . . . leave much to the credit side of Poe" (*AQ,* 693).

Quinn also held Poe in high esteem as a literary artist and made an extensive study of the full range of his literary activities as an editor, journalist, poet, novelist, short story writer, literary theorist, critic, and philosopher. He valued Poe as a poet and idealist thinker rather than as a fiction writer, and this is reflected in the six pages he gives to "Al Aaraaf" compared with the two pages on *Pym.* He was not very responsive to Poe's humor and satire; for instance, he dismissed "How to Write a Blackwood Article" as "interesting now mainly to those who seek Poe's sources" (*AQ,* 272) and was uneasy over Poe's exploitation of horror themes, preferring the gentler "Eleonora": "When the mood is spiritual, as in 'Eleonora,' the intellect yields to its guidance and the result is ideal. When the mood is horrible, as in 'Berenice,' the thought becomes diseased, and the intellect, being subverted to the mood, has no restraining influence" (*AQ,* 329). He also argued from deep conviction that *Eureka* (which had been scorned as nonsense by Woodberry) was the climax of Poe's creative achievement, a triumph of poetic, philosophical, and scientific analysis. Poe's vision of the universe in *Eureka* seemed to Quinn to be a "strangely modern" foreshadowing of the great discoveries of modern science, and he anticipated that it would be valued in years to come: "When that spiritual progress is fully understood, then perhaps at last *Eureka* will come into its own" (*AQ,* 557).

Through Quinn's work, most of the important facts of Poe's life were made known, and the distortions and errors perpetrated by earlier biographers were cleared up. In contrast to the outcast and reprobate of Griswold's legend or the emotionally disturbed neurotic created by Krutch and Bonaparte, Quinn emphasized Poe's normality and his strengths—his capacity for hard work, his brave struggles with poverty and a constitutional weakness for drink, his friendships, loyalties, and sense of responsibility toward his family. He argued that *Eureka* and "The Poetic Principle" prove that Poe's mental faculties did not diminish toward the end of his life; nor did his lyric gifts or his uncompromising commitment to his literary ideal: "It is for this great refusal, for his willingness to lay all things on the altar of his art, that Poe is most to be respected" (*AQ,* 695).

WORKS CITED

Allen, Hervey. *Israfel: The Life and Times of Edgar Allan Poe.* 2 vols. New York: George H. Doran, 1926.

———. *Israfel: The Life and Times of Edgar Allan Poe.* New York: Farrar and Rinehart, 1934.

Bandy, W. T., ed. *Edgar Allan Poe: sa vie et ses ouvrages.* Trans. Charles Baudelaire. Toronto: U of Toronto P, 1973.

———. "Dr. Moran and the Poe–Reynolds Myth." *Myths and Reality: The Mysterious Mr. Poe.* Ed. Benjamin F. Fisher IV. Baltimore: Edgar Allan Poe Society, 1987, 26–36.

Baudelaire, Charles. *Baudelaire on Poe.* Trans. Lois Hyslop and Francis Hyslop. State College, PA: Bald Eagle P, 1952.

Bayless, Joy. *Rufus Wilmot Griswold.* Nashville: Vanderbilt UP, 1943.

Benton, Richard. "Friends and Enemies: Women in the Life of Edgar Allan Poe." *Myths and Reality: The Mysterious Mr. Poe.* Ed. Benjamin F. Fisher IV. Baltimore: Edgar Allan Poe Society, 1987, 1–25.

Bonaparte, Marie. *Edgar Poe, étude psychanalytique.* 2 vols. Paris: Denoël et Steele, 1933.

———. *The Life and Works of Edgar Allan Poe: A Psycho-Analytic Interpretation.* Trans. John Rodker. London: Hogarth Press, 1949.

Burroughs, John. "Mr. Gosse's Puzzle over Poe." *Dial* 15 (Oct. 1893): 214–15.

Carlson, Eric W., ed. *The Recognition of Edgar Allan Poe.* Ann Arbor: U of Michigan P, 1966.

———. *Critical Essays on Edgar Allan Poe.* Boston: G. K. Hall, 1987.

Cooke, Philip Pendleton. "Edgar Allan Poe." *SLM* 14 (Jan. 1848): 34–38. Rpt. in Carlson 1966, 21–28; Walker, 269–76.

[Daniel, John Moncure]. "Edgar Allan Poe." *SLM* 16 (Mar. 1850): 172–87. Rpt. in Walker, 356–76.

Didier, Eugene. "Life of Edgar Allan Poe." *The Life and Poems of Edgar Allan Poe.* New York: W. J. Widdleton, 1877.

Forclaz, Roger. "Psychoanalysis and Edgar Allan Poe: A Critique of the Bonaparte Thesis." *CE* 1987, 187–95.

[Fuller, Hiram]. "A Sad Sight." *New York Evening Mirror,* July 20, 1849. Rpt. in Moss, 69–70.

Gilfillan, George. "Edgar Allan Poe." *Galleries of Literary Portraits.* Vol. 1. Edinburgh: James Hogg, 1856.

Gill, William F. *The Life of Edgar Allan Poe.* London: Chatto and Windus, 1876.

Graham, George R. "The Late Edgar Allan Poe." *Graham's Magazine* 36 (Mar. 1850): 224–26. Rpt. in Walker, 376–85.

Griswold, Rufus Wilmot. "Edgar A. Poe." *The Poets and Poetry of America.* Philadelphia: Carey and Hart, 1842.

[———]. "Ludwig." "Death of Edgar Allan Poe." *New York Tribune,* Oct. 9, 1849. Rpt. in Carlson 1966, 28–35; Walker, 294–302.

———. "Memoir of the Author." *The Works of the Late Edgar Allan Poe.* 3 vols. New York: J. S. Redfield, 1850–1853, 1: xxi–lv, 3: vii–xxxix.

Ingram, John Henry. "Memoir of Poe." *The Works of Edgar Allan Poe.* Vol. 1. Edinburgh: Adam and Charles Black, 1874.

———. *Edgar Allan Poe: His Life, Letters and Opinions.* 2 vols. London: John Hogg, 1880.

James, Henry. "Baudelaire." *French Poets and Novelists.* London: Macmillan, 1878. Rpt. in *REAP* 1966, 65–67.

Krutch, Joseph Wood. *Edgar Allan Poe: A Study in Genius.* New York: Knopf, 1926.

Lauvrière, Emile. *Edgar Poe, sa vie et son oeuvre: Étude de psychologie pathologique.* Paris: F. Alcan, 1904.

Lawrence, D. H. "Poe." *Studies in Classic American Literature.* New York: Boni, 1923, 93–120. Rpt. in *REAP*, 110–27.

Lowell, James Russell. "Our Contributors—No. xvii. Edgar Allan Poe." *Graham's Magazine* 27 (Feb. 1845): 49–53. Rpt. in *REAP*, 5–17; Walker, 156–68.

———. *A Fable for Critics.* New York: G. Putnam, 1848.

Miller, John Carl. *Building Poe Biography.* Baton Rouge: Louisiana State UP, 1977.

———, ed. *Poe's Helen Remembers.* Charlottesville: UP of Virginia, 1979.

Moran, John J. *A Defence of Edgar Allan Poe.* Washington, D.C.: W. F. Boogher, 1885.

Moss, Sidney P. *Poe's Major Crisis.* Durham, NC: Duke UP, 1970.

Neal, John. "Edgar A. Poe." *Portland Daily Advertiser,* April 26, 1850. Rpt. in Walker, 385–93.

Phillips, Mary E. *Edgar Allan Poe, The Man.* 2 vols. Philadelphia: John C. Winston, 1926.

[Poe, Edgar Allan]. "Edgar Allan Poe." *Philadelphia Saturday Museum,* Mar. 4, 1843. Rpt. in Pollin 1993, 163–71.

Pollin, Burton R. *Essays and Outlooks: Essays on Great Writers.* New York: Gordian P, 1986.

———. "Frances Sargent Osgood and *Saroni's Musical Times:* Documents Linking Poe, Osgood, and Griswold." *PoeS* 23 (Dec. 1990): 27–36.

———. "Poe's Authorship of Three Long Critical and Autobiographical Articles of 1843 Now Authenticated." *American Renaissance Literary Report* 7 (1993): 139–71.

Quinn, Patrick F. *The French Face of Edgar Poe.* Carbondale: Southern Illinois UP, 1957.

Rice, Sara S., ed. *Edgar Allan Poe: A Memorial Volume.* Baltimore: Turnbull, 1877.

Robertson, John W. *Edgar A. Poe: A Psychopathic Study.* New York: Putnam, 1923.

Stoddard, R. H. "Memoir." *Poems by Edgar Allan Poe.* London: Routledge, 1875.

Thompson, John R. *The Genius and Character of Edgar Allan Poe.* Ed. James A. Whitty and James H. Rindfleisch. Richmond: Garrett and Massie, 1929.

Walker, Ian M., ed. *Edgar Allan Poe: The Critical Heritage.* London: Routledge, 1986.

Whitman, Sarah Helen. *Edgar Poe and His Critics.* New York: Rudd and Carleton, 1860.

Whitman, Walt. "Edgar Poe's Significance." *Specimen Days & Collect.* Philadelphia: Rees Welsh, 1882–1883. Rpt. in *REAP*, 73–76.

Willis, Nathaniel Parker. "Death of Edgar A. Poe." *Home Journal* (Oct. 20, 1849). Rpt. in Carlson 1966, 35–41; Walker, 305–13.

Wilmer, Lambert. *Merlin; Baltimore, 1827; Together with Recollections of Edgar A. Poe by Lambert Wilmer.* Ed. with intro. by Thomas O. Mabbott. New York: Scholars' Facsimiles and Reprints, 1941.

Woodberry, George E. *Edgar Allan Poe.* American Men of Letters Series. Boston: Houghton Mifflin, 1885.

———. *The Life of Edgar Allan Poe, Personal and Literary.* 2 vols. Boston: Houghton Mifflin, 1909.

2

Modern Poe Biography and Its Resources

ALEXANDER HAMMOND

In their introduction to *The Poe Log: A Documentary Life of Edgar Allan Poe 1809–1849* (1987), Dwight Thomas and David K. Jackson justly observe that "Poe has attracted more than his share of biographers, drawn no doubt by his constant struggles with poverty and alcoholism, and by the drama inherent in his ill-fated romances with women and his verbal battles with literary contemporaries." In addition, they warn that many available accounts of Poe's life are "journalistic," that biographers' hypotheses about his sex life are necessarily speculative, that popular assumptions about his "drug addiction" have no ground in reliable evidence, and that myths about his lack of recognition by contemporaries are false (ix–x). For those attempting serious study of Poe's life for the first time, these cautionary notes are especially important.

For such inquirers, this chapter begins with a practical set of suggestions for preliminary entry into the daunting mass of available scholarship on Poe's life; the emphasis here is on brief, reliable readings that foreground Poe's literary career. The second section (portions of which are adapted with permission from my 1982 essay "On Poe Biography") offers an evaluative overview of the scholarly resources for modern study of Poe's life, with an emphasis on orienting the reader toward the documentary and interpretive dimensions of biographical scholarship since the 1940s. The last section focuses on two recent biographies—Jeffrey Meyers's *Edgar Allan Poe: His Life and Legacy* (1992) and Kenneth Silverman's *Edgar A. Poe: Mournful and Never-Ending Remembrance* (1991), the latter the first full-scale scholarly biography on Poe since 1941— and points toward biographical questions opened up by recent critical attention to issues of race and gender in Poe's writings.

PRELIMINARIES

In Thoreau's *Walden,* we are urged to "work and wedge our feet downward through the mud and slush of opinion, and prejudice, and tradition, and delusion, and appearance . . . till we come to a hard bottom and rocks in place, which we call *reality,* and say, This is, and no mistake." Poe's biographers occasionally take similar rhetorical stances toward the recovery of "hard" evidence used to dismantle old, and build new, representations of their subject. Thoreau is not, of course, advocating naive empiricism, nor are most serious biographers of Poe; the textual and material traces of any life are inevitably incomplete, such evidence does not interpret itself, and the "real" Poe is always an irrecoverable absence, however much his presence may seem accessible through biographers' representations. All biographical Poes are creative constructs, but some clearly have foundations with more "rocks in place" than others.

Perhaps the most trustworthy brief introductions to Poe's life and career are the chronological outlines in two widely available editions of his work: T. O. Mabbott's "Annals" ("Written primarily for those who have not made an extensive study of his life") in his *The Collected Works of Edgar Allan Poe: Vol. 1, Poems,* and G. R. Thompson's shorter "Chronology" in his *Edgar Allan Poe: Essays and Reviews* (an updating of a similar chronology in Thompson's 1970 *Great Short Works of Edgar Allan Poe*). Published in 1969 and 1984, respectively, these chronologies provide useful, highly reliable schematizations of Poe's complex life, career, and writings.

In conjunction with them, I would urge use of Michael J. Deas's *The Portraits and Daguerreotypes of Edgar Allan Poe* (1989), which comprehensively collects all known visual images of the writer, and of John Ward Ostrom's 1982 article, "Edgar Allan Poe: His Income as Literary Entrepreneur." The latter offers a succinct summary of the pitifully small income that Poe realized from his year-by-year efforts to support himself and his small family as author, editor, and lecturer. Ostrom estimates that Poe's *lifetime* earnings from these labors totaled only $6,200 (in 1980 dollars, the equivalent of $55,800 cumulative return for the years 1833 through 1849), a striking index of the poverty that haunted his professional life.

To reinforce the importance of seeing the biographical Poe in the context of the literary marketplace in which he labored, I next recommend reading I. M. Walker's "Introduction" to *Edgar Allan Poe: The Critical Heritage* (1986) and Bruce Weiner's *The Most Noble of Professions: Poe and the Poverty of Authorship* (1987). These works provide factual and interpretive expansions on the outlines of Poe's literary career mentioned before, with particular emphasis on how the production and reception of his writings were conditioned by audiences, publishing and reviewing mechanisms, and his own attitudes toward authorship. They are also valuable because, like Mabbott's *Annals* and Deas's *Portraits,* they strongly establish the contingency of any account of Poe's life upon both the biographer's frame of reference and the adequacy of his or her assessments of the validity and meaning of documentary evidence (points strikingly reinforced by Deas's precise archaeology of surviving pictorial images of Poe).

For a brief, reliable, interpretive narrative of Poe's life and career, I suggest that students turn to G. R. Thompson's 1979 "Edgar Allan Poe" entry in *Antebellum Writers in New York and the South* (vol. 3 of *Dictionary of Literary Biography*). Again, this work treats the composition and publication of Poe's poems, tales, and critical writings as the primary events in its narrative of the life. The forty-eight–page overview effectively combines a narrative of Poe's psychological and intellectual development with a well-proportioned account of his efforts as a "man of letters" to "unify" the "disparate roles of poet, writer of fiction, theoretical critic, practical critic, reviewer, journalist, editor, and philosopher" (249).

As I argued in "On Poe Biography," a major strength of Thompson's narrative is its recognition that biographers shape the lives they reconstruct. Thus he calls the reader's attention to his own interpretive emphasis on the paradoxical "self-division" and "obsessive quest for unity" in Poe's "fragmentary life" (250). He frames his explanatory constructs as heuristic devices—"Byronic models are useful formulations for Poe" (253) or "One of the more coherent explanations of Poe's fragmented life is that which casts him as an actor imitating various personalities"—and acknowledges their limitations—"The player analogy seems to explain a great deal, but not all the facts of Poe's life fit the interpretation equally well" (250). And he consistently foregrounds the possibility of alternate readings of both Poe's texts and the patterns he finds in his life. The result is that, at the end of this narrative, the reader recognizes that Thompson's final, categorically expressed claims about Poe's intellectual and aesthetic quests are contingent on the interpretive frameworks set forth in the narrative itself:

In [Poe's] creative, critical, and philosophical writings his romantic program was nothing less than to resolve all apparent contraries of the world into unity: the life and death impulses of existence; the apparent irradiation and collapse of a pulsating universe; the paradoxes of time and space, of matter and energy, of the rational and irrational; the seeming oppositions of the material and the immaterial, of the serious and the comic, of logic and imagination, of science and poetry. His works and his career are brilliant records of that inconclusive quest. (294–95)

Although many book-length introductory biographies on Poe are available, their reliability is often questionable; I urge beginning with the works noted previously because they foreground Poe the writer and stress the importance of scholarly skepticism in approaching reconstructions of Poe's life. The documentary and interpretive poles of such reconstructions are traced in the following section, which offers an overview of, first, the resources that have emerged from the long history of scholarly efforts to recover a "hard" foundation of biographical evidence about Poe's life and, second, the interpretive tasks and narrative choices that biographers face in attempting to link Poe's writings to the public and private experiences of the man himself.

DOCUMENTARY AND INTERPRETIVE RESOURCES

The earliest biographical accounts of Poe's life involve efforts to clear away both accidental and deliberate obfuscations, the latter of which might be said to begin with Poe's own systematic rewriting of his life story, especially in the "biographical" accounts he created in 1842 and 1843 (see A. H. Quinn, 370–75; Silverman, *Poe,* 196–97; Pollin, "Poe's Authorship"). The record was further clouded by the distortions, fabrications, and forgeries perpetrated by his "literary executor" and editor, Rufus Wilmot Griswold, particularly in the "Memoir" he included in his 1850 edition of Poe's works (see A. H. Quinn, 646–77 especially; for a brief, contextual overview of the growth of Poe biography from Griswold forward, see Walker, 44–59).

John C. Miller's *Building Poe Biography* (1977) and *Poe's Helen Remembers* (1979) offer a dramatic record of British biographer John Henry Ingram's struggles to gather the materials that went into the first carefully researched nineteenth-century accounts of Poe's life—Ingram's partisan "Memoir" of 1874 and two-volume *Edgar Allan Poe: His Life, Letters, and Opinions* of 1880. As Miller argues, Ingram's "efforts and publications not only laid the foundations for Poe biography but they also erected most of the superstructure, for every biographical account of Poe that has been published from 1874 to this date owes most of its contents to Ingram's discoveries and publications about Poe" (*Building Poe Biography,* xv). Miller's carefully edited volumes document how Ingram "amass[ed] the largest and most valuable collection of primary source materials for Poe biography that anyone had ever owned," reveal how profoundly the impulse to rebut Griswold shaped Ingram's acquisition and selective use of these materials, and emphasize how many "foundation stones" (xvi) of Poe biography consist of problematic, contradictory accounts of his behavior and personality by contemporaries.

Jay B. Hubbell's "Biography" section on Poe in the 1981 edition of *Eight American Authors: A Review of Research and Criticism,* edited by James Woodress, can be consulted for a brief summary of subsequent scholarly contributions to the growth of modern Poe biography (see also Walker, 53–63). Certainly the most notable contribution after Ingram's was George E. Woodberry's balanced, careful two-volume *The Life of Edgar Allan Poe, Personal and Literary* of 1909. In this expansion of his 1885 one-volume biography of Poe, Woodberry could build upon documents assembled in James A. Harrison's seventeen-volume *Complete Works of Edgar Allan Poe* of 1902, which included a gathering of the correspondence. The full extent of Griswold's forgeries would persist uncorrected, however, until the publication of Arthur Hobson Quinn's *Edgar Allan Poe: A Critical Biography* in 1941, a study that drew on the full range of previous Poe scholarship (including groundbreaking work in the 1920s and

1930s by Killis Campbell, David K. Jackson, and James Southall Wilson) and served as the standard literary biography of Poe for the next half century.

One indication of the thoroughness of Quinn's scholarship is that, thirty years after this biography appeared, Jay B. Hubbell could still describe it as "the best factual account we have" (10). Indeed, its strengths as a source book and reference tool are many: working from primary sources, Quinn encyclopedically cites (and often reproduces) the documents on which he bases his conclusions; effectively, if not always gracefully, describes the relevant economic, social, literary, and familial contexts of Poe's career and personal life; and explicitly presents the grounds on which he challenges or accepts the reliability of contemporary and posthumous accounts of Poe's character and behavior. Among its particular contributions, the biography offers masses of new material about the stage careers of Poe's parents, strong arguments for rejecting accounts of the "Mary Devereaux" courtship (196–97), and equally convincing reasons for accepting testimony by T. D. English that Poe did not have an opium habit (350). It also offers scholars full texts of numerous letters to and from Poe, some new, many otherwise available only in scattered printings or manuscript; it restores accurate texts of other letters commonly printed in earlier biographies with silent excisions; and, most spectacularly, it demonstrates with double-column printings the full range of Griswold's tampering with his own and Poe's correspondence.

Quinn's biography, as reviewers early recognized (see, for example, Wilson), had major weaknesses, many of which can be attributed to the naive empiricism with which the biographer interpreted the complexities of Poe's inner life—or rather, the displaced, fragmentary traces and textual residue of those complexities. Note, for example, Quinn's prefatory claim for the transparency of Poe's opaque, rhetorically conditioned letters: "Poe's own letters are so interesting and reveal his nature so clearly that it seems to me impertinent to paraphrase them" (iii). As might be predicted from the assumptions about the self-evident meaning of textual evidence here, Quinn dismisses most prior efforts to construct interpretive models of his subject's personality as nonempirical: "Around his name has accumulated a mass of rumor, conjecture, psycho-analysis, and interpretation based upon imagination rather than *fact*. To picture Poe as he really was, it is necessary for a biographer to examine all these speculations but it is not necessary to trouble the reader with them" (vii; italics mine). Clearly, Quinn fails to recognize that his own "picture" of Poe "as he really was" is as contingent on interpretive assumptions as the reconstructions he dismisses so casually.

In place of analysis of the puzzling dynamics of Poe's personality and behavior, Quinn instead offers normalizing defenses of his "character" and moral values, a nineteenth-century tactic that Poe's most recent biographers have finally abandoned. As a result, he constructs a highly partisan but unconvincing representation of the author as a loving husband, a hard-working head of household, a principled professional journalist with "lofty standards"—which he must occasionally prostitute to help support Virginia (694)—and a "patrician" with a "willingness to lay all things upon the altar of his art" (695). Even though the biographer records numerous behaviors that contradict this portrait (Poe's drinking problems, his manipulation of personal and literary relationships, his self-pitying and self-justifying distortions in letters, his posturing and often-questionable displays of learning in reviews and essays, his vindictiveness), Quinn largely fails to offer any coherent explanation for them, resorting, instead, to explaining away such evidence in terms of the press of circumstance or the "weaker side" of the "duality of Poe's nature" (693).

The biography's interpretations of Poe's writings are only slightly more effective than those of his personality. Quinn gives us little sense of Poe's intellectual development or evolving vision of life, and his readings of the creative work, which stress sources and thematic paraphrase, are not convincingly connected to the figure who wrote them. Not unexpectedly, the biographer's approach to Poe's character produces only simplistic explanations for the author's intellectual positions and creative work: "we owe his poetry and prose" to Poe's great "capacity for feeling both happiness and unhappiness" (81); "throughout his career, Poe was to develop in many forms the four themes of pride, love, beauty, and death. They are all in his first poem, and to any student of his life, they are natural selections. He was a worshipper of beauty, his capacity for love was unusual, his pride . . . was intense, and his preoccupation with death was constant" (125).

Richard D. Altick asserts that "the basic postulate of modern literary biography is that there is an essential connection between the person and the artist, that the personality of the writer and the events of his life have a demonstrable relevance to the psychic forces, however defined, that produce his art" (11). Quinn, evidently reacting against what he saw as the excesses of early psychoanalytic biographers, clearly sidesteps the necessary interpretive risks of making such connections, however hypothetical, between Poe's inner life, his experiences, and his writings.

While scholars continue to consult Quinn's biography as a kind of encyclopedic reference work for relevant data about particular periods and events in Poe's life, such use requires caution. The most efficient method of testing and updating Quinn's gatherings and judgments of evidence is to cross-check with entries in Thomas and Jackson's 1987 *Poe Log*. Furthermore, in the years following Quinn's work, the scholarly contributions to the documentary basis of Poe biography have been massive. Standard, indexed guides to this scholarship include *Edgar Allan Poe: A Bibliography of Criticism 1827–1967* by J. Lasley Dameron and Irby B. Cauthen, Jr. (1974) and *Edgar Allan Poe: An Annotated Bibliography of Books and Articles in English 1827–1973* by Esther F. Hyneman (1974), which can be updated with the periodic "Poe Bibliography" and "International Poe Bibliography" listings in *Poe Studies* (a cumulative subject index for 1969–83 appears in volume 17, for 1984–88 in volume 24, and so on); with the annual Poe entries in the *MLA International Bibliography;* and, since

1963, with the yearly assessments of work on Poe in *American Literary Scholarship: An Annual.*

For directly working with the primary documents of Poe biography, a variety of archival guides are available. The most general remains J. Albert Robbins's *American Literary Manuscripts* of 1977; the Lilly collection at Indiana University is described in David A. Randall's *The J. K. Lilly Collection of Edgar Allan Poe: An Account of Its Formation,* the Koester collection at the University of Texas at Austin in Joseph J. Moldenhauer's *A Descriptive Catalog of Edgar Allan Poe Manuscripts in the Humanities Research Center Library,* and the massive nineteenth-century Ingram collection in John C. Miller's *John Henry Ingram's Poe Collection at the University of Virginia.* Miller's guide has been updated, expanded, and corrected in a second edition by John E. Reilly; particularly important is the new subject, title, and name index, which functions as an annotated guide to the contents of the entire collection, which are available on nine reels of microfilm. Finally, prior to its sale, H. Bradley Martin's important private collection was described in Sotheby's 1990 auction catalog, *The Library of H. Bradley Martin* (Richard Kopley prepared the commentary on the Poe holdings; G. Thomas Tanselle provided an overview of the library's significance).

Modern scholarship on the documentary foundation of Poe biography has led to scholarly editions of his letters, poetry, tales, and prose writings, as well as to carefully edited compilations of reviews and other contemporary responses to Poe's work and life. Because Poe left no diaries, John Ward Ostrom's edition of Poe's letters constitutes perhaps the most fundamental tool for exploring connections between Poe's public and private lives. The opening paragraph of Ostrom's "Revised Check List of the Correspondence of Edgar Allan Poe" (*Studies in the American Renaissance,* 1981) highlights the sustained commitment that has kept his original, meticulously edited *Letters of Edgar Allan Poe* of 1948 updated for more than thirty years:

This Revised Check List . . . makes available in one location all the pertinent material from the Check List in my edition of *The Letters of Edgar Allan Poe,* 2 vols. (Cambridge: Harvard University Press, 1948); two supplements: *American Literature,* 24 (November 1952): 358–66, and 29 (March 1957): 79–86; a third supplement appended to the 1966 reprinting of the 1948 *Letters* (New York: Gordian Press); the fourth supplement: *American Literature,* 45 (January 1974): 513–36; and, subsequently, materials that have come to my attention. (169)

This 1981 "Check List" is a necessary adjunct to careful use of Ostrom's *Letters;* it offers new solutions to a variety of cruxes of dating and provenance in the 1966 edition and updates citations of the locations of printed and manuscript texts of both sides of Poe's correspondence. For subsequent updatings, the best reference guide is *The Poe Log,* which prints one previously unpublished letter (371), offers full or partial reprints of many others, and provides in its "List of Sources" a convenient means of finding published texts of letters (both to and about Poe) by his contemporaries.

Reliable texts of Poe's poems, fiction, critical essays, and journalistic writings, as well as information about the biographical and literary sources, textual history, and material conditions that shaped their production and reception, are necessary foundations for serious study of both his life and his works. The latter information is most readily accessible in the extensive apparatus and annotations of two interrelated scholarly editions of Poe's writings: T. O. Mabbott's *The Collected Works of Edgar Allan Poe* (1969–1978), which covers the poems (vol. 1) and the tales and sketches (vols. 2–3); and Burton R. Pollin's *The Collected Writings of Edgar Allan Poe* (1981–1986), which covers the long fiction (vol. 1), the essays/note collections such as "Pinakidia" and "Marginalia" (vol. 2), and the writings for *The Broadway Journal* (vols. 3–4). To supplement these collections, Patrick F. Quinn's *Edgar Allan Poe: Poetry and Tales* (Library of America, 1984) offers the best available edition of Poe's *Eureka: A Prose Poem*, while G. R. Thompson's *Edgar Allan Poe: Essays and Reviews* (1984) in the same series provides the fullest compilation and most reliable texts of the critical essays and reviews not yet included in Pollin's ongoing *Collected Writings*.

Obviously, modern editions have largely, but not wholly, replaced Harrison's textually unreliable *Complete Works of Edgar Allan Poe* of 1902 (Harrison's inclusion of an April 1836 *Southern Literary Messenger* review of two books on slavery as Poe's has been a particular source of continued controversy; for an overview and a convincing argument against the attribution, see J. V. Ridgely's "The Authorship of the 'Paulding-Drayton Review' "). In using Harrison's edition for biographical and source-study research, Pollin's computer-generated index, *Dictionary of Names and Titles in Poe's Collected Works,* is a vital tool. All of these editions provide a means of concretely documenting Poe's reading and responses to his intellectual and cultural milieu and may be supplemented with a wide variety of particularized source and influence studies of individual works. (Illustrative collections of such studies include Burton R. Pollin's *Discoveries in Poe* and Benjamin Franklin Fisher IV, ed., *Poe and His Times: The Artist and His Milieu*; for a cautionary reminder about the character of Poe's access to the sources and learning reflected in his writings, see Pollin's useful "Poe's Life Reflected through the Sources of *Pym*.")

In addition to editions of Poe's letters and writings, modern scholars have assembled a variety of carefully edited compilations that organize and reprint documents about particular aspects and periods of the writer's life. Deas's recent *Portraits and Daguerreotypes* has been discussed. An earlier example is Sidney P. Moss's *Poe's Major Crisis: His Libel Suit and New York's Literary World* (1970), which collects and annotates interrelated documents from 1846 and 1847 concerned with Poe's lawsuit against the *New York Mirror*. Like Moss's compilation, Dwight Thomas's massive 1978 dissertation, "Poe in Philadelphia, 1838–1844: A Documentary Record," is a genetic predecessor of his and David K. Jackson's *Poe Log* of 1987, but both remain useful supplements to the latter because of the relatively more ample space available to their compilers for commentary and reproduction of primary documents.

Thomas's massive dissertation, for example, offers "a comprehensive compilation of documents" that provides a "kaleidoscopic chronicle" of Poe's Philadelphia period and "a reasonably detailed account of the activities of his Philadelphia associates." To make the work serve as an "encyclopedic reference tool for the scholar" (vi–vii), Thomas includes an elaborate topic, name, and title index and a "Directory" featuring (1) reminiscences of Poe's life in Philadelphia and (2) brief biographical and bibliographic sketches of "Poe's Philadelphia associates, acquaintances, and correspondents" and of "the one hundred and thirty-two American literati" mentioned in Poe's "Autography" articles (x–xi). The compilations by both Moss and Thomas juxtapose chronological records of Poe's personal and professional life with documents that record his public reception and reputation. In Moss's words, they both emphasize that "Poe has to be projected against his background if he is to be understood" (vii).

I. M. Walker's 1986 compilation, *Edgar Allan Poe: The Critical Heritage,* is an equally vital documentary resource for studying responses to Poe the writer. Identifying reviewers and providing contextual information necessary for judging their perspectives, Walker includes "all the significant reviews and critiques of Poe and his work [from 1827 through Griswold's edition of 1850] . . . together with many minor and even desultory notices" and "such items as letters, publicity devices, biographical accounts, obituary notices and Poe's own prefaces—in short, anything that could be helpful in shedding light on Poe's contemporaneous reputation as a writer and literary personality, or on the chaotic literary environment in which he created his art" (xv).

Since the original 1951 edition of Jay Leyda's *The Melville Log: A Documentary Life of Herman Melville,* Poe scholars have recognized the value of a similarly comprehensive assembly of excerpted and ordered documents for Poe biography. The compilations by Moss, Thomas, and Walker are obviously partial versions of such a work, which was fully realized in 1987 with the publication of Thomas and Jackson's *The Poe Log: A Documentary Life of Edgar Allan Poe 1809–1849.* With a concise, necessary minimum of explanation and interpretive commentary, this carefully indexed work offers an 859-page chronological ordering of "the verifiable facts of Poe's life as revealed in excerpts from contemporary documents: the letters he wrote or received, newspaper reports, magazine articles, reminiscences, and legal records. . . . The compilers have attempted to include as much relevant material as possible; and while they could not exhaust all potential sources of information, they may justly claim to have prepared a more comprehensive and reliable account than has hitherto been available" (x). The *Log* also offers the fullest available "register" of Poe's contributions to particular newspapers and magazines, as well as an extensive section of "Biographical Notes" on persons "frequently mentioned in the text" (xi).

This monumental work both draws upon and independently evaluates the mass of biographical and bibliographical scholarship and primary documents referenced in its "List of Sources" (for a convenient overview of the compilers' many independent contributions, see the review by J. Lasley Dameron and Thomas C. Carlson). *The Poe Log,* I should stress, is not simply a reference work: it is also a specialized form of biography that privileges readers' direct engagement in the documentary record itself, sets forth the historical divergence in contemporary responses to Poe's personality and professional career, and formally acknowledges that multiple interpretations of his life and career are not simply possible but inevitable. In sum, the work is both an indispensable resource for the study of Poe's life and career and an essential complement for interpretive narrative biographies of the author.

Although little evidence is ever gathered independently of interpretive concerns, the preceding contributions to the "factual" base of Poe biography may be distinguished from those aimed more explicitly at constructing and defending interpretive models of his life. Richard D. Altick has suggested that the modern literary biographer faces "the overriding question of how to apportion attention and establish the relation between the man's outer and inner lives and, in the case of the latter, between his general emotional and intellectual tendencies and those which bore most directly upon his literary production" (378–79). However dated their methodology, the often crude psychoanalytic accounts of Poe's life written in the 1920s and 1930s made serious efforts to deal with Altick's "overriding question," one which Quinn's 1941 biography, as we have seen, generally avoided.

For psychoanalytic biographers, Poe's personality is deeply marked by the death of his mother before he was three years old, by the still earlier disappearance of his father, and by his childhood and adolescent years as an orphan raised but never formally adopted by the family of John Allan. While the effects of these experiences (including hypotheses of sexual impotence and latent necrophilia) vary with the interpreter, most see their influence in patterns of repetition in his relationships with women and in the recurring subject matter of his writings. To quote an exemplary passage from Joseph Wood Krutch's reductive, pathologizing *Edgar Allan Poe: A Study in Genius* of 1926: "Just as [Poe's] whole life was a struggle, conducted with all the cunning of the unconsciousness, against a realization of the psychic impotence of his sexual nature, so was it a struggle also against a realization of the mental instability to which [that impotence] gave rise" (22).

Of such early studies, Marie Bonaparte's massive *The Life and Works of Edgar Poe: A Psycho-Analytic Interpretation* of 1933 (1949) justifiably remains the most influential, although it is vital to consult it through the lens of later scholarship. Her interpretations of the life experiences are based on severely dated biographical information, her arguments assume she can unambiguously recover the unconscious processes and determinants that explain Poe's manifest behaviors and art, and her readings almost entirely ignore the genres, literary contexts, and nonbiographical sources of Poe's writings. (See Roger Forclaz's "Psychoanalysis and Edgar Allan Poe: A Critique of the Bonaparte Thesis" on the weaknesses and internal inconsistencies of Bonaparte's application of psychoanalytic theory, and Shoshana Felman's "On Reading Poetry: Reflections on the Limits and Possibilities of Psychoanalytical Approaches" for a critique of both Bonaparte's methodology and that of critics who respond by insisting on Poe's conscious control of his art; both "fail precisely to account for the dynamic *interaction* between the *unconscious* and the *conscious* elements of art" [143].) In spite of its methodological limitations, however, later scholars have returned again and again to Bonaparte's study in efforts to reinterpret the compulsive repetitions that she finds in Poe's life and writings (see Patrick F. Quinn's *The French Face of Edgar Poe,* Roger Asselineau's *Edgar Allan Poe,* Daniel Hoffman's *Poe, Poe, Poe, Poe, Poe, Poe, Poe,* Sybil Wuletich-Brinberg's *Poe: The Rationale of the Uncanny,* and the studies gathered in Joseph P. Muller and William J. Richardson's *The Purloined Poe: Lacan, Derrida & Psychoanalytic Reading,* to name just a few examples).

One of the most important biographical studies to update early psychoanalytic approaches to Poe was N. Bryllion Fagin's 1949 *The Histrionic Mr. Poe,* an attempt to supply the interpretive center that Quinn's biography obviously lacked. Focusing on the theatrical qualities in Poe's life and art and implicitly influenced by the stress on ego mechanisms and coping strategies in neo-Freudian thought, Fagin formulated the general dynamics of Poe's personality in terms of a self-division between the gentleman "unprovided with the means needful to maintain the life of one" and "the repressed strolling player":

Both were unhappy, because neither was permitted to function naturally, and each sought compensations and made adjustments: the gentleman by facing the world with insolent pride, by wearing his shabby attire with meticulous dignity, and by turning himself into a literary histrio: the player by turning the world itself into a stage. (32)

As various commentators have observed, Fagin's study rather overextends its application of this model for Poe's personality. Nevertheless, his view of the writer as self-divided, as a role-player who dons masks as a strategy of self-protection and engages in kinds of theatrical performance in both his life and art, has proved to be remarkably influential for subsequent Poe critics, especially those who emphasize duplicity, irony, and self-detachment in Poe's fiction and prose. Fagin's views inform, for example, Michael Allen's emphasis on Poe's literary role-playing in *Poe and the British Magazine Tradition* (1969), as well as much of the "ironist" tradition in Poe criticism (for a listing and representative sampling of the work of such critics, see Dennis Eddings's 1983 collection, *The Naiad Voice: Essays on Poe's Satiric Hoaxing*).

Fagin's relatively specialized biography places strong emphasis on Poe's career as a journalist and critic, a concern shared by a wide variety of critical studies written after 1941 that can be broadly classified as "biographical." Such works range in character from Perry Miller's *The Raven and the Whale* (1956), a vivid (if now dated) narrative account of New York's literary politics of the 1840s and Poe's role in them, to Claude Richard's *Edgar Allan Poe: Journaliste et Critique* (1979), an exhaustive analytical account of the foundations and development of Poe's critical practice and poetics that stresses the theological character of his aesthetics and the rationalism of his methods (for a detailed evaluation, see Patrick F. Quinn's 1980 review). Numerous such specialized studies, written both before and after Quinn's 1941 biography, are cited by the compilers of *The Poe Log*. From their extensive "Listing of Sources," I select just two illustrative examples (for discussion of others, see my 1982 "On Poe Biography").

Sidney P. Moss's *Poe's Literary Battles: The Critic in the Context of His Literary Milieu* (1963) sees Poe as a reformer who fought journalistic campaigns against the literary coteries of his era and their practice of "puffing" the productions of allies in newspaper and journal reviews. The study, organized topically, emphasizes that Poe's critical positions as a reviewer must often be understood as tactical moves on the literary and cultural battlefronts of his era. The approach anticipates recent studies of particular works by Poe that contextualize his stance as author or critic in ideological, cultural, or economic terms (see, e.g., Bruce Weiner's *Most Noble of Professions* [1987] and the Poe chapters in Michael T. Gilmore's *American Romanticism and the Marketplace* [1985], Leland S. Person's *Aesthetic Headaches: Women and a Masculine Poetics in Poe, Melville, & Hawthorne* [1988], Cynthia S. Jordan's *Second Stories: The Politics of Language, Form, and Gender in Early American Fictions* [1988], Kenneth Dauber's *The Idea of Authorship in America* [1990], and Stephen Railton's *Authorship and Audience: Literary Performance in the American Renaissance* [1991]).

In contrast to studies that place primary emphasis on the contextual factors that shaped Poe's writing practices, Robert D. Jacob's *Poe: Journalist and Critic* (1969) offers an inside narrative of the dialectically evolving critical and theoretical positions in Poe's reviews and essays. For Jacobs, Poe "as a working critic looked backward toward the mechanistic psychological aesthetic of the previous century and forward toward the dynamic organicism of the romantic period" (viii); ultimately, Jacobs claims, "Poe was unique among nineteenth-century American critics because he not only evaluated literary works but also developed an aesthetic theory and a theory of nature to support it" (447). Jacobs's final chapters stress Poe's efforts—especially in the angelic dialogues, "Mesmeric Revelation," the late theoretical essays, and the cosmological speculation of *Eureka*—"to formulate a consistent theory of the universe that would correlate with his aesthetics" (414).

Full-length, conceptually oriented studies of Poe's critical and journalistic career such as Jacobs's and Claude Richard's move toward the equivalent of intellectual biographies of the author. Of course, any critical discussion that attempts to account for the intertextual congruences among different works in

Poe's canon necessarily presupposes some interpretive model, however limited, of the biographical Poe. Models that stress the author's philosophical perpectives are perhaps most apparent in critical studies like Jacobs's that deal with the place of *Eureka* in Poe's thinking and art (see book-length works by Edward H. Davidson, G. R. Thompson, David Halliburton, David Ketterer, Kent J. Ljungquist, John T. Irwin, J. Gerald Kennedy, Michael J. S. Williams, and Joan C. Dayan for examples by critics with strongly divergent approaches). The degree of coherence that critics find in Poe's intellectual and aesthetic perspectives varies, of course, as does the weight given them in assessing his literary career and writings. For an argument on the importance of taking a holistic perspective, see Eric Carlson's "Frames of Reference for Poe's Symbolic Language," which offers a particularly useful guide to studies finding an organic relationship among Poe's symbolism, his theory of literature, and "his philosophic perspective or general outlook on life" (207).

Obviously, modern Poe biographers face difficult choices, especially in apportioning attention and interpretation in a narrative that attempts to deal simultaneously with Poe's private and public experiences, his personal and professional relationships, his writings, the contexts in which he wrote, and the evolution of his intellectual and aesthetic perspectives. Between the publication of Quinn's 1941 biography and the appearance of Silverman's in 1991, the problem of focusing and organizing overall accounts of Poe's life has largely fallen to those who aim to introduce Poe to general audiences. In some cases, like Geoffrey Rans's dated but well-researched *Edgar Allan Poe* of 1965, authors attempt only brief narratives of the life as preface to introductory overviews of the writings (Rans's strategy is particularly effective because of his running metacommentary on the strengths and weaknesses of prior biographical interpretations). Whatever their strategy, such introductory narratives of Poe's life must be used with caution: most deal very selectively with the range of Poe's writings, and errors of fact seem almost inevitable, especially when the work of earlier biographers is drawn on without being thoroughly tested against current scholarship.

To cite a few examples from efforts by reasonably careful authors, William Bittner's *Poe: A Biography* (1963) overlooks available evidence for rejecting the legend that Poe left *Graham's Magazine* because he found Griswold occupying his chair, and Julian Symons's *The Tell-Tale Heart: The Life and Works of Edgar Allan Poe* (1978) misses scholarship that debunks Poe's inflated account of the reception of his 1844 "Balloon Hoax." More serious traps await the unwary readers of popularizations such as David Sinclair's *Edgar Allan Poe* (1977), which advances a psychoanalytic interpretation of the writer that misrepresents his contemporary reputation and reception, and especially Wolf Mankowitz's *The Extraordinary Mr. Poe: A Biography of Edgar Allan Poe* (1978), which serves up a vivid pastiche of most of the unreliable reminiscences, legend, and "gossip" that A. H. Quinn tried so hard to strip away from the author's life.

The problem of narrative design is variously solved in these accounts. Symons's strategy is both extreme and illuminating: he divides his text into "The Life" and "The Work," which allows him to avoid serious assessment of how Poe's private and public experiences conditioned the concerns and intellectual and aesthetic positions in the creative work and criticism. Attention to historical and cultural context is highly restricted, interpretation of Poe's personality is minimized, and psychological and "symbolic" approaches to the writings are rejected as illegitimate. By avoiding interpretation at almost every level, Symons's biography achieves an unquestionable chronological clarity and topical orderliness, albeit at the expense of almost any other kind of coherence.

The example of Symons illustrates a contention that Altick's discussion of literary biography explores at length: narrative and organizational demands inevitably confront literary biographers with reductive choices, most simply in the quantity of information to be included, most significantly in the level and extent of interpretive engagement with the documentary materials from which they are built and with the writings they attempt to explain. In the next section, the choices made by Poe's two most recent biographers are examined.

THE MEYERS AND SILVERMAN BIOGRAPHIES

Jeffrey Meyers's recent *Edgar Allan Poe: His Life and Legacy* (1992) has both strengths and limitations as a narrative shaped to interest general readers. It is expressively written and clearly indexed and documented, with a nice touch for selecting telling passages from letters and other texts; it draws usefully on *The Poe Log* and other major scholarly compilations; it creates a vivid representation of the drama of Poe's private and public life; and it has relatively few errors of fact (but see Burton R. Pollin's 1992 review, "Another Poe Biography," 42–43, for a specialist's listing).

On the other hand, Meyers's positioning of his voice invites little testing of his interpretive process, which he effaces behind a biographer's voice that advances authoritative, rarely qualified conclusions about Poe's personality and behaviors, his writings, and the parallels between his life and literary career and those of other writers. The unelaborated statement of his principle of selection in dealing with the writings is illustrative: "Since the quality of Poe's poems, stories, and criticism . . . varies enormously, I have concentrated on his best work and ignored the rest" (xii). Meyers's interpretive descriptions of what he considers Poe's "best work" offer accessible critical perspectives and selective summaries of their autobiographical elements, sources, and subsequent influence, but often the stance tends toward flat judgments that discourage rather than invite exploration of the multiple interpretive potentials of the texts under discussion.

In his notes, Meyers points out that he completed his study before the 1991 publication of Silverman's much longer biography (357). Meyers's own review of the latter work can be consulted for a list of his interpretive disagreements with Silverman. In it, he makes clear the more limited aims of his own forth-coming biography: "There is still room, however, for a shorter, less psycho-analytical, and more dramatic narrative ... which would emphasize [Poe's] recurrent pattern of striving for a goal in journalism, friendship, or marriage and then destroying his prospects just as he was about to achieve it" ("A Wretched Genius," 586). The narrative impulse to represent Poe "dramatically" clearly informs Meyers's biography, as does the intention to emphasize "self-destructive" patterns in Poe's life. To account for the dynamics of such behav-iors, Meyers early offers his readers a vivid, synthesized overview of Poe's character (57–59), although again readers are not alerted to the hypothetical and contingent nature of this reconstruction. In sum, while this is clearly the most thorough of the many introductory Poe biographies (and the only one still in print), it is best used with the Pollin review, with a cautious sense of skepticism about its interpretive certainties and with a recognition that the "drama" and range of Poe's intellectual life are, at best, a secondary focus.

Silverman's *Edgar A. Poe: Mournful and Never-Ending Remembrance* is written by a scholar who approaches Poe with impressive credentials in Amer-ican literary scholarship (but without a prior record of work focused on this particular author). His labors, it is widely recognized, have produced the first comprehensive scholarly biography devoted to Poe since A. H. Quinn's. Sil-verman builds this work from both the cumulative body of biographical schol-arship on the author and a fresh reexamination of the archival and documentary records; Kent J. Ljungquist's review, "Memory and Mourning," as well as Richard Kopley's in *American Literature* provide useful summaries of the new findings that result.

In 1941, Quinn aspired, as had most serious Poe biographers before him, to make his work double as a repository for large samples of the evidence from which it was built (indeed, Quinn often substituted reproductions of documents for interpretive engagement). Silverman obviously recognized that such a strat-egy in the 1990s would not only drown the narrative of the life in an ocean of primary material but also ignore the existence of Ostrom's *Letters,* the *Poe Log,* and other editions and compilations.

Clearly dedicated to writing biography as interpretive narrative, Silverman reproduces primary evidence selectively, rarely quotes text in blocks, relegates extended summaries or perspectives on selected works (including *Pym* and *Eu-reka*) to eight appendixes, and shapes a well-proportioned account that folds back upon itself whenever necessary to deal with the writings or with simulta-neous and overlapping threads in Poe's personal and professional life. Without masking the incompleteness of the record or his interpretive role in reconstruct-ing it, Silverman masterfully juxtaposes inner and outer narratives of his sub-ject's life in ways that systematically illuminate the tensions and connections among Poe's evolving (and often contradictory) needs, motives, and intellectual commitments; his behaviors, relationships, and writings; and the people and cultural institutions that both shaped the author's personal and professional life and so often resisted the demands he made of them.

Unlike Quinn, Silverman does not begin this biography by justifying his overall strategy or choices of emphasis, does not conclude with a grand synthesis, and does not announce in his text the specific contributions to new understanding recorded in his notes (the method of documentation, which draws efficiently on the *Poe Log,* is thorough, unobtrusive, but frankly challenging for casual use). Perhaps as a consequence, reviewers may have placed more weight than he intended on the chapter subtitled "Remarks on Childhood Mourning" (68–78), in which he briefly steps back from his narrative to offer some broad perspectives on the dynamics of Poe's personality.

Acknowledging in notes his debt to Marie Bonaparte's early insights into "the pervasive effects of mourning on Poe's life and writing" (464), Silverman in this chapter draws on current psychoanalytic accounts of "childhood mourning" to formulate the hypothetical effects of Poe's early loss of his mother, effects that he finds consistent with the "cluster of dead-alive persons, still-moving landscapes, and deathly dread-longings" that dominate "not only Edgar's three slim volumes of [early] poems but also . . . his entire literary career. Much of his later writing, despite its variety of forms and styles, places and characters, is driven by the question of whether the dead remain dead" (76). Finding in the writer an "underlying denial of death" (77), Silverman suggests that much of Poe's career "may be understood as a sort of prolonged mourning, an artistic brooding-on and assemblage of the fantasies activated by an ever-living past," by memories of a loss that "no product of his imagination would put to right" (78).

In advancing this model, Silverman insists that it functions as an explanatory heuristic in his narrative, not as the sole way in which the evidence can be explained:

The inability of young children to mourn the death of a parent perhaps seems but one of many ways, if any are needed at all, to account for Poe's odd, intent imaginings about death. As this biography is not an argument but a narrative, no attempt will be made to "prove" that the psychoanalytic prototype of the bereaved child applies to him, still less to examine by its light his every word and action. The narrative does often recur to his ideas about death. Yet it does so not in order to demonstrate the truth of a particular view of their origins, but because he continued to pore over them. His absorption becomes increasingly evident, however interpreted. (77–78)

The qualifications here are important: without avoiding the biographer's obligation to make sense of his subject, Silverman resists imposing simplification where he finds complexity, certainty where he finds unresolvable questions. Characteristic of his interpretive stance is the formulation of the contrast between Poe's early claims to "independence of thought" in the preface to his 1831 *Poems* and the borrowings in both that preface and the poems themselves:

To point out the contrast is not to overlook his youth, nor his steeping himself in and absorbing the poetry of his time, nor especially the fact that his poems, taken whole and as a group, read as distinctly his. Yet like his early imitation of Byron, his various pseudonyms, and his appropriating his brother's adventures, Edgar's ease in taking over and passing off as his own the ideas, opinions, and expressions of other people does imply a feeling of not being someone definite. As perhaps the outcome of many early shifts from caretaker to caretaker, it suggests a sense of deficiency in himself, and envy toward others he thought more adequate. (72)

In my view, such careful reconstructions of the uncertain boundaries of Poe's sense of self and of the complex emotional and intentional dynamics of his personal and professional behaviors are a central strength of this impressive biography (best seen, perhaps, in Silverman's remarkably convincing explications of Poe's letters).

Silverman's emphasis on the importance of biographical and psychological factors in explaining the genesis and character of Poe's public writings and intellectual positions has received mixed responses from Poe critics. Compare, for example, the enthusiastic reviews by Kopley and Daniel Hoffman ("Life Was One Long Midnight Dreary") with Ljungquist's and Eric Carlson's more qualified assessments. The latter, for example, finds insufficient attention to recent critical perspectives in Silverman's discussions of the writings and argues that the biography does not fully "realize that for Poe death is most significant when joined with the theme of rebirth to a higher, creative, moral, or cosmic consciousness ('death as metamorphosis' Poe called it)." On the other hand, Carlson does find in the biography's comments on Poe's self-styled transcendentalism and on works such as "Mesmeric Revelation" that Silverman "comes close to sensing that Poe as artist developed beyond a mournful Memory to an authentic philosophic perspective and symbology ('well-articulated aesthetic principles' 1994:165)" (1994:238–39).

From a different perspective, Ljungquist argues that "Silverman downplays what emotional distance Poe may have had from loss, death, and mourning"; thus, even though the biographer finds in Poe a "penchant for self-dramatization and masking," he sees "direct emotional investment rather than emotional distance" and ironic detachment in much of the creative work—an emphasis that runs counter to the line of modern Poe criticism that stems from Fagin and especially from the work of G. R. Thompson. Ljungquist concludes, "In sum, the volume may offer a welcome and authoritative gathering of biographical discoveries that have appeared since Quinn's biography; it does not present an analogous synthesis of Poe criticism over the same span of time" (42).

In my own view, one index of Silverman's strength as a biographer is his resistance to what must have been a strong temptation to synthesize such established, if divergent, lines in modern Poe criticism as Carlson and Ljungquist emphasize. These approaches, like much twentieth-century critical discourse on Poe, have generally weighted biographical and psychological explanations far less heavily than conceptual and contextual ones in accounting for the genesis and character of the author's writings. Choosing not to engage directly with the range of critical debate about most Poe texts, Silverman, instead, places renewed emphasis on the importance of understanding recurring features of the writings in terms of the biographical experiences and memory-haunted personality of the subject who produced them—and thus implicitly challenges critics to test alternative explanations against his own biographically grounded readings. (For a useful summary of key points of his critical position, see Silverman's 1993 "Introduction" to *New Essays on Poe's Major Tales,* 15–24.)

Silverman's biography offers a particularly fruitful resource for certain recurrent topics of critical debate about Poe, especially those dealing with gender issues in his writings. Compare, for example, Silverman's views on Poe's representations of women (summarized in the introduction just cited) with J. Gerald Kennedy's "Poe, 'Ligeia,' and the Problem of Dying Women" (a related essay in the same volume). Together, these pieces advance an alternative to Jordan's and Person's recent feminist rereadings of Poe; Kennedy does so explicitly by stressing, in Silverman's words, "how Poe's fictional treatment of the deaths of beloved women . . . betrays an underlying revulsion and rage" (24). See also the responses to Silverman in recent essays by Joan Dayan, Jacqueline Doyle, and Monica Elbert in Michael Williams's "Poe and Gender" issue of *Poe Studies/Dark Romanticism.* In terms of another recurrent issue in Poe criticism, Silverman devotes relatively little space to exploring Poe's ideological and political positions on race, especially those in *Pym,* but the biography's unblinking summaries of Poe's support for slavery, opposition to abolitionism, and racist characterizations of blacks in the tales and *The Journal of Julius Rodman* (see 206–7, 405–6, 484n.) are important starting points for assessing recent debates about critical attention to Poe's attitudes toward slavery—see, for example, John Carlos Rowe's "Poe, Antebellum Slavery, and Modern Criticism," J. V. Ridgely's critique of attributions of the Paulding-Drayton review to Poe, and Dayan's "Amorous Bondage: Poe, Ladies, and Slaves."

In conclusion, I would observe that Silverman's biography offers us a Poe with warts in place, a Poe that stands in sharp contrast to Quinn's idealized, if beleaguered, gentleman artist and critic, as well as a Poe less rationalistic, less emotionally detached from the recurrent concerns and images in his fiction and poetry, and less sure of the consolations envisioned in such works as *Eureka* than many Poe critics have argued for. Silverman does not flinch from taking interpretive risks (or from going against the grain of well-established approaches to Poe's work) in reconstructing connections among Poe's life experiences, psychological makeup, and writings. The rigor and thoroughness that Silverman brings to this all-important task of the literary biographer, whatever one's view of his choices of emphasis and analytical approach, make this a biography that will inevitably shape critical discourse on Poe for years to come.

WORKS CITED

Allen, Hervey. *Israfel: The Life and Times of Edgar Allan Poe.* 1926. Rpt. in New York: Farrar and Rinehart, 1934.

Allen, Michael. *Poe and the British Magazine Tradition.* New York: Oxford UP, 1969.

Altick, Richard. *Lives and Letters: A History of Literary Biography in England and America.* Rpt. in Westport, CT: Greenwood, 1979.

Asselineau, Roger. *Edgar Allan Poe.* Minneapolis: U of Minnesota P, 1970.

Bittner, William. *Poe: A Biography.* Boston and Toronto: Atlantic Monthly P, 1963.

Bonaparte, Marie. *The Life and Works of Edgar Poe: A Psycho-Analytic Interpretation.* Trans. John Rodker. London: Imago, 1949.

Carlson, Eric, ed. *Critical Essays on Edgar Allan Poe.* Boston: G. K. Hall, 1987.

———. "Frames of Reference for Poe's Symbolic Language." Carlson, *Essays,* 207–17.

———. [New Poe Criticism and Biographies.] Rev. of *Edgar Allan Poe: His Life and Legacy,* by Jeffrey Meyers, and *Edgar Allan Poe: Mournful and Never-Ending Remembrance,* by Kenneth Silverman. *American Notes and Queries* 7, no. 4 (Oct. 1994): 235–240.

Dameron, J. Lasley, and Thomas C. Carlson. "A Documentary Life of Poe." Rev. of *The Poe Log* by Dwight Thomas and David K. Jackson. *Poe Studies/Dark Romanticism* 21 (1988): 44–46.

Dameron, J. Lasley, and Irby B. Cauthen, Jr. *Edgar Allan Poe: A Bibliography of Criticism 1827–1967.* Charlottesville: UP of Virginia, 1974.

Dauber, Kenneth. *The Idea of Authorship in America: Democratic Poetics in America from Franklin to Melville.* Madison: U of Wisconsin P, 1990.

Davidson, Edward H. *Poe: A Critical Study.* Cambridge: Harvard UP, 1957.

Dayan, Joan. "Amorous Bondage: Poe, Ladies, and Slaves." *AL* 66 (1994): 239–73.

———. *Fables of Mind: An Inquiry into Poe's Fiction.* New York: Oxford UP, 1987.

Deas, Michael J. *The Portraits and Daguerreotypes of Edgar Allan Poe.* Charlottesville: UP of Virginia, 1989.

Eddings, Dennis, ed. *The Naiad Voice: Essays on Poe's Satiric Hoaxing.* Port Washington, NY: Associated Faculty P, 1983.

Felman, Shoshana. "On Reading Poetry: Reflections on the Limits and Possibilities of Psychoanalytical Approaches." Muller and Richardson, 133–56.

Fisher, Benjamin Franklin, IV, ed. *Poe and His Times: The Artist and His Milieu.* Baltimore: Edgar Allan Poe Society, 1990.

Forclaz, Roger. "Psychoanalysis and Edgar Allan Poe: A Critique of the Bonaparte Thesis." Carlson, *Essays,* 187–95.

Gilmore, Michael T. *American Romanticism and the Marketplace.* Chicago: U of Chicago P, 1985.

Halliburton, David. *Edgar Allan Poe: A Phenomenological View.* Princeton: Princeton UP, 1973.

Hammond, Alexander. "On Poe Biography: A Review Essay." *ESQ* 28 (1982): 197–211.

Harrison, James A., ed. *Complete Works of Edgar Allan Poe.* 17 vols. Rpt. in New York: AMS P, 1965.

Hoffman, Daniel. "Life Was One Long Midnight Dreary." Rev. of *Edgar Allan Poe: Mourning and Never-Ending Remembrance*, by Kenneth Silverman. *New York Times Book Review*, December 22, 1992, 1, 17–19.

———. *Poe Poe Poe Poe Poe Poe Poe*. New York: Doubleday, 1972.

Hubbell, Jay B. "Edgar Allan Poe." *Eight American Authors: A Review of Research and Criticism*. Ed. James Woodress. Rev. ed. New York: Norton, 1981, 3–36.

Hyneman, Esther F. *Edgar Allan Poe: An Annotated Bibliography of Books and Articles in English 1827–1973*. Boston: G. K. Hall, 1974.

Irwin, John T. *American Hieroglyphics: The Symbol of the Egyptian Hieroglyphics in the American Renaissance*. New Haven, CT: Yale UP, 1980.

Jacobs, Robert D. *Poe: Journalist and Critic*. Baton Rouge: Louisiana State UP, 1969.

Kennedy, J. Gerald. *Poe, Death, and the Life of Writing*. New Haven, CT: Yale UP, 1987.

———. "Poe, 'Ligeia,' and the Problem of Dying Women." *New Essays on Poe's Major Tales*. Ed. Kenneth Silverman. New York and Cambridge: Cambridge UP, 1993, 113–29.

Ketterer, David. *The Rationale of Deception in Poe*. Baton Rouge: Louisiana SUP, 1979.

Kopley, Richard. Rev. of *Edgar Allan Poe: Mournful and Never-Ending Remembrance*, by Kenneth Silverman. *AL* 64 (1992): 373–74.

Krutch, Joseph Wood. *Edgar Allan Poe: A Study in Genius*. New York: Alfred Knopf, 1926.

The Library of H. Bradley Martin. New York: Sotheby's, [1989].

Ljungquist, Kent. *The Grand and the Fair: Poe's Landscape Aesthetics and Pictorial Techniques*. Potomac, MD: Scripta Humanistica, 1984.

———. "Memory and Mourning." Rev. of *Edgar Allan Poe: Mournful and Never-Ending Remembrance*, by Kenneth Silverman. *Poe Studies/Dark Romanticism* 25 (1992): 40–42.

Mabbot, T. O., ed. *The Collected Works of Edgar Allan Poe*. 3 vols. Cambridge: Harvard UP, 1969–1978.

Mankowitz, Wolf. *The Extraordinary Mr. Poe: A Biography of Edgar Allan Poe*. London: Weidenfeld and Nicolson, 1978.

Meyers, Jeffrey. *Edgar Allan Poe: His Life and Legacy*. New York: Scribner's, 1992a.

———. "A Wretched Genius." Rev. of *Edgar Allan Poe: Mournful and Never-Ending Remembrance*. *Virginia Quarterly Review* 68 (1992b): 583–86.

Miller, John C., ed. *Building Poe Biography*. Baton Rouge: Louisiana State U, 1977.

———. *John Henry Ingram's Poe Collection at the University of Virginia*. 2d ed. by John C. Reilly. Charlottesville: U of Virginia Library, 1994.

———. *Poe's Helen Remembers*. Charlottesville: UP of Virginia, 1979.

Miller, Perry. *The Raven and the Whale*. New York: Harcourt Brace, 1956.

Moldenhauer, Joseph J. *A Descriptive Catalog of Edgar Allan Poe Manuscripts in the Humanities Research Center Library*. Austin: U of Texas, 1973.

Moss, Sidney P. *Poe's Literary Battles: The Critic in the Context of His Literary Milieu*. Durham: Duke UP, 1963.

———. *Poe's Major Crisis: His Libel Suit and New York's Literary World*. Durham: Duke UP, 1970.

Muller, Joseph P., and William J. Richardson, eds. *The Purloined Poe: Lacan, Derrida & Psychoanalytic Reading*. Baltimore and London: Johns Hopkins UP, 1988.

Ostrom, John Ward. "Edgar Allan Poe: His Income as Literary Entrepreneur." *PoeS* 15 (1982): 1–7.

———. ed. *Letters of Edgar Allan Poe.* 2 vols. Rev. ed. New York: Gordian P, 1966.

———. "Revised Check List of the Correspondence of Edgar Allan Poe." *Studies in the American Renaissance 1981.* Ed. Joel Myerson. Boston: Twayne, 1981, 169–255.

Pollin, Burton R. "Another Poe Biography." Review of *Edgar Allan Poe: His Life and Legacy,* by Jeffery Meyers. *Poe Studies/Dark Romanticism* 25 (1992): 42–43.

———. ed. *The Collected Writings of Edgar Allan Poe.* 4 vols. Boston: Twayne, 1981 (vol. 1); New York: Gordian P, 1985–1986 (vols. 2–4).

———. *Dictionary of Names and Titles in Poe's Collected Works.* New York: Da Capo P, 1968.

———. *Discoveries in Poe.* Notre Dame, IN: U of Notre Dame P, 1970.

———. "Poe's Authorship of Three Long Critical and Autobiographical Articles of 1843." *American Renaissance Literary Report: An Annual* 7 (1993): 139–71.

———. "Poe's Life Reflected through the Sources of *Pym.*" *Poe's Pym: Critical Explorations.* Ed. Richard Kopley. Durham: Duke UP, 1992, 95–103.

Quinn, Arthur Hobson. *Edgar Allan Poe: A Critical Biography.* 1941. Rpt. in New York: Cooper Square, 1969.

Quinn, Patrick F. "The Critical Mind of Edgar Poe." Rev. of *Edgar Allan Poe: Journaliste et Critique,* by Claude Richard. *PoeS* 13 (1980): 37–40.

———. ed. *Edgar Allan Poe: Poetry and Tales.* New York: Library of America, 1984.

———. *The French Face of Edgar Poe.* Carbondale: Southern Illinois UP, 1957.

Railton, Stephen. *Authorship and Audience: Literary Performance in the American Renaissance.* Princeton: Princeton UP, 1991.

Randall, David A. *The J. K. Lilly Collection of Edgar Allan Poe: An Account of Its Formation.* Bloomington: Indiana UP, 1964.

Rans, Geoffrey. *Edgar Allan Poe.* Writers and Critics Series. Edinburgh and London: Oliver and Boyd, 1965.

Richard, Claude. *Edgar Allan Poe: Journaliste et Critique.* Paris: Librairie C. Klincksieck, 1979.

Ridgely, J. V. "The Authorship of the 'Paulding–Drayton Review.'" *PSA Newsletter* 20, no. 2 (Fall 1992): 1–3, 6.

Robbins, J. Albert, comp. *American Literary Manuscripts: A Checklist of Holdings in Academic, Historical, and Public Libraries, Museums, and Authors' Homes in the United States.* Athens: U of Georgia P, 1977.

Rowe, John Carlos. "Poe, Antebellum Slavery, and Modern Criticism." *Poe's Pym: Critical Explorations.* Ed. Richard Kopley. Durham: Duke UP, 1992.

Silverman, Kenneth. *Edgar A. Poe: Mournful and Never-Ending Remembrance.* New York: HarperCollins, 1991.

———. "Introduction." *New Essays on Poe's Major Tales.* Ed. Kenneth Silverman. New York and Cambridge: Cambridge UP, 1993, 1–26.

Sinclair, David. *Edgar Allan Poe.* Totowa, NJ: Rowman and Littlefield, 1977.

Symons, Julian. *The Tell-Tale Heart: The Life and Works of Edgar Allan Poe.* New York: Harper and Row, 1978.

Thomas, Dwight. "Poe in Philadelphia, 1838–1844: A Documentary Record." Diss. University of Pennsylvania, 1978.

Thomas, Dwight, and David K. Jackson. *The Poe Log: A Documentary Life of Edgar Allan Poe 1809–1849.* Boston: G. K. Hall, 1987.

Thompson, G. R. "Chronology." *Edgar Allan Poe: Essays and Reviews.* New York: Library of America, 1984, 1473–81.

———. "Edgar Allan Poe." *Antebellum Writers in New York and the South.* Vol. 3. *Dictionary of Literary Biography.* Detroit: Gale Research, 1979, 249–97.

———. *Poe's Fiction: Romantic Irony in the Gothic Tales.* Madison: U of Wisconsin P, 1973.

Walker, I. M. "Introduction." *Edgar Allan Poe: The Critical Heritage.* Ed. I. M. Walker. London and New York: Routledge and Kegan Paul, 1986, 1–63.

Weiner, Bruce. *The Most Noble of Professions: Poe and the Poverty of Authorship.* Baltimore: Enoch Pratt Free Library and Edgar Allan Poe Society, 1987.

Williams, Michael J. S., ed. "Poe and Gender." *Poe Studies/Dark Romanticism* 26 (1993): 1–44.

———. *A World of Words: Language and Displacement in the Fiction of Edgar Allan Poe.* Durham, NC: Duke UP, 1987.

Wilson, James Southall. Rev. of *Edgar Allan Poe: A Critical Biography,* by Arthur Hobson Quinn. *AL* 14 (1942): 168–71.

Woodberry, George E. *The Life of Edgar Allan Poe, Personal and Literary.* 2 vols. Boston: Houghton Mifflin, 1909.

Wuletich-Brinberg, Sybil. *Poe: The Rationale of the Uncanny.* New York: Peter Lang, 1988.

Part II

POE'S WRITINGS

3

The Poems: 1824–1835

ELIZABETH PHILLIPS

The natural voice for the young Poe was poetry. Many of the best early poems were written by the time he was twenty-two. Comparing them to the later verse, some critics hold the opinion that there are little or no development and perhaps a misbegotten music from first to last. Other critics, giving more attention to the tales and to Poe's aesthetics, rarely consider the poetry apart from them. While that approach may be illuminating, it neglects the sense of trials by which Poe tested and proved himself as a poet. The lines of force in the evolution of the work are not consistent or continuous; there are starts and stops and returns for rewriting. The first poems are also more diverse in kind, richer thematically, and more varied prosodically than is apparent in studies of them as illustrations of Poe's a posteriori poetics. The experimental quality of the verse from 1825 to 1835 merits consideration as it developed before the poet became a professional critic.

THE CRITICS' RESPONSE

Two noteworthy essays concentrate on the early verse. In "The Self and the World: Poe's Early Poems" (1977), Robert D. Jacobs traces changes in the poet's rhetorical strategies for displacing the "I" who suffers and tells (in 1827) by an "I" who relates his distress to phenomena that are general or at least less idiosyncratic (in 1829) and finally by his mature idiom—a pictorial mode representing speculation about the human condition (1832). G. R. Thompson, in "Circumscribed Eden of Dreams: Dream Vision and Nightmare in Poe's Early Poetry" (1984), explores Poe's epistemological problems vis-à-vis the Platonic idea of supernal and transcendent loveliness, even if rarely glimpsed by the earthbound poet. In Thompson's view, the darkening and demonic destruction of Poe's visionary experience leaves only the aesthetic as that which stands closest to the angelic vision.

Edward H. Davidson, in "The Necessary Demon: The Poetry of Youth," the first chapter of *Poe: A Critical Study* (1957), characterizes Poe as an imaginative seeker investigating the "inner world" of reality, the romantic dilemma of self-awareness, the agony of isolation, and self-annihilation—"narrow and static" themes that persisted throughout his life.

Notes on individual poems supplement prefatory essays in Richard Wilbur's *Poe* (1959), Eric W. Carlson's *Introduction to Poe: A Thematic Reader* (1967), and Thomas O. Mabbott's *Collected Works of Edgar Allan Poe: Vol. 1: Poems* (1969). For Wilbur, Poe's vision of poetry entails his "refusal of human emotion and moral concern," "the symbolic destruction of material fact," and negation of "all that he could of the world and worldly self" (39). Carlson gives a central place to Poe's cosmic myth: an unending, dynamic process of creation, dissolution, and rejuvenescence in which "Spirit works through Man." In this context, "Poe endows uncorrupted Youth with something like a race-unconscious," including "dreams" of an ideal by which the poet is haunted. This motif in the 1827 poems "reflects mainly Youth's aspirations toward perfection," but the dream becomes, by 1829, "a vision of supernal Beauty, . . . the Edenic world of poetic harmony and imagination, from which 'passionate' man has fallen" (xxiv). Mabbott, pointing out that Poe wrote the poems before the theoretical work, keeps "purely aesthetic criticism" to a minimum but considers him a lyric poet who wanted "to arouse our best emotions by contemplation of beauty and power." Personal experience deepened Poe's feelings and "heightened his art" but should not be unduly emphasized (xxii–xxx).

Several books on Poe as a literary figure include discussions of selected early poems. Geoffrey Rans, in *Edgar Allan Poe* (1965), analyzes the poet's practice and vision, which by 1829 had "nothing tentative about it" (6). Rans privileges poems that tend to be "symbolic"—by which he means that "the poet does not set out . . . to explain or account for his vision . . . but must try to create it, in *effect*" (41). In *Edgar Poe the Poet* (1969), Floyd Stovall, maintaining that Poe's "theory and practice are so closely related neither can be understood without the other" (16), directs attention from the biography toward analysis of the texts, whereas in *Poe Poe Poe Poe Poe Poe Poe* (1972), Daniel Hoffman's approach is biographical, psychological, and literary. David Halliburton in *Edgar Allan Poe: A Phenomenological View* (1973) explores "the need for transcendence and affirmation" (46), Poe's challenge to himself "to answer darkness with light" (191) in poems that "body forth" autonomous experiences (4). Kenneth Silverman, as the title of *Edgar A. Poe: Mournful and Never-Ending Remembrance* (1991) suggests, traces a preoccupation with death and the afterlife through eighteen of the early poems, many of which disclose a "personal content" as well as "an unfamiliar inner life difficult to grasp" from the known details of the poet's life or his letters (40, 70, passim). Jeffrey Meyers, in *Edgar Allan Poe: His Life and Legacy* (1992), comments briefly on themes and judges the quality of twelve of the early poems; he concludes that the 1831 volume, "an impressive achievement for a young man of twenty-two, was the best written, thus far, by an American poet" (53). Meyers extracts, usually verbatim, the relevant commentary from the book for his essay, "Edgar Allan Poe," in the *Columbia History of American Poetry* (1993).

Other recent (1987) essays, "The Heart of Poe and the Rhythmics of the Poems" by Claude Richard and " 'A Strange Sound, as of a Harp-String Broken' " by David Murray, offer new approaches drawing on work from all periods of Poe's career. Richard analyzes Poe's paradoxical imagination, the "revelatory value" of nonverbal signifiers, and the ultimate aim of his poetry: "to perceive Being as rhythm" and, therefore, "to found the legitimacy of poetry on a rhythmic concept" (195). Murray is concerned with "the separation of language and the real world, and of the real world and the ideal world in Poe's poetry." His language, however, has "a *dual* role as a divider and a connector of discontinuous realms, but gains its special existence from its relation to both" (137–38).

EARLIEST POEMS: 1824–1827

Poe seems to have begun writing verse primarily for amusement. "Oh, Tempora! Oh, Mores!" (1825?), the earliest extant poem of any length, was first published in 1868 (*M* 1, 8–9). In comical heroic couplets, he satirizes the manners of the day and ridicules the dandy. Poe's impudent ironies turn on the trope of the dandy's "cat's eyes," before which the poem aims to "hold a glass/ And let him see himself a proper ass" (*M* 1, 12, lines 87–88). Although this satire "has been with difficulty accorded a place" in the canon, the verse reflects "one element in the mind of even the youthful Poe: a sense of propriety, or ordonnance, of eighteenth century discipline struggling for expression" (Davidson, 3); it is also commended for the poet's "skill in imitation" (Silverman, 24).

Two other juvenile poems are a flirtatious lover's "complaints" for the albums of young women. "To Margaret" (1827–1828) is a literary game—a "parodic cento"—in which the poet pretends a disadvantage. He charges Margaret with having been seduced to "foul revolt" and preferring "squalid wit" to "true wisdom" and "honorable rhyme." Poe deliberately misquotes from "masterpieces" such as Milton's *Paradise Lost,* Cowper's *The Task,* and Pope's *Essay on Criticism,* noted alongside the patchwork of excerpts (*M* 1, 14–15). The interplay between lines and titles is ingenious as well as original. By comparison, "To Octavia" (1827) is commonplace in its lightly ironic expression of the writer's struggle to forget the woman's power over him and does not match the sense of fun in "To Margaret" but anticipates a theme that recurs in later lyrics.

"Tamerlane" (1827)

The title poem of Poe's first volume, published anonymously when the author was eighteen, is a dramatic monologue of 406 lines. After reworking or dropping many lines, presumably in 1828, Poe again shortened the poem to 243 lines and included the much-changed version in *Al Aaraaf, Tamerlane and Minor Poems* (1829). There was also an 1831 version, but the 1829 "Tamerlane" was to be the final form (*M* 1, 24–25) and is the best known. One sees, however, the emergence of Poe as a poet in "Tamerlane" of 1827. It is Poe's first extended use of a "confessional" narrative voice, adopted later for many of the tales.

The monologue of the dying Tamerlane, speaking to a "holy father," is singularly undramatic. The diction is formal, old-fashioned, and occasionally archaic. The pace is measured and, as Jacobs observes (1969, 194–95), often distinguished by extended temporal balance (equalizing "the time of a given foot with others in the line" or "throughout an entire sentence"). The rhyming, though conventional, is accomplished, generally unobtrusive, and rarely strained, in either matched pairs or quatrains with alternating correspondences. The poem, Halliburton concludes, is "a narrative . . . trying to become a lyric" (8).

Tamerlane's contemplative moments frequently veer toward rationalizations of his behavior; and since there are only two questions from which to infer anything but acquiescence or silence on the part of the priest, there is really no one to gainsay the monologist. On that score alone, he is given the habit of commanding attention in a characteristically egocentric way. A mountain lad (a lowly cottager), he describes himself as "of kingly mind—/ And a proud spirit, which hath striv'n/ Triumphantly with human kind" (*M* 1, 27–28, lines 35–37).

Ambitious and willful, he sacrificed hallowed love ("passionate and divine") to become the "great" unhallowed ruler of half the world. Oh, he dreamed that the young girl he had loved from childhood would be his bride and queen; when he returned home to "crown" her, she was dead. In the "diadem'd" outlaw's brooding disquisition on youthful love and the memory of his experience, it is *his* desire, *his* "wild career," *his* vision, *his* power of which he speaks. Admitting to having deceived her and recalling that he left without a farewell, he says that he was ignorant of "woman's heart." Tamerlane's egoism has destroyed the visionary ideal; his deceit has violated her trust and love.

The tale told, Tamerlane ends with a rhetorical flourish as he reflects upon the city where he rules, but, hearing the sound of revelry and light voices coming over him as if it were not his dying hour, he declares that power imparts its venom secretly: "Nothing have I with human hearts" (*M* 1, 37, line 346).

"Tamerlane" is often read in relation to Poe's "unhappy love" for Sarah Elmira Royster, who—during his time at the University of Virginia—became affianced to someone else (*M* 1, 24). Davidson argues that Poe is indulging in a dream legend in order to write about himself—"the only subject Poe ever had." The revisions, however, "diminish the theme of the arrogant, triumphant self because of the obvious disparity between the subject in the poem and the conditions in Poe's own life.'' The poem is a projection ''of a mind which is neither anguished nor penitent; it is a mind which is, quite simply, seeking some means of self-expression'' (4–6). In contrast, Jacobs reads the poem as a ''narrative of a consciousness that attempts to account for an ontological failure by citing a wrong choice among conflicting inclinations'' (1977, 647). Jacobs finds that ''the significant changes between 1827 and 1829'' simplify Tamerlane's character and focus more precisely on ''his opposing impulses.'' In the original version, it is ''hard to tell'' which is his more serious regret—losing his childhood sweetheart or ''the drying up of his sensibilities.'' The 1829 '' 'Tamerlane' intensifies the character's psychological conflict and emphasizes'' his abandoning ''both love and beauty for personal magnitude'' (1977, 650–52).

Other Poems (1827)

A group of lyrics completes *Tamerlane and Other Poems* (1827). Their quality is uneven. They are, in Thompson's view, ''primarily self-conscious manipulations of literary conventions'' (30). The lyrics, however, are not mere distillations of the work of poets from whom Poe learned his craft. While their influences show, they provided him exercises in thinking for himself and making poems that were recognizably his own.

"Song"

(''I saw thee on thy bridal day''). Although ''Song'' depicts a stock situation, Poe rescues it from banality. By changing the ''I'' of the opening stanzas to ''him'' in the closing stanzas, the persona distances himself from the woman and the intimacy they once shared. Admittedly uncertain of the meaning of ''a kindling light'' in her eye—''all of loveliness my aching sight . . . could see''— he thought her blush ''perhaps'' a sign of shame and wanted to believe it was for *him* in whose breast the ''glow'' had ''raised a fiercer flame.'' The balladic reprise, ''Though happiness around thee lay, / The world all before thee,'' is muted by the singer's perceptions, which convey simultaneously unspoken feelings, restrained passion, and an acute sense of loss.

"Dreams"

In this seminal poem, Poe becomes an inquisitor of dreams: sorrowful, pleasurable, chilling, or happy ones because of their ''vivid coloring of life.'' The poem, to Stovall, ''is a juvenile imitation of Byron'' and reveals ''such things as would-be unhappy boys are made of'' (202); to Rans, ''dreams are presented as the only way to a vision of ultimate reality'' (48). But talking about dreams— even in rhymed couplets and fairly regular iambic pentameters—is less imaginative than depicting them.

"Visit of the Dead"

Perhaps inspired by a scene in Byron's *Manfred,* Poe's "Visit" and the effectively revised "Spirits of the Dead" (1829) testify to the sovereign power the dead have over the thoughts of one bereft. The tones of the poem are solemn and quiet in keeping with the presence of the spirits of the remembered dead. Their will overshadows all else in the solitude of night when the stars—"red orbs"—burn without relief. The breath of God is still, and the mist upon the hill is unmoving, betokening the mysterious "visions" that, unlike the dew, will not vanish. The ambience of the poem is sustained by its musical structure with subtle variations in the prevailing iambic pentameter.

"Evening Star"

This poem is a revision of Thomas Moore's "While Gazing on the Moon-Light" in which the moon is milder, nearer to the earth, and "more dear" than the brighter, lone, distant glory of "Each proud star." Poe describes slavish stars that shine pale through the light of the brighter, cold moon—"her beam on the wave"—and turns to address the brilliant Evening Star: "more I admire/ Thy distant fire, / Than that colder, lowly light" (*M* 1, lines 21–23). The verse is less prosaic and more intricate in its structure than Moore's. Beginning with a dissonant five lines of which three are unrhymed, Poe's lyric moves through another five lines of which one is unrhymed and continues with the harmonies of full rhymes for fourteen lines that culminate in affirmation of the superior beauty of the emblematic star—"the light of the visionary ideal" (Carlson, 557).

"Imitation"

Contending with "interminable pride—/ A mystery, and a dream," the persona doubles back to say the dream was "fraught/ With a wild, waking thought/ Of beings" he would not have seen had he let them pass by "With a dreaming eye" (lines 1–10). He sighs, then almost shrugs off the fact that the hope, the light time, the worldly rest, and the thought he cherished earlier have vanished. The poem is an imitation of Byron's "Dream" of a woman whose love he failed to win as well as his sense of the discrepancies between human aspirations and one's significance. "Imitation" is uneasily phrased, its rhymes occasionally strained, and the title suggests that the sentiments are not altogether genuine.

"Stanzas"

The epigraph of the poem, originally untitled (*M* 1, 76–78), is inexactly quoted from "The Island" by Byron in response to "Nature's universal throne," which for Poe is God's throne. Knowing the power that a secret communicant with Earth drew from sun and stars, Poe suggests there is more of sovereignty in the moonbeam than ancient lore has revealed and wonders whether that wild light may be "the unembodied essence" of a fleeting thought. Its very transience, like the sound ''of a heart-string broken,'' awakens us from apathy to see the common things that ''lie/ Each hour before us'' (lines 21–25). Recipients of a vision of beauty given by God, the high-spirited—who otherwise would fall from life and Heaven—have triumphed over godliness and wear the consequent power ''as a crown.'' The ottava rima, with occasional extra unaccented syllables to lighten the cadence, is probably indebted to the heroic verse of Byron's *Don Juan*.

''The Happiest Day''

In a lyric cry from a ''sear'd and blighted heart'' to be still, Poe echoes a phrase from Byron's lines on his thirty-sixth birthday. But the persona's knowledge that ''the happiest day—the happiest hour'' of his life are over is inseparable from the memory that the brightening glance of pride and power was alloyed by an awareness of their capacity to injure. The poem is rhythmically accomplished: the longer lines of each quatrain in tetrameters diminishing to trimeters and frequent dimeters in accord with the motif of lost hope that power and pride assure.

''The Lake: To—''

Inspired by a natural scene near Norfolk, Virginia, and ''A Ballad: The Lake of the Dismal Swamp'' by Thomas Moore, Poe evokes an emptier and lonelier place than that in Moore's ballad, suggested by the story of a young man who, having lost his mind upon the death of a girl he loved, disappeared. Since he frequently said that she was not dead but had gone to the Dismal Swamp, it was supposed he followed her and died there. Poe assumes the point of view of another young man. Beginning awkwardly, the persona recalls the place, gropes to express the nuances of feeling it aroused, and ends in an elegiac strain. With a few bold strokes, Poe suggests the beauty, isolation, and quiet of the ''wild lake.'' Sensing full well the terror and the reality of death in the poisoned waves of the lake, he pays homage to a darkened mind, whose heroism was that his ''wild'ring thought could even make/ An Eden of that dim lake'' (lines 21–22).

Tamerlane's final assertion, ''Nothing I have with human hearts,'' seems in marked contrast to the ''fellow feeling'' that is the motive for this lyric. As Thompson says, ''[T]he awakened imagination of the speaker, creatively sharing the delusion of the lover while maintaining some distance from him in the dramatized imagining of him, can also transmute terror and sorrow and death into loveliness: the complex response to the physical scene results in the poem itself'' (41). Poe rewrote ''The Lake'' and included it in the 1831 text of Tamerlane's soliloquy but later printed the poem as a separate lyric. The fact that Poe thought of it in relation to ''Tamerlane,'' however, makes it a fitting conclusion to the first book of poems. They compose, as Silverman notes, ''a portrait of the artist as a young man'' (39, 41).

POEMS FIRST COLLECTED IN 1829

Receiving no critical response to the 1827 poems did not prevent Poe from writing new ones. The second volume, *Al Aaraaf, Tamerlane, and Minor Poems. by Edgar A. Poe,* published late in 1829, is distinguished by evidence of the twenty-year-old author's coming of age.

"Sonnet—to Science"

Introducing *Al Aaraaf,* the poet's first sonnet is appropriate. Wilbur commends its "lucid logical progression and its air of being public speech" (9). Hoffman thinks it worthy of being included in selections of sonnets by the great English masters of the genre (38). Meyers judges it "the most accomplished poem in the second volume" (1992, 42; 1993, 77). The sonnet is both disciplined and original.

In it, Poe protests the rapacious power of Science, symbolized by the Vulture, in conflict with freedom of the imagination. Having dragged the virgin goddess Diana from her chariot, the predatory bird has swooped to earth to drive both wood nymphs and water nymphs from their natural habitats, the faeries from the grass, and the poet himself from beneath the tamarind tree. The ultimate question, then, is what a poet can make of the diminished freedom.

Poe's structuring of the sonnet bears scrutiny. The vulture, belonging to the real world, is the dominant figure in both the octave and the sestet. But in the sestet, as Thompson points out, the poet re-creates the mythological images "in the very act of their passing, so that the poem becomes a celebration of the poet's imagination" and thereby triumphs over the "predication of the destruction of poetry" (42). While Poe uses the fixed form of fourteen iambic pentameter lines, he follows the practice of many sonneteers in the liberties he takes within the pattern. The opening trochee and the pull to turn iambs into spondees in the first line introduce a barrage of accusatory questions for which "the rhythm is . . . varied" and "the stresses those of natural speech" (Stovall, 208). The rhyme scheme, too, is expressive. Using the Spenserian sonnet, Poe changes it slightly in the first four lines of the sestet, where the expected *c d c d* becomes *d* ("car") *e* ("wood") *d* ("star") and an echoing *e* ("flood"); and the tones are bound together by the hard consonants at one with the thematics. The young Poe was not a jingle man.

"Romance"

Titled "Preface" in 1829, "Romance" is of interest for its relation to Poe's poetic development. John Neal, a contemporary, thought it "the best thing" in *Al Aaraaf* (*M* 1, 127); Hoffman included the verse among the early poems that "transcend the conventions of the time" (36).

Poe associates "Romance" with both nonverbal music and language. Loving "to nod and sing, / With drowsy head and folded wing," Romance has been to the poet "a painted paroquet/ . . . a most familiar bird" from whom the child learned to say his alphabet and "to lisp"—the verb is a perfect choice for beginning speech—his "very earliest word." The adjective "painted" suggests a work of art, but, as Jacobs notes (616), Poe most likely intends the brightly colored Carolina parakeet (once common in the southern states). To think of the bird "among green leaves as they shake/ Far down within some shadowy lake" when the poet was "a child with a most knowing eye" is pleasing. But that time is past.

"Of late" indicates the change, and tension builds in clusters of run-on lines. The tonalities in the progression from the memory of the gentle bird that "loves to nod and sing" to the thunderous "eternal Condor years" with "no time for idle cares" are transfigured in the trope of "an hour with calmer wings" that "flings" its down upon the adult poet's imperiled spirit. Because he cannot forget the parakeet—calling attention to itself as the one irregular word in the poem's rhyme scheme—it is all the more imperative that he seize the precious little time he has for a different music: "My heart would feel it to be a crime/ Unless it [the heart] trembled with the strings" of the poet's lyre.

Wilbur reads "Romance" as "a straightforward account of how the poet was robbed by Time of his original imaginative wholeness" (131). To Stovall, romance was for Poe "as a boy, . . . imitative, a parakeet, and a painted one besides, which suggests that the sentiments expressed in the earliest poems were insincere," whereas "romance as it appeared to him in his more mature years . . . is a real bird, not a painted one, and . . . not a parakeet but a bird that sings its own individual song and through it expresses its genuine nature and feelings" (207–8). Carlson thinks that "Poe renounces the Romantic conception of poetry as diversion and rhetoric . . . in favor of impassioned wisdom and disciplined feeling" (563). There is, however, a continuity between the child's educative experience and the vocation of the poet.

"Al Aaraaf (1829)"

Predicated on a belief in creative freedom, "Al Aaraaf" is an extraordinary poem. "This cosmic myth," Carlson says, "constitutes the major poetic expression of Poe's Neoplatonic philosophy of Beauty" (558). "What is more interesting," to Murray, "is the extent to which Poe uses language not to write *about* this Platonic conception of absolute beauty, but to embody it, or rather, to find a verbal *equivalent* to it" (138).

Al Aaraaf, "from the Arabians" (viz., the Koran), is a wandering star, a "world afar" both in space and time after the imagined destruction of the earth. (A star, Poe notes, appeared suddenly in the heavens in 1572, was observed by Tycho Brahe, attained a brilliancy surpassing that of Jupiter, and suddenly disappeared [*M* 1, 92]). The stellar realm, therefore, must be "imagined," too. "Apart from Heaven's Eternity—and yet how far from Hell" (2, line 173), the star is inhabited (Poe explains) by spirits who, having chosen it "as their residence, do not enjoy immortality—but after a second life of high excitement, sink into forgetfulness & death—" (*M* 1, 92). The poem, permeated with images of music and light, ethereal and nearly insubstantial, is daring without being flamboyant and engaging without being intense. Al Aaraaf—"yon lovely earth/ When sprang the 'Idea of Beauty' into birth" (1, lines 30–31)—is Poe's supreme fiction.

The principal figures in the poem are personifications of perceptive modes: the maiden Goddess Nesace "is associated with the perception of beauty, seen here as a religious devotion" (Jacobs, 653); her handmaiden Ligeia, "whose harshest idea/ Will to melody run" (2, lines 102–3), keeps watch over the divine spirit of harmonious correspondence in "the music of Nature" (*M* 1, 93–94); the angel Ianthe and her seraph-lover Angelo (Michelangelo), the goodly spirit who half-wished "to be again of men" (2, line 226), are creatures of passion.

The action begins with Nesace's kneeling in a shrine of "Fair flowers, and fairy! to whose care is given/ To bear the Goddess' song, in odors, up to Heaven" (1, lines 80–81). As God's messenger, she awaits his reply: "A sound of silence on the startled ear/ Which dreamy poets name 'the music of the sphere' " (1, lines 124–25). The message God entrusts to Nesace—"the word-bearer"—is, as Richard says, "primarily inhibitive. 'Be,' orders the God of Poetry, . . . 'To ev'ry heart a barrier and a ban' " (1, lines 148–49). The interdiction is "to counteract the destructive effect of the heart" (197). Singing to awaken the beautiful Ligeia, Nesace, in turn, entrusts her with the task of summoning the Aaraafians to eternal sleep: "Sweet was their death—with them to die was rife/ With the last ecstasy of satiate life—" (2, lines 168–69). It is Nesace's hope, Stovall thinks, to "save these beings of other worlds from the guilt of man and so from condign punishment" (110). But Ianthe and Angelo fall: "Heaven no grace imparts/ To those who hear not for their beating hearts" (2, lines 176–77).

In an extensive analysis of the poem, Stovall posits three structural elements: "a religious motif, . . . concerned with man in his relation to the authority of God" (103); the conception of Al Aaraaf as the "abode for which Poe sometimes longed, where apart from the passions of the heart and the excitements of the mind, the weary spirit may find rest in an eternity of dreams" (110); and the presentation "allegorically" of Poe's theory of poetry (116), based on the "desire to apprehend supernal beauty" beheld by the poet in "visions." "Al Aaraaf is the realm of beauty, and the spirits who dwell there are artists, lovers of beauty, whose duty it is to reveal to men the true nature of God" (118); the story of Angelo and Ianthe illustrates that passions may cause the ruin of artists by distracting them from . . . the creation and dissemination of beauty" (120).

For Richard, "Angelo and Ianthe, lovers not even in the flesh, cannot hear the voice of Nesace embodied in Ligeia's song. They will be damned," and "the cause of the fall is not so much 'passionate love' as the actual deafening sound of 'the beating of their hearts.' " Theirs "is not a metaphysical damnation of 'passionate man' but the downfall of the artist. . . . The wages of the heart's passion are the loss of *poetic* grace'' and ''the definitive blurring of the glorious vistas opening up on a perpetually desired and perpetually lost 'Eden.' '' To Richard, then, ''the cadence of a living heart deafens the poet who can no longer perceive the sublime 'echoes' which are the soul of true poetry'' (197–98). But, in Silverman's reading, ''Death permeates 'Al Aaraaf' '' as well as ''other early poems'' and invades ''their language and imagery'' (72).

''Al Aaraaf,'' in Hoffman's view, provides ''a more convincing imaginative experience and a much more adept show of versification'' than ''Tamerlane'' (36–37). The young poet ''was able to handle complex conceptions in his verse and to vary the texture of that verse.'' In Part 1, ''the normative line is first, octosyllabic couplets, then pentameter couplets, with the interposition of a lyrical interlude in alternately rhymed trimeter-dimeters'' (39). When God speaks from eloquent silence, ''the eternal voice'' gives commands ''in couplets of Miltonic grandeur'' (40). Part 2 ''consists of pentameter couplets with the interposition of another lyric, this time in anapestic dimeters.'' The whole work ''runs to 422 melodious lines'' (39). Other readers hold dissenting opinions: The poem is ''obscure and elliptical in places,'' although the ''basic action is simple'' (Silverman, 56); or the poem is ''suffused with a fashionable Romantic melancholy and . . . melodramatic incoherence''; Poe's ''most turgid and opaque poem,'' characterized by murky style, . . . specious reasoning, . . . and vague theme,'' that is, a ''failure'' (Meyers 1992, 41, 181, 214, 239; 1993, 176–77).

''Minor Poems'' (1829)

The remaining poems in the volume are of interest as experiments in tone. The parting song, ''To— —'' (''Should my early life seem . . . a dream—'') returns in lines 9–12 to a point made in ''Imitation'' (1827) that there are ''beings . . . / Whom my spirit had not seen/ Had I let them pass me by/ With a dreaming eye.'' ''To— —'' and ''A Dream within a Dream'' (1845) share the image of the persona's standing on the seashore watching the sand slip through his fingers to ''the deep,'' whereas the speaker in ''Imitation'' seems finally not to care. In the 1845 lyric, acknowledging that his days have been a dream, he weeps that he cannot grasp the grains of golden sand as they ebb away, and asks if *all* is not illusion within illusion, ''To— —'' is rebellious. The tone ranges from sarcastic to defiant.

Mirror images for reciprocal love in ''To the River [Po]'' are delicately and playfully drawn without the poet's betraying their significance. The tone is affectionate. To Silverman, ''the poem sees works of art as at once shiningly transparent and complex'' (57).

''To M—'' (''I heed not'') attempts to be nonchalant. It is, however, unclear whether the persona is speaking to a woman who has hurt him or speaking about her to someone else. The tone is ironic as he turns to chiding M, who ''meddles'' with his fate—even when he uses an endearing term (''sweet'') or the vocative "lady," he seems ungracious. Reducing the poem's twenty lines to eight for "To—," Poe changes the tone: the speaker takes heed gratefully, in fact, mourns, that "she" sorrows for his fate.

"Fairy-Land"

In the last poem of this volume, Poe's imagination has free rein. A dim, shadowy, tear-soddened night-landscape is palely illuminated as "Huge moons there wax and wane/ Again—again—again—/ . . . Forever changing places"; one "more filmy than the rest" (and therefore "best") showers light over every drowsy thing. Come morning, the fairies awake to see "their moony covering" soaring in the skies "Like—almost anything—/ Or a yellow albatross—" and "They use that moon no more/ For the same end as before—/ Videlicet a tent—/ Which I think extravagant." It seems, as Wilbur says, "wasteful to use a perfectly good moon only once" (132). The butterflies of earth, however, "seek the skies" and "come down again" to bring a specimen of the moon's light upon "their quivering wings."

One's sense of tone is especially pertinent in reading the poem. Davidson sees it as "an apocalyptic vision" (31); Carlson, "surrealistic dream" (563); Halliburton, "whimsical" (185). To Wilbur, it is a successful example of Poe's humor, with traces of self-mockery (131). Stovall thinks the transforming art of illusion is the theme, the butterflies symbolizing artists (*M* 1, 12). The quick pacing, capers with simile and rhyme, stylistic incongruities, and the visually sensitive correspondence between butterflies and moonlight dispel the gloom and, as if by legerdemain, culminate in surprise.

FUGITIVE VERSES

Two "fugitive verses" from the years 1829–1831 are acrostics written in the album of a cousin, Elizabeth Rebecca Herring. Poe, clever fellow that he was, must have enjoyed writing these *jeux d'esprit,* which show off a youthful gift for bantering. A quatrain, "To Isaac Lea," seems a reply to criticism or an inquiry from Lea and reflects on a cause to which the poet is pledged. The succinct statement, in a natural and vigorous rhythm, leaves little to the imagination except the inference that the cause is poetry and the disappointment Poe must have felt over a failure to interest Lea in publishing the *Al Aaraaf* volume. "Lines on Joe Locke" was provoked by Poe's experience at West Point, where the reluctant cadet was said to have amused himself by "Pasquinading the Professors." The verse, depending on accurate timing and puns, is of slight interest other than that it is the only surviving example of lampoons for which Poe was remembered at the academy. Meyers comments: "a tame squib—rather than biting satire" (1992, 50; 1993, 178–79).

"Alone"

Written in an autograph album about 1829 and published posthumously without a title in 1875, the poem is now referred to as "Alone" (from the line "And all I lov'd—I lov'd alone—''). The verse owes debts to Byron's "Prisoner of Chillon" (who is "Lone—as solitary cloud") and *Manfred* (whose "Spirit walked not with souls of men"). "Alone" begins by explaining that "From childhood's hour I have not been/ As others were—I have not seen/ As others saw—I could not bring/ My passions from a common spring—" (lines 1–4) and ends with the revelation of the "mystery which binds me still/. . . . the cloud that took the form/ (When the rest of Heaven was blue)/ Of a demon in my view—" (lines 12, 20–22). "Alone" is a liberating exercise. The poem runs freely along in irregular measures—punctuated by the rhetorical dashes and almost never slowed by the rhymed couplets. The rush of energy, the theme, and the imagery suggest that the author is Poe.

For Allen Tate, "Alone" is the symbolic matrix in a study of Poe as "a forlorn demon gazing at himself in the glass"; the narcissistic "I" in a "wilderness of mirrors" is, in Tate's view, a description of most of the fictional heroes (1981, x-xi; 1968, *Essays,* 387). Hoffman writes that, although there are Byronic echoes in "Alone," the poem is "Poe's own work, his destiny, his woe: the Alienated Poet come to life." Hoffman concludes that the poem *qua* poem is "nearly a success"; while the language is commonplace but clear and open, it "modulates, by the end, to the intensity of early William Blake" and transcends the conventions of the time (36).

POEMS BY EDGAR A. POE–SECOND EDITION

Published in 1831 by the New York firm of Elam Bliss, *Poems* begins with a "Letter to Mr.—" ("Letter to B—" when it was reprinted in 1836), an apologia for *some* of the early verse.

What, Poe asks, is the end of existence? "Happiness," which is another word for "pleasure." Poetry, then, as Wallace Stevens would reassert, must give pleasure. Poe discusses qualities he appreciates in the work of a few poets: the "glimpses of extreme delicacy (delicacy is the poet's own kingdom)" in the early Wordsworth; "all that is airy and fairy-like" in Shakespeare's *A Midsummer Night's Dream* and *The Tempest*; James McPherson's "gorgeous, yet simple [nature] imagery, where all is alive and panting with immortality"; and the volcanic power—"the very darkness bursting from the crater. . . . fire and light . . . weltering below" in the poetry of Coleridge (Harrison, xxxviii–xliii).

The letter, at last, gives a teleological definition of poetry. In contrast to the object of a work of science, which is truth, the immediate aim of both romance and poetry is pleasure; but romance has as its object a *definite,* and poetry an *indefinite,* pleasure attained by the difference between "perceptible images with definite and *in*definite sensations," respectively. Music is the means of creating indefinite sensations. Therefore: "Music, when combined with a pleasurable idea, is poetry" (Harrison, xliii). The reader is left to puzzle over what is for Poe "a pleasurable idea."

Reaction to the "Letter" varies: Rans thinks the implied aesthetic is expressed

"with wit and precision" (19); Jacobs considers it "a jejune performance, disorganized and irresponsible" but "well enough managed" (1969, 59); Silverman, "meandering" although "an important statement of aesthetic principles"
(69). Poe's predilections, Rans continues, account for poems as different as the
early "Song" ("delicacy"), "Fairy-Land" ("all that is airy and fairy-like"),
the first stanza of "Romance" ("gorgeous yet simple nature imagery"), and—
at least one new poem—"The Doomed City" (Coleridgean "volcanic power").
But it requires Poe's own "sleight-of-hand" to say that all of the poems are
accounted for or to include all of them in the theoretical package. While there
are qualities in "Tamerlane," for instance, connected with those to which the
"Letter" refers, depiction of character is not one of them. Furthermore, although
there are indefinite sensations, there is a dearth of perceptible images in the
"dream" poems. Poe's after-the-fact theorizing works best in relation to *Al
Aaraaf,* for which I suspect it was intended to plead.

For the 1831 edition of poems, he "made few changes, almost all of them
abortive, in 'Al Aaraaf' " (*M* 1, 98). "Romance" was titled "Introduction"
and extended from twenty-one to sixty-six lines, but Poe later dropped forty-
three of them, perhaps because they were "extremely personal" (*M* 1, 156). He
also later wisely retained the more unified original version of "Fairy-Land,"
which he had lengthened from forty-five to sixty-four lines—forty-four of which
are entirely new—for this volume (*M* 1, 161). The important new poems in the
book are "To Helen," "Israfel," "Irenë" (rewritten as "The Sleeper"), "The
Valley of Nis," and "The Doomed City."

"To Helen"

An example of the poet's successful integration of subject and form, the poem
was a tribute to Jane Stith Stanard (to whom he referred as "Helen Stanard"),
the mother of his friend Rob when they were boys in Richmond. Bearing the
name of the heroine celebrated as the most beautiful woman of ancient times
and remembered in Marlowe's words as the "face that launched a thousand
ships," she is for Poe the embodiment of a compelling ideal vision: quiet grace,
classical beauty, poise, and *caritas.*

The poem, following a simple narrative line, is allusively complex. A "weary,
way-worn" traveler, having roamed "desperate seas," affirms Helen's power
to draw him like a victorious bark over fragrance-ladened waters to his home-
land. His identity has been much debated—the poet, Eros, "an exhausted but
victorious Greek Warrior" (Meyers, 1992, 17; 1993, 181), and Everyman,
among those suggested. He is an archetypal figure, the male wanderer who keeps
before him the image of a woman as muse and guide waiting faithfully for him
to return to "the glory that was Greece" (the sacred country of classical art)
and "the grandeur that was Rome" (the great architecture of the Eternal City).
As he beholds her, standing statuelike with a lamp in hand at "yon window,"
he exclaims to himself, "Ah, Psyche, from the regions which/ Are Holy-Land!"

Although he is safely "home" and she is in clear view, she does not move and he beholds her from a distance. Will she, the woman whom the boy Cupid loved but also the anima, breath, and soul, having sustained him as he wandered, remain both close and forever distant? That is the "romantic" essence of the quest for ideal or spiritual beauty.

The lyrical economy and balance in the perfected form of the poem are in keeping with what Stovall terms Poe's "impulse to classicism" (173). "It is perhaps in 'To Helen,' " Lynen observes, "that Poe's essential action is most gracefully managed" (261). Meyers thinks it "Poe's most beautiful elegiac love lyric" (1992, 17; 1993, 181).

"Israfel"

Poe modified the epigraph, "And the angel Israfel who has the sweetest voice of all God's creatures," for the 1831 poem, to read "And the angel Israfel, whose heart-strings are a lute" for the final version. The poem draws a contrast between the heavenly Israfel, who sings "so wildly well" and the "sustained banality" (Hoffman, 36) of the mortal poet in "a world of sweets and sours." Complementing "To Helen," the vision in "Israfel" is of the ideal poetic realm. In the poet's heaven, deep thoughts are a duty, Love is a grown-up God, and the glances of the Houri (the alluring nymphs of the Mohammedan paradise) are imbued with the beauty of a star; but whether the wise Israfel's song is of grief or joy, hate or love, the spiritual purity of the music is paradoxically not without his burning measure, the trembling, living heart strings that are a lute. "And the giddy stars are mute."

The little comic note, "giddy stars," anticipates the poet's quip that earthly flowers are "merely—flowers" and the witty play in the allusion to the Platonic allegory of the cave—the shadow of Israfel's "perfect bliss" is the "sunshine" of the imperfect world of humankind. Poe speculates finally, with wry humor, that if the two poets could exchange places, the angelic poet might sing less well, while the mortal poet might surpass the song he has written in praise of Israfel. The poem, in Mabbott's view, is "one of Poe's great accomplishments" (171). Meyers comments that it is "mysteriously incantatory" and confirmation that "Poe found in Romantic poetry an artistic correlative for his own unhappy life" (1992, 51, 52; 1993, 179, 180).

"Irenë" (1831) and "The Sleeper" (1831–1845)

"Irenë" (Eirēnē is the Greek personification of Peace [*M* 1, 179]) and "The Sleeper" (1845) are two markedly different versions of the same poem, in which Poe writes on a motif that is said to have obsessed him: the death of a beautiful woman.

"Irenë" begins with a "song" of the soaring moon; an attentive persona observes the soporific influence of the moon on the peaceful landscape and states the poem's first theme—"All beauty sleeps": Irenë sleeps. The meaning of Irenë's sleep is slowly revealed, and another theme emerges—"The lady sleeps: the dead all sleep—/ At least as long as love doth weep." Irenë has been interred; the mourners have departed. When "light laughter chokes the sign" of grief, her indignant spirit returns to the pure waters of a remembered lake and "sinks within (weigh'd down by wo)/ Th' uncertain, shadowy heaven below." But the persona observes "the untrodden grass." (He does not say she has not disturbed the ground over which she has moved.) The only sound he hears is the keening ("Ai! ai! alas! alas!") of the flowers as the night winds pass. Poe later unfortunately excised the passage (lines 41–59). There is a break between it and the concluding lines (60–74); the repetend, "The lady sleeps," serves as a bridge to the third and final theme: may she rest in the peace of the honored dead. The bereaved narrator prays that there will be for Irenë a fitting burial chamber, more holy if more melancholy than the grave to which she was consigned and forgotten. As a last confirmation that she is loved, he remembers her as a living child, throwing "many an idle stone" against the "sounding door" of a tomb that often "flung its black/ And vampyre-winged pannels back/ Flutt'ring triumphant o'er the palls/ Of her old family funerals" (lines 67–74).

" 'Irenë' fails," Jacobs thinks, "to come to any sort of thematic focus" (1977, 664), whereas "The Sleeper" has the coherence of only two themes and a single voice. "Irenë" is, however, developed as a musical composition. Its three themes are closely related by variations in the refrain also employed in "The Sleeper," but in "Irenë" there are vocal subtleties—the narrative and elegiac voice consonant with the loving but ineffective voice of the guardian moon and the lament of the flowers—that "The Sleeper" lacks.

Poe's aim in "The Sleeper," Halliburton says, "is to 'elevate' the work" by reversing "the tendency to let nature take the place of a human presence" and "by placing" the death of Irenë against "a religious background": " 'Heaven have her in its sacred keep . . . poor child of sin!' " (91–92). For Carlson, the "constancy of her grieving lover (the speaker) transfigures Irenë into a symbol of ideal peacefulness of spirit" (567). To Lynen, however, "The Sleeper" illustrates "Poe's favorite device of beginning with a moody bit of scene setting, so ominous in its effect that the action that wells up from it seems illusionary from the outset" (257).

A comparison of the impressionistic elements in both versions of the poem suggests that the imagery is flawed. For instance, while "the lily lolls on the wave," "tinted shadows rise and fall," or "icy worms" creep about in "Irenë," the lily lolls, shadows are "like ghosts," "the pale sheeted ghosts go by," and the worms are "soft" in "The Sleeper." These are Poe's tags that encourage readers to find him, as Hoffman does, "tasteless" (20). Both versions, nevertheless, signal Poe's striving for a transposition of an "idea" into a state of being that the poem itself—through situation and scene, visual and vocal imagery—symbolizes.

"The Valley of Nis" (1831) and "The Valley of Unrest" (1831–1845)

Poe fully realized the new mode in the revisions of the poem retitled "The Valley of Unrest." Incantatory and musically impressionistic, it is the kind of poem in which Poe's French admirers saw his "genius." Stéphane Mallarmé placed "The Valley of Unrest," for example, among "the most significant" of the verse and said the poem was "unquestionably stamped with the seal of spiritual maturity" (Alexander, 64).

The poem is a trope for the transformation from an Edenic peace to a state of restlessness. When Poe deleted sixteen introductory lines of "Nis," he "eliminated almost all of the story" and "some of the clearer allusions" (*M* 1, 190). In "Nis," landscape imagery, without being "unrealistic," becomes gradually alive with movement—culminating with the moon that shines unsteadily by night and the sun that reels by day. In "The Valley of Unrest," nothing there, save the airs that brood over the solitude, is motionless; the imagery becomes "surreal." The trees that "palpitate like chill seas" and the clouds "that rustle through the unquiet Heaven" are driven by no wind. But to call the poem (as critics do) surrealistic or dreamlike is inadequate. The imagery does violence to laws of natural phenomena—the sky is "terror stricken"—yet there is no evident sense of panic, and the terror is not that felt during cataclysmic events. The terror is, rather, the consciousness of incessant motion without a moment's peace. "The human condition," Carlson observes, "is one of unrest, reflected in nature itself, which weeps ['perennial tears'] for man's tragic loss of innocence and of Eden" (563). That reading recalls the opening of "The Valley of Nis": "Far away—as far at least/ Lies that valley as the day/ Down within a golden east—/ All things lovely—are not they/ Far away—far away?" (lines 2–5).

"The Doomed City" (1831) and "The City in the Sea" (1831–1845)

The doomed city is "Far down within the dim west." Death dominates the scene; a frightful calm and melancholy pervade the strange city that lies isolated—"all alone"—in a "long night-time." Drawing its idea from Sodom and Gomorrah (*M* 1, 204), condemned by God, the poem depicts, Jacobs notes, "a world without motion"—"the good and the bad, and the worst, and the best/ Have gone to their eternal rest," "Time-eaten towers . . . tremble not," the waters of the sea lie "resignedly" (lines 4, 10, 12), and "the only perceptible form of energy is a light that streams up from the sea, 'a wilderness of glass.' " If, as Jacobs says, "things do not move in space," Time "moves: 'the very hours are breathing low,' and upon the death of Time, the city sinks into Hell" (1977, 662).

Poe made "a few minor alterations" when the poem was reprinted as "The

City of Sin'' in 1836 (*M* 1, 198), but ''The City in the Sea'' is noticeably different from the original. By cutting the closing anticlimactic couplet (''And Death to some happy clime/ Shall give his undivided time.'') of ''The Doomed City,'' Poe ends ''The City in the Sea'' with a grand finale. *As* the inert city—without resistance, without an earthly sound—begins slowly to sink ''down and down'' and ''to settle hence, / Hell rising from a thousand thrones/ Shall do it reverence'' (lines 51–53). Hearing the hissing of the poem's last words die away, one has a *frisson de terreur* that, again, no naturalistic description is likely to effect.

The ''conventional suggestion'' of a damned city, Jacobs points out, is also ''muted. . . . God is simply absent. . . . The death-world, in spite of its display of human accomplishments—domes, spires, kingly halls, temples, and towers—is frozen'' in space. ''Nothing descends from above—the realm of being; and the only illumination proceeds from below—the realm of nothing'' (1977, 663). For Carlson, ''This symbolic poem has less to do with Sodom and Gomorrah than with the classical Hades. Unorthodox rather than Christian, the image of the city . . . owes much to legends of such buried cities as Ys'' (564). Although Poe carefully details what Rans calls a ''fantasia of architectural glories,'' the ''city's foundation is never established. . . . The scene is richly ambiguous: it is a place of 'eternal rest' but its serenity is 'hideous.' '' The poem, Rans continues, ''is a triumph of the indefinite in the mixture of effects of horror and fulfillment; its ending is a catastrophe without a tragedy''; and because ''no single interpretation will completely reduce the poem to statement,'' Poe has made ''The City in the Sea'' something ''much greater. . . . It is a created event frighteningly whole in itself'' (56). ''The City in the Sea,'' in Lynen's view, ''is perhaps the most impressive of all the poems'' (252).

Poems of 1832–1835

When Poe said in 1845 that ''events not to be controlled have prevented me from making, at any time, serious efforts in what, under happier circumstance, would have been the field of my choice,'' the remark certainly pertains to the years 1832–1835. He had begun writing prose fiction, for which there was a market, and he had less time for verse. There are few poems from the period, and only two are well known.

"To One in Paradise" (1833).

This poem is admired for its simple melody and images in the voice of a romantic poet: ''Thou wast all to me, love, / For which my soul did pine—/ A green isle in the sea, love, a fountain and a shrine.'' Upon the loss of the dream, the poet's emotion becomes perfervid, the ''song'' exclamatory: ''alas! alas!'' or ''No more—no more—no more—/ (Such language holds the solemn sea/ To the sands upon the shore)/ [No More] Shall bloom the thunder blasted tree/ Or the stricken eagle soar!'' Then the excitement subsides; the last stanza is a denouement in which the disconsolate poet tells the woman that his days are trances but that he dreams nightly of her gray eyes and her dancing by eternal streams (*M* 1, 215).

Poe added a fifth stanza to the poem for its inclusion in "The Visionary" (1834), where the narrator "discovers" it to be in the handwriting of the protagonist—modeled on Lord Byron. Retained in all versions of the tale (later, "The Assignation"), the stanza is omitted in separately published versions of the poem (*M* 1, 212–13). The additional lines account for the grief of the poem's persona: the young woman he loved had been married "to titled age and crime!"

The poem seems unlabored, as if written without hesitancy and as if it is the culmination of years of brooding that began with "Tamerlane." While Poe had other themes, he is particularly identified with disappointment in love and its loss. The mournful *o*'s and the repeated "alas! alas!" that amplify the vowels and sibilants of the title "To One in Paradise" are qualities also especially associated with Poe's poetry; and, after scanning the iambic trimeters for displacements of expected stresses and natural exchanges of appropriately lighter or stronger rhythms, Stovall concludes that the lyric form as well as the theme "is characteristic of Poe's early period" (217).

"The Coliseum."

The second memorable poem of 1833 is Poe's first work in blank verse. An apostrophe in the voice of a pilgrim to the colossal amphitheater, once the embodiment "of pomp and power" but now testament to Time's corrosive change, the poem is, as Wilbur notes, "a bit of mutability rhetoric" (137). The pilgrim himself is altered and humbled in the tiring search for "springs of lore." Kneeling in silence, he contemplates the significance of the great symbol of classical antiquity. The poem, in Wilbur's reading, does not merely assert "that ancient Rome still strongly influences our minds and our culture." The poet's subject "is *all Ruin*; and the 'prophetic' power of the Ruin . . . is its power to exalt the spirit" (138). The crumbling stones, blackened, grayed, and pallid in the dim night, answer in echoes—"as Melody from Memnon" to the light of morning—the pilgrim's question about the meaning of these broken images left to him. Within "a cluster of negations," the stones insist that not all the attributes (power, magic, wonder, mysteries, memories) have been lost and thereby affirm for the pilgrim a vision to shore against the ruins (Halliburton, 108). In Silverman's view, "the inner theme of the poem is rebirth—the coliseum is a survivor of death" (92).

The emotion in "The Coliseum," in Halliburton's view, is "of a controlled and practiced kind. It is a public emotion" in a "Ciceronian or rhetorical mode that is more or less self-consciously public." It was "audible for the first time" in "Oh, Tempora! Oh, Mores!," when the youthful author tried on "the jacket of eighteenth century wit, only to find it too tight for his taste" (105). For Stovall, the "tone of sonorous melancholy" in "The Coliseum" is "but a deepening of the one we have heard in earlier verse. Poe here displays such a command of blank verse that one wonders whether, after all, his genius was exclusively lyrical'' (216).

POLITIAN: 1835

Poe's major work in blank verse is the short, tragic drama *Politian,* with which the early period of the poet comes to a halt in 1835. Having begun employment on *The Southern Literary Messenger,* where he published five scenes of the play, Poe never finished it; but Mabbott, who edited a composite of extant versions of the text, thinks it ''needed only a few lines to be completed'' (*M* 1, 241).

Reading like a libretto for an Italian opera, the play is set in a Roman palace, its garden, and the Coliseum. The primary events reveal the characters' response to the excessive power of their emotions: Castiglione's guilt for having betrayed Lalage and Politian's resolve—after falling in love with her—to avenge her honor.

Poe indicates an aptitude for drama in more than one scene. Castiglione, for instance, is visited by a companion who offers him a choice of gifts: twelve bottles of good wine or a sackcloth bundle and a tub of ashes as if in the theater of the absurd. Castiglione chooses the wine. Lalage, secluded for months in a palace apartment, is unable to quiet the conflicts in her soul. At ''war with God,'' she rejects penitence, prayer, and crucifix but defiantly draws a cross-handled dagger and raises it high as symbol of ''the deed—the vow'' to which she swears (Scene IV, line 104), starkly countering Castiglione's faithlessness and foretelling the end. The involvement of Politian, the world-weary traveler, in the plot is, then, inevitable. Overhearing the plaintive yet sweet voice of a woman singing a familiar song, he later encounters her in the garden. The change from the moment of his being captivated by Lalage's voice to quickening love for the singer is both theatrical and poetic. They long to flee together to a life of joyful freedom in the new world, the golden west a thousand leagues away. But ''the deed is to be done'' and cannot be escaped, however tempting the vision of happiness (Scene VII, lines 655–74) where ''Eros'' shall ''be all'' (line 677).

As the action closes in, Politian awaits the arrival of Castiglione and his betrothed at the marriage altar in the interior of the ruins of the Coliseum, the play's most operatic setting. Poe adapts the poem ''The Coliseum,'' with its sparse, almost spectral images of a shattered world, as a soliloquy for Politian. The sense of ruin and abandonment, of glories lost, of empty and pervasive desolation—all signify the hero's mood; the spirit of the place oppresses him, but the awareness of the mystery of the cold stones gives him strength for retribution.

The play has received less favorable attention than it deserves. For Stovall, the style is derivative, the plot melodramatic; Politian ''never comes to life'' (216). To Rans, the work ''is not of the first interest'' as poetic drama but shows

Poe's use of a situation "to satisfy his own preoccupations"—a man "shut out from common passions," Lalage "transformed into unearthly loveliness," and the America to which they hope to escape "transformed into Poe's paradisiac ambition" (60–61). Meyers criticizes Poe's imitation of "the hackneyed and tedious conventions of Jacobean tragedy," "the wooden hero, archaic style," and "the pointless repetition of banalities" that suggest "the astonishing awfulness of the play" (1992, 76, 77; 1993, 182, 183). Poe has moved, nevertheless, from the depiction of a self-absorbed Tamerlane of 1827 to an old-fashioned hero willing to sacrifice himself on the "altar of love."

The verse from 1825 to 1835 reveals not only the frustrated hopes but also the exceptional gifts of the poet. The fine, sensitive, and often subtle effects that he realized when he was free to explore the pleasures of poetry without trimming his talents for the marketplace are often overlooked. Yet, critic after critic has found early poem after early poem to praise. Although, in most instances, the poem commended by a critic of a particular persuasion is not that chosen by other readers, a gathering of the separate favorable judgments by attentive students of the first poems speaks well for Poe.

The daring, originality, and skill evident in the variety of poetic modes that he tried suggest the value he placed on a *range* of styles. Attention to Poe's ideas has frequently resulted in neglect of his stylistics. When they have been discussed, the tendency is to cite lapses in taste. For example, Robert von Hallberg, after comparing only two brief passages from *Politian* and discussing Poe's criteria for good writing, remarks that his "interest in stylistic range was a fascination for what he must have known he thoroughly lacked as a poet" (92). Poems as different as "I saw thee on thy bridal day" and "The Coliseum," however, belie the claim that he lacks stylistic versatility.

Poe, as W. H. Auden observed, "was interested in too many poetic problems and experiments at once for the time he had to give them" (xi). In learning what Auden calls the poet's trade, the young writer took risks. There is, for instance, nothing like the imaginative "Al Aaraaf" in nineteenth-century American literature. But there are also pedestrian poems. There are those to which he returned more than once in an effort—with or without success—to strengthen them. Like Robert Lowell, Poe treated even his printed work as "manuscript" by often revising it for republication. It is in the craft that Poe's tormented perfectionism is perhaps most visible. "To strive for perfection," Halliburton observes, "is to affirm," to say "yes, if not in thunder, at least with a certain insistence" (190–91).

WORKS CITED

Alexander, Jean. *Affidavit of Genius: Edgar Allan Poe and the French Critics. 1847–1924.* Port Washington, NY: Kennikat, 1971.

Auden, W. H. "Introduction." *Edgar Allan Poe: Selected Prose and Poetry*. New York: Holt, 1950.

Carlson, Eric W. *Introduction to Poe: A Thematic Reader*. Glenview, NY: Scott, 1967.

Davidson, Edward H. *Poe: A Critical Study*. Cambridge: Belknap of Harvard UP, 1957.

Hallberg, Robert von. "Edgar Allan Poe, Poet-Critic." *Nineteenth-Century American Poetry*. Ed. A. Robert Lee. London: Vision; Totowa, NJ: Barnes and Noble, 1985.

Halliburton, David. *Edgar Allan Poe: A Phenomenological View*. Princeton: Princeton UP, 1973.

Harrison, James A. *The Complete Works of Edgar Allan Poe*. Vol. 7. New York: Thomas Y. Crowell, 1902.

Hoffman, Daniel. *Poe Poe Poe Poe Poe Poe Poe*. Garden City, NY: Doubleday, 1972.

Jacobs, Robert D. *Poe: Journalist & Critic*. Baton Rouge: Louisiana State UP, 1969.

———. "The Self and the World: Poe's Early Poems." *Georgia Review* 3 (Fall 1977): 638–68.

Lynen, John F. *The Design of the Present*. New Haven, CT: Yale UP, 1969.

Mabbott, Thomas Ollive. *Collected Works of Edgar Allan Poe: Poems*. Vol. 1. Cambridge: Belknap of Harvard UP, 1969.

Meyers, Jeffrey. *Edgar Allan Poe: His Life and Legacy*. New York: Charles Scribner's Sons, 1992.

———. "Edgar Allan Poe." *Columbia History of American Poetry*. Ed. Jay Parini and Brett C. Miller. New York: Columbia University P, 1993.

Murray, David. " 'A Strange Sound, as of a Harp-String Broken': The Poetry of Edgar Allan Poe." *Edgar Allan Poe: The Design of Order*. Ed. A. Robert Lee. London: Vision; Totowa, N.J.: Barnes and Noble, 1987.

Richard, Claude. "The Heart of Poe and the Rhythmics of the Poems." *Critical Essays on Edgar Allan Poe*. Ed. Eric W. Carlson. Boston: G. K. Hall, 1987.

Silverman, Kenneth. *Edgar A. Poe: Mournful and Never-Ending Remembrance*. New York: HarperCollins, 1991.

Stovall, Floyd. *Edgar Poe the Poet*. Charlottesville: UP of Virginia, 1969.

Tate, Allen. *The Complete Poetry and Selected Criticism of Edgar Allan Poe*. New York: New American Library, 1968, 1981.

———. "Our Cousin, Mr. Poe." *Essays of Four Decades*. Chicago: Swallow, 1968.

Thompson, G. R. "Circumscribed Eden of Dreams: Dream Vision and Nightmare in Poe's Early Poetry." Baltimore: Enoch Pratt Library, Edgar Allan Poe Society, and U of Baltimore Library, 1984.

Wilbur, Richard, "Introduction." *Poe: Complete Poems*. New York: Dell, 1959.

4

The Poems: 1836–1849

DWAYNE THORPE

Poe did not relinquish a career in poetry willingly. Nevertheless, under threat of starvation, he did abandon what was for him "not a purpose, but a passion" (*PQ* 18), becoming, for three-fourths of his career, "essentially a magazinist" (*O* II, 326): reviewer, editor, and tale-writer. The meteoric success of "The Raven" (1845), of course, linked his name at once with poetry; but by that time, in a life plagued by poverty, grief, failure, and self-destruction, there was no energy or time to begin again. Moreover, there were persistent doubts. His contemporaries usually invoked that vague word *genius* in evaluating his poetry, but always with reservations (see, for instance, Lowell, Higginson, and Whitman in *REAP*; 9–12, 67–70, 73–76). Others have been unwilling to concede even a qualified "genius." Aldous Huxley's well-known charge of "vulgarity," for instance (31–37), was shared by others (Winters, 93–122; Asselineau, 40).

Outside America, Poe's poetry has evoked epoch-making responses, most markedly in France, among both poets (P. Quinn) and critics (Alexander). But at home, only a rare voice has hailed his poetry. Symptomatically, the influential have been ambivalent. Thus, Eliot at first paraphrased James's disparaging view and said he could "never be sure" whether Poe had influenced him—even though the influence of the Poe-inspired French *symbolistes* is obvious (Eliot 1949, 327)—but later chose Poe, with Twain and Whitman, as one of the three defining "landmarks" of Amerian literature (Eliot 1965, 53). Auden edited an anthology of Poe's work, but his remarks gently explain the flaws in Poe's poetry, echoing Eliot (Auden, v–xvii). Richard Wilbur, in many ways the best contemporary critic of Poe, having analyzed his work in a number of essays and even edited the poems, nevertheless declared his aesthetic "insane" (Wilbur 1959, 120). Academic criticism provides a striking picture of neglect. In any given year, critics produce dozens of analyses of Poe's fiction but almost none of his poetry; and most essays are analyses of single poems, not attempts to view the poetry as a whole.

The poems have been well edited on three occasions (Campbell, Stovall, Mabbott), but the absence of book-length studies "speaks volumes." Almost none exist, and the most recent, now a quarter of a century old, is a collection of previously published essays (Stovall 1969).[1] Poe, by contrast, continually strove to return to poetry and gave the best efforts of his final years to it— including his great prose poem, *Eureka.* This was not simple tenacity or vanity. His poetry through 1831 was remarkable for youthful promise. By the age of twenty-two, he had already published three volumes containing "Sonnet—To Science," "To Helen," "Israfel," "The Valley of Unrest," and "The City in the Sea." After 1833, he produced a remarkable, though small, body of work, including some of the best-known poems in the language: "To One in Para-dise," "The Haunted Palace," "The Raven," "The Bells," "Ulalume," "For Annie," and "Annabel Lee."

This contrast between Poe's passion for his poems and the critics' indifference to them is the essential fact confronting anyone who studies them, and it needs to be understood. Critics have neglected Poe's poetry partly because he wrote so little of it; partly because his best fiction is very good, indeed; partly because the poetry has primarily influenced non-English poets; but chiefly because it runs against the stream. This is most obvious in his insistent musicality. Poe defined poetry as "the rhythmical creation of beauty" (*T,* 78) even as Emerson was laying down a new law that "it is not metres, but a metre-making argument that makes a poem"; and twentieth-century American poets have built on the image, not the musical phrase. By Poe's standards, his finest achievement is "Ulalume," whose evocative music resists comprehension. But critics have usu-ally attended only to meaning, so that commentary on "Ulalume" has been a repeated exercise in interpretation (cf. Davidson, Carlson, Jacobs, Omans, Sto-vall 1969, and Rans).

Poe's poetry explores longings for the eternal in a world of time, as becomes clear in "The Poetic Principle" (1848), his analysis of the dialectic of poetry as a consequence of the tripartite nature (Pure Intellect, Taste, and Moral Sense) of "the world of mind."[2] There follows his major definition of the nature of poetry:

An immortal instinct, deep within the spirit of man, . . . a sense of the Beautiful, . . . a thirst unquenchable. . . . It is no mere appreciation of the Beauty before us—but a wild effort to reach the Beauty above . . . and thus . . . through a certain, petulant sorrow at our inability to grasp *now,* wholly, here on earth, at once and for ever, those divine and rapturous joys, of which *through* the poem, or *through* the music, we attain to but brief and indeterminate glimpses. (*T,* 77)

Here he argues that the true poet attempts to transcend the Beauty of the here and now in his quest for "glimpses" ("psychal fancies" or intuitions), "brief and indeterminate" though they may be. To some ironist critics, this passage seems to admit the futility of attempting to escape the world of time, being left with rearranging the components of the world into novel combinations. "We struggle, by multiform combinations among the things and thoughts of Time, to attain a portion of that Loveliness whose very elements, perhaps, appertain to eternity alone" (*T*, 77). Novel, musical combinations elevate the soul momentarily, producing melancholy as glimpses of the ideal fade into a recognition that time cannot be escaped. "After the lapse of half an hour, at the very utmost, it flags—fails—a revulsion ensues—and then the poem is, in effect, and in fact, no longer such" (*T*, 71). It should be noted, however, that a "glimpse" of half an hour allows for a substantial visionary experience. Poe's poems turn repeatedly on three major concepts: art as a pursuit of the ideal; the destructive power of time; and the inherent connection of beauty with melancholy.

For nearly a decade after 1833, his poems were sometimes connected with fiction. "The Coliseum" (1833) was written at the same time as "MS Found in a Bottle" and is directly related to it, both through the tale's narrator, that "dealer in antiquities" whose "very soul has become a ruin" (*M* 2, 145), and through the subject of both works: the awakening of the soul by scenes "imbued with the spirit of Eld" (*M* 2, 144). That same year, he began to embed poems within tales, as keys to their "under or mystic current" of meaning (*M* 2, 406). "To One in Paradise" (1833) forms the climax of "The Assignation"; "The Haunted Palace" (1839) is the key to "The Fall of the House of Usher"; and "The Conqueror Worm" (1843) illuminates the nihilism of the revised "Ligeia." These poems are indispensable in revealing the meanings of the tales.

POEMS: MIDDLE AND LATE

"The Haunted Palace" (1839)

The narrator of "The Fall of the House of Usher" was the first "reader" to realize that "The Haunted Palace" is the key to Roderick Usher's state of mind: the terror that is "not of Germany, but of the soul" (*PQ*, 129). It is entirely possible that Poe wrote the tale to accommodate the poem rather than the other way around, though critics have usually reduced it to a tool for interpreting the tale. One essay about Poe's poetry, for instance, confines its commentary on "The Haunted Palace" to the statement that it "first appeared in Poe's finest story . . . and expresses the themes of the story in poetic form," followed by four paragraphs summarizing the plot of the tale without further comment on the poem (Meyers 1993, 184). But the poem can stand on its own.

As Richard Wilbur has noted (1959), the poem uses a conceit to represent a disordered mind as a palace fallen into ruin after the overthrow of its king. The palace's "head," "two luminous windows," door of "pearl and ruby," and singing "spirits," portray a singer and embody a lost harmony of mind and soul that existed in "the olden / Time long ago" (lines 11–12). The unseen king, Porphyrogene, was once surrounded by dancing spirits; but that music that

Poe elsewhere called "an all-sufficient education for the soul" (*M* 2, 610) is now broken and discordant. In the world of ruin, "the greenest of our valleys" (line 1) has changed from shelter to imprisoning circle (Poulet); and the king's wit and wisdom have faded into the music of this poem: melancholy rhythms that recall "a dim-remembered story / Of the old-time entombed" (lines 39–40). The accompanying tale reflects the same disaster in its decaying landscape, fissured house, moribund family, split twins, and divided hero whose lute produces only wild fantasias.

Poe declared that he meant the poem "to imply a mind haunted by phantoms—a disordered brain" (*O* 1, 161), and both poem and tale have been frequently misread in attempts to discover a specific cause for the downfall of the king and the madness of Usher. Poe envisioned not clinical disorder but the dissolution of primal harmony (Halliburton, 117). The mind is overthrown by "evil things in robes of sorrow" (line 33), is discordant, not ill. "The Haunted Palace," as its two-part structure shows, laments the fall into time, the discovery that "then" (the lost time of the radiant palace) is sundered from "now" (the ruined palace). In that great disaster, unity was lost. Thus, the poet can only suggest what it was, using metaphor and music to conjure impressions of "the greenest of our valleys" (line 1). Music *now* cannot be the same as music *then*. Then it effortlessly blended wit and wisdom; now it is broken even in its artistry, and Poe's verse captures restlessness through ever-changing, unpredictable combinations of anapests, iambics, trochees, and dactyls; lines that shift from tetrameter to trimeter to dimeter; and alternating masculine and feminine rhymes that are imperfect ("valleys/palace," "dallied/pallid") almost as often as perfect. The fragmented melody of Usher's melancholy fantasia shows how Eden was lost. Its artful struggle to recapture the lost vision is both the means by which we see Usher's hopelessness and a profound statement of the loss of unifying vision for the modern poet.

"The Conqueror Worm" (1843)

Poe again used a poem to illuminate an "under-current of meaning" when he included "The Conqueror Worm" in the revised "Ligeia," revealing mortal despair in what many read as a tale of ideality. Perhaps Poe had changed his mind about the idealism of the tale; or perhaps some factor (such as the complimentary but obtuse letter from Philip Pendleton Cooke) had convinced him that his darker meaning was unclear. But, in either case, this, the most nihilistic of Poe's poems, uses allegory not to reveal meaning but to reduce it to "a dim-remembered story." Describing a play with an audience of angels, the poem concludes that "the play is the tragedy, 'Man,' / And its hero the Conqueror Worm" (lines 39–40). Life is reduced to a drama so remarkable for its lack of meaning that readers have sometimes accused Poe of violating the presumably transcendent theme of "Ligeia" (Stovall 1969, 219). The characters are without individuality or even free will. "Mere puppets" danced about at the will of invisible puppet masters; they bumble their way through an incoherent "motley drama" (line 17) about a

> Phantom chased forever more,
>> By a crowd that seize it not,
> Through a circle that ever returneth in
>> To the self-same spot,
> And much of Madness, and more of Sin,
>> And Horror the soul of the plot. (lines 19–24)

As Fagin points out (150), the poem's five stanzas correspond to the five acts of a tragedy; but the play is a tragedy only by courtesy, for its hero is not one of the mimes but the worm itself, a "crawling shape" that enters in the last act and devours the actors. The metaphor of life as a play, used from Elizabethan times on to portray an orderly universe, here stands order on its head (Lubbers, 378). Behind the drama is no "great chain of being" with a benevolent God holding the top link but "vast formless things / That shift the scenery to and fro, / Flapping from out their Condor wings / Invisible Wo" (lines 13–16). It is the first absurdist drama: *Waiting for Godot* with a melodramatic finale; and Poe's metaphor of the stage-flat world as a "scenic solitude" (line 28) suggests there is nothing behind the scenery. The angels who begin and end the poem underline the absence of divinity, for they do nothing but observe, affirm, and frame the drama. The actors are "Mimes, in the form of God on high" (line 9), echoing the language of Genesis, but this is just as ironic as the opening announcement of "a gala night." God is the final, formless horror, and the human drama a miniature version of a cosmic one. The drama begins at the end of time, "Within the lonesome latter years," and ends when the stage lights (the stars) go out. From this circle of destruction there is no exit.

The music is inventively cacophonous, subjecting the eight-line stanza of "The Conqueror Worm" to disconcerting rhythmic variations paired with sledgehammer stresses, obsessive rhyme (four "b" rhymes in each stanza), shrieks ("It writhes!—it writhes!," line 29), and mimetic effects (such as the gasping rhythm of "While the orchestra breathes fitfully").

"Sonnet—Silence" (1839)

But Poe's poems of despair and nihilism are not simply keys to his tales. "Sonnet—Silence," for instance, stands alone, though its "twin" motif is parallel to "William Wilson," written at about the same time. Here, Poe treats silence as a "twin entity." The "corporate Silence," death, "dwells in lonely places, / Newly with grass o'ergrown" and is not to be feared. "No power hath he of evil in himself" (line 11). Its twin and shadow, however, is different. Though Stovall believes the poem distinguishes the death of the body from the death of the soul (Stovall 1969, 218), John Hollander reads it more accurately as a "romantic" attempt to introduce into sound something beyond sound (89). The second silence is never named because it is literally unnameable. Words like *nothingness* merely clothe a missing body. Like the attempt of Ligeia's husband to define the power of her eyes as their "expression," these are words "of no meaning, behind whose vast latitude of mere sound we intrench our ignorance of so much of the spiritual" (*M* 2, 313). The incapacity of words and need for a strategy of suggestion are a subject to which Poe repeatedly turned, beginning with his assertion in the 1831 "Letter to Mr.— —" that poetry must produce "*indefinite* sensations, to which end music is an *essential,* since the comprehension of sweet sound is our most indefinite conception" (*PQ,* 17) and climaxing with his statement in *Eureka* (1848) that all words we use to speak of God and spirit are "by no means the expression of an idea—but of an effort at one" (*PQ,* 1272). "Sonnet—Silence" implies that some words merely suggest; or, as semantics reminds us, at that level of abstraction, all words are constructs or metaphors. (For "suggestiveness" in Poe's poetry, see Richard Wilbur's essay in *Critical Essays on Edgar Allan Poe,* ed. Carlson.)

"The Bells" (1848)

Suggestiveness is the hallmark of Poe's verse. Since poetry is about what cannot be named, its essence lies in evocative music, and his poetry is a gallery of strategies of suggestion, each one new. "The Bells," for instance, is a tour de force that expresses meaning entirely through musicality. The author of a popular book on public speaking had suggested to Poe that a poem for recitation, offering great variety of vocal expression, could achieve both fame and profit (*M* 1, 410), and Poe responded with this virtuoso exploration of onomatopoeia. But "The Bells" is considerably more than sound effects. Inattentive readers hear in it only the sounds of four different kinds of bells, and even expert readers (Auden; Stovall 1969) sometimes miss the point. As the poem moves from silver to gold to brass to iron, its tonal shifts evoke attendant emotions, settings, and activities, and finally the shape of a life divided into four stages: courtship, marriage, crisis, and mourning. Meaning wells up from music, the bells that mark the stages of life. This can be seen in the evolution of a single line through the poem's four stanzas.

> *What* a world of merriment their melody foretells!
> . . . . .
> *What* a world of happiness their harmony foretells!
> . . . . .
> *What* a tale of terror, now, their turbulency tells!
> . . . . .
> *What* a world of solemn thought their monody compels!
>
> (*M* 1, 435–37)

The slide from merriment to solemnity accompanies a shift from future to present, the fatal "now," and ends with a new verb marking the power of time to force the mind. "Melody" and "harmony," the music before the fall, dissolve here as in "The Haunted Palace."

The metamorphosis of this line reveals the pattern of the poem: a pattern noted by readers who attend to the music's variations (P. Williams, 25). As time overshadows the carefree life of the opening, so it dominates the poem's expanding stanzas. The first stanza has fourteen lines, the second twenty-one, the third thirty-four, and the last forty-four. The first two stanzas, describing the happiness of life before knowledge of loss, have less than half the length of the last two. Thus, structure weights the poem toward darkness.

"A Dream within a Dream" (1849)

A late work—a revision of a youthful poem so different from its original that there is no recognizable connection—carries dissolution into the very fabric of identity. The subject of the poem is mutability, embodied in two symmetrical stanzas that portray two linked scenes. In the first, two lovers are parting forever. In the second, the solitary narrator strives hopelessly to grasp grains of sand. The point lies in the ironic resemblance of lovers and sand, both fleeting. To emphasize the irony, Poe treats the first stanza with calm, controlled language, reserving emotive emphasis for the second, dominated by expletives, exclamation points, passionate repetition, and intense adjectives. Those elusive sand grains naturally suggest an hourglass, the traditional metaphor of time, whose ineluctable changes reduce both sand and lovers to mere "dream" images. As the refrain lines, which link the two scenes, have it, "what we see" (external reality) "and seem" (internal identity) are both "but a dream within a dream" (*M* 1, 452), at a double remove from reality. If existence is only a hall of self-reflecting mirrors, concepts of cause and consequence break down utterly, leaving only a rhetorical question: a dilemma in which neither idealism nor empiricism is imaginatively acceptable.

But if time in Poe's poems is a shapeless force that first divides soul from thought, then swallows self, universe, and God, its opposite, the ideal, may offer no solace. Though some readers (e.g., Auden, Baudelaire, Bonaparte, Buranelli, Hoffman, Krutch, Lawrence, Tate, Wilbur, Winters) see Poe's dream poems as a pursuit of "The summer dream beneath the Tamarind tree" (*M* 1, 91), they express a late, though reluctant, realization that, in their very nature, Romantic ideals are doomed to disillusionment for lack of the disciplined creativity and integration of a genuine "transcendent vision." This final, 1849 version restates this more deeply felt tragic realization of the earlier versions without the bold defiance of 1829. While the Platonist finds ideal beauty beyond time, Poe examines it only within time—and its effects are not encouraging. His mature poetry, like his fiction, contains many indications that the dream may be a trap. For instance, his characteristic symbol of the supernal, the dream maiden, at times haunts the mind, leaving a legacy of tormented dream and memory, as in "To Zante" and "The Raven"; whereas others—"Ulalume," "The Sleeper," and "Annabel Lee"—represent those powers of consciousness ("world of mind") that provide sustenance and revived potential, far more than mere echoes of a vanished harmony.

"To Zante" (1837)

This poem connects the dead maiden with a green island in the sea, recalling "the greenest of our valleys" and the nameless maiden of "To One in Paradise" (1833). The island is fair, gentle, radiant, charming; but because it is associated with a maiden who is "no more," it holds only memories of "entombed hopes" and so has become "accursed ground" (*M* 1, 311). Carlson summarizes the theme of the poem: "Memory of past joy brings only a bitter sense of loss" (1967, 564). But more than emotion is at stake. The poem is as much metaphysical as psychological, dramatizing the conflict of mortal and visionary realms. Man cannot maintain continual contact with the transcendent; neither can he forget it. As in "To One in Paradise," the loss of radiance makes it impossible to go forward or back. There the narrator was lost in "trances" and "dreams." Here the reaction is more bitter. In both poems, the issue is not death but the long shadow death acquires from the luminous ideal.

"Bridal Ballad" (1837)

The issue returns in a companion piece, a dramatic monologue that presents the same experience from the point of view of a bride striving to convince herself that, although her first love has died, marriage to another has made her happy. Like a Poesque version of Joyce's Gretta Conroy remembering the dead Michael Furey, Poe's woman can never be free of the shadow of "the dead d'Elormie," as her ironic, repeated insistence that she "must be happy now" makes obvious (*M* 1, 308).

Taken together, these poems raise the question of the mind's responsibility for its own yearnings: a large factor in Edward H. Davidson's estimate of Poe as "a 'crisis' in the Romantic and the symbolic imagination" (1957, ix). The similar experiences and contrasting reactions of these narrators suggest an answer. Both have suffered irreplaceable loss, but while one hides her feelings to insist that she is "happy," the other curses the very ground of his former happiness.

"The Raven" (1844)

Poe's sometimes ironic treatment of narrators in his tales has been the focus of critical attention for a number of years, but little has been said about the narrators of his poems, even though many of them are clearly not Poe. Almost all critics, however, have recognized the crucial role of the narrator in "The Raven," and there is general agreement that he creates his own fate. There is good reason to think so. The narrator of "The Raven" is a young man drained by grief, superstitiously seeking release in "forgotten lore," and terrorized by rustling curtains. As he answers a tapping at the door, he unwittingly reveals himself.

> Deep into that darkness peering, long I stood there wondering, fearing,
> Doubting, dreaming dreams no mortal ever dared to dream before;
> But the silence was unbroken, and the stillness gave no token,
> And the only word there spoken was the whispered word, "Lenore?"
> This I whispered, and an echo murmured back the word, "Lenore!"
> Merely this and nothing more. (*M* 1, 365–66)

An ear that can change the echo of a question into an exclamation would need no commentary if the punctuation were not so often altered, removing both the question mark and Poe's remarkably subtle suggestion. The narrator's reaction to the raven is predetermined by his tendency to exaggerate (changing the raven from a mere bird to something from "the saintly days of yore"—line 38) and to personify and project meaning onto his surroundings. Coals are not coals but reminders of Lenore as "each separate dying ember wrought its ghost upon the floor" (line 8). The raven is no mimic but speaks his single word "as if his soul in that one word he did outpour" (line 56). Even lamplight cannot simply fall on the cushion but must fall "gloating o'er" it (line 77). One can see why Davidson reads the poem as a case study of a mind watching its own disintegration (1956, 496), for all meaning in the raven's single word is created by the narrator's questions, as Poe pointed out in "The Philosophy of Composition," his commentary on the poem, which makes the ironic distance between author and narrator obvious. In an orgy of self-destruction, "that species of despair which delights in self-torture" (*T,* 19), the young man conjures a fate of which he is both maker and victim.

Yet, the poem is more than a case study, for the student sinks not into madness but into despair (Carlson, 567). Poe concludes "The Philosophy of Composition" by pointing to the "undercurrent" of meaning in the narrator's shriek, "Take thy beak from out my heart, and take thy form from off my door" (line 101). These words "dispose the mind to seek a moral in all that has been previously narrated" (*T,* 25): to see raven, chamber, and student as symbolic. As a symbol, the raven is no delusion but "emblematical of *Mournful and Never-Ending Remembrance*" (*T,* 25). The picture of the raven squatting on the bust of Pallas symbolizes learning (or scholarship, possibly wisdom) overmastered by grief, mournful remembrance. To free oneself from the memory of Lenore would be to escape the enclosed chamber; but the haunted vision of the past has locked the door.

"The Raven" is not merely psychological, nor can the narrator's final paralysis be dismissed as derangement. As in "The Haunted Palace," discordant world and fragmented mind are interchangeable, and the narrator's obsession is just as objective as subjective. The "nevermore" of Lenore's death tolls through the poem like the bell of time, echoing in every stanza by those insistent (and audacious) "or" rhymes. Moreover, the poem's setting in December, at midnight, in the midst of a tempest, in a small chamber that is the only spot of light amid overwhelming darkness, suggests that the threat of nothingness is real, not something the narrator has "made up." The shadow of the bird of darkness is a symbolic bit of a larger darkness threatening to blot out the brightness briefly glimpsed in Lenore. Whether one sees that darkness as the shadow of time or the shadow within matters less than seeing that outer and inner shadows are twins (as in "Sonnet—Silence"); for memory, the shadow within, is, of all the mind's attributes, the one most formed by time.

It is also intimately connected with the ideal, for *what* is remembered is the connection with the supernal, "the rare and radiant maiden whom the angels name Lenore" (line 11). The narrator is destroyed by his obsessive attachment to an ideal powerless to aid but powerful to haunt. The opposite of nepenthe is Lenore. The ideal in its own nature *may* be eternal, but, in this world, beauty takes only vanishing forms and is never free of mortality. Lenore's angelic beauty touches the strings of ideality in the student but is snatched away almost as soon as it is perceived, leaving a gnawing doubt that eternity exists.[3] The narrator's questions spring from that doubt. His inability to know whether the raven is bird, demon, or prophet—to know what, if anything, lies beyond time— turns the ideal into torment. Thus, the narrator is not insane but shattered because his universe is disjointed.

"Lenore" (1843)

Despair, however, is not a necessary reaction to duality; and in "Lenore" (not the same radiant maiden as in "The Raven"), Poe had already portrayed death as the occasion for triumph. *This* Lenore's lover refuses to weep, recognizing death as an escape from earthly envy and slander. Lenore is not to be mourned because she has been taken "to friends from fiends . . . / From Hell unto a high estate within the utmost Heaven." Thus "tonight my heart is light: —no dirge will I upraise, / But waft the angel on her flight with a Paean of old days!" (*M* 1, 337).

"For Annie" (1849)

According to Mabbott, commentators are disagreed on whether or not the narrator of this late poem is dead. Mallarmé, says Mabbott, was "certainly right" in holding the narrator to have been "so ill as to fancy himself in the first moments of death but has been revived by the presence and affection of Annie," the decisive passage being in line 16, 'might *fancy* me dead' (*M* 1,

454). Lines 71–78 can hardly apply to a corpse by any stretch of the imagination. From an ironic view, which assumes a dead narrator, this poem is comparable to Dickinson's "posthumous" poems and Poe's "The Colloquy of Monos and Una" (1841). From this view, the opening lines suggest a recovery from illness; but death is the recovery, life the illness ("the fever called 'Living' / Is conquered at last"). Death is serenity, not cessation. But Wilbur points out that "Living" here is a state of Hellish torment, a state of uncontrollable, degrading passion (1959, 150). The reader may "shudder to look at me, / Thinking me dead" (lines 93–94), but only because he does not understand death, in which the soul survives, awake to a "dream of the truth." "A very few / Feet under ground" is a spiritual spring, "a water / That quenches all thirst" (lines 38–41).

The allusion to John 4: 14 does not make "For Annie" a Christian poem but reveals Poe's connection to the poetic line, descending from Christian Platonism and the conventions of courtly love, which saw the love of woman as the gateway to salvation. In his dying moment, cradled on the breast of Annie, the narrator has achieved union with her love, and his heart is now "brighter / Than all of the many / Stars in the sky": beyond passion or change because "It glows with the light / Of the love of my Annie—/ With the thought of the light / Of the eyes of my Annie" (lines 99–102). Annie, refined from woman to eyes to light to thought, is Poe's heroine of the spirit: an earthly symbol of the "glories beyond the grave" (*T*, 77), which he had identified as the impetus behind poetry in "The Poetic Principle," written no more than six months before this poem. Other aspects of the poem connect the progress of the speaker with the poetic process in that essay. Thus, he moves beyond both thought and passion—"the fever / That maddened my brain" (lines 27–28) and the "Torture of thirst / For the napthaline river / Of passion accurst" (lines 34–36)—into a vision that satisfies the "tantalized spirit" (line 53). One critic, deploring that explication and biography have been the only foundations for reading the poem, draws attention to its combination of genres (romantic lyric and dramatic monologue) and concludes that "Annie is being praised not merely by being idealized but by being transformed into a kind of hallucination" (Armistead, 3). But this ignores the speaker's death-cleansed condition. What he beholds is vision, not hallucination, as beauty and truth become one: the "dream of the truth / And the beauty of Annie" (lines 69–70). In "The Colloquy of Monos and Una" and still earlier in "Al Aaraaf," the immortal vision is signaled in the "language-of-flowers books of his day" by which novel sensations, "fancies" of the odors of flowers, "A rosemary odor, / Commingled with pansies—/ With rue and the beautiful / Puritan pansies" (lines 63–66) are communicated to the reader. Wilbur explicates these flowers: myrtle for "Love" (here a symbol of poetic Beauty suitable to the Uranian Venus), the rose "Beauty," pansies Thoughts, rosemary Fidelity or Remembrance, rue Grace or Purification (1959, 150–51). A subtle music, mixing internal rhyme and anapests, produces a rhythm both graceful and ever-shifting. Poe's later poetry rarely grants such serenity, however. In its own realm, the ideal embodied in the eyes of Annie is life-enchancing; inside mutability, it is ambiguous: an idea explored in "Ulalume" and "Annabel Lee" (which uses the anapests of "For Annie" to achieve a very different effect).

"Ulalume" (1847)

"Ulalume" presents another psychic conflict, which, in its resolution, suggests another way of going beyond "The Raven" toward unity, not least in its use of musicality. A key poem in the Poe canon, it is also, as George Saintsbury said, "the prearranged and never-to-be-wholly-done-away-with battleground—the Belgium . . . of Poeian criticism" (321). It is the poem that led to Huxley's charge of "vulgarity" (32); that Poe's contemporaries found nearly incomprehensible (*M* 1, 415); and that Auden reduced to an experiment sacrificing sense to sound (x). None of those reactions can withstand scrutiny. Mabbott points out that many have considered it the greatest of all Poe's poems. "It must be read aloud or sounded to the 'inner ear' and indeed it was composed for recitation" (1: 409). To Woodberry, it was "the most spontaneous, the most unmistakably genuine utterance of Poe" (*M* 1, 415). A close reading reveals not only a coherent narrative (Jacobs) but also significant meaning from a variety of viewpoints: allegorical (Miller); psychological (Carlson 1963); phenomenological (Halliburton); and philosophical (Omans). A close reading also reveals a rationale for the poem's overpowering music.

The poem presents a narrator deeply divided, walking and debating with "Psyche, my Soul" as with another person. He finds himself near dawn on an October night passing through a sorrowful and vaguely threatening landscape. Venus is rising, and its associations with warmth and love draw him forward in the form of Astarte, whom Psyche mistrusts. But the narrator persuades her to follow him, and they walk toward the light, only to discover the door of a tomb that he recognizes as that of his "lost Ulalume." Now the cause of the divided self, the loss of memory, and the soul's mistrust of Astarte becomes clear. The tomb holds the narrator's dead love, whom he had "forgotten" until the light of Venus led him to it. The final stanza states his and Psyche's belief that "pitiful" and "merciful" ghouls (censors of the unconscious) had, out of pity, tried to bar the way to the secret of the tomb—had they not "drawn up the spectre of a planet . . . This sinfully scintillant planet / From the Hell of the planetary souls?"

Psychologically, then, the poem is a study in repression. The narrator has taken the same course as the student in "The Raven," but with success, finding "surcease of sorrow" by repressing the memory of Ulalume's burial. Venus Astarte, however, changes everything. Her promise of peace is false, for the goddess of love inevitably leads to the repressed memory. There are two conflicting loves here: Venus Astarte of the passions and Ulalume the supernal (Jacobs, 441). But the supernal seems to perform no saving act. Having lost Ulalume, the narrator has suppressed that memory, dividing mind from soul and seeking consolation from Astarte with Psyche's consent (he "tempted her" and "conquered her scruples"). But if allegiance to Ulalume does not dispel his sorrow, as his heart once more grows "ashen and sober . . . withering and sere," he has recovered his "lost Ulalume," that is, his psychal-supernal Self symbolized by Ulalume.

Halliburton and Silverman have both pointed out, though for different reasons, that much of Poe's thought arises from conflicting responses generated by loyalty to the dead, and here is the heart of that dynamic. Set on Allhallow's eve, the death of the year, the poem also takes place near dawn, with its implication of rebirth and reaffirmation. Another reading sees the new day as pushing the calendar deeper into autumn, just as the anniversary of Ulalume's burial marks off one more year. But, with his revived memory, the final stanza brings a full recognition by the narrator and Psyche (speaking in unison for the reunited Self) not only of death but, more significantly, of the rediscovered Ulalume (as symbol), whom he had been about to betray. The parallels to "Ligeia" are obvious.

This struggle of the soul to rise above rational meaning and earthly experience is reflected in the overwhelming music, which may seem vulgar to those seeking restraint but essential to the poetry of ecstasy, which embodies struggle, not grace: "excites, by elevating the soul" (T, 71). "The Vulgarity of Poe," Aldous Huxley's notorious attack on "Ulalume" for, in Carlson's words, "its allegedly gross defects of trite diction, heavy meter, overuse of rime and cloying sounds, and general effect of theatricality" was followed in 1937 and 1938 by similar detractions by Yvor Winters and Cleanth Brooks/Robert Penn Warren out of "blindness to the symbolic-impressionistic nature of this poem" (Carlson, 1963, 22–23). Carlson's detailed analysis—"Symbol and Sense in 'Ulalume' "—claimed that an evaluation of this poem must take into account its dramatic structure, symbolism, and psychological meaning. Under a section entitled "Symbolism," the first stanza is described as "an impressionistic prelude . . . full of overtones in its repetends and invented symbols. As a panel of mystery, its very vagueness or 'indefinitiveness' makes for a desirable artistic delay." A good reading depends on due attention being given to tone color, pitch, and changes of pitch; the sonority of *sober* and *October* is reinforced by *Auber*. *Auber* and *Weir* and so on are as much sound-symbols as actual names (29). In 1958, William Van Doorn insisted that, in "Ulalume," Poe's use of tone, repetition, monotony, and made-up sound words was entirely functional, not the gaudy rhetorical embellishment Huxley assumed it to be. In his article, Carlson quoted a long passage from Van Doorn, with examples from the poem, in which monotony of tone and rhythm is justified for its trance-inducing effect, in keeping with the poem as a subconscious "memory" (27).

"The Sleeper" (1849)

The task of fusing mortality and beauty is daunting. Poe revised "The Sleeper" nine times between 1831, when it was called "Irenë," and 1849, when he made his last microscopic changes. Mabbott notes that Poe listed this poem among his best, with the latest (1849) version preferred by anthologists. But what makes it one of the best—the theme or vision? the verse form? the music? It certainly exemplifies Poe's belief that "the death of a beautiful woman is, unquestionably, the most poetical topic in the world." Using the same valley landscape as "The Haunted Palace," the poem's couplets (a form Poe rarely used) play on the same metaphor as in "For Annie": the metaphor of death as sleep, or sleep as seeming-death, either of which represents a release into serenity, peace of mind and spirit. A moldering lakeside ruin wrapped in fog and a lady lying beneath a canopy both seem to slumber, but the final version gradually reveals this to be more than slumber in any literal sense: "All Beauty sleeps!—and lo! where lies / Irenë, with her Destinies" (lines 16–17). The first version contained some rather clumsy moral indignation aimed at those who forget the dead, but, after 1841, Poe excised everything that would distract from his delicate ironies, which seem to have influenced the very similar "Bells for John Whiteside's Daughter." The poem is altogether striking; yet, at the climactic moment, some readers stumble over the line "Soft may the worms about her creep" as morbid or absurd. However, the final lines recover with one of Poe's strongest combinations: the adult narrator accepting the finality of death at the grand family vault. "Oh, may her sleep, / As it is lasting, so be deep!"

"To Helen" (1849)

Mabbott speaks of this as a "major poem" and "a poem of distinction" celebrating "one of the great romances of literary history" (441, 444). Mrs. Sarah Helen Whitman was a widowed poetess when Poe met her in Providence in 1848. He first caught sight of her in 1845 in her garden as he was passing by near midnight. It is, therefore, as Wilbur says, a "vision poem" of a windless, moonlit summer night. Poe sent Mrs. Whitman a copy with this note: "The poem contained all the events of a *dream* which occurred to me soon after I knew you. Ligeia was also suggested by a *dream*—observe the eyes in both tale and poem" (Wilbur 1959, 148–49). From a full moon, "There fell a silvery-silken veil of light, / With quietude, and sultriness, and slumber/" on the upturned faces of roses "That gave out, in return for the love-light / Their odorous souls in an ecstatic death." Against this romantic background, Helen is seen as "half-reclining" in white on a violet bank—her face upturned in sorrow. Then all disappeared "Save only the divine light in thine eyes/ Save but the soul in thine uplifted eyes" . . . with their "fathomless capacity for love." Only those eyes remained "to illumine and enkindle/ My duty *to be saved* by their bright light"—the stars I kneel to both night and day—"two sweetly scintillant / Venuses, unextinguished by the sun!"

The transcendent power of this symbolic dream poem of the "eyes" of another "Helen," this time a real person, is unmistakable. But that fact does not make it entirely autobiographical. "Her eyes become," Wilbur notes, "as do the eyes of Ligeia—the poet's key to a visionary world" (1959, 149). To insist, as one critic has, that the Helen of both "To Helen" poems is dead flies in the face of the text and the theme, missing the whole point in an effort to find irony in poems that are central expressions of Poe's psychal transcendentalism. In form, the poem moves gradually from the larger scene to a focus on Helen and finally, as all else disappears from view, on her eyes, eyes that are more symbolic than actual. This poem-in-process exemplifies Poe's interest in idea (theme) as realization, found also in Poe's prose, for example, "The Road to Landor's Cottage" (Dayan, 104–29).

"Annabel Lee" (1849)

This last poem is sometimes seen as a response to the death of Virginia, though it is not, any more than "Ulalume" merely expresses Poe's guilt feelings about courting Mrs. Whitman. Real disservice is done to Poe's work by the assumption, perennial and predictable as spring peepers, that his works are simply keys to his biography.[4] Nothing could more thoroughly sabotage his artistry. Poe did write some autobiographical poetry: a species of cavalier poem much admired in the antebellum South; and Byron's ability to write dashing, cavalier lyrics doubtless was one of the features that cast a spell over the young Poe. He never entirely deserted the genre, and his later life is sprinkled with compliments, flirtations, impromptus, and appreciations addressed to various ladies: "To [Violet Vane]," "Stanzas [To F.S.O.]," "To Marie Louise Shew," and so forth. But these were acts of social grace rather than serious poetry, and none of his better work is of that sort.

"Annabel Lee" is not autobiography but a work of completed art with roots in his first published poem, the 1827 "Tamerlane." There the dead, ideal maiden first appeared, her eyes equated with heaven, her loss blamed on a superhuman power, her love described in almost the same phrase: a love "such as the angel minds above / Might envy" in the first poem (*M* 1, 30); and such "a love that the winged seraphs of Heaven / Coveted her and me" in the last (*M* 1, 479). Such motifs were "in progress" and developed in various forms during the intervening twenty-two years. "Annabel Lee" is the climax of a career, not a response to Virginia's death.

The poem's anapests create an artful *valse triste:* a lovely melody and haunting rhythm that have made it almost as well known as "The Raven"; and its treatment of the refrain, blended into the poem rather than compartmentalized, along with its handling of incremental repetition, raises the ballad form to high art. These aspects of the poem are directly linked to the "suggestive undercurrent" of meaning in Poe's identification of it as "a ballad" (*O* 2, 438): a song that tells a story. The story is both ancient and sentimental; but Poe's ending gives fidelity a new twist.

> And so, all the night-tide, I lie down by the side
> Of my darling, my darling, my life and my bride

> In her sepulchre there by the sea—
> In her tomb by the sounding sea. (lines 38–41)

It would be distasteful to call the poem a hymn to necrophilia (though Princess Bonaparte would approve), but we must make something of that stanza. Yet readers regularly miss the point because of the poem's music, which is just as vital as its psychology. For this ballad merges the radiance of the supernal with the darkness of death to achieve the melancholy Poe identified as his goal in "The Poetic Principle." "Annabel Lee" is a triumph of the Poe method. To look at the elements of death and beauty—or, more accurately, death and love/fidelity—in isolation is to see two different poems. The dark elements may seem pathetic or even grisly, but since the loved girl died "many and many a year ago," the speaker is not a desperate or mad youth but a grown man "recollecting in tranquility" what he once possessed.

> The angels, not half so happy in Heaven,
>   Went envying her and me—
> Yes!—that was the reason (as all men know,
>   In this kingdom by the sea)
> That the wind came out of the cloud by night,
>   Chilling and killing my Annabel Lee. (lines 21–26)

These haunting lines rely on insistent rhythm, parenthesis, restrained use of rhyme, and strong metaphor.

The tone and point of view, in short, are devotional. Love of the dead is portrayed not as a pathological obsession, but as symbolic of simple fidelity to outraged innocence. The maiden, an ideal fantasy, lives only "to love and be loved" (line 6) without passion: pure enough to be a child, noble enough to inhabit a kingdom, lofty enough to shame a seraph. Her enduring power identifies her with transhuman beauty and love, and Poe applies all his favorite words to her: *angels, soul, moon, dreams, stars, eyes,* even *a love that was more than love,* his familiar shorthand for the sublime.

"Annabel Lee" is, of course, more subtle than "Ulalume" in its combinations of sound. The delicacy of "a tomb by the sounding sea" does not force itself on the reader as does "Astarte's bediamonded crescent"; and the brazen combination of alliteration, assonance, and consonance in "sinfully scintillant planet" is very different from the unobtrusive alliteration, consonance, and simple internal rhyme of "the moon never beams without bringing me dreams." But they have a common goal: the use of music to suggest the soul's yearning for a world beyond time and fate.

In "The Philosophy of Composition," Poe wrote that "Beauty . . . in its supreme development invariably excites the sensitive soul to tears. Melancholy is . . . the most legitimate of all the poetical tones" (*T,* 17). He was at one with his time in that belief, which is why the young Ruskin sounds exactly like him:

"[W]hat is most musical will always be found most melancholy; and no real beauty can be obtained without a touch of sadness" (Ruskin, 18). The dead maiden was one symbol of the ideal beyond human reach, and music was Poe's most powerful tool in making those "novel combinations" that would convey suggestions denied to description, didacticism, and intellection.

But music, though essential, was only one form of invention. Once he had used a form, stanza, or effect, he rarely returned to it, and his revisions almost always replace regular stanzas and repeated elements with novel effects (as, for instance, in "Bridal Ballad," where he turned the seven regular six-line stanzas of the original into five, all different). Nor are his evocations of the ideal limited to ethereal maidens. Two final poems demonstrate that other kinds of visions can be equally elusive, ambiguous, and powerful.

"Eldorado" (1849)

The subject of this poem is a "gallant knight" who rides through life without finding his goal, until at last a shadow falls over his heart, linking Eldorado with the prospect of failure, even death. Like the student putting his questions to the raven, the knight asks a pilgrim Shadow where Eldorado may be and elicits the concluding stanza:

> "Over the Mountains
> Of the Moon,
> Down the Valley of the Shadow,
> Ride, boldly ride,"
> The shade replied,—
> "If you seek for Eldorado!" (*M* 1, 463)

Arthur Quinn read this poem as symbolizing the gold rush, and Mabbott as "a cheerful comment" on it. But the antimaterialist point could scarcely be missed in 1849, when Eldorado was California (Pollin, 231). The point lies deeper than mistrust of the gold rush, however. More significantly, as Eric W. Carlson has noted, it reflects Poe's outlook on life, as expressed, for example, in a letter to Frederick W. Thomas on February 14, 1849:

For my own part, there is no seducing me from the path. I shall be a *Litterateur*, at least, all my life; nor would I abandon the hopes which still lead me on for all the gold in California. Love, fame, the dominion of intellect, the consciousness of power, the thrilling sense of beauty, the free air of Heaven, exercise of body and mind with the physical and moral health which result—these and such as these are really all that a poet cares for:—then answer me this—*why* should he go to California?" (*O* 2, 426–27)

This statement of faith was expressed also in Poe's 1842 review of Longfellow's "Excelsior," which Poe sums up approvingly as depicting "the *earnest upward impulse of the soul*—an impulse not to be subdued in Death. . . . The poet holds in view the idea of never-ending *progress.*'' So, Carlson sums up the final stanza of ''Eldorado'' as an ''unqualified and unambiguous assertion of ideal faith . . . a sense of the finality and purity of the Ideal'' (233).

For some other readers, the poem casts a dark ''Shadow'' in each of the poem's four stanzas, until it finally comes to mean possible ''death,'' and its link (through repeated rhyme) with Eldorado makes the goal as ambiguous as Poe's dead maidens. Is the pilgrim shadow's advice comforting or ironic? Does the pilgrim have spiritual authority, or is he still on his quest, no closer to the goal than the knight? Does the poem demonstrate Poe's belief in idealism (Carlson 1961) or his rejection of idealism (Coad)? Does it show ''the futility of pursuing the ideal, yet the impossibility of happiness without pursuing it'' (Stovall 1931, 61)? Or is it altogether ambiguous and ironic (Sanderlin)? In Poe, only two things about the ideal are clear: it may not be realized in this world, but the soul is not free to give up the search.

''Dream-Land'' (1844)

Here is a literal view of the world of dreams, the report of a newly wakened sleeper. What he has seen in that world ''Out of SPACE—out of TIME'' is such a mixture of things that it is simply ''wild,'' ''weird,'' and ''sublime.''

> Bottomless vales and boundless floods,
> And chasms, and caves, and Titan woods,
> With forms that no man can discover
> For the dews that drip all over;
> Mountains toppling evermore
> Into seas without a shore;
> Seas that restlessly aspire,
> Surging, unto skies of fire;
> Lakes that endlessly outspread
> Their lone waters—lone and dead—
> Their still waters—still and chilly
> With the snows of the lolling lilly. (*M* 1, 344)

The wild mixture pits conflicting images against each other: falling succeeded by climbing and liquids linked with fire. The chief quality of this dream-region is confusion. It cannot be viewed directly; memories of it are often more frightening than beautiful; and one can no more understand it than one can penetrate eternity. The magic in such poetry, as Wilbur justly says, ''consists in starting the imagination and then not stopping it. . . . Poe's strategy here is analogous to that of the Zen Buddhist who contemplates a logical contradiction in hopes of short-circuiting the intellect and so inviting a mystic illumination'' (1959, 33–36). Poe used dream as he used music: as the meeting ground of soul and mind or, as a modern psychologist would say, of the conscious and the unconscious, where the ''King'' forbids ''the uplifting of the fringed lid.'' Except for the lines quoted before, however, the literal description, as Mabbott notes, is "founded on experience" with dreams, as other passages in Poe's poems and tales illustrate. If "[n]othing is inconsistent with this in the poem," as Mabbott rightly comments (*M* 1, 342–43), then the poem can be accepted without ambiguity as revelatory of the nature of dreams. The use of "ultima Thule" here is "purely figurative" (*M* 1, 345), as is "Eldorado." Even this difficult poem is no exception to the conclusion that the late poems are most rewarding to the reader who is sensitized by a knowledge of Poe's work as a whole, that is, by a knowledge of his perspective on life and art.

NOTES

1. I do not mean to overlook the major voices. They certainly do exist, as the rest of the chapter makes clear. W. H. Auden, Charles Baudelaire, Killis Campbell, Eric W. Carlson, Edward H. Davidson, Daniel Hoffman, T. O. Mabbott, Floyd Stovall, Allen Tate, G. R. Thompson, Richard Wilbur, and William Carlos Williams have all mapped out positions. But the point remains that the list of major contributors to the analysis of Poe's fiction would be ten times as long.

2. I have already analyzed the ideas summarized here in "The Limits of Flight: Poe and 'The Poetic Principle,' " *Topic* 30 (1976).

3. Not all critics see Poe's women as symbols of the supernal. A few still treat them as biographical reflections. Critical reactions to Poe's women are, in fact, a touchstone to general shifts of critical assumptions. Poe's contemporaries tended to see them as simple embodiments of the ideal; those around the turn of the century tended to emphasize Poe's treatment of women as "unhealthy"; those from the 1920s to the 1950s were heavily influenced by a psychoanalytic approach; and those after the 1950s have tended toward symbolic readings not only of Poe's women but of everything in his work.

4. Recent examples are Kenneth Silverman's generally masterly biography, 1991; and, less Freudian, Jeffrey Meyers's 1992. Their purpose, to interpret Poe's life, naturally justifies a biographical reading, but their readings sometimes seriously distort the poems.

WORKS CITED

Alexander, Jean. *Affidavits of Genius: Edgar Allan Poe and the French Critics, 1847–1924*. Port Washington, NY: Kennikat P, 1971.

Armistead, J. M. "Poe and Lyric Conventions: The Example of 'For Annie.' " *PoeS* 8, no. 1 (June 1975): 1–5.

Asselineau, Roger. *Edgar Allan Poe*. Minneapolis: U of Minnesota P, 1970. (One of a pamphlet series.)

Auden, W. H., ed. "Introduction." *Edgar Allan Poe: Selected Prose, Poetry, and Eureka*. New York: Rinehart, 1950.

Baudelaire, Charles. Trans. and ed. Lois Hyslop and Francis E. Hyslop, Jr. *Baudelaire on Poe*. State College, Pa.: Bald Eagle P, 1952.

Bonaparte, Marie. *The Life and Works of Edgar Allan Poe: A Psycho-Analytic Interpretation*. Trans. John Rodker. London: Imago, 1949.

Buranelli, Vincent. *Edgar Allan Poe*. New York: Twayne, 1961.

Campbell, Killis, ed. *Poems of Edgar Allan Poe*. New York: Ginn, 1917.

Carlson, Eric W. "Frames of Reference for Poe's Symbolic Language." *Critical Essays on Edgar Allan Poe*. Boston: Hall, 1987, 207–17.

———, ed. *Introduction to Poe: A Thematic Reader*. Glenview, IL.: Scott, Foresman, 1967.

———. "Poe's 'Eldorado.' " *Modern Language Notes* 76 (Mar. 1961): 232–33.

———, ed. *The Recognition of Edgar Allan Poe*. Ann Arbor: U of Michigan P, 1966.

———. "Symbol and Sense in Poe's 'Ulalume.' " *AL* 35 (Mar. 1963): 22–37.

Coad, Oral Sumner. "The Meaning of Poe's 'Eldorado.' " *Modern Language Notes* 59 (Jan. 1944): 59–61.

Davidson, Edward H. *Poe: A Critical Study*. Cambridge: Harvard UP, 1957.

———, ed. *Selected Writings of Edgar Allan Poe*. Boston: Houghton Mifflin, 1956.

Dayan, Joan. *Fables of Mind*. New York: Oxford UP, 1987.

Eliot, T. S. "American Literature and the American Language." *To Criticize the Critic*. New York: Farrar, Straus, and Giroux, 1965, 43–60.

———. "From Poe to Valéry." *Hudson Review* 2 (Aug. 1949): 327–42.

Fagin, N. Bryllion. *The Histrionic Mr. Poe*. Baltimore: Johns Hopkins UP, 1949.

Gargano, James W. "The Question of Poe's Narrators." *College English* 25 (Dec. 1963): 177–81.

Granger, Byrd Howell. "Devil Lore in 'The Raven.' " *PoeS* 5 (Dec. 1972): 53–54.

Halliburton, David. *Edgar Allan Poe: A Phenomenological View*. Princeton: Princeton UP, 1973.

Hoffman, Daniel. *Poe Poe Poe Poe Poe Poe Poe*. Garden City, NY: Doubleday, 1972.

Hollander, John. "The Music of Silence." *Prose* 7 (Fall 1973): 79–91.

Huxley, Aldous. "Vulgarity in Literature." *Poe: A Collection of Critical Essays*. Ed. Robert Regan. Englewood Cliffs, NJ: Prentice-Hall, 1967, 31–37.

Jacobs, Robert D. *Poe: Journalist and Critic*. Baton Rouge: Louisiana State UP, 1969.

Krutch, Joseph Wood. *Edgar Allan Poe: A Study in Genius*. New York: Knopf, 1926.

Lawrence, D. H. "Poe." *Studies in Classic American Literature*. New York: Boni, 1923, 93–120.

Lubbers, Klaus. "Poe's 'The Conqueror Worm.' " *AL* 39 (Nov. 1967): 375–79.

Mabbott, Thomas Ollive, ed. *Collected Works of Edgar Allan Poe, I: Poems*. Cambridge: Harvard UP, 1969.

Meyers, Jeffrey. *Edgar Allan Poe: Life and Legacy*. New York: Macmillan, 1992.

———. "Edgar Allan Poe." *The Columbia History of American Poetry*. Ed. Jay Parini. New York: Columbia UP, 1993, 172–202.

Miller, James E., Jr. " 'Ulalume' Resurrected." *Philological Quarterly* 34 (Apr. 1955): 197–205.

Omans, Glen A. "Poe's 'Ulalume': Drama of the Solipsistic Self." *Papers on Poe: Essays in Honor of John Ward Ostrom*. Ed. Richard P. Veler. Springfield, OH: Chantry Music P, 1972, 62–73.

Pollin, Burton R. "Poe's 'Eldorado' Viewed as a Song of the West." *Prairie Schooner* 46 (Fall 1972): 228–35.

Poulet, Georges. "Edgar Poe." *The Metamorphoses of the Circle*. Trans. Carley Dawson and Elliott Coleman in collaboration with the author. Baltimore: Johns Hopkins UP, 1966, 182–202.

Quinn, Arthur Hobson. *Edgar Allan Poe: A Critical Biography*. New York: Appleton-Century, 1941.

Quinn, Patrick F. *The French Face of Edgar Poe.* Carbondale: Southern Illinois UP, 1957.

Rans, Geoffrey. *Edgar Allan Poe.* Edinburgh: Oliver and Boyd, 1965.

Robinson, David. " 'Ulalume'—The Ghouls and the Critics." *PoeS* 8 (June 1975): 8–10.

Ruskin, John. *The Works of John Ruskin.* Eds. E. T. Cook and Alexander Wedderburn. London: George Allen, 1903. New York: Longmans, Green, 1907. "Early Prose Writings 1834–1843."

Saintsbury, George. "Poe." *Prefaces and Essays.* London: Macmillan, 1933, 314–23.

Sanderlin, W. Stephen, Jr. "Poe's 'Eldorado' Again." *Modern Language Notes* 71 (Mar. 1956): 189–92.

Silverman, Kenneth. *Edgar A. Poe: Mournful and Never-Ending Remembrance.* New York: HarperCollins, 1991.

Stovall, Floyd. *Edgar Poe the Poet.* Charlottesville: UP of Virginia, 1969.

———. "Poe as a Poet of Ideas." *University of Texas Studies in English* 11 (1931): 56–62.

———, ed. *The Poems of Edgar Allan Poe.* Charlottesville: UP of Virginia, 1965.

Tate, Allen. "Our Cousin, Mr. Poe." *Essays of Four Decades.* Chicago: Swallow P, 1968, 385–400.

———. "The Poetry of Edgar Allan Poe." *Sewanee Review* 76 (Apr.–June 1968): 214–25.

Thompson, G. R. *Poe's Fiction: Romantic Irony in the Gothic Tales.* Madison: U of Wisconsin P, 1973.

Thorpe, Dwayne. "The Limits of Flight: Poe and 'The Poetic Principle.' " *Topic* 30 (1976): 68–80.

Wilbur, Richard. "The House of Poe." *Poe: A Collection of Critical Essays.* Ed. Robert Regan. Englewood Cliffs, NJ: Prentice-Hall, 1967, 98–120.

———, ed. "Introduction." *Poe.* New York: Dell, 1959, 7–39.

———. "Poe and the Art of Suggestion." *UMSE,* new series, 3 (1982): 1–13.

Williams, Paul. "A Reading of Poe's 'The Bells.' " *Poe Newsletter* 1 (Oct. 1968): 24–25.

Williams, William Carlos. "Edgar Allan Poe." *In the American Grain.* New York: New Directions, 1956, 216–34.

Wilson, Edmund. "Poe at Home and Abroad." *New Republic* 49 (Dec. 8, 1926). Rpt. in *The Shores of Light.* New York: Farrar, Straus, and Young, 1952, 179–90.

Winters, Yvor. "Edgar Allan Poe: A Crisis in the History of American Obscurantism." *AL* 8 (Jan. 1937): 379–401. Rpt. in *Maule's Curse.* Norfolk, Conn: New Directions, 1938, 93–122.

5

The Tales: 1831–1835

RICHARD P. BENTON

THE FOLIO CLUB TALES

Edgar Allan Poe's career as a writer of short fiction began in July 1831, when he submitted five tales to a literary contest held by the *Philadelphia Saturday Courier*. Although none of these tales captured the prize, the *Courier* thought they all merited publication. Consequently, they all appeared successively in the pages of the *Courier* from January 14 through December 1, 1832. In the order of their appearance, the five stories were "Metzengerstein"; "The Duc de L'Omelette"; "A Tale of Jerusalem"; "A Decided Loss" (later, "Loss of Breath"); and "The Bargain Lost" (later, "Bon-Bon"). One tale, "The Duc de L'Omelette," was reprinted at this time by the *Minerva* and the *Literary Gazette*.

Thus encouraged, Poe continued to write short stories. By May 1833, he added six more stories to his original five. He proposed having the eleven tales collected into a single volume, to which he gave the title of *Eleven Tales of the Arabesque*. He queried the Buckinghams, proprietors of the *New England Magazine*, regarding the publication of the whole in their periodical, submitting a new tale called "Epimanes" as representative of the collection. He also explained to them that the tales were conceived of as being "read at table by eleven members of a literary club" and were "followed by the remarks of the company upon each" (*O* 1, 53). However, the Buckinghams apparently declined publication, although no reply from them—if one was made—is extant.

However, when, in the summer of 1833, the Baltimore *Saturday Visiter* offered a prize of fifty dollars for the best tale submitted in its forthcoming literary contest, Poe entered the six unprinted tales. This time, however, he changed the title of his volume to *The Tales of the Folio Club*. The judges chose his "MS.

Found in a Bottle'' as the best tale, and it appeared in the *Visiter* for October 19, 1833. In reporting the winner of the fiction prize, the judges advised Poe to seek publication of the whole volume of eleven tales. Poe asked his friend the Baltimore novelist John Pendleton Kennedy to help him in this endeavor. Hence, Kennedy sent the volume to his own Philadelphia publishers, Carey, Lea, and Blanchard, specifically to Henry Carey. Eventually, Carey declined to publish the volume, seeing no profit in it because the American public much preferred novels to volumes of short stories. However, to help Poe out, Carey sold "MS. Found in a Bottle" to the *Gift,* an annual, in which it did not appear until the 1836 issue. Carey also sold "The Visionary" (later, "The Assignation") to *Godey's Lady's Book,* in which it was published in January 1834.

When Thomas W. White of Richmond, Virginia, launched the new literary magazine the *Southern Literary Messenger* in May 1834, Kennedy urged Poe to write for it. Poe wrote "Hans Phaall" especially for the *Messenger.* He also informed White of his unpublished Folio Club collection, specifying that "Lionizing" belonged to the volume. Further, Kennedy wrote White in April 1835, suggesting that he might find it to his advantage to give Poe some permanent employment. By July 1835, Poe's tales "Berenice," "Morella," "Hans Phaall," and "The Visionary" had appeared in the *Messenger.* In August, White hired Poe to assist him in editing the magazine. By the September issue, Poe's "Bon-Bon," "King Pest," and the fine "Shadow—A Parable" had appeared in the *Messenger.* Although Poe's "Siope—A Fable" is known to have been one of the original Folio Club tales, it was not published until late 1837 in the annual *The Baltimore Book for 1838.*

In December 1835, White asked an admirer of Poe's work, New York novelist James Kirke Paulding, to recommend the Folio Club tales to the new publishers, Harper and Brothers. In March 1836, Paulding reported to White that Harpers had rejected Poe's volume. They gave as their principal reason, he explained, the obscurity of the tales, which would, they believed, "prevent ordinary readers from comprehending their drift, and consequently from enjoying the fine satire they convey," requiring, as they did, considerable "familiarity with various kinds of knowledge which they do not possess, to enable them to relish the joke," and he added, "[T]he dish is too refined for them to banquet on" (*PoeL,* 193).

This particular judgment by culturally literate contemporaries of Poe is perhaps the most important commentary on the original eleven Folio Club tales, for it defines the *double audience* that Poe addressed: the culturally literate few and the culturally limited many. It shows Poe's attitudes toward his material and toward his readers in the light of his wide scholarship and learning, his "half serious, half funny" turn of mind, and his penchant for *secret writing*— for mystery, ambiguity, conundrums, cryptograms, hieroglyphs, anagrams, obscure allusions, foreign languages, pedantries, logical traces, puns, hoaxes, jokes—in short, for deception and cunning one-upmanship.

As for the whole intention and plan of the eleven-tale frame, these were set forth in detail in 1833, when Poe prepared an Introduction for the volume, which is extant in manuscript form in the Houghton Library at Harvard University. It was first printed in 1902 by James A. Harrison in his edition of Poe's *Complete Works* 2, xxvi–xxix and reprinted in *M* 2, 200–207.

The Introduction is supposedly written by the "newest member" of the Folio Club, who met with the other members at the home of Mr. Rouge-et-Noire. According to the writer, the members of the club meet every Tuesday evening. They are, he declares, "a mere junto of Dunderheadism," being as stupid as they are ugly. Most of the members have pseudonyms, which are followed by a brief description of each: Mr. Snap, the president of the club, is "a very lank man with a hawk nose . . . formerly in the service of the Down-East Review"; Mr. Convolvulus Gondola, "a young gentleman who had travelled a good deal"; De Rerum Naturâ, Esq., "who wore a very singular pair of green spectacles"; "a very little man in a black coat with very black eyes"; Mr. Solomon Seadrift, "who had every appearance of a fish"; Mr. Horribile Dictû, who has "white eyelashes" and had graduated at Göttingen; Mr. Blackwood Blackwood, a writer for foreign magazines; Mr. Rouge-et-Noire, "who admired Lady Morgan"; "a stout gentleman who admired Sir Walter Scott"; Mr. Chronologos Chronology, "who admired Horace Smith, and had a very big nose which had been in Asia Minor"; and the newest member—the narrator—unnamed and undescribed (*M* 2, 205).

With the maturation of Poe scholarship, Poe's Folio Club tales became an important problematic with a number of scholars. They sought to ascertain how many tales rightly belonged to the volume planned before Poe gave up hope of publishing it, which tales they were, and what arrangement Poe had made of them. Further, since it was evident that Poe meant each member of the Folio Club to represent a real author, including himself, these scholars sought to identify them. Since it was evident that the tales that could be associated with the Folio Club collection were varied in their modes—parody, satire, romantic irony, burlesque, straight romance, quiz, hoax, Gothicism, science fiction, or whatnot—whether intended to be taken as funny, serious, or half funny and half serious, these scholars attempted to determine these things as well as to decide who or what in a tale was being treated, either in ridicule or with respect and admiration.

The number of tales associated with the Folio Club project has ranged from the original *eleven* tales Poe submitted to the literary contests of 1831 and 1833 to the *fourteen* tales published in the *Messenger* by the fall of 1836, when Poe tried unsuccessfully to get two publishers to issue his volume, which this time he had apparently increased to *seventeen* tales. Poe now gave up hope of publication. No volume of Folio Club tales as such ever was published. Indeed, readers had to wait until 1840 before Poe's first volume of collected tales came out under the title of *Tales of the Grotesque and Arabesque*. In respect to the Folio Club problematic, most scholars have been content to deal only with the original eleven-tale frame.

THE TALES OF 1831-1835

"Metzengerstein" (1832)

Subtitled in its second printing "A Tale in Imitation of the German," it is set in Hungary in the forested region of Transylvania. The time would seem to be after the expulsion of the Turks in 1763. The plot is concerned with the hatred generated by an ancient feud between two noble Germano-Hungarian families, one of purely German origin, represented by young Frederick, Baron Metzengerstein, the other of mixed Saracen blood, represented by old Wilhelm, Count Berlifitzing.

Frederick cultivates his hatred by frequently contemplating an imposing tapestry which hangs on the wall of the Metzengerstein castle. It depicts an episode from the battle of Monács in 1526, when the invading Turks destroyed the Hungarian army. Featured is a gigantic horse and its unseated rider, a Saracen ancestor of Berlifitzing, being stabbed by a dagger in the hand of a Metzengerstein. When the young Frederick becomes sole proprietor of the family fiefdom, he likes to perpetrate evil deeds. The stables of old Wilhelm, Count Berlifitzing, are discovered in conflagration. Viewing the tapestry, Frederick thinks he sees the huge horse change its position and assume a human expression. At the same time, his shadow on the wall mimes the position assumed by his ancestor on the tapestry. Wilhelm loses his life in the stable fire, and Frederick comes into possession of a huge horse of mysterious origin. He rides this charger wildly about his demesne from dawn until dark, otherwise shutting himself up in his palace and avoiding social contacts.

One day on returning from one of his wild rides, Frederick has lost control of the big charger. It leaps over the gateway and moat of the castle, which is now on fire, to bound up its "tottering staircases" and disappear with Frederick into "a whirlwind of chaotic fire."

As a parody "in imitation of the German," "Metzengerstein" is surely not a satire designed to ridicule the *Shauerroman* but to pay homage to it. Poe meant to show that he could write a terror tale as good as the German tales admired by his contemporaries. Such type of tale often appeared in the pages of *Blackwood's*. Hence, "Metzengerstein" can be treated seriously as a romance, as David R. Hirsch and Eric W. Carlson have done. Hirsch proposed that the story deals with the dualism of body and soul. He further proposed that the horse and rider embody the turbulent state of a romantic artist's subconscious. Carlson treated this Gothic story thematically, seeing its "Gothic devices and plot" supportive of "a serious moral theme: the evil of pride and arrogant power brings about self-destruction by retributive forces from within" (306). Earlier, Benjamin Franklin Fisher IV had objected to the placing of this story "among Poe's burlesques and hoaxes such as 'Loss of Breath,' 'A Tale of Jerusalem,' or 'How to Write a Blackwood Article,' which lampooned authors and fads of Poe's own day." Its prose, Fisher pointed out, in its revised version "is not nearly so overwrought as that of the first version" ("Not a Hoax"). On the contrary, G. R. Thompson maintains that the tale is "an intended parody of the Gothic mode" that uses absurdist techniques in a "unified pattern of satiric irony" ("Absurdist Techniques"). Alexander Hammond fully accepts Thompson's reading ("Reconstruction").

Although Poe scholars have proposed several sources for Poe's story, none have been a controlling factor. More akin to "Metzengerstein" than these is Walter Scott's translation of Gottfried August Bürger in *The Chase and William and Helen* (1796). "The Chase," Scott's title for Bürger's "Der wilde Jüger" (1786), features a mad German count obsessed with riding his horse to the hunt every day, including Sundays. He ends up breaking God's laws and losing his own soul. "William and Helen," Scott's title for Bürger's "Lenore" (1773), features a German specter-knight killed in Bohemia at the conclusion of the Seven Years' War in 1763. The specter-knight rides his horse from the battle-field to his sweetheart's village. He takes her aboard his horse and wildly transports her to the land of death. In his translation, Scott *changed the locale to Hungary* and the time of the action to the fourteenth century.

The teller of Poe's tale, of course, is Mr. Horribile Dictû ("Horrible to Tell"), who has "white eyelashes" and had "graduated at Göttingen." He can be identified with Augustus Wilhelm von Schlegel, who became the chief spokesperson of the German Romantic school. He had graduated at Göttingen, where he had studied under Bürger, a professor there. Wilhelm's younger brother was Frederick von Schlegel, the chief theoretician of the Romantic school and a Sanskrit scholar and student of Hinduism, whose goal is liberation from the cycle of rebirth, or metempsychosis.

Therefore, Poe's tale is told by Wilhelm von Schlegel in the manner of Bürger, and it is not a happenstance that the names of his characters are Frederick and Wilhelm. Although the tale was imperfect in style in its original version, Poe's assiduous revising—noted by Fisher—made the final version, as Mabbott declared, a masterpiece. Nevertheless, despite the tale's seriousness, it is not without its "jokes": the titled names of the principal characters are both "phony" and "funny." Horribile Dictû is the opposite of mirabile dictu (wonderful to tell). The tale may be viewed as a quiz on Scott and other such Germanophiles, including contributors to *Blackwood's*.

"The Duc de L'Omelette" (1832)

This may be Poe's most skillfully wrought piece of humor. The place of the principal action is hell, although the locale of the duke's death—worked in by flashback—is Paris. The time of both actions is that of the French kingdom restored—that is, the reigns of Louis XVIII and Charles X. The protagonist is the foppish, debonair, Epicurean French nobleman the duc de l'Omelette. His antagonist is the Devil.

The plot is simple. Having died of disgust at the sight of the nakedness of

an undressed ortolan served at his dinner without its customary paper panta-
loons, the duke finds he has been conveyed to the sumptuous apartment of the
Devil in hell. Although its furnishings include statues and paintings of erotic
female nudes, and voluptuous music floats through the air from an unknown
source, when the duke sees the red fires of hell glowing through the apartment's
windows, terror, like a _coup de foudre,_ strikes him. He realizes that he must act
promptly if he is to be free again.

Concluding that the Devil is an Epicure and adventurer like himself, the duke
decides to tempt him with a conditional wager: if the duke wins, the Devil will
set him free; if the Devil wins, the duke will be ''doubly damned.'' Having read
in some authority that the Devil could never refuse an invitation to gamble at
cards, the duke suggests that they play _rouge et noire._ The Devil accepts, but
the duke wins.

Obviously, Mr. Rouge-et-Noire is the teller of this tale. Kenneth L. Daughrity
has demonstrated conclusively that Mr. Rouge-et-Noire is to be identified with
the author, journalist, and dandy N. P. Willis. Founder and editor of the Boston-
based _American Monthly Magazine,_ he conducted a department called ''The
Editor's Table.'' Inviting his readers to share the hospitality and exquisiteness
of his editorial rooms, Willis described them in detail for his readers. Since,
according to Poe, Mr. Rouge-et-Noire ''admired Lady Morgan,'' Daughrity
noted that Willis had overpraised the Irish novelist's _Book of the Boudoir_ in the
American Monthly for November 1829.

Thus, the teller of ''The Duc de L'Omelette'' is N. P. Willis, who tells it in
the manner of Lady Morgan. The story is both a parody and a burlesque in
which Poe not only quizzed Willis but also mimicked Lady Morgan's fatuous
style to reflect on Willis's literary taste.

"A Tale of Jerusalem" (1832)

Mabbott characterized this story as a ''harmless buffoonery on a very old
theme'' (_M_ 2, 41). He meant the very old custom of the Jewish proscription
against the eating of the flesh of a pig because the pig is not a ruminant as
required by Mosaic law in the Torah (or Pentateuch). Hence, as an ''unclean''
animal, the pig was also unfit for ritual slaughter.

The locale of the tale is Jerusalem. The time is 63 B.C., when Pompey the
Great (Cnoeus Pompeius, 104–48 B.C.) laid siege to Palestine with his Roman
army. The plot has to do with a practical joke the Romans played on the Jewish
defenders. Having agreed to supply the Jews with lambs for religious sacrifice,
the Romans realize that the defenders are using them to supplement their sparse
food supply, thus thwarting the attackers in their effort to starve the Jews into
submission. Legalists like the Jews, the Romans therefore substitute pigs in place
of lambs, thereby in their view observing the _letter of the law_ of Pompey's
agreement while preventing the Jews from using the pigs for food. In the table

of contents for his 1842 collection he called *Phantasy Pieces,* Poe retitled this story "A Pig Tale." This proposed volume, however, was never printed.

This tale of Jerusalem is a parody and a burlesque. The teller of the tale is apparently Mr. Chronologos Chronology, "who admired Horace Smith, and had a very big nose which had been in Asia Minor." Traditionally, a "big nose" had been the stereotypic physical feature Gentiles had employed to distinguish Jews in a Christian community. Hence, Mr. Chronologos Chronology would seem to represent the Jewish journalist, playwright, and politician Mordecai M. Noah, who initially supported Andrew Jackson and served as U.S. consul to Tunis. Noah's hobby was Jewish history, and he may have admired the historical novels of Horace Smith such as *Zillah, a Tale of Jerusalem* (1828). According to James Southall Wilson, it is Smith's manner that Poe parodies in this unusual tale. At the same time, he quizzes Major Noah.

Unlike Mabbott, however, Edward H. Davidson was offended by "A Tale of Jerusalem." He called it "a rather graceless story," which he believed "smacks of popular . . . anti-Semitism" (*Poe,* 147).

"A Decided Loss" (1832)

This seems but a first draft for the later "Loss of Breath" (1835). The subtitle of "A Decided Loss" was "A Tale a la Blackwood," but with the 1856 version of "Loss of Breath," the subtitle was changed to "A Tale Neither in nor out of 'Blackwood's' " (*M* 2, 61), Poe apparently preferring on the second run to be oblique rather than direct. In a letter to his mentor, the novelist John Kennedy, dated February 1836, Poe described "Loss of Breath" as an intentional satire aimed at "the extravagancies of Blackwood" (*PoeL,* 191). Following the appearance of this fantastic tale in the *Messenger* for September 1835, the New York *Courier and Enquirer* called it "a capital burlesque of the wild, extravagant, disjointed rigmarole" with which *Blackwood*'s "is so redundant" (*PoeL,* 180).

The locale of the action is Philadelphia, and the time is 1830. The protagonist—surely an antihero—is Mr. Lackobreath, and his antagonists are his wife, Mrs. Lackobreath; her lover, Mr. Windenough; and the motley crowd. The plot hinges on the calamity—and the complication—of Mr. Lackobreath's loss of breath while berating and condemning his wife for her association with Mr. Windenough. The action of the tale consists of Mr. Lackobreath's efforts to recover his breath. However, these frantic efforts are complicated by his subjection to other possible calamities—such as being hanged by the neck until dead.

The irony of it all is that when Mr. Lackobreath discovers his lost breath, it is in the possession of Mr. Windenough. He is, therefore, obliged to make a bargain with his rival.

Clearly, this story was designed to be told by Mr. Blackwood Blackwood. But this name does not refer to the real proprietor of *Blackwood's*—namely,

William Blackwood. It refers to someone "more Blackwood than Blackwood." This person is most likely "the wayward Irishman," William Maginn, a forceful man on the staff of *Blackwood's,* who became famous for writing burlesques characterized by racy, realistic dialogue. He was largely responsible for conferring on the magazine its typical tone. Therefore, Maginn tells the story in the manner of the typical Blackwood "extravaganza."

Although no one has mentioned it, it is patent that in "Loss of Breath" Poe indulges in double entendre in presenting a plight occurring in a *ménage à trois* of husband, wife, and lover and that a "lack of breath" refers to sexual impotency and a "wind enough" to sexual potency. In the American magazine world of Poe's time, such a light treatment of this subject was strictly verboten. If any contemporary readers understood this "undercurrent of meaning"—as some surely did—they never uttered a word in writing.

"Bon-Bon" (1835)

The original version of this tale, *The Bargain Lost* (1832), was a mere anecdote. Poe was sufficiently dissatisfied with it that he rewrote it almost completely, making changes and adding material. He changed the locale from Italy to France and his hero's nationality from Italian to French. His rewriting and expansion made "Bon-Bon" into a comic masterpiece rivaling his "The Duc de L'Omelette."

The action in "Bob-Bon" takes place inside the Câfé de Bon-Bon in the city of Rouen, in northwestern France. The time is the period when skeptical and materialist philosophers flourished in France, that is, the mid-eighteenth century. The characters are Pierre Bon-Bon, a *restaurateur-philosophe* of Rouen, both a gourmet and a composite of three real *philosophes*—La Mettrie, Helvetius, and d'Holbach. His antagonist is the Devil, who pretends to be Epicurus. The narrative structure of the story is in the form of dialogue or colloquy, for the dramatic interest lies entirely in the conflict of ideas and the exchanges of wit between Bon-Bon and the Devil. As mouthpieces for the ideas they convey, these characters are stylized caricatures. Bon-Bon is short and possesses a small head and a large stomach. He wears a colorful costume. The Devil is tall and lean. He has a lofty forehead, a pale complexion, and fanged teeth, and his swallow-tailed coat shows evidence of a tail underneath. Although the Devil wears "green spectacles," he has never had eyes in his head. When the story begins, Bon-Bon is described as a *philosophus gloriosus*. But his failure to inveigle the Devil into making a pact with him, that is, his "lost bargain," transforms him into a *philosophus ridiculosus*.

The idea in "Bon-Bon" that the Devil is an Epicure who feeds on men's souls Poe derived from Francisco de Quevedo's *El Sueño del infierno* (1608; "The Vision of Hell"), most likely in an English translation.

The teller of "Bon-Bon" is De Rerum Naturâ, Esq., "who wore a very singular pair of green spectacles." This is the Devil as Lucretius-Epicurus, for the Roman author of *De rerum natura* ("On the Nature of Things") expresses in his poem the materialist philosophy of Epicurus. In "Bon-Bon," the Devil attempts to pose as Epicurus. As Alexander Hammond pointed out, the assumption that souls may be eaten is "a comic embodiment of the argument of *De Rerum Natura* that the soul is composed of atoms and is therefore material." This tale is perhaps best taken as Poe's "version of the Faust story as Satan himself might tell it" (Hammond, "Reconstruction," 28).

"Epimanes" (1836)

In 1833, Poe sent this tale to the *New England Magazine* to represent his collection *Eleven Tales of the Arabesque,* but it and the whole volume were rejected. "Epimanes" was not published until it appeared in the *Messenger* for March 1836. In 1840, the tale became part of Poe's first volume of collected stories, *Tales of the Grotesque and Arabesque,* but, with it, the tale had a new title, "Four Beasts in One—The Homo-Cameleopard." Mabbott called "Four Beasts in One" one of the best of Poe's grotesque tales (*M* 2, 117).

The locale of the story is the city of Antioch. Located on the Orontes River, Antioch was the capital of ancient Syria. The time is 175 B.C. This was during the reign of the Selucid king, Antiochus IV, who was called "Epiphanes" (God Manifest) and also "Epimanes" (Madman). Strongly Hellenistic in his attitude, Antiochus's efforts to suppress Judaism brought about the Wars of the Maccabees.

Poe's tale concerns Antiochus's military adventures, his massacre of a thousand Jews, and his cultivation of the mob—which worships him as a divinity. The narrative structure consists of a series of tableaux to be viewed at the scene by the reader guided by the unnamed narrator. He addresses the reader as "friend" and invites him to join him in the streets of ancient Antioch at a good vantage point. There the two will witness the events, the sights, and the sounds of history in the making. This unusual narrative approach is a parody of what had been used by Horace Smith in his *Tales of Early Ages* (1832).

Two general themes emerge from Poe's story—one anthropological, the other political. The first has been stated well by Davidson, who saw the story revealing "the bestial nature of man which lies just beneath the surface of civilization" to suggest that "man is the destructive beast, whereas the animals are humane" (*Poe,* 152). On the other hand, according to Mabbott, Poe's beast fable illustrates "the baseness of the ancient mob—shared by its modern counterpart" (*M* 2, 117). William Whipple proposed that "Four Beasts in One" is a political allegory—an attack on President Andrew Jackson and his policies (81–95). Although today Jackson is regarded as the symbol of democracy, in his time his opponents regarded him as a monarch who cultivated "mobocracy." In contemporary political cartoons, he was referred to as "King Andrew" and even as "Richard III."

"Four Beasts in One," then, is a fable and a farce; it is also a moral fantasy

and a political allegory. Who the teller of this tale is, is not clear. It may be
Major Noah, but it seems more likely, in the light of the political allegory
scenario, that Mr. Snap, that is, the American journalist and novelist John Neal,
may be the right choice, telling it in the manner of Horace Smith.

"MS. Found in a Bottle" (1835)

Of it, Mabbott declared: "This story is a masterpiece in the literal sense of
the word. By winning a prize contest it set its author on the way to lasting
fame" (M 2, 130). Although the tale mocks the popular fictional sea voyages
of the time and makes fun of the outlandish speculations of Captain John
Symmes, it is Poe's first science fiction tale and proposes a serious philosophical
theme. The narrator is Mr. Solomon Seadrift. His name mocks two heroes of
fictional sea adventures—Sir Edward Seaward, the hero of English novelist Jane
Porter's *Sir Edward Seaward's Narrative of His Shipwreck . . .* (1831), and Captain Adam Seaborn, the pseudonym adopted by Captain John Cleve Symmes in
authoring his science fiction novel entitled *Symzonia—A Voyage of Discovery*
(1820). Under the guise of fiction, however, Symmes proposed a theory he
actually believed in.

"MS. Found in a Bottle" is the story of an extraordinary sea voyage from
the island of Java, in the Greater Sundra Archipelago, south by east into the
South Pacific Ocean to the western coast of Antarctica, which consisted of gla-
cier and shelf ice and was in the vicinity of the South Magnetic Pole. The voyage
takes place in the early nineteenth century. In the story, Poe makes use of
Symmes's theory that the earth is hollow, open at both ends, and inhabitable
within. Symmes was quite serious about this theory. With James McBride, he
published a serious description of it in *Symmes' Theory of Concentric Spheres*
(1826). He also tried to convince the U.S. government to outfit a naval expedition to survey the South Pacific in an effort to prove his theory.

That Symmes is identifiable with Seadrift is shown "when the narrator daubs
the word 'DISCOVERY' on a sail," thus signifying that his adventure is "A
Voyage of Discovery." This is "the subtitle of *Symzonia* and a phrase that
occurs repeatedly in its text" (Hammond, "Reconstruction," 29). Hence, "MS.
Found in a Bottle" is a parody of currently popular fictional sea voyages told
in the manner of Captain Seaborn (John Cleve Symmes), whose pseudoscience
is being quizzed in Poe's first science fiction story. But apart from illustrating
Symmes's theory of holes at the poles, the story develops two other themes: the
legend of the Flying Dutchman and the possibility of "transcendental discovery" and its consequences, the latter the theme that Poe perhaps took the most
seriously.

At the conclusion of the story, the narrator discovers that the gigantic mystery
ship on which he has grown old is *in a current* and contained by "stupendous
ramparts of ice, towering away into the desolate sky, and looking like the walls
of the universe." The ship "thunders on to the southward with a velocity like

the headlong lashing of a cataract.'' Though horrified, his curiosity overcomes his despair. He is sure he is ''hurrying onwards to some exciting knowledge—some never-to-be-imparted secret, whose knowledge is destruction.''

"The Visionary" (1834; later, "The Assignation")

This is perhaps Poe's most beautiful and picturesque story. Mabbott called it ''the most romantic story Poe ever wrote'' (*M* 2, 148). The story deals with the Western code of ''romantic love'' as originated and developed by the trouba-dours and courts of love of the Middle Ages. It concerns a romantic triangle involving an English poet, the young Marchesa Mentoni, and her old husband. It is Poe's personal, imaginative, and creative conception of what he deemed would have been a fitting conclusion to the life of Lord Byron—an assignation with a beautiful woman in a suicide pact. Poe's romantic triangle was based on the actual triangle of Lord Byron, the young Countess Quiccioli, and her old husband. For his Byronic material, he owed a debt to Thomas Moore's *Letters and Journals of Lord Byron, with Notices of His Life* (1830), including the poem written by the English poet in the story, which parodies lines that Byron wrote for his early love, Mary Chaworth (see Benton, ''Is Poe's 'The Assignation' a Hoax?''). Benjamin Franklin Fisher IV and David Ketterer (both 1986) have supported the tale's seriousness.

Because of what some critics have called the story's ''inflated bathos'' or ''operatic style,'' ''The Visionary'' has caused confusion in the minds of its commentators—some holding that it is a lampoon of romanticism, others that it is to be taken as sincere, genuine romanticism on the part of Poe. As for those who take the former position, Eric W. Carlson has commented, they must reckon ''with Poe's preference for the visionary Hero, the classic Hellenic heroine, the conventional villain, the symbolic rescue, the arabesque apartment, the love poem'' and ''the final suicide pact'' (309). Furthermore, although the typical parody is taken by most critics to be destructive in aim, that is not necessarily always so; parodies have been written in order to honor a style or a work, to conserve and perpetuate it. Ezra Pound has done this in several of his *Cantos,* as Canto 49 honors the Chinese-Japanese lyric poetry tradition. Such parodies tend to be not only creative but personal.

''The Visionary'' is not a satire or burlesque in its ''ludicrous sentimental-ism,'' as Edward H. Davidson concluded (*Poe,* 153). On the contrary, it is a remarkable tribute to a poet whose life mirrored his poetry, who was to Poe at the time of writing his poet-hero. In the tale, he gave free rein to his own penchant for Byronism, which he had had to suppress because of objections voiced against it by his foster father. The teller of the tale is easily identified by Poe's choice of pseudonym, Mr. Convolvulus Gondola, ''a young gentleman who had travelled a good deal.'' This is so even apart from Poe's playing with the name of the English statesman Sir Thomas More to echo that of the Irish poet Thomas Moore, Byron's friend. In 1819, Moore made the journey down the Grand Canal in Venice to Byron's Palazzo Mocenigo, located not far from the Rialto Bridge. ''The Visionary,'' then, is told by Moore not to ridicule but to honor Byron's romanticism.

"Lionizing" (1835)

This is one of Poe's most effective farces and contains a lively humor. Contemporary readers understood its main theme clearly. James Kirke Paulding called it ''one of the most happy travesties of the coxcombical egotism of travelling scribblers I have ever seen'' (*PoeL*, 159). The Richmond *Compiler* of the day saw it as a satire ''upon the rage for making a Lion of every contemptible pretender to fashion, or small authorship'' (*PoeL*, 181). Critics of the time generally referred to ''Lionizing'' as a ''burlesque'' or an ''extravaganza.''

The action of ''Lionizing'' takes place in ''Fum-Fudge,'' that is, London. As Hammond recognized, the tale apparently follows the early career of the novelist and politician Benjamin Disraeli (''Poe's 'Lionizing' '' and also ''Reconstruction'').

During the period from 1822, when Disraeli quit the study of law in a lawyer's office in London, to 1835, when he became a member of the Tory or Conservative Party, he consistently failed in his endeavors except for the success he enjoyed with the publication of his novels, *Vivian Grey* (1826) and *The Young Duke* (1831). In 1831, Disraeli was introduced by his friend the novelist Edward Bulwer-Lytton, author of the popular *Pelham* (1828) and *Paul Clifford* (1830), into the salons of Lady Blessington, which she held either in her London home, Seamore Place, in Mayfair, or at Almack's Assembly Rooms, in King Street, St. James's, London. At Lady Blessington's salons, Disraeli met other literary persons on the fringes of upper-class society. He sought to create a sensation by wearing extravagant dress and by studding his conversation with wit, sarcasm, and paradox.

Richard P. Benton suggested that ''Lionizing'' was aimed at the literary circle surrounding Lady Blessington, which included Bulwer-Lytton, Disraeli, and the American N. P. Willis, and that Poe was slapping particularly at Willis's social climbing and self-puffery ('' 'Lionizing' ''). But G. R. Thompson (''On the Nose'') argued for the influence of Bulwer-Lytton's *Pelham* on Poe's tale, and he proposed that Bulwer-Lytton was most likely the teller of it. In this last proposal, Thompson seems correct. The narrator does appear to be Bulwer-Lytton, the Folio Club's ''newest member'' and the author of the prologue to the *Tales*. But he tells the story in the manner of Disraeli, the influence of the latter's *Vivian Grey* being pronounced.

"Shadow—A Fable" (1835; later subtitled "A Parable")

This is so pictorial, musical, and choice in its language that it might be regarded as a prose poem. Woodberry held it as ''the most noble and most artistic expression of Poe's imagination during the first period of his career" (*M* 2, 187).

The locale of the action is the city of Ptolemais in Byzantine Egypt. This is presumably Ptolemais Theon on the Red Sea, of which Pliny the Elder reported in his *Natural History* that "for ninety days in midsummer the sun at noon cast no shadow" (*M* 2, 192). The time of the action is during the reign of Byzantine emperor Justinian when the plague struck Egypt in A.D. 542.

The plot is simple. The Greek Oinos tells the story in a memorial left behind at his death. In a company of seven, he is assembled at a wake for their dead friend Zoilus, a victim of the pestilence. As the seven drink Chian red wine and make merry, they discern the Shadow of death emerge from the black draperies of the hall to come to rest upon the "brazen doorway." The seven are afraid to look the Shadow in the face but, with eyes cast down, inquire of him his name and abode. He replies in a single voice, which soon, however, changes into the tone of a multitude of beings, including those of "many thousand departed friends." The story combines great beauty with the terror associated with the thought of death.

Although Poe critics have called attention to the story's style as resembling the styles of the King James Bible, of Edward Bulwer-Lytton, and of Thomas De Quincey, Burton Pollin has clearly shown the predominant influence on it of Thomas Moore's philosophical romance of third-century Egypt, *The Epicurean* (1827) ("Light on 'Shadow' "), Moore's only attempt at prose fiction. Pollin was convinced that Poe's "Shadow" was intended as a quiz on the Irish poet and biographer of Byron bedecked "in Gothic and Oriental trappings." It is a story told by the "very little man in a black coat with very black eyes"— namely, by Edgar Poe himself—in the manner of Thomas Moore. It is a parody but not a satire—it honors Moore. Pollin rightly speaks of "Shadow" as "so beautifully wrought that it has appeared to Poe critics as a serious and profound commentary on the power of the symbolized Shadow of death to provoke terror and horror in the hearts of men" (170).

"Siope—A Fable" (1838; later, "Silence—A Fable")

This is regarded as a companion piece to "Shadow—A Parable," both considered prose masterpieces. In the first publication of "Siope" in the *Baltimore Book,* the title included the notification "in the manner of the Psychological Autobiographists." Most noted of these English authors were Edward Bulwer-Lytton, Benjamin Disraeli, and Thomas De Quincey. In his story, Poe owed a good deal to Edward Bulwer-Lytton's tale "Monos and Daimonos—A Legend," and it may be said that Poe's story is told in the manner of Bulwer-Lytton. But it is one of the most cryptic of Poe's stories, and it has baffled numerous readers.

Although the locale of the action appears to be Central Africa somewhere on the Congo River, and the time seems to be the heyday of the Roman Empire, these basic facts appear to have little meaning because the story is really a dreaming—indeed, a dream-within-a-dream: it is a fable or fairy tale that observes itself. In this fabulous dream, Poe objectifies his own two selves—his "ordinary self," that is, himself as a professional man of letters, and his "artistic self," that is, himself as artist ruled by his creative imagination. In the story, Poe objectifies his "creative self" as the Demon of the Imagination, and a dramatic spectacle is put before the eyes of the observing author, who sees himself cast in this drama as Everyman. As such, he is the solitary explorer of the "Dark Continent," which is the Universe, Nature, and Man. He seeks, it appears, some clue that will unlock the secret of universal existence, but this is a Perilous Realm, and the discovery of the secret may be fatal.

Hence, playing the role of Everyman dressed as a citizen of ancient Rome, Poe, disgusted with mankind, "clings to the rock of reality in the valley named DESOLATION. Although terrified by the presence of wild beasts and buffeted by thunderstorms, he holds steadfastly to his position on the rock, undeterred by the danger of death. However, when he sees that the name of the valley has changed from DESOLATION to SILENCE, he becomes completely unnerved. Now he realizes that NOTHINGNESS was and still is as possible as BEING. Rising in terror on his rock, he flees into the distance. This action concludes the Demon's drama.

From his vantage point in the wings of the stage, the author-spectator steps to the forepart of the stage and addresses another witness, the reader. He informs him that the terror and flight of the Roman underlines the moral of the Demon's drama. He tells the reader that he regards this drama as more marvelous than the stories told by the Magi. He notes, too, that, at the end of the drama, the Demon "fell back within the cavity of the tomb and laughed." But, he says, "I could not laugh. And the lynx which dwelleth forever in the tomb, came out therefrom, and lay down at the feet of the Demon, and looked at him steadily in the face." In this manner, Poe's "Silence" expresses mankind's ANGUISH OF BEING.

Other views of "Silence" have been expressed by G. R. Thompson (" 'Silence' ") and Alice M. Claudel. Thompson saw it as an ironic work in the "Absurdist tradition," and Claudel considered it a satire aimed at the New England transcendentalists. What is certain is that this dream landscape is no optimist's paradise; it may be not only contingent but absurd.

"Berenice" (1835)

This is one of Poe's most sensational and horrible tales. Some readers have found it too horrible, and Poe himself confessed it to be such.

On a literal level, it is the story of the monomania of a young English aristocrat, Egaeus, who violates the grave and the fragile body of his prematurely buried cousin, Berenice, by the extraction of all of her thirty-two white teeth.

However, on an allegorical level, it is a story of head versus heart. Egaeus is a man of pure intellect with a complete absence of feeling for other human beings. He spends his time meditating on objects he has abstracted from the material world. Reality to him is like a tour through a gallery of abstract art. In contrast, his lovely cousin, Berenice, is a woman of feeling. She is loving, sensitive to the concrete physical world around her, enjoying the outdoors and nature, and glad to be alive. Although Egaeus is aware of her fondness for him, to him she is but beauty in the abstract rather than a person to be loved.

When Berenice falls ill with epilepsy, and her beauty of person begins to deteriorate to the point of the grotesque, Egaeus becomes fascinated and then obsessed with her teeth, which he abstracts into *ideas.* His monomania in this respect causes him to commit the horrible act he does after the supposedly dead Berenice has been buried in her grave.

Eric W. Carlson has viewed "Berenice" from the interesting angle of "an allegory of the bipart self suffering a radical split. . . . In extracting her teeth . . . Egaeus (the heartless intellect) violates the very unity of mind and heart that his fragmented self so desperately seeks to recover" (310).

"Berenice" does not seem connected with the original eleven *Tales of the Folio Club.*

"Morella"

The appearance of this tale in the 1835 *Messenger* brought about a mixed response. The Augusta (Georgia) *Chronicle* thought it "one of the best of those wild and gloomy exhibitions of passion, heretofore belonging . . . to . . . the German school of romance." On the other hand, the Richmond *Compiler* saw it as "the creation of a fancy unrestrained by judgment and undirected by design," ending in "a sore and unmerited disappointment" (*PoeL,* 156f.). However, Poe himself thought it was one of his best tales to that date (*PoeL,* 183). It was a more complex variation of the same theme as "Berenice" and a preparation for Poe's greater masterpiece, "Ligeia." This theme has to do with an obsession with rational empiricism and an absence of human feeling to the point that one is transformed into a mental vampire and repeats the sin of Adam as well as that of Faust.

When the unnamed narrator meets Morella, he is impressed with her erudition and powerful intellect. He marries her with a view of becoming her pupil, picking her brain, and knowing her mentally but not physically. The fires that burn in him are not those of Eros, and he "never spoke of love, or dreamed of passion." But there is a gender difference. She is a woman. Although greatly his superior intellectually, she attaches herself exclusively to him.

Morella has evidently been educated at the Academia Istropolitana at the Hungarian city of Pozsony (German Pressburg). She introduces her husband to the secret speculations of the Pythagoreans—especially to their doctrine of metempsychosis—to the pantheism of Fichte (his *Ich-heit*) and Schelling's view of identity (*Identität*). But he is a Lockean and cannot follow her into such esoteric realms. Nevertheless, he seeks to suck the lifeblood of her power and knowledge from her. When he looks into her eyes, however, he is shocked. He begins to understand—at least vaguely—that she holds his ignorance "of the flowers and the vine" against him, that sense knowledge—"earth knowledge"—is but a ladder to spiritual knowledge—"heavenly" knowledge—and that the supreme good is to become *godlike.* She regards him as one "of the sons of Earth and Life," whereas she is one of "the daughters of Heaven and Death." His scrutinizing, empirical analysis of her—his mental vampireness—has killed her love for him. Now he hates her and longs for her death. She wills to die while giving birth to a daughter. But he will be punished for his sin, for his life after her death will be sad.

Morella dies, and an instant later her daughter is born. Her father raises his daughter to her majority, and she is baptized. When conferring her name on her, he is impelled to name her "Morella," and he realizes now that there has occurred a transmigration of souls.

Poe's character of Morella was based on a Spanish prodigy, Julian Morella, who was noted for her extensive learning at the age of twelve. She later became a nun at the convent of Prasedia at Avignon. She died in 1653.

The basis of Poe's plot was derived from Henry Glassford Bell's story "The Dead Daughter" (*The Edinburgh Literary Journal,* January 1, 1831). However, Poe added to it and completely transmuted it into his own.

"King Pest the First" (1835)

Upon its appearance, this story was subtitled "A Tale Containing an Allegory." Whatever the allegory, as a story it is a grotesque and a burlesque. Indeed, it is in the modern mode called *"l'humeur noire,"* or an effort to make the repulsive funny. His success in this way has been a matter of controversy among critics. It was well received by some of Poe's contemporary readers, as, for instance, the Richmond *Compiler,* which commented: "In King Pest, the evils and maladies attendant upon intemperance are well portrayed in the Allegorical personages who group around the drinking table of the monarch 'Tim Hurly-gurly' " (*PoeL,* 181). Commentators have differed widely in their opinions of it. Constance Rourke in her *American Humor* (1931) viewed it as "one of the most brillant pure burlesques in the language," whereas Eric W. Carlson recently declared its black humor "so extreme that it ceases to be funny" (74). But its humor is political as well as literary and is dated.

"King Pest" takes place in fourteenth-century London, in the parish of St. Andrews, during the reign of Edward III, when the Black Death, or bubonic plague, was devastating the city. Two sailors, a tall, slim man named Legs and a short, stout man named Hugh Tarpaulin, have overstayed their welcome at an alehouse by drinking more than they can pay for. Hence, they are forced to flee at midnight, the landlady of the Jolly Tar in hot pursuit.

The sailors manage to escape by taking refuge in a broken-down undertaker's shop built over a wine cellar. In the shop, they find a monarch and his consort, King and Queen Pest, together with their retainers, Arch Duke Pest-Iferous, Duke Pest-Ilential, Duke Tem-Pest, and Arch Duchess Ana-Pest, all sitting around a table, royalty and nobility drinking from skulls. All six persons are in varied stages of intoxication and in poor health. Each person is titled, named, and described so that one physiological feature is exaggerated and thus emphasized. They are making merry by drinking in honor of their "unearthly sovereign . . . whose name is Death."

The sailors' inquiries and remarks insult their royal hosts, who sentence each of them to drink a gallon of Black Strap (cheap wine) in honor of their unearthly sovereign. The sailors refuse, and a brawl develops. The sailors overcome the monarchs and their retainers and escape with two of the noblewomen.

What the allegory of "King Pest" consists of has largely been ignored by modern commentators. In an allegory worked out by a pupil of Mabbott's, Lynne Chaleff, each one of the "pesty" persons sitting drinking around the table represents some character type. For instance, King Pest, who has a high forehead, represents a man of intellect who fails to do anything with it; Queen Pest, who has a big mouth, is a gossip; Arch Duke Pest-Iferous, who has large ears, is a sot; Duke Pest-Ilential, who has goggle-eyes, sees all but recoils from the world; Arch Duke Tem-Pest, who is cheeky, is deserving of nothing; and Arch Duchess Ana-Pest, who has a long nose, is a bad poet who is overcurious (*M* 2, 255).

However, William Whipple proposed that "King Pest," like "Four Beasts in One," was a satire directed against President Andrew Jackson and Jacksonian equalitarian democracy. Foes predicted chaos during the reign of "King Andrew." King Pest the First is described as the "President of the Table." He is tall and gaunt, with a yellow complexion and a lofty forehead, his head decorated with sable-hearse plumes. This is General Andrew Jackson, seventh president of the United States (1829–1837), to his admirers the greatest hero of his day but to his opponents "King Andrew" and even "Richard III." The story takes place in "the parish of St. Andrews." When at midnight, the two sailors are pursued by the landlady of the Jolly Tar, they flee "down a dark alley in the direction of St. Andrew's Stair." The stairway of Jackson's home named "The Hermitage," near Nashville, Tennessee, was named "St. Andrew's Stair." The undertaker's shop, therefore, must be the kitchen of the White House, and the other persons are the members of the Jackson "family," including some members of Jackson's Kitchen Cabinet. Queen Pest, the lady with the big mouth, is Peggy Eaton, the wife of Secretary of War John Henry Eaton, whose chastity Jackson defended; Arch Duke Pest-Iferous, who has large ears, is Amos Kendell, fourth auditor (< L. *audire,* to hear) of the Treasury; Duke Pest-Ilential, who has goggle-eyes, is Francis Preston Blair, Sr., assistant editor of the Frankfort (Kentucky) newspaper, *The Argus* (giant with a hundred eyes), and editor of the *Washington Globe* (< L. *globus,* ball; hence, related to "bulging" or "goggle"-eyes); Duke Tem-Pest, who is cheeky, is Secretary of War Eaton, whose wife became the center of a teapot *tempest* that split the president's cabinet wide open; and Arch Duchess Ana-Pest, the diminutive, *haut-ton* lady who is consumptive, is Emily Donelson, Jackson's acting First Lady (his wife, Rachel, died ten weeks before his inauguration). Emily died of consumption in December 1836.

Hammond considered "King Pest" one of the original eleven Folio Club tales. He proposed that it is told by Washington Irving in the manner of Sir Walter Scott ("Reconstruction"). For other work on the Folio Club Tales, see Hammond, "Tales."

For work on the Folio Club problematic by European scholars, see Claude Richard, "Le Contes du Folio Club et la Vocation Humoristique," in *Configuration Critique d'Edgar Allan Poe,* ed. Claude Richard (Paris: Minard, 1969), and Sybille Haage, *Edgar Allan Poes 'Tales of the Folio Club' Versuch der Rekonstruktion einer zyklischen Rekenerzählung* (Frankfurt am Main/Bern/Las Vegas: Peter Lang, 1978), a monograph that traces the development of the Folio Club plan, and her Edgar Allan Poe, *"Tales of the Folio Club" and Three Other Stories,* ed. with Introd. (Frankfurt am Main/Bern/Las Vegas: Peter Lang, 1978), Haage's reconstruction of the Folio Club volume.

The importance of Poe's Folio Club plan to his training and development as a writer and critic can hardly be overestimated—especially as this period pointed to his future artistry.

WORKS CITED

Benton, Richard P. "Is Poe's 'The Assignation' a Hoax?" *Nineteenth Century Fiction* 18 (1963): 193–97. Rpt. in *The Naiad Voice.* Ed. Eddings (1983).

———. "Poe's 'Lionizing': A Quiz on Willis and Lady Blessington." *Studies in Short Fiction* 5 (1968): 239–44.

Carlson, Eric W. "Edgar Allan Poe." In *American Short-Story Writers before 1880.* Ed. Bobby Ellen Kimbel, with William F. Grant. Detroit: Gale Research, 1988, 303–22. (Dictionary of Literary Biography, vol. 74.)

Claudel, Alice M. "What Has Poe's 'Silence' to Say?" *Ball State. University Forum* 10 (1969): 66–70.

Daughrity, Kenneth L. "Poe's Quiz on Willis." *AL* 5 (1933): 55–62.

Davidson, Edward H. *Poe: A Critical Study.* Cambridge: Harvard UP, 1957.

Fisher, Benjamin Franklin, IV. "The Flights of a Good Man's Mind: Gothic Fantasy in Poe's 'The Assignation.'" *Modern Language Studies* 16 (1986): 27–34.

———. "Poe's 'Metzengerstein': Not a Hoax." *AL* 42 (1971): 487–94.

———. "To 'The Assignation' from 'The Visionary' and Poe's Decade of Revising." *Library Chronicle* 39 (1973): 89–105.

———. "To 'The Assignation' from 'The Visionary' (Part Two): The Revisions and Related Matters." *Library Chronicle* 40 (1976): 221–51.

Hammond, Alexander. "Edgar Allan Poe's *Tales of the Folio Club:* The Evolution of a Lost Book." *Library Chronicle,* 41 (1976): 13–43.

———. "Poe's 'Lionizing' and the Design of *Tales of the Folio Club.*" *Emerson Society Quarterly* 18 (1972): 154–65.

———. "A Reconstruction of Poe's 1833 *Tales of the Folio Club.*" *PoeS* 5 (1972): 25–32.

Harrison, James A., ed. *Complete Works of Edgar Allan Poe.* 16 vols. New York: Thomas Y. Crowell, 1902. Rpt. in New York: AMS P, 1965.

Hirsch, David R. "Poe's 'Metzengerstein' as a Tale of the Subconscious." *UMSE* 3 (1982): 40–52.

Ketterer, David. "The Sexual Abyss: Consummation in 'The Assignation.' " *PoeS* 19 (1986): 7–10.

Mabbott, Thomas Ollive, ed. *Collected Works of Edgar Allan Poe.* 3 vols. Cambridge: Belknap P of Harvard UP, 1969–1978.

Ostrom. John Ward, ed. *The Letters of Edgar Allan Poe.* 2 vols. Cambridge: Harvard UP, 1948.

Pollin, Burton R. "Light on 'Shadow' and Other Pieces by Poe, or, More of Thomas Moore." *Emerson Society Quarterly* 18 (1972): 160–70.

———. "Poe's 'Diddling': More on the Dating and the Aim." *PoeS* 9 (1976): 11–13.

Rourke, Constance M. *American Humor: A Study of the National Character.* New York: Harcourt Brace, 1931.

Thomas, Dwight, and David K. Jackson. *The Poe Log: A Documentary Life of Edgar Allan Poe 1809–1849.* Boston: G. K. Hall, 1987.

Thompson, G. R. "On the Nose—Further Speculations on the Sources and Meaning of Poe's 'Lionizing.' " *Studies in Short Fiction* 6 (1988): 94–96.

———. "Poe's Flawed Gothic: Absurdist Techniques in 'Metzengerstein' and the *Courier* Satires." In *New Approaches to Poe.* Ed. Richard P. Benton. Hartford, CT: Transcendental Books, 1970, 38–54.

———. " 'Silence' and the Folio Club: Who Were the 'Psychological Autobiographists'?" *Poe Newsletter* 2 (1969): 123.

Whipple, William. "Poe's Political Satire." *University of Texas Studies in English* 35 (1956): 81–95.

Wilson, James Southall. "The Devil Was in It." *American Mercury* 24 (Oct. 1931): 215–20.

6

Comic Satires and Grotesques: 1836–1849

STUART LEVINE AND SUSAN F. LEVINE

Although most of the Poe stories in this group are dated and topical, they spring back to life if the reader is provided explanations of context and of Poe's allusions and references. That the stories have some success even without these aids is testimony that Poe is a very good storyteller.

Good critical studies include Fagin on theatrical aspects, Mooney on comedy (1961, 1962), Thompson on Poe's irony, Levine (1978) and Reynolds on Poe and society; essays edited by Eddings; annotations by Mabbott (1978); and annotated editions by Levine and Levine (1976, 1990) and Galloway.

Several of these stories resemble popular journalism, but within a fictional frame that functions as a box to hold amusing tidbits. Such stories include "The Thousand-and-Second Tale of Scheherazade," "Some Words with a Mummy," and "The Business Man." Others of this type—"Three Sundays in a Week," "Diddling," "The Spectacles," and "Thou Art the Man"—treat several topics personally significant for Poe: a hopeful young man; a young man engaged in a courtship; a young man with a wealthy relative; the likable and hearty person revealed as a cheat and a fraud. Poe's difficulty with his prosperous stepfather, John Allan, provides autobiographical resonance.

COMIC SATIRES

"Mystification"

(June 1837, *American Monthly Magazine;* 1840, *Tales of the Grotesque and Arabesque;* December 27, 1845, *The Broadway Journal*)

Poe often reused stories, generally reediting them for each publication. His revisions of "Mystification" show the interplay among varied and overlapping motives behind much of his work. They hardly affect the plot: a consummate hoaxer who sees the absurdity of student duels picks a quarrel with Hermann, a dueling-code fanatic, hurls wine by way of an insult, and urges "P—," the narrator, to offer his services as second. Then, instead of actually dueling, he refers Hermann to an incomprehensible dueling treatise, which, he says, explains why the duel need not occur. Hermann, too vain to admit his inability to understand (the book is a deliberate hoax, meant to be unreadable), accepts the "explanation."

In 1837, "Von Jung the Mystific," as "Mystification" was first called, contained American references—"Gotham" among them—which Poe later removed. We know why they were present: Poe had panned Theodore S. Fay's recent novel, *Norman Leslie,* which contained an episode that Poe's tale seems to mock. Poe and Fay were engaged in a verbal duel. The wine-of-insult in Poe's story (in the revised form, in which it is usually read) is hurled not at the character Hermann but at Hermann's mirror image. That puzzling detail was not puzzling to contemporaries. It is a holdover from Poe's earlier intention, for the *New York Mirror* was Fay's newspaper and had run some blather puffing *Norman Leslie,* along with the portion of *Norman Leslie* that "Von Jung/Mystification" parodies. Ever alert to plagiarism real or imagined, Poe had damaging evidence in this case, for Fay had largely borrowed his dueling chapter from another writer's work (Levine and Levine 1990, 454; *M* 2, 291–92; Pollin 1972b; Moss 1953, 1963). "Von Jung the Mystific" in 1837, then, was an attack on puffery, literary cliques, and third-class talents.

Poe's revisions make "Mystification" much less specific. A reader unaware of its original text and original target sees simply an attack on the absurd aristocratic custom of dueling. Indeed, the story even has interesting biographical implications. It is set in Germany, at "G—n," seat of a dissolute university. Poe did not know Germany but had attended the University of Virginia during a dreadful period when academic life was badly disrupted (there was even a murder) in ways that connect to "G—n." Biographers speculate that Poe's own difficulties at the University of Virginia had to do with the pseudoaristocrats there. Poe often took antidemocratic stands; his story "Mellonta Taunta," for instance, mocks American national political confidence and pretensions. Yet, "Mystification" in final form (there is an intermediate stage, 1840, called "Von Jung," then the usually reprinted 1845 "Mystification") depends for its effect upon its readers' healthy democratic biases against ugly aristocratic customs. Poe's alterations suggest, first, that his feud with Fay was old news and, second, that dissolute students and the stupid *Code Duello* were still good copy.

The contradictions between Poe's frequently snobbish pseudoaristocratic stance and the populist flavor of this story will not reconcile. Poe *is* inconsistent. So are most people, but writers leave records of it.

"How to Write a Blackwood Article/A Predicament"

(November 1838, *The American Museum of Science, Literature and the Arts,* with titles "The Psyche Zenobia"/"The Scythe of Time"; 1840, *Tales of the Grotesque and Arabesque,* with the title "The Signora Zenobia"; July 12, 1845, *The Broadway Journal,* as "How to Write a Blackwood Article"/"A Predicament")

Poe casts this tale in an old form of literary satire in which a writer in a tight spot turns to someone more knowledgeable for advice about how to succeed in an established literary genre. Poe likely had two "how-to-do-it" satires in mind when he wrote this burlesque of the practices of sensational fiction writing—the Prologue to Part One of Cervantes's *Don Quixote,* in which Cervantes had his "author" beg advice from a friend about how to deck his work in proper literary finery, and Frederick Marryat's "How to Write a Fashionable Novel," in which a poor student author, who knows nothing of "fashionable" life, is hard-pressed to produce a "fashionable" novel under contract and asks *his* friend what to do. The satires are very different, but in each the friend says, in effect, "Don't worry—just remember these simple formulas and start writing" (Levine and Levine 1986).

Such satire is funny for readers who know the formulas and clichés of the genres being satirized. Though Poe knew and admired *Blackwood's Edinburgh Magazine,* he knew also that the "intensities," the special stories of sensation that it had pioneered, had often fallen into the hands of less gifted writers than *Blackwood's* best and that formulas were easy to copy badly. "Mr. Blackwood's" advice to the Signora Psyche Zenobia is filled with errors and misattributions, but it is not impossibly bad advice—Poe, after all, followed it himself in some of his best work. It's just that Poe, unlike Zenobia, had the skill to make literary art of the formulaic materials, the "recording" of exaggerated sensations, the parade of conspicuous erudition, and so forth. So "How to Write a Blackwood Article/A Predicament" documents Poe's professional attitude toward his material. High art often results when genius comes to commercial entertainment, as Shakespeare to Elizabethan popular theater, Keaton to silent film comedy, Verdi to Italian opera, or Poe to magazine fiction.

"Blackwood/Predicament" does more than satirize magazine fiction. It echoes other things Poe wrote, reflects his biases, carries on his battles.

Circumstantial evidence suggests to Thomas H. McNeal that Zenobia is a caricature of Margaret Fuller, scholar, literary critic, and "leading female light" among the New England transcendentalists, writers at whom Poe often sniped. Specialists are not certain that McNeal is right; Poe invented Zenobia before Fuller was famous. It *is* interesting that when Hawthorne in 1852 wrote a novel about these transcendentalists, he named his female lead Zenobia and was so certain that readers would take her for Fuller that he inserted a careful disclaimer.

There is no point in trying to hide Poe's offensive racism. His references to blacks, as here, are almost universally stereotyped, condescending, even sneering. As Rans puts it, Poe's "response to corruption took many forms, but never that of a publicly offered melioristic solution" (71).

Poe's works overlap and interpenetrate. The feud with Theodore Fay and the New York *Mirror* noted before, for example, is also reflected here when Poe has Mr. Blackwood refer to the famous "Slang-Whang." Poe got that name from a fable in the New York *Mirror* in which "Slang-Whang" is a Chinese editor who hits the brandy bottle and may, indeed, be Poe himself, since staff at the *Mirror* bore him a grudge (Pollin 1972a). "Blackwood/Predicament" also shares allusions with, among others, "The Literary Life of Thingum Bob, Esq.," "The System of Dr. Tarr and Prof. Fether," and "Never Bet the Devil Your Head,"[1] a list that should suffice to make us take seriously Poe's comment that his whimsical fiction aimed at multiple targets. He blazed away in all directions and sometimes even called in fire upon himself.

"The Man That Was Used Up"

(August 1839, *Burton's Gentleman's Magazine;* 1840, *Tales of the Grotesque and Arabesque;* 1843, *Prose Romances of Edgar Allan Poe;* August 9, 1845, *The Broadway Journal*)

This story is opaque to most modern readers. Even the redoubtable Thomas Ollive Mabbott shows honest head scratching in *Collected Works* (2, 376–77). Sometimes Poe stories were obscure to readers, even editors, in his day. But this one is obscure only today, because its targets were topical.

A nervous narrator who cannot bear even "the slightest appearance of mystery" is bewildered by the mysteries surrounding General John A.B.C. Smith. Unable to obtain an explanation, he calls on Smith himself. Smith is a bundle on the floor. When to the bundle are added artificial body parts, he appears as a precise and handsome hero; he has lost limbs, bosom, scalp, eyes, and palate in "the Late Bugaboo and Kickapoo Campaign."

Edgar Poe was one of the editors of *Burton's Gentleman's Magazine* when it published this tale. "The Man . . ." was thus extremely topical, for the famous conspiracy trial of Captain Daniel Mann, as Varner has shown (77), was still in progress, and any reader up on gossip and daily news would have responded to the references to "*Captain* Mann" in the middle paragraphs. Poe's main target, though, was Vice President Richard M. Johnson, as Whipple (1956) convincingly demonstrated. Behind the violence in "The Man . . ." was a terrible and well-known historical fact. During the Battle of the Thames in 1813, there had been an especially sickening passage of butchery in a swamp. Johnson fought courageously, killed the famous Chief Tecumseh (neither "Kickapoo" nor "Bugaboo" but Shawnee) and sustained severe and repeated wounds. That courage, those wounds, and his consequent stature as a hero were potent campaign assets. Whipple (92) quotes a contemporary: Johnson was "[a] man upon crutches; his frame all mutilated; moving with difficulty yet an object of patriotic interest with everybody.''

Hence, the incidents of destruction or self-destruction.[2] But the label ''political satire'' fails to get it all, for Poe always had multiple intentions. Social satire, especially of excessive respect for appearance, is obvious, as is pure literary play. Poe plays as he constructs patterns of any sort, even the patterns of destruction and self-destruction. They are not present merely because Johnson was associated with violence: they are evidence of artistic craft.

''The Devil in the Belfry''

(May 18, 1839, *Saturday Chronicle and Mirror of the Times;* 1840, *Tales of the Grotesque and Arabesque;* November 8, 1845, *The Broadway Journal*)

The 1840 anti-Martin Van Buren campaign song with the famous line ''Van, Van's a Used Up Man,'' connects with ''The Man That Was Used Up'' (*M* 2, 377). Van Buren is also a butt of ''The Devil in the Belfry'' (Whipple 1956). Poe introduced numerous details to make contemporaries think of the president.[3] But the story is not therefore a political satire, for Poe said that such stories hit out in all directions. Ethnic and racial humor, often ugly, appears regularly in Poe—antiblack humor in the Blackwood pair, humor at the expense of Native Americans in ''The Man That Was Used Up,'' and here caricature of the Dutch less affectionate than Washington Irving's.

Moreover, Poe's literary play, his pleasure at creating connections, seems more important than is any single ''target'' of satire. To illustrate: the comically orderly and punctual Dutch community in this story is disrupted by a bringer of chaos, the Devil in the Belfry. He is associated with things Irish. As Whipple explains, this is because Van Buren's political power in New York was based on the well-organized Irish vote. But Poe also alludes frequently to Thomas Carlyle's *Sartor Resartus* (Levine and Levine 1976, 355–56). Poe's two satirical lines coalesce in the Irish jig at the end, for Carlyle's book devotes a late chapter (Book 3, Chap. 10) largely to the Irish and concludes with a paragraph about ''[a]ll too Irish mirth and madness.''[4]

Imagery that connects to *Sartor Resartus* cannot exactly be called a private joke. Carlyle was, after all, famous. Many readers would know *Sartor Resartus,* just as most would know about Van Buren. As Eddings and his capable colleagues conclude (see 158ff.), Poe's playfulness is important for understanding his literary character.

''Why the Little Frenchman Wears His Hand in a Sling''

(1840, *Tales of the Grotesque and Arabesque;* September 6, 1845, *The Broadway Journal*)

''It's on my wisiting cards,'' says the Irish narrator, ''Sir Pathrick O'Grandison, Barronitt.'' Ignorant and pretentious, he means to court ''the purty Misthress Tracle." But he has a competitor, a French dancing master. A comic misunderstanding is the total plot: seated on either side of the lady on a sofa, each holds a hand behind her back and is delighted by the warm responses to squeezes. Then the lady gets up, and the men discover they are holding each other's hands.

Poe apparently planned "Frenchman . . ." as another whimsical literary burlesque for "Tales of the Folio Club," this time mocking the writing of Lady Sydney Morgan. Poe had done stage-Irish before: in 1836 he "used up" the author of a novel called *Ups and Downs,* using heavy brogue in his review. Most Folio Club stories were written earlier, but although "Frenchman . . ." was first published in 1840, it fits the pattern.

Ethnic or foreign dialect humor appears often in this period. A *New York Mirror* piece from late 1836 used French dialect and told of a Frenchman getting cheated (*M* 2, 462); Lady Morgan's *Florence Macarthy: An Irish Tale* (1818) includes a scene close enough to "Frenchman . . ." to have given Poe the idea of noncommunication between an Irishman and a Frenchman.[5] Moreover, Lady Morgan's overfondness for French was notorious. In "Blue-Stocking Revels," Leigh Hunt wrote of her

> So he kissed her, and called her "eternal good wench";
> But asked why the devil she spoke so much French?

"Frenchman . . ." is essentially a dialect joke.

Poe had a weakness for both misidentifications and stage effects. A vain young man who won't wear his glasses mistakes a very old woman for a young one in "The Spectacles." A narrator implausibly mistakes a tiny bug close to his face for a vast monster in the distance in "The Sphinx." As Fagin showed, Poe thought in stage terms. In the familiar story "The Masque of the Red Death," Poe constructs a corridor that serves only as a source of lighting. He likely visualized "Why the Little Frenchman . . ." as stage comedy. Theater of the time was filled with set-piece episodes of the sort. Indeed, Mooney (1962) sees farce and vaudeville in much of Poe's comedy. One "source" is less important than "sources," for the story grows out of popular culture, ethnic stereotyping, and popular theater.

"The Business Man"

(February 1840, *Burton's Gentleman's Magazine;* August 2, 1845, *The Broadway Journal*)

This story's first title, "Peter Pendulum, the Business Man," implies care and measurement. We remember that Poe satirizes being methodical in "The Devil in the Belfry." That the title is alliterative was one hint that led Mabbott to conclude that Poe was parodying the popular *Charcoal Sketches,* a collection of sketches about eccentric, complaining misfits by Joseph C. Neal (1808–1847),

Philadelphia journalist. Unlike Poe's burlesque, Mabbott concludes, Neal's piece showed "wry compassion for his characters" (*M* 2, 480–81).

Poe's is thoroughly journalistic, apparently a takeoff on a journalistic book by a journalist that plays off the sort of urban gossip becoming a staple of American newspapers in that era. Peter tells us that he has been relieved of his intelligence by a blow on the head: even in a sketch this slight, Poe provides a rational explanation for strange behavior. Peter now equates intelligence with insanity. A "genius," anyone, that is, who pursues an even moderately useful or skilled profession, is to him an "ass," while a scoundrel and parasite is a "business man." In such satire, the author carries to extremes some tendency noticed in the news. Art Buchwald uses the formula regularly today. Poe would have made a good satirical columnist.

Poe was an urban writer and a product of new print media. This tale should be compared to the equally urban "Diddling" and to "The Man of the Crowd." Perhaps because the latter seems more important, its journalistic texture is generally overlooked: at its beginning, the narrator, in a coffee shop, reads the classifieds!

"Never Bet the Devil Your Head"

(September 1841, *Graham's* as "Never Bet Your Head"; August 16, 1845, *The Broadway Journal* with present title)

Poe answered Joseph Evans Snodgrass's question about intention here (letter [*O* 1, 183], September 19, 1841), saying this was not an attack on the Transcendentalists' *Dial*. Rather, "the tale in question is a mere Extravaganza . . . hitting right & left at things in general." After a whimsical introduction in which Poe's narrator plays with the argument that every story must have a moral and with the assumption that his do not, he tells the life of his friend Toby Dammit, "a sad dog" brought up wrong: his mother intended to administer the beatings that would have ensured that Toby grew up right. She was, alas, left-handed, "and a child flogged left-handedly had better be left unflogged." Poor Toby developed a habit of asserting his certainty through oaths, especially, "I'll bet the Devil my head."

Walking over a covered bridge with the narrator, Toby says that he'll bet the Devil his head that he can jump over the turnstile they encounter at the far end. The Devil appears, Toby accepts the challenge, and Toby, with a running start, leaps up, executing the mandatory midflight pigeonwing. But darkness above the stile conceals a sharp bar and Toby bounces back, deprived of his head, with which the Devil departs.

As Mabbott notes, the sketch is not taken very seriously and is rarely reprinted. But it is a well-written literary comedy—the opening especially—that, as Poe said, is not aimed at anything in particular except humor.

The whimsical ending is probably worth quoting, especially since few readers, even among Poe scholars, have read the tale with any patience.

He did not long survive his terrible loss. The homoeopathists did not give him little enough physic, and what little they did give him he hesitated to take. So in the end he grew worse, and at length died, a lesson to all riotous livers. I bedewed his grave with my tears, worked *bar* sinister on his family escutcheon, and, for the general expenses of his funeral, sent in my very moderate bill to the Transcendentalists. The scoundrels refused to pay it, so I had Mr. Dammit dug up at once, and sold him for dog's meat.

Homeopathic physicians tried to cure patients with minute doses of whatever had made them ill. The lesson "to all riotous livers" is a parody of a ministerial cliché. Really, we know nothing about Toby's riotous living. The "*bar* sinister" is very witty. In heraldry, a *bar* sinister indicates illegitimacy, but poor Toby was killed by the sinister bar in the darkness above the stile. The story doesn't say much—it is primarily a vehicle for whimsy—but it says at least that people who attempt high-flying "stiles," who cut pigeonwings in midair, do so at their peril. Surely, the closing reference to the "Transcendentalists" suggests a connection, since Poe objected to their abstruse ("high-flying"), metaphysical writings.

"Three Sundays in a Week"

(November 27, 1841, *Saturday Evening Post* as "A Succession of Sundays"; May 10, 1845, *The Broadway Journal*)

This is another story out of the texture of American journalism. Poe had seen "Three Thursdays in One Week" in the *Philadelphia Public Ledger* for October 29, 1841 (Levine and Levine 1976, 503, following A. H. Quinn and F. N. Cherry; *M* 2, 648), about anomalies involving the international date line—cross it in one direction and gain a day; cross it the other and lose one. So Poe invents a love story in which hard-hearted grand-uncle Rumgudgeon denies the young narrator permission to marry cousin Kate until three Sundays come in a week, something the lovers arrange by bringing in two seamen who traveled around the globe in opposite directions; each therefore perceives a different "Sunday."

How close the tie is to journalism is suggested by Poe's tinkering with the title. He published the piece first less than a month after the *Ledger* item, calling it "A Succession of Sundays," probably to avoid echoing the article. But when he ran it again, in *The Broadway Journal* for May 10, 1845, he called it "Three Sundays in a Week," figuring probably that enough time had elapsed or perhaps forgetting his source, recalling only a catchier title in the back of his mind.

The calendar anomaly should have a familiar ring for readers who remember what Sunday supplements were like a few decades ago, for journalists long remained fond of such matters. "Curiosities" filled the popular press in Poe's day, and Poe seems as fascinated by them as were contemporaries.

Notes in *Collected Works* and *Short Fiction* identify different ways in which the story ties, through allusions, to other aspects of popular culture: references to a popular lecturer Poe thought a windbag and to slang, some of it vulgar.

Mabbott (*M* 2, 658, n. 5) notes of being told that the bride comes with her "plum," that a plum means £100,000. But "her plum" meant also what vulgar slang now calls "her cherry." Poe's sexual humor often has a nasty sexist flavor.

Sensational biographers who read Poe as though his work came from a patient on the psychiatrist's couch and assume that the heated manner of Poe's more famous and intense stories shows how compulsive is the artistic process for him should pay more attention to stories such as this, in which the autobiographical implications are really quite strong but in which there is no evidence of compulsion—only whimsy and play. For the narrator's situation is sufficiently similar to Poe's own to deserve comment: both are orphans brought up by an "uncle" whose relation to his ward is strained. Both guardians are wealthy but tight-fisted, and each orphan marries an unusually young cousin (Levine and Levine 1976, 546, n. 6).

"Diddling"

(October 14, 1843, *Saturday Courier* as "Raising the Wind; or Diddling Considered as One of the Exact Sciences"; January 14, 1845, *Lloyd's Entertaining Journal* and September 13, 1845, *The Broadway Journal* as "Diddling")

Diddle means *defraud,* and one could argue that this is less a story than a magazine item about frauds that contains, in its latter portions, narrative (fictional) illustrations. Apparently, journalists still exploit accounts of fraud: notorious impostors hire ghost writers and sell their life stories.

"Diddling" ties strongly to theater. Its author was English, but there was a New York edition in 1804, followed by American productions. Its first title, "Raising the Wind . . . ," was slang for getting together some money. That version was published in Philadelphia; Philadelphia saw a very recent performance of James Kenney's farce "Raising the Wind" (1803); in it is a character named Jeremy Diddle. Poe did not borrow much else from the play beyond the personality of the character (Pollin 1969). Quinn (1941, 712) notes that Poe had a very close personal tie to the play. Poe's actor father appeared in it "at least three times." We guess that Poe shortened the title both for simplicity and because, although "Raising the Wind" was a popular play, fashions in slang change.

Unlike many Poe satires, "Diddling" "works" without extensive explication, probably because straightforward accounts of frauds are entertaining. Explication, however, adds resonance. In the first paragraph, for example, Poe says that Jeremy Bentham has "been much admired by Mr. John Neal." That is simply a fact; Neal's *The Yankee and Boston Literary Gazette* for July 1829 contained "a picture and eulogistic notice of Jeremy Bentham, with a motto from Bentham" (*H* 5, 210). There is still more to it: in an odd sense, Neal (1793–1876) was the "author" of "Diddling." "Diddling" was a Folio Club tale, to have been told by a "Mr. Snap." As Hammond and others have noticed, "Mr. Snap is a caricature of John Neal."

"The Spectacles"

(March 27, 1844, *The Dollar Newspaper;* November 22, 1845, *The Broadway Journal*)

A foolish young man, too vain to wear the glasses he needs, falls in love with a person he thinks is a lovely young woman: she is his great-great-grandmother. Very slight stuff, generally considered one of Poe's weaker pieces. What Poe thought he was about, however, is clear, for a number of his stories attempt to translate to fiction procedures, material, and attitudes more familiar in theatrical context.[6]

We suggested in *Short Fiction* that were "The Spectacles" "a light theatrical comedy instead of a short story," readers would more likely be comfortable with it and its foolish hero, recognizing "him as the sort of silly romantic youth to whom Gilbert and Sullivan generally assigned their tenors." Although, as Poe himself came to see, "The Spectacles" is too long (Mabbott noticed Poe's apology for its length when Poe reprinted it in *The Broadway Journal* in 1845 [*M* 3, 884]), it enjoyed some contemporary success, probably because it shared familiar material with those farces, operas, and operettas that "poke fun at romantic illusion about love, the 'electrical' love-at-first-sight, the idea of one-true-love-and-no-other, [and] the infatuated hero who will die if separated from his beloved" (Levine and Levine 1990, 323).

What happens in "The Spectacles," then, is only as absurd as popular farces. The genre survives in 1930s and 1940s Hollywood comedies and television today. Perhaps audiences laugh more readily at elaborate, improbable fantasy in performance than in print. Literary histories credit Poe with being a pioneer, indeed, an inventor, of short story form. It is worth remembering that the conventions of that form were not securely established in 1844. The inventor tried a number of experiments that puzzle us now because short fiction has usually followed other conventions—many of which he invented, too. Yet, this story and its relatives[7] were not simply abortions, for they, too, surprisingly, have descendants in short fiction. Jorge Luis Borges, for instance, strongly influenced by Poe, like Poe, experimented with absurd and grotesque stories.

SOCIAL SATIRES/MYSTERIES

"Thou Art the Man"

(November 1844, *Godey's Lady's Book*)

From 1930s Hollywood movies, we recognize the handsome but untrustworthy-looking chap we meet here; he tended in that era to wear a thin moustache. If the movie were a detective story, he had a way of looking guilty, whether or not, in the grand explanatory scene at the end, he turned out to have "dunnit." Mabbott probably exaggerates in saying this story "is outstandingly important in literary history, for it is ancestral to so much later entertaining fiction" (*M* 3, 1042). Later authors of offbeat detective stories do not acknowledge "Thou

Art the Man'' as their model, as do those who, like Arthur Conan Doyle and other successors, patterned their detective heroes on Poe's Dupin.

''Thou Art the Man'' concerns a young dandy, Pennifeather, who has reason to want his wealthy relative dead and who is framed by that relative's newfound and likable friend, good old Charley Goodfellow. So ''Thou Art the Man'' is a detective story, but it is at least equally a satire on small-town manners and gullibility. It is another good corrective for writers who guess at Poe's personality by analyzing only more feverish stories. This one has as much to teach, for the relationship between Barnabus Shuttleworthy and his nephew forcibly evokes that between John Allan and his ward Edgar Poe. A contrivance to make Mr. Shuttleworthy's corpse sit up to accuse the murderer is Gothic claptrap, but the plot says most basically that sunny people like Charley Goodfellow may turn out to be liars and murderers, while waxy ne'er-do-wells, misunderstood, maligned, may at heart be worthy and innocent. The fairy tale formula ''happily ever afterwards'' emphasizes the reversal of expectations. Poe sometimes preached that art had nothing to do with morality, and, as noted in the case of ''Never Bet the Devil Your Head,'' he mocked the idea of stories with ''morals.'' Yet, here is a plain moral: rakish young men may be nice guys; cronies of the establishment, scoundrels.

"The Oblong Box"

(September 1844, *Godey's Lady's Book;* December 13, 1845, *The Broadway Journal*)

Puzzled by the secretive and erratic behavior of an artist friend traveling on the same ship, the narrator investigates, building a theory to explain why his friend has taken three staterooms, protects his new wife from social contacts, keeps an oblong box in his cabin, and acts strangely. The amateur detective's conclusions are all wrong. The supposed bride is a servant; the box contains the body of the real wife, who had suddenly died. Unwilling to leave the oblong box, the artist dies when the foundering ship must be abandoned.

Vierra, Mabbott (*M* 3, 919–21), and *Short Fiction* (1990, 249–50) suggest sources in news items and Poe's reading. Cool in tone, the story is evidence ''that whether Poe's horror is 'from Germany' or 'of the soul,' he could turn it on and off at will'' (Levine and Levine 1976, 154). The narrator is normal, not obsessed, motivated by curiosity and strong tea, not madness, drugs, hypersensitivity, alcohol; the artist acts from grief and love. The tale is neither morbid nor ''gothic,'' just sad.

LITERARY SATIRES

"The Angel of the Odd"

(October 1844, *Columbian Magazine*)

Oddest of odd stories is ''The Angel of the Odd,'' but it is characteristic Poe even in its oddness: though it seems unnecessary to make an extravaganza credible, Poe provides his usual margin of credibility. Thus, before the narrator first encounters the angel of the odd, he confesses that he had been eating rich food, drinking strong red wine, and, worse, reading absurd happenings in his newspaper. So the reader understands that when the angel appears, when wildly improbable catastrophes beset the narrator, it is not merely that the angel has his revenge—the truffled food, potent spirits, stultifying reading, and absurd news items speak as well.

Claude Richard labels "The Angel . . ." literary satire. Poe slaps at writers and various literary attitudes (see Levine and Levine 1976, 500–501, nn. 2, 5, 9, and 10 especially). Poe's label, however, was "extravaganza." For us, the surrealistic coincidences in the dream sequence seem as much the "point" as is the literary humor. Poe blazed a path here for surrealists. His wild humor is akin to material that has been successful in media other than literature: comparably surreal compoundings of comic catastrophes occur in silent film comedies. To some extent, Poe was probably reacting to bizarre comedy in contemporary theater.

Moreover, "The Angel . . ." also takes a characteristic swipe at the national belief in meliorism (Gerber). So it is not just a literary satire.

Gerber also showed that there is comparable material in contemporary periodicals. We would add that that is true of almost everything that Poe wrote. Rarely is his matter original. If one feels that most of what was in the popular prints was junk, then one might say that Poe, like avant-garde Parisian artists in the 1920s, found a way to make art of junk. To be fair, not everything around Poe was "junk," and many of his ideas came from different kinds of sources. The comparison is nevertheless apt, and the label "surrealist" surprisingly appropriate for some of Poe's work.

"The Literary Life of Thingum Bob, Esq."

(December 1844, *Southern Literary Messenger*; July 26, 1845, *The Broadway Journal*)

This story is about an incompetent poet who becomes a force in New York literary circles by learning how the game is played, then playing it. The play is dirty.

Thingum Bob's name is a variant spelling for "Thingumabob," something one has forgotten the name of. A "Lady Jane Thingumabob" appears in Thomas Moore's *The Fudges in England* in an appropriate context (Pollin 1972a). We are told there of "a literary man who edits 'live authors as if they were posthumous.' " Poe's Thingum has neither ancestry nor education. Ignorant of Dante, Shakespeare, Homer, or Milton, he doesn't know a Creek from a Greek. (Poe's snobbery and racial condescension are unfortunately evident.)

George Graham, like Thingum Bob, bought up and combined magazines; like Bob, he was a *very* minor poet—even the indefatigable Thomas Ollive Mabbott, who devoted a lifetime of antiquarian scholarship to Poeiana, found only one Graham poem. But Graham was not Poe's main target in this comic, angry, affectionate piece. Poe was after the whole petty world of American magazines. Since we are not Americans of that era, however, if we read the story without some help, we may not find it interesting, let alone humorous. Given adequate notes, students report that this more than other Poe work induces a sense of time travel; it is a window on Broadway in the 1840s.

Fiercely competitive, insecure about their artistic worth, limited in popularity and influence, American literary magazines had to create an illusion of importance to survive. Their editors were, indeed, guilty of the faults that Poe exaggerates in Thingum Bob, such as the tendency to see "the Literary History of America" in terms of their own careers. Whipple (1957) identifies one target of Poe's sarcasm. Lewis Gaylord Clark began in 1844 publication of the *Literary Remains of the Late Willis Gaylord Clark,* his twin. Poe's "Thingum Bob" represents Willis, but, since Willis is dead, Poe's real target is Lewis and the system of reciprocal back scratching prevalent in magazine and book publishing. Note the similarity in titles. "Thingum" is still alive (Whipple errs here), but Poe includes "late" (i.e., deceased) in his subtitle to make clear that he has the Clarks' *Literary Remains* in mind. A reader of "Thingum Bob" in the *Broadway Journal* would have seen the connection—a piece about Willis was in the same issue!

Poe attacks "puffing," overpraising the work of friends, who then reciprocate in *their* magazines. So Thingum Bob's introduction to literature involves "puffery"—his father rewards the editor-poet who praises his hair oil. When Poe arrived in New York in 1844, he encountered varied puffery for Lewis Clark's edition of his brother's work.

There is another related target: Poe's dispute with Lewis Clark stems largely from Poe's famous hostile review of Theodore Fay's *Norman Leslie.* Fay fought back in a satire aimed at Poe: he called Poe "Bulldog," made him editor of "The Southern Literary Passenger," and said that Poe hated successful novelists because publishers rejected Poe's works. Poe responded with this tale. Pollin (1972a) convincingly explains its relationship to Fay's piece. Clearly, Poe had Fay in mind as well as the Clarks; clearly, the tale is another multiple-targeted foray against the New York cliques.

A web of allusions ties it to Poe's experience. There is a little dispute over precisely what connects to what, but scholars agree that Poe's reading—Thackeray, Cooper, Dickens, and Byron among contemporaries—affects the story, as does popular culture, from patent medicines to horse races. Poe's own writings (such as "The Cask of Amontillado" and his 1849 poem "The Bells") may be plainly heard.

SATIRES OF MODERN REFORM

"The System of Doctor Tarr and Prof. Fether"

(November 1845, *Graham's Magazine*)

"During the autumn of 18—, while on tour of the extreme Southern provinces of France," Poe begins, "my route led me within a few miles of a certain *Maison de Santé*, or private Mad-House, about which I had heard much, in Paris, from my medical friends." The narrator asks for a tour. He has heard that this asylum operates on the soothing system—patients, dressed in ordinary clothes, are closely observed but not confined. Unknown to the narrator, rebellious inmates have taken over; Poe's plot turns on that circumstance.

Specialists disagree on Poe's intentions. Whipple (1954) thinks there is satire here aimed at Dickens, while to Benton, the target is Nathaniel Parker Willis, for both had published pieces on the innovative asylum, and both had recently offended Poe. Our impression is that Poe as usual had several purposes, that his attitudes toward literary rivals mixed with his attitudes toward other matters.

Poe is essentially illiberal. The "Blackwood/Predicament" story, whatever its other targets, is antifeminist and racist.[8] He was consistently skeptical or hostile toward humanitarian reform. One cannot defend his attitudes by saying that they are part of a conservative philosophy. That Poe believes that humanity does not "progress" is not offensive. That he snickers at attempts to remedy the abuses of slavery or at inhumanity toward the insane is.

"The System . . ." is consistently contemptuous of reform. Poe associated reform movements with one another and with the largest American reform movement of his century, abolitionism. The repeated references in this story to the "South," where, "Parisians" say, residents are "peculiarly eccentric," to the obvious failure of reform, to the idea that tar and feathers was how to treat "inmates," and to the inmates' band playing "Yankee Doodle"—all suggest that, whatever its other targets, "The System . . ." is intended to allegorize America, the South, and slavery. On this subject, Poe is reactionary.

Poe had firsthand experience with the fear of slave uprisings (Levine 1984); that persistent Southern fear seems to be present here, too, for the "inmates" *have* taken over, treating their former masters cruelly. They are not the equals of the citizens of the "South" of "France" but can easily outwit bleeding-heart reformers. They can be "cunning"—cunning enough to hoax the stupid narrator. These are personality traits that antebellum Southern accounts of slave personality usually stress—cunning, childlike behavior, eccentric aping of elite white folks' ways. "Paris" thus seems to represent the North; the "South" of France, the South; the inmates, slaves.

The story is, alas, consistent with other Poe works on social statement.[9]

... AND CURIOSITIES

"The Thousand-and-Second Tale of Scheherazade"

(February 1845, *Godey's Lady's Book;* October 25, 1845, *The Broadway Journal*)

Poe's motto for this, "Truth is stranger than fiction," expresses his plan. Scheherazade, having, through her thousand tales of the bizarre, mythical, and wonderful, kept the king from his vow to take a new wife each day and kill her come morning, now on the thousand-and-second day drops fantasy for fact. She describes scientific and technological wonders.

Such is Poe's simple "frame," though he carves into it a few jokes and digs at familiar targets, including the Reverend Rufus Griswold. The king's vow becomes a running joke: the king has "fulfilled . . . [it] for many years to the letter, and with a religious punctuality and method that conferred great credit upon him as a man of devout feelings and excellent sense." Why did Scheherazade remain alive after the first night? "The king's curiosity . . . prevailing, I am sorry to say, even over his sound religious principles, induced him for this once to postpone the fulfillment of his vow."

But into this frame Poe places odd and wonderful "facts" (not always correct[10]), ranging from technological wonders such as the telegraph to principles of physics. Scheherazade's truthfulness is more than royalty can bear; it costs her life, but all is in fun, and the frame is just an excuse to display modern wonders. Plainly, Poe was as interested in the curiosities and as proud of the accomplishments as was any booster of progress.

So we confront another contradiction: in "Mellonta Tauta" Poe shows that progress seen from the perspective of a thousand years in the future is not impressive, warning against temporal chauvinism. But here in "Scheherazade," quite the opposite. Poe's inconsistency is like that of Mark Twain, who, Sherwood Cummings noted, mocked the "sirens of progress" one day and was enchanted by their strains the next.

Poe provided no fewer than thirty-four footnotes, mainly to explain the modern "facts" to which Scheherazade fancifully alludes. His major source for these notes involves another contradiction. In "Three Sundays in a Week" we hear of "Dr. Dubble L. Dee," that is, LL.D., whom Mabbott identifies as the popular science lecturer Dionysius Lardner. Poe, unimpressed, lambasted Lardner in print, but in "Scheherazade," Poe was in his debt, for Poe's footnote information comes largely from Lardner (Mabbott 1943).

"Some Words with a Mummy"

(April 1845, *American (Whig) Review*; November 1, 1845, *The Broadway Journal*)

This is a superior example of Poe's journalistic work. The foolish plot pro-

vides a fictional framework in which Poe presents interesting and unusual information—"curiosities." Some friends bring a surplus museum mummy to life
and have "some words" with him. Scientific wonders and modern technology
impress the mummy not at all; things were better in ancient Egypt. "Some
Words" suggests how very strong were Poe's ties to his time and place; it shows
both fascination and a certain detachment. Like Twain, he was at once caught
up in the excitement of new technology and new science and, in another mood,
skeptical that "progress" meant anything.

Poe's frame story itself was topical. Exciting Egyptological archaeology and
scholarship followed Napoleon's Egyptian campaigns. When Poe and his friends
on the *New York Sun* put out their spurious extra that contained Poe's "Balloon
Hoax," they had it share the front page of the *Extra Sun* with an article on
Egyptology, still good copy in 1844 (that page is reproduced in Levine and
Levine 1976, 551). "Some Words" plays on a popular topic. A comic actor, a
famous diplomat-cum-Egyptologist, phrenologists, and a clothing store proprietor all stroll through "Some Words," which also contains local New York City
jokes, as well as humor based on popular subjects, patent medicines, and even
advertisements.

No profound research went into Poe's tale; as usual, he lifted information
from any handy source—much of the technical material came from the *Encyclopedia Americana.*

Poe's narrator encounters the ancient Egyptian in a dream brought on by too
much rich food. Readers of more "serious" stories know the device: some agent
or condition produces an unusual state of mind, giving the reader the option of
concluding that the experience described is hallucinatory. Thus, some Poe characters tell us that they are mad (or madly insist that they are perfectly sane);
others are terrified into supernormal states. Some take drugs; others overindulge
more prosaically, as in the green tea binge in "The Oblong Box" or the gluttony
here. Seeing the device in this light story makes a good corrective to the writings
of psychoanalytical critics who see Poe's art as compulsive. For every vision
induced by madness or fever there exists one from too much cheese and stout.

"The Sphinx"

(January 1846, *Arthur's Ladies Magazine*; 1851 *The American Keepsake*)
"The Sphinx" is not very important, largely because its underlying idea, that
someone could mistake an insect crawling before the eye (indeed, a sixteenth
of an inch away) for a distant monster approaching is neither plausible nor very
interesting. Eyes don't focus that way. What *is* interesting is the odd mixture of
slight with serious material. Cholera is not a joke; American urban dwellers—
Poe's career was urban—were all too familiar with its horrors.

Poe's narrator, as usual in such stories, has made himself hypersensitive by
reading books likely to "force into germination whatever seeds of hereditary
superstition lay latent in [his] bosom." When the narrator tells his host what he

thinks he has seen, the host quickly figures out what has happened and enters into a philosophical discussion on the importance of getting proper perspective. His example has to do with "the influence to be exercised on mankind at large by the thorough diffusion of Democracy," a subject on which Poe had strong—if contradictory—feelings.

A couple of paragraphs later, the host reads the narrator "a school-boy account" of the bug that the narrator has seen. There follows an entire paragraph of quotation; only Poe specialists see the private joke, because Poe quotes Thomas Wyatt's *A Synopsis of Natural History* (Philadelphia, 1839), a book that Poe probably ghostwrote, having been hired by Professor Wyatt (Heartman and Canny)!

Trace a horrific or morbid topic throughout the Poe canon, and one finds that for each apparently obsessive, heated story, there is one that is cool and detached. So "The Sphinx" shares fear of epidemics with "The Masque of the Red Death." Similarly, Madeline Usher is buried alive in the serious "The Fall of the House of Usher." But in "The Premature Burial," burial alive is dealt with humorously by a narrator who learns that obsessive fears are foolish and resolves not to read any more scary stories—and then, turning to the reader, adds, "such as this one." Just so here in the cases of "The Masque" and "The Sphinx." Indeed, perhaps the comparison of two is more revealing, for while fear of burial alive has about it the flavor of sensational journalism, fear of urban epidemics was widespread and rational. Not many people are accidentally entombed alive, while thousands of Americans died of cholera. Poe, we should insist, is *not* his fear-crazed narrators, certainly not the foolish narrator of "The Sphinx," who, frightened by creepy books about omens and epidemics, thinks he sees a monster. But he saw only a bug. There is no ambiguity; the wild vision is *not* real. It was a bug, nothing but a bug.

Some modest conclusions seem possible. First, these Poe stories grow directly out of the texture of America in Poe's day, its intellectual life, politics, popular culture, technology, journalism, and entertainment.[11] Second, most of them have more than one purpose. A "political satire" is also a literary joke, a detective story is also a satire on small-town life, and so forth. Third, several stories make one skeptical of interpretations of Poe that stress compulsive, "haunted" behavior, for his choice of topics was more commercial than obsessive, his treatment of horror more whimsical than crazed. Fourth, Poe at work is Poe at play. The playfulness of these tales is evident to readers who have access to adequate annotation of the topical, political, and personal allusions.[12] This has very important implications for all of Poe's work, for having seen whimsy here, one begins to notice it elsewhere, even in pieces that have been regarded as "serious"—in his literary criticism, for example, or in his more famous short stories. Poe is not the author he is popularly supposed to be; he is much more interesting and complicated, and he is always witty.

NOTES

1. These tales allude to the Society for the Diffusion of Useful Knowledge (SDUK), to Lord Brougham, and to Willis Clark. Although casual readers would never catch the last, it is plainly there—Willis Clark's pen name in the *Knickerbocker* magazine was "Ollapod" (Whipple 1957). There is also an allusion shared with "Never Bet the Devil Your Head" in the person of William Ellery Channing II (Levine and Levine 1976, 501, n. 6). Poe's "serious" tales also echo in his humorous work; the echoes are not limited to allusions. Ljungquist, for instance, notices that Poe connects great height with sublimity (50); that association is present both in "A Predicament" and in Poe's writings that deal with landscape.

2. Smith admires "man-traps and spring-guns," instruments of inadvertent self-destruction. Wherever the narrator seeks information about Smith, violence confronts him. In church, man "cometh up and is cut down like a flower." At the theater is Othello, who, having killed his wife, kills himself. At cards, people talk of Captain Mann, "either shot or hung" for a jewel. Even while dancing, he hears of Byron's Manfred, who, consumed with guilt, yearns not only for death but for eternal oblivion. When the narrator's friend Sinivate (Cockney for "insinuate") brings up Captain Mann again, the narrator responds, "Captain Mann be damned!"

3. Whipple's argument is summarized and explicated in Levine and Levine 1976, 355. See also, 430ff.

4. Another connection to *Sartor Resartus* is noted in *M* 2, 363.

5. Pollin (1972a) notes humorous dialect in Thomas Moore's *The Fudges in England* (1835), apparently known to Poe. Galloway's annotations, often informative, are especially useful for this tale (249).

6. Poe thought in theater terms. Thus, as already noted, "The Masque of the Red Death" uses traditional stagecraft; in the essay "explaining" how he wrote "The Raven," Poe uses the analogy of shifting sets and creating effects to the craftsmanlike side of poetic composition. "King Pest" is built upon a mode of nineteenth-century theater, and the present story, "The Spectacles," is both theatrical in conception and largely set in a theater. N. Bryllion Fagin's *The Histrionic Mr. Poe* stresses Poe's conscious dramatization of his own life. Rourke, always valuable, makes cogent suggestions (181) on this topic.

7. Mabbott identifies several contemporary stories that use similar ideas (*M* 3, 883–84).

8. Bernard Rosenthal discusses Poe's pro-slavery views.

9. Characteristically, it also shares texture, turns of language, and allusions in other tales—for example, a reference to a Bellini opera in "The Spectacles" (Levine and Levine 1976, 619, n. 2; *M* 3, 1022, n. 2); a reference to Lord Brougham with "The Literary Life of Thingum Bob." Very significantly, the latter reference appears also in the equally illiberal "Blackwood/A Predicament" pair (Levine and Levine 1976, 920, n. 18; *M* 3, 1023, n. 17).

10. Levine and Levine (1976, 541, n. 39) explain how Poe muffs a demonstration of the principle of interference in rays of light.

11. See Reynolds's discussion of "*assimilation* and *transformation*" (7) and Poe as product of his age (47, 226, 231, 243, 524–33, 531); cf. Levine (1978).

12. Mooney (1961) points out that Poe flags his comic intention by certain indicators

in the plot, but the indicators do not always apply to flights of whimsy in apparently serious pieces. There is some nonsense, some pure play, in about every Poe work. Much involves echoing—repeating phrases or passages in unexpected contexts, wordplay, slipping in allusions that perhaps he never thought a reader would "catch." Dayan, interestingly, finds such behavior compulsive, on one hand, and related to Poe's conception of the cosmos, on the other. A very different approach to the mixture of elements in Poe is G. R. Thompson's; he argues that Poe employs "Romantic Irony" in the German philosophical sense.

WORKS CITED

Benton, Richard P. "Poe's 'The System of Dr. Tarr and Prof. Fether': Dickens or Willis?" *Poe Newsletter* 1 (Apr. 1968): 7–9.

Cherry, Fannye. "The Source of Poe's 'Three Sundays in a Week.' " *AL* 2 (Nov. 1930): 232–35.

Cummings, Sherwood. "Mark Twain and the Sirens of Progress." *Journal of the Central Mississippi Valley American Studies Association* 1, no. 2 (Fall 1960): 17–24.

Dayan, Joan. *Fables of Mind: An Inquiry into Poe's Fiction.* New York and Oxford: Oxford UP, 1987.

Eddings, Dennis W., ed. *The Naiad Voice: Essays on Poe's Satiric Hoaxing.* Port Washington, N.Y.: Associated Faculty Press, 1983.

Fagin, N. Bryllion. *The Histrionic Mr. Poe.* Baltimore: Johns Hopkins UP, 1949.

Galloway, David, ed. *The Other Poe: Comedies and Satires.* Harmondsworth, Middlesex, England: Penguin Books, 1983.

Gerber, Gerald. "Poe's Odd Angel." *Nineteenth Century Fiction* 25 (June 1968): 88–93. Cited in *M* 3, 1098.

Hammond, Alexander. "A Reconstruction of Poe's 1833 Tales of the Folio Club." *PoeS* 5 (Dec. 1972): 25–32.

Heartman, Charles, and James Canny. *A Bibliography of First Printings of the Writings of Edgar Allan Poe.* Hattiesburg, Miss.: Book Farm, 1940.

Levine, Stuart. *Edgar Poe: Seer and Craftsman.* Deland, Fl.: Everett/Edwards, 1972.

————. "Poe and American Society." *Canadian Review of American Studies* 9, no. 1 (Spring 1978): 16–33.

————. "Masonry, Impunity and Revolution." *PoeS* 17, no. 1 (1984): 22–23.

Levine, Stuart, and Susan F. Levine. " 'How to' Satire: Cervantes, Marryat, Poe." *Modern Language Studies* 16, no. 3 (Summer 1986): 15–26.

————, eds. *The Short Fiction of Edgar Allan Poe: An Annotated Edition.* Indianapolis: Bobbs-Merrill, 1976; Champaign-Urbana: U of Illinois P, 1990.

Ljungquist, Kent. *The Grand and the Fair: Poe's Landscape Aesthetics and Pictorial Techniques.* Potomac, Md.: Scripta Humanistica, 1984.

Mabbott, Thomas Ollive. "Poe and Dr. Lardner." *American Notes & Queries* 3 (Nov. 1943): 115–17.

————, ed. *The Collected Works of Edgar Allan Poe.* Vols. 2 and 3. Cambridge: Harvard UP, 1978.

McNeal, Thomas H. "Poe's *Zenobia:* An Early Satire on Margaret Fuller." *Modern Language Quarterly* 11 (June 1950): 205–16.

Mooney, Stephen. "The Comic Intent in Poe's Tales: Five Criteria." *Modern Language Notes* 76 (May 1961): 432–43.

————. "The Comic in Poe's Fiction." *AL* 33 (Jan. 1962): 433–41.

Pollin, Burton. "Poe's 'Diddling': The Source of Title and Tale." *Southern Literary Journal* 2 (1969): 106–11.

————. "Poe and Thomas Moore." *ESQ,* no. 63 (June 1972a): 166–73.

————. "Poe's 'Mystification': Its Source in Fay's *Norman Leslie.*" *Mississippi Quarterly* 25 (Spring 1972b): 111–30.

————. "Poe's 'Diddling': More on the Dating and the Aim." *PoeS* 9, no. 1 (June 1976): 11–13.

Quinn, Arthur Hobson. *Edgar Allan Poe: A Critical Biography.* New York: D. Appleton-Century, 1941.

Rans, Geoffrey. *Edgar Allan Poe.* Edinburgh and London: Oliver and Boyd, 1965.

Reynolds, David. *Beneath the American Renaissance: The Subversive Imagination in the Age of Emerson and Melville.* New York: Alfred A. Knopf, 1988.

Richard, Claude. "Arrant Bubbles: 'The Angel of the Odd.' " *Poe Newsletter* 2 (Oct. 1969): 46–48.

Ridgely, J. V. "The Authorship of the 'Paulding-Drayton' Review." *PSA Newsletter* 20, no. 2 (Fall 1992): 1–3, 6.

Rosenthal, Bernard. "Poe, Slavery, and the *Southern Literary Messenger:* A Reexamination." *PoeS* 7, no. 2 (Dec. 1974): 29–38.

Rourke, Constance. *American Humor/A Study of the National Character.* New York: Harcourt Brace, 1931. Rpt. in Tallahassee, Fl., 1986.

Thompson, G. R. *Poe's Fiction: Romantic Irony in the Gothic Tales.* Madison: U of Wisconsin P, 1973.

Varner, Cornelia. "Notes on Poe's Use of Contemporary Materials in Certain of His Stories." *Journal of English and Germanic Philology* 32 (Jan. 1933): 77–80.

Vierra, Clifford C. "Poe's 'Oblong Box': Factual Origins." *Modern Language Notes* 74 (Dec. 1959): 693–95.

Whipple, William. "Poe's Two-Edged Satiric Tale." *Nineteenth Century Fiction* 9 (Sept. 1954): 121–33.

————. "Poe's Political Satire." *Texas University Studies in English* 35 (1956): 81–95.

————. "Poe, Clark, and 'Thingum Bob.' " *AL* 29 (Nov. 1957): 312–16.

7

Tales of the Human Condition

WILLIAM GOLDHURST

Although no single concept or line of development may be traced in these tales, they do treat such related themes as death and dying, the nature of the afterlife, and the place of man in the universe. Unquestionably, with the exception of "The Premature Burial" and "The Lighthouse," these tales of the human condition manifest a progression from simple to complex and from a spirit of inquiry into metaphysical questions to assured definition. All show Poe in the process of intellectual and artistic maturing. Poe's tales in this category were initially published in this order: "MS. Found in a Bottle" (1833), "Shadow" (1835), "Silence" (as "Siope—A Fable" 1838), "The Conversation of Eiros and Charmion" (1839), "The Colloquy of Monos and Una," "The Island of the Fay," and "A Descent into the Maelstrom" (all 1841), "Mesmeric Revelation" and "The Premature Burial" (both 1844), "The Power of Words" (1845), and "The Lighthouse" (c. 1849 in manuscript; first published in 1909).

TWO FABLES: "SHADOW" AND "SILENCE"

"Shadow" (1835) and "Silence" (1838) are often considered companion pieces because of their similarity in prose style, their brevity, and their "fable" character or intent. Of the two, "Shadow" is more concrete, with its real (though somewhat allegorical) characters and its implied theme of death delivering a sober message to the living, whereas "Silence" is more symbolic and allegorical, with its African setting and prototypical human figure. Both tales, as we shall see, contain religious imagery. Despite the evidence of Poe's serious intentions, a critical controversy has developed with reference to the tone of these tales.

G. R. Thompson thinks "Silence" and "Shadow" are parodies of Bulwer-Lytton, DeQuincey, and "the psychological autobiographists" referred to in the headnote to "Silence." With drunkards in "Shadow" and "shrieking water lilies" in "Silence," he writes, these tales reflect the author's intention to fill the Folio Club series (1833–1836) with "tales of a bizarre and whimsical character" (*TPoe*, 169). David Ketterer finds Poe's prose style in "Shadow" to be overwritten or disingenuous but the tone and content of the fable to be serious rather than satirical or parodic. Ketterer believes the story "pushes against the frontiers of mortality in an attempt to glimpse what is beyond" (146). For "Silence," Ketterer works out an intricate allegorical interpretation: the Roman figure, confronted by the Demon, suggests Satan's temptation of Christ in the Wilderness. As Christ resisted the rewards proffered by the fallen angel, so the Roman withstands storm and bizarre animals; but, threatened with nothingness ("silence"), he flees (147–48).

Benjamin Franklin Fisher denies that "Silence" is a satire or parody. A close study of the revisions Poe made in sequential drafts of "Silence" shows the author's altering the tone in the direction of serious symbolic fiction, beyond the conventional Gothic or typical parodic. Fisher concludes that "Silence" is a serious psychological study rather than a humorous or hoaxy exercise (64–69).

Perhaps the most insistent voice in reading "Silence" as comic satire is Alexander Hammond, who believes the tale is a self-parody, the original title of which—"Siope"—is an anagram for IS POE. The question of Poe's intended tone here is suggested by the author's prologue to a group of early stories called "Tales of the Folio Club." Comic members of this group were to assemble for the purpose of telling stories, followed by criticism and "ratings" at the conclusion. These remarks, Hammond believes, indicate the satiric purpose of the tales involved (*PoeS*, 5, 26). However, as Eric Carlson has emphasized, (1988, 307), Poe referred to "most" of these early stories as "intended for half-banter, half-satire," singling out only "Lionizing" and "Loss of Breath" as "satires properly speaking." The satire/parody school of critics tends to ignore the fact that Poe included a reference to more serious intentions—to illustrate a range of "imaginative faculties"—in the Folio Club collection (307). Carlson considers "Silence" and "Shadow" tales that exemplify this impressionistic use of "imaginative faculties." Burton Pollin thinks that Poe's original concept for "Shadow" might have been satiric, but his innate creativity invested the narrative with "poetic charm and emotional intensity" that lift it out of the category of parody (1972a, 170).

In an illuminating essay on "Shadow," Joseph Defalco treats the tale as an allegory about body and spirit. The death of Zoilus (body) causes Oinos (Everyman) to seek comfort in self-reflection (the polished table top). The climax occurs when Shadow appears, but the effect is more than emotional shock; the full impact of the denouement is related to an observation in *Eureka* where Poe says individual identity is lost at death. Shadow's message, says Defalco, has a more appalling effect than the introduction of a simple *memento mori* (643–48). Defalco's reading of this early story should be supplemented by Poe's statements about identity in the later work, *Eureka*. The loss of individual identity is part of the process of assimilation into supernal One-ness, or, in other words, part of the transition from ordinary existence into Godhead (*PQ,* 1358).

Some aspects of ''Shadow'' resemble Baroque or modern painting techniques. Notice the seven sitters' recognition of their own fears by the mirror image of each companion in the tabletop illuminated by candlelight (chiaroscuro) and the very deft positioning of Shadow as he emerges from the sable draperies exactly at the place where the notes of music seemed to have disappeared—in a surrealistic sound-sight transformation. Characterization in this tale, though necessarily rudimentary, is also of more than passing interest. The image of Oinos attempting to dispel the gloom by means of wine and song, then gradually desisting as he yields to the compelling stare of the ''corpse at the feast'' is surely an effective blend of the two emotions involved—terror and self-transformation. At the same time, Poe's conclusion adds an element to previously established Gothic conventions. As Kenneth Silverman observes:

Gothic fiction aimed at creating the presence of something that suspends and calls into doubt the laws of the universe. As in Morella's rebirth through her daughter or the appearance of the many-voiced shade in ''Shadow,'' it implied that the terrors of the world we know are driven by something unknown and unknowable beyond them (112).

''Silence'' is a more problematic story. As we have seen, interesting interpretations have been advanced by various scholars, yet certain details seem to have been overlooked that, when assembled, tend to indicate an overall meaning that has not been sufficiently emphasized. Eric Carlson has observed: ''[T]he Roman figure of Man is unafraid of his own loneliness and of the desolation and stormy hostility of nature. When confronted by a silent universe empty of life, however, the spirit of Man shudders and flees in terror'' (1972, 10). The many religious references in the tale—the Magi and the Sibyls, the use of the place-name DoDona (an ancient site where priests gathered), and the messages engraved on rocks (as was the practice in several ancient religions)—suggest a religious theme in which the spirit of Man confronts divine silence. Possibly Poe is implying that dignified man (the Roman) would like to believe but requires a ''sign.'' God's answer, of course, is silence (as in Revelation, when the seventh seal is broken, and there is a silence in heaven). Without any visible or physical evidence, Man is therefore free to choose whether to believe or not to believe, free to make this important decision on his own. This freedom, as later (existentialist) philosophers would confirm, terrifies or, at the very least, discomfits the individual. Poe's parable is a forerunner of the twentieth-century dilemma of faith, an issue explored in T. S. Eliot's *The Waste Land* and Ingmar Bergman's *The Seventh Seal.* There is no internal evidence whatever that ''Silence'' is a spoof or a hoax or a satire on foreign authors. It is quite simply too significant and compelling in its seriousness to be considered comic.

THE COLLOQUIES: PSYCHAL VISIONS

I next discuss "Mesmeric Revelation" (1844) and "The Power of Words" (1845). In "The Angelic Imagination," Allen Tate places much emphasis on the metaphysical dialogues (Ransom's term). Tate constructs a kind of development chart that illustrates Poe's thought from "Eiros and Charmion" to *Eureka*. In "Eiros and Charmion," Tate sees Poe predicting the end of the world as "a moral and logical consequence of the condition to which man has previously brought himself" (242). "Monos and Una," he writes, adumbrates a philosophy of "impressive extent and depth" (244). "The Power of Words" reflects the "full angelic vision" in Poe's perspective. In "Frames of Reference for Poe's Symbolic Language," Eric Carlson quotes Tate as a starting point for understanding Poe's philosophy by way of the ideas implicit in the dialogues. Both critics tend to see Poe's thought graduating from literal and concrete to metaphysical and transcendent. In a different essay, Carlson places "Eiros and Charmion" in a category he calls existential—in which Poe's emphasis is on the disintegration of the self, with a prospect of reintegration. "Mesmeric Revelation" belongs in a different category Carlson terms psychal-transcendental, in which Poe voices his faith in the realization of transcendent modes of reality. Stories in this category, which includes "Monos and Una," show human aspiration toward divinity. According to Carlson, Poe's central theme is "the rediscovery of the lost psychal power essential to every man" (1972, 11–20). Poe's transcendental perspective is analyzed in detail by Ottavio M. Casale in "Poe's Transcendentalism."

Alice Chandler, in a study of Poe's dreamers, thinks "Mesmeric Revelation" achieves a "mending" of the Cartesian breach between matter and spirit. By making these elements "continuous," says Chandler, Poe invents a new kind of dreamer—a person who moves from waking reality to the dream state without radical denials of self. David Halliburton's lengthy discussion of these tales is largely summary, but he concludes that, in "Eiros and Charmion" and "Monos and Una," death is both ontological and heuristic—in the sense that superior knowledge is possessed by one of the characters, while a "coming to know process" is always implied on the part of the listener. Halliburton also observes that destruction in the dialogues is never disastrous; the victims, in some manner or form, always survive (378–80).

In a study of "The Fall of the House of Usher," Wendy Flory reminds us that Poe considered pure contemplation and intuition the highest mental activity, as stated in "Monos and Una." In Poe's epistemology, the soul is impeded by flawed understanding but is "purged" of the impediment at death. Thus, after the death of the body, the human intellect has access to "poetic contemplation and majestic intuition." With imperfections removed and the best avenue to understanding accessible, the prospect for acquiring knowledge is limitless (17).

Comparatist criticism has noted contemporary corollaries for these apocalyptic tales. Curtis Dahl's "The American School of Disaster" enumerates the nineteenth-century literary and artistic works exploiting the popular taste for the disaster genre. Most relevant to present purposes is James G. Percival's poem "The Vision" (1821), in which a fiery star approaches and envelops Earth in a mantle of flame and then moves on, leaving behind darkness and destruction (Dahl, 386). T. O. Mabbott's discussion of "Eiros and Charmion" includes the appearance of comets and meteors in Poe's day as possible inspirers of the tale, along with a literary source, S. Austin, Jr.'s story "The Comet" (1839). A detailed, full-length study of the apocalyptic theme in our literature is Douglas Robinson's *American Apocalypses,* in which the critic remarks that Poe (along with Emerson) is the author of "definitive forms of the American apocalypse." Says Robinson: Poe defined the "range of issues" that must be dealt with "if American experience is to make sense" (xiv–xv). In this respect, Poe is central to the genre, and his apocalyptic fiction has more longevity than the comparable works of his contemporaries because he invested the sensational content with serious themes.

"The Conversation of Eiros and Charmion" (1839) describes the thoughts and feelings of the multitude as the catastrophe impends. This format not only affords Poe an opportunity to depict terror and panic but also provides him with an occasion for an ironic treatment of the role of reason. The wise men in the story predict no harm or danger, and the theologians agree. But on the second day into "the planet's influence," the people feel pain, then terror, then loss of hope: "Eiros and Charmion" is thus a study in mass hysteria. The descriptions of luxuriant foliage, the lurid light, and awesome sound—so reminiscent of Hiroshima—lend an eerie dimension of prescience to Poe's narrative, while also implying a skeptical attitude toward savants, scientists, and theologians in a time of crisis. Years later, an English reviewer, conscious of the tale's thought as well as action, remarked that "The Conversation of Eiros and Charmion" is "full of terror and instruction, true to philosophy and holy writ" (*PoeL,* 621). A point remains to be made concerning the names used in this story. As the Levines discovered, Eiros and Charmion were derived from Jacob Bryant's *Mythology,* where the two names are glossed as attendants upon Cleopatra, signifying the rainbow and the dove, God's signs of wonder and continuation after the flood (146). In other words, these names connote survival after destruction.

"The Colloquy of Monos and Una" (1844) also reveals Poe's visionary orientation as Monos is born again into a life of "heightened intuitive consciousness," again implying a philosophic perspective emphasizing man's transcendental and (in Carlson's words) "psychal potential" (1987, 211). Second, in "Monos and Una," Poe uses the occasion to criticize American culture and society. Monos tells Una, among other things: "[T]he fair face of Nature was deformed. . . . Green leaves shrank before the hot breath of furnaces . . . we worked out our own destruction in the perversion of our taste, or rather in the blind neglect of its culture in our schools . . . and the odd idea of Universal Equality gained ground" (*M* 2, 610). Plato's idea of education was not only ignored but repressed. In brief, democratic government, industrialization, pollution of the environment, and technical education were all contributing to the downfall of civilization, as Monos perceived it. In order to survive, Monos says, man must be "born again." Presumably, Poe has in mind an earlier agricultural, rather than industrial, way of life with government in the hands of an educated aristocracy.

"Mesmeric Revelation" (1844) is an essaylike tale that is thematically linked to "The Power of Words," "The Facts in the Case of M. Valdemar," "The Colloquy of Monos and Una," and *Eureka*. All contain elements of Poe's pseudoscientific propositions about the afterlife, the cosmos, and the nature of deity. "Mesmeric" and "Valdemar" pursue the same road to these metaphysical secrets, namely, through hypnosis, or, more properly speaking, by way of mesmerism. As Doris Falk observes in her article "Poe and the Power of Animal Magnetism"—essential for an understanding of these associated tales—critics have long suffered from erroneous assumptions about Poe's use of the term *mesmerism*. While most scholars—not to mention the general public—think mesmerism means hypnosis, Falk's research reveals a much more complex and occult definition, which, in Poe's hands, emerges as far more than "putting someone under." The mesmerist believed that "animal magnetism" was a pervasive force that accounted for the power of magnets as well as the fixed position of the stars. The mesmerist attempted to "tap the flow of magnetic fluid"—something akin to electricity—that was present in the human body and activated the muscles. The fluid entered through the will. Poe's "Mesmeric," "Valdemar," and "Tale of the Ragged Mountains" reflect these beliefs, which, at their peak, were circulated and debated in the 1840s, as recorded by Slater Brown in *The Heyday of Spiritualism*. Falk says Poe's "Mesmeric" belongs to a genre she calls "dream vision or prophecy." Most contemporary examples of this genre were frivolous, but Poe adapted the conventions to his own purposes, which meant showing how "deep mesmerism" could enable the "sleep waker" to scrutinize and report upon eternal questions concerning the nature of the deity and man's relation to God (Falk, 536–38, 543–45).

In Poe's tale, the progress of the thought is almost as important as its content. What is God? asks the questioner. I cannot tell, replies Mr. Vankirk. But he can tell, and he does tell, little by little. Poe's advice to the writer of short stories—that the drama must be introduced gradually—applies here with some force. The reader realizes almost immediately that Vankirk is in a highly unusual—perhaps a unique—mental state that enables him to convey messages of momentous philosophic import. By a process of question and answer and occasional doubt ("I could not have said this; it is an absurdity"), Poe builds the theory step by step: (1) God is unparticled matter; (2) unparticled matter is Mind; (3) what we call spirit is actually infinitely rarified matter; (4) unparticled matter in motion is Thought; (5) such Thought creates; (6) in order to create individual beings, God "incarnated" portions of the divine mind; (7) the human body is imperishable; (8) in death, the rudimentary body undergoes metamorphosis into the perfected state or "ultimate body"; (9) the "ultimate condition . . . is of unlimited comprehension in all points but one—the nature of the volition of God'' (*M* 3, 1037); and (10) the mesmeric state is similar to the perfected state, when the rudimental life is ''in abeyance.''

Poe compressed these ideas, using similar language, in letters to James Russell Lowell (July 2, 1844) and to Thomas Holley Chivers a few days later, and the theory is implied in the closing passages of *Eureka* (1848). In light of these reiterated statements, it would seem self-evident that ''Mesmeric'' contains Poe's serious reflections on the issues aforementioned.

G. R. Thompson thinks otherwise. He believes the story is ''a parody of occult metaphysics'' (1973, 153). Thompson singles out some of Vankirk's assertions, which, out of context, appear silly. In addition, this critic finds examples of self-contradiction, paradox, circular reasoning, and irony—all pointing toward the conclusion that Poe knew he was writing humor and not serious philosophy. But what of the letters to Lowell and Chivers, which state unreservedly that the theories in ''Mesmeric'' are Poe's own? Thompson replies by pointing out that, in other contexts, Poe made slurring remarks about both contemporaries—suggesting that he might have been ''hoaxing'' them in his correspondence. Finally, in ''Marginalia,'' Poe wrote that Swedenborgians had taken every detail in ''Mesmerism'' to be factual, while actually ''the story is pure fiction from beginning to end'' (157). In this remark in ''Marginalia,'' most likely Poe was referring to the action of the tale, which is to say that Vankirk and the hypnotist existed only as ''pure fiction''—but fiction that obviously reflects Poe's deeply held convictions.

The Poe Log reproduces interesting reactions to ''Mesmeric Revelation'' on the part of editors and critics. The story prompted a number of disclaimers: ''[I]t proves not to be the 'magnetic revelation' it claims for itself, but simply the production of its author's own brain'' (*PoeL*, 573). A London weekly, by way of contrast, reprinted the tale with an introduction declaring that ''it bears internal evidence of authenticity'' (*PoeL* 596).

''The Power of Words'' (1845) constitutes a clarification, as it were, of the human spirit's activities in the ''perfected'' state mentioned in the previous postmortem dialogues. In ''Power,'' Poe emphasizes and describes the soul's quest for knowledge once the rudimentary state (life on earth) has been transcended. Happiness, says Agathos, consists of acquiring knowledge, but it is not given even to the perfected condition to know everything. Heaven is a place that affords ''infinite springs at which the soul may allay the thirst to know, which is forever unquenchable within it'' (*M* 3, 1212). Agathos next informs Oinos that God creates all things initially but that all creation afterward is non-divine or ''secondary.'' This thesis leads, in turn, to assumptions about the ''creative force'' of each movement or action: these forces may be seen as ''impulses upon the air'' or ''impulses upon the ether,'' the latter being ''the great medium of creation'' (*M* 3, 1215). These formulations prepare the reader for the story's dramatic climax. Since words are a form of motion, and all motion has power, ''the power of words'' is by no means an unreasonable concept.

Agathos then reveals that he "spoke" the earth into existence, at a time when he was in a troubled state of mind over frustration in love. Earth's flowers are therefore "unfulfilled dreams" and earthquakes are "heart's passions" (*M* 3, 1215). Mabbott identifies a parallel passage in *Eureka,* where Poe speaks of the infinite vibrations set up by even the smallest human action (*M* 3, 1210).

To Burton Pollin, Poe's use of the phrase *the power of words* reflects the author's devotion to language, especially in its creative aspects (1980, 6). Allen Tate says Poe borrowed from Pascal the concept that "the slightest movement affects the whole of nature"; only Pascal added a point about "the moral check on human power," which Poe chose to ignore (250). Tate further claims that "Power" endows man with the power of God. David Halliburton criticizes Tate's interpretation by claiming that Agathos "expresses a creative power he neither originates nor controls." Furthermore, says Halliburton, Tate's conclusion about the divinity of the human condition is premature, since Poe elevated man to that eminence only in the later work, *Eureka* (391).

"The Premature Burial" demonstrates (1) Poe's fascination with the "buried alive" theme; (2) his unique ability to blend horror with humor; (3) a foreshadowing of his mature cosmology; and (4) deliberate craftsmanship in short story construction. About the first point, Mabbott lists seven other stories containing hints of Poe's preoccupation with the theme of living interment and adds that Poe probably dreamed about or imagined a similar fate for himself (*M* 3, 953). Stuart Levine disagrees, claiming that the repetition of the theme reflects not personal trauma but professional self-interest; as both Levine and Mabbott document, premature burial was a popular subject (Levine, 246). Second, G. R. Thompson thinks Poe is hoaxing his readers in this story—by making victims of them through their gullibility—and then concluding with a "ludicrous event" (1970, 47). Arnold Goldman adopts a more complex view of the tale. In an article entitled "Poe's Stories of Premature Burial," Goldman states that the tale in question—by way of the early sequence of grim examples culminating in the comic episode at the end—embodies all Poe's "buried alive" stories and scenes. According to this critic, "Premature" demonstrates that the deadly serious as well as the comic and all "postures" in between can coexist in one sensibility. Third, Goldman also believes that "Premature" looks forward to the philosophical perspective of *Eureka,* where the grave holds no terrors for the enlightened (60–63). Eric Carlson agrees; he thinks the story traces the pattern of "death as metamorphosis" leading to redemption, a concept basic to Poe's mature thought (personal communication, 1992).

Fourth, the structure of "Premature" deserves added critical attention, which it has received from Stuart Levine, who says: "[N]ever was there a piece in which the reader's mental furniture was more carefully arranged by the author. Here is no emotional rush of terror-filled language, but a calculated, premeditated construction of a single effect" (246). Levine might have added a point about characterization in the tale and how it merges skillfully with the structure. Because Poe wishes his narrator to suffer confusion in the final episode, he plants this sentence midway in the story: "Upon awaking from slumber, I could never gain, at once, thorough possession of my senses, and always remained, for many minutes, in much bewilderment and perplexity" (*M* 3, 963). For all its expertise in execution, however, and its beautiful closing paragraph, the tale suffers from occasional woeful lapses in tone. Early on, Poe is describing the case of a Baltimore housewife who exhibited all the appearances of death and was buried in some haste owing to fear of rapid decomposition. Three years later, when the family vault was opened, the skeleton fell upon the interloper. Investigation revealed that the lady had awakened in the coffin, had struggled so vigorously that the box had fallen from its shelf to the floor, where it splintered and allowed the contents to make its way to the locked door of the vault. Salvaging a piece of wood from the wrecked coffin, the lady commenced to bang on the door; while thus occupied, she either swooned or died, which Poe summarizes by observing: "Thus she remained, and thus she rotted, erect" (*M* 3, 957).

But "Premature Burial" ends on a somewhat positive note: In the culminating, near-death experience, the narrator realizes that Good may come from Evil—"I became a new man, and lived a man's life." Yet, as Hawthorne also warned, "the grim legion of sepulchral terrors cannot be regarded as altogether fanciful. . . . they must be suffered to slumber, or we perish" (*M* 3, 969).

SEA TALES

"MS. Found in a Bottle" (1833) was awarded first prize in a contest sponsored by the *Baltimore Saturday Visiter* in 1833. Poe submitted six stories for consideration, including "MS.," comprising a collection he proposed to call "Tales of the Folio Club" (never published as such). The judges were impressed with Poe's genius and issued a statement to that effect. In addition to the fifty-dollar prize, Poe gained the friendship of John P. Kennedy, who proved influential in securing an editorial position for the novice author. This extremely important passage in Poe's life is documented in detail in *The Poe Log* (129–36).

Critical opinion on this tale seems disparate and varied in the sense that scholars focus on different aspects of Poe's maritime narrative. Richard Wilbur believes the vortex (which swallows up the ship at the conclusion) represents "the loss of consciousness and the descent of the mind into sleep" (157). Wilbur interprets each stage of the hero's journey as a step in the process leading from the waking state to the hypnagogic state to deep sleep. The ship's departure represents the mind's "withdrawal" from wakefulness, the drowning of crew and captain symbolizes the "growing solitude of reverie," and so on. Poe remarked that the state between waking and sleeping was filled with vivid images—what Wilbur calls "the visionary condition *par excellence*" (265).

David Halliburton focuses on past–present references, which create a paradoxical tone in "MS." (248–56). The paradoxical quality of ship and crew noted

by Halliburton, says Ketterer, is a sign of transcendence similar to that found
in the description of decor in "The Assignation." Ketterer's analysis is inconclusive; but the reader gathers that he believes "MS." to be a study of spirit
travel from time to eternity (119–24). Douglas Robinson in *American Apocalypses* says that the sea voyage tales—"MS.," "Descent," and *Pym*—contain
the significant theme of "movement from one level of material existence to
another, from the human to the angelic" (111). Both Ketterer and Robinson see
"MS." as a vehicle for expressing the progress of the soul from the ordinary
to the psychal-transcendental visionary state, a thesis mapped out in detail by
Wilbur and Carlson. J. Gerald Kennedy takes a more down-to-earth view of the
story's climax, claiming that the "mystery of the 'southern pole' becomes in
this symbolic journey synonymous with death itself, as a powerful current carries
the ship into an immense . . . whirlpool where the narrator . . . reports the ship
'going down.' In 'MS.' as in *Pym,* the end of the manuscript seems to coincide
either with revelation or annihilation, but Poe refuses to disclose the ultimate
meaning of the blankness at the end of the page" (Kennedy, xvi).

Clark Griffith thinks "MS." is a turning point in Poe's relationship to traditional Gothic effects. Mrs. Radcliffe and Horace Walpole deploy extraordinary
circumstances to alarm and dismay the men and women in their fictions. Poe
also uses extraordinary circumstances, says Griffith, but "now, for the first time
the narrator speaks of strange 'conceptions' which are arising from inside his
mind." The tale, with its emphasis on internal feelings and sensations, shows
Poe modifying the earlier Gothic mode. Still, the tale is a long way from abandoning the externals—as Poe progresses in the direction of "psychologizing the
Gothic" (Veler, 22).

Alexander Hammond emphasizes Poe's dependence upon Symmes's *Symzonia: A Voyage of Discovery* (1820) as a source for "MS." Hammond believes
that Poe, like Symmes, is hoaxing his audience (i.e., members of the Folio Club)
with a far-fetched tale that includes an implied journey to the center of the earth!
(*PoeS*, 5, 25–32). Other sources for the tale, according to researchers quoted by
Mabbott, include "The Rime of the Ancient Mariner" by Coleridge and a short
story by Simms entitled "A Picture of the Sea" (*M* 2, 130–34). As Jeffrey
Meyers points out, Joseph Conrad was impressed by "MS.," comparing Poe's
realism with Coleridge's (in "Rime of the Ancient Mariner"):

The indifference of Coleridge's animated corpses to the living people resembles the
indifference of the secular ghosts in the overgrown ship in E. A. Poe's impressive version
of the Flying Dutchman. A very fine piece of work—about as fine as anything of that
kind can be—and so authentic in detail that it must have been told by a sailor of a
sombre and poetical genius in the invention of the phantastic. (1992, 66–67)

In my opinion, "MS. Found in a Bottle" is best seen as a variation on the
theme of the American "breakaway" from society. Edward H. Davidson notices
the type in his discussion of Dupin:

He belongs to the people and yet he must make his great decision or undergo the major trial in the waste places or in the solitude of the anguished soul. He is one of us; yet he must, to express himself, go above, away from, or beyond our commoner range of experience in order to bring his message, the fire from heaven, the solution to the crime. (214)

The narrative pattern commences with departure from home, from family and friends and familiar surroundings, then proceeds to a dramatic event or decision that propels the protagonist into strange territory, where he sojourns—for either a specified or indefinite period of time. In some versions of the story, the hero *chooses* to break away, as in Hawthorne's "Wakefield," an account of a perverse husband who elects to leave his wife, without explanation or good reason, to live in a nearby neighborhood for twenty years, after which time he returns home. In other versions, the hero is swept into his adventure willy-nilly, as in Poe's "MS." Still another example is Irving's "Rip Van Winkle," in which the initiate goes willingly, but without knowing what mysterious experience is in store. Finally, there is the folkloric variety, in which an ignorant individual utters some sort of blasphemy and is punished by being removed from his routine existence; such is the fate of "Peter Rugg, the Missing Man" (1824) by William Austin. Peter is delayed one night by a heavy storm and impatiently curses the elements. "Let the storm increase," he says. "I will see home tonight or may I never see home!" Thereafter, he travels the roads around Boston, always heading for his village and never arriving—except once years later, when he finds everything changed and unfamiliar (Austin, 11).

In these tales, as in the initiation ritual they resemble, the *desorbitado* is expected to return home a wiser man, matured and educated by his hardships and his sojourn in strange lands. Ironically, Rip, after spending time with Henry Hudson and his crew, returns home the same old simpleton, and Wakefield has apparently learned nothing from his misadventure. Peter Rugg has virtually no intellectual dimension to begin with and certainly none after flitting around Boston for twenty years. The experience of the Poe narrator, by way of contrast, emphasizes learning and intellectual *discovery*—a word, in fact, that is treated in the tale as an early climax. What does the narrator learn? Primarily, he learns the effect on his mind of his extraordinary situation—that is to say, the sensation of being invisible to the curious crew, the evidence of extreme old age in the captain's face, the possibility that the porous wood of the ship's timbers is alive and growing—the cumulative impact of all this leading to a kind of superrespect for "the spirit of eld." (Note that the old Swede tells the narrator that the ship will grow like the body of a living seaman.) The narrator's acute curiosity, coupled with his sensitivity to impressions, reinforces the idea that "MS." dramatizes a learning experience.

Stories of *desorbitados* probably reflect political developments as the country passed from colonial to independent status. Drastic change of this sort would seem to send particularly naive individuals "out of orbit," so to speak. Rip and

Peter Rugg return to once-familiar scenes now changed both obviously and subtly; this is not the world they knew! Hawthorne is making a different, but related point: citizens of the new republic had better stay faithful to the old values for fear of being alienated if once they "step aside." But Poe is using the convention to dramatize the mental experience of being out of time itself. Note also how provincial the other stories seem in terms of setting: all the protagonists sojourn "in strange lands" within walking distance of home! Poe takes us not only to foreign ports on far-flung seas but into extraordinary states of awareness. Thus, Poe's variation on the dropout or breakaway narrative is not to be taken as a story of alienation from conventional society (as are all the other examples considered here) but rather implies a "rising above" ordinary thought and life patterns. In this sense, "MS." aligns with the transcendental or "higher consciousness" implications of Poe's metaphysics.

"A Descent into the Maelstrom" (1841) has elicited more interesting criticism than any of the other Poe tales reviewed in the present chapter. It is one of Poe's profoundly suggestive stories; the author's use of a double narrator is an intriguing and sophisticated device, and each detail of the maritime adventure seems laden with significance, inviting allegorical interpretation despite Poe's qualified aversion to allegory. Furthermore, the themes implicit in "Maelstrom" reflect and parallel themes in other important Poe tales and in *Eureka.* In the Poe canon, "Maelstrom" is unquestionably of major importance; in American short fiction up to that time, only a few stories are as expertly executed or as significant.

T. O. Mabbott describes the process by which Poe created his tale from various sources: a story in *Fraser's Magazine* for 1834 entitled "The Maelstrom: A Fragment"; various articles in the *Encyclopedia Britannica;* portions of *The Mariner's Chronicle* (1834); possibly others (*M* 2, 575–76).

A cosmological interpretation is offered by Richard Finholt, who argues that concepts in "Mesmeric Revelation" and later in *Eureka* give depth to the "Maelstrom" narrative: according to all three texts, either explicitly or implicitly, God is "Matter in motion" or Thought; and each individual is a differentiated particle of the original Unity. The characters are caught—suspended— (in "Maelstrom") between attraction and repulsion or between struggling to stay out, and the irresistible pull downward toward the center of the abyss. The story thus depicts God as manifest in the great whirlpool, and the action projects an image of man's place in the universe. Finholt says the seamen move from the periphery of God's mind to its center; and the sailor telling the story survives because he establishes crucial "unity" with the watery environment; his mental "lucidity" is "one with" the mind of God; his deserting the boat and entering the whirlpool are obvious acts of "returning to original unity." The elder brother perishes because he is a slave to sense, instinct, and emotion—elements that do not allow for lucidity. The surviving brother, in determining his own fate, approximates the divine mind (87–95).

Finholt says the rainbow perceived by the surviving mariner represents God's promise that the whirlpool will be the pathway between time and eternity (88). Because "rainbow" signified survival in Poe's "Eiros and Charmion" (indirectly by use of the title character's name), the literal rainbow in "Maelstrom" might be intended to signify the same hopeful outcome for the fisherman "in the depths." This interpretation is derived from the Levines' gloss ("rainbow and dove"), as found in Bryant's *Mythology*.

If by "lucidity" Finholt means intuitive insight, then he would be in agreement with Gerard M. Sweeney, who claims that Poe's survivor is saved by "taste" (poetic intellect) rather than reason. Caught in the maelstrom, the surviving brother observes the beauty of the whirlpool; he seems strangely detached, amused even—all this suggesting poetic appreciation or aesthetic perception as the state of mind that assures survival. Sweeney points out that Poe never claims man can control nature but that stories like "Maelstrom," "The Pit and the Pendulum," and the Dupin series suggest that poetic insight is the avenue to understanding (effecting, in a sense, a *union-with,* as Dupin becomes one with the criminal, the man in the pit becomes one with his tormentors—by feeding the rats—and the surviving mariner becomes one with the whirlpool) (22–25).

Jonathan Auerbach, in *The Romance of Failure,* devotes much attention to Poe's first-person narrators and the identity of the author himself, with special emphasis upon "The Man of the Crowd." According to Auerbach, in "Descent," personal identity is obliterated by the voyage into a "fearful vortex or abyss, an expression of Poe's desire to return to the womb, according to psychoanalytically inclined critics." Auerbach adds that in "Maelstrom" and in "MS. Found in a Bottle," the first-person narrator "moves toward some primal union with God prior to self-consciousness" (34). Kenneth Egan, Jr., however, believes that too many critics treat Poe as a deep thinker, rather than as an artist; to correct the false emphasis, Egan focuses on the imagery used in "Maelstrom." Offering an alternative to Finholt's "lucid moment" and Sweeney's "taste" as keys to survival, Egan wants us to consider Poe's use of the funnel, moon, and surface of the water as keys to the main theme of *perspective.* The hero, says Egan, progresses from blindness to blurred perception to illumination—the degree of his understanding depending on his distance or detachment from the object of contemplation. Moonlight penetrates to the depths, "seeing" all at once and without difficulty, because of its cosmic perspective. As the whirlpool subsides, man, moon, and funnel meet at the surface, suggesting that the man has attained "the elucidating perspective of the moon," which is to say he perceives things now from a universal vantage point (157–62).

Brief reference might be made to Mark Hennelly, Jr., and Jules Zanger, both of whom offer Freudian interpretations. Hennelly sees the plight of the mariner as a reflection of a return-to-the-womb fantasy (9). Zanger thinks "Maelstrom" can be grouped with "Morella," "Ligeia," and "MS. Found in a Bottle"—all of which dramatize the theme of forbidden knowledge. The whirlpool is the female image, while the descriptions of the females' eyes in the other stories suggest female sexuality. Zanger believes that sexual references in Poe imply both horror and fascination (541).

Overall, criticism of "Maelstrom" tends to fall into two categories: cosmological, which finds elements of Poe's mature reflections on man, God, and the universe; and Freudian, which uses the approach (now largely discredited) employed by Marie Bonaparte in the 1930s. Students should read Roger Forclaz's "Psychoanalysis and Edgar Allan Poe: A Critique of the Bonaparte Thesis" for a convincing criticism of Bonaparte's assumption that Poe tales are an expression of repressed neurosis.

"The Island of the Fay" (1841) was published the same year as "Monos and Una" and "Maelstrom"; this tale shares something of the themes of both the colloquy and the sea story, with an additional suggestion of prescient psychological insight. To the Levines, the tale implies "linked analogies" in an occult world in which everything is animate and God-like (3). Halliburton thinks time-diction ("during") is set off against place-diction ("within"), suggesting the assimilation of time and space that leads to the Fay's demise. But the tale is more affirmative than melancholy, says this critic; the experience has benefited the narrator by showing him a higher level of being—intermediate between human and divine. The Fay seems mutable, says Halliburton; though brief, her life is not extinguished at the end but is absorbed into the Godhead (354–56).

Kent Ljungquist has a contrasting view: "The Island of the Fay" is satirical, a parody of fairyland writing. Ljungquist bases this interpretation on Poe's critical writing and assumed attitudes in "Sonnet: To Science" and "Fairyland," along with internal details in "Island," such as the narrator's "lying under a shrub and having a snooze" (Ljungquist's diction). Comparing the tale with the two earlier poems, this critic believes these works were meant to serve as an admonition to the poet to get down to something substantial (269).

Burton Pollin has done some serious digging into the background of the illustration that accompanied "Island" on initial publication. He finds that Sartain's engraving derived from sketches done by the English artist John Martin, who left graphic designs for waterworks to be channeled into London from an outlying river. Pollin compares the original graphic with the later magazine illustration and finds considerable "adjustments" and changes, suggesting that Poe did not write the story "to order" after being shown the picture, as has often been claimed, but rather had a hand in altering the original sketches to suit the needs of the narrative.

David Ketterer's interpretation is of a piece with his general view of what went on in the mind of Poe during this period of creativity. Ketterer believes that Poe craved "release" from human limitations (e.g., space, time, and personality) and adopted a strategy of pretense or "deception" in presenting reality. Inevitably, he adopted a half-waking perception that was essentially solipsistic and led to the blurring of distinctions between light and dark, reality and image, even life and death (106–8). In "Island," says Ketterer, shadows and water, light and shade, fairy and landscape—all these contrasting substances exist in a state of fusion reflecting Poe's solipsistic perception. Ketterer might have related this "fusion" process to the discussion on the final pages of *Eureka,* where it forms an essential part of Poe's cosmology. Such a tie-in would undoubtedly improve Ketterer's "reading" by aligning it with Poe's mature perspective. Something should also be said for Poe's "painterly" techniques in fiction. When an artist creates an image of light blending with dark or a human figure merging into, say, a waterfall, the implication is not that the painter has a warped or impaired view of reality; rather, he is striving for a certain effect by way of shape, value, hue, composition, and so on.

Patrick Quinn thinks the tale is of major importance in understanding Poe's imagination but cautions that the story must be read in conjunction with "The Oval Portrait." The key passage, says Quinn, occurs when Poe describes the shadows of the trees being absorbed into the stream, just as in the later story the model's vitality is absorbed into the painted portrait. The theme is "construction and destruction inherent in the same process, even the creative process of art" (262–66).

Overall, it seems fair to say that critics have paid too little attention to the details of the action in "The Island of the Fay." The essence of Poe's fable is twofold: (1) assumptions about the universe and human perception with (2) a creature who symbolizes the reality of those assumptions. The Fay additionally represents certain truths about a particular psychological condition. As regards the first part, Poe's language is couched in mythic terms that suggest a cyclical universe. Matter, "instinct with life," is part of God. The living universe may be imaged as time cycles (era within era) and space cycles (the rings of Saturn). Time-space cycles encompass everything, with cycle-within-cycle describing the reality of minute as well as cosmic activities—from anthills to solar systems— in a way that implies the center of things—an all-important concept more fully developed in *Eureka.* The center is the condition of Unity, the Oneness of being that is Poe's God. These formulations in Part One (some of which are implicit) prepare the narrator for the events to be witnessed in Part Two. The Fay comes out of the darkness and disappears back into it; she is a part of the living universe. Her passing around the islet suggests the cyclical movement that characterizes activity in Poe's universe. Now a dimension is added: the Fay's cycles suggest a psychological process as well as an ontological one—alternating as she does between joy and dark melancholy, which gradually deepens. This depiction anticipates what modern psychologists would call the manic-depressive personality. The story is the kind of undertaking in brief space that only Poe could bring off successfully; it is a poetic masterpiece in prose rich in philosophical and psychological implications.

"The Lighthouse" (ms. 1849) is a fragment, left incomplete by Poe probably at the end of his life. It was part of the collection of manuscripts and other papers given to Griswold at Poe's death; one page became separated from the rest, and the complete text was not published until 1942. Mabbott gives a complete account (*M* 3, 1388–89). Both Mabbott and Burton Pollin believe Poe was influenced by contemporary interest in lighthouse improvement and construction (Pollin 1970, 150–51). The Levines think the protagonist, who after some difficulty secures a government position and who finds more faith in his trusty dog than in all society, is perhaps "emblematic" of Poe himself (629).

The story is told in diary form, with only three entries. The first describes the efforts of the narrator's sponsor to secure him a position as solitary keeper of a lighthouse in some unspecified northern country. The narrator claims he is "a noble of the realm" and considers himself fortunate to be the sole proprietor. However, he is a bit fearful about "keeping his head" under the pressure of isolation; his remark concerning the "peculiar echoes" in the cylindrical walls suggests that he is "jumpy" or maybe a bit hallucinatory. (Up to this point, the story is incredibly reminiscent of Stanley Kubrick's 1979 film *The Shining*.) The first entry also mentions the narrator's large, faithful dog, Neptune. The brief second entry expresses the narrator's joy at being alone; he says he has found true satisfaction in solitude. The third entry describes the dimensions and construction of the lighthouse, then expresses some fear of hurricanes and high seas, and closes with the ominous observation that "the basis on which the structure rests seems to me to be chalk" (*M* 3, 1390–92).

Mabbott says there is no doubt the lighthouse is doomed. I think it likely that the narrator will go through extreme emotions that he will write down very factually (at least as he *perceives* what is happening); that he will either perish in a huge tidal wave—or survive everything by way of ingenious resourcefulness; and that Neptune will either save his master or rescue the diary for posterity. It is not at all unlikely that, if Poe had finished "The Lighthouse," it would be linked thematically to "MS." and "Descent." That is to say, the solitary lighthouse keeper would experience some sort of consciousness expansion and/or witness secrets of nature in her very violent manifestations. In the end, perhaps, there would be some kind of fusion with the whirlwind.

In conclusion, Poe's "tales of the human condition" seem to be ultimately hopeful and optimistic. The metaphysical dialogues assert the survival of the human spirit, its creativity and hunger for knowledge. These tales transcend the popular "Christian consolation" formulas of his day to propose a serene afterlife where the essential activity is the pursuit of understanding and happiness. The sea stories stress human consciousness expansion, resourcefulness, the awareness of danger, and an ontological-psychological cycle of existence. The "Premature Burial" leads us from fear to safety, from the contemplation of horrors to common sense and a revived eagerness for living.

This is not to sentimentalize Poe. If "Shadow" might well be called a "grim reminder" story, it may also be seen as a healthy reprimand to those whose frivolity is auspiciously inappropriate. If "Silence" emphasizes the intolerables, it also assumes that the best of us deserve better. If "The Island of the Fay" has its dark side, it also has its bright side. If the hero of "The Lighthouse" is in a threatening situation, at least he is not to be thought of as an innocent—in the sense of ignorant—victim or a coward.

Ralph Waldo Emerson's faith in the infinite potential of the American citizen is reflected in odd ways in Poe, who also believed in the ability of his characters to cope with life's difficulties. Yet, Poe's people are beset with crises undreamed of in the mind of his New England contemporary. Emerson's common man existed in Nature, which (in most cases) meant the sunshine. Poe takes us inside the whirlpool, into the pits of the Inquisition, into the darkness of the grave, the depressive side of neurosis, the despair of shipwreck, the vision of *nada*, the destruction of our physical world. Still, the Poe hero survives and transcends most of these potentially disastrous circumstances to emerge wiser, stronger, and, in some cases, emotionally serene. Poe's vision of the human spirit is basically affirmative.

Scholarly work on such a varied body of fiction is bound to be somewhat miscellaneous, but the best critiques tend toward affinity (if not uniformity) regarding basic, positive aspects of Poe's perspective. His vision of human potential, his perspective on "man's fate," his cosmology—all emphasize human capabilities for higher, perfected modes of thought and existence. Ketterer notes Poe's narrators' striving for a condition "above and beyond" the ordinary. DeFalco sees the Poe hero in transition from a lower to a higher state. Halliburton finds a movement from human to angelic, while Finholt believes Poe's characters can move from the periphery to the center of God's consciousness. Poe is no Emersonian optimist; he does not endorse the infinite potential of the common man. But, in Poe's mind, the sensitive, courageous, aware individual can overcome human imperfection.

Among the most interesting and insightful critiques surveyed for this chapter are DeFalco's on "Shadow," Ketterer's on "Silence," Finholt's on "Maelstrom," and Wilbur's on the vortex. Finholt's is an example of ideal Poe criticism. Critics especially strong on scholarly research leading to improved understanding of Poe stories include the Levines on Jacob Bryant, Doris Falk on mesmerism, and Clark Griffiths on "MS." Eric Carlson, Burton Pollin, and Goldman, among others, have been especially helpful in correcting false leads in Poe scholarship. Finally, Carlson's tracing of Poe's sequential development in "Poe's Vision of Man" seems to be the most viable overall view of Poe's achievement as a thinker. My own preference, in Poe studies as in scholarly work on any American author, is the cross-referential comparison and contrast to similar works by contemporaries. Poe then emerges in startling clarity.

WORKS CITED

Auerbach, Jonathan. *The Romance of Failure.* New York: Oxford UP, 1989.
Austin, William. "Peter Rugg, The Missing Man." *American Short Stories of the Nineteenth Century.* London: Dent, 1974.
Brown, Slater. *The Heyday of Spiritualism.* New York: Hawthorne Books, 1970.

Bryant, Jacob. A New System, or, an Analysis of Ancient Mythology, 1774–1776. London, 1807.

Carlson, Eric W. "Poe's Vision of Man." *Papers on Poe*. Ed. Richard P. Veler. Springfield, Ohio: Chantry Music P, 1972.

———. "Frames of Reference for Poe's Symbolic Language." *Critical Essays on Edgar Allan Poe*. Ed. Eric W. Carlson. Boston: G. K. Hall, 1987.

———. "Edgar Allan Poe." *Dictionary of Literary Biography*. Vol. 74. Detroit: Gale Research, 1988.

Casale, Ottavio M. "Poe's Transcendentalism." In *The Transcendentalists: A Review of Research and Criticism*. Ed. Joel Myerson. New York: MLA, 1984.

Chandler, Alice. "The Visionary Race: Poe's Attitude toward His Dreamers." *Emerson Society Quarterly* 60 (1970): 73–81.

Dahl, Curtis. "The American School of Disaster." *American Quarterly* 11 (Fall 1959): 380–90.

Davidson, Edward H. *Poe: A Critical Study*. Cambridge: Belknap P of Harvard UP, 1957.

Defalco, Joseph M. "The Source of Terror in Poe's 'Shadow—A Parable.' " *Studies in Short Fiction* 6 (1969): 643–48.

Egan, K. V., Jr. "Descent to an Ascent: Poe's Use of Perspective in 'A Descent into the Maelstrom.' " *Studies in Short Fiction* 19 (1982): 157–62.

Falk, Doris. "Poe and the Power of Animal Magnetism." *PMLA* 84 (1969): 536–46.

Finholt, Richard D. "The Vision at the Brink of the Abyss: 'A Descent into the Maelstrom' in the Light of Poe's Cosmology." *Georgia Review* 27 (1973): 356–66.

Fisher, Benjamin Franklin, IV. "The Power of Words in Poe's 'Silence.' " *University of Pennsylvania Library Chronicle* 41 (1976): 56–72.

Flory, Wendy S. "Usher's Fear and the Flaw in Poe's Theories of the Metamorphosis of the Senses." *PoeS* 7 (1974): 17–19.

Forclaz, Roger. "Psychoanalysis and Edgar Allan Poe: A Critique of the Bonaparte Thesis." In Carlson, *Critical Essays*.

Goldman, Arnold. "Poe's Stories of Premature Burial: 'That Ere Kind of Style.' " *Edgar Allan Poe: The Design of Order*. Ed. A. Robert Lee. London and Totowa, N.J.: Vision and Barnes and Noble, 1987.

Griffith, Clark. "Poe and the Gothic." *Papers on Poe*. Ed. Richard P. Veler. Springfield, Ohio: Chantry Music P, 1972.

Halliburton, David. *Edgar Allan Poe: A Phenomenological View*. Princeton UP, 1973.

Hammond, Alexander. "A Reconstruction of Poe's 1833 *Tales of the Folio Club*." *PoeS* 5, no. 2 (1972): 25–32.

———. "Further Notes on Poe's Folio Club Tales." *PoeS* 8 (1975): 38–42.

Hennelly, Mark, Jr. "Oedipus and Orpheus in the Maelstrom: The Traumatic Rebirth of the Artist." *PoeS* 9 (1976): 6–11.

Ketterer, David. *The Rationale of Deception in Poe*. Baton Rouge: Louisiana State UP, 1979.

Levine, Stuart. *Edgar Poe: Seer and Craftsman*. DeLand, Fla.: Everett/Edwards, 1972.

Ljungquist, Kent. "Poe's 'Island of the Fay': The Passing of Fairyland." *Studies in Short Fiction* 14 (1977): 265–71.

Meyers, Jeffrey. *Edgar Allan Poe: His Life and Legacy*. New York: Scribner's, 1992.

Poe, Edgar Allan. *Letters*. Ed. John Ward Ostrum. New York: Gordian P, 1966.

———. *The Short Fiction: An Annotated Edition.* Ed. Stuart Levine and Susan Levine. Urbana: U of Illinois P, 1976.

———. *Collected Works.* Ed. Thomas Ollive Mabbott. 3 vols. Cambridge,: Harvard UP, 1978.

———. "Eureka." *Poetry and Tales.* Ed. Patrick F. Quinn. New York: Library of America, 1984.

Pollin, Burton. *Discoveries in Poe.* Notre Dame: U of Notre Dame P, 1970.

———. "Light on 'Shadow' and Other Pieces by Poe; Or More Thomas Moore." *Emerson Society Quarterly* 18 (1972a): 166–73.

———. "Poe's Illustration for 'The Island of the Fay': A Hoax Detected." *Mystery and Detection Annual.* Beverly Hills, Calif.: Donald Adams, 1972b.

———. *Poe, Creator of Words.* Bronxville: Nicholas T. Smith, 1980.

Quinn, Patrick F. *The French Face of Edgar Poe.* Carbondale: Southern Illinois UP, 1971.

Robinson, Douglas. *American Apocalypses: The Image of the End of the World in American Literature.* Baltimore: Johns Hopkins UP, 1985.

Silverman, Kenneth. *Edgar Allan Poe: Mournful and Never-Ending Remembrance.* New York: HarperCollins, 1991.

Sweeney, Gerard M. "Beauty and Truth: Poe's 'A Descent into the Maelstrom.' " *PoeS* 6, no. 1 (1973): 22–25.

Tate, Allan. "The Angelic Imagination." *The Recognition of Edgar Allan Poe.* Ed. Eric W. Carlson. Ann Arbor: Michigan UP, 1970.

Thomas, Dwight, and David Jackson. *The Poe Log.* Boston: G. K. Hall, 1987.

Thompson, G. R. "Poe's 'Flawed' Gothic: Absurdist Techniques in 'Metzengerstein' and the Courier Satires." *Approaches to Poe: A Symposium.* Ed. Richard P. Benton. Hartford: Transcendental Books, 1970.

———. *Poe's Fiction: Romantic Irony in the Gothic Tales.* Madison: Wisconsin UP, 1973.

Veler, Richard P., ed. *Papers on Poe: Essays in Honor of John Ward Ostrom.* Springfield, OH: Chantry Music P, 1972.

Wilbur, Richard. "The House of Poe." *The Recognition of Edgar Allan Poe: Selected Criticism.* Ed. Eric W. Carlson. Ann Arbor: Michigan UP, 1970.

Zanger, Jules. "Poe and the Theme of Forbidden Knowledge." *AL* 49 (1978): 533–43.

8

Tales of Psychal Conflict: "Berenice," "Morella," "Ligeia"

Eric W. Carlson

These tales were part of Poe's *Tales of the Grotesque and Arabesque* (1840) and obviously represent the "arabesques," or those in which "the singular [was] wrought out into the strange and mystical," as he described them. Mainstream Poe biography and criticism have accepted this grouping, as in Arthur H. Quinn's recognition of thirty-six of sixty-eight tales as arabesques, the three in the title of this chapter, among others, being labeled "supernatural arabesques" (*AQ*, 292–307). In the Definitive Edition of 1894–1895, Stedman singled out the "Romances of Death" group, which he said might be called "Pastels" or "Impressions" or "Petits Poèmes en Prose." (*The Works of Edgar Allan Poe*, 346).

Stedman might also have praised other subgroups of the "supernatural arabesques" for their distinctive style and co-relation of parts, but it was not until 1959 that Richard Wilbur at the close of his Library of Congress lecture on "The House of Poe" said: "Poe is a great artist, and I would rest my case for him on his prose allegories of psychic conflict. In them, Poe broke wholly new ground, and they remain the best things of their kind in our literature. . . . I think he will have something to say to us as long as there is civil war in the palaces of men's minds" (*REAP*, 277).

David Halliburton in his *Edgar Allan Poe: A Phenomenological View* (1974) treated several of these tales under "Tales of Women" (199–229). In recent years, feminist studies of these stories have concentrated more or less negatively on Poe as allegedly patriarchal in his treatment of women characters (see Chapter 18 on "Feminist Re-Visioning"). John Irwin devotes only a few pages to "The Dying Woman Stories" in *The Mystery of a Solution* (Chaps. 24, 25).

These tales dramatize positive themes as well as psychic conflict; they are accompanied (e.g., *Pym*) or followed not only by stories of demonic compulsion, crime, and punishment but also by the colloquies (1839–1845), "The Island of the Fay" (1841), and "Mesmeric Revelation" (1841). Chapter 7 in the present book reveals that Poe's central theme is a quest, psychal and cosmic, for a supernal Beauty and unifying, transcendental Truth. The tales of psychic conflict, often referred to as moral allegories, are indeed psychomoral or psychotranscendental.

Clark Griffith in "Poe and the Gothic" explained that these tales are in line with the mainstream "visionary" critical perspective that led to "a genuinely new Gothic." In "MS. Found in a Bottle" (1833), the protagonist's "Discovery" of "an entire new order of experience" implies a shift from the "mere man" of traditional Gothic to the "Creative Man" (Griffith) of the neo-Gothic. It marks a return from "outer wonder" to "the dark, secluded interiors of eighteenth-century fiction . . . suggestive of the human mind itself" (22–23).

"BERENICE"

The first example of this psychologizing of the Gothic appeared in "Berenice" (*Southern Literary Messenger,* March 1835). Despite its long neglect by critics, it is recognized today as a Faulknerian "memory" narrative unmatched in its time. From its first publication, the shocking impact of the climax caused "many readers [to] find the tale too repulsive by far" (*M* 2, 207). On April 30, Poe replied to Thomas W. White, publisher of *SLM,* who had expressed some complaints over this story: "A word or two in relation to Berenice. Your opinion of it is very just. The subject is by far too horrible. . . . The Tale originated in a bet that I could produce nothing effective on a subject so singular, provided I treated it seriously. . . . I allow that it approaches the very verge of bad taste— but I will not sin quite so egregiously again" (*L* 1, 17). The full text of this long letter, however, makes clear that Poe felt justified in using the style and manner characteristic of the sensational fiction in the magazines. Mabbott calls the style magnificent (*M* 2, 207). Although Poe did not alter or omit the "too repulsive" extraction of Berenice's teeth throughout ten years and three editions, in the 1845 version, he removed four paragraphs describing Egaeus's visit to the encoffined Berenice in her bedchamber, where he noticed a movement of a finger under her shroud, and under the broken band over her mouth "the livid lips wreathed into a species of smile and . . . once again there glared upon me in too palpable reality, the white and glistening, and ghastly teeth of Berenice" (*M* 2, 217). Apparently, this Gothic passage could be sacrificed as unessential to the plot despite its symbolic value.

D. H. Lawrence's famous essay on Poe's "love" stories was first published in 1919, then revised for his collection of *Studies in Classic American Literature* (1923). Lawrence saw reflected in this tale Poe's own desire for the unison, the flowing, the heightening of life against nature's limitations. "Hence the man in *Berenice* must take possession of the irreducible part of his mistress. '*Toutes ses dents étaient des idées,*' he says. Then they are little fixed ideas of mordant hate, of which he possesses himself'' (1923, 685). To Lawrence, Berenice's teeth symbolize her hatred, suggested by the earlier description—''long, narrow, and excessively white, with the pale lips writhing about them''—as seen by Egaeus in his monomania. But Lawrence fails to follow through with the full context and meaning of the teeth. As Egaeus ''pondered upon'' them at length, he ''assigned to them in imagination a sensitive and sentient power, and even when unassisted by the lips, a capability of moral expression . . . I felt that their possession alone could ever restore me to peace, in giving me back to reason'' (*M* 2, 216). In his mind, the teeth without the ''writhing lips'' have become symbolic of Berenice's *moral* nature and, as such, are a continuing reminder to him of what he has lost or destroyed. This theme recurs in several of the tales of psychal conflict.

Many years passed before academic scholars began to come to terms with this story. Patrick Quinn states, ''Astonished, taken aback, confused by such things as 'Berenice,' critics and scholars in this country have tried to explain Poe's stories by explaining them away.'' His strange stories have an ''enigmatic quality that is not readily analyzed.'' Quinn then quotes as valid Baudelaire's view that ''the Poe character . . . is Poe himself. And his women . . . they too are Poe.'' This insight, Quinn concludes, leads us ''not to the books Poe read but to the mind that read them'' (218–20). But here both Baudelaire and Lawrence seem to have fallen into the fallacy of confusing Egaeus with Poe.

As Clark Griffith reads this story, the narrator Egaeus is both ''projector and voice,'' for whom ''realities are the realities of his own making,'' especially in his obsession with the teeth. The Gothic wonders of this tale have been internalized into a ''psychic state,'' a stream of consciousness, a process by which the perceiving mind in the horror stories originates the terror. So to read them, ''as though they were notes composed from within is often to clarify and enrich the stories'' (23–24).

David Halliburton read ''Berenice'' as a drama of consciousness and victimization, thus inverting the transcendental affirmation of the poems. Egaeus is ''an outside observer of an activity that takes place, paradoxically, inside himself'' (200). His room, in which he was born and from which he cannot escape, symbolizes his monomania, his lack of vitality, his pathological attentiveness to trivial details in his surroundings. The teeth ''preserve the numinous attributes of the original object (the living Berenice)'' and symbolize ''*des idées*,'' memories of a vague, platonic preexistence in which, if recovered, he might again be happy and whole (202–5).

Theodore Ziolkowski's ''The Telltale Teeth: Psychodontia to Sociodontia'' explores the role of human teeth in cultural, historical, as well as literary and psychological contexts. As an image of sex and beauty, the tooth (or teeth), we are told, appears in modern literature (Dostoevsky, Thomas Mann, Graham Greene, Gunter Grass, et al.), the Bible, folklore, and primitive myth. But the limited commentary on ''Berenice'' (113–14) is merely incidental to Ziolkowski's social-historical focus.

Elizabeth Phillips, in "Mere Household Events: The Metaphysics of Mania," devotes several pages to the illness of Egaeus as understood in Poe's day. Drawing chiefly on Isaac Ray and Benjamin Rush, Phillips concludes that Poe apparently "hashed together material from more than one source," especially from Rush, who noted that murders by the deranged are "usually committed by near relations, and friends, and often by persons of the most exemplary moral and religious characters . . . and sometimes by persons under the influence of delusive opinions in religion" (quoted, 119).

Jules Zanger's "Poe's 'Berenice': Philosophical Fantasy and Its Pitfalls" is one of the best interpretive "Berenice" essays to date. Although recognizing that this tale fails to integrate its Gothic surface plot with its "serious and coherent substructure of meaning," Zanger realizes that Egaeus's world consists not only of clearly defined opposites—health and illness, reason and insanity—but also of two different periods of consciousness, namely, reality and fantasy. Egaeus is a sane man describing a period of madness in his past, a rational man making a comprehensible statement of his own lapse from rationality" (137). Such a lapse is described in the fourth paragraph beginning "In that chamber [the library] was I born." After this first section comes the main narrative that Egaeus *now* regards as an aberration of living too long in the "stagnation" of a dreamlike state. The polarization of Egaeus's two worlds is reflected in the two main characters—Egaeus, the cloistered, immobile, miserable one seeking the permanent and eternal through contemplation, and Berenice, graceful, energetic, outgoing until her illness subtly changes her personality both physically and "morally." Meanwhile, Egaeus becomes obsessed with her teeth, which he likens to *idées,* so called after Plato's Ideas—the absolutely True, Good, and Beautiful essences or forms beyond all change, time, and sense perception. The gruesome climax (when Egaeus, confusing her teeth with *des idées,* removes them) results from the frailty of human reason, according to Zanger. But isn't Egaeus's lack of love for Berenice the primary cause of what follows? For Zanger, the story fails: the narrative details are either too shocking or too difficult to relate to the undercurrent of meaning; yet it is a significant achievement in that the young Poe here attempted "to transform the sensational gothic fiction of the period that preceded it into a genuine fantasy of ideas" (141).

In 1987, two ambitious thesis studies appeared. J. Gerald Kennedy in *Poe, Death, and the Life of Writing* contended that Poe "deconstructs the idealized deathbed scene" of his day by inscripting "a symbolic transcendence of mortality." Seeing death as "the crux of being" and intuiting its intrusion into consciousness, Poe foresaw the "post-Christian" despair and nihilism of a later age. But Kennedy does not view "Berenice" in this context. As a "visionary" (in the psychological sense only), Egaeus, the protagonist, suffers an "inversion" of reality and illusion; to him, Berenice was, in the words of the text, "not as a being of earth, earthy, but as the abstraction of such a being; not as a thing to admire, but to analyze; not as an object of love, but as the theme of the most abstruse although desultory speculation" (quoted 78). As Berenice's illness grows progressively worse, there occurs an "appalling distortion of her personal identity": her once black hair becomes a vivid yellow, her eyes lifeless, and her teeth "long, narrow, and excessively white, with the pale lips writhing about them." Writhing with "mordant hate," as Lawrence put it? How these teeth signify "the problem of death" Kennedy does not clarify, and the story's ending is ignored altogether.

In her *Fables,* Joan Dayan considers "Berenice" in the context of *Eureka* as " 'A New World of Philosophy' " to serve as a philosophical baseline for her anti-Romantic readings. She regards her view of *Eureka* as the opposite of Wilbur's: to him, *Eureka* is Poe's cosmic vision in which imagination is the mode of creative realization in maintaining or recovering psychic harmony (Wilbur, 8–9); to Dayan, *Eureka* is "an indeterminate philosophy . . . inseparable from a severely Calvinist theology" (19). Poe's belief in "a radically physical world . . . deconstructs the romantic sublime" of the Transcendentalists, which is replaced by "sceptical realism" in his thinking about poetry, perception, fiction, and self-identity (24, 26). In the end, however, true to her own post-modernism, Dayan dismisses Poe's "perspectival game" as impossible of any determination, Poe deflating his own stated truths with his new language of "mereness," with "new ambiguities and double talk" and the "sophistical delusions" of speculative cosmogonizing.

In Part III, Dayan concentrates on tales that she regards as "largely ignored in Poe criticism" in "an attempt to question and complete the established Poe canon." A section on "The Identity of Berenice" (135–58) deals with the first of three early Gothic tales representing the breakdown of "the law of identity." Of these, "Berenice" is Poe's "most violent sabotage of the reveries of idealism" (136). Egaeus is satirized as a speculative visionary whose "transcendent idea" sees Berenice as an abstraction to be analyzed, not loved. The pulling of her teeth is a total extraction of her identity and a mark of his derangement. The antecedents of this mania are cited as Augustine, Locke, and a poem by Catullus. These digressions, typical of Dayan's comparatist criticism, still leave unanswered "what Poe intends by the cruel and seemingly gratuitous violence to human identity." This problematic ending leads to a confused question: in his disorder and her distortion, whose identity is at stake? To Dayan, the merging of her teeth and his "ideas" results in a denouement in which Egaeus "quite literally" becomes Berenice. Whether those scattered, "irradiated objects become the remnants of an impossible purity . . . idols of a cold and perfect clarity," or Berenice's teeth, or "the resurrected remains of memory, . . . the real effect is that of unending transformation" (155). Another case of multiple choice?

Kenneth Silverman in his recent biography describes "Berenice" and "Morella" as "subtle psychological studies" of attempts to deal with the loss of loved ones through "avoidance and denial, told in eerie, disturbed tones by the traumatized survivors." Egaeus, the victim of his own lack of self-knowledge, wonders how "from beauty I have derived a type of unloveliness [unhappiness].'' More precisely, the reader might ask, is it not Egaeus's *lack of love* that causes the disintegration of Berenice, as also occurs in Henry James's ''The Beast in the Jungle''?

Jacqueline Doyle's ''(Dis)Figuring Women: Edgar Allan Poe's 'Berenice,' '' a long analytical critique, views the tale from a feminist perspective, arguing that ''Poe embodies a radical critique of the patriarchal poetic tradition . . . [especially] the disfiguring power of the rhetorical figures . . . which have enslaved the female body and silenced the female voice'' (13).

"MORELLA"

This tale appeared in the April number of the 1835 *SLM,* a month after ''Berenice.'' An extant manuscript copy, though incomplete, probably dates from late 1834 or early 1835, with a plot based on ''The Dead Daughter'' by Henry Glassford Bell. In December 1835, Poe referred to ''Morella'' as his best tale (*M* 2, 221–24). If written before ''Berenice,'' along with the other tales of women or psychic conflict, first importance should be attached to paragraph four, where the narrator's ''theological morality'' is defined in terms of two ''identities.'' One is ''the wild Pantheism of Fichte; the modified palingenesis [metempsychosis] of the Pythagoreans; and above all, doctrines of *Identity* as urged by Schelling, [which] were generally the points of discussion presenting the most of beauty to the imaginative Morella.'' The other identity is the rational consciousness of a person (as defined by Locke) that distinguishes him ''from other beings that think, and giving him his personal identity.'' The first is ''the *principium individuationis*—the notion of that identity *which at death is or is not lost forever,* was to me—at all times, a consideration of intense interest'' (226–27).

After an opening paragraph introducing the narrator-protagonist as a man of ''deep affection'' but one who did not speak of passion nor think of love, Morella is presented as a powerful intellect who acts as his guide in the study of German mystical literature. But when, ''poring over forbidden pages, I felt a forbidden spirit enkindling within me—would Morella place her cold hand upon my own, and rake up from the ashes of a dead philosophy some low, singular words, whose strange meaning burned themselves in upon my memory.'' After hours of listening to ''the music of her voice,'' he felt terrified at ''those too unearthly tones.'' Unable to respond to the ideal and mystical writings, he could no longer bear her wan fingers, low musical voice, and melancholy eyes—a weakness she called Fate. Were the psychic (psychal) insights and powers of these mystical writings a threat to his orderly, shallow, rational way of thinking, his ego-centered, loveless existence, his ''proper identity''—and therefore ''forbidden'' to him? Or were they forbidden by the church of that time? ''Yet was she woman, and pined away daily.'' Meeting her ''meaning eyes,'' he became giddy as if gazing into an ''unfathomable abyss.'' When he longed for her decease, he became furious over its delay as "her gentle life declined." Then one autumn evening, she said: "I am dying, yet shall I live . . . her whom in life thou didst abhor, in death thou shalt adore" (232). After her death, their daughter did, indeed, become the object of his fervent love—while still in her infancy, he had noticed "the wisdom or the passions of maturity . . . hourly gleaming from its full and speculative eye" (234).

More disturbing and even terrifying to him were other resemblances of daughter to mother: her smile, her eyes (looking down into his soul), her wan fingers, high forehead, ringlets, musical tones of speech, and expressions of the dead Morella. For two decades, she remained rigidly secluded and nameless, called "My child" and "My love" by her father. But at her baptism he involuntarily named her "Morella," at which she fell prostrate, crying out "I am here!"—evidence of her transmigrated soul. As his life darkened, he lived for Morella only—but she died, "and with my own hands I bore her to the tomb; and I laughed with a long and bitter laugh as I found no traces of the first, in the charnel where I laid the second—Morella" (236). Morella and her daughter seem to represent what Poe in "the world of mind" ("The Poetic Principle") termed "taste" or "poetic intellect." In contrast, the narrator stands for "the harsh mathematical reason," abstract knowledge or thinking, and the technical arts (technology). The resulting psychic conflict threatens our individuation and our humanizing fine arts in education, as described in "The Colloquy of Monos and Una" (1841). There, Poe put in a plea for "the sentiment of the natural" in order to abolish "the rectangular obscenities" of the "Art-scarred surface of the Earth."

Patrick Quinn identified metempsychosis as one of the themes Poe explored through "the life of a great ontological imagination" in a "voyage of the mind" (274). In "Morella," this theme is linked with Poe's conception of "death as a transmutation of life—'the painful metamorphosis' he called it" (273).

In the "Tales of Women," David Halliburton sees the main woman character as of superior erudition and powerful volition, "the woman displaying a volition that conquers time, the male representing a resistance that suffers defeat" (219). The psychic conflict occurs within an "ontological economy" of only two persons at one time; when her child is born, Morella dies, but she is "the one who is constant in change, the perfect continuous being [through] the force of her will, and her dominion over time" (221). With Morella's survival, the narrator becomes conscious of an absolute presence: "Morella has transcended the condition of womanhood; she is an incantation, a primal and timeless rhythm, a name: it is with the enunciation of Morella's name that each of the last three sentences ends . . . the articulation of sacred feeling . . . high and absolute purpose" (222–23).

G. T. Thompson, in *Poe's Fiction*, refuses to deal with either "Berenice" or "Morella" as serious tales. The former is dismissed as a lampoon of the tale of compulsion, in which the narrator suffers an "absurd obsession" with Berenice's teeth and has "become totally imbued with the Gothic horrors and weird philosophical (transcendental) mysticism of the day." In "Morella," "the major insinuated irony of the ostensibly supernatural . . . lies in the suggested madness of the narrator." In this reading, Thompson thinks that Poe provides motive and ambiguity enough to suggest that the narrator may have murdered his wife and daughter. But the only evidence for "corroboration of the [this] psychological reading" is a notorious case in Spain of a father charged with the homicide of his learned daughter, Juliana Morella (*M* 2, 168, 236, n. 5).

David Ketterer (1979) equates Morella with "the ideal arabesque state" as the narrator gazes into the abyss of her eyes, "the entire event, presumably, being symbolic of the meaningless distinction between life and death" (188).

Martin Bickman's earlier major essay in *Poe Studies* for December 1975 was ignored by Ketterer, although it had already shed new light on "Morella" ("Animatopoeia: Morella as Siren of the Self," reprinted in *The Unsounded Centre*, 58–78). Taking a Jungian approach, Bickman defines the conflict within the psyche between the conscious and the unconscious, subject and object, and so on, creating an imbalance or division in the "self." Later in life, the ego is to be reintegrated with the rest of the self, a process called "individuation." In the conclusion to *Eureka,* the identity of the One "tends to become, operationally at least, the unity of the entire psyche, the self. Poe stands at a crucial junction where metaphysics begins to turn into a phenomenology of consciousness . . . and where spiritual aspirations and eroticism are seen as expressions of the same movements of mind." According to Jung, the "anima or female soulmate represents both an urge to life and a secret knowledge or hidden wisdom, which contrasts most curiously with her irrational self in nature" (quoted, 29). When Morella (his anima) seeks union with the narrator's self, he is so unprepared for this ecstasy that the "unearthly tones" of her musical voice became "tainted with terror." To him, Morella's "wild tales and thrilling theories" were both exciting and terrifying. Morella is mainly interested in the transcendental "identity" of Fichte and Schelling whereas the narrator leans toward Locke's rationalistic philosophy. Although there is no place for reincarnation in these authors, the narrator focuses on the transmigration of souls after death— a release from the death–rebirth cycle into a merger with the One (30), as hinted in the epigraph of this tale. When the narrator looks into the mirror-eyes of the daughter Morella, he sees an "unfathomable abyss," that is, "the lost promise of an identity between the individual and the universe and between the ego and the self" (31). When Morella cries out, "I am here," his ego is so weak, he is unable to integrate, and his anima collapses into the unconscious in "a dark, perverse, regressive reflection of the luminous self-awareness that accompanies proper individuation . . . the psychic transformation" described symbolically in the next-to-last paragraph of "The Poetic Principle" (*H* 14; 290–91) and in the vision of the narrator's wife in "Ligeia" (e.g., the analogies of the growing vine). " 'Morella,' then, is a delineation of the very subtle but very real differences between creative mysticism and psychosis, between individuation and dissolution. . . . integral to this theme [of dissolution] is a complementary vision of psychic expansion of an extended and balanced soul that is at one with itself and the universe'' (32).

Joan Dayan in a chapter on "The Naming of Morella" (in *Fables of Mind*) again finds that Poe's rhetoric "engages one in a fierce seesaw motion between apparent opposites" (171): body or matter versus spirit or idealism. Poe is said not to be an essentialist, despite the violence of his language in a radical departure from surface Platonism. In his own words, "Abstractions may amuse and exercise, but take no hold on the mind. . . . The will may assent—the soul—the intellect never" ("Mesmeric Revelation," *M* 3, 1031). Poe's narrator is "literally undone by the 'idea' of woman," Dayan writes, as in "Morella," where he is haunted by a name, and "the name takes revenge on the namer" (171). In the baptismal rite, the name—in "a visible conversion *in process*—brings to life the bodily reincarnation of what the narrator had tried so hard to empty of its worldly weight" (172). The carnal reality has triumphed over the abstract Idea of woman. But, as Bickman and others have realized, the conflict here resolves into the theme of the psychal continuum and the power of psychic transformation, not mere bodily reincarnation.

"LIGEIA" (1838)

T. O. Mabbott (1978) calls "Ligeia" "a masterpiece of Poe's elaborate early style, surpassing the longer narratives written earlier, and to be surpassed, if at all, only by 'The Fall of the House of Usher.' " In a letter of January 8, 1846, Poe referred to it as "undoubtedly the best story I have written," and, on August 9, 1846, he wrote, " 'Ligeia' may be called my *best* tale." It was so carefully revised that, again in Mabbott's opinion, "it must be regarded as a thoroughly conscious and complete work of art." Some literal-minded readers had difficulty with the ending; and, in response, Poe conceded that "I should have intimated that the *will* did not perfect its intention—there should have been a relapse . . . and Ligeia . . . should be at length entombed as Rowena," adding that he would "suffer 'Ligeia' to remain as it is." However, when, in 1843, he inserted "The Conqueror Worm" into the text, he implied, in effect, that the human will could not conquer death (*M* 2, 306–7).

"Ligeia," the third of these three tales of psychic conflict, is a culmination of the quest theme in the two preceding stories in which the narrator's unloving possessiveness and rationalism block the capacity for love and the "sentiment of the natural." In each instance, the husband becomes the victim of his own failure of love and respect for his wife and suffers the bitter consequences of that failure. In "Morella" and "Ligeia," however, there is the further realization of a rebirth of psychal continuity and harmony, as symbolized in these tales.

Sarah Helen Whitman in *Edgar Poe and His Critics* (1860) praised "Ligeia" for its sumptuous imagery, rhythmical cadences, "weird metempsychosis," and "psychal attraction which transcends the dissolution of the mortal body and oversweeps the grave; the passionate soul of the departed transfusing itself through the organism of another to manifest its deathless love" (*CE*, 59).

George Bernard Shaw in 1909 singled out "Ligeia" as "unparalleled and unapproached. There is really nothing to be said about it: we others simply take off our hats and let Mr. Poe go first" (*CE*, 89).

D. H. Lawrence likens the narrator in "Ligeia" to a vampire of the mind, whose probing analysis left Ligeia passive with horror. Yet she lusted after "more beastly KNOWING"; thus she and Poe "sinned against the Holy Ghost that bids us all laugh and forget, bids us know our own limits. . . . It is a ghastly story of the assertion of the human will, the will-to-love and the will-to-consciousness, asserted against death itself. The pride of human conceit in KNOWLEDGE" (1923, 83, 85). "Ligeia," Lawrence holds, "is not a free person. She is just a phenomenon with which Poe strives in ill-omened love. . . . She is not a woman. She is just a re-agent, a reacting force, chimerical almost" (*CE* 1919, 93). She is consumed by inordinate love, unlike "creative love," in which "there is a recognition of each soul by the other. . . . But in Poe and Ligeia such balance is impossible. Each is possessed with the craving to search out and *know* the other, entirely; to know, to have, to possess, to be identified with the other. . . . And not until too late does she realise that such identification is death" (1919, 95). After Ligeia's death and the marriage to Rowena, his memory of Ligeia returned—"Ligeia, the beloved, the august, the entombed. I revelled in recollections of her purity," and so on. When Ligeia rises up from the corpse of Rowena and opens her eyes, Ligeia and the narrator are reunited. "Henceforth the two are one, and neither exists. They are consumed into an inscrutable oneness" (97).

Without any reference to Lawrence or Marie Bonaparte, who preceded them, two renowned Poe scholars, Margaret Alterton and Hardin Craig, published their superb Poe text-anthology, *Edgar Allan Poe: Representative Selections* (1935) for the American Writers Series. In its long Introduction, four pages (xciv–xcvii) are devoted to the theme, plot, and characterization in "Ligeia." Ligeia's luminous eyes, related to the circle of analogies, are seen as suggestive of "the cycle of life and death and life again" and of the transmigration theme in "Morella." After the marriage of the narrator to Rowena, "the canvas is crowded full with symbolic action and symbolic detail: the fantastic marriage chamber, the second wife's dress, the slight sounds in the lofty room," and so on. This is one of the earliest recognitions of Poe as a symbolic writer.

Roy B. Basler in "The Interpretation of 'Ligeia' " took issue with those earlier critics who ignored the contextual emphasis of the tale on "the hero's obsession, madness, and hallucination . . . entirely natural, though highly phrenetic, psychological phenomena." A. H. Quinn, for instance, "ignores the most obvious evidence of the nonrational theme and motivation of 'Ligeia,' preferring to see it as a tale of the supernatural." The narrator's "erotic obsession" leads to his "symbolic deification of Ligeia as a sort of personal Venus Aphrodite who personifies the dynamic urge of life itself but who, because of the hero's

psychic incapacity, cannot reveal to the narrator the 'forbidden knowledge' . . .
of the power and mystery of the entire universe'' (Kesterson, 85–87). To Basler,
the epigraph from Glanville expresses the narrator's, not Ligeia's, ''fierce obsession'' to conquer death. Up to her death, he has adored her ''in an erotomania
primarily sensual (though frustrated by a psychic flaw) and hence projected into
a symbolic realm of deity and forbidden wisdom.'' Following her death, however, his obsession becomes an intense megalomania motivated by his will to
restore her to life in another body through a process of metempsychosis. Mur-
dering Rowena in his intense longing for the beloved, beautiful, pure, ethereal
Ligeia, he imagines the actual poison to be ''three or four large drops of a
brilliant and ruby-colored liquid'' distilled from the atmosphere. As for the ending, Basler regards it as ''artistically perfect and unassailable if the story is
understood to be that of a megalomaniac, a revelation of obsessional psychology
and mania'' (92). Given the hero's obsession in the first half of the story and
his megalomania in the second half, to Basler, ''the concluding paragraph remains aesthetically as utterly incomprehensible to me as it was to Philip Pendleton Cooke, if the story is merely a story of the supernatural'' (95).

Clark Griffith in ''Poe's 'Ligeia' and the English Romantics'' proposed a
view of this tale as a satire and a burlesque. Because it was published in the
same year as ''How to Write a *Blackwood* Article'' and shortly after ''Silence,''
both of which Griffith regarded as satires of Transcendentalism, he concluded
that ''Ligeia'' also must be another such satire, despite the lack of evidence
other than its Gothic background, its lush prose, and ''its inarguable irony.''
Actually, only one-tenth of ''*Blackwood* Article'' deals with Transcendentalism,
and the verbal echoes of ''Silence'' fail to prove anything. To Griffith, the
narrator is a sly psychopath through whom Poe mocks Ligeia's spiritual depths
by the circle of analogies and other ''oddly incongruous details.'' Presumably
because this essay impressed only the ''irony'' critics, it received no mention
in Griffith's later piece on ''Poe and the Gothic'' (see later), which perceives
Poe's Gothic as ''genuinely new.''

James Schroeter's ''A Misreading of Poe's 'Ligeia' '' is easily the longest,
most analytical, and most systematic treatment of this tale, largely in reply to
Basler's argument of 1944 (see earlier) but also to the ''incomplete'' and ''misleading'' interpretations accumulated over the years. Those interpretations are
divided into (1) the older ones by Cooke, Woodberry, and Hamilton and (2) the
more recent readings by Lawrence, Bonaparte, Basler, and Griffith. (The absence
of Wilbur's name from this list indicates that his text introduction to Poe of
1962 [see later], with its inside essay on ''Ligeia,'' appeared too late for consideration by Schroeter either for its symbolic interpretation or its ''perspective''
approach.) All deny that the story is primarily about Ligeia and her triumph
over death, and all, according to Basler, assume that the story should be read
literally but that ''the statements in the story are merely symptoms of a deeply
buried meaning . . . , which must be reconstructed with the aid of facts and
theories drawn wholly from outside the story'' (392–93). All of the recent in-

terpretations are said to be "a peculiarly twentieth-century misreading of 'Ligeia,' but perhaps the most injurious is the one by Roy Basler . . . because it has been widespread and influential" since 1944 (see earlier). Basler's theory of the narrator as mad has "gone uncontested, been uncritically accepted, or been copied whole cloth," even though Basler regards it as "totally incompatible" with his "rational" view (398).

Schroeter's detailed analysis of Basler's interpretation cannot be adequately summarized in this space, but a close reading of Schroeter's critique will reward the reader with a better comprehension of the story from the contrasting perspectives of these critics as applied to the narrative action, the opening and closing scenes, the characters, especially the narrator and Ligeia, the choice of metaphors and names, the passage from Glanville, the Poe–Cooke correspondence, and so on, realizing that Schroeter had the great advantage of being able to attack Basler's published critique, whereas Basler had only his brief response published in *PMLA* for December 1962, page 675. In that brief rejoinder Basler objects to Schroeter's reference to "errors in fact and judgment," as if the word *fact* here could refer to anything but fiction. Similarly with Basler's theory of the narrator as mad: Basler notes that "beautiful, clear, and cogent sequences" have been known to follow. Differences on three other relatively minor matters are aired. Schroeter concludes the exchange with the view that the Glanville quotation is not the narrator's, as Basler claimed; only Ligeia, not the narrator, makes the idea work; to the narrator it remains " 'mysterious' and opaque."

In 1962, Richard Wilbur offered another textbook introduction to Poe in *Major Writers of America*. This essay is one of the most lucid, insightful, and integrated critiques of the time. Ten pages are devoted to "Ligeia" because, in Wilbur's view, the story is so central to Poe's thought, so characteristic of his method, and so much an index of his symbolism that it opens up the fiction in general. The typical Poe story is, in its action, an allegory of dream-experience; it occurs within the mind of a poet; the characters are not distinct personalities but principles or faculties of the poet's divided nature; the steps of the action correspond to the successive states of a mind moving into sleep; and the end of the action is the end of a dream (58). Therefore, the reader is likely to find the undercurrent of meaning in the symbolism of the hypnagogic dream state, that "condition of semi-consciousness in which the closed eye beholds a continuous procession of vivid and constantly changing forms . . . the visionary condition *par excellence.*" These "glimpses of the spirit's outer world . . . arise . . . where the confines of the waking world blend with those of the world of dream" ("The House of Poe," repr. *REAP*, 265). As an example, Wilbur offered this summary interpretation of "Ligeia": "The lady Ligeia, for example, stands for that heavenly beauty which the poet's soul desires; while Rowena stands for that earthly, physical beauty which tempts the poet's passions. The action of the story is the dreaming soul's gradual emancipation from earthly attachments—which is allegorically expressed in the slow dissolution of Rowena. The result of this process is the soul's final, momentary vision of the heavenly Ligeia" (*REAP*, 275).

Without labeling it as such, this process is clearly transcendental from beginning to end, both to Poe and to Wilbur.

Poe's use of indefinitiveness as an artistic device ("a definitiveness of vague and therefore of *spiritual effect*" in "Marginalia," December 1844) was, Wilbur wrote, to "estrange the reader from mundane fact and meaning, and presumably set him adrift toward the spiritual and dim . . . in 'Ligeia' it is sustained throughout by the narrator's uncertainties" (*Responses*, 5). Ligeia's musical voice is explained in terms of Milton's siren and the "music of things," and her eyes, which "delighted and appalled" the narrator, are made meaningful in the context of "the well of Democritus" in the epigraph to "The Descent into the Maelstrom" (*Responses*, 52–53). The narrator's retreat to the abbey, the decor of the bridal chamber, and his resort to opium are seen as ways of withdrawing from the temporal and physical and earthly until the volition of Ligeia and the narrator's "gazing" alters Rowena. Then Ligeia waxes as Rowena wanes. Under the golden chain of the censer—the purifying fire of imagination—Ligeia "at last reopens her profound eyes" (58).

Also in 1962, James W. Gargano took issue with Lawrence's "psychological assault on 'Ligeia,' " though accepting his treatment of the story as "a suggestive and symbolic complex" and not literally, as "an admittedly puerile and shabby Gothicism" (337–38). According to Gargano's reading, the hero escapes into an Ideal realm until his vision is eclipsed by the dismal abyss of reality, when he attempts to compensate for the loss of Ligeia through wild, ecstatic fantasies only to become disillusioned by them (symbolized by Rowena). Finally, he attempts to resurrect Ligeia, his dream ideal, who is appropriately vague, mysterious, strangely beautiful, and wildly passionate—"an apotheosis of the poetic vision. As he soars into a transcendent, mystical realm of the beautiful and the spiritual Ideal, the narrator experiences Ligeia as 'a huge metaphor for his romantic version of a Platonic heaven.' " Although all such visions are " 'through a psychal necessity, transient' " and of " 'a wisdom too divinely precious not to be forbidden!' " the narrator cannot admit that they are irrecoverable. Yet, he is forced "to descend from the peaks where eternal values immutably reign into a world that is fragmented, dreary, and mutable," where he is threatened with "incipient madness" (339). When the poetic or ideal world gradually reemerges, he wills more and more life into his vision of Ligeia ("passionate waking visions of Ligeia") until "symbolically, each wild meditation on Ligeia is an assertion of the narrator's [subconscious] desire and will." But Poe "knows only too well that the wages of protracted romantic self-indulgence are self-deception and ultimate madness" (341–42).

Donald Barlow Stauffer in his study of "Style and Meaning in 'Ligeia' and 'William Wilson' " analyzed these two tales in terms of their style as related to meaning and theme. The style of "Ligeia" is described as incantatory, especially the rhythm and sound effects of the opening paragraphs, which establish the tone of the entire narrative. The strong rhythmic pattern of the first sentence, for example, stands in marked contrast to the opening sentence of "The Man

Who Was Used Up.'' Other noticeable stylistic elements are parallelism, repetition, inversions, "the genitive of possession" (e.g., "the person of Ligeia"), and parenthetical constructions variously to create the mood or an archaic tone or to heighten "a sense of the mysterious, the irrational and the unreal." Later in the story, a more rational, measured style appears in the description of the English abbey; but as he comes closer to Ligeia in memory, the narrator's style is marked by inversions, repetitions, exclamations, questions, italics, dashes, capitals—largely "the language of emotional and dramatic involvement." Parenthetical expressions are "part of Poe's deliberate effort to give the narrator's emotions an air of verisimilitude . . . in a highly ordered, highly formal prose." "Ligeia," the most poetic of the tales, takes place in "Poe's mythical region of absolute unity of matter and spirit. . . . Like the words in Poe's poetry, the words in 'Ligeia' are symbolic. . . . Poe . . . is forced to use 'a circle of analogies' rather than direct statement." Hence, the exotic, archaic style is appropriate for the momentary suspension of rational faculties lulled by haunting, irrational melodies (120).

In 1966, John Lauber reacted against the continuing flood of symbolic readings in "A Plea for Literalism." He argued that "Ligeia" "makes perfect sense when read literally, and Poe gives no clear hint that it should be read otherwise."

Heedless of Lauber's plea, James M. Cox perceived Ligeia as a hallucinated aspect of the narrator's imagination in a

perverse disintegration of the psyche. Only by killing Lady Rowena, the blond and blue-eyed empty beauty . . . can the narrator resurrect his lost Ligeia. Through the disintegration of the Lady Rowena and the rank artifice of gothic machinery surrounding her, the fragile yet dark intensity of Ligeia is brought to life. This does not mean that Ligeia is the vital dark lady of mythical power and passion. . . . She is the repressed will, the diseased passion, lying beneath the sterile image of Rowena. . . . What the story marvelously succeeds in doing is to define the relation between the two empty traditions Poe inherited and burlesqued: the gothic world of vampires and the romantic world of maidens. (79–80)

Eric W. Carlson in "Poe's Vision of Man" and *Papers on Poe* applied the "philosophic perspective" approach of Allen Tate in "The Angelic Imagination" and of Richard Wilbur's (1959 and 1962). Poe's psychal transcendentalism was clearly set forth in several of his major essays: "Mesmeric Revelation," "Marginalia" essay 150 on "psychal fancies," *Eureka,* and "The Poetic Principle." In the "Marginalia" essay, Poe described his "sleep-waking" intuitions as "psychal impressions" (*P* 2, 257–59; *H* 16, 87–90; cf. Wilbur's "The House of Poe" on hypnagogic dreams). In a parallel study, Doris V. Falk described the power of animal magnetism in Poe's three mesmeric tales as "psychedelic," operating "within the mind as a unifying and illuminating force" (537).

"Ligeia" dramatizes the narrator's struggle to achieve such a peak experience through a shared study with Ligeia of "the many mysteries of the transcendentalism in which we were immersed,'' presumably, as in ''Morella,'' the writings of Fichte, Schelling, and other German idealists of the time. In ''The Colloquy of Monos and Una,'' Monos speaks of being ''born again,'' probably through knowledge gained from trances and other occult means rather than through orthodox faith. He says of ''born again'' that they are ''the words upon whose mystical meaning I had so long pondered, rejecting the explanation of the priesthood, until Death himself resolved for me the secret.'' In addition, there is the account of Poe's absolute refusal to retract the pure pantheism of *Eureka* despite the disapproval of the orthodox John Henry Hopkins, Jr., Mrs. Shew, and the spiritualist Sarah Helen Whitman (*PoeL,* 730–31, 745–46).

When, in the final scene, Ligeia is resurrected, the narrator is struck by the power of ''the full, and the black, and the wild eyes of my lost love,'' implying a reunion with the Ligeia of the ''luminous'' eyes. He has now, momentarily at least, become whole again, reintegrated with his psyche or anima, and with the Divine Will, ''the great will pervading all things by nature of its intentness.'' The search for, and sometimes the realization of, this psychotranscendent will became the central theme of Poe's writings. In 1972, Carlson's lecture ''Poe on the Soul of Man'' suggested the affinity of Poe's ontology with similar new ideas in the counterculture revolution of the 1960s, the humanistic or third force psychology of Abraham Maslow, the human potential movement, the women's liberation movement, and the new feminist psychology, ''possibly of first importance in understanding Poe's deep and mysterious women characters'' (4).

Clark Griffith in ''Poe and the Gothic'' contrasted the ''genuinely new Gothic'' of Poe's psychological tales with the traditional physical Gothicism of Walpole and Mrs. Radcliffe. In the word *Discovery* (in ''MS.''), Poe hinted at a new order of experience that marked the transition of the terrifying from ''the spectacle'' to ''the spectator or perceiving mind,'' as in, for example, the narrator in ''Berenice,'' ''Usher,'' and ''Ligeia'' (22–24). This new strategy ''operates as the means of discovering relevance, pattern, even a certain sort of beauty and ideality in objects which, left to themselves, would be 'essentially fixed and dead.' In their downward journeys Poe's characters are 'granted a kind of glory' . . . during a single transcendent moment . . . they have the privilege of calling up out of their very beings a totally new order of reality'' (25–26). Thus was the *new Gothic* confirmed.

G. R. Thompson in *Poe's Fiction* dealt at length with ''Ligeia'' but from an entirely different perspective, that of so-called Romantic Irony as he derived it from Tieck, the Schlegels, and other nineteenth-century German sources. This irony he regarded as characteristic of Poe's career as a satirist from beginning to end, claiming that ''the ironic mode and the ironic vision of the later tales . . . are implicit in the early satires . . . Poe exploited the terrors of the absurd as an ironically detached artist, exploring perverse human psychology in a perverse, absurd universe'' (67). ''Gothicist critics,'' as non-ironic critics were dubbed, were said to have viewed Poe as ''merely the schizophrenic genius of the demoniac imagination'' (7). In advocating ''a new way of reading Poe," however, Thompson begged the critical issue by holding that "[f]lat statements or commitments in Poe are only seeming . . . controlled by a prevailing duplicity or irony in which the artist presents us with slyly insinuated mockery of both ourselves as readers and himself as writer." Irony was nothing less than the device by which Poe faced his obsession with death, murder, and so on, and the fear of "total annihilation in a meaningless universe" as set forth in *Eureka* (7, 9), referred to as "Poe's most colossal hoax" (194).

Thompson defined Poe's technique in the Gothic tales as one of "deceptive tripleness" on the supernatural, the psychological, and the satiric-ironic levels; and if "the reader is deceived by a satiric and mocking Gothic tale, he is properly served" (77). Since direct evidence for the psychologically explained Gothic is "scanty," Thompson claims that Poe's exchange in 1839 with Philip P. Cooke regarding the ending of "Ligeia" is ambiguous: the original version included the supernaturalist event—"the hideous drama of revivification." But, one might add, whether the final scene ended too soon without Ligeia's relapse back to Rowena seems beside the point, the dramatic climax occurring (in Poe's words) "with a sudden half-consciousness, on the part of the narrator, that Ligeia stood before him." The ending works on the symbolic level; its meaning is prepared for by all that precedes. Supernatural or natural realism is secondary to the consistent pattern of intended meaning in the unfolding narrative, and that can be measured only by the baseline of Poe's perspective. In the heavily semi-Gothic and semi-Druidical decor of Rowena's funereal bridal chamber, Thompson sees only "obsessive delusion" and arabesque deceptiveness. The narrator's opium addiction, to induce trance realization of Ligeia, is attributed to "the delusive madness of the narrator" (92), an unfounded assumption. This pervasive assumption of satiric intent challenges the deeper understanding of the perspectivist approach, however intriguing the verbal parallels may be. "Poe's insinuated mockery of transcendentalism and mysticism" (of Coleridge, Swedenborg, and the New England transcendentalists) ignores the real psychic conflict between the rationalistic Lockean ego and the transcendental, deeply intuitive self of Schelling and Fichte, as revealed in "Morella."

David Halliburton's *Edgar Allan Poe: A Phenomenological View* (1973) was the first and only full-length study of Poe with a phenomenological approach. Paul Brodtkorb, Jr., had applied the same method to *Moby-Dick* in his 1965 study. This European methodology derives from Husserl, Sartre, Heidegger, and others. Halliburton's introductory chapter defines this approach as "standing open to the work, by taking what comes as it comes," identifying with the creating consciousness of the main or point-of-view character (27). The final, cosmic vision of *Eureka* is a positive affirmation that the universe is God, who, in turn, is immanent in man. *Eureka* is Poe's essay on the sublime, not a hoax on the gullible reader. As if in reply to the ironic-satiric critics, Halliburton issued this caution:

The hunt for concealed ironic messages has a way of leading the critic indefatigably on. . . . Raise the suspicion that the author is pulling your leg, and it becomes difficult to take him seriously at any time. No reader wants to seem a fool by missing the joke. . . . The temptation today . . . is to infer comic intention where it does not in fact exist. This attitude alienates the serious work from its own identity. (229–30)

The so-called Gothic tales, in keeping with Poe's work as a whole, are in the main serious, not comic or ironic.

In the second-paragraph description of Ligeia as "an airy and spirit-lifting vision," her chin is prominent in suggesting "the fullness and the spirituality of the Greek"; her large, brilliant black eyes radiate an unearthly beauty; these and other images are symbolic of her transcendental beauty and power of will, especially "the wild desire for life." To Halliburton, "the narrator does not seek possession for its own sake; he would possess in order to transcend" and "to watch the lady die is to watch her going back to the sources of life" (209). The bridal chamber, "the spatial complement of the narrator's consciousness," is the medium, both physical and mental, for seeing reality, the medium for "the struggle of dream and reality . . . of death and life" (211). In this primal conflict, Ligeia's powerful intelligence survives death in returning and taking over the body of Rowena (212–13). Halliburton seems to assume that the narrator's struggle is to call back the spirit of Rowena in his "passionate waking visions of Ligeia," in which "volition plays no role." This "perceptual struggle" is both psychological and rational and "supernatural and mystical, which sees in terms of a gradually overpowering reality [216]. . . . the indestructible identity of Ligeia, defeating death, has regained . . . the living person," recognizable by her energy, expansion, and vitality—"real life . . . of the insistent, eternal, confrontative female presence" in her "continuity of life and supremacy of will." In thus experiencing vicariously "the reality of transcendence woman has proved, through the force of her will, that life is everlasting" (218).

David Ketterer in *The Rationale of Deception,* a study of "arabesque" motifs and themes in Poe, identifies the arabesque designs in Lady Rowena's bridal chamber as similar almost point for point to the room in "The Visionary" ("The Assignation")—in its shape, tinted glass, golden chain and censer, and arabesque, phantasmagoric draperies. "The dimensions of time and space give way to a new dimension that will allow Ligeia's return from the dead. The room itself, properly perceived, is the means of her resurrection" (41). The conflict is as between "the arabesque ideal" (Ligeia) and "the mundane world" (Rowena); between the Glanvill epigraph on the will to live and death's finality ("The Conqueror Worm"). Ketterer agrees with Richard Wilbur that Ligeia and Rowena symbolize "the narrator's apprehension of the nature of reality," and, in further describing Ligeia's perception and studies, Poe's transcendental philosophy is acknowledged (190). Ketterer cites Basler as sensing that it's the narrator's, not Ligeia's [?], will to conquer death that motivates the story. Basler's error is carried over into a view of the bridal room as a death chamber where Rowena is supposedly poisoned by the narrator.

Maurice J. Bennett in *"The Madness of Art: Poe's 'Ligeia' as Metafiction"* (1981) cites some of his forerunners in the study of "the relation between Poe's metaphysics and the formal structures of his fiction": Tate, Wilbur, Molden-hauer, Carlson, E. Arthur Robinson, and others. The subtitle here is not used in a postmodernist context: Poe's "aesthetics and metaphysics successfully unite" as mental processes are dramatized in constant flux (5). These ideas are identified by judicious summaries from Poe's criticism: his belief in intuitive perception ('the sudden glancing at a star'), in the primary place of music or tone in poetry, in the transcendental level of realization ('elevating excitement of the soul,' Supernal Beauty), and in the "simplicities" of nature (stars, rivers, lakes, a woman's eyes, voice, love) as the "texture" of Poe's art. The epigraph Bennett reads as a metaphor of the triumph over death—"an escape into the ideal world of poetry" (3). Ligeia is not only a classical "goddess of harmony" but an embodiment of the spiritual and ideal. More specifically, the metaphors and images that surround her concretize her as a link to Poe's conception of poetry (3). "The narrator's madness should not be read . . . as literal derangement for which nearly all the tale's commentators have taken it" but as "the divine afflatus . . . a temporary madness"—the conventional romantic metaphor for "the exalted intensifications of consciousness" granted the poet (3–4). The "flux and reflux" of poetic inspiration is represented by Ligeia's entering and exiting from the narrator's chamber. Bennett's interpretation also convincingly deals with the marriage to Rowena, her chamber, his drug use, and the final scene of Ligeia's transformation.

Joan Dayan's twenty-page essay on "Ligeia" appeared in her *Fables*. Here, as elsewhere, her ironic perspective is evident in both the view that "Poe's hyperbolic praise for Cooke's theory of a final transition signals Poe's ironic intent" (175) as well as the sense that "the ending is really a perspectival anomaly" (189). "The transaction between Ligeia and Rowena is an episte-mological problem to be solved . . . in Ligeia's mock-heroic quest for knowledge through remembrance (178–79)." Ligeia's apparent triumph is turned on its head by "The Conqueror Worm." Though Dayan grants that, at the end, Lig-eia's "opening eyes could signal his [the narrator's] own awakening . . . an awakening that returns him to the identity that has swelled and shrivelled throughout the tale, the ending. . . . is really a perspectival anomaly. . . . Lady Ligeia's superb hair becomes a hag's removable wig" [!] (191).

Dayan ends on the positive suggestion that reading back to these tales from *Eureka* would enable them to be judged as convertible with the cosmos (192). How this is possible is far from clear if "Poe betrays the high cost of such tran-scendental realization through the narrator's madness and the lady's death" (135).

J. Gerald Kennedy's seventeen-page essay on "Poe, 'Ligeia,' and the Prob-lem of Dying Women" consists of a closely reasoned analysis of "Ligeia" as "the definitive projection of Poe's tortured thinking about women." With echoes of feminist and postmodern ideologies, Kennedy quotes Andre Breton on Woman idealized as "Truth, Beauty, Poetry—she is All: once more all under the form of the Other. All except herself" (232–37). But this reduction of Woman to an abstract Platonic Ideal omits the three-dimensional psychal conflict and transcendentalism in "Ligeia" and "Morella." Kennedy rightly emphasizes that "woman's love" was, for Poe, "the essential source for bliss, security, and life itself" and that the poems seem to "incarnate the idea—or ideal—of Woman," as in "Al Aaraaf," where Ligeia represents "the idea of musical (or poetic) creativity." In other poems, especially "For Annie," Poe celebrates the nurturing, protective, restorative, maternal power of woman's love. Kennedy quotes the passage on "the beauty of woman" in "The Poetic Principle" with its concluding reference to man's worshiping that beauty "in the faith, in the purity, in the strength, in the altogether divine majesty—of her love." Kennedy and other ironist critics, however, fail to note that, in this context, "the beauty of woman" is more than an empty abstraction—whether of Truth, Beauty, or Poetry—and more than the theme of "death and beauty" that some feminist critics insistently invoke. Poe's use of the term *beautiful*, it should also be noted, is in keeping with Webster's definition: "*beautiful*, the most comprehensive, applies to what stirs a heightened response of the senses and of the mind on its highest level." As an example of this meaning, Webster might have quoted Poe's famous dictum that "the death of a beautiful woman is, unquestionably, the most poetical topic in the world." Poe hints at this meaning in summing up Ligeia's beauty as *spiritual* and like *the spirituality of the Greek*. Kennedy contends that the narrator's idealization of Woman is based on dependency: "Within this neurotic paradigm, the absolute power of Woman (who in 'Ligeia' represents beauty, learning, and will) is the inverse effect of the male's utter helplessness." But to claim that this helplessness leads to outrage and violence against women throughout Poe's fiction is to miss the desperate *inner* desire of the male ego for a recovery of *love-will-spirituality* as symbolized by the Ligeia self. Kennedy calls up biographical support from the death of Elizabeth Poe, Frances Allan, Virginia Poe and from Poe's search for love among his lady friends (Shew, Ellet, Osgood, Shelton, Richmond, Whitman) as real life parallels to the women in the fiction. Kennedy also recognizes the "symbolic opposition" between "the raven-haired mystical Ligeia" and "the blonde, Anglo-Saxon Rowena," with Ligeia further characterized as of an "essentially poetic nature . . . and an incomparable loveliness . . . and an indefinable expression which brings to mind transcendental analogies resembling poetic metaphors" (120). The death of Ligeia leads to "a psychic crisis," and, in "a moment of mental alienation," the narrator marries Rowena, whom he soon comes to loathe and hate in his longing for Ligeia. "Rowena remains a nonentity," says Kennedy. After her death, the narrator gazes on Rowena's body with "a bosom full of bitter thoughts of the one only and supremely beloved!" Through the charged moment of transformation, the hated Rowena becomes the beautiful and beloved Other, fusing the two wives into "a beautiful undying woman." Kennedy undercuts these affirmative conclusions, however, by crediting the transformation to "the mechanism of dependency-desolation-retribution" alone, instead of to the positive, dynamic power of Ligeia's will.

WORKS CITED

Alterton, Margaret, and Hardin Craig. *Edgar Allan Poe: Representative Selections.* New York: American Book Co., 1935.

Basler, Roy B. "The Interpretation of 'Ligeia.' " *College English* 5 (April 1944): 363–73.

Bickman, Martin. "Animatopoeia: Morella as a Siren of the Self." *PoeS* 8 (December 1975).

Carlson, Eric W. "Poe's Vision of Man" (MLA 1969 and *Papers on Poe,* 1972). Carlson's 1972 lecture "Poe on the Soul of Man" (Baltimore, 1973).

Cox, James M. "Edgar Poe: Style as Pose." *Virginia Quarterly Review* 44 (Winter 1968): 67–89.

Doyle, Jacqueline. "(Dis)Figuring Women: Edgar Allan Poe's 'Berenice.' " *PoeS* 26, nos. 1, 2 (June–Dec. 1993).

Gargano, James W. "Poe's 'Ligeia': Dream and Destruction." *College English* 23 (Feb. 1962): 337–42.

Griffith, Clark. "Poe's 'Ligeia' and the English Romantics." *University of Toronto Quarterly* 14 (Oct. 1954): 8–25.

———. "Poe and the Gothic" in Veler, ed., *Papers on Poe* (1972).

Halliburton, David. *Edgar Allan Poe: A Phenomenological View.* Princeton: Princeton UP, 1973.

Irwin, John. *The Mystery to a Solution . . .* Baltimore: Johns Hopkins UP, 1994, Chaps. 24, 25.

Kennedy, J. Gerald. "Poe, 'Ligeia,' and the Problem of Dying Women." In Kenneth Silverman, ed., *New Essays on Poe's Major Tales,* 1993.

Lauber, John. " 'Ligeia' and Its Critics: A Plea for Literalism." *Studies in Short Fiction* 4 (Fall 1966): 28–32.

Phillips, Elizabeth. "Mere Household Events: The Metaphysics of Mania" in *Poe: An American Imagination.* Port Washington, NY: Kennikat P, 1979.

Schroeter, James. "A Misreading of Poe's 'Ligeia.' " *PMLA* 76 (Sept. 1961): 397–406.

Stauffer, Donald Barlow. "Style and Meaning in 'Ligeia' and 'William Wilson.' " *Studies in Short Fiction* 2 (1965): 316–20.

Wilbur, Richard. "Edgar Allan Poe." In *Major Writers of America,* 1962. Vol 1. Repr. in *Responses,* 1976.

———. "The House of Poe." *The Recognition of Edgar Allan Poe.* Ed. Carlson.

The Works of Edgar Allan Poe. Ed. E. C. Stedman and G. E. Woodberry. Definitive Edition of 1894–1895. Chicago: Stone and Kimball, 1903. Scribner's, 1914.

Zanger, Jules. "Poe's 'Berenice': Philosophical Fantasy and Its Pitfalls." In *The Scope of the Fantastic . . .* Ed. Robert A. Collins and Howard D. Pearce. Westport, CT: Greenwood P, 1985, 135–42.

Ziolkowski, Theodore. "The Telltale Teeth: Psychodontia to Sociodontia." *PMLA* 91 (Jan. 1976): 9–22.

9

Tales of Psychal Conflict: "William Wilson" and "The Fall of the House of Usher"

ERIC W. CARLSON

"WILLIAM WILSON"

This psychological tale of conscience, of the avenging moral Double, has been a favorite of young and old, general readers and specialists alike. Silverman notes that "its complex delineation of Wilson's habits of thought . . . Thomas Mann admiringly compared to the 'psychological lyricism' of Dostoyevsky" (150). Edward Davidson in his *Poe: A Critical Study* sees William Wilson as "the clever man of the world who, however, in order to succeed in the world, must destroy an essential part of himself, his soul or spirit" (199). With only his mind as a guide, he is immune to society. religion, and moral principle; the second Wilson is "not really a moral conscience, but is merely another being in the moral wilderness of Wilson's life . . . in a world wherein the only criterion is success" (199).

Donald Barlow Stauffer in "Style and Meaning in 'Ligeia' and 'William Wilson' " identified the close, functional relationship of style to meaning in the second of these tales. Told rationally and logically, its style is "highly ordered, marked by connectives and transitional elements, balanced and periodic sentences, a relatively high level of abstraction, little concrete imagery . . . , few vivid adjectives, and a precision of diction." The dominant eighteenth-century *ordonnance* quality is reinforced by parallelism, a measured rhythm, abstract diction, long sentences—all in all, a formal, measured, yet leisurely neoclassical style (324). Exceptions are the first and last paragraphs, the first being marked by an oratorical style heightened by rhetorical questions, apostrophes, inversions, repetitions, dashes, and archaic diction. The closing paragraphs alternate between the incantatory and the rational, with the last paragraph ending in the strong moral tone of *"You have conquered, and I yield. Yet henceforward art thou also dead . . . in my death, see by this image, which is thine own, how utterly thou hast murdered thyself"* (324–25, 328–29).

James W. Gargano in *New Approaches to Poe,* focused on "Art and Irony in 'William Wilson.' " The confused narrator is seen as so perversely blind to his own motivations as he relates the story of his life—fleeing from his namesake, the "estranged part of himself"—that he becomes a victim of "self-deception and self-destruction." He becomes, archetypically, another example of psychic conflict: of man's quarrel with "a potential ally and a sure source of strength." In externalizing this inner self as the villain, he resorts to acts of self-humiliation and self-torture ending in suicide. Before the climax, Wilson's moral dilemma and decline are traced through the symbolic use of light and darkness in the dormitory room and at Oxford as well as in the description of the schoolmaster and the "architectural nightmare" of the academy building with all its irregularities and subdivisions. Added to these is the carnival in Rome, where the masked characters suggest hidden intentions in a psychological masquerade. In conclusion, Poe showed that "once his protagonist has abdicated his kinship to his namesake, his life becomes a never-ending masquerade of motive and identity . . . the culminating symbol in the tale is a 'mirror' in which Wilson sees the murdered masquerader as, simultaneously, a separate identity and himself" (22).

G. R. Thompson in his *Poe's Fiction* echoes Gargano in describing this tale as "a dramatization of the ultimate perversity of self-vexation and destruction," with the mirror taken as "a symbol of the illusory nothingness on the other side of appearances." Thompson seems caught between reading the tale as a "man's confrontation, supernaturally, with his own soul" and "the delusive but perversely persistent confrontation of a guilt-ridden mind with itself," the narrator remaining ambiguous (170).

David Halliburton's phenomenological reading, published in the same year (1973), derives from Poe's affirmative philosophy of the potential Self dramatized by his "great ontological imagination" (*PQ,* quoted, 305). The story is the guilt-ridden narrator's confession of willful evil actions that he attributes to an external *fatality* beyond his control. Another powerful force is the old school building, with its innumerable lateral branches suggestive of Poe's belief in man's limited capacity to know. The third "mediator of the beyond" is the second Wilson "bringing to mind dim visions of my earliest infancy . . . at some epoch very long ago." In "refusing to face the incriminating gaze of the other," Wilson I rejects the potential for the good and the godly in himself (300–303). Here, Halliburton translates the psychomoral narrative into an inner monologue of the first Wilson's struggles with guilt and a growing sense of "the gaze of the others as it is refracted not only in the gaze of the second Wilson, but in my own. . . . My guilt is internalized social rejection" (303). His guilt is compounded by his failure to recognize, to remember, and to comprehend his confrontations, occurring in symbolic dimness or darkness. "When William Wilson's moment of recognition finally comes, it comes through a *combination* of the improbable, the circumstantial, and the psychological." When he sees the mirrored "reality" of the other, then he sees the reality of himself. "In seeing the truth of his being embodied in another—he ceases to exist" (308).

Eric W. Carlson (" 'William Wilson': The Double as Primal Self") defined the psychic conflict as one between a shadow self and a decadent public personality. The unfolding spiritual autobiography is developed by symbolic representations of the harsh, suppressive system in school and community and the gradual revelations of the nature of Wilson II as the potential for moral decency in Wilson I. This alter ego turns out to be an acquaintance from "some epoch very long ago—some point of the past even infinitely remote" (37)—similar to the vague memory of the narrator's platonic preexistence in "Usher" and "Ligeia" (see Bickman in previous chapter). In keeping with the subliminal nature of these dim visions, they occur in darkness or semidarkness. At the end, Wilson I, still blind to his self-deception, clings to the idea of some "fatality" of circumstance, some "wildest of all sublunary visions" as the cause of his moral destruction. But the perceptive reader senses that Wilson's Double represents the potential for harmony of Intellect, Taste, and Moral Sense in the "world of mind," as Poe defined it (40).

Thomas Joswick, in a twenty-five-page essay titled "Who's Master in the House of Poe? A Reading of 'William Wilson,' " applies the ironic illusion of Wilson's mastery to the reader. The "reserved irony of the tale, if brought forward, could make for a disturbing question: what if Poe's story is really about how a reader's linguistic mastery of ethical tales such as this one signifies his own ethical dilemma?" (227). First, one must determine exactly what Wilson's failure was. Worse than his lack of conscience is "the egotism at the heart of his snobbery," as shown by his disgust over his "very common" name. This self-will replaces the social will, and, with it, he mimics lawful authority. In this drama of psychal conflict, there is "a complex plotting of antagonistic forces . . . dramatic images for life [that] suggest a lurking necessity under the appearances of things" (233). The truth of Wilson's divided self escapes him, though it obtains in the world at large as "the straightforward opposition between snobbish egotism and conscientious regard for others" (234). As social will, the latter is represented by the rigid social controls at the academy, symbolized by its very exterior (high brick wall, a gate with jagged iron spikes, and so on) and by the "terror-inspiring" Dr. Bransby and his *sanctum.* Realizing the hypocritical doubleness of social will thus embodied, Wilson senses that he is at the mercy of its official language—"the 'arbitrary dictation' that systematizes the conventions of ethical terms and oppositions." In Part 2, Joswick compares Poe's story with Paul's letter (to the early Christian church at Rome) "with its brilliant insights into the ethical language and situations required to bring the 'law of sin' out of hiding." "William Wilson" offers a perspective on how this law of sin abides in systemized ethical conventions and complicity: Poe's little story, conning us into a sense of mastery of it, "might in the end be Poe's own lesson about lim-

its—the difference between the mastery of a language and the misery of a life
... isn't that difference what we'd like to say is exactly what all of Poe's
writing is about?'' Maybe our mastery of ethical conventions is no greater
than Wilson's in our desire for '' 'some little oasis of *fatality* in this wilderness of error' '' (245, 247).

"THE FALL OF THE HOUSE OF USHER"

This tale is the best known and most popular of Poe's if only because most
often anthologized since 1847, when Griswold chose it for his *Prose Writers of
America*. To Poe, it was one of his ''best tales'' (nine in all), along with ''Ligeia'' and ''William Wilson.'' Its popularity has been matched by countless academic essays and critical studies, including several collections. Thomas
Woodson, the editor of one such collection (1969), points out that ''no work of
Poe's has so haunted later artists and readers. It led Debussy to attempt the
musical setting of 'a symphony on psychologically developed themes,' and later
an opera, which obsessed him for years, but was never accomplished'' (3). One
of the most recent is the radio opera by Philip Glass performed by the American
Repertory Theatre on October 29, 1988, in Cambridge, Massachusetts. The
opera calls for three singing parts and a twelve-piece orchestra, as well as dialogue and dream sequences. Effective use of the musical score runs through two
acts of five scenes each. Jean Epstein's silent film in 1928 and Roger Corman's
technicolor version in 1960 were attempts to translate the story into images,
with limited success. Roderick Usher's paintings have been likened by Paul
Ramsey to modern abstract art, especially their ''strange invention . . . uncanny
illumination, and foreshadowing'' (Woodson, 3).

In the abstracts that follow, a certain sameness or repetition of motifs is
apparent, giving support to a degree of consensus regarding theme, character,
symbolism, narrative point of view, and so on, often with fine distinctions.
Beyond this consensus, the reader will find some marked differences in critical
approach and interpretation, which add to the flavor.

As with ''Ligeia'' D. H. Lawrence in 1919 and 1923 offered a bold, original,
psychosexual reading of ''Usher,'' probably the first to see the Roderick–
Madeline relationship as an incestuous one that causes Roderick to suffer a
breakdown of ''the true centrality'' of his self, leaving him oversensitive to
sounds and effects in an extreme ''vibration of inorganic consciousness'' (1923,
88). In their exclusive passion, Roderick ''devours'' his sister until she dies.
''He knew his love had killed her . . . [but] unwilling and unappeased she rose
once again'' and 'fell heavily inward' upon him in a final death-embrace.
Lawrence sums it up as ''lurid and melodramatic but true . . . a ghastly psychological truth . . . the Ushers betrayed the Holy Ghost in themselves. They would
love, love, love, without resistance . . . they would be as one thing . . . the Holy
Ghost says you must *not* be as one thing with another being. Each must abide
by itself, and correspond only within certain limits.'' The Holy Ghost is many

gods inside us, gods who come and go. Poe was doomed: "[H]e died wanting more love, and love killed him. A ghastly disease, love. . . . He told us plainly how it was, so that we should know" (1923, 89, 91–92). From Lawrence's essay to 1949, there were few notable Poe studies of this tale. Marie Bonaparte in her psychoanalytic study of Poe applied an extremely Freudian interpretation to the tales, as, for example, in this passage:

> [T]he deeper meaning of this sinister tale lies in the fate of Usher. Poe is *punished* for having betrayed his mother in loving Madeline–Virginia. Usher–Poe is *punished* for not having dared to seek and rewin his babyhood mother when, like Annabel Lee, men bore her away, and also for his silence and acceptance, in his childish incomprehension of death. Usher–Poe is *punished* for his sadism, as shown in the way Usher treated his sister. Finally, Usher–Poe is *punished* for his infantile incestuous wishes toward his mother, as witness all the quotations from the *Mad Trist* . . . the dragon, symbol of the father, is killed and the mother set free to belong to the victorious son. (240)

This heavy-handed psychoanalyzing left most Poe readers entirely unconvinced and engendered a devastating exposé of its fallacious assumptions and weak analysis (see Roger Forclaz, in *CE,* 187–95).

Darrel Abel, one of the first analytic critics in this century, led the way with "A Key to the House of Usher," revealing the subtlety of Poe's art as an anticipation of Kafka without the latter's obscurities. To Abel, the setting served to suggest a receptive mood and to supply details suggestive of decadence and remoteness: the house with its ominous crack and setting (tarn, vapor, "evil sedges," and fungi) reflected Usher's "distempered ideality." Usher himself suffered from hypochondria, introverted vitality, isolation, hyperacuity of the senses, morbid fears, and finally a collapse into madness. Madeline, his twin, intensified his isolation. A psychic conflict between Life-Reason (the "heavenly, organic, harmonious" qualities) and Death-Madness raged for the possession of Roderick, as depicted also in "The Haunted Palace." Roderick's tragedy was due not only to his fatal introversion but to his ineffectual and late summoning of his friend. When he shrieks, "Madman!" he has crossed the line into insanity, after which he is carried down by the collapse of the house. Throughout, this tale operates by "parallel symbolic suggestions . . . alternative explanations, nat- ural and supernatural, of the phenomena set forth" and by "a common-sense witness gradually convinced in spite of his determined scepticism, to accept imaginatively the supernatural explanation. The tale is a consummate psycho- logical allegory . . . its method is so concealed that the too casual reader may take the impressions to be meretricious" (185).

Allen Tate's "Our Cousin, Mr. Poe" appeared at the end of 1949. In it, Tate accepted Lawrence's incest theme as both literal and symbolic:

> The American case against Poe, until the first World War, rested upon his moral indifference, or his limited moral range. The range is limited, but there is no indifference;

there is rather a compulsive, even a profound, interest in a moral problem of universal concern. His contemporaries could see in the love stories neither the incestuous theme nor what it meant, because it was not represented literally. The theme and its meaning as I see them are unmistakable: the symbolic compulsion that drives through, and beyond, physical incest moves towards the extinction of the beloved's will in complete possession, not of her body, but of her being; there is the reciprocal force, returning upon the lover, of self-destruction. Lawrence shrewdly perceived the significance of Poe's obsession with incestuous love. (Carlson casebook, 44)

When Roderick thinks Madeline has died from his possessing her inner being and puts her into the "tomb," she resists his hypertrophied will and returns in "the unquiet spirit" of a vampire (not the Bram Stoker variety). Her *will to know* has reciprocated on the inner being of her brother: "[T]hey must achieve spiritual identity in mutual destruction," and, together with the house, "the central dramatic situation moves toward spiritual unity through disintegration" (casebook, 47), paralleling the thesis of "annihilation" in *Eureka*. In the history of the moral imagination in his century, Tate concludes, "Poe occupies a special place. No other writer in England or the United States, or, so far as I know, in France, went so far as Poe in his vision of dehumanized man" (47). In a brief sequel to this article, Tate and Gordon called Poe an artist in "insight symbolism" and summed up Usher as the prototype of the Joycean and Jamesian hero in his "hypertrophy of sensibility and intellect in a split personality" (repr. in Carlson casebook, 48–49).

Leo Spitzer's "A Reinterpretation of 'The Fall of the House of Usher' " replied to Cleanth Brooks and Robert Penn Warren's treatment of this tale in their *Understanding Fiction*. They viewed it as inducing "nightmare" and "horror for its own sake" and for lacking "tragic quality, even pathos." The protagonist, they held, is wanting in both free will and rational decision, and his sister in a struggle against her doom. The sense of gloom is "played up" excessively because of Poe's "own morbid interest in the story" (a clear case of a biographical reading by these two New Critics) (351, repr. in Carlson casebook, 56). Actually, Poe's "attitude of doomedness," Spitzer noted, "was at the time a new step forward in the psychological study of hitherto neglected recesses and arcana of the human mind" (57).

In his response, Spitzer followed the line of thought already established by Lawrence, Abel, and Tate, enriched by his own depth of analysis and original insights. Madeline was seen as "the true male and last hero of the House of Usher" (353, repr. in Carlson casebook, 58). She resists the curse of the incestuous, sterile love of the last of the Ushers. She personifies the will-to-live, life-in-death, in contrast to the passive Roderick, representative of death-in-life, the death wish. The narrator's function is to make real Usher's fear, his consciousness of fear itself, and his premature anticipation of terrible events, especially Madeline's and his own death. Out of fear of his approaching death, he buries his sister in hysterical haste. Given his schizoid condition, in which nerves and intellect act separately, Usher is reduced to pure sentience, without the power of reason, and to ''pure abstraction'' as in his painting, enforced by the black-white pattern of the floors, the draperies, and the effect of ''the *physique* of the gray walls . . . upon the *morale* of his existence'' (58–63). This latter aspect of ''atmosphere'' Spitzer developed into a five-page inside essay in which he drew upon his knowledge of linguistics, comparative literature, and the history of ideas. He traces the term *atmosphere* to seventeenth- and eighteenth-century concepts of vapor or air exhaled from the body of a planet or a part of it and then extended to be in the planet's sphere of influence and later the sphere within which the attractive magnetic or electric force acts (cf. Faraday's ''field''). Meta-phorically, in English, 1797–1830, it came to mean the '' 'surrounding mental or moral element, environment' '' and '' 'an extensive atmosphere of conscious-ness.' '' Spitzer: ''I would surmise that Poe's concentration on the *visible* aspect of 'atmosphere' is his peculiar contribution,'' and ''It is my conviction that we cannot understand the achievement of Poe unless we place his concept of 'atmo-sphere' within the framework of ideas concerning *milieu* and *ambiance* which were being formulated at his time. . . . The theory of the time was that the or-ganic being must be explained by the environment just as the environment bears the imprint of this being.'' Thus, with Poe ''atmosphere'' is ''the perceptible manifestation of the sum total of the physical, mental, and moral features of a particular environment and of the interaction of these features'' (359; casebook, 64–65). In his conclusion, Spitzer remarks, ''Our critics [Brooks and Warren] are wrong in reading Poe only 'emotionally,' not 'conceptually' '' (362; case-book, 68).

Maurice Beebe in ''The Universe of Roderick Usher'' took a hint from Allen Tate that because ''Poe's symbols refer to a known tradition of thought, an intelligible order in *Eureka,* we are justified in trying to interpret Poe's fiction in the light of his cosmology. . . . Both [''Usher'' and *Eureka*] are built on a structural and thematic pattern of unity-radiation-diffusion-return to unity'' (147). It might be said that the 1839 tale anticipated the 1848 essay. Beebe then proceeds to identify through detailed correlations of the two texts how *Eureka* clears up ambiguities in ''Usher'' (148). The cosmology, for instance, is closely analogous to Poe's theory of the short story: the preestablished design of the tale and the universe as a plot of God; the cosmic process of radiation and expansion likened to plot development with each element related to every other; the analogy between the line of cosmic diffusion and the Usher House atmo-sphere of gloom; the tarn as ''the oneness or nothingness from which all has emerged and to which all must return''; the fissure as ''the diffusion split be-tween Roderick and Madeline''; and so on with the painting, the vault, Roderick, Madeline, and others.

Roderick's action is the peak of the self-diffusion, the beginning of a return to a concentrated oneness . . . by burying his sister alive, he tries to stop the diffusion . . . the diffusion has been carried to the point of self-annihilation . . . the diffused particles re-main and begin their return upon him. . . . The last sentence suggests a return to the original unity: "the deep and dank tarn at my feet closed sullenly and silently over the fragments of the House of Usher." (158–60)

Patrick Quinn, one of our finest Poe scholars and critics over the past forty years or more, best known for *The French Face of Edgar Poe,* devoted a chapter to "Usher" under the title "That Spectre in My Path." The narrator is identified as having a curious kinship with Usher—a boyhood companionship—and as providing the point of view for the reader, though failing to see beyond appearances. The visible realities are only clues to the inner forces engaged in a "fatal conflict." The terrifying image reflected in the tarn suggests that "the evil influences operative in the story derive from the recesses of Usher's mind" (240; casebook, 77). The images of sterility and rankness in the first part of the story are "emblematic of the family line of the Ushers." Similarly with the motif of "radiance" in the poem, the painting, the vault, and "the faintly luminous gaseous exhalation which hung about and surrounded the mansion." This unnatural atmosphere becomes "finally redolent of moral corruption" followed by the premature burial of Madeline, an act that "in intention if not in deed was incestuous" and indicative of the split personality (241–44; casebook, 78–79). Here, as a reversal of "William Wilson," the warfare within Roderick is "waged by his consciousness against the evil of his unconscious" as he tries to dispose of "an integral part of himself." But his malady has gone too far, as shown by his ghastly pallor and lost luminosity of eye as he vainly tries to dispose of his counterpart self (245–46; casebook, 80–81).

Edward H. Davidson, author of *Poe: A Critical Study,* begins with a summary of what he calls Poe's "moral cosmology," in which "pain is the basis for life, and death is the only release from the grotesque condition of 'perversity.' . . . The universal metaphysic is tripartite: body, mind, and soul. Every element and form in the cosmos . . . is constituted so that it has three separate organisms and functions . . . intricately interrelated" (193–94; casebook, 83). This tripartite conception was derived from Andrew Combe, Spurzheim, and Horace Binney Wallace. The mind, the only link between the body and the soul, mediates between them. The external house, then, is like the body; the dark tarn mirrors the mind. In the psychic drama, Usher represents the mind or intellect, now diseased, too long separated from the physical or sensual side (twin sister). The tale depicts "the total disintegration of a complex human being." When Madeline returns from the coffin to embrace her brother, body and mind are reunited in death. Thus, through the pictorial method, Poe makes "the physical world of nature experience the drama more intensely than can any human being" (195–98; casebook, 84–86). More intensely, perhaps, but not more intensively in the way demonstrated by Abel and Spitzer. Furthermore, Davidson overlooks Poe's own tripartite "world of mind" divided into the faculties of Intellect, Taste, and Moral Sense, as set forth in "The Poetic Principle"—a better clue to the allegorical intention in this tale.

Richard Wilbur, in "The House of Poe," (1959; repr. in *REAP,* 1966) introduced his hypnagogic dream interpretation of Poe's allegorical tales of psychic conflict, with ''The Fall of the House of Usher'' as his primary example. In these psychodramas, ''certain scenic or situational motifs'' recur, especially *enclosure* or *circumscription.* William Wilson ''seems never to set foot out-of-doors,'' and Roderick Usher has not for many years ventured forth from his mansion, which is isolated by a stagnant lake and a large barren tract—suggestive of the isolation of the poetic mind in a visionary state (260–61). After an analysis of ''The Haunted Palace'' as symbolizing the effect on the poetic soul of the corrupting forces of the external world, Wilbur turns to the ''Usher'' story, in which he equates the house with the body of Roderick and its dim interior with his visionary mind. The narrator's journey is understood as a dream toward his inner and spiritual self, Roderick Usher, whom the narrator reaches by way of reverie or dream representing the hypnagogic state, ''the visionary condition *par excellence''* (264–66). Usher's improvisations on the guitar—rapid, wild, novel—imply hypnagogic experience, and his abstract paintings ''quite simply *are* hypnagogic images.'' Usher's library of books from all times and tongues is another ''concrete symbol of the timelessness and placelessness of the dreaming mind.'' The decayed condition of the house signifies that the narrator ''has very nearly dreamt himself free of his physical body and of the material world.'' At the end, when the house disintegrates, it is because Roderick has become ''all soul . . . it *is* possible for the poetic soul to shake off this temporal, rational, physical world and escape, if only for a moment, to a realm of unfettered vision'' (267). But to read the story in a psychomoral context, as most do, not as a conflict of poet and the world, leads to different meanings and conclusions, as, for instance, when Madeline is seen as representing the Moral Sense in Poe's faculty psychology, rather than physical Beauty. Wilbur's view that the final paragraph implies a plunge into subliminal madness and also ''a foreview of the soul's reconstitution and purification in death'' recognizes the ending to be both negative and positive (''Introduction,'' 26–28). But can it be both?

By far the most objective and detailed analysis of ''Usher'' was E. Arthur Robinson's ''Order and Sentience in 'The Fall of the House of Usher.' '' In over 10,000 words, Robinson continued A. H. Quinn's study of the structure, form, recurrent ideas, character relationships, rigorous pattern of thought and thematic development, and rational elements. An early footnote reveals his familiarity with Auden, Beebe, Davidson, Abel, Krutch, and the subconscious, the arabesque, and the phantasmagoric. The house and landscape, for example, involve the supporting concept of ''sentience,'' an unusual but key idea perceptible as atmosphere (cf. Spitzer, earlier), giving rise to a psychic conflict between Roderick and the ''living quality of the house'' (70–71). The second line of action is the physical deterioration of Roderick Usher, his image in ''The Haunted Palace,'' his intensified physical senses, and ''certain parallels between Poe's philosophic writing and Usher's psychological being.'' As these are more or less familiar to readers of this chapter, there is no need to restate them here.

In the fourth line, however, the theme of sentience links "Usher" with *Eureka,* that is, identity with God through the "diffused Matter and Spirit of the Universe" (*H* 9; 164–68). This view is posited on "a cyclic and recurring creation," an expanding universe, each creature within the universe in ordered relationship to it. With increased heterogeneity comes Conscious Intelligence, and with intensified "sentience" the organic system rushes to its End. Usher's is "the story of man's fall, and any emergence into a newly self-creative, expansive existence is left unexpressed" (71–74). On the symbolic level, Robinson accepts Davidson's view of the tale as "a profound inner drama," Roderick representing the intellectual aspect of man, and Madeline the physical (which is not an accurate application of the three-part "world of mind"). Of the Freudian approach and the incest theory, Robinson says "there is little outright evidence of this sort of thing," only mysterious allusions to "evil things" and "pestilent" vapour and "want of moral energy." The sexual element seems secondary compared to "the excessive cultivation and individuation" of Usher's powers. (To Patrick Quinn, Madeline does not symbolize incestuous desire but the "dark, under side" or unconscious "evil" in Usher.) Usher and Madeline are less separate elements of human nature than "aspects of a single state of being . . . as intensified paralysis" tending toward disintegration (75–79). The theme is duplicated in the structure and style. The narrator provides a bridge between Usher and the reader, being a kind of "pre-Jamesian confidant." The message of "Usher" is not a hopeful one: intensified "heterogeneity and sensitivity become too exquisitely attained" to coexist through their very acuity and for lack of order on the whole (80–81).

In his introduction to this tale, Mabbott quotes a fine passage from Woodberry on the unity of design of "Usher" (*M* 3, 392). Then Mabbott offers his own scenario because "some details [in the tale] have proved puzzling":

The House of Usher has only one soul which has its abode in the mansion and in the members of the family. Roderick Usher is aware of this, although his sister may not be, and he has concluded that since they are twins, and childless, this soul is interdependent with them and the building. Hence, if one dies, all must perish together. Roderick also fears that he is going mad, and so summons his friend, the only person he trusts who has no part in the fate of his ancient house. Both brother and sister are dying: the latter seems to die first, but the former is sure that she is still alive because he is. He avoids her actual burial by a temporary intombment. He reads books which deals with unusual ideas about the relation of matter to spirit, of doubles, and of demoniac possession. (394–95)

This excerpt suffices to illustrate how literal is Mabbott's reading compared to the allegorical interpretations of Wilbur and others. Mabbott rejected D. H. Lawrence's incest theory, Bailey's vampire hypothesis—"Madeline is certainly not an orthodox vampire"—and Lyle Kendall's view of Madeline as a succubus (396).

Vampires and Atmosphere

In his short article (1963) on the vampire motif in "Usher," Lyle H. Kendall, Jr., charged that symbolic, psychological, and *Eureka*-related readings have overlooked that "it is a Gothic tale, like 'Ligeia,' and that a completely satisfactory and internally directed interpretation depends on vampirism, the hereditary Usher curse. Madeline is a vampire—a succubus—as the family physician well knows and as her physical appearance and effect upon the narrator sufficiently demonstrate" (450; Woodson, 99).

J. O. Bailey in "What Happens in 'The Fall of the House of Usher'?" posed a question, How is it that the "psychic and supernatural influences" on the narrator and Roderick, even driving Roderick mad and destroying the house, are concealed? Poe's first device for concealment was to have the story told by a narrator, a rationalist and a skeptic, who rejects supernatural evidence. Allen Tate thought that Poe had used materials from vampire lore, and Bailey holds that Roderick's library contained books on how to understand and combat it (445–58/100–102). Among the kinds of vampirism identified by Bailey are

atmospheric vampirism: dead vegetation around the house, the "pestilent and mystic vapor," the house as a "psychic sponge" draining Roderick's vitality, the demonic vampirism of the house, the "extravagant, mystic, spiritualistic, and terror literature" in Roderick's library, all concerned with "the idea that spirit is extended throughout all matter"; vampire-caused storms, this one not without numerous characteristic symptoms; the heavy doors of the house opening by themselves; at the end, perhaps they all die at the same instant, with Roderick's soul saved, after all, by the innocuous thousand waters, and the curse lifted; and

human/vampiric powers: Roderick's "peculiar sensibility of temperament," "a constitutional and family evil" illness, Roderick's cadaverous complexion, his "morbid acuteness of the senses," Roderick's preserving Madeline's body in the vault because she may be possessed by a vampire spirit, and he may wish to exorcise that evil spirit; "the scarcely intelligible" sympathies shared by the twins and with the house; Madeline's miraculous escape from the airtight vault; Madeline's heart beating with a heavy vampiric beat; Madeline in her bloodied white robes like a "white and blood-stained tooth poised to plunge into Roderick's life-stream"; finally, "the somewhat erotic embrace of its victim, the prone position for the kill, and the moan of pleasure are commonplaces of vampire lore"; "as Roderick dies, Madeline and the House die, for their source of vitality is cut off."

In his conclusion, Bailey observes, "We need not suppose that in using this material to plot a piece of fiction Poe believed in vampires." But he states that if his reading is valid, it has some biographical significance, and he offers a few speculations. An allegorical reading he considers to be outside this study (448–65; casebook, 106–19). At no time does Bailey or Kendall place the events and characters in the context of Poe's philosophic perspective. Obviously, Poe drew upon the Gothic tradition for his setting, characters, and story line; but to fill out that surface narrative, as Kendall and Bailey do, is not to interpret its undercurrent of meaning.

I. A. Walker, turning away from vampirism as well as allegory, demonstrated "The Legitimate Sources of Terror in 'The Fall of the House of Usher' " by documenting two important "German" motifs in the tale: "the sinister black tarn which dominates the environment, and Madeline Usher's return from the tomb to destroy her brother" (586). The tarn not only is part of the Gothic decor but also contributes to Roderick's destruction. The crack as a house–man symbol represents the imminent collapse of Roderick. The "atmosphere" around the house and tarn, in a special nineteenth-century physical sense, is "a kind of sphere formed by the effluvia, or minute corpuscles emitted from them" (the Rees *Cyclopedia,* 1819; cf. Spitzer earlier) and accounts for the effect of the *physique* of the walls and towers on the *morale* of Roderick. Walker's main original contribution is his analysis of "Febrile Miasma," the gases from stagnant water or decayed matter and their effects on mind and body as documented by Benjamin Rush, Isaac Ray, and Thomas C. Upham's *Elements of Mental Philosophy* (1837). The effect on Roderick is evident in his slow pulse and lowered blood supply and the alternating depression and excitement of his mental state. Madeline's return from the tomb has generally been accepted as literal fact, a tribute to Poe's skill as a writer; but it does not mean that Madeline actually returned from the vault. "The purpose of the tale is to explore mental derangement rather than to present an elaborate Gothic horror story, and the terror it contains is psychological not 'German.' . . . Roderick is not killed by his sister, but is literally terrified to death by his environment and his distorted imagination" (588–92).

Herbert F. Smith explored further the theme of "sentience" (cf. earlier, the 1961 article by E. Arthur Robinson) in "Usher's Madness and Poe's Organicism: A Source," which traced Poe's indebtedness to Richard Watson's *Chemical Essays,* vol. 5 and preface. A footnote added by Poe to the 1840 version of "Usher" listed the "other men" who shared Roderick's belief in "the sentience of all vegetable things." But, as Smith notes, Roderick "believed not merely in the capacity of plants to *feel,* but also in their capacity to organize themselves in the non-organic materials around them," especially the stones of the mansion, the decayed trees, the tarn, into "a new organic unity" able to create a distinctive atmosphere. In other words, "apparently inorganic matter is only an inert form of larger life" (380–81). Watson maintained that the three kingdoms—mineral, vegetable, and animal—were not separated by "systematic distinctions" but similar or analogous in their "locomotive powers," their "perception" (response to light and touch), their reproductive processes, and so on. In *Eureka,* Poe's views of the universe resemble Watson's, though Poe ranges further—into cosmology, physics, psychology, metaphysics (Smith, 382–87). In "Usher," Roderick's "madness is centered around the biological phenomenon which might be described as 'colonial organicism,' symbiosis, or mutualism . . . an example of aberrant *microcosmic* organicism" (387). In "Usher," vegetable sentience is simply a part of the argument for "the organic relatedness of *all matter,* . . . and not merely matter but mind as well." In the end, the Usher hubris rushes to a complete unification and annihilation in an act of "perfect, but insane, solipsism . . . in his insanity [he] forgets the Neoplatonic lesson of moral character. . . . The same factor, included in *Eureka,* keeps that essay from being a document of despair" (388–89).

Joseph J. Moldenhauer's comprehensive essay on "Murder as a Fine Art: Basic Connections between Poe's Aesthetics, Psychology, and Moral Vision" provided a much-needed integration of Poe's three-part perspective, the "symbolic structure" of his aesthetic, and his fiction and poetry, with an emphasis on "a center of meaning or a unified design underlying the polar modes of imagination," an "extraordinary anticipation of modern psychology," and a "singularly self-consistent vision" (285). Most interesting is his "concept of Beauty as the focus of an apocalyptic religion" (287–88). In the tales of terror, the narrator-protagonists are artists, among them, of course, Roderick Usher. In "Usher," the instinct for oneness is dramatized by "repeated doublings on the literal and symbolic planes . . . the house and its mirror image in the tarn; the Usher family and the Usher mansion"; Roderick and Madeline; Roderick's life-urge and death-wish; etc. Roderick's love for Madeline is incestuous but it has "no overt erotic component." "The 'going down' of Poe's protagonists symbolizes a return to the mother, to soporific warmth and darkness, to the womb. But this is no more than, and perhaps finally less than, the achievement of an artistic perfection in death" (291, 295).

Eric W. Carlson in "Poe's Vision of Man" (1972) defined Poe's central perspective as unified not by death but by the theme of "spiritual rebirth or rediscovery of the lost psychal power" latent in every man and woman seeking fullest self-realization (20). "Usher" (17–19) was identified as Poe's most complex embodiment of his psychal transcendentalism. The three characters are seen as symbolic of the tripartite self, Roderick and Madeline as complementary, Roderick the amoral and overrefined artist whose lack of vital "moral energy" has left him weak, introverted, and decadent; Madeline, the psychal potential and will—Roderick's suppressed twin. Key symbols of Roderick's character are his eye—"large, liquid, and luminous beyond comparison"—his weak chin suggestive of "a want of moral energy," the disorder of his books and instruments indicative of a lack of vitality and rational control, his wild improvisations, and his fanciful abstract paintings. Latent strength is suggested by "the lofty and enshrouded figure of the Lady Madeline of Usher" when she appears on the "threshold" as the suppressed revenant, the psychomoral self. In his later lecture, "Poe on the Soul of Man," Carlson concluded that the fatal embrace of Madeline bearing Roderick to his death implies the deadly consequence of their unresolved psychal conflict (19–20).

John F. Lynen's long chapter on Poe (205–71) in *The Design of the Present* deals, in part, with "Usher," which is regarded as Poe's "most precise and elaborate enactment of the return to unity." He is critical of Wilbur for turning this unity-of-the-universe theme into "a mere psychological allegory" of Poe's capacity for creating a dream of world destruction. Thus, the dream reuniting Usher with Madeline is, to Wilbur, "a foreview of the soul's reconstitution and purification in death" ("Introduction," 27–28). Yet, if the writings are as unified as Wilbur claims, they cannot be inconsistent with *Eureka*, with its unity of mind and matter. By intuition, the visionary self realizes in the *tendency* of things the whole design of reality and the final unity. The plot of "Usher," Lynen continues, shows that "the world of mind and the world of matter are in truth one realm . . . in the process of developing toward an annihilating unity." In "Usher," the narrator is "shaken by the suspicion that the world has a mind of its own. In *Eureka*, Poe confirms that nightmarish suspicion by coolly describing how, as entities merge, the multiple selves combine to reconstitute God's personality, which is not a mind distinct from the world but a unitary being that supersedes both . . . to foreshadow . . . that final stage of history when mind and world have been replaced by a different kind of being" (235–36).

Two valuable collections of critical essays on "Usher" appeared at this time. The first, a paperback from Prentice-Hall (1969) edited by Thomas Woodson with a twenty-one-page biographical, historical, and critical introduction, contained passages by noted critics and nine key essays or excerpts. All but one of these essays are considered in this chapter. The second paperback was edited with introduction by Eric W. Carlson. It contains the full text of the story and fifteen essays and excerpts ranging from Lawrence to Cox. Especially useful as study and teaching aids are seventeen paragraphs of suggestions for papers, long and short, plus recommended critical articles. The Introduction of six pages consists of editor's key questions and quoted "perspective" passages on Poe's "world of mind," supernal Beauty, "psychal fancies," the two "identities," and "genius," along with brief suggestive comments on "Ligeia," Roderick, Madeline, and the main theme.

Poe Studies 5, no. 1 (June 1972) was devoted entirely to "The Fall of the House of Usher": reviews of six essays, two essay collections, one casebook, and a checklist of criticism since 1960. The lead essay of over seven double-column pages by Barton Levi St. Armand is entitled "Usher Unveiled: Poe and the Metaphysic of Gnosticism." Because this article is discussed in the chapter on Poe and alchemy by Randall Clack, only a few highlights are given here. St. Armand begins with T. S. Eliot's suggestion that if unjustly negative views of Poe as a thinker are replaced with an integrated view of his work as a whole, we see "a mass of unique shape and impressive size to which the eye constantly returns" ("From Poe to Valéry"). Or, in St. Armand's words, we see "an incredibly detailed and a profound metaphysic," namely Gnosticism, suppressed in the early centuries by the dogmatic church at the Council of Nicaea, among others. The symbolic language of Gnosticism is similar to images in Poe's poems and tales, such as a God of the Abyss and a fallen world. At that time, there were two competing mystical traditions: Neoplatonism and Gnosticism. As a hermetic philosophy, Gnosticism sought to liberate the soul or primal spirit through an act of *gnosis*. St. Armand shows that, in "Usher," there are both an aesthetic unity and "an intriguing and wholly respectable metaphysical unity as well" (1–2). St. Armand proceeds to analyze such occult details as the House, the landscape, the "Mad Trist," Usher, the vault, his painting, Madeline and her final collapse upon Roderick in a "liberating embrace . . . he has become pure soul . . . one with the hidden god—he has achieved *gnosis*" (3–7).

David Halliburton's twenty pages (278–99) on "Usher" in his *Edgar Allan Poe* are focused on the narrator's consciousness as defined by the opening pages of atmospheric description in terms of images, sentence structure, "ontological structure," and the narrator's "illusion of illusion" (278–83). The house and Roderick are analyzed in depth and related to sentience and organicism, with credits to Herbert Smith, Maurice Beebe, and E. Arthur Robinson. "The ontological economy remains, as in the tales of women, an economy of two . . . Roderick and Madeline, who form the primal couple." Just as diffused particles tend to return to their primal oneness, so Usher, near the end of his diffusion, prepares for his dissolution or return to oneness (285–89). In the climactic *reunification,* Madeline's overpowering will brings about the physical convergence with Roderick: "[B]ody to body, the pair fall from life as we know it to life as we know it not" (292). Nature (the storm, the atmosphere) is dominant over the Ushers. Halliburton sees the final fall of the Ushers as an "inward-tending, self-completing . . . embrace brought to its own peculiar perfection . . . and terror-producing effect" (207). He sees it also as an "absolute Irrelation" (*Eureka*) in which "a power numinous, vast, unknown draws me not so much *to* itself as *back within* itself . . . to one's original state: it is, in a word, to go home" (298). "The fall of the House of Usher is the fall of being—through matter—into the gulf beyond" (299). This conclusion shows that Halliburton is aware of Poe's kind of transcendentalism.

At the heart of "Usher," G. R. Thompson (*Poe's Fiction*) finds "an essential ambiguity, carefully insinuated and carefully wrought." Then he remarks that what he has to offer are "principally addenda" to "Darrel Abel's brilliant analysis of the tale as a psychodrama of the mutual hysteria of the narrator and Roderick Usher" (see earlier, Abel 1949]. Within the primary structural context "the subjectivity of the narrator" is said to hold in tension the other structures, notably the pattern of doubling and redoubling. The traditional Gothic elements of fear, madness, and death are introduced by the death's-head image of the house in the tarn, which Poe intended to be the central image of the tale. Similarly, the strange painting of the vault reflects "the death and burial of consciousness and rationality themselves . . . of Usher's internal void . . . spiralling further to the mocking irony of the ultimate theme of nothingness, which is all the mind can truly know . . . an over-all structure mirroring the pattern of the universe itself, as expressed in *Eureka*" (88–90). "Mocking irony" is also found in the "Mad Trist," which is an "absurd parody of a medieval romance . . ." (93), in Madeline's escape from the tomb (94), and in Usher's arabesque face, which ''provides a major clue to the irony insinuated into, under, and around the apparent Gothic surface of the story'' (95). However, this assumption that such ''ludicrous'' Gothic details are intentionally ironic overlooks Poe's caution against misconstruing an author's ''incredibilities'' (1836 review of *Sheppard Lee*. See earlier, chapter 14). The consensus of the preceding critiques regards the narrator as a man of common sense, at times puzzled or skeptical but not ''completely deranged.''

David W. Butler in his 1976 *AL* article, ''Usher's Hypochondriasis: Mental Alienation and Romantic Idealism in Poe's Gothic Tales,'' took issue with modern critics who have failed to identify Usher's illness correctly and thus have obscured the rich parallels between medical and romantic theories of the mind. For Butler, Walker's argument for miasmic poisoning can readily be subsumed by the medical descriptions of hypochondriasis (1). Medical contemporaries of Poe denied a causal relation between insanity and creative imagination, especially ''authentic private visions of a transcendent order.'' It is not clear that Poe denied such visions, given ''the continuing conflict between psychological and mystical explanations of Poe's Gothic tales'' and the deliberate parallel presentation of the scientific and the romantically idealistic (2–3). Butler expressed his indebtedness to Herbert F. Smith and his source (see earlier, *AL*, 1967). With the death of Roderick and Madeline, the ''sympathetic'' mansion disappears into the tarn. This annihilation may, in romantic terms, be said to bring them ''into unity with the realm of pure mind . . . through the absolute dissolution of the real in order to achieve complete union with ideality'' (10–11). But because we do not know whether the narrator can be believed and whether the doctors are right or wrong, this tale ''brilliantly indicates, in terms of both the scientific and the romantic psychology of his time, just how difficult the discernment is to come by'' (12).

David Ketterer, in his *The Rationale of Deception in Poe,* also regards ''Usher'' as a tale that may be interpreted in natural or supernatural terms if the various readings are held in suspension. The tale is ''a sentient ideogram and Poe's finest experiment in the technique of fluid fusion''; it is impossible to impose ''fixity'' on a shifting arabesque and ''phantasmagoric'' surface (193). This indeterminate quality is marked by a tension between parallels: Usher's poem and the tale itself; the painting and the actual vault; Madeline as a projection of Usher's ''madness''; the ''Mad Trist'' and the meeting with Madeline (Mad-eline); and so on. Finally, the arabesque images or dreams are indistinguishable from the perceptual actuality when ''the waters of the tarn (the arabesque world) close over the grotesque human state as symbolized by the actual house.'' The house poised over the tarn waits for the ''lapse'' from the everyday into ''arabesque life'' (194). Madeline pulls Usher toward ''arabesque reality'' while the narrator resists—the tension between deception and fusion, the vulgar and the spiritual all occurring within Usher's mind as psychic conflict (197). Ketterer's study is the most thorough documentation of Poe's transcendental *arabesque* motifs in his tales.

In *Ruined Eden of the Present: Hawthorne, Melville and Poe,* edited by G. R. Thompson and Virgil L. Lokke, three essays represent a continuing debate on "Usher" between Thompson and Patrick Quinn. In the first, "A Misreading of Poe's 'The Fall of the House of Usher,' " Quinn questions Thompson's claim (in his chapter in *Poe's Fiction* discussed earlier) that Poe as an ironical author intended his narrator here and elsewhere to be "unreliable." In all, Quinn takes up four points: the appearance of the house, the narrator's experience, the ending of the story, and its theme. "I shall try to show that in this case it may be the critic of the story rather than its narrator whose reliability is more open to question" (304).

Thompson's likening the house to a skull-like face strikes Quinn as implausible ("extremely difficult to visualize"), and the claim that it dominates the tale is not correct. As for the experience of the narrator, Quinn registers three objections to the face-facade theory on grounds of its being inaccurate and unconvincing. A close reading citing key passages also reveals that the narrator does not suffer a collapse into "a frenzy of terror" or a progressive deterioration of mind or feeling (304–10). As to "What Happened to the House," Quinn analyzes and rejects Thompson's notion that the house was blown up by a lightning-caused explosion of stored gunpowder, though no lightning flashes were visible. Finally, as to the theme, only a mentally stable narrator could sense the thematic drift as Thompson describes it (310–12).

In rebuttal, Thompson followed with "Poe and the Paradox of Terror: Structures of Heightened Consciousness in 'The Fall of the House of Usher' " (313–40), in which he stressed that his reading of this tale is "central to my whole approach to Poe's fiction" (313). But when Thompson claimed that he was simply following Darrel Abel's belief that the narrator undergoes an "increasing subjective involvement," Quinn retorted that this was *not* Abel's position. Quinn responded to Thompson's long and detailed reply in his own final, short rebuttal, " 'Usher' Again: Trust the Teller!" (341–63). In it, he devoted three pages to *Abel vs. Thompson,* documenting Abel's view that it is Usher's story as reported by the "matter-of-fact" narrator. For Thompson, it is not—it is mainly about an emotionally unstable narrator whose revelations are the source of irony (342–44). Of course, Quinn documented his own view of the narrator's experience and state of mind, concluding that "the narrator's sanity and *savoir-faire* are three times tested . . . and they survive . . . he keeps his wits" (347). Quinn also noted that Thompson's last pages are written as if Quinn's demurs have been disposed of, and the narrator's unreliability demonstrated (352).

In " 'The Fall of the House of Usher': An Apocalyptic Vision,'' James W. Gargano, following the lead of Allen Tate and Maurice Beebe (1956, earlier), examined the relationship between the theme and Poe's cosmological-philosophic views as a unique context for the narrative action and for "the major characters' unique emotions and their inability to explain their ordeal." Poe's concern with eschatological issues is expressed through the narrator's "apocalyptic vision of the destruction of the world . . . the predetermined collapse of separateness and identity into unity'' as the Usher mansion and its occupants disappear into the tarn. This preoccupation with the End of the World was also evident in ''The Conversation of Eiros and Charmion'' three months later (December) than ''Usher'' (53). Disagreeing with Darrel Abel's view of the narrator as providing ''a mere point of view for the reader to occupy,'' Gargano calls this tale ''the ironic drama of a tormented soul adrift in a universe no longer stable or comprehensible . . . [in short,] mankind's cosmic plight'' (54). The narrator is also confronted by ''the physical and psychic breakdown of one man, Roderick'' and ''the end of a once-eminent historic dynasty'' and the seemingly sinister destructive power of nature. Because of the narrator's conventionalized, even closed, mind, the reader is drawn in to participate as a third consciousness observing the narrator-observer (54–55). In the very first paragraph, the narrator surrenders to ''a panicky distrust of reason,'' returning to rationality only as a refuge from the ''facts'' (55). The disintegrating Usher estate is seen as ''a vast living web'' of sick occupants, blighted premises, sentience, and the power of fate or death. ''Usher represents Man in the last stage of his existence,'' but he lacks ''the prophet's second sight'' into that fact. Verbal similarities in ''Usher'' and ''Eiros and Charmion'' indicate a close relationship in theme and mood (57–60). ''Poe's ironic rendering of the narrator's apocalyptic vision'' differs from ''the ultimately hopeful prophecies [of ''Eiros'' and *Eureka*] ''because Poe gives no hint of a future existence that may reduce the fatal storm to the proportions of a cosmic incident'' (61–63).

Terry Heller's ''The Entrapped Critic'' appeared in *The Delights of Terror;* another chapter is devoted to ''Anticlosure: Poe's 'Ligeia.' '' These essays are based on the concepts of aesthetic distance (Ingarden) and the phenomenology of reading and ''the implied reader'' (Iser). The text offers the implied reader a role, a point of view, a world, and a culture, whereas the naive reader is carried away by his enthusiasm, to rejoice, hope, or suffer (2–5). Even so, readers of ''Ligeia'' must rearrange their interpretation to include Ligeia's transformation: ''Ligeia emerges as monstrous'' to the implied, entrapped reader, says Heller.

Without Poe's philosophic perspective with which to read this allegorical tale, Heller faults the text for its ''lack of information'' and the critics for invoking the narrator as the source of ''dreams'' and hallucinations. In ''The Fall of the House of Usher,'' anticlosure entraps the implied and the real readers. Although Roderick and Madeline are seen as ''impenetrable'' mysteries, the sentient house transforms Usher in body and soul into a mirror of itself, and Usher dominates the narrator. But to say that Usher, the narrator, and Madeline ''have been placed alive in the tomb. For them, this is the human condition'' seems too pat a leap to the metaphysical level, as is also true of the next vision, this time of '' 'the full, setting, and blood-red moon,' '' taken to mean that ''[t]he universe is a coffin unnaturally lit from within'' (135–36). How is the implied reader to free himself or herself from this narrator? asks Heller. The story ends with dreamlike visions but no explanation for the final image of the house disappearing into the tarn. Speaking of critics who have taken the tale as "a metaphysical dream-allegory in which the narrator is confronted by an opportunity to achieve transcendental union with the universe," Heller singles out E. W. Carlson (introduction to his casebook) and Richard Wilbur (in "The House of Poe") as proponents of this view. A half dozen other critics—Davidson, Martindale, Saliba, Stein, Spaulding—are said to "see the tale more as a psychological dream-allegory in which various characters stand for different components of the personality." To Heller, these interpretations are said to have too many gaps, are too abstract, and so on. Heller deplores the trend in "recent Poe criticism . . . of forcing every Poe text into too simple a conformity with 'Eureka.' " Wilbur's view of "Usher" is summed up as "an intellectual abstraction" and an "intellectual sanctuary," quite contrary to Wilbur's subtle and sophisticated readings. Because they do not "drain the tale of the real terror," Thompson, Ketterer, and Bachinger are praised, oddly enough, for leaving the reader in "the 'limbo' of ambiguity" (142–43). The lack of resolutions in the tale "makes the role of implied reader obsessive and intolerable. The role has no end, no last word" (146).

In Respect to Egotism by Joel Porte has a chapter on "Poe: Romantic Center, Critical Margin." The section on *Eureka* (98–105) calls that essay "a cosmogony, a cosmology, an apocalypse, and a theodicy, all in the form of a 'prophetical and poetical rhapsody,' " which Poe claimed to be both true and beautiful because of its consistency. After the initial act of creation, the subsequent process of diffusion continues until the many are pulled back by gravity into the apocalyptic unity or point of beginning. "This pagan Neoplatonic scheme of cyclical movement from unity to dispersion and back again" (101) Schelling spoke of in 1811 as "the journey back to the lost paradise, or golden age, which is the restoration of a lost unity of the human intellect with itself and with nature." In 1814, Wordsworth made a similar call for transforming the ancient paradise into present reality. Porte claims that Poe's journey is "ever downward, 'to the end.' " His ultimate metaphoric sound motif in much of the fiction is the ominous *rushing* noise, as when Madeline amid the *rushing* gust collapses in death upon her brother, and as the fissure of the House widens, the walls are "*rushing* asunder." Similar uses of this motif occur in "Ligeia," *Pym,* and *Eureka.* "The frantic rushing together finishes in a 'rushing asunder' that leaves everything uncreated." In this last essay-romance (*Eureka*), Poe attempted to "produce something like a unified field theory of cosmic love and death in the guise of a scientific treatise . . . but one must take it for what it is—Romantic mythmaking, not veritable gospel astrophysics" (102–3). In respect to the ending in "Usher," Porte suggests that Poe intended the reader to experience the "spiritual effect" of terror at the catastrophic events, delight at the *efflorescence* of language, and recognition of the theme of *thanatos.* But do not the concluding images of "the mighty walls rushing asunder" and "the long tumultuous shouting sound like the voice of a thousand waters" imply that the powers of nature are "rushing" to their predestined End of that cycle and the point of Beginning within the larger epic cycle of renewal—of Life, Life, within Life? If all this is not explicitly implied by the text of "Usher," it turned up as "the law of periodicity" ten years later in *Eureka* (1848), where the atoms are described as "*rushing* toward their own general centre . . . with their spiritual passion for oneness . . . into a common embrace" (quoted 102). Also to the point is Porte's citation from *Pym*, published in 1838, prior to "Usher" (September 1839): "[M]ost spectacularly, Arthur Gordon Pym experiences both 'the final bitterness of the *rushing* and headlong descent' into the arms of Dirk Peters and his more final '*rushed*' movement into the 'embraces of the cataract' and its mysterious 'shrouded human figure' of a perfect and perfectly terrifying whiteness" (102). This pervasive intertextual context throws new light on the intended meaning of the symbolic ending of both "Usher" and *Pym*," which share with *Eureka* the key words *rushing* and *embrace* as positive, not negative, metaphors. This entropic culmination of the process of creation and expansion-contraction, followed by a new Big Bang, is confirmed by modern astrophysics, as described in the Life in the Universe Special Issue of the *Scientific American* for October 1994. (See also Clack 384 and St. Armand 377; *PoeS* 5, 116–7.)

WORKS CITED

Abel, Darrel. "A Key to the House of Usher." *University of Toronto Quarterly* 18 (January 1949): 176–85.

Bailey, J. O. "What Happens in 'The Fall of the House of Usher'?" *AL* 35 (Jan. 1964): 445–66.

Beebe, Maurice. "The Universe of Roderick Usher." *Personalist* 37 (Spring 1956): 147–60.

Brooks, Cleanth, Jr., and Robert Penn Warren. "On 'Usher.' " *Understanding Fiction.* New York: F. S. Crofts, 1943, 202–5.

Butler, David W. "Hypochondriasis: Mental Alienation and Romantic Idealism in Poe's Gothic Tales." *AL* 48 (1976): 1–12.

Carlson, Eric W., ed. *Poe: The Fall of the House of Usher.* Charles E. Merrill Literary Casebook with editor's introduction and with essays and excerpts ranging from Lawrence to Cox. Columbus, Ohio: Charles E. Merrill, 1971.

———. " 'William Wilson': The Double as Primal Self." *Topic* 30 (Fall 1976): 35–40.

Chandler, Alice. "The Visionary Race": Poe's Attitude toward His Dreamers." *New Approaches to Poe.* Ed. Richard P. Benton. Hartford: Transcendental Books, 1970, 73–81.

Gargano, James W. "Art and Irony in 'William Wilson.' " *ESQ* 60 (Fall 1970): 18–22. Repr. in *New Approaches to Poe.* Ed. Richard P. Benton.

———. " 'The Fall of the House of Usher': An Apocalyptic Vision." *UMSE*, new series 3 (June 1982): 53–63.

Griffith, Clark. "Poe and the Gothic." In *Papers on Poe.* Ed. Veler. 1972.

Griswold, Rufus Wilmot. *The Prose Writers of America.* Philadelphia: Carey and Hart, 1847.

Heller, Terry. "The Entrapped Critic: Poe's 'The Fall of the House of Usher.' " In *The Delights of Terror* (1987), 127–46.

Joswick, Thomas. "Who's Master in the House of Poe? A Reading of 'William Wilson.' "
    Criticism 30, no. 2 (Spring 1988): 225–47.
Kendall, Lyle H., Jr. "The Vampire Motif in 'The Fall of the House of Usher.' " *College
    English* 24 (Mar. 1963): 450–53.
Poe Studies 5, no. 1 (June 1972): special issue on "The Fall of the House of Usher":
    reviews of six essays, two essay collections, one casebook, and a checklist of
    criticism since 1960. The lead essay is St. Armand's on Gnosticism.
Porte, Joel. "Poe: Romantic Center, Critical Margin." *In Respect to Egotism* . . . Cam-
    bridge: Cambridge UP, 1991.
Robinson, E. Arthur. "Order and Sentience in 'The Fall of the House of Usher.' " *PMLA*
    76 (Mar. 1961): 68–81.
St. Armand, Barton Levi. "Usher Unveiled: Poe and the Metaphysic of Gnosticism."
    Poe Studies 5 (June 1972): 1–8.
Smith, Herbert F. "Usher's Madness and Poe's Organicism: A Source." *AL* 39 (Nov.
    1968): 379–89.
Spitzer, Leo. "A Reinterpretation of 'The Fall of the House of Usher.' " *Comparative
    Literature* 4 (Fall 1952): 351–63.
Stauffer, Donald Barlow. "Style and Meaning in 'Ligeia' and 'William Wilson.' " *Stud-
    ies in Short Fiction* 2 (Summer 1965): 316–30. Repr. in *CE,* 113–27.
Thompson, G. R., and Virgil L. Lokke, eds. *Ruined Eden of the Present: Hawthorne,
    Melville and Poe.* 1981.
Walker, I. A. "The Legitimate Sources of Terror in 'The Fall of the House of Usher.' "
    Modern Language Review 61 (Oct. 1966): 585–92.
Wilbur, Richard. "The House of Poe." *The Recognition of Edgar Allen Poe.* Ed. Carlson.
———. "Introduction" and "Notes" to *Poe.* The Laurel Poetry Series. New York: Dell,
    1959.
Woodson, Thomas, ed. *Twentieth Century Interpretations of The Fall of the House of
    Usher.* Englewood Cliffs, N.J.: Prentice-Hall, 1969.

10

Dream Texts: The Narrative of Arthur Gordon Pym and The Journal of Julius Rodman

GRACE FARRELL

Early in 1838, having been relieved of the editorship of *The Southern Literary Messenger* a year earlier and having moved from Richmond to first one, and then another, lodging in New York City, Edgar Poe relocated his family to a boardinghouse in Philadelphia, where he, Virginia, and Mrs. Clemm proceeded to starve. Contemporaries report that they were " 'literally suffering for want of food' and forced to live 'on bread and molasses for weeks together' " (*PoeL,* 248). On July 19, 1838, Poe wrote to James Kirke Paulding, newly appointed secretary of the navy, pleading for a job: "Could I obtain the most unimportant Clerkship in your gift—*any thing, by sea or land*—to relieve me from the miserable life of literary drudgery to which I now, with a breaking heart, submit, and for which neither my temper nor my abilities have fitted me, I would never again repine at any dispensation of God" (*PoeL,* 248). Eleven days later, on July 30, Harper and Brothers published Poe's first novel, *The Narrative of Arthur Gordon Pym;* this and the unfinished *Journal of Julius Rodman,* published serially in 1840, constitute Poe's only attempts at long fiction. They depict journeys, by sea and by land, that would test the will of anyone who undertook them if he or she had vowed never to question the dispensations of his or her God.

Pym depicts a series of sea voyages, a preliminary sail on board the small craft *Ariel* followed by journeys on the *Grampus* and the *Jane Guy,* which, as its extended title indicates, involve mutiny, murders, shipwrecks, starvation, cannibalism, gangrenous wounds, conflagration, and an apparent final absorption into "a chasm [which] threw itself open to receive us" (*P* 1, 206). *Pym* is an exploration of extremes—in geography, in endurance, and in consciousness—and *Julius Rodman,* too, involving a journey up the Missouri River and west over the Rocky Mountains, is an exploration "beyond the extreme bounds of civilization," a tour to " '*an unexplored region,*' " a place not located on any map (*P* 1, 565, 521). *Rodman* seems quite a bit tamer than *Pym* only if we fail to recognize its subtle terrors, such as those pointed out in David Ketterer's discussion of the juxtaposition in *Rodman* of idyllic retreats and treacherously shifting sandbars, the one the object of enraptured yearning, the other indicative of the deceptive nature of reality (1979, 141–45). As Edward H. Davidson suggested, both narratives "begin at the same place in the creative imagination— with the facts of a voyage or a journey to unexplored lands. One remains earthbound and text-confined to its sources, which Poe quite ruthlessly copied, extracted, or revised; the other, *Pym,* takes off from its sources, comes back to them for supporting details, and then transforms and makes them into art'' (156).

THE JOURNAL OF JULIUS RODMAN

The Journal of Julius Rodman begins with an introduction that records details of westward exploration from 1749 to 1832 and explains the reasons the manuscript, which purports to be a true account of explorations made during 1791–1794, prior to the Lewis and Clark expedition of 1804–1806, came to light only in 1840. As in so much of Poe's fiction, Rodman's travels begin with multiple deaths and displacements. Rodman is doubly displaced—from his ancestral home in England in 1784 and from his Kentucky home after the deaths in the fall and winter of 1790 of his entire family. These displacements lead him to yet another: the motivation for the journey, we are told, is "a desire to seek, in the bosom of the wilderness, that peace which his peculiar disposition would not suffer him to enjoy among men. He fled to the desert as to a friend'' (*P* 1, 522). The manuscript, too, is displaced and misplaced—it is displaced in memory, written many years after the journey's end, and it is lost on the road in transit to an explorer who was to have undertaken the expedition thereafter completed by Lewis and Clark. Many more years are to pass before it is found, three months prior to publication, in the secret drawer of a bureau owned by Rodman's grandson. How it got there is never known.

Running through the narrative is the intense friendship between Rodman and Andrew Thornton:

I never, at any period of my life, felt so keenly as I then did, the want of some friend to whom I could converse freely, and without danger of being misunderstood. The sudden loss of all my relatives by death, had saddened, but not depressed my spirits, which appeared to seek relief in a contemplation of the wild scenes of Nature; and these scenes and the reflections which they encouraged, could not, I found, be thoroughly enjoyed, without the society of some one person of reciprocal sentiments. Thornton was precisely the kind of individual to whom I could unburthen my full heart, and unburthen it of all its extravagant emotion, without fear of incurring a shadow of ridicule, and even in the certainty of finding a listener as impassioned as myself. (*P* 1, 537)

While the manuscript is written from Rodman's memory, the journey is undertaken as his meditation, and the background of the narrative is filled with the storytelling of Thornton. Linking memory, meditation, and storytelling, *Rodman* is yet another example of Poe's inward turn of narrative. Thornton, like Rodman and like Poe, tells tales "of his adventures and hardships in the wilderness— recounting them with a strait-forward earnestness which left us no room to doubt their truth; although indeed, many of them had a marvellous air" (*P* 1, 532). Such a description could as easily be applied to Rodman's story and, indeed, to the stories of Poe. Poe's art mimicked life so well that *The Journal of Julius Rodman* was presumed to be authentic by the librarian to the Department of State, who cited *Rodman* in the U.S. Senate Documents, 1839–1840 (Jackson 1974).

The journey begins exuberantly with high spirits, lush scenery, and plentiful food, but hardships are soon introduced. The travelers are attacked by Sioux Indians, whom they defeat with one shot of their cannon; they run turbulent currents and navigate precipitous cliffs; and they witness the agonized drowning of vast numbers of buffalo. The novel ends after the explorers survive a gruesome attack by enormous brown bears. The *Saturday Courier* reviewed the first chapter, calling it " 'one of the most extraordinary narratives ever penned' " (*PoeL*, 287), but subsequent chapters received little recognition, and Poe never completed the narrative, leaving Rodman "stranded in Montana in May 1792 with thousands of miles to go before reaching the promised Yukon" (*P* 1, 509).

Poe probably completed the first three chapters of *Rodman* by December 1839 (*P* 1, 509) and began its publication, anonymously, as a serial in *Burton's Gentlemen's Magazine,* for which Poe had become assistant editor in June 1839. He mapped out a round-trip for Rodman, from Missouri, across the Rockies, as far north as the Yukon and back again (*P* 1, 509). Projected for twelve installments, the novel ran for six, from January through June 1840, when Poe left the employ of the magazine after a falling out with William Burton. Poe's authorship of *Rodman* is confirmed in his June 1, 1840, letter to Burton (*PoeL,* 298).

The sources of both *"Pym"* and *Rodman* have been extensively examined, particularly by Burton F. Pollin, and are best summarized in his 1981 edition of *The Imaginary Voyages.* This volume is unequaled as the most complete source of valuable information on the composition, early reception, and publication history of these works. For *Rodman,* Poe borrowed liberally ("largely plagiarized," according to Stuart Levine 1960) not only from Irving's *Astoria,* which he also used for *Pym,* but also from the journal of Lewis and Clark, whose expedition Julius Rodman's supposedly preceded (*P* 1, 513–14). Although unpolished, *Rodman,* writes Pollin, shows "occasional gleams of Poe's genius" (*P* 1, 515).

To date, *Rodman* has received scant critical attention. Stuart Levine (1960) saw Rodman not only as a hero who is self-exiled from society but as a Jew who is an outsider in a hostile world. He compares Rodman to Ishmael, whose quest is also motivated by loneliness, and argues convincingly that the cast of characters introduced by Poe boded well for a serious study of isolation and artistic perception. But the promise was unfulfilled, and the reader "swindled" (253) by the plagiarized pistache that follows. Edwin Fussell included a discussion of the novel in his volume *Frontier: American Literature and the American West,* concluding that "Poe has simply nothing to say, and quickly collapses into the trivial and inane, as in the ridiculous picture of himself, or his factotum Rodman, cavorting in the prairie" (161). Taking a different approach from that of Levine, John J. Teunissen and Evelyn J. Hinz stated that the novel not only is a successful hoax but, in its liberal use of sources, is a satire on the plagiarism common to the popular narratives of western exploration. An interesting postmodern view was given by Stephen Mainville in an essay that built upon French metafictionist readings of *Pym* to define the literal and metaphorical frontier in *Rodman,* as well as in *Pym,* as the space "between the meaningful and the interpretable" (361). Kent Ljungquist (1984) remarked that "the basic paradox of *Julius Rodman* involves the desire to write a story about an eighteenth-century landscape garden in the framework of an American wilderness setting" (14). The tone of the novel shifts from the rapture of a heroic quest to that of "a leisurely, scenic tour" (13). Liliane Weissberg, influenced by Foucault's notions of authorship and editorship, played with the text's editorial lineage from the fictional Rodman through the real Poe—who is the real author of the text as well as its fictional editor and the real editor of *Gentlemen's Magazine*—through the real Burton Pollin, who established the first complete, authorized version of the text since its initial journal publication.

Like the wide-open spaces that Rodman set out to investigate, *The Journal of Julius Rodman* offers scholars considerable little-trod territory to explore. Mainville and Ljungquist suggest productive lines of inquiry that could be expanded. Mainville's essay foregrounds the issue of meaningful design in nature and the human capacity to articulate it. Ljungquist's discussion of the landscape and the wilderness could be pursued in regard to American Edenic myths and to the gentrification, by the nineteenth century, of the seventeenth-century notion of the errand into the wilderness. In addition, as I have previously suggested, *Rodman* could be explored in terms of the narratology of displacement and memory, of loss and secrets.

THE NARRATIVE OF ARTHUR GORDON PYM

Sources, Publication, Reception

Firsthand accounts of disasters at sea, like the narratives of westward exploration, constituted a popular genre in the nineteenth century, and Poe borrowed liberally from them for *The Narrative of Arthur Gordon Pym.* Among many other sources, Poe used Benjamin Morrell's *Narrative of Four Voyages,* Jeremiah Reynolds's *Voyage of the Potomac* and *Address on the Subject of a Surveying and Exploring Expedition,* as well as John L. Stephens's *Incidents of*

Travel in Egypt, Arabia Petraea and the Holy Land, and Gesenius's *Hebrew and English Lexicon of the Old Testament.* Through Reynolds, Poe most probably learned of the atrocious mutiny on board the Nantucket whaler, the *Globe,* details of which appear as plot elements in *Pym* (Beegel). Again through Reynolds, Poe became familiar with John Cleves Symmes's *Symzonia* and his "holes at the poles" theory, which postulated the earth's hollow core (*P* 1, 17–28), a theory that could account for Pym's disappearance into the "embraces of the cataract" (*P* 1, 206). J. Lasley Dameron (Kopley 1992) has demonstrated William Scoresby's 1823 *Journal of a Voyage to the Northern Whale-Fishery* to be a most probable source for the final details of *Pym,* concluding that the ending, even the strangely veined waters and the final vision of the monumental white figure, is an accurate description of physical phenomena. In addition, the hieroglyphics on the island of Tsalal may have a source in contemporary accounts of Viking expeditions (Moldenhauer 1992).

Pym was planned as a serial publication, and two installments appeared under Poe's name in January and February 1837 in *The Southern Literary Messenger,* from which Poe, earlier, had been dismissed as editor. He did not continue the series with *SLM* but instead made arrangements with Harper and Brothers to publish *Pym* in book form, which, when it did appear, included a preface signed by A. G. Pym explaining that the first installments published as fiction under the name of "Mr. Poe" were not fiction but were the facts of Pym's own adventure, which he was now willing to continue to tell under his own name. In May 1837, *Knickerbocker Magazine* announced that *Pym* was "nearly ready for publication" (*PoeL,* 244), and Harper and Brothers made application for copyright on June 10, 1837. But the volume was not announced by Harper's until the following May and not published until the end of July 1838 (Heartman and Canny, 39).

Although Killis Campbell reported that a letter from Harper's dated February 20, 1839, indicated that fewer than 100 copies were sold in the United States during the first year after publication (49, n. 3), a portion of that letter in the *Poe Log* reads more ambiguously: " 'We are inclined to think that "Pym" has not succeeded or been received as well in this country as it has in England. When we published the work, we sent 100 copies of it to London—And we presume they have been sold. In addition to which we understand that an English edition has been printed' " (260). *Pym* was printed in London by Wiley and Putnam in 1838, with a third London edition appearing in 1841. It first appeared in France, translated by Baudelaire, in 1858 (Heartman and Canny, 39). In 1974 and 1975, Burton Pollin published his discoveries of nineteen contemporary reviews of *Pym* and clearly demonstrated his thesis that Poe's novel was neither ignored nor condemned by reviewers. For instance, in September 1838, while *Burton's Gentleman's Magazine,* which was to hire Poe as assistant editor within a year, wrote, " 'We regret to find Mr. Poe's name in connexion with such a mass of ignorance and effrontery' " (*PoeL,* 254), *Family Magazine,* distributed in New York, Boston, and Philadelphia, exclaimed: " 'Commend us to Arthur

Gordon Pym! He is a genius and his *adventures* rare and wonderful' '' (Pollin 1975, 33–34).

Professor Pollin has collated a bibliography of over 320 translations, adaptations, and reprints from around the world, suggesting that "the book has by no means fallen into neglect or out of print at any time" (1978, 93). The novel's influence on such writers as Melville, Baudelaire, Jules Verne, H. P. Lovecraft, Henry James, H. G. Wells, Fuentes, Pynchon, Nabokov, Barth, and others has been well discussed (*PQ* 1952; Seelye 1967; Haverstick 1969; Santraud 1972; LeClair 1973; Watson 1975; Farrell Lee 1978, 1992; Tintner 1978; Berressem 1982; Rainwater 1983; Levine 1984; Ljungquist 1985; Zanger 1986; Barth 1989, 1992). In recent years, *Pym* has come to be seen by some as central to Poe studies. Criticism devoted to *Pym* has been unusually voluminous: ninety critical articles were produced between 1950 and 1980, with that number close to doubling in the decade since then. See especially surveys of criticism compiled by Douglas Robinson (1982) and David Ketterer (1992). The winter 1978 issue of *American Transcendental Quarterly,* edited by Richard Benton, was entirely devoted to *Pym,* and during the 150th anniversary of its publication, a four-day conference on "*Arthur Gordon Pym* and Contemporary Criticism" was held on Nantucket Island, from which Pym began his adventures. The first volume devoted solely to *Pym* includes selected essays from that conference under the title *Poe's Pym: Critical Explorations,* edited by Richard Kopley.

Genesis, Structure, Unity, Genre

The literary history of *The Narrative of Arthur Gordon Pym* has been beset by controversy in almost every particular. Not only crucial aesthetic conclusions but facts concerning its genesis and publication history have been debated. Questions regarding its structure and unity have been closely tied to its genesis. Although it has been stated that, until the 1960s, critical response to the novel presumed upon its structural unity (Ketterer 1992), as early as 1948 Alexander Cowie had declared the novel a failure *unless* we approach it as a succession of episodes (302). In the early 1960s, Sidney Kaplan (1960) and L. Moffitt Cecil (1963) argued that *Pym* is essentially two disjointed, superficially fused tales. "They remain unnaturally yoked together. The *Grampus* story wants climax and conclusion, and the *Jane Guy* story, so placed that it might be expected to serve for both, can really supply neither" (Cecil, 240). In 1966, Sidney Moss cited *Pym* as a "literary patchwork" (85) occasioned by Poe's decision, after serial publication of the initial episodes in *SLM,* to continue serialization of an expanded novel, and that same year, Joseph Ridgely and Iola Haverstick presented detailed evidence charting the course of Poe's writing that identified five distinct stages of development:

(1) the *Southern Literary Messenger* text, composed in late 1836 and published in the January and February, 1837, issues; (2) the material following the end of the *Messenger*

segment up through the close of Chapter IX, written in April–May, 1837; (3) Chapters X through XV, put together probably in late 1837 and early 1838; (4) Chapter XVI to the conclusion, with the omission of Chapter XXIII and the final "Note," composed between March and May, 1838; and (5) Chapter XXIII and the "Note," added to the text in July, 1838. (64)

They concluded that "the story lacks a controlling theme and has no incontrovertible serious meaning—symbolic, psychoanalytic, existentialist, racist, or otherwise. The subtle readings of recent commentators . . . depend upon emphasis on certain chosen elements at the expense of consideration of the *whole* text. No amount of straining can bring all its disparate elements into a consistent interpretation" (80). The following year, Moss wrote that only after Poe had begun to publish the tale serially did he decide to expand it into a novel, and he thus proceeded to develop the Jane Guy section. Moss contends that those who have found unity of theme in *Pym* have merely discovered a thematic relation between two tales, a not uncommon occurrence among the works of Poe, and concludes that structural flaws preclude any thematic interpretation.

Recently, scholars have reassessed both facts and conclusions concerning the genesis of *Pym*. Alexander Hammond (1978) questioned the Ridgely/Haverstick assumption that it was because Poe failed to supply a completed manuscript that Harper and Brothers applied for copyright in June 1837 but did not publish the novel until July 1838. Hammond contends that the manuscript was complete by the copyright date but that the financial panic of 1837 resulted in a decision by Harper's to delay publication. In "Growth of the Text," Ridgely challenges the import of Hammond's conclusions, while modifying some of his earlier views: he posits four discrete stages in the composition of *Pym,* is less emphatic about precise dates, and is more open to serious critical readings. Ridgely twice mentions that Poe moved from New York to Philadelphia in August 1838, implying that he did so only after the composition of *Pym* was completed. However, the *Poe Log* cites early 1838 as the time of Poe's move (248). Using sources that he newly identified, Richard Kopley (1987) presented arguments that Poe may have begun to write the first chapter of *Pym* as early as mid- to late February 1836, rather than quite late in 1836, as Ridgely and Haverstick contend (162–63 n. 14). Hammond and Kopley contend that *Pym* was more carefully planned than has previously been thought the case. The implications of the genesis and publication controversy touch upon the reasonableness of scholarly approaches that see unifying patterns in the work.

In 1974, Professor Ridgely enlarged the debate by bringing the question of genre to bear upon it. Critical approaches have presumed that the work is an imaginary voyage or a verisimilar voyage narrative or a true voyage narrative, a picaresque or a tale of terror, a bildungsroman, an initiation story, a mythic quest, a satire, a hoax, a racist allegory, a biblical allegory. Ridgely suggested that the tale's hoaxing tone delimits its genre and ought to restrain critical "overingenuity" (8). Jules Zanger (1986) argued that *Pym* is composed of two genres:

travel literature with its scientific detail and even-toned narrative and the Gothic with its horror and fantastic mystery. A scientific reading of the ending would reduce the fantastic elements of the novel to madness, while a visionary reading devalues the scientific. Poe's challenge was to exploit the fantastic while satisfying an audience that demanded rational explanations.

Attempts to restrain readings of *Pym* through genre delimitations or reiterations of its flaws have largely failed. Poe himself, in a letter to William Burton dated June 1, 1840, referred to his novel as a "very silly book" (Ostrom: 1, 130). Perhaps he did so only in reaction to Burton's scathing criticism of *Pym* as an "impudent attempt at humbugging" (*PoeL,* 254). In any event, his own assessment has not curtailed serious critical approaches to *Pym*. They are multifold.

Critical Approaches

Surveys of Pym *Criticism.* Valuable bibliographies of *Pym* criticism include those compiled by Frederick Frank (1981), Douglas Robinson (1985), and David Ketterer (1992). Frank's is organized around editions, source studies, and interpretive and analytic essays and includes annotations of each entry. Robinson organized criticism published between 1950 and 1980 around six foci: *Pym's* relation to Poe, its relation to Poe's world, narrative symbolism, narrative unity, the narrator's relation to the author, and the problematic frame. Moving through criticism published from 1980 to 1990, Ketterer adopted Robinson's format, isolating three approaches (reception, source, and influence studies) and eleven distinct readings (psychoanalytical, mythic, psychological, existential, social commentary, *Eureka*-inspired, formal and compositional, hoax, satiric and ironic, deconstructive, and visionary). Read out of context, any multiplication of distinctions, because it focuses on details of difference, may seem to simplify the complex interrelatedness of *Pym* scholarship and to obscure its broader outlines. Much work on *Pym* and myth, for instance, involves, in central ways, not only psychological and/or psychoanalytical readings but also visionary and *Eureka*-inspired readings as well as source study, and Ketterer is careful to point this out. The surveys have done substantial work in the area of classification and distribution that does not need to be repeated here. The aim of the present study is the opposite, although complementary, undertaking of integration with a focus on the dynamics at play in the heterogeneous dialogue of *Pym* scholarship.

Early Studies. The earliest critical responses to *The Narrative of Arthur Gordon Pym* were based on either the assumptions of verisimilitude or the foregrounding of the text's symbolic patterns. This chapter's sketch of a genealogical tree of subsequent critical approaches to *Pym* finds sociohistorical and New Historical readings linked to the former and all other readings, in their manifold diversity, linked (even negatively through their opposition) to the latter. The former include those of Henry James, F. O. Matthiesen, Alexander Cowie, and

W. H. Auden; the latter include studies of the novel's thematic patterns: Marie Bonaparte's *Edgar Poe: Sa vie, son oeuvre—Étude psychanalytique,* Patrick F. Quinn's "Poe's Imaginary Journey," and Edward H. Davidson's *Poe: A Critical Study.* Gaston Bachelard (1944) called for a dual approach, stressing both verisimilitude and symbolism.

Although, in 1878, Henry James wrote that "an enthusiasm for Poe is the mark of a decidedly primitive stage of reflection. . . . Baudelaire thought him a profound philosopher, the neglect of whose golden utterances stamped his native land with infamy. Nevertheless, Poe was much the greater charlatan of the two, as well as the greater genius" (60); he also praised "a wonderful tale . . . which was a thing to show, by the way, what imagination Americans *could* have—the story of the shipwrecked Gordon Pym." In a preface for the 1907–8 edition of *The Golden Bowl,* James, while appropriating the ending of *Pym* for his own novel, declared Poe's work to be a failure; it fails "because it stops short, and stops short for want of connexions. There *are* no connexions; not only, I mean, in the sense of further statement, but of our own further relation to the elements, which hang in the void; whereby we see the effect lost, the imaginative effort wasted" (1934, 257). Burton Pollin (1973) has detailed the "changing relationship" between Poe and James, while Adeline R. Tintner (1978) pointed out that James's very appropriation was a measure of his appreciation. Stephen Donadio (1986) has argued that James's "insistence on literary closure" (91) is what led to his refusal to accept the ending of *Pym* as an artistic achievement. "James's aesthetic predilections (which are essentially—though hardly simply—those of literary realism) are in most important respects antithetical to those of the author of the shifty, inconsistent *Narrative*" (92).

Bonaparte's 1933 psychobiographical approach (available in translation in England in 1949 and in the United States in 1954) treated Poe's work as symptomatic of his presumed psychopathology. It may seem dated to any post-Lacanian reader and, as Roger Forclaz contended, reductive and contradictory (1987) or even "dangerous" (1964). Forclaz maintains that if Poe's art is merely the product of psychopathology, then its importance is limited to the autobiographical, excluding cultural and aesthetic, significance. He points out the flaws in Bonaparte's method, especially in its "suppression of contradictions," and concludes that while Jungian depth psychology can illuminate the psychological dimension of Poe's work, Bonaparte's use of Freudian psychology distorts the facts of Poe's craftsmanship. Still, Bonaparte's analysis of *Pym* isolated patterns and themes upon which many serious readings of the novel were built. Patrick F. Quinn called her a "highly gifted reader" (1957, 22). Her reading, classically Freudian, is oedipal: Pym's voyage is a revolt against the Father and a return to the Mother. He strikes out against paternalistic authority while sailing maternal, amniotic seas. The ships aboard which Pym voyages and the island caverns he explores are maternal bodies, and his are fantasies of returning to the womb. The anxiety activated by such incestuous desires is displaced into the castrative potential of teeth: those of Tiger, the pet dog who turns on Pym, or of Dirk Peters, his companion, or of the totem birds, which circle overhead screaming "Tekeli-li!" (the once perplexing scream that has now been identified as the title of a play in which Poe's mother had a role [Jackson and Pollin, 1979]), or of the sharks that tear apart Pym's boyhood companion after he has lost his gangrenous leg to the castrative power of the maternal sea. Returning to the womb is a risky business! Thus does Pym approach and avoid it throughout his journey. But return he does in the ultimate episode: the caverns on the island of Tsalal Bonaparte likens to the womb; the very water is like maternal blood on which the fetus survives; and, as Pym and Dirk Peters rush into the embrace of a gigantic, shrouded human figure, the hue of whose skin is of perfect whiteness, the womb fantasy is revived, and the wish is finally fulfilled. The two "sons" are permitted entry into the milky white but, alas, cold and dead body of the mother (290–352).

Apart from Bonaparte, verisimilitude was the aesthetic standard against which most of the earliest critics measured *Pym,* and the critical conclusions reached were often a function of how strongly one insisted on mimetic readings. Gaston Bachelard, in *La Psychanalyse du feu* analyzed Poe as a poet of darkened, stagnant waters that comsume life. In 1944, Bachelard introduced a reedition of Baudelaire's 1858 translation of *Pym,* urging readers to remain open not only to the text's verisimilitude but to the dream components and the fantasy. The poles of verisimilitude and of dream broadly sketch the parameters of *Pym* criticism throughout the twentieth century. "Literature, divided between the fantastic and the real, between free invention and servile description, too often ignores intermediary and blended forms that are nonetheless the forms of the living imagination. *The Narrative of Arthur Gordon Pym* helps us reunite, through numerous themes, the real and the imaginary" (18). Bachelard briefly introduced elements that were to become important in later readings of *Pym,* including myth and Jungian analysis, as well as social commentary and a vision of a hostile universe.

In *Literary History of the United States* (1946), F. O. Matthiessen acknowledged those aspects of *Pym* that have remained the source of both its condemnation and its praise:

On one level these adventures of young Arthur and his friend Augustus, who survive mutiny and delirium and the sight of sea gulls gorging themselves on human flesh, are merely the last word in adolescent fantasy. But the imaginative effect of the compulsive horror of whiteness, as the voyagers are driven at the close farther and farther into the uncharted Antarctic, relates back to Coleridge's albatross and forward to Melville's "whiteness of the whale," and is on the level kindred with both. (329)

Alexander Cowie's *The Rise of the American Novel* also made passing reference to *Pym*'s probable influence on Melville, including a discussion of verisimilitude in *Pym.* He pointed to Poe's preface, his use of New England and Virginian settings, and his knowledge of seamanship and exploration as attempts to claim authenticity for a story that contains elements of "phantasmagoria." Cowie remarked that *Pym* "contains passages as gripping as Poe ever wrote" (302) and that "granted its defects, it exhibits flashes of genius that have interested many special students of the craft of fiction" (305). Two years later, W. H. Auden included *Pym* in his 1950 anthology of Poe's work for Rinehart Press, calling it "one of the finest adventure stories ever written" (vii).

Patrick F. Quinn acknowledged his debt to Marie Bonaparte and to Bachelard in "Poe's Imaginary Journey," an essay that Edward H. Davidson, in turn acknowledging his debt to Quinn, called "brilliant." Quinn stated that what Baudelaire, Bonaparte, and Bachelard knew was that "Poe's singular gift was to probe into the caverns of the psyche and to bring up to the level of imaginative literature the dark scrolls—of fear, guilt, and obsession—that those caverns contain" (1957, 26). Quinn contended that *Pym* is "strictly organized and skillfully developed. Its architecture takes the form of a set of episodes in each of which a revolt and overthrow occur. Like a schematic image of the sea itself, the narrative line of this oceanic adventure follows a pattern of crest and trough, and at each crest the new conflict that has been preparing is resolved in violence" (182–83). Quinn's work is important not only because he deepened the insights available from the French critics but because he anticipated those critics whose focus is on myth and quest literature, on Poe's irony and hoaxing, and on postmodernist concerns with indeterminacy. Quinn argued that *Pym*'s design involves a pattern of revolt and a recurring theme of deception, deception that defines the world of the novel as marked by "an incessant struggle between reality and appearance. Pym is caught up in a life in which nothing is stable, in which nothing is ever really known. Power and authority are repeatedly overthrown; expectation and surmise can anticipate only false conclusions" (181). Pym's journey, Quinn maintained, is a "voyage of the mind" (201).

Quinn also discussed the novel's many parallels with *Moby-Dick,* and he raised other issues that became important in the work of later critics, such as perverseness, the doppelgänger, the novel's inconsistencies, and the bifurcation of the hero into Pym and Augustus and later into Pym and Peters. As Frank put it, this essay is "a point of departure for modern *Pym* criticism and a mandatory essay for all *Pym*-ologists" (125).

Davidson (1957), building upon Bonaparte's focus on revolt and on death and rebirth and upon Quinn's focus on revolt and deception, isolated four themes: deception, self-loss, death, rebirth. He, too, viewed the novel as a voyage of the mind, "a study of emerging consciousness" (160). Long before the metafictionists and postmodernist critics appropriated, for their very different ends, issues of epistemology and self-reflexivity, Davidson wrote that

Poe steadily defines and sharpens the point of perception until all else fades before the intensity with which a Pym-self regards the world and itself. This self-as-imagination begins with the real, substantial world, follows the poetic direction of penetrating and destroying that world, and then goes even farther in order to set up on "the other side" certain symbols and keys to the mind's perception of reality. The book is indeed finished. . . . However ill-organized it may be, *Pym* is a study of the emergence and growth of the knowing and thinking self. (160–61)

Unlike the postmodernists who later zeroed in on Pym's dissolving world, Davidson affirms the reconstruction of "symbols and keys to the mind's perception of reality." Like the myth critics who built upon his work, Davidson associated the quest for self in *Pym* with the quest for Unity in *Eureka* and discussed *Pym* as a quest for primal origins, concluding that "*The Narrative of Arthur Gordon Pym* is a curiosity in Romantic symbolism: its main burden is the ultimate submergence and loss of man to the world of infinitely variable forms which Romanticism posited" (179–80).

   Being or Nothingness? The early symbolists provided what Eric Carlson called a "transcendental-symbolic" framework for reading Poe (1987, 215). They could claim for their progeny the bulk of *Pym* criticism, which either springs from, or is in opposition to, their own. Two divergent perspectives— one positing a redemptive affirmation, the other emphasizing its loss—characterize the poles between which most of these readings of *Pym* move. For instance, while Davidson suggested that Pym's movement toward self-discovery culminates in an illuminating vision of Unity, later explored in *Eureka,* Walter E. Bezanson, in "The Troubled Sleep of Arthur Gordon Pym" emphasized Pym's drive toward self-extinction rather than self-knowledge. Pym's is a "passive abandonment" to "dream power" (171). Charles O'Donnell's "From Earth to Ether: Poe's Flight into Space" discussed *Pym* in terms of "the dread of annihilation and the unfolding search for unity" (87) but concurred with Davidson that Poe's "movement from *Pym* to *Eureka* is from the perceptual to the conceptual . . . throughout his work he is concerned with the problem of identity" (91). In 1969, John F. Lynen, Peter J. Sheehan, and Richard A. Levine each discussed Pym's emergence of consciousness at the moment of annihilation. Lynen read the ending of *Pym* in the context of *Eureka,* with its final movement toward "new knowledge, a vision of the All in which the self disappears" (227). Sheehan maintained that the conscience or reason (Dirk Peters) continually saves the imagination (Pym) in the process of the soul's growth toward consciousness, "a growth which will be complete at the moment in which the soul perceives its own destruction, losing itself in the reunification with the One" (67). Levine discussed the conscious/unconscious dichotomy enscribed by imagery of above/below, high/low which indicates a "symbolic and unconscious journey downward through the levels of the human soul" (31). Pym's is a purgative journey, Levine suggests, a descent into evil before a final passage into purity and whiteness: "from shadow to light to salvation" (31).

   The two major books on Poe published in 1973, David Halliburton's *Edgar Allan Poe: A Phenomenological View* and G. R. Thompson's *Poe's Fiction: Romantic Irony in the Gothic Tales,* clearly define the forked path down which Pymologists travel—one emphasized transcendence and wholeness; the other foregrounded irony and led to issues of hoaxing and indeterminacy. In his *Southern Literary Journal* review, Patrick F. Quinn distinguished between the two: Halliburton's concern is with Poe's theme of affirmation, Thompson's with the possibility of nothingness. Halliburton's volume is one of the most comprehensive analyses of Poe's transcendental vision, a vision that affirms cosmic unity. Repeatedly, Halliburton maintains, Poe delivers Pym from Nothingness until, at the end, Pym reaches the longed-for moment of unifying transcendence, a moment Poe would again reach for in *Eureka*. While Halliburton discussed the ending of *Pym* as a transcendent vision, Thompson wrote that "what Pym discovers at the pole, as he moves through a world before time, is a final deceptive perversity of fortune, the final grotesquerie in the journey toward 'discovery' of the self" (182). Like Quinn and Davidson before him, Thompson regarded "the experience of the inner mind" (176) as central to *Pym,* but unlike his predecessors, he viewed Pym's attempts "to discover the primal facts of existence and of the self" (176) to be futile. Thompson argued that Pym's journey inverts the usual path toward death and maturation, as he regresses into that final amniotic sea. He climbs into his coffin on the Grampus, and, while he "seems to undergo a resurrection," he "actually regresses further and further into unbeing. . . . Whatever God there may be in the universe, if any, has moved Pym from darkness to whiteness, from nothing to nothing, and mockingly exacted a perverse vengeance for some unknown offense" (183). Combining the Gothic and the satiric, Thompson saw Poe as creating a "Romantic irony" that both expresses and protects himself from his own dark obsessions. To Poe, the novel is both silly and serious, because Poe the ironist always mocks what he takes quite seriously.

Visionary Journeys. That the urge toward transcendence or toward revelation and self-knowledge motivates Pym's journey is the contention of those critics who have focused on the mythic foundations to the novel's patterns of death and rebirth and of the return to primal origins. In 1960, Walter Bezanson established in detail the recurring pattern of deaths and rebirths in *Pym.* Charles O'Donnell's 1962 essay noted that Pym's voyage runs a suggestive nine months and that "his ultimate symbolic birth into knowledge of the eternal is preceded by many symbolic deaths and rebirths" (87). Joel Porte concluded that "ultimately Pym's ontogenic voyage to primitive lands and beyond suggests a phylogenic voyage to the past of mankind, a journey to the beginning of consciousness and to that core of fear at the heart of the interior self. From the restraints of the modern world Pym journeys back to absolute freedom and seemingly to non-being, as omnipotent primitive fantasies finally overwhelm his frail reason" (93–94). In *Poe Poe Poe Poe Poe Poe Poe,* Daniel Hoffman wrote that *Pym,* edging "inexorably toward apocalypse" (259), is "the Total Voyage of Discovery" (260) through which Pym "enters the womb of the world itself, from which he was born, and is reborn" (272).

In my 1972 and 1978 studies of Poe's appropriation of mythic archetypes, I linked the death/rebirth motifs with the myth of the eternal return and the pattern of descent into hell to argue for the structural integrity of the novel. *Pym* "re-vitalizes an archetype found throughout religious mythology, the descent into Hell, and utilizes the structure of a sea voyage, a familiar post-Jungian image of the collective unconscious, to voyage into the recesses of the human psyche and journey backward in time to the origins of creation" (1972, 24). Similarly, in his introduction to the Godine edition of *Pym* the following year, Richard Wilbur wrote of the shrouded white figure: "[T]o the reader who understands that the tale is covertly a dream of spiritual return, the figure will be recognizable as Anthropos, or the Primal Man. . . . In other words, the figure stands for the coming reunion of the voyager's soul with God—or what is the same thing— with the divinity in himself' " (xxiv). Seeing Pym's voyage as a fictive pre-cursor of *Eureka,* I discussed his final vision as "at once annihilistic and re-demptive. The world pulls in upon itself, annihilating all that is, sinking at once into a chasm of Nothingness; but it is a chasm which throws itself open as if to embrace. It is the chasm of Unity and the embrace of God" (1978, 77).

Paul J. Eakin's "Poe's Sense of an Ending" also viewed the novel as a pattern of deaths and resurrections. *Pym* is one in a series of Lazarus stories in which Poe was in pursuit of ultimate knowledge, beyond the death experience. Pym confronts such knowledge in the final white vision. John Hussey separated Pym, who experiences the journey but fails to understand it, from "Mr. Poe" of the foreword, who shapes those experiences and gives them meaning. Building on O'Donnell, Wilbur, and others, Hussey elucidated "the nearly perfect symme-try" of the novel and the "succession of falls into the unconscious (or death), followed by new surges of power and energy until finally it is readied for its ultimate goal—a mystical union with divinity" (29–30).

Substantiating the interpretations of these earlier critics, Ana Maria Hernandez argued that Poe, as well as Hawthorne and Melville, was very much aware of mythological syncretism, important in Europe since the 1770s, which empha-sized the interrelatedness of all creation and concerned itself with origins and primal myth. Poe knew the theories of Jacob Bryant's *A New System, Or an Analysis of Antient Mythology,* 1774–1776. (See also Levine and Levine 1975 and Ljungquist 1985.) He probably knew George Stanley Faber's treatise *On the Origin of Pagan Idolatry,* both because Faber was a disciple of Bryant and because his work was widely popular in New England in the 1830s and 1840s. Faber discussed the Magna Mater as the melding of all the Pagan goddesses into a figure of the great mother and the earth who often assumed the form of a ship. She sprang from the sea but was born from a sacred mountain from which flowed the rivers of Paradise. Hernandez believes that Poe "deliberately employed and artfully elaborated" (9) upon symbols discussed by Faber.

Kent Ljungquist, in his essays and book on Poe's landscape aesthetics, also made use of Bryant's *Mythology.* He examined "the aesthetic dimension of sublimity" in order to "illuminate Poe's thematic purposes" in *Pym* (1978, 76). With reference to Bryant and the tradition of Romantic Titanism, which Ljung-quist maintained Poe probably knew from Keats and Shelley, he argued that the gigantic white figure at the end of *Pym* is a Titan: "somewhat less mysterious and more seriously grounded in a mythological tradition" (1985, 253). It "represents the search for sublime knowledge that exists beyond the veil of space-time existence" (1984, 60).

Discussing images of the Uruboros, the snake that forms a circle by swallowing its own tail and that "stands for cohesion, assimilation, primal unity" (65), Barton Levi St. Armand treated themes of transformation and repetition in *Pym*. With reference to Jung and Neumann, St. Armand linked the Uruboros to creation myths and maternal archetypes: "Here, too, beginning and ending merge and in the primal sea which washes the fetus, life is renewed and the cycle of existence continued. The womb is a 'natural' symbol of eternity as is the sea itself, and it is upon the sea that the drama of Arthur Gordon Pym is played out. . . . The world of *Pym* is a prenatal one" (68–69).

Curtis Fukuchi maintained that "a providential design informs the narrative as a whole. . . . The human plots and counterplots in the narrative are played out against this divine plot, and their repeated collapse suggests the inadequacy of materialistic quests" (147). Fukuchi used Poe's source in Morrell, who called for "the exploration of 'the secrets of the great Creator' " (155), to argue that *Pym* is a voyage of repeated providential salvation.

In a series of essays (1980, 1982, 1987), Richard Kopley combined a study of biographical and biblical allusions in *Pym* to make what is perhaps the most emphatic argument for the novel's unity of design. "All three levels of *Pym*," Kopley suggested, "the literal, the autobiographical, and the biblical—concern loss and recovery" (1987, 158). He elaborated upon O'Donnell's literal reading of the shrouded human figure at the end of the novel as "a figurehead, sail, or prow of a ship blown toward him by the new winds from the south" (O'Donnell, 90) and argued that the mysterious figure is the reemerging ship, the *Penguin,* coming again, as it had in the novel's preface, almost to destroy and then to rescue Pym. These symmetrical penguins, self-reflecting icons, mirror the center of the novel: the death of Augustus. It is that moment of death, Kopley claimed, to which Pym wished to return so that he might die along with his friend. Linking Augustus to Poe's brother Henry and arguing that Poe's focus in *Pym* is through Henry to his mother, Kopley concluded that the final shrouded figure is both brother and mother. In a subsequent essay, Kopley suggested that the shrouded figure is an emblem of Christ.

Myth criticism persists in *Pym* studies. In a well-documented essay on Poe's knowledge and use of Celtic myths and Arthur legends, "Poe's Reading of Myth: The White Vision of Arthur Gordon Pym," Carol Peirce and Alexander G. Rose III present intriguing links between a variety of Arthurian elements and *Pym.*

Darker Visions. Although Quinn and Davidson had early defined, or redefined, a transcendental vision inherent to Pym's voyage, there are elements of darkness implicit in Quinn's emphasis on deception, revolt, and violence as well as in Davidson's focus on a revelation that comes only at the moment of annihilation. In addition, proceeding from Thompson's ironic reading, other "dark" readings had begun to persist as a kind of shadow side to the explicitly affirmative tradition defined by Quinn and Davidson and continued by Halliburton and others. In her 1966 essay, "Possibilities in *Pym,*" Helen Lee wrote that the novel demonstrates how any "pursuit of the meaningful brings destruction rather than understanding" (1153), and she viewed Poe's pretense that *Pym* is a factual account as "an echo of the hoaxes of human experience itself, which seems such an infinitely well-organized physical mechanism but which eventuates in nothingness" (1153). The hoaxical elements of *Pym*—that the first installments were published as fiction, that the novel was published with a preface purporting the fiction to be fact, that the endnote attempted, in matter-of-fact tone, to explain the unexplainable, and so on—were noted by early commentators and discussed by Quinn and later by Evelyn Hinz. Joel Porte concluded that "*The Narrative of Arthur Gordon Pym* finally defies circumscription of meaning, demonstrating how in Poe's hands the romance of New World adventure could become an illimitable allegory of self-exploration—a symbolic journey that ends only because it is truncated and that issues, not in the expected self-knowledge, but in an apocalypse of cosmic mystery" (94). On a less apocalyptic note, Burton Pollin, in his introduction to *Pym* in *The Imaginary Voyages,* cited the novel's inconsistencies as evidence of Poe's parodic intent and stated that "in general, Poe was never concerned with consistency of characterization nor subtlety of motivation. There is no reason to lament the lack of psychological depth in *Pym;* juvenile fiction and sea tales rarely contain these elements" (10).

Josie Campbell (1970) discussed Poe's vision of a world so dark that deception and violence are appropriate responses to it. Building upon Quinn's discussion of Pym's "will-to-disaster" (1952, 181), Joseph Moldenhauer argued that the life-giving creative imagination triggers a death-wishing perverse response. At the end, "dying to life, they are born into death" (278). The very "logic of the *Narrative* is," he wrote, "the convertibility and even identity of destruction and deliverance" (271). William Peden defined *Pym* as "a dark voyage from which there is no return, an existentialist trip from nothingness to nothingness. . . . Poe has created his own special province where the real, the unreal, and the surreal coalesce or coagulate: inscape from which all familiar signs eventually are obliterated or removed and over which only Death 'looks gigantically down' " (89).

Robert Carringer (1974) considered Poe's impulse to "delimit space" (508) as a device to entrap and bury the protagonist, rather than enlighten and free him. *Pym* combines the expansion of a sea voyage with the restriction of multiple enclosures, but, instead of fusing these "contradictory tendencies" into a "single psychological drive, a destructive quest for ultimate knowledge" (514), Poe alternates from one extreme to the other. While building upon the work of Quinn and Davidson, Harold Beaver, in his "Introduction" to the Penguin edition of *Pym,* stressed deception and hoaxing as central to Poe's vision in *Pym.*

He saw the primary theme of the novel as the disintegration of a dual self—composed first of Augustus and Pym and then of Pym and Peters—as it moved from innocence to experience and was "reborn to life-in-death, from which there is no turning back" (30).

Postmodern Criticism. While Cecil, Moss, Ridgely, and Haverstick declared that there was no unified meaning in *Pym,* for decades other critics have defied such pronouncements in myriad ways and have found a multitude of unifying themes and patterns. Postmodern theorists have declared the debate over unity of meaning to be beside the point because unity is a nostalgic illusion anyway—meaning cannot be determined, and the more indeterminate the text, the better.

In 1973, Paul Eakin had noted that the existence of meaning is not in doubt in *Pym,* "but rather man's capacity to apprehend it. . . . Whether Poe's endings take the hero to the brink of the abyss or plunge him into the gulf beyond, they all confirm that Poe and his heroes believe in a significant universe; they believe in its buried treasure and they dream of the man who could find it out and cry 'Eureka!' to an astonished world" (21). Precisely this dream of crying "Eureka!" to an astonished world is what is at stake in the critical controversies involving *Pym.* Both the traditional, or neo-Romantic, critics who argue for unity of meaning in the novel and those critics of its composition who fault it for lack of a unified design operate out of a context that values "buried treasure": the hidden meaning at the center of a unified pattern of form and theme. But those critics loosely grouped as postmodern are concerned with all that disrupts such unity. Their interests lie in irony, parody, and self-reflexivity, in texts that do not close, and in the indeterminacy of meaning. John Carlos Rowe wrote that "forever holding out the promise of a buried signified, *Pym* offers a sequence of forged or imitation truths: delivered messages, deciphered hieroglyphs, a penultimate vision. And yet the inability of each successive sign to present its truth is ironically disclosed, increasingly entangling any reading in the signifying web it attempts to unravel" (1977, 104). Thus whereas Richard Kopley speaks of the *key* to *all* of Poe's *Pym* (1987, 151), Judith Sutherland argues that "in fact, there is no key" (12).

A series of studies of *Pym* as metafiction, published primarily in France during the late 1960s and 1970s, presents an image of Pym literally edging in and out of the typeface or moving between and betwixt lines of the text, readings that remind one of Mallarmé's "Un coup de dés," which begins with words slowly emerging from the whiteness of the page and ends as they slowly sink back into whiteness. In these readings, *Pym* is about itself—a self-reflexive text. In "*Le Caractère singulier de cette eau,*" Jean Ricardou read the Tsalalian dichotomy of black and white as black ink imposed on white paper. Maurice Levy's "*Pym, Conte Fantastique?*" discussed the embrace of the final white figure as a fall into the abyss of a final white page. In the tradition of Poe's own "A Predicament," Maurice Mourier's "*Le tombeau d'Edgar Poe,*" mocking the critical enterprise in its search for meaning in texts, facetiously argued that the strange shapes of the caverns on Tsalal and the engravings on the walls spell the names of Poe and Pym. Daniel A. Wells's essay "Engraved within the Hills: Further Perspectives on the Ending of *Pym*" failed to cite Mourier but seemed to take him quite seriously, making the point that the Tsalalian episode is intentionally self-reflexive: in spelling out his own name in the caves, Poe points a finger at his own handwriting on the walls and "at the artificiality of the entire construct" (14). "Here," wrote Wells, "as in experimental contemporary fiction, emphasis on the artificiality of art can create self-annihilating artifacts" (15).

The intriguing critical play of the French commentators became a darkly ironical matter in the hands of American deconstructionists: DeFalco, Rowe, Ketterer, and Kennedy followed the lead of G. R. Thompson's ideas concerning Poe's "Romantic irony." Joseph DeFalco (1976) discussed "Pym's failure to perceive that the nature of reality cannot be penetrated by mind in any direct way" (64). As John Carlos Rowe (1977) put it, "What is in fact inscribed at the heart of the island is the doubleness of writing which we have seen enacted as the major theme of the work. The chasms present themselves as signs of the darkness and ambiguity in which man finds himself imprisoned" (115).

The hoaxical elements of *Pym* became thematic material for critics probing Poe's pre-postmodernist concerns. As J. Gerald Kennedy (1976) wrote, "Deception constitutes both the medium and the message: the reader's encounter with a treacherous text mirrors the narrator's encounter with a duplicitous world, and both experiences point toward a realization that man's search for truth and meaning culminates not in transcendent harmony but cognitive confusion" (42). Kennedy maintains that, for Poe, experience is double and truth is problematical:

Poe's hoaxes pose the epistemological question of how one can determine rationally the meaning of perceived phenomena. . . . For Poe, the hoax apparently embodied his conception of man's relationship to the phenomenal world: the pursuit of meaning confirms only the deceptiveness and inaccessibility of truth. The universe is not merely the plot but the hoax of God. (1976, 44)

So if Poe hoaxes his readers, these critics maintained, it must be remembered that the universe hoaxes us all. David Ketterer (1979) wrote that Poe operates on "the belief that in relation to a sensed visionary reality everyday reality constitutes one gross deception" (xii–xiii).

The insights of Bonaparte, Patrick Quinn, Davidson, and those who built upon them are quite apparent in the work of John T. Irwin, although, clearly, appropriated for far different interpretive ends. What Halliburton called the "space beyond the word" (269) was central to Irwin's influential *American Hieroglyphics*. He echoed the work of the earlier French metafictionists and, by integrating that work into his appropriation of previous scholarship on mythic patterns in *Pym* (especially, O'Donnell, Porte, and Farrell Lee), brought the myth criticism into a postmodern context. Irwin discussed the "endlessness of the quest for origins, the limitlessness of seeking an ultimate limit" (113):

That Pym's voyage to the pole is a symbolic quest for the origin of writing, a quest
embodied in the written narrative's own oblique questioning of its origin (its unexplained
"being in existence"), is subtly evoked by Poe's displacement [*sic*] of the dangers of
the abyss from the act of exploring to the act of writing. It is not that the writing stops
with the interruption of the voyage but that the voyage stops with the interruption of the
writing. Writing in search of its origin *is* the self-dissolving voyage to the abyss. (91)

Paul Rosenzweig, in an important essay on the problematical nature of truth in
the novel, contended that "*Pym* reflects the inability of meaning, on every level,
to assert or declare itself, and of any end to complete itself despite man's constant search—whether he be adventurer or reader—for enduring meaning"
(139). Even the note at the novel's end, which seeks to explain the sudden
cessation of the narrative, "has one continual thrust—a search for meaning"
(147), but it succeeds only in creating further mystification.

   J. Gerald Kennedy wrote that *Pym* "presents itself as unreadable; the letter
from Augustus to Pym finally becomes, in fact, a synecdoche of the novel,
manifesting its excruciating doubleness: one side contains a legible but confounding inscription, while the other reveals an essential blankness—the absent
meaning of an effaced, incommunicable message" (1983, 133–34). Later in *Poe,
Death, and the Life of Writing*, Kennedy theorized that *Pym* "grimly illustrates
the way that Poe projects nature and phenomenal experience as an unintelligible
text in which death figures as the ultimate cipher" (155). In his introduction to
The Narrative of Arthur Gordon Pym of Nantucket and Related Tales (1994),
Kennedy agrees with Patrick F. Quinn that because it incorporates "many of
Poe's most characteristic and obsessive themes" (xiv), *Pym* is the "crucial text"
in understanding Poe. Kennedy posits a "philosophical split at the heart of the
narrative" between belief in a caring God whose providential plan lies behind
the vicissitudes of life and trust in the pagan concept of *fortuna* with its implication of absurd unpredictability (xiii). *Pym* is "a composite of the desires and
anxieties, the dreams and realities, which have become synonymous with Poe's
vision of our moral predicament" (xx). In *The Narrative of Arthur Gordon Pym
and the Abyss of Interpretation* (1995) Kennedy goes on to discuss *Pym* and
the myriad interpretations that it has spawned as indicative of the human struggle
for meaning in the face of meaninglessness:

Has Pym been rescued by a heavenly form . . . or vaporized by an author racked by
private frustrations? This is the enigma of *Pym* that haunts the reader, for the novel
enacts the metaphysical crisis of modernity itself: the longing for faith before the great,
silent void of nonbeing . . . Poe's novel prefigures the spiritual dilemma that now conditions our reading of the protagonist's struggle against meaninglessness. (13)

Of course, Kennedy, in stressing the struggle for meaning and the will to believe,
has constructed yet another meaning for the text. His abyss is not the void; it
is quite full of possibilities for meaning.

Some postmodern critics have had a less bleak view of the possibility of making meaning out of the text. In *American Apocalypses,* Douglas Robinson, with both a decidedly Derridean approach as well as a mythic perspective, raises the interpretive act to salvific heights. He writes that artistic or philosophical acts ''in terms of their apocalyptic hopes, may . . . project [human beings] into a transfigured beyond'' (122). Dennis Pahl in his 1989 book-length study gave a deconstructionist reading that did not simply declare that meaning is dead but suggested that we might be invited to invent for ourselves new meanings:

> [I]n attempting to locate the meaning of the white mist that Pym encounters, critics have in a sense repeated Pym's quest for ultimate truth and knowledge. . . . by creating a gap or space into which (let us say) the reader must voyage, [Poe] makes ironic the very idea of bringing the text to a successful closure—with a correct meaning. For the ''white light of revelation'' is really no revelation at all; it simply marks the absence around which the reader is allowed to construct his own interpretive discourse, filling in the blank space with his own sort of fiction. What Poe's text accomplishes here is not to represent an ultimate knowledge of the self, but rather to lay down the conditions upon which such a knowledge is possible: thus to see how ''truth''—and more specifically, the truth of the self—is not discovered, but invented. (41–42)

Pahl might want to reassess whether the white light of revelation, even as he defines it—as the absence around which the reader's interpretive discourse is constructed—is simple and is no revelation at all. That space of possibility may provide far more revelation than an essentialist message engraven in the text. Irwin's point that meaning is often determined ''by an unperceived shadow which the reader's own self casts upon the text'' (1988, 13; see also Irwin's essay in Kopley 1992) need not imply that an acknowledgment of the self-reflexive nature of those shadows precludes finding within them a knowledge both of self and of the possibility of meaningful design in the world.

One can acknowledge that *Pym* is an open-ended text and that its meaning may be indeterminate without dead-ending in a vision of the void. G. R. Thompson's extensive ''Romantic Arabesque, Contemporary Theory, and Postmodernism: The Example of Poe's *Narrative* (also, Kopley 1992), part of which was presented as the keynote address at the *Pym* Conference on Nantucket Island, provides a rereading of *Pym* that draws insights across theoretical lines without single-mindedly succumbing to a nihilistic vision. While he questions the assumption that the patterns in *Pym* are inherently meaningful, Thompson discusses indeterminacy in *Pym* as ''framed'' and thus somewhat stabilized. Like arabesque carpets, the novel uses elaborately repetitive patterning to frame a bit of infinity, and, while what is within the frame may not be inherently meaningful, it points to more than is contained; it gestures toward the possibility of meaning.

Cultural Studies. While the early symbolists influenced the bulk of *Pym* criticism, the assumptions of verisimilitude inform, or are examined by, cultural studies of *Pym* that have quietly persisted over the last four decades. One strand of studies has focused on Poe's racism. In 1946, F. O. Matthiessen had written, "Poe went so far as to deplore the French Revolution, to defend slavery as 'the basis of all our institutions,' and to assume the scorn held by the propertied classes for the democratic 'mob' " (328). In *The Power of Blackness,* Harry Levin read the ending of *Pym* as an allegory of racial hatred: "[F]or Poe, whose symbols claim to be actualities, [black and white] are charged with basic associations which are psychological and social" (120). Poe's animosity toward blacks is evident, according to Levin, when, connecting the language of the Tsalalian natives with the biblical handwriting on the wall, "we are warned against a divided kingdom, which stands in danger of being given over to dark-skinned interlopers" (122). Bezanson also discussed the "ominous and lamentable theme of black-white racial hatred" (169), as did Sidney Kaplan, who maintained that the revelation that Poe reached for in *Pym* "went deeper than contempt for the Negro" (xxv) in its assumptions that slavery was divinely ordained. To Kaplan, the message "*I* have graven it within the hills, and my vengeance upon the dust within the rock" is not biblical, though it is meant to sound so. Linking the Tsalalian episode of *Pym* with Poe's knowledge of Hebrew through his access to Gesenius's *Hebrew and English Lexicon of the Old Testament,* Kaplan explained that the island natives speak a form of primitive Hebrew. Not only are all the principal names Hebrew variations on blackness, but "the world of Tsalal is black to its core—so quintessentially black that it is divided by 'chasmal differences' from whiteness in any form. The sea around it is 'extraordinarily dark'; its fauna and flora are black; its granite and soil, the very dust in the bowels of its earth are black" (155). Kaplan saw the Jane Guy section of the novel as an allegory of black/white hatred.

Leslie Fiedler (1962), who discussed the novel as archetypally American in its escape from domesticity into wilderness, also saw in it a revelation of America's racial fears. Harold Beaver (1975) wrote that "as a Virginian in the 1830's [Poe] was obsessed not only by Antarctic fantasies but racial fantasies, not only by Polar expeditions but a black-white polarity that was riddling the whole nation with tension" (15). Furthermore, he stated that Poe "deliberately played on Southern hysteria, by suggesting that blacks, far from timid, were both a sly and warlike people; that quite apart from subversion without, the South should be constantly on its guard against treachery within" (17). That same year, Eric Mottram contended that *Pym* is "deeply western" and "deeply American" (32) and very much about domination and submission across a color line: "the total structure of the novel is embedded in the genesis of slavery" (48).

In a restatement of the earlier affirmative/transcendental view, John Limon (1983, 1990) placed Poe in the midst of the nineteenth century's debate between science and art, with "Sonnet—to Science," *Pym,* and *Eureka* as the key texts in his argument. While other critics, most notably O'Donnell (1962), Lynen (1969), Farrell Lee (1972), Halliburton (1973), and Wilbur (1973), had discussed *Pym* as a precursor of *Eureka,* Limon's project was to move in the reverse direction, using *Eureka* to create retrospectively an intellectual context for the interpretation of *Pym*. He defines Poe's use of the nature-philosophic tradition (*Naturphilosophie*) of Hegel, Schelling, and Oken, which co-opts science by spiritualizing nature and which accounts for diverse polarities in the empirical world, even while positing spiritual Unity, by viewing all polarity as a function of the unifying polarity of subject-object. The *Naturphilosphen* attempt to deny the gaps between science and literature led to a conflation of genres, such as Poe's *Eureka*—a scientific essay that claims to be a poem—a conflation that mirrors that of scientific data and spiritual teleology—gravity and electricity are functions of an "aesthetic God" (1990, 20). *Eureka*, Limon writes, "creates a universe that pulses between multiplicity and unity, writing cosmically his fissiparous misanthropy and his all-embracing narcissism, a single syndrome with alternating effects" (1990, 24). Poe diverged from *Naturphilosophie* in his view of history; while Schelling believed that history was a progressive revelation of the absolute, Poe saw history as an emptying out of all material possibilities, a retreat back to, rather than a progressive revelation of, the spirit. To demonstrate how Poe situates *Pym* out of the linear progression of history, Limon takes as his own the myth-based readings established by Bezanson, O'Donnell, and Farrell Lee (1972). His reading, therefore, is not new, but the intellectual context in which he places the reading is. His conclusions are at odds with postmodern reconsiderations of Poe's racism, for he sees the ending of the novel as an allegory of *Naturphilosophie's* polarities.

Recently, Dana D. Nelson and John Carlos Rowe (1992) have enlarged the discussion of Poe's racism. Rowe suggests that the focus of both New Critics and postmodern deconstructionists on language and texts and writing has enabled them to avoid the issue of racism. He argues that the importance of Poe's Southernness and his pro-slavery sentiments have been neglected because the hierarchies of power, which Poe's antebellum politics sought to reaffirm, are contiguous with those of "the postbellum politics of aesthetic language and its powerful hierarchies of verbal competency and cultural 'literacy' " (138). Nelson gives a detailed reading of "Colonialist motives" in *Pym,* citing the white supremacist undertones and concluding that the novel "is not solely about absence of meaning, but about the impulses—social, political, economic—that undergird the construction of any system of meaning" (108).

In his study of the American romance, *Dreaming Revolution* (1993), Scott Bradfield includes a reading of *Pym* that extends the discussion of racism to include that of class. He treats Poe as "a furious reactionary" (73) who opposed bourgeois revolution as a threat to aristocratic government and imperial expansion. He goes on to link Poe's political ideology with his cyclic and apocalyptic cosmology but diminishes his argument appreciably when he connects it with the review of Paulding's "Slavery in the United States," which is no longer thought to be by Poe (see Ridgely 1992).

A variety of other cultural contexts have been the topic of recent essays. Alexander Hammond (1992) places *Pym* in the changing context of the nineteenth-century literary marketplace, where the feeding frenzy of the reading public finds its analogue in the novel's modes of cannibalism. He contends that eating is a trope for reading and writing: when Augustus scrawls his note to Pym in blood, he uses a toothpick for a pen! J. Gerald Kennedy (1992) "fleshes out" his discussion of putrefaction, demonstrating how Poe decomposes "the myths and pieties of nineteenth-century culture," including those that posit a benevolent deity, the legitimacy of colonial exploitation, and white racial superiority (174). Nineteenth-century mourning conventions and twentieth-century grief theories inform my study of *Pym* and *Moby-Dick,* linking Poe's unabated mourning to his construction of meaning in *Eureka*'s cosmology: "So pervasive is Poe's search for his own lost parent that just such a search becomes central to the very workings of the universe. The entire cosmos is locked in mourning" (Farrell, in Kopley 1992, 116). David H. Hirsch discusses *Pym* as a prescient fiction that, in its violent disfigurations, anticipates "the inversion of values that characterizes our post-Auschwitz age" (150).

Decades of Poe scholars have demonstrated that *The Narrative of Arthur Gordon Pym* is indeed what Douglas Robinson called "the interpreter's dream-text" (1982, 47). Neither the early pronouncements by Ridgely or Moss denying the text's meaningful design nor the later pronouncements by postmodernists precluding any design of meaning have impeded or negated fifty years of scholarship. The complex openness of the novel will most likely continue to provide scholars with a field large enough to absorb a wide variety of critical approaches.

WORKS CITED

Auden, W. H. "Introduction." *Edgar Allan Poe: Selected Prose and Poetry.* New York: Rinehart, 1950.

Bachelard, Gaston. "Introduction." *Aventures d'Arthur Gordon Pym.* Trans. Charles Baudelaire. Paris: Stock, 1944.

———. *La Psychanalyse du feu.* Paris; Librairie Gallimard, 1938. *The Psychoanalysis of Fire.* Trans. Alan C. M. Ross. Boston: Beacon P, 1964.

Beaver, Harold. "Introduction." *The Narrative of Arthur Gordon Pym.* New York: Penguin, 1975.

Beegel, Susan F. " 'Mutiny and Atrocious Butchery': The *Globe* Mutiny as a Source for *Pym.*" In Kopley, *Poe's Pym,* 7–19.

Bezanson, Walter E. "The Troubled Sleep of Arthur Gordon Pym." *Essays in Literary History.* Ed. Rudolf Kirk and C. F. Main. New York: Russell, 1960, 149–75.

Bonaparte, Marie. *Edgar Poe: Sa vie, son oeuvre—Étude psychanalytique.* Paris: Denoel et Steele, 1933. Trans. John Rodker. *The Life and Works of Edgar Allan Poe: A Psychoanalytic Interpretation.* London: Imago, 1949.

Bradfield, Scott. *Dreaming Revolution: Transgression in the Development of American Romance.* Iowa City: U of Iowa P, 1993.

Carlson, Eric W., ed. *Critical Essays on Edgar Allan Poe.* Boston: G. K. Hall, 1987.

Carringer, Robert L. "Circumscription of Space and the Form of Poe's *Arthur Gordon Pym.*" *PMLA* 89 (1974): 506–16.

Cecil, L. Moffitt. "The Two Narratives of Arthur Gordon Pym." *Texas Studies in Language and Literature* 5 (1963): 232–41.

Cowie, Alexander. *The Rise of the American Novel.* New York: American, 1948.

Davidson, Edward H. *Poe: A Critical Study.* Cambridge: Harvard UP, 1957.

DeFalco, Joseph M. "Metaphor and Meaning in Poe's *The Narrative of Arthur Gordon Pym.*" *Topic* 16 (1976): 54–67.

Donadio, Stephen. "Emerson, Poe, and the Ruins of Convention." *Emerson and His Legacy: Essays in Honor of Quentin Anderson.* Eds. Stephen Donadio, Stephen Railton, and Ormond Seavey. Carbondale: Southern Illinois UP, 1986, 84–106.

Eakin, Paul J. "Poe's Sense of an Ending." *American Literature* 45 (1973): 1–22.

Faber, George Stanley. *On the Origin of Pagan Idolatry.* London: F. C. Rivingtons, 1816; New York: Garland, 1984.

Farrell, Grace. "Mourning in Poe's *Pym.*" In Kopley, *Poe's Pym,* 107–16.

———. "*Pym* and *Moby-Dick:* Essential Connections." *American Transcendental Quarterly* 37 (1978): 73–86.

———. "The Quest of Arthur Gordon Pym." *Southern Literary Journal* 4 (1972): 22–33.

Fiedler, Leslie A. *Love and Death in the American Novel.* New York: Stein, 1960. Rev. ed., 1966.

Forclaz, Roger. "Un Voyage Aux Frontières de L'Inconnu: Les Aventures d'A.G. Pym, d'Edgar Poe." *Études de Lettres* 7 (1964): 46–58. Trans. Gerald Bello. *American Transcendental Quarterly* 37 (1978): 45–55.

Frank, Frederick S. "Polarized Gothic: An Annotated Bibliography of Poe's *Narrative of Arthur Gordon Pym.*" *Bulletin of Bibliography* 38 (1981): 117–27.

Fukuchi, Curtis. "Poe's Providential *Narrative of Arthur Gordon Pym.*" *ESQ* 27 (1981): 147–56.

Fussell, Edwin. *Frontier: American Literature and the American West.* Princeton: Princeton UP, 1965.

Halliburton, David. *Edgar Allan Poe: A Phenomenological View.* Princeton: Princeton UP, 1973.

Hammond, Alexander. "The Composition of *The Narrative of Arthur Gordon Pym:* Notes toward a Re-Examination." *American Transcendental Quarterly* 37 (1978): 9–20.

———. "Consumption, Exchange, and the Literary Marketplace: From the Folio Club Tales to *Pym.*" In Kopley, *Poe's Pym,* 153–66.

Hernandez, Ana Maria. "Poe, Pym and Mythological Symbolism in Cortazar's First Novel." *Gypsy Scholar* 4 (1977): 5–16.

Hinz, Evelyn. " 'Tekeli-li'.: *The Narrative of Arthur Gordon Pym* as Satire." *Genre* 3 (1970): 379–99.

Hirsch, David H. " 'Postmodern' or Post-Auschwitz: The Case of Poe." In Kopley, *Poe's Pym,* 141–52.

Hoffman, Daniel. *Poe Poe Poe Poe Poe Poe Poe.* London: Robson, 1973.

Hussey, John P. " 'Mr. Pym' and 'Mr. Poe': The Two Narrators of 'Arthur Gordon Pym.' " *South Atlantic Bulletin* 39 (1974): 22–32.

Irwin, John T. *American Hieroglyphics.* New Haven, Conn.: Yale UP, 1980.

———. "The Quincuncial Network in Poe's *Pym.*" In Kopley, *Poe's Pym,* 175–87.

Jackson, David K., and Burton Pollin. "Poe's 'Tekeli-li'." *PoeS* 12 (1979): 19.

Jackson, David K. "A Poe Hoax Comes before the United States Senate." *PoeS* 7 (1974): 47–48.

James, Henry. *The Art of the Novel.* Ed. R. P. Blackmur. New York: Scribner's, 1934.

———. *French Poets and Novelists.* London: Macmillan, 1878.

Kaplan, Sidney. "Introduction." *The Narrative of Arthur Gordon Pym.* New York: Hill, 1960. Rpt. in Robert Regan, ed. *Poe: A Collection of Critical Essays.* Englewood Cliffs, N.J.: Prentice-Hall, 1967.

Kennedy, J. Gerald. " 'The Infernal Twoness' in *Arthur Gordon Pym.*" *Topic* 16 (1976): 41–53.

———. "Introduction." *The Narrative of Arthur Gordon Pym of Nantucket and Related Tales.* New York: Oxford UP, 1994.

———. "The Invisible Message: The Problem of Truth in *Pym.*" In *The Naiad Voice.* Ed. Dennis W. Eddings. Port Washington, N.Y.: Associated Faculty P, 1983, 124–35. Revision of " 'The Infernal Twoness.' " *Topic* 16 (1976): 41–53.

———. *The Narrative of Arthur Gordon Pym and the Abyss of Interpretation.* New York: Twayne, 1995.

———. *Poe, Death, and the Life of Writing.* New Haven, Conn.: Yale UP, 1987.

———. "*Pym* Pourri: Decomposing the Texual Body." In Kopley, *Poe's Pym,* 167–74.

Ketterer, David. *The Rationale of Deception in Poe.* Baton Rouge: Louisiana State UP, 1979.

———. "Tracing Shadows: *Pym* Criticism, 1980–1990." In Kopley, *Poe's Pym,* 233–274.

Kopley, Richard. "The Hidden Journey of *Arthur Gordon Pym.*" *Studies in the American Renaissance: 1982.* Ed. Joel Myerson. Charlottesville: UP of Virginia, 1982.

———. *Poe's Pym: Critical Explorations.* Durham: Duke UP, 1992.

Lieber, Todd. *Endless Experiments: Essays on the Heroic Experience in American Literature.* Columbus: Ohio State UP, 1973.

Limon, John. "How to Place Poe's *Arthur Gordon Pym* in Science-Dominated Intellectual History, and How to Extract it Again." *North Dakota Quarterly* 51 (1983): 31–47.

———. *The Place of Fiction in the Time of Science.* New York: Cambridge UP, 1990.

Ljungquist, Kent. "The Descent of the Titans: The Sublime Riddle of *Arthur Gordon Pym.*" *Southern Literary Journal* 10 (1978): 75–92.

———. *The Grand and the Fair: Poe's Landscape Aesthetics and Pictorial Techniques.* Potomac, Md.: Scripta Humanistica, 1984.

———. " 'Speculative Mythology' and the Titan Myth in Poe's *Pym* and Melville's *Pierre.*" *Sphinx* 4 (1985): 250–57.

Lynen, John F. *The Design of the Present: Essays on Time and Form in American Literature.* New Haven, Conn.: Yale UP, 1969.

Mainville, Stephen. "Language and the Void: Gothic Landscapes in the Frontiers of Edgar Allan Poe." *Genre* 14 (1981): 347–62.

Matthiessen, F. O. "Edgar Allan Poe." *Literary History of the United States.* Vol. 1. Ed. Robert E. Spiller et al. New York: Macmillan, 1946.

Moldenhauer, Joseph J. "Imagination and Perversity in *The Narrative of Arthur Gordon Pym.*" *Texas Studies in Literature and Language* 13 (1971): 267–80.

———. "*Pym,* the Dighton Rock, and the Matter of Vinland." In Kopley, *Poe's Pym,* 75–94.

Moss, Sidney. *"Arthur Gordon Pym* or the Fallacy of Thematic Interpretation." *University Review* 33 (1967): 299–306.

―――. "A Conjecture Concerning the Writing of *Arthur Gordon Pym.*" *Studies in Short Fiction* 4 (1966): 83–85.

Mottram, Eric. "Poe's *Pym* and the American Social Imagination." *Artful Thunder*. Ed. Robert J. DeMott and Sanford E. Marovitz. Kent, Ohio: Kent State UP, 1975, 25–53.

Mourier, Maurice. *"Le tombeau d'Edgar Poe."* *Esprit* 12 (1974): 902–26.

Nelson, Dana D. *The Word in Black and White: Reading "Race" in American Literature, 1638–1867*. New York: Oxford UP, 1992.

O'Donnell, Charles "From Earth to Ether: Poe's Flight into Space." *PMLA* 77 (1962): 85–91.

Ostrom, John Ward, ed. *The Letters of Edgar Allan Poe*. Cambridge: Harvard UP, 1948. Republished with three supplements (New York: Gordian, 1966); fourth supplement, *American Literature* 45 (Jan. 1974): 513–36.

Pahl, Dennis. *Architects of the Abyss: The Indeterminate Fictions of Poe, Hawthorne, and Melville*. Columbia: U of Missouri P, 1989.

Peden, William. "Prologue to a Dark Journey: The 'Opening' to Poe's *Pym.*" *Papers on Poe: Essays in Honor of John Ward Ostrom*. Springfield, Ohio: Chantry Music P, 1972, 84–91.

Peirce, Carol, and Alexander G. Rose III. "Poe's Reading of Myth: The White Vision of Arthur Gordon Pym." In Kopley, *Poe's Pym*, 57–74.

Pollin, Burton R. "A Comprehensive Bibliography of Editions and Translations of *Arthur Gordon Pym.*" *American Transcendental Quarterly* 37 (1978): 93–110.

―――. "Poe and Henry James: A Changing Relationship." *Yearbook of English Studies* (1973): 232–42.

―――. "Three More Early Notices of *Pym* and the Snowden Connection." *PoeS* 8 (1975): 32–35.

―――, ed. *Edgar Allan Poe, The Imaginary Voyages: The Narrative of Arthur Gordon Pym, The Unparalleled Adventure of One Hans Pfaall, The Journal of Julius Rodman*. Boston: Twayne, 1981.

Porte, Joel. *The Romance in America: Studies in Cooper, Poe, Hawthorne, Melville, and James*. Middletown, Conn.: Wesleyan UP, 1969.

Quinn, Patrick F. "Poe's Imaginary Journey." *Hudson Review* 4 (1952): 562–85. Rpt. in *The French Face of Edgar Poe*. Carbondale: Southern Illinois UP, 1957.

―――. "Poe: Between Being and Nothingness." *Southern Literary Journal* 6 (1973): 81–100.

Reynolds, Jeremiah. *Voyage of the United States Frigate "Potomac" Around the World*. New York: Harper, 1835.

―――. *Address on the Subject of a Surveying and Exploring Expedition to the Pacific Ocean and South Seas*. New York: Harper, 1836.

Ricardou, Jean. *"Le Caractère singulier de cette eau."* *Critique* (1967): 718–33. Trans. Frank Towne. *PoeS* 9 (1976): 1–6.

Ridgely, Joseph V. "The End of Pym and the Ending of *Pym.*" *Papers on Poe: Essays in Honor of John Ward Ostrom*. Springfield, Ohio: Chantry Music P, 1972.

―――. "The Growth of the Text." *Edgar Allan Poe, The Imaginary Voyages: The Narrative of Arthur Gordon Pym, The Unparalleled Adventure of One Hans Pfaall, The Journal of Julius Rodman*. Ed. Burton R. Pollin. Boston: Twayne, 1981.

———. "Tragical-Mythical-Satirical-Hoaxical: Problems of Genre in *Pym*." *American Transcendental Quarterly* 24 (1974): 4–9.

Ridgely, Joseph V., and Iola S. Haverstick. "Chartless Voyage: The Many Narratives of Arthur Gordon Pym." *Texas Studies in Literature and Language* 8 (1966): 63–80.

Robinson, Douglas. *American Apocalypses: The Image of the End of the World in American Literature*. Baltimore: Johns Hopkins UP, 1985.

———. "Reading Poe's Novel: A Speculative Review of *Pym* Criticism, 1950–1980." *PoeS* 15 (1982): 47–54.

Rosenzweig, Paul. " 'Dust Within the Rock': The Phantasm of Meaning in *The Narrative of Arthur Gordon Pym*." *Studies in the Novel* 14 (1982): 137–51.

Rowe, John Carlos. "Poe, Antebellum Slavery, and Modern Criticism." In Kopley, *Poe's Pym*, 117–40.

———. "Writing and Truth in Poe's *The Narrative of Arthur Gordon Pym*." *Glyph* 2 (1977): 102–21. Rpt. in *Through the Custom House*.

St. Armand, Barton Levi. "The Dragon and the Uroboros: Themes of Metamorphosis in *Arthur Gordon Pym*." *American Transcendental Quarterly* 37 (1978): 57–71.

Sheehan, Peter J. "Dirk Peters: A New Look at Poe's *Pym*." *Laurel Review* 9 (1969): 60–67.

Sutherland, Judith. *The Problematic Fictions of Poe, James, and Hawthorne*. Columbia: U of Missouri P, 1984.

Teunissen, John J., and Evelyn J. Hinz. "Poe's *Journal of Julius Rodman* as Parody." *Nineteenth-Century Fiction* 27 (1972): 317–38.

Thompson, G. R. "The Arabesque Design of *Arthur Gordon Pym*." In Kopley, *Poe's Pym*, 188–216.

———. *Poe's Fiction: Romantic Irony in the Gothic Tales*. Madison: U of Wisconsin P, 1973.

———. "Romantic Arabesque, Contemporary Theory, and Postmodernism: The Example of Poe's *Narrative*." *ESQ* 35 (1989): 163–271.

Vitanza, Victor J. "Edgar Allan Poe's *The Narrative of Arthur Gordon Pym*: An Anatomy of Perverseness." *Études anglaises* 27 (1974): 26–37.

Weissberg, Liliane. "Editing Adventures: Writing the Test of *Julius Rodman*." *Modern Fiction Studies* 33 (1987): 413–30.

Wells, Daniel A. "Engraved within the Hills: Further Perspectives on the Ending of *Pym*." *PoeS* 10 (1977): 13–15.

Wilbur, Richard. "Introduction." *The Narrative of Arthur Gordon Pym*. Boston: Godine, 1973.

Zanger, Jules. "Poe's Endless Voyage: *The Narrative of Arthur Gordon Pym*." *Papers on Language and Literature* 22 (1986): 276–83.

11

Moods of Mind: The Tales of Detection, Crime, and Punishment

THOMAS JOSWICK

The amateur detective and the criminal madman—one coolly rational, the other either nervously prolix or grimly laconic about often grisly brutalities—are among Poe's most popular creations and account for much of the view promoted by Rufus Griswold that Poe's "realm was on the shadowy confines of human experience, among the abodes of crime, gloom, and horror" (55). Popular as they have been, however, Poe's iconic figures of crime and detection are much more than sensational portraits intended to thrill the public. They show two sides of the solitary self bracing against the horrors that threaten unexpectedly close to home in his fiction.

Poe's detective, on one hand, triumphs over sinister and, at times, maniacal violence by virtue of his self-reliance and native know-how, dazzling readers in the process with those skills at pragmatic observation and intuitive insight that have been passed along to all his literary descendants. His is an independent mind upon which nothing is lost and that balks at nothing, and his ratiocinative heroics have been described as Poe's "allegory of how the mind may impose its interior logic on exterior circumstances" (Davidson, 221)—the detective as "a kind of Platonic embodiment, a sedentary mastermind whose very lack of physical exertion emphasizes the mastery of mind over the material world" (Irwin, xvi). In contrast, the confessional tale of Poe's criminal madman grimly mocks the belief that the mind could be master even of its own designs. The madman succumbs to compulsions of a deep torment: his is a mind divided against itself, obsessed with phantoms of its own hidden devising and betrayed into self-exposure and self-destruction by an uncontrollable impulse to confess.

Striking as their differences are, the detective and the criminal madman together reveal the complexity of the psychomoral imagination underlying Poe's craft, making his tales far different from other crime fiction against which he competed for an audience (see Reynolds, 225–48). For one thing, moral agency in Poe's tales is not adequately accounted for by any neat polarization between a virtuous will and depraved desires, nor is the mind adequately explained by an exact opposition between reason and impulse. Instead, madman and detective alike are more often given to complex "*moods* of mind" (*M* 2, 638), under the sway of which reason and impulse, will and desire contend with each other to define the central drama of the tale. The detective himself, for example, may be driven by obsessions and the desire for revenge that characterize the madman, while the latter's destructive impulses may, at times, "operate in furtherance of good" (*M* 3, 1223) as unlikely agents of justice. Not a stable polarization, then, but a principle of "convertibility," to use Joan Dayan's term (36), gives form to moral agency in Poe's fiction.

Yet, while complementary in their study of human character, the ratiocinative and confessional tales are distinct in their narrative forms, and Poe's legacy to modern literature has been, in large part, the careful designs of those forms. Thus, while Poe moved readily from one form to another, I discuss the tales of detection together, followed by the tales of crime and punishment, in order to assess the narrative strategies of each group. I turn first, however, to "The Man of the Crowd." A study of what its narrator calls "deep crime," this tale introduces in Poe's fiction a metaphysical speculation about crime and human character, the implications of which inform the narrative structures of the later tales.

THE MYSTERY OF "DEEP CRIME"

"The Man of the Crowd"

Published in December 1840, "The Man of the Crowd" marks a turning point in Poe's treatment of crime. Its narrator asserts that in the human heart may be "some secrets which do not permit themselves to be told" and that, due to such an internal interdiction, "the essence of all crime is undivulged." Impulses to confess apparently contend against this profound secretiveness of the heart but are futile once "the conscience . . . [has taken] up a burden so heavy in horror that it can be thrown down only into the grave" (*M* 2, 507). The "essence" of crime, this speculation suggests, may have elicited Poe's interest for how its burdens test what in the self resists exposure—what resists the knowledge and control of both self and others.

The story develops when the narrator is motivated by "moods of the keenest appetency" (*M* 2, 507) to track down the secret of crime, to confront it and know it. These moods border on the obsessive. Feeling "enchained" by the "wild effects" of observing a turbulent violence beneath the collective anonymity of a London crowd, the narrator sees a mysterious figure emerge and is suddenly possessed by "a craving desire . . . to know more of him" (*M* 2, 511). His attempts to know what might remain beyond telling require reading the stranger's inner character from exterior signs, but this reading, in turn, requires identifying with the stranger, leading the narrator unconsciously to imitate the one he desires to know. Masking himself with a handkerchief, he pursues the stranger into the haunts of London, arriving back where he started, however, no more certain than when he began of whatever secret the stranger may possess. He concludes only that the stranger, frantic in his apparent need of the crowd but incommunicado in its midst, is "the type and genius of deep crime" (*M* 2, 515), his wandering to and fro a fitting emblem of his secret burden. More important, however, the narrator himself is transformed. Having begun by "amusing [himself]" with observations, he ends "wearied unto death"—the end, we may assume, of his "craving desire . . . to know."

The mystery of "deep crime" remains unsolved, and for that reason Bruce I. Weiner argues that "The Man of the Crowd" is a more profound work than the ratiocinative tales, being an instance of what Poe called "that metaphysical art in which the souls of all *mysteries* lie" (*T*, 244). Yet, much of what makes for mystery in this tale also informs the later tales, especially the fascinating bond between the narrator and the "genius of deep crime." Patrick F. Quinn first identified the stranger as the narrator's double (229–32); they are joined by a bond neatly portrayed when the narrator first sees the stranger through a window pane on which is reflected his own image, so that he sees "in the specular mystery of the other, the image of himself therein contained" (Byer, 237). Such a double exposure of self is an emblem of the agon central to Poe's fiction— what Richard Wilbur calls "a soul's fathoming and ordering of itself" ("Edgar Allan Poe," 62). In the tales of crime and detection that follow "The Man of the Crowd," the capacities of the soul to fathom itself—and to resist and deceive itself—are further explored in the ordeal of self-recognition that distinguishes Poe's fiction: a solitary self confronting an adversary who turns out to be the self's own double.

THE TALES OF DETECTION

A Form Invented by Poe

Arthur Conan Doyle once wryly remarked that "the monstrous progeny of writers on the detection of crime" must be "ascribed" to Poe (117). While some historians of detective fiction point to influences from Voltaire's *Zadig,* Godwin's *Caleb Williams,* and the *Mémoires* of the French detective Vidocq (who is dismissed as a "good guesser" in "The Murders in the Rue Morgue" [*M* 2, 545]), most accede to Doyle's pronouncement and to Dorothy Sayers's judgment that "the general principles of the detective-story were laid down forever" in the tales of Poe (72). Howard Haycraft and Robert Lowndes, for example, have traced to Poe's tales thirty-two techniques of plot, setting, and characterization that are now standard conventions of detective fiction.

Poe's inventions took such a firm hold on the genre because they effectively sustain suspense, as a British reviewer recognized early on, "solely by the nature of the evidence, and the inferences to be adduced from it" (*Critical Heritage,*

221). In the first important study of Poe's detective fiction, J. Brander Matthews likewise noted that Poe's originality consisted in shifting attention from the sentimental possibilities of plot to the intellectual acuity of the detective, whose subsequent analysis of events reveals the hidden tissue of logic or stratagem within them and becomes thereby the central interest in the story (85–86). With this shift, crime becomes an aesthetic problem: "an amusement" for the detective (*M* 2, 546), shared with an admiring companion, the narrator of the tale, who passes along the aesthetic pleasure—now a mixture of his own earnest amazement and the detective's lucid analysis—to the reader.

The reader's reception of the "amusement" was also cagily anticipated by Poe's compositional strategies. As the detective explicates the clues to the narrator, the reader's response is modeled by the narrator's excitement over a surprisingly *internalized* discovery: "I seemed to be upon the verge of comprehension, without power to comprehend—as men, at times, find themselves upon the brink of remembrance, without being able, in the end, to remember" (*M* 2, 555). This sensation of an idea emerging in the act of reading is the preconceived effect that Poe considered essential for a truly original work. He argued that such a work combines "the pleasurable effect of *apparent* novelty" with the reader's "egotistic delight" in identifying his own "half-formed" and "unexpressed" ideas with those gradually clarified in the tale (*T*, 581). The resulting "bond of sympathy" between author and reader is especially strong for devotees of detective fiction, for, as Poe remarked, the reader "is made to confound the [detective's] ingenuity . . . with that of the writer of the story" (*O* 2, 328)—a confusion that must afford the writer plenty of "egotistic delight" as well.

While sustaining an aesthetic "amusement," however, the narrative method also allowed Poe exploration of such pressing issues to him as the province of reason, the human longing toward transcendental unity, the structure of language and its relation to consciousness, and the adversarial relations between self and others in a "nation of self-made men," as Donald E. Pease argues, bereft of traditional forms of religious and secular authority, increasingly set at rivalrous odds with one another, and increasingly devoted to self-aggrandizement in the instant (187). Thus, unlike most detective fiction, Poe's tales are not exhausted by a single reading to learn "whodunit." In these tales, Davidson concludes, "are presented Poe's most consistent social and moral views, all together amounting almost to a 'system.' . . . They were moral, philosophical, and as autobiographical as Poe ever became" (213).

TWO DUPIN TALES

"The Murders in the Rue Morgue"

The first tale featuring the Chevalier C. Auguste Dupin, Poe's shrewd detective, appeared in the April 1841 issue of *Graham's Magazine*. Revisions on the manuscript indicate that Poe worked on the story right up to its typesetting, including the brilliant stroke of changing the street name from Rue Trianon-Bas to Rue Morgue (Asarch, 83). Two months earlier, he had completed "Eleonora" (*PoeL,* 319), a tale that speculates "whether madness is or is not the loftiest intelligence—whether much that is glorious—whether all that is profound— does not spring from disease of thought—from *moods* of mind exalted at the expense of the general intellect" (*M* 2, 638). A similar speculation about "loftiest intelligence" stands at the beginning of "Rue Morgue," and a similar suggestion about the disease of thought appears later when Dupin is described in one of his own "moods" of analysis (*M* 2, 533). Like "moods of the keenest appetency," the phrase *moods of mind* suggests that passional motives accompany the detective's cool rationality and "rich ideality." The narrator, for example, insists that the analytic powers associated with "ideality" are known only by their effects (cf. *Essays,* 510), and foremost among these are the "liveliest enjoyment" they give the one who possesses them and the special excitation and advantage they give him in those enterprises "where mind struggles with mind" (*M* 2, 529). The discourse on analysis, then, is not so much about an abstract faculty (though it is that, too) as about an entire mood of the mind, informing and determining its engagement with the world—its inward retreat from it and its struggle for mastery over it.

In the tale, Dupin's analysis, indeed, masters all—from the associative patterns of his companion's most private thought to the enigma of a language that the principal nationalities of Europe cannot decipher. His abilities to "inhabit" another's consciousness and to interpret a sequence of facts as signs in a unified, intentional design have led several critics (including Stauffer, Halliburton [237– 45], Levine [1972, 167], and Ketterer [1979, 245]) to amplify Davidson's argument that Dupin is "the supreme artistic ego: everything external to himself can be made to fit the theoretical, ideal logic" (221). Wilbur has carried this argument furthest, claiming that Dupin represents, for Poe, an "omniscient solipsism": "He is a godlike genius who, possessing the highest and most comprehensive order of mind, includes in himself all possible lesser minds, and can therefore fathom any man—indeed, any primate—by mere introspection" ("Edgar Allan Poe," 62).

Dupin's mastery of mind, however, is not without ambiguities. Early on, he confides that while not "particularly attentive," he remembers details distinctly because "observation has become with [him], of late, a species of necessity" (*M* 2, 535), as if darkly hinting at inner compulsions to which his will is merely contingent. Later, he triumphs precisely by reversing the subjection of will to necessity: what appear to be random events are recast into the logic of his analytic discourse with the insistence that his deductions "are the *sole* proper ones, and that the suspicion arises *inevitably* from them as the single result" (*M* 2, 550). As Burton Pollin has shown, however, the inventory of logical possibilities does not warrant Dupin's singular conclusions; in fact, if Pollin is right, Poe may be slyly undermining the "supposititious Dupin" (*O* 2, 338) throughout the tale. Regardless of a possible hoax in the tale, however, the necessity Dupin claims for his analysis—that, by adhering to his line of thought, "all apparent impossibilities *must* be proved to be not such in reality" (*M* 2, 552)—derives less from a logical order within events than from his own willful mastery over the all too senseless, because unmotivated, accidents of events.

By translating brutal events into a discursive order, Dupin can remain unperturbed by what most unsettles the narrator and readers: the horrifying violence of an "Ourang-Outang" that uncannily resembles the violence of human mastery. With a "*mood* of mind" detached because triumphant over senseless events, Dupin returns to the sanctuary of his own thought once the horror is explained. The world of sensational shocks and murderous impulses is left for the reader to wonder and tremble at. And well the reader should, according to Pease, who argues that the reader's "will to sensation" has been covertly indulged by Dupin's rational analysis of all the intimate details of a lurid crime and that, when the moral agency of the detective is withdrawn, "the reader . . . is left to contemplate his own complicity in crime, constituted by the very act of reading" (185). The "amusement" of the tale, then, is not wholly innocent, and, by exposing a hidden complicity, the tale effectively critiques the culture of sensationalism.

"The Mystery of Marie Roget"

In this tale, Poe risked using his fictive detective as a "pretense" for his own "rigorous analysis" (*O* 1, 201) of clues in the murder case of Mary Cecilia Rogers, whose battered body was discovered floating in the Hudson River on July 28, 1841. On June 4, 1842, Poe had his "Sequel to the Murders in the Rue Morgue" ready (*PoeL*, 369–70) but could not arrange its publication until November. In a detailed historical analysis, John Walsh carefully examines Poe's strategic use of newspaper accounts in the tale, including the deft revisions Poe made following the November installment to accommodate stories that Mary Rogers had died of a botched abortion, a possibility Poe still alluded to in 1848 (*O* 2, 356). Despite, however, the self-congratulatory footnotes supplied to the 1845 version, which Walsh demonstrates were clever hoaxes, Poe did not convincingly solve the mystery of Mary Rogers—nor has anyone else.

As for the tale itself, Sayers maintains that, having fewer imitators, "Marie Roget" "is the most interesting of all [Poe's tales] to the connoiseur" (82), while Richard P. Benton argues that it is a "mixed form" of colloquy, tale, and essay, in which Poe ridiculed the "thinking of the Jacksonian common man" (1969, 147). Poe himself claimed that "Marie Roget" "reveals the whole secret of [the] mode of construction" for the tales of ratiocination (*T*, 872), referring perhaps to the structure of Dupin's reasoning: proof for his intuited hypothesis lies in reasoning inductively from those "collateral or circumstantial events" (*M* 2, 752) that tend to conceal the truth by their very marginality. Poe may have been referring also, however, to Dupin's provocative claim about "the doctrine of chance." In scientific reasoning about the future, Dupin asserts:

"*Accident* is admitted as a portion of the substructure. We make chance a matter of absolute calculation" (*M* 2, 752). In "Marie Roget," "a series of scarcely intelligible *coincidences*" (*M* 2, 724) is subsumed into the aesthetic necessity of design and preconceived effect, making the reciprocity of chance and calculation that Dupin claims for scientific analysis a structuring principle for the tale of ratiocination. Reason triumphs in the ratiocinative tale precisely because nothing, in short, is left to chance despite appearances to the contrary.

"The Gold-Bug"

Having first sold this tale to *Graham's* for fifty-two dollars in late 1842 or early 1843, Poe later withdrew it in order to enter it in a contest in the *Dollar Newspaper* (a fortuitously appropriate title to carry the tale), where it was published in two installments in June 1843. It was enormously successful and continued as Poe's most popular story throughout the nineteenth century; Arthur Conan Doyle, for one, later credited it for shaping his own tastes and literary bent (124).

Poe indicated that his intention was "to write a popular tale: money, and the finding of money being chosen as the most popular thesis. In this he endeavored to carry out his idea of the perfection of the plot, which he defines as . . . that, in which we are never able to determine whether any one point depends upon or sustains any one other" (*T*, 869). According to J. Woodrow Hassell, the result of Poe's efforts is "a romantic narrative, in which realism and fantasy are in general nicely blended" (180), and, when they are in conflict, violations of verisimilitude are concealed by Poe's skill at creating "an atmosphere of a kind of inevitability" to events (180). Thus, as if fulfilling the "doctrine of chance" advanced in "Marie Roget," Poe aims at "the perfection of plot" in this tale by making what is accidental appear to depend on, as well as to sustain, what is necessary. A series of unlikely events leads the hero, William Legrand, to uncover a cryptogram that apparently admits to but one meaning (see, however, Kempton), which, once deciphered, leads directly to fabulous wealth, freeing Legrand from the "perverse moods of alternate enthusiasm and melancholy" to which the prior loss of a family fortune had subjected him. The reciprocity of cause and effect—from Legrand's own moods and intuitions, to the fortuitous character of events, to the necessity determined by the "views of Fate," and back again—is conveyed by the circular logic of the term *fortune* in the story. As Legrand explains, having been "irresistibly impressed with a presentiment of some vast fortune impending" (or perhaps it was more "a desire than an actual belief"), he is led to conclude that a "bug is to make [his] fortune . . . [s]ince Fortune has thought it fit to bestow it upon [him]" (*M* 3, 833, 815)—a perfectly symmetrical gratification of desire that Poe calculated would appeal to his readers' most treasured fantasy.

Baudelaire, for one, was delighted by the symmetry, finding in the visionary Legrand a confirmation that a lucid logic might justify the imagination's desires:

"For the treasure is found! *It was not a dream* . . . this time it is a *real* treasure, and the decipherer has indeed won it" (69). In a reading that shows Poe's "adeptness in the philosophy of alchemy," Barton Levi St. Armand demonstrates how "[i]t is actually Legrand's Romantic imagination which helps accomplish the multiplication of the gold-bug into Captain Kidd's treasure" (5). Yet, the base of the alchemical transmutation is not altogether forgotten, for, if the fantastical fortune is made to appear the necessary result of destiny, imagination, and good ole American entrepreneurial character, the logic of transmutation becomes suspect once we recall that it leads as surely to the skeletal remains of those who fell victim to Captain Kidd's ruthlessness as to the talismanic relics of his treasure.

Another approach to the tale's symmetrical structure is Jean Ricardou's, according to which the plot and stylistic features refer to "the laws of the text" that generate the meaning readers enthusiastically seek as if it were a fabulous treasure. The treasure itself, however, cannot be appropriated because the text's ultimate referent is an act of writing that "both establishes the meaning and contradicts it" (39). Vying intepretations, then, that seek a hidden meaning deep in the text show, instead, the effects of those structures of language that the tale raises for self-conscious reflection. Michael J. S. Williams, for example, shows that Legrand succeeds as an interpreter by recognizing that "the relationship between word and referent is ultimately arbitrary" (128) and that "meaning is created by conventions of use and context" (130). In a more general study of Poe's cryptography, Shawn Rosenheim argues that the model of semiotic operations that the cryptograph implied led Poe to the "reluctant realization that every decoding is another encoding, and that the crypt of the letter can't be penetrated in an attempt to extract its immanent meaning" (381). But if the profound depth of "immanent meaning" is unavailable, Poe's detective stories "exploit the fact that there is an almost seamless joining of the represented world of the stories to the signs of the representation itself" (385). In that symmetry of representation, the triumph and discovery are all the author's. The receptivity of Poe's tales to such structuralist and poststructuralist analysis "may rest largely on [Poe's] insistence on their textuality" (24), as Joseph G. Kronick concludes, and, with its emphasis on codes, misreadings, coincidental signs, mispronunciations, and decipherment, "The Gold-Bug" is indeed a tale whose "textuality" is foregrounded.

"Thou Art the Man"

Comic in tone, this tale (completed by late spring 1844 [*PoeL* 463]) borders on parody of the Dupin stories. Nonetheless, it added several conventions to the repertoire of detective fiction, including the criminal's planting false clues while parading his innocence before an unsuspecting public, a ballistics report used as empirical evidence, and the detective's wily but extravagant psychological strategies to trick the criminal into confession. The story, moreover, begins with the narrator's scoffing at a gullible public that has mistaken for a miracle his outrageous trick of having a corpse appear to have popped back to life; like Dupin, this detective arrives to dispel any credence in a supernatural intervention into human affairs, demonstrating how events can be explained, if not by "the Calculus of Probabilities" (*M* 3, 724), then by a hoaxer's ploys.

"The Purloined Letter"

A few months prior to its publication in September 1844, Poe commented that "The Purloined Letter" was, "perhaps, the best of [his] tales of ratiocination" (*O* 1, 258). It develops what the earlier tales hint are the darker sides to Dupin's character, especially his motives for personal revenge and his identification with the criminal mind that makes for a disturbing complementarity between him and his adversary.

If the difficulty in "Rue Morgue" was owing to the *outré* nature of the crime, the difficulty in "The Purloined Letter" is that the facts of the crime are too simple and self-evident. Everything that usually makes for mystery is out in the open: the identity of the thief, the mode of his theft, and the fact of his still possessing the purloined letter are all known. With the mystery on the surface, however, the surface itself requires analysis, since Poe plots it to indicate a bond between Dupin and his adversary, the Minister D—, who is identified as a sort of monstrous excess, like the orangutan in "Rue Morgue," because he "dares all things, those unbecoming as well as those becoming a man" (*M* 3, 976). The bond is confirmed by Dupin's choice of a citation from Crébillon's *Atrée* as his "signature" (see Riddel, 140) on a counterfeit letter left for the minister. The citation refers to a deadly design of violation and revenge, a plot in which cause and effect sustain reciprocal acts of violence. In this final gesture, as Liahna Klenman Babener concludes, Poe exposes "a deep affinity between Dupin and his archrival . . . [that] calls into question the customary ethical norms of the detective tale" (333).

In his "Seminar on 'The Purloined Letter' " (1966), Jacques Lacan also analyzes the repetition of scenes and the affinities of characters to one another in those scenes as defined by their (in)abilities to see the purloined letter. Not concerned with the moral depth or psychology of characters, Lacan advances, instead, a revision of Freud's "repetition compulsion" by a complex theory of language and intersubjectivity based on his analysis of the tale's structure: subjectivity for Lacan is defined not by some psychological "depth" but by the structural positions in a symbolic order—positions exemplified by the characters in "The Purloined Letter." The triangular (oedipal) pattern of these positions is the crux of Jacques Derrida's critique of Lacan (see *The Purloined Poe*). Derrida argues that Lacan ignores the tale's two scenes of narration and thereby is blind to the uncanny doubling in the tale—a doubling that finally resists and subverts the normalization of Lacan's imposed structure. The issues between Derrida and Lacan are best defined first by Barbara Johnson in "The Frame of

Reference'' (in *The Purloined Poe*) and then by John Irwin in *The Mystery to a Solution*. These studies show not only how "reciprocal opposites" inhere in the critical debate of the tale but how Dupin's own analysis of his adversary's mind depends on an internal "psychic otherness," as Irwin puts it (25), an internal difference Poe evoked between thinking and "a consciousness which always accompanies thinking" (*M* 2, 226).

The popular reception, however, never accounted for the darker sides to Dupin's character. According to John G. Cawelti, because Dupin is apparently able "to harmonize the hidden cravings of the mind . . . with tremendous rational order and self-discipline" (104), he had a special appeal to middle-class readers who sought to reconcile in fantasy the discordant values of middle-class reality (individualistic aggression in the marketplace opposed to a submissive morality in domestic life). Poe's own comments indicate that he did not share the reasons for regarding the tales of ratiocination as highly as the public did: "[They] owe most of their popularity to being something in a new key," he said. "[P]eople think them more ingenious than they are—on account of their method and *air* of method. In the 'Murders in the Rue Morgue,' for instance, where is the ingenuity of unravelling a web which you yourself (the author) have woven for the express purpose of unravelling?" (*O* 2, 328). J. Gerald Kennedy has concluded that Poe abandoned the detective form out of dissatisfaction with the limits of ratiocination—"an intellectual system out of touch with the problems of human fallibility and mortality" (195). Yet, far more than clever technique gives these tales their lasting prominence in Poe's work. Analysis may define how the detective's "reason feels its way . . . in its search for the true" (*M* 2, 548), but it is more significant as the expression of a "*mood* of mind" of what the narrator fancies might be "a double Dupin—the creative and resolvent" (*M* 2, 533). At once aloof and darkly implicated in the mystery his reason seeks to unravel, Poe's detective is a hero of "the Bi-Part Soul"—a complex portrait of human character not to be reduced to mere ingenuity.

THE TALES OF CRIME AND PUNISHMENT

Griswold credited Poe with eminent success "in the metaphysical treatment of the passions" (55), having in mind, no doubt, popular tales of crime and punishment such as "The Tell-Tale Heart" and "The Pit and the Pendulum." These tales focus on the workings of law and moral order in a psyche often characterized by obsessive "*moods* of mind" and usually at conflict with itself. In the tales of crime, moreover, Poe presents the psychic conflict in a confessional form that distinguishes this fiction from that of his contemporaries. As Allen Tate argues, "Poe is the transitional figure in modern literature because he discovered our great subject, the disintegration of personality, but kept it in a language that had developed in a tradition of unity and order" (1959, 439). For Poe's narrators, the confessional form becomes primarily an anguished register for forces (psychological, social, moral) over which they can no longer exercise authority and into which they can no longer attain insight. What order may lie beyond the horizon of the narrator's consciousness may be communicated only indirectly through the irony of the narrative situation. These tales, then, carry forward Poe's diagnosis of cultural collapse that Eric W. Carlson has identified as a central burden of Poe's writing during the early to the mid-1840s ("Poe's Vision," 12–13) and presage, as Joseph J. Moldenhauer argues (see later), Poe's search for a "unitary theory of metaphysics" in his later cosmological writings.

The compositional strategy of these tales relies on what Poe called the "power of simulation." "A writer must have the fullest belief in his statements," Poe wrote, "or must simulate that belief perfectly, to produce an absorbing interest in the mind of his reader" (*T*, 873). Poe's confessional narrator is a creation of simulated belief. He is presented as if he were "firmly impressed with the truth, yet astonished at the immensity, of the wonder he relates, and for which, professedly, he neither claims nor anticipates credence" (*T*, 402). He addresses an interlocutor (either an implied audience or a nameless, silent character in the tale) with an earnest commitment to tell the truth no matter how incredible that truth might seem. But Poe's simulation of belief has ironic consequences. The narrator's truth-telling ultimately succeeds, if at all, only by virtue of his own blindness to what he has to tell: if he is the example (victim or agent) of some astonishing truth as he claims, he is so only because he himself does not see how what he says reveals something other—and perhaps opposite—of what he intends.

This deeply embedded structure of irony in these tales has permitted two kinds of readings. James W. Gargano, for example, sees in the irony a "comprehensive intelligence critically and artistically ordering events so as to establish a vision of life and character which the narrator's very inadequacies help to 'prove' " ("Poe's Narrators," 165), as in "The Black Cat," where the telling point is "the narrator's fatuous denial of a moral order at the same time that the reader observes its unfaltering operation" (Gargano, " 'Black Cat,' " 91). On the other hand, G. R. Thompson claims that the "substantive" irony shows the true horror of Poe's fiction, for it amounts to the only sane method of confronting and surviving the truth of a "perverse" and "absurd" universe in which events are disconnected, meaning is opaque, and life's cruel secret is that all is nothing (*TPoe*, 176). Against such antithetical claims for Poe's final meaning, however, Kennedy has recently argued that Poe's narrative irony in these tales expresses "a site of conflict" where characters vie for the authority of language to silence their rivals, to whom, nonetheless, victors are always bound by a return of violence through language against themselves (*Poe*, 1987, 114–44). Claims for mastery over Poe's tales, thus, might well be cautioned by the rivalrous conflict over authority dramatized in the tales themselves.

"The Masque of the Red Death"

In a review published in the May 1842 issue of *Graham's,* Poe claimed to have detected in Hawthorne's "Howe's Masquerade" "something which resembles a plagiarism—but which *may be* a flattering coincidence of thought" to his own story "William Wilson" (*T,* 575). Given that Hawthorne's tale appeared a year before Poe's, Robert Regan contends that Poe's charge—or acknowledgment of a "flattering" imitation—was an invitation to the astute reader to detect that it was actually Poe who had done the culling from Hawthorne and had done it in the very tale that Poe had chosen to appear along with his review of Hawthorne—"Mask of the Red Death. A Fantasy." Regan claims that Poe's "duplicity" shows how closely tied Poe's fiction was to his criticism, how in the one he might illustrate or parody what he critiqued in the other.

In the review of Hawthorne, however, Poe also provided his clearest definition of the tale form: an artistic construct unified by an economy of preconceived effects. No story better illustrates that definition than "The Masque of the Red Death." The rhythmical sentences; the symbolism of the seven rooms, all in different colors, with blue in the east and black in the west; the domination of order by the chimes and the pendulum swing of the ebony clock in the western room—all convey the sense of the plot's inevitable progression to a climax. It is a tale, however, of self-imprisonment by the very *"mood* of mind" expressed in the aesthetic structure. Prince Prospero, whose *"august taste"* gave shape to the lavish palace, seeks to control the horrible reality of the Red Death by closing it out from the realm of his authority. He succeeds, however, only to ensure its presence within and his subjection to it. His ornate abbey, with all its bizarre beauty, is, in effect, "the foolproof Gothic dungeon from which no prisoner escapes," as David Halliburton has put it (311).

More than the architect of his own imprisonment, the Prince is an executioner, for his authorial control precipitates the death of all he encloses with him. Douglas Robinson argues that "the key act of (self)-recognition for Prospero is the act of murder, specifically a ritual murder or sacrifice in which he seeks to protect his enclave from outside contagion . . . by eliminating an image of the undesirable" (205). Such violence done to ensure security and self-mastery links "The Masque" to Poe's later tales of murder and revenge. For all its "novel effect," the most powerful allure of the "castellated abbey" is Prospero's claim that "security [is] within" (*M* 2, 671), yet the desire for security against death prompts in Prospero an impulse that betrays the self to all that makes human life contingent and insecure. The moment of self-recognition comes when he rushes "in rapid impetuosity" to expel the figure of the Red Death, only to fall "prostrate in death" before it. The Red Death has come "like a thief in the night" (*M* 2, 676), a reference to St. Paul's caution against confidence in human powers: "[T]he day of the Lord so cometh as a thief in the night. For when they shall say, Peace and safety; then sudden destruction cometh upon them" (1 Thessalonians 5:2–3).

"The Pit and the Pendulum"

By the time "The Masque" appeared, Poe had probably already completed "The Pit and the Pendulum" (*PoeL*, 370), though it appeared later in *The Gift* (142). He drew upon popular conventions of those minute accounts of sensational experiences that he had satirized in "How to Write a Blackwood Article," but he transformed all his sources into a harrowing tale of condemnation and punishment whose ordeal pushes the narrator to the brink of an abyss at once internal and cosmic. In this tale, as David H. Hirsch explains, Poe "re-infuses" the imagery of a cosmic Judgment Day with "naturalistic coherence by offering it as a representation of . . . a consciousness-of-reality in the process of crumbling" (647).

Throughout, the narrator details his efforts to grasp fleeting "psychal fancies" (*T*, 1383) at the margins of consciousness, those faint "impressions eloquent in the memories of the gulf beyond" that he retains from a deep swoon in the beginning of the tale (*M* 2, 682). These mental glimmerings escape him, but just when death seems most certain, and a "keen, collected calmness of despair" comes over him, he is able to retrieve the "unformed half of [an] idea of deliverance" and free himself from the path of the descending pendulum (*M* 2, 693). Salvation thus appears to depend on a form of knowledge, as it had in "A Descent into the Maelstrom" (1841). But the "unconquerable desire—*to know*," which Poe says forms an essential part of the imagination (*T*, 510) and which saves the narrator of "A Descent," serves only to intensify the "hideous moral horrors" in "The Pit and the Pendulum." The narrator is "Free!—and in the grasp of the Inquisition" (*M* 2, 695)—a recognition of human limitation that Hirsch compares effectively to Camus's sense of "absurd freedom" (641). Final release comes only in the form of a deus ex machina. As the narrator falls "fainting, into the abyss," repeating the swoon with which the story begins, only the outstretched arm of the suddenly intervening General Lasalle can save him. It seems an entirely accidental salvation, apparently as unmotivated as the initial condemnation. Hirsch concludes, however, that the ending's apocalyptic imagery transforms a tale of despair into one "of transcendent hope" (650), that "the transcendence downward resolves into a transcendence upward" (651). The apocalyptic imagery, in other words, allows hope and salvation, as well as reinforces a sense of contingency and absurdity in human affairs.

"The Tell-Tale Heart"

The awful powers of the Inquisition to scrutinize and torture the narrator of "The Pit and the Pendulum" are internalized in this tale (first published in January 1843) by a single character who is both their agent and victim. Mabbott suggests a probable source for the story is a portion of Daniel Webster's speech in a notorious murder case that Poe seems likely to have noticed when working on "Marie Roget":

He has done the murder. No eye has seen him, no ear has heard him. The secret is his own, and it is safe!

Ah! Gentlemen, that was a dreadful mistake. . . . True it is . . . that 'murder will out' . . . [that] the guilty soul cannot keep its own secret. It is false to itself; or rather it feels an irresistible impulse to be true to itself. . . . The secret which the murderer possesses soon comes to possess him. . . . It has become his master. . . . It must be confessed, it will be confessed. (*M* 3, 790)

Poe's narrator, however, seems driven less by a guilty conscience than by a frenzy of fears he cannot directly acknowledge, and both the murder and subsequent confession act out these deeper torments. He denies his own "mortal terror" by simulating control over time and space and by impersonating "Death" itself (the narrator significantly capitalizes the word) to be rid of a threat that is simultaneously without and within. The impressionistic style— with its rushed and staggered syntax, its repetitions and qualifications, its insistent address to the auditor—suggests a hysteria barely in control. He may be schizophrenic, mistaking the ticking sound of "death watch" beetles for the beating of the old man's heart (Reilly, 4), or his insanity may derive from an obsessive fear of death, fantasized as a gaze (the Evil Eye) similar to the old man's (Davis, 996–97). In the end, the internalized powers of Inquisitorial inspection and torment overtake him and lead him to a self-destructive confession, directing the violence back to the source of those fears from which it had been originally deflected.

"The Black Cat" and "The Imp of the Perverse"

The moral tenor of Poe's confessional form is best defined by these two tales (August 1843; July 1845). Each includes a discourse on "the spirit of PERVERSENESS" as "one of the primitive impulses of the human heart" (*M* 3, 857), and, in each, a narrative irony complicates any decisive conclusion since the "primitive impulse" leads to both crime and retribution. The narrators are held accountable for the evil they choose by the same inner impulse that accounts for their choice in the first place. Thus, contrary to utilitarian theories that moral choice is an extension of self-interest, the concept of perverseness rests on the assertion that actions of moral consequence (good or evil) are motivated by an "unfathomable longing of the soul to . . . offer violence to its own nature" (*M* 3, 852).

Because perverseness is so at odds with self-interest, its "necessity," according to one narrator, has been overlooked "by all the moralists. . . . In the pure arrogance of the reason, we have all overlooked it" (*M* 3, 1219). Noting that the tone is "uncannily like the sound of philosophy as established by Descartes, as if Poe's prose were a parody of philosophy's," Stanley Cavell has read in the tales of perverseness a critique of "pure reason," arguing that the imp of the perverse, like a form of persistent skepticism, shows the limits of reason as the ground for certainty about self and the world (120–44). Each narrator initially delights in the "absolute security" (*M* 3, 1224) that his "cunning" has gained for him—only in the end to feel that security shattered by an impulse contrary to his "self-interested" reason. The "pure arrogance of the reason" would even "dictate purposes to God" (*M* 3, 1219), but victims of the imp, having first aspired to the place of God, come to know better.

An early review from Princeton College called "The Imp of the Perverse" "humbug philosophical" (*PoeL,* 602), and any favorable comments avoided philosophical issues. Evert A. Duyckinck, for instance, praised Poe's psychological realism "in representing, with the utmost exactness, and in sharpest outlines, the inward life of beings, under the control of perverse and morbid passions" (Walker, 187), but he strictly limited perverseness to "the phenomena of insanity" (190). "The Black Cat," in particular, no doubt demonstrates Poe's acute insights into the "psychology of the abnormal" (Halliburton, 342). Its narrator may appeal to supernatural causes to explain his actions, but his "homely narrative" clearly reveals that deep disturbances in his relations to others are at the root of his derangement. From early childhood, he has substituted the affections of animals for what he calls "the paltry and gossamer fidelity of mere *Man*" (*M* 3, 849). That substitution, as Daniel Hoffman has shown, expands to include his fascination for, and anxiety about, sexual desires and culminates in his murder of his wife—as if that "had been his unacknowledged purpose all along" (237).

Yet, while these narrators are studies in psychological disorders, perverseness is explored as more than a form of lunacy. It belongs to that field of inquiry called *theological morality* (*M* 2, 226), and perhaps the best approach to the philosophical and psychological issues lies along the direction Patrick F. Quinn points to by comparing perverseness to Sören Kierkegaard's concept of dread. Like Poe's imp, dread demands an oxymoronic definition: it is a "sympathetic antipathy" for evil that results in an apparent lack of accountability, but a lack that "ensnares" the individual in the evil he both desires and abhors (1957, 160–66). The compulsive attraction and abhorrence form one principle, which is fundamental to Poe's moral imagination.

"The Cask of Amontillado" and "Hop-Frog"

In these last tales of crime, the murderer escapes retributive punishment, and some readers have seen in them Poe's own fantasy of revenge against personal antagonists and an unsympathetic public. "The Cask of Amontillado" (November 1846) was composed while Poe was embroiled in a thoroughly mean-spirited feud over what he called the "critical *gossip*" in his "The Literati of New York City" (*O* 2, 332). The feud raged on during the summer of 1846, peaking in July, when Poe filed a libel suit against two newspapers for publishing an article asserting that he had committed forgery (see Moss, 220–34). That "The Cask of Amontillado" shows Poe's working out of his immediate emotions in this feud, as Mabbott concludes, "can hardly be doubted" (*M* 2, 1253), but the tale's extraordinary power derives more from the relentless irony embedded in the rivalry—or "perfect hate," in D. H. Lawrence's view (100)—it depicts.

According to Lawrence, "The lust of Montresor is to devour utterly the soul of [his rival] Fortunato" (100), and, in the end, his revenge does appear grimly triumphant. As Kennedy shows (*Poe* 1994, 138–43), Montresor prevails by effectively silencing Fortunato: his puns echo Fortunato's words and divert the intended meaning to one to suit his own purpose, while his mocking repetition of Fortunato's last cries of anguish and pleas for mercy deprive them of any communicative effect, thereby emptying them, too, of any meaning. In short, Montresor's revenge appears so triumphant because he controls language. Or does he? Walter Stepp notes that "the 'mocking echo' motif" is "the most suggestive of the two men's relationship" (450), in that Montresor is forever bound to the rival whose name resembles his own. Kennedy argues that by recounting events in a confessional narrative, Montresor becomes the victim himself of the very irony of language he plays upon—"the psychological captive of his own perfect strategy" (142). More, Lawrence concludes that "the result is the dissolution of both souls, each losing itself in transgressing its own bounds" (100). Finally, Benton has recently argued that Poe's use of the physical sciences in the tale expands its irony of psychological entrapment to a cosmic irony of life entrapped by death ("Poe's 'The Cask' ").

In "Hop-Frog" (March 1849), the unexpected victim of Poe's irony might well be the reader, for the tale is a "moral fantasy," to use Davidson's term, about the violence concealed within desires for just retribution. This kind of fantasy is a tale "so obviously a fable" that the reader is initially beguiled into enjoying its emotional ploys, only later to be "betrayed into self-recognition" as "the fantasy moves toward disgust" (Davidson, 151, 153). In the tale, the cruel humor of a king and his ministers provokes their long-suffering court jester (Hop-Frog) to outdo their cruelty with his own righteous revenge and terrifying form of humor. Ordered to produce "characters" for a masquerade ball, Hop-Frog dresses the king and ministers as orangutans, but, at the height of their frolic, he manages to set the costumed royalty ablaze before the eyes of their appalled subjects. The unholy mingling of personal vengeance and social justice in the scene calls to mind a comment from Poe's "Marginalia": "What can be more soothing, at once to a man's Pride and to his Conscience, than the conviction that, in taking vengeance on his enemies for *in*justice done him, he has simply to do them *justice* in return?" (*T*, 1461). Yet, however appealing to self-esteem such revenge might be, the "power of simulation" central to Poe's art in the tales of crime and punishment intervenes at the end, undermining Hop-Frog's triumph by revealing in its reign of terror the bestial and gratuitous violence that a fantasy of self-justification may conceal and indulge. Just as Poe's madmen become victims of their own self-aggrandizement, the reader, initially beguiled by the fantasy in "Hop-Frog," is left to acknowledge the self-deception and dubious moral purpose at its source.

CRITICAL PERSPECTIVES

While Poe conceded that his tales were shaped, in part, by the necessities that made him "essentially a Magazinist" (*O* 1, 270), his "vision of things," Wilbur reminds us, was from first to last "cosmic in extent" ("Edgar Allan Poe," 48). Critical inquiries into the tales of crime and detection have demonstrated that "cosmic" reach by exploring the relation of Poe's narrative forms to his philosophical, ethical, psychological, and ideological perspectives.

Wilbur himself, for example, argues that Poe's vision was "a Neo-Platonic one of the soul's conflicts, trials, and cosmic destiny" (1967, 133). He sees in Dupin a portrait of how the soul prevails by relying on "a supra-logical faculty, infallible in nature" (134), and studies by Davidson, Ketterer, Levine, and Irwin bear out that Dupin's mode of analysis is more intuitive than merely calculating, as much cosmological as it is psychological; in Irwin's words, the "ongoing mystery at the heart of [Poe's] three detective tales [is] . . . the puzzle of self-consciousness," but in *Eureka* this mystery is also "the central puzzle of the universe" (400). For Davidson in particular, the ratiocinative plot offers a Poesque "glimpse into ideality": the disruption of order caused by the crime is overcome by the detective's imaginative apprehension of "the total, primal calculus of relationship" to which the crime itself belongs (217–18). Joseph J. Moldenhauer elaborates this "primal calculus" by showing that Dupin's intuitive powers link him to Poe's ideal "poet-critic": each seeks a perfect unity, defined in Poe's metaphysics as the design of material conditions to return to (or die back into) a primordial oneness, from which to spring again into the "abnormal" relations of material forms. Moldenhauer concludes that, in the tales of terror, murder "constitutes a radical but fundamentally aesthetic solution to the problem of disunity . . . in a fragmented universe" (292), so that beneath the horror and ethical dilemma is an aesthetic and cosmic value: "[T]he murderer is born into the only genuine life, which is the fixed aesthetic order or 'poem' of death" (296). For John F. Lynen also, the anguish of Poe's characters has an important ethical dimension. Since the "universal order" is at distinct odds with the mortal self's interest to perpetuate its individuality, the extreme ordeals of the characters are the very means to apprehend "the good toward which [the] whole of life is directed" (216–17). Poe's cosmology, then, has proved central to the "transcendental-symbolic" readings of his work that, from responses as early as Baudelaire's, have become, in Eric W. Carlson's words, "a solid baseline from which new triangulations can emerge" ("Frames of Reference," 216).

Interested less in Poe's metaphysical vision, however, than in the existential moods and conflicts rendered in his fiction, Kennedy argues that the "perception of death as an absolute horizon of existence" is the key to Poe's aethetics (1987, 211). The position is similar to Harry Levin's sense that Poe's tales are "notes from underground" whose structural ironies serve Poe's "bold attempt to face the true darkness" of human fate (163–64), but Kennedy contends further that

Poe conferred on writing "a quasi-mystical power derived largely from its capacity to resist death" (1987, 212). If in language can be created a separate "world of words" resisting the mortality that flesh is heir to, Poe explores that world, as Michael J. S. Williams maintains, only to discover an instability within the concepts that a reliable order depends on. Williams is especially effective in detailing the relationship between self and language that underlies the identity of Poe's narrators, a relationship that disturbs the "conviction of the unity and stability of personal identity" (18).

Close readings of the rhetoric of Poe's tales, however, need not cross into speculations about cosmic design or self-identity. Especially noteworthy among the variety of such close readings are the New Critical studies of narrative structure by James Gargano, the phenomenological investigation of imagery and characterization by David Halliburton, the structuralist account of self-reflexivity in "The Gold-Bug" by Jean Ricardou, the narratological account of authority in "The Purloined Letter" by Ross Chambers, and the reader-response study of "The Black Cat" by Terry Heller. Such readings demonstrate the conscious craftsmanship of Poe's most popular tales and confirm Poe's belief that, while high critical merit could not assure a large popularity for a truly original work, what popularity it did achieve was "the legitimate result of certain well-understood critical propositions reduced by genius into practice" (*T,* 226).

Psychological studies of the tales of crime and detection are also abundant. Dostoevski admired Poe for "the marvelous acumen and amazing realism" with which he described "the inner state" of characters placed in extraordinary situations (78), and, according to Robert Schulman, the critic's business is to learn from Poe's own "unusually specific and profound understanding of the processes of obsession, displacement, hatred, and self-hatred" (259). Many studies, however, gloss Poe's own understanding with twentieth-century psychoanalytic theories. While loose applications of Freudian terminology to describe the repressed content of the tales have resulted in interesting accounts of character motivations (see Hoffman), Shoshana Felman rightly warns against reductive readings that assume a "clinical reality" outside the text as its cause and the final arbiter of its meaning (143). Instead of "the *application* of psychoanalysis *to* literature," Felman recommends investigating "their *interimplications in* each other" (153), and she maintains that such investigation is the critical enterprise of Lacan's "Seminar on 'The Purloined Letter' " (see earlier). *The Purloined Poe* contains the essays by Lacan, Derrida, Johnson, and Felman, along with a valuable editors' "Overview" that makes it an essential textbook for Poe studies engaging the complexities of poststructuralist thought.

Finally, Poe's relation to his culture has received increasing attention. David S. Reynolds provides a rich description of the popular forms of crime literature against which Poe's own fiction should be compared. He argues that popular fiction of the day maintained a moral neutrality about crime (178), at best attributing crime to an uncontrollable evil in depraved characters, while Poe's fiction "was simultaneously a full enactment of the popular Subversive imagination and a careful containment of it,'' free from the ''mob fantasy'' and ''moral confusion'' that characterized the popular literature of sensationalism (230). On the other hand, studies by Cawelti, Porter (1981), Bloom, and Knight hold that Poe's detective fiction participates in the dominant ideology even as it appears on the surface to be opposed to it, especially in the way it reassures readers that potentially dangerous and morally unsettling disturbances of the social order can be transformed into something completely under control (Cawelti, 105). Cynthia S. Jordan, finally, maintains that the detective fiction shows Poe to be ''a writer of feminist sensibility'' (5), his fiction thus running counter to repressive attitudes toward women in his culture. All these cultural studies reveal the double burden Poe's writing has carried: his fiction has been both accomplice and antagonist in the development of cultural attitudes toward violence, law, and punishment.

These varied approaches gauge very well the critical interest that the tales of crime and detection sustain and the centrality they have in Poe's canon. In the last year of his life, Poe wrote to a friend that he considered literature ''the most noble of professions'' and ''the dominion of intellect'' and ''consciousness of power'' its greatest rewards. As the critical heritage attests, it was the allure, the dimensions, and the ambiguity of these rewards that Poe explored in the tales of crime and detection. In ''the dominion of intellect,'' no character appears more masterful in Poe's fiction than his detective nor anyone so self-deceived as the criminal madman, while ''consciousness of power'' describes equally well the detective's triumphant satisfaction and the madman's abject misery. These popular characters have lasting significance in Poe's fiction, then, because, in many ways, they are iconic figures for the complex art that gave them form.

WORKS CITED

Asarch, Joel Kenneth. ''A Telling Tale: Poe's Revisions in 'The Murders in the Rue Morgue.' '' *Poe at Work: Seven Textual Studies.* Ed. Benjamin Franklin Fisher IV. Baltimore: Edgar Allan Poe Society, 1978, 83–99.

Babener, Lianhna Klenman. ''The Shadow's Shadow: The Motif of the Double in Edgar Allan Poe's 'The Purloined Letter.' '' In Muller and Richardson, eds., *The Purloined Poe,* 323–34.

Benton, Richard P. '' 'The Mystery of Marie Roget'—A Defense.'' *Studies in Short Fiction* 6 (1969): 144–51.

———. ''Poe's 'The Cask' and the 'White Webwork Which Gleams.' '' *Studies in Short Fiction* 28 (1991): 183–94.

Bloom, Clive. ''Capitalising on Poe's Detective: The Dollars and Sense of Nineteenth-Century Detective Fiction.'' *Nineteenth-Century Suspense: From Poe to Conan Doyle.* Ed. Clive Bloom et al. London: Macmillan, 1988, 14–25.

Byer, Robert H. ''Mysteries of the City: A Reading of Poe's 'The Man of the Crowd.' '' *Ideology and Classic American Literature.* Ed. Sacvan Bercovitch and Myra Jehlen. New York: Cambridge UP, 1986, 221–46.

Cavell, Stanley. *In Quest of the Ordinary: Lines of Skepticism and Romanticism.* Chicago: U of Chicago P, 1988.

Cawelti, John G. *Adventure, Mystery, and Romance: Formula Stories as Art and Popular Culture.* Chicago: U of Chicago P, 1976.

Chambers, Ross. *Story and Situation: Narrative Seduction and the Power of Fiction.* Minneapolis: U of Minnesota P, 1984.

Davis, Robert Con. "Lacan, Poe, and Narrative Repression." *Modern Language Notes* 98 (1983): 983–1005.

Dostoevski, Fyodor M. "Three Tales of Edgar Allan Poe." In *CE,* 77–79.

Doyle, Arthur Conan. *Through the Magic Door.* New York: McClure, 1908.

Felman, Shoshana. "On Reading Poetry: Reflections on the Limits and Possibilities of Psychoanalytic Approaches." In Muller and Richardson, eds., *The Purloined Poe,* 133–56.

Gargano, James W. " 'The Black Cat': Perverseness Reconsidered." *Texas Studies in Literature and Language* 2 (1960): 172–78. Rpt. in *Twentieth Century Interpretations of Poe's Tales.* Ed. William L. Howarth. Englewood Cliffs, N. J.: Prentice-Hall, 1971, 87–93.

Griswold, Rufus W. "Memoir of the Author." In *The Works of Edgar Allan Poe.* Vol. 1. New York: Redfield, 1850. Rpt. in *CE,* 52–57.

Hassell, J. Woodrow, Jr. "The Problem of Realism in 'The Gold-Bug.' " *AL* 25 (1953): 179–92.

Haycraft, Howard. *Murder for Pleasure: The Life and Times of the Detective Story.* New York: D. Appleton-Century, 1941.

Heller, Terry. *The Delights of Terror: An Aesthetics of the Tale of Terror.* Urbana: U of Illinois P, 1987.

Hirsch, David H. "The Pit and the Apocalypse." *Sewanee Review* 76 (1968): 632–52.

Irwin, John T. *The Mystery to a Solution: Poe, Borges, and the Analytic Detective Story.* Baltimore: Johns Hopkins UP, 1994.

Kempton, Daniel. "The Gold/Goole/Ghoul Bug." *ESQ* 32 (First Quarter 1987): 1–19.

Kennedy, J. Gerald. "The Limits of Reason: Poe's Deluded Detectives." *AL* 47 (1975): 184–96.

———. *Poe, Death, and the Life of Writing.* New Haven, Conn.: Yale UP, 1987

Knight, Stephen. *Form and Ideology in Crime Fiction.* Bloomington: Indiana UP, 1980.

Kronick, Joseph G. "Edgar Allan Poe: The Error of Reading and the Reading of Error." In *Southern Literature and Literary Theory.* Ed. J. Humphries. Athens: U of Georgia P, 1990 206–25.

Lacan, Jacques. "Seminar on 'The Purloined Letter.' " *The Purloined Poe,* 28–54.

Lowndes. Robert A. W. "The Contribution of Edgar Allan Poe." *The Mystery Writer's Art.* Ed. Francis M. Nevins, Jr. Bowling Green: Bowling Green U Popular P, 1970, 1–18.

Matthews, J. Brander. "Poe and the Detective Story." *The Recognition of Edgar Allan Poe.* Ed. Eric W. Carlson. Ann Arbor: U of Michigan P, 1966, 81–93.

Moldenhauer, Joseph J. "Murder as a Fine Art: Basic Connections between Poe's Aesthetics, Psychology, and Moral Vision." *PMLA* 83 (1968): 284–97.

Pease, Donald E. *Visionary Compacts.* Madison: U of Wisconsin P, 1987.

Pollin, Burton R. "Poe's 'Murders in the Rue Morgue': The Ingenious Web Unravelled." *Studies in the American Renaissance: 1977.* Ed. Joel Myerson. Boston: Twayne, 1978, 235–59.

Porter, Dennis. "Of Poets, Politicians, Policemen, and the Power of Analysis." *New Literary History* 19 (1988): 501–19.

————. *The Pursuit of Crime: Art and Ideology in Detective Fiction.* New Haven, Conn.: Yale UP, 1981.

Regan, Robert. "Hawthorne's 'Plagiary': Poe's Duplicity." *Nineteenth-Century Fiction* 25 (1970–1971): 281–98.

Reilly, John E. "The Lesser Death-Watch and 'The Tell-Tale Heart.' " *ATQ* (1969): 3–9.

Ricardou, Jean. "Gold in the Bug." Trans. Frank Towne. *PoeS* 9 (1976): 33–39.

Riddel, Joseph N. "The 'Crypt' of Edgar Poe." *Boundary 2* 7, no. 2 (1979): 117–44.

Rosenheim, Shawn. " 'The King of "Secret Readers" ': Edgar Poe, Cryptography, and the Origins of the Detective Story." *English Literary History* 56 (1988): 375–400.

St. Armand, Barton Levi. "Poe's 'Sober Mystification': The Uses of Alchemy in 'The Gold-Bug.' " *PoeS* 4 (June 1971): 1–7.

Sayers, Dorothy L. "Introduction." *The Omnibus of Crime,* 1929. Rpt. in *The Art of the Mystery Story: A Collection of Critical Essays.* Ed. Howard Haycraft. New York: Grosset and Dunlap, 1946, 71–109.

Schulman, Robert. "Poe and the Powers of Mind." *English Literary History* 37 (1970): 245–62.

Stauffer, Donald Barlow. "Poe as Phrenologist: The Example of Monsieur Dupin." *Papers on Poe: Essays in Honor of John Ward Ostrom.* Ed. Richard P. Veler. Springfield, Ohio: Chantry Music P, 1972, 113–25.

Stepp, Walter. "The Ironic Double in Poe's 'Cask of Amontillado.' " *Studies in Short Fiction* 13 (1976): 447–53.

Walsh, John. *Poe the Detective: The Curious Circumstances behind "The Mystery of Marie Roget."* New Brunswick: Rutgers UP, 1968.

Weiner, Bruce I. " 'That Metaphysical Art': Mystery and Detection in Poe's Tales." *Poe and Our Times: Influence and Affinities.* Ed. Benjamin Franklin Fisher IV. Baltimore: Edgar Allan Poe Society, 1986, 32–48.

12

The Science Fiction and the
Landscape Sketches

DAVID E. E. SLOANE AND MICHAEL J. PETTENGELL

INTRODUCTION

Roughly grouped under the heading of "science fiction" and "landscape sketches" are the balloon hoaxes—"Hans Pfaall," "Mellonta Tauta," and "The Balloon Hoax"; the science fiction piece "Von Kempelen and His Discovery"; the mesmeric sketches—"The Facts in the Case of M. Valdemar," "A Tale of the Ragged Mountains," and "Some Words with a Mummy"; and a series of landscape pieces—"The Landscape Garden," "Morning on the Wissahiccon," "The Domain of Arnheim," and "Landor's Cottage." Virtually all of the tales and sketches discussed in this chapter are developed through some kind of journey. Unless further evidence of Poe's intention is brought forth about the nature of this travel, however, it may prove extremely difficult, if not impossible, to determine whether Poe's intent was to create "arabesques" (Ketterer 1974), inward journeys to visionary consciousness (Wilbur), or hoaxes (Thompson 1973). All the theories differ in their appeal depending on how a given reader emphasizes different components. Richard Wilbur, in his justly famed "House of Poe" lecture, contended that Poe's works were consistent in their symbolic representation of an inward journey into a "hypnagogic" state—the sleep-waker's state of psychomachia and dream vision—where the psychic conflicts of the soul's quest toward a higher state are projected. Wilbur recognized the hypnagogic state in Poe's "Marginalia" entry on "psychal fancies" as those "glimpses of the spirit's outer world" during the dream state between waking and sleeping (29).

Richard Wilbur's view provides an appealing starting point for a discussion of Poe's science fiction and landscape writings, stretching as they do from "Hans Pfaall" in 1835 through "Landor's Cottage" in 1849. By extension, some of these stories burlesque contemporary American life and still project this alternative state, as in "Hans Pfaall." The landscape sketches fit into the chain of stages of matter by being physical interpolations on Earth—and thus necessarily limited and imperfect—of a higher state. Wilbur notes that Earth as fallen away from God's "perfection of composition" has lost its first beauty in proportion to man's loss of perception of the beautiful (23). Poe's landscape sketches elevate the reader to the highest level of earthly perception. The science fiction stories address parallel issues of man's physicality and the horror of his physical dissolution almost literally—"Valdemar" most notably—or bring the reader into a critical perspective on the egocentric factuality of Western science, as in "Mellonta Tauta." Characteristically, Poe writes in several of his hoaxes in such a way as to make his own allegorical intention overobvious, but, each time he rejects the factual American mind-set, he leaves traces of an alternative way of knowing as an intriguing leitmotiv behind the surface events of the story or sketch.

Other approaches besides Wilbur's are open to the student of Poe's science fiction and landscape sketches, many of them quite compatible, even though different. David Ketterer's generic approach to the stories as science fiction in *New Worlds for Old,* for example, finds that the balloon hoaxes, "A Tale of the Ragged Mountains," and "Von Kempelen" can be associated with either April fooling or "Wellsian dystopia," as he sees "Mellonta Tauta." If the tales are not primarily science fiction, since they tend not to take themselves seriously, they are at least apocalyptic in nature, vision, and philosophy, showing Poe welding the rationale of science fiction to transcendental reality (Ketterer 1974, 72–74). Eric Carlson's "Frames of Reference for Poe's Symbolic Language" describes a number of avenues that also must be considered in relation to this particular set of stories. The philosophic-aesthetic approach to the landscape sketches is naturally attractive, especially considering Poe's fondness for, and interest in, interior and landscape design, noted by many of the sources cited later. Likewise, the Romantic-ironic critics have found substantial evidence supporting their readings of the stories as puzzles for readers trying to untangle the author's intention from the unreliability of the narrator or by critics misreading Poe's intricacy where the stories are laden with clues to Poe's real intention. As cultural documents, the stories also provide clear insights into Poe's attitude toward contemporary American society, as in "Morning on the Wissahiccon" and "Mellonta Tauta." Alfred Kazin, in *A Writer's America: Landscape in Literature,* flatly asserts that Poe's "landscapes were issued from his mind alone, consistent with Wilbur" (66–67).

THE BALLOON HOAXES

"Hans Pfaall"

First appearing in the *Southern Literary Messenger* as "Hans Phaall—A Tale" in June 1835, Poe's earliest balloon story was reprinted without his name attached in the *New York Transcript* shortly thereafter, September 2–5, as "Lunar Discoveries, Extraordinary Aerial Voyage by Baron Hans Pfaall." *Poe Log* cites two balloon ascension items in 1833–1834, one by Poe's uncle-in-law Henry Heering, to suggest the contemporaneity of the topic, and Poe's own "The Balloon Hoax" in the *New York Sun* almost a decade later. Interest in balloon voyages was widespread, the first English Channel crossing having taken place in 1785, with an American aboard. Critics generally enjoyed the burlesque of the contemporary balloon mania, praising Poe for both imagination and execution. Because the *New York Sun* published Richard Adams Locke's comparable "moon-story" during the last week of August 1835, a minor controversy arose (*PoeL*, 166), which led to the *Transcript*'s reprinting and caused Poe to add a note to the tale in *Tales of the Grotesque and Arabesque* (1840) defending the originality of the tale. Despite concerns by Poe regarding the comparison to Locke, subsequent scholarship has found more similarities between Poe's story and George Tucker's *A Voyage to the Moon,* published in 1827 (Posey, Bailey). Poe may have intended to create a subtle satire of Tucker's work, as he follows its plot closely, but offers stupid, uncooperative lunarians rather than the conventional satire of American culture based on the life of the more intelligent inhabitants discovered by Tucker's hero; also, the envelope of the tale undercuts its truthfulness by suggesting that Pfaall never left Earth (Wilkinson 1966). Other sources provided scientific verisimilitude and were direct sources, including Sir John Herschel's *A Treatise on Astronomy* (1834) (Campbell, Ketterer 1971, Pollin 1981).

Burton Pollin's "Introduction" and "Notes" to his reprinting of "The Unparalleled Adventure of One Hans Pfaall" offer a definitive discussion of the sketch and its background, including the sources cited earlier. "Leaves from an Aeronaut," from the January 1835 *Knickerbocker Magazine* and "Aerostation" from *Rees's Cyclopedia* are added to the list of notable sources (Pollin, 370–71), which are echoed in phrases and ideas. A "Note" was added to the later reprintings of the tale, "padded . . . out with a learned analysis of the French translation of Godwin's *Man in the Moon*" (376–77). Pollin concludes that although Poe was interested in perfecting the "scientific ambiance" of the tale, he was surprisingly lax in grammatical precision: "Having written it in haste, he seemed disinclined to polish it" (378). Nevertheless, Pollin finds it ambivalent about science, even though he disagrees with the contention by Bailey and others that it is a parody of romantic moon voyages (367–69).

"Hans Pfaall" allows the critic several avenues of approach. Ronald Wilkinson's identification of the story as a parody-travesty of the Tucker novel makes good sense of the farcical meeting with the lunarians and the otherwise over-obvious ending, exposing the fraud. Poe was attempting to make the moon voyage itself the convincing part of the story and was rejecting the overt moralizing of Tucker by turning the moon people into travesties (Wilkinson 1966, 336). Without addressing the matter of Poe directly, American interest in lunarians can be dated back at least to the publication of a short-lived periodical named *Moonshine* in 1807, and undoubtedly before. Poe's description of the

Rotterdammers has other resonances. With more than passing similarities to the style of Washington Irving in treating the residents of Gotham in his Knicker-bocker history, the first pages of the story satirize New York, and two articles have contended that the story is a comedy or political satire (Greer, Reiss). From yet another direction, David Ketterer, in arguing that Hans died, went to Hell, and is reborn at the end of the story, identifies passages on cloud formations, Hans's doppelgänger on the moon, and hypnagogic landscape visions that place this story comfortably within Wilbur's construct of an internal journey, in this case, with obvious travesties of the external empirical world of Hans and of the earlier sources Poe may burlesque. Hans himself speaks of the incipient madness that he feels as he begins his journey into the clouds, thus aligning his experience with other, more serious Poe figures. Emerging from the mist, Hans sees Earth as a landscape only. Traces of human habitation have vanished, and the Earth is now appropriately depopulated and mysteriously beautified. Whether Hans is a science fiction hero or one making a journey to an inward truth of human affairs, Earth looks better when distance obscures mankind. At the other end of the journey, however, more overtly satiric elements come into play. Following the bouleversement in which the moon's gravity replaces the Earth's, Hans must cut loose his car and fall into a lunar civilization populated by grinning idiots, one of whom—unless he is an earless dwarf from Bruges employed as part of a hoax—bears Hans's petition for a pardon for his crimes. The petition sequence, compounded of science fantasy and travesty, is a characteristic Poe response to the deliberate men of science and politics who act as Hans's foils in receiving his message. Addressing the "overwise," who may include readers taken in by the foolscap balloon into an overly credulous analysis of the story, Poe offers readers an interpretive puzzle. He writes in a manner that may suggest duplicity regarding his universal theory, for he seems overly obvious in announcing that "hoax, with these sort of people, is, I believe, a general term for all matters above their comprehension." Hans, with his balloon papered over with old newspapers from Earth, may be a fake, but there may be hidden in his tale a "disguised account of Pfaall's transference from conventional reality to arabesque reality" (Ketterer 1974, 72). The story may be neither a direct hoax nor a literal piece of science fiction, but rather a compound carrying multiple philosophical implications. Thus, the story implicates readers as well as Rotterdammers who either accept or reject Earth and moonscape too literally.

"The Balloon Hoax"

Between "Hans Pfaall" and "Mellonta Tauta" stands the now boldly titled "The Balloon Hoax," first printed in the *New York Sun* on April 13, 1844, as a broadside, to considerable excitement and a rush for copies that were sold for as much as fifty cents each, according to Poe. As one of the most realistic hoaxes of its day, Poe's account of Monck Mason's flight across the Atlantic Ocean to land on the beach at Charleston, South Carolina, was written in the style of a journalistic flash, and since the *Sun* extra edition gave all the signs of being a real newspaper scoop, it is not surprising that a sensational sale, 50,000 claimed, was the result (*PoeL* 457–62). Lively debate followed in the papers, with references made to Locke's moon hoax of ten years earlier; Poe was not identified as the author until nine months later. As Mabbott's notes and commentary on the sketch make clear, names of real balloonists and the author Harrison Ainsworth, as well as passages following closely Monck Mason's *Account of the Late Aeronautical Expedition* from England to Germany in 1836 (noted originally by Scudder), provided verisimilitude (*M* 3, 1084–88). Poe even uses the same device of a dramatic reversal of direction as Monck describes to provide the dramatic crux of his story (*M* 3, 1086, n. 19). Poe also drew on a description of Mason's machine from *Alexander's Express Messenger* of February 21, 1844, "to add realism to his description of the construction of the 'Victoria,' " as he used Mason's voyage for the actual journey (Wilkinson 1960).

Scholarship has been concerned, reasonably enough, with the nature of Monck Mason's report, possible sources, and surrounding events of the story's publication and acknowledgment as a hoax (Brigham, Wimsatt, Mabbott), but room for a more literary appreciation exists. Falk has made an interesting connection between Poe's undermining his hoax and the self-destructiveness of his characters in the 1844 period. According to an account by Thomas Low Nichols, Poe had a glass of wine and appeared outside the publisher's door on the day of the story's publication to announce to a mob of would-be buyers that the story was a hoax (Falk 1972, 48). Poe's relationship to his own story might thus be called into question, and more might be done in focusing on the juxtaposition of the practical man, Mason, and the visionary, Ainsworth. Even where Poe translated more or less directly from Mason's real account into Ainsworth's supposed postscripts, the language Ainsworth uses is unduly stilted and calls into question his visionary ability in understanding the "sublimating" quality of the experience. Traces of sublime landscapes and the wispy clouds that elsewhere identify the hypnagogic state appear in the story, but only the passages reputedly added by romancer Harrison Ainsworth to the factual records presented by Mason carry out suggestions of this state; taken as a hypnagogic state, however, the Ainsworth portions fit the theory extremely well, even in subordination to the verisimilitude of the hoax. Poe's wonderful pun, in fact, codifies the situation for "quidnuncs" of all sorts: "If, on the other hand, any circumstances should cause undue levity, and consequent ascent, this levity is immediately counteracted by the additional weight of rope upraised from earth" (*M* 3, 1024). Poe ironically makes the empirical and transcendent pull against each other, a formula reflected in the human spirit elsewhere in the canon.

"Mellonta Tauta"

This tale first appeared in *Godey's Lady's Book* in February 1849, completing the series of balloon hoaxes, unless we grant separate status to Mabbott's "A

Remarkable Letter,'' a version of material in ''Mellonta Tauta'' quarried from
paragraphs 11–25 of *Eureka* (*M* 3, 1310–19). Woodberry has identified it as a
humorous rewriting of other Poe pieces and notes its similarity to the introduction to *Eureka* (327); comparisons to *Pym* are also appropriate, as Ljungquist's
discussion of the story makes clear (80–82), and, as a caricature of Western
epistemology, it reaches from ''Aries Tottle'' through the ''Ettrick Shepherd,''
using the name of James Hogg to allow a punning foray against the ''Baconian''
school. Social satire is clearly the focus of Poe's intention, but the story is also
intriguing in light of the Wilbur thesis. Overtly, the sketch is a diary kept on a
futuristic monthlong balloon journey in 2848 with ''odious pleasure seekers''
in which almost the first observation is that no invention exists to visit the human
pericranium as opposed to jog-trot travels in the sky. The April 3 entry repu-
diates the Hoggish procedure by facts, an error by ''Amriccans'' and others that
was ''analogous with that of the wiseacre who fancies that he must necessarily
see an object the better the more closely he holds it to his eyes.'' Pundita, the
writer of the sketch, seems anti-individualistic in the extreme—applauding the
recognition by her age that an individual does not exist and later decrying
the ''prairie dog'' philosophy that ''all men are born free and equal'' as flying
''in the very teeth of the laws of *gradation*'' (*M* 3, 1293, 1299). The correspondent concludes with an attack on Mill's contention in natural logic that ''a
tree must be either a tree or not a tree,'' undercut by the simple remark *why,*
leading to the writer's stated preference for the ''Soul that loves nothing so well
as to *soar*'' over the ''preposterous proscription'' of all other paths than the
''creeping'' and ''crawling'' schools Pundita identifies. Thus, embedded in the
idea of the balloon flight and its visions—which ultimately comes to the reader
as a message in a bottle, like other mysterious Poe messages of otherworldly
experiences—is the announced predilection for something very like the intuitive
state rather than the epistemological methods of induction and deduction of
Western thought or their political counterparts in democratic polity. Pundita—
whose name may be a pun on pundit—rises naturally enough to the climax,
beginning with ''Eureka!'' on April 8, just before plummeting into the sea when
the balloon breaks, and provides a splendid attack on the Knickerbocker savages
who lived in twenty-story buildings on a narrow island destroyed by earthquakes
in 2050 and subsequently become Paradise—the Emperor's principle pleasure
garden. The travesty culture of the savages is given over to monument-rearing
and sausage-making, the latter activity done with Cornwallis's body after his
surrender, according to Pundita. But does Pundita reflect the internal vision
behind Poe's own eye? The brief heading of the sketch signed by Edgar A. Poe,
''To the Editors of the Lady's Book,'' claims that he offers a translation by an
obvious caricature name for Andrew Jackson Davis, the ''Poughkeepsie Seer,''
of a bottled manuscript floating in the ''Mare Tenebrarum,'' a sea visited only
by transcendentalists; all of these references indict the manuscript by associating
it with mystics despised by Poe. Confusing John Stuart Mill with Joe Miller
reduces the philosopher to the level of an old jest book, famous for the triteness

of its jokes and the supposed stupidity of Joe, the reputed author. Thus, this late sketch is given over to broad caricaturing of Poe's philosophical adversaries. Mabbott's notes, relying on his own and Pollin's research, highlight Poe's attack on contemporary politicians as well, including the corrupt New York politician Richard Riker and the rhetorician Thomas Hart Benton (*M* 3, 1309n.). Pundita's confusion of the undersubscribed and unfinished Washington monument in New York with an indication of "intention" suitably burlesques sham patriotism. Ljungquist finds the imagery and diction of *The Narrative of Arthur Gordon Pym* retained but, otherwise, the story diminished, the descent into an awesome cataract deflated to a tumble into the sea. His brief but convincing analysis finds the conclusion of the story to travesty the Titans of *Pym,* making of them "objects of satirical abuse" (80–82).

A SCIENCE-FICTION HOAX

"Von Kempelen and His Discovery"

Published only two months after "Mellonta Tauta" in *The Flag of Our Union* for April 14, 1849, this tale would seem a natural companion to the moon hoaxes and belongs to both the hoax and the science fiction categories. The text does, indeed, refer to the story as having "an amazingly moon-hoax-y air." Mabbott documents Poe's intention to offer a quizzing corrective to the Gold Rush fever sweeping the nation since the discovery of gold at Sutter's Mill (*M* 3, 1355–56). Allusions to the elements of a hypnagogic state also appear: the discovery of a means of changing base metals to gold is fabricated high up in a house of seven stories, under the mansard no less, in a neighborhood featuring "a labyrinth of narrow and crooked passages," another of Poe's frequent allegorical indications of a higher consciousness. Von Kempelen, like Hans Pfaall, had problems with his creditors prior to his amazing reversal and seems to have escaped through his technical devices. Thus, the story has many elements connecting it to the pattern established in the balloon stories and suggestive of the transcendent state.

In "Von Kempelen," antimony is being turned to gold at this mysterious higher elevation, just as the imagination transmutes facts, and concomitant with the story's reference to Sir Humphrey Davy's notebooks, putatively the source of the idea—by chance, since they should have been destroyed due to Davy's being "morbidly afraid of *appearing* empirical." The other indication of inspired fraudulence dominating mechanism lies in the naming of the inventor, and Poe is at pains to directly relate the name of the alchemist to Maelzel's automaton-chess-player, which Poe had dealt with elsewhere. (Sidelights on Von Kempelen and Maelzel's chess player appear in Evans, who cites Poe's emphasis on psychology in identifying a human mind as the simple mechanism that regulates the machine; the relationship here is primarily in the acknowledged carryover by Poe of the name for its suggestiveness.) Poe's tongue-in-cheek conclusion—that Von Kempelen has "actually realized, in spirit" the chimera of the philosopher's stone—has the perverse consequence of raising the value of lead by 200 percent. The pattern of the story is remarkably consistent with the other hoaxes burlesquing the success of fraud over the gullible factual mentality.

Burton R. Pollin's *Discoveries in Poe* devotes a chapter to Poe's own involvement with "Von Kempelen," adding several points of interest to the story. He suggests, for example, that slighting reference to Mr. Kissam of Maine may refer to Poe's irritation with his would-be protégé, George W. Eveleth of Brunswick, Maine. Eveleth seemed to have developed a cosmological theory rivaling Poe's *Eureka,* and Pollin proposes this as the annoyance that triggered the statement that the interloper was rivaling the discovery of a way to transmute base metals into gold (Pollin, 181–83). Also noted is the translatability of "azote" and "protoxide" into nitrous oxide, or laughing gas, a clever indication of the hoax (178–79). In toto, Pollin describes the tale as motivated, in part, by the "sheer exuberant humor of his inventiveness" (173) but achieving "the culmination of Poe's efforts in the field of the literary hoax" (166), a comment that justifies a careful interpretive reading. Since the story can be approached through philosophic, biographical, historical, or literary-analytical avenues, as well as bearing traces of the descent/ascent themes of Wilbur's approach, it offers a rich field for speculative reading.

TALES OF MESMERISM

Poe's interest in science has been thoroughly documented, but mesmerism provided Poe with a particularly Gothic means of fabricating the hypnagogic state in which special spiritual revelations might be brought forward. In his letter to James Russell Lowell dated July 2, 1844 (*O* 1, 256–58), Poe provided an astonishingly succinct cosmogony that establishes the likeness of his own philosophy to some tenets of the pseudoscience that claimed that a magnetic influence could be exerted between individuals for medical purposes. He even included his pessimistic view of mankind as not progressing, which does much to explain his ironic attitude toward the responses of the masses of men to the alchemic and balloon hoaxes. In terms consistent with "Mesmeric Revelation," he proposes that men and other things are rudimentary "individualizations of unparticled matter," explaining how the worm becomes the butterfly, and the sleep-waker sees ghosts; gradations of particulate matter rarefy toward, but can never make the leap over to, the creative thought of God lying outside the material. Spiritualism as such, for Poe, was an absurdity, as God's volition was unknowable, but it is easy to see from the foregoing how magnetic influence could be transmitted between organizations of particles. As Doris Falk notes, however, the three tales—"Mesmeric Revelation," which Poe told Chivers carried a statement of "my own faith" (*O* 1, 259), "The Facts in the Case of M. Valdemar," and "A Tale of the Ragged Mountains"—form a compact group that seems defined by its special subject matter but takes on added meaning when considered in the broader context of other poems and tales and *Eureka* (Falk 1969, 536). Poe's theories can also be related to ideas propounded by Benjamin Rush and George Combe, particularly Combe's *The Constitution of Man* (New York: Fowler and Wells, 1835). Both medical men, whose works were instrumental in the developing mental sciences from the humane treatment of insanity through the pseudoscience of phrenology, are classed among the rational empiricists who found the human mind part of a holistic continuum of physical and mental causes, effects, and influences; Poe had drawn on their works for ideas and imagery from "Berenice" through "The Fall of the House of Usher." Sidney Lind has satisfactorily documented Poe's reliance on Chauncey Hare Townshend's *Facts in Mesmerism,* using his understanding of metempsychosis to suggest that Bedloe's story is actually a study of hypnotic influence—a limited scientific event—by Dr. Templeton on Bedloe rather than a study of metempsychosis, as is "Ligeia" or "Morella" (1085). "The Facts in the Case of M. Valdemar" and "A Tale of the Ragged Mountains" are our focus here.

"A Tale of the Ragged Mountains"

First published in *Godey's Lady's Book* in April 1844 and subsequently reprinted in the *Columbia Spy* on April 24 and revised in the *Broadway Journal* the following year, this tale describes the fate of Mr. Augustus Bedloe, of indeterminate background and melancholic disposition, who is maintained during his neuralgic attacks by his friend and mesmeric enthusiast, Dr. Templeton. Ultimately, Bedloe—killed by a poisonous, snakelike leech used by Dr. "Templeton"—is revealed to be a conversion of Mr. Oldeb, killed by a poisoned Bengalee arrow to his forehead in an Indian uprising. The tale shows the galvanic power of the doctor in taking over Bedloe's body, as the narrator reveals fully and finally through the device of a typographical error in the newspaper death announcement of Bedloe, where the similarities become obvious. Bedloe enters into his sleep-waking state through the use of morphine and, in "Indian summer," encounters the strange misty gorges and scenery typical of that time of year as he journeys through a thousand vague fancies into a dream state that takes him to the vision of Benares and Oldeb's death. A state bordering on the hypnagogic is a major component of the story, submerged in the mesmeric components of Poe's storytelling apparatus. Within Bedloe's dream revelation is encapsulated Oldeb's experience, which includes a vision from his embattled kiosk of a gay palace overhanging a river; Oldeb dies in entangling narrow, recessive streets when his right "temple" is struck by a "writhing creese of the Malay" as he attempts to battle through the maddened mob to the palace. Thus, Oldeb's quest is reflected in Bedloe's journey through the landscape of the Ragged Mountains, and both are, in some way, a creation of Dr. Templeton. The hypnagogic analysis corresponds comfortably with the view of the story as a mesmeric-Gothic tale based on Dr. Templeton's imagination, conjoined with animal magnetism, as elaborated by Lind and Falk. Lind has strongly argued the case for seeing the story as a hoax on the narrator, who does not see that Templeton's hypnosis of Bedloe is the real causative factor, rather than mesmerism. G. R. Thompson has also held that the story is a hoax, the narrator being the dupe and the reader being offered a series of clues that should reveal the truth of the real nonmesmeric relation between the two. The tale is thus comparable to the other ratiocinative tales of the period (Thompson 1969). Falk has argued, however, that animal magnetism provides a means by which patient and magnetizer come closer to a recognition of a higher state of unparticled matter, and, placing more emphasis on the shocks felt by Templeton, she finds the story closer to "Mesmeric Revelation" (542–43, 546).

"The Facts in the Case of M. Valdemar"

"This repulsive masterpiece," as Mabbott called the story, circulated as a credible hoax, to Poe's own surprise (*M* 3, 1228–32). Sent by a Boston mesmeric practitioner to England, it was reprinted in London in 1846 as a truthful account entitled *Mesmerism "In Articulo Mortis,"* although it had already appeared in the *American Review* of December 1845 as "The Facts of M. Valdemar's Case." Horace Greeley professed surprise that anyone was credulous enough to take the sketch as fact, but this seems to have been the case (*PoeL,* 603, 605, 617, 632, 727), despite seemingly obvious evidence that the tale was a hoax in the details of the story (Thompson 1973, 158–60, 174). Regarding the story simply as fiction, Elizabeth Barrett sent a copy of "Valdemar" to Robert Browning, commenting that it showed more power than Poe's poems, particularly in the ending details (*PoeL,* 620). Lind describes "The Facts in the Case of M. Valdemar" in relation to Townshend's *Facts in Mesmerism* as "a logical, pseudo-medical case-study, once the impossible premise has been granted" (1091–93). One premise that Lind cannot so easily grant is that the description of the decay in Valdemar's lungs leading to his death—the death from which mesmeric influence has detained him—could come only from an autopsy made impossible by the rapid dissolution of the dead man upon the release from mesmeric power. Falk notes that Poe departed from the mesmerists in this sketch by not bringing any retributive consequences to bear on the mesmerist who thus experimentally suspended death, for mesmeric theory suggested that the magnetist would be more strongly galvanized than the subject (539). The mesmerist narrator is involved as a horrified observer but is otherwise physically distanced, and the story actually offers less explicit cosmological or philosophical ideology than do the more articulated tales, for Valdemar tells the listeners nothing more than the fact of sleeping between life and death. The evidence of a journey downward, however, appears in the description of Valdemar twice as a "sleep-waker" who speaks, after death, as from "a vast distance, or from some deep cavern within the earth." The quality of Valdemar's voice adds to the terror.

Part of the impact of the tale lies in the reasonable attempt to use mesmeric influence to diminish physical pain, a worthy medical objective. The fact— ''Facts''—that a further suspension of the dying process takes place constitutes the violation of natural law. Valdemar's story can be a journey into a deeper state of consciousness or of a horrific in-between state artificially suspended by scientific intervention, first accounting for his repulsive death scene, rightly admired by Elizabeth Barrett as an unusually gruesome Gothic event, and the even more gruesome consequent dissolution upon release from the mesmeric state. With this tale, Poe completed a display of the depth of communication possible through particulate matter from deeper consciousness in a man of nervous temperament and creative literary ability, but, in this story, too weakened to communicate explicitly about the translation taking place.

THE LANDSCAPE SKETCHES

In 1923, Norman Foerster mentioned Poe's name only once in *Nature in American Life* (New York: Macmillan, 1923, 221) in an introduction to a chapter on Lanier, whereas, today, criticism accords substantial and thoughtful discussion to Poe's landscape sketches. The landscape sketches have a special place in the Poe canon. They reflect an idealistic reaching for a more perfect spiritual state. ''The Domain of Arnheim'' might be man's most significant attempt to organize nature into a more perfect state and thus rise above the chaotic forces of a disorganized world. Kent Ljungquist's *The Grand and the Fair: Poe's Landscape Aesthetics and Pictorial Techniques* sheds light on the sublime and ideal components of eighteenth- and nineteenth-century ideology that contributed directly to these landscape visions, tracing elements of the philosophy of Locke and Burke's concept of the ''delightful horror'' of some scenery as an influence on the Gothic school (17–28). Kant is also identified as a significant influence by his identification of the sublime as residing in man's imagination rather than in external nature (22–24). The attendant interest in the picturesque, notably in England from 1730 to 1830, reached its strongest expression in the American literary tradition in the 1840–1850 period, and American nationalism may have played some part in translating the idea of landscape-as-literary-device into landscape as a means of self-definition, involving a number of complexly related influences balancing sublimity, grandeur, and size (28–52). Yet, Ljungquist often finds a darker, more ironic element in these sketches. Ljungquist's readings may be considered concurrently with recognition of Poe's symbolism and his seeking to express the implications of his psychal transcendentalism in physical realms. Conjoined readings give a remarkably suggestive study of the sketches at the historical-aesthetic and moral-philosophical levels. ''Mere'' landscape architecture, thus, may fall short of the sleep-waking state but may still express crucial conceptions in Poe's aesthetics. Gloomier views of the sketches taken by several recent scholars, including Thompson, Dayan, and Ljungquist, even argue an element of hoax or parody in some elements of the stories.

"The Island of the Fay"

First printed in *Graham's* in 1841, it has been called a "prose poem, almost perfect in its tone" (*AQ*, 313–14) but without the moral thrust of "The City in the Sea," from which it borrowed and altered a couplet: "So blended bank and shadow there, / That each seemed pendulous in air—." However, the overt statement of Poe's inclusive philosophy of the "colossal members of one vast animate and sentient whole" universe (*M* 2, 600) would seem to offer a philosophical position: "cycle within cycle . . . revolving around one far-distant centre which is the Godhead" (*M* 2, 601). In its conclusion, *Eureka* states this same theme, providing a context for interpreting this story as directly consistent with Poe's cosmogony. The later pages of the story take the reader into a "dreamy vision" in which the lights and shadows play upon, and excite, the fancy of the narrator, musing with half-shut eyes, until he sees the Fay, representing at a higher level of consciousness the nature of man's life progressing from elastic joy through compressed symbolic cycles of day and night, aging to care, uncertainty, and "the region of the ebony flood"—death. Because the narrator has established that human life would mar the scene, the sleep-waking vision is presented in terms of the landscape and the accelerated cyclical movement of the Fay from light to dark around the island.

Critics disagree over the interpretation of the sketch. Mabbott accepts it directly as a "charming fantasy" (*M* 2, 597). John Sartain's 1841 engraving of the same name in *Graham's Magazine* was accompanied by Poe's tale as a plate article, although Poe may have influenced Sartain's engraving as well as responding to it (*M* 2, 597, 597n). Ljungquist regards the sketch as a parody of the conventional Romantic landscape viewer. He finds an implication from the once-attached "Sonnet—To Science" that the narrator may be an unoriginal thinker, imposing imagination on the scene rather than truly entering it (110–19). Dayan has described the vision of the Fay as a weakness in the narrator. The narrator's exulting over the scene: " 'If ever island were enchanted,' said I to myself 'This is it' "—may also be honest appreciation; it might not suggest a too-easy merging of nature and mind—an error in his philosophy (Dayan, 80–93). Dayan contends that the story ends with "the paradox of a deepening that is simultaneously a fading or diffusion" (92). Yet, Poe's statement of a cosmic philosophy appears neither ambiguous nor ironic when taken as the vision of a dreamer in a half-waking state: the symbolic dream pattern is consistent with the cyclical view of man-in-nature.

"Morning on the Wissahiccon"

Not published until 1844 in *The Opal: A Pure Gift for the Holy Days*, two years after "The Landscape Garden," it may yet provide the best entry into the group of sketches specifically centered on landscape: "The Landscape Garden," first printed in *Ladies Companion* (October 1842), "The Domain of Arnheim," a partial revision of the previous story, published in *Columbian Lady's and Gentleman's Magazine* for March 1847, and "Landor's Cottage," subtitled "A Pendant to 'The Domain of Arnheim,' " when it was published in *The Flag of Our Union* on June 9, 1849. "Morning on the Wissahiccon" has been identified as another of Poe's plate articles, this one accompanying J. G. Chapman's "Morning," which showed an elk in romantic scenery, and Poe later referred to the story as "The Elk" (*M* 3, 860). It begins with a paean of praise for the western American scenery, which is "a realization of the wildest dreams of paradise" missed by the lazy traveler and the British traveler alike. To the narrator, "beauty" is the only characteristic of such scenery; it does not show the "sublime." The real traveler may seek simpler scenes in neglected byways. Here the narrator journeys through the winding banks of the Wissahiccon to where he envisions only the red man and the elk trod, without picnickers, "the Demon of the Engine," or commerce. But it turns out that the half-slumbering dream vision of the elk that bound up the teller's whole soul in admiration is only the chance sighting of an escaped pet of a wealthy English landowner.

Two conflicting analyses of the sketch are plausible. The noble elk may be seen as completing the vision of nature unspoiled—a heroic image of bygone wilderness beauty and grandeur. The ending thus rounds out that theme. Alternatively, the sketch might seem a self-burlesque in which the poet seeking an easy hypnagogic state deceives himself. The viewer is off-guard; he shares the laziness of the masses of travelers, like the English travel writers whom he decries but to whom he is connected when he incorrectly romanticizes the superannuated elk of the English family's artificial landscape design. The later renaming of the story "The Elk" might thus further focus attention on the ironic ending. Because the narrator had talked of the elk as representative of his visionary red men in protest against the utilitarian changes around the stream, the discovery that the elk is itself the pet of the English landowner is ironic. All the attitudes of the teller are called into question by the outcome. Even the stealthy Negro is a negative element in this "snare in the bower of bliss" (Dayan, 103). Dream visions are not to be so easily realized, nor is the Thoreau-like dissent from society to be so simplistically validated. The other sketches show more complexity in design and are less susceptible to dual interpretations.

Opinions of the meaning of the three other sketches vary widely. Sheldon Liebman has proposed that Poe's heroes actually apply Poe's theory of poetic experience, each becoming "the man of genius who must ultimately translate his experience into concrete form," and such an idea might throw a highly positive light on the stories (582–83, 592). Ljungquist, however, finds that "Arnheim" and "Landor's Cottage" are somewhat ironic, revealing Ellison's "jejune perfectibilitarian notions" in the former sketch and a veiling of the narrator's perceptions, "rather than availing insight," in the latter (131, 137). Some critics have contended that the prevailing direction into enclosed space and spatial suspension was a journey into the imagination and, by extension with stories like "Usher," into madness (Baym, 48–52). Others see the sketches as clear declarations that the artist can bring order to inchoate nature (Jacobs, 412–13); among the most positive are E. W. Pitcher and Elizabeth Phillips, who see them as idealizations of the artist's ability to rationalize the world. Joan Dayan claims that the sketches "derealize" language, and landscape becomes "a natural spectacle turned into artistic emblem" (110, 113). Matter and spirit are thus proved to be interchangeable, and Poe's use of biographical elements, scientific discourse, the picturesque, and philosophical citations all widen the focus on the universal problem of spirit, matter, and truth of mind, which form their real subject (128–29).

"The Landscape Garden"

"The Landscape Garden" is primarily a definition of landscape gardening as an art form. Mabbott sees the story as "pure beauty" without sadness or humor, citing Poe's comment to Helen Whitman that the later version of the sketch had much of his own soul in it (*M* 2, 700–701). The story may hold several ironic points in regard to Poe's general philosophy, not the least of which is the overly fortunate and self-confident Ellison, committed as he is to artifice. Since the narrator takes the role of admiring listener, as in the "Ragged Mountains" sketch, there is little room for a demur, however, and an interpretation of the story as ironic is therefore speculative. A. H. Quinn takes the sketch at face value, concluding that Ellison is seriously intended as the artist who "adds creatively a new charm" (*AQ,* 359). Eschewing poetry and art, Ellison's object is practically to embody a highly spiritual ideal in the perfect landscape. Yet, the doctrines of Ellison might also imply that the absence of defects is a rejection of "grovelling herd instinct," not the true sense of the Almighty Design, which includes the most savage. The sketch thus holds some teasing contradictions. Ellison surmises that a class of invisible beings might exist for whom God ordered the whole earthly landscape garden, after all, which throws into doubt all of man's changes (*M* 2, 708–9), but his own theories seem presented without irony or any demur from the narrator.

"The Domain of Arnheim"

This later elaborated sketch used the twelve paragraphs of the previous piece to make up its first fifteen paragraphs, although Poe carefully edited and tightened up by deleting many adjectives, as Mabbott points out. Poe broadens the theory of the naturally imperfect landscape to suggest that a poet of pecuniary resources might add design interest that was spiritual and artistic, uniting beauty, magnificence, and *strangeness* (*M* 3, 1276). Ellison acquires a spot close to human habitation, since he is not a misanthrope, and accepts the challenge to produce something in nature shorn of distance and unique in spiritual beauty. As soon as the idea of achievement is offered, Ellison himself is removed from the scene by death, so that the narrator then conducts the reader into Arnheim.

"The Domain of Arnheim" fits Liebman's model well in one critic's thoughtful comparison to Samuel Johnson's happy valley "Amhara" in *Rasselas*. By contrast to Poe, Johnson's literalism and Christianity led to a flight from death and the valley, whereas Poe looked toward unity and oneness to be achieved by the true poet Ellison, who created a world hovering between man and God (Jeffrey). Arnheim is entered by a stream that is reminiscent of the Wissahiccon in the earlier story, however, and this might put the reader on guard. Nevertheless, here the river, seeming to have no floor, resembles a state of suspension between heaven and earth as it reflects the sky and the landscape. Literal detail dominates the latter part of the sketch: a journey into perfection is under way: river debris is absent in this modified nature without a dead branch; nature is also falsified, as the narrator knows in describing a hill's shape that has been changed by man, but without leaving a trace of his workmanship—yet, such an artistic distortion was accounted for as being the function of the landscape architect/poet. Indeed, the miracle of Arnheim is that it is fully an artistic construction of genius.

E. W. Pitcher interprets Arnheim's symbolism as reflecting Poe's cosmogony. The river approach to Arnheim, noting the twisting descent into a half-waking torpor—analogous to Wilbur's sleep-waking state, perhaps—and the transfer from a larger vessel into an ivory canoe, is analogous for Pitcher to abandoning the physical body and entering a dream state, suggesting fairy presences (30–31). Finally, in the mazelike channel and with overhanging clouds, the "fairy bark" brings the traveler westward toward the sun and ultimately beyond death, if the analogy is maintained, to the golden doors and the "dreamlike intermingling" of landscape elements, to the semi-Gothic, semi-Saracenic splendor of the palace in air. This experience is the artist's imaginative representation of a state like the hypnagogic. It is a symbolic artifact, as the last golden door and the semi-Gothic, semi-Saracenic ruins assure us. It shows man's ability to create something like a higher state; it is not clear that the narrator enters a higher consciousness at the end of the landscape journey, although Poe may have intended this idea. Poe may also have been objecting to the pedestrian view of landscape, arguing for a more soulful creation (Sanford, 55–59). Sharon Furrow has noted that the journey is an "allegory of the power of poetry to take us nearer the ideal" and follows the pattern of the hypnagogic state defined by Wilbur, but she also speculates that Poe had difficulty making the natural represent the spiritual or psychological state (25–26). If Ellison is simply Poe's spokesman, as E. W. Pitcher contends (27), the artificiality of the gardening act is oddly compromised, for the domain is thrown open to the masses after the brief life, Fay-like, of its creator. Poe's aesthetic as reflected by Ellison has been closely identified with Christian and classical values and with nineteenth-century American values of expansionist capitalism and history by Jules Zanger. The role of the poet in perfecting the corrupted natural world shows clear affinities with other Poe stories: a unifying vision returns the viewer at its climax to the "Garden [of Eden] come again" (Zanger, 95–96). Zanger particularly stresses that Ellison is a man of action and capital and thus representative of the man of his day, entering the "Arcadian American garden without despoiling it" (98–99), but Ellison is hardly representative in his wealth and perspective as Poe describes his situation. Joan Dayan, on the other hand, focuses on the reciprocal displacements in the indeterminate views culminating in the mirror/lake. She contends that the hedging of language in the physical descriptions, assessed in light of Poe's contempt for the intellect's "monomaniac grasping at the infinite" in *Eureka,* leads to the conclusion that the story is a caricature in which "Poe mimes the visionary's supernatural dream" (96–107). Various critics have noted that Dayan's analysis does not lead easily to the symbolic or allegorical level of interpretation (Carlson, "Poe: II," 109).

"Landor's Cottage"

The last sketch in this series, first published in *The Flag of Our Union* on June 9, 1849, begins with more of the evident machinery of the hypnagogic state—the mist, undulating road, and unfamiliar setting—but also features grass that "we" seldom see out of England and the total absence of any impediments, twigs, or dead twigs—material notable by its absence. Unlike the previous two sketches, this one features a walk into the area, culminating in a visit to Landor's cottage itself in its secluded vale, presided over by Annie, representing "womanliness" and "romance." Thus, Poe's applied vision of physical loveliness takes precedence over didactic theory. One critic sees Poe challenging the assumptions of Andrew Jackson Downing's *Treatise on Landscape Gardening* (1841), with which he was familiar and which he may have been attempting to debate in 1842 by submitting the first sketch in the series to *The Democratic Review,* which had favorably reviewed Downing (Hess). Although Poe's sketch seems to outline his own philosophy unequivocally, some critics still find ambiguity. Rather than seeming to be visions on the inner eye, the walk into the area of the cottage gives the feeling of a coup d'oeil characteristic of the externality and contrivance of the *pittoresque* scene. Details of trees and lakes dominate, down to the "clear heaven below" reflected in the perfect lakelet. The words, often describing things by what they are not, "derealize" nature as an aspect of God (Dayan, 110). Yet, aspects of the story coincide with Poe's personal statements of landscape aesthetics as recited to Mrs. Whitman (*M* 3, 1326–27), or so it appears, and the sketch is a simpler natural realization of the principles behind the creation of Arnheim (Rosenfeld, 264–65). Again and again, the narrator emphasizes the "neatness," the picturelike quality of the poetic scene, leading to Annie and her "Romance" and inside the house to the decorative forms contrived by the guiding genius of Mr. Landor consistent with the external site of the house. The conclusion leads back in a circle to the earliest piece in the series. Joan Dayan has forcefully contended that the piece "is a difficult exercise in incongruity." Poe's balancing between the "neat and graceful on the one hand, and the *pittoresque,*" on the other, his speaking of the sun moving "as if" with a "*chassez,*" his references to artifice in scenery (111–

14), all point toward a massive reconstruction of language that implies the protean effects of a creator or sorcerer "behind the scenes." She proposes that the tales in the series actually lead not to heaven but to hell in their grotesquely affected language and representation. Poe, she argues, wants us to notice the shift from "representation to enchantment" as a "clanking of gears" (114) in the mechanics of storytelling. Language and space are inverted again and again, and the landscape designs are altered and changed by reversals of language and ambiguities of phrasing (96–105, 110–12, 128). To Dayan, Annie's appearance at the end of the sketch is one of many dissolving views that confirm the hypothesis that the levels of landscape offer the reader different levels of interpretation, some textual and some biographical and psychological, which finally "neutralize" each other and undercut their own meaning (129). To most critics, however, Landor's cottage as described in the sketch is an idealization of Poe's cottage at Fordham (*AQ,* 506–9). Mabbott has also identified the descriptions of a perfect room in "The Philosophy of Furniture" (1840) with this sketch, further grounds for seeing the sketch as Poe's own ideal (*M* 2, 494–95).

The seeming directness of the landscape sketches, at variance with the dreamy disorder of some of the Gothic horror and detective stories, ought to present the analyst with fewer problems of authorial intention. Arthur Hobson Quinn, the biographer and traditional critic, implies a link directly to Poe himself through a strong likeness between "Arnheim" and Poe's own practice of canoeing on the Wissahiccon (*AQ,* 531), and perhaps Poe identified so fully with these river experiences that they caused his landscape visions to be more focused expressions of the artist's potential for re-creating his world in a more perfect order, Dayan's interpretation notwithstanding. In any event, taken together with the science fiction and the balloon hoaxes, they belong to a species of art above the level of factual reporting. The critic who brings new insights to these issues, as does Pitcher, or brings forth further evidence will have expanded our understanding of Poe's intention. Perhaps these stories are consistent, after all, with Poe's sense that the universe was subservient to man's control only in art transforming nature, especially in landscaping (Halliburton, 356–63). A true encounter with the creative design lying behind the physical world, as in "Arnheim," could occur in the deeply felt responses to nature by the poet/artist of landscape form. So, too, might a true cosmic awareness be revealed in the ultimate mystery lying behind the deaths of Valdemar, Pfaall, and their ilk and in the more exuberant expressions of worldly disorder and dissolution seen in the science fiction tales and hoaxes. The major critical judgments fall into two categories, the more convincng one taking the sketches as serious works of art symbolic of Poe's ideas on cosmic order and disorder, the other seeing them as implying the unknowability of what lies beyond the physical state of man. These different themes will continue to be addressed as Poe scholars further define Poe's philosophical perspective. Richard Wilbur's thesis continues to appeal to the analyst in taking the stories as comprehensible literary allegories, and later criticism tends to add to, rather than detract from, the value of his insights into Poe's use of the hypnagogic state as discussed at the outset of this chapter, even though some studies seem to move in alternative directions. In fact, most theories are compatible with Wilbur's insights, and he remains a reliable guide to Poe's achievements in this subgenre.

WORKS CITED

Bailey, J. O. "Sources for Poe's *Arthur Gordon Pym,* 'Hans Pfaall,' and Other Pieces." *PMLA* 57 (1942): 513–35.

Baym, Nina. "The Function of Poe's Pictorialism." *South Atlantic Quarterly* 65 (1966): 46–54.

Brigham, Clarence S. *Poe's "Balloon Hoax."* Metuchen, N. J., 1932.

Campbell, Killis. "Poe's Reading." *Texas Studies in English* 5 (1925): 166–96.

Carlson, Eric W. "Frames of Reference for Poe's Symbolic language." In *Critical Essays on Poe*. Boston: G. K. Hall, 1987.

————. "Poe: II, New Critical Studies." *American Notes and Queries,* new series, 1 (1988): 108–10.

Dayan, Joan. "The Poet in the Garden." *Fables of the Mind: An Inquiry into Poe's Fiction*. New York: Oxford UP, 1987, 80–129.

Evans, Henry Ridgely. *Edgar Allan Poe and Baron Von Kempelen's Chess-Playing Automaton*. Kenton, Ohio: International Brotherhood of Magicians, 1939.

Falk, Doris V. "Poe and the Power of Animal Magnetism." *PMLA* 84 (1969): 536–46.

————. "Thomas Low Nichols, Poe, and the 'Balloon Hoax.' " *Poe Newsletter* 5 (1972): 48–49.

Furrow, Sharon. "Psyche and Setting: Poe's Picturesque Landscapes." *Criticism* 15 (1973): 16–27.

Greer, H. Allen. "Poe's 'Hans Pfaall' and the Political Scene." *Emerson Society Quarterly* 60 (1970): 67–73.

Halliburton, David. *Edgar Allan Poe: A Phenomenological View*. Princeton: Princeton UP, 1973.

Hess, Jeffrey A. "Sources and Aesthetics of Poe's Landscape Fiction." *American Quarterly* 22 (1970): 177–89.

Jacobs, Robert D. "Poe's Earthly Paradise." *American Quarterly* 12 (1960): 404–13.

Jeffrey, David K. "The Johnsonian Influence: *Rasselas* and Poe's 'The Domain of Arnheim.' " *Poe Newsletter* 2 (1970): 26–29.

Kazin, Alfred. *A Writer's America: Landscape in Literature*. New York: Knopf, 1988, 66–67.

Ketterer, David. "Edgar Allan Poe and the Visionary Tradition of Science Fiction." In *New Worlds for Old*. Garden City, N. Y.: Anchor, 1974, 50–75.

————. "Poe's Usage of the Hoax and the Unity of 'Hans Pfaall.' " *Criticism* 13, no. 4 (1971): 377–85.

————. "The Ultimate Life, I–III." *The Rationale of Deception in Poe*. Baton Rouge: Louisiana State UP, 1979, 206–15.

Liebman, Sheldon W. "Poe's Tales and His Theory of the Poetic Experience." *Studies in Short Fiction* 7 (1970): 582–96.

Lind, Sydney. "Poe and Mesmerism." *PMLA* 62 (1947): 1077–94.

Ljungquist, Kent. *The Grand and the Fair: Poe's Landscape Aesthetics and Pictorial Techniques.* Potomac, Md.: Scripta Humanistica, 1984.

Mabbott, Thomas Ollive. *Collected Works of Edgar Allan Poe.* Vols. 2–3. Cambridge: Harvard UP, 1978.

Phillips, Elizabeth. "The Imagination of a Great Landscape." *Edgar Allan Poe: An American Imagination, Three Essays.* New York: Kennikat, 1979, 53–96.

Pitcher, E. W. "The Arnheim Trilogy: Cosmic Landscapes in the Shadow of Poe's *Eureka.*" *Canadian Review of American Studies* 6, no. 1 (1975): 27–35.

Pollin, Burton R. "Poe in 'Von Kempelen and His Discovery.' " In *Discoveries in Poe.* Notre Dame: U of Notre Dame P, 1970, 166–89.

———. "The Unparalleled Adventure of One Hans Pfaall." *Collected Writings of Edgar Allan Poe.* Vol. 1. Boston: Twayne, 1981, 366–506.

Posey, Meredith N. "Notes on Poe's 'Hans Pfaall.' " *Modern Language Notes* 45 (1930): 501–7.

Reiss, Edmund. "The Comic Setting of 'Hans Pfaall.' " *AL* 29 (1957): 306–9.

Rosenfeld, Alvin. "Description in Poe's 'Landor's Cottage.' " *Studies in Short Fiction* 4 (1967): 264–66.

Sanford, Charles L. "Edgar Allan Poe: A Blight upon the Landscape." *American Quarterly* 20, no.1 (1968): 54–66.

Scudder, H. H. "Poe's 'Balloon Hoax.' " *AL* 21 (1949): 179–90.

Thompson, G. R. "Is Poe's 'A Tale of the Ragged Mountains' a Hoax?" *Studies in Short Fiction* 6 (1969): 454–60.

———. *Poe's Fiction.* Madison: U of Wisconsin P, 1973.

Townshend, Chauncey Hare. *Facts in Mesmerism.* New York: Harper and Brothers, 1841 [London, 1840]. (Lind believes that Poe used the London, 1844 reprinting.)

Tucker, George [Joseph Atterly, pseud.]. *A Voyage to the Moon.* New York: Elam Bliss, 1827.

Wilbur, Richard. "The House of Poe." *Anniversary Lectures/ 1959.* Washington, D.C.: Library of Congress, 1959, 21–38. Repr. in *The Recognition of Edgar Allan Poe.* Ed. Eric W. Carlson. Ann Arbor: U of Michigan P, 1967, 254–77.

Wilkinson, Ronald Sterne. "Poe's 'Balloon Hoax.' " *AL* 32 (1960): 313–17.

———. "Poe's 'Hans Pfaall' Reconsidered." *Notes and Queries* 13 (1966): 333–37.

Wimsatt, W. K., Jr. "A Further Note on Poe's 'Balloon Hoax.' " *AL* 22 (1951): 491–92.

Woodberry, George E. *Edgar Allan Poe.* Boston: Houghton Mifflin, 1885.

Zanger, Jules. "Poe's American Garden: 'The Domain of Arnheim.' " *ATQ,* no. 50 (1981): 93–102.

13

The Essays and "Marginalia": Poe's Literary Theory

BEVERLY R. VOLOSHIN

This chapter treats the literary and aesthetic theories that Poe expressed in his essays and "Marginalia."[1] These exhibit his wide-ranging familiarity with intellectual currents of his era, as well as his remarkable synthetic and inventive capacities. Poe's theoretical writings provide ways of reading his poetry and fiction and are an important part of his oeuvre in their own right. They have had an almost continuous influence on literary theory and literary creation from Poe's moment to ours.

After his early venture in poetry, Poe hoped to make his career in the magazines as an editor and literary journalist. Indeed, he wrote most of his essays for magazine publication. In the 1830s, the number of magazines in the United States expanded greatly, offering new opportunities for a profession in letters; at the same time, this literary marketplace was a volatile and insecure world, as Poe's career amply demonstrates. Though Poe was often a productive editor and writer, his income from his literary labors was always meager, and he often found himself out of work. While recognized in his own time as an important critic, Poe seldom had a free hand in what he wrote for the magazines and never realized his dream of editing his own independent magazine. Still, Poe used the magazine format to work out a set of aesthetic and critical ideas that, in its ambitiousness, complexity, and originality, is almost unique in the United States in the antebellum period.[2]

EDITIONS

I refer mainly to the essays and reviews in G. R. Thompson's edition of *Essays and Reviews,* which supersedes the corresponding volumes of Harrison's edition. Thompson drops some texts erroneously attributed by Harrison to Poe and includes others more recently established as Poe's. Thompson's edition has the virtue of compactness, yet, for scholarly purposes, it has certain limitations. It is not a complete edition but an ample selection of Poe's nonfictional prose, and, because of the format, Thompson's notes are sparse. The reader can still turn with profit to F. C. Prescott's notes in his selection of Poe's critical writings, and, for "Marginalia" and related writings, one should consult the texts and notes in Burton R. Pollin's edition of *The Brevities*. Finally, in the Thompson edition, the arrangement of the material by topic and the absence of a comprehensive table of contents make it difficult for the reader to locate items and to trace the development of Poe's ideas.

APPROACHES TO POE'S LITERARY THEORY

One of the traditional approaches to Poe's critical and aesthetic theories is the study of sources, influences, and development. Of the many studies in this field, three long, scholarly works should be remarked in particular. The earliest of these is Margaret Alterton's *Origins of Poe's Critical Theory,* which identifies those readings that appealed to Poe and the "broad lines of thought [that] grew up in his mind as a result of these congenial interests" (3). Alterton focuses on the principle of unity as Poe derived it from the British periodicals, the criticism of Augustus Wilhelm Schlegel, and the criticism of Coleridge. This idea of unity, which Poe initially embraced as a literary aim, came to have wider import in *Eureka* as Poe fashioned a cosmology that paralleled and subsumed his literary theory. Robert D. Jacob's *Poe: Journalist and Critic* argues that "Poe as a working critic looked backward toward the mechanistic psychological aesthetic of the previous century and forward toward the dynamic organicism of the romantic period" (viii). Jacobs details the eighteenth-century inheritance, particularly that of the Scottish commonsense philosophers. The most recent of the major scholarly works is Claude Richard's *Edgar Allan Poe: journaliste et critique,* a massive European dissertation that charts Poe's literary tastes and his career as a literary journalist and analyzes his literary theories. Richard's discussion of Poe's notions of ideality, beauty, and effect is particularly valuable, and he reassesses what Poe made of the theoretical writings of Coleridge and Schlegel. Like other influential critics of Poe such as Richard Wilbur, Maurice Beebe, and Joseph J. Moldenhauer, Richard reads Poe's aesthetics in the light of his last work, his cosmological prose-poem, *Eureka.* Unlike Jacobs, Richard sees Poe as a critic who aspired to a coherent and unified literary theory.

Poe's literary theory can be understood as a coherent set of ideas by examining it in terms of what M. H. Abrams has called the orientation of critical theories (3–29). Poe consistently rejects the didactic and the mimetic critical orientations. The end of the work is not to instruct, but to give pleasure, which Poe also characterizes as the apprehension of beauty. The aim of poetry is beauty, not truth as correspondence to reality. While the tale might admit of truth as representation, that is not a requisite. Even when Poe admits representation or content, it is not for its own sake but as a means toward an end. Poe also rejects the expressive critical orientation of Romanticism, for, although the poem might be the expression of the poetic sentiment in the poet, it need not be. Since the purpose of the poem or tale is to stimulate an effect, the work could as well be the result of the writer's calculation. The work, then, is seen by Poe as a construction, a mechanism, an interrelated system of elements any of which may be regarded as cause or effect of any of the others; the purpose of this system is to stimulate an effect. Poe's doctrine of effect is usually expressed in transcendental terms, such as *"an elevating excitement of the Soul,"* and can thus be located within the field of Romantic literary theory (*T*, 93). But Poe's antididactic, antimimetic, and antiexpressive critical orientation; his doctrines of construction and of effect; his vision of the text as a system—these features of his critical and creative work are modernist. Or, if one does not wish to date modernism to so early a period, these are among the features of Poe's theory that would figure in literary modernism. These features appealed to, and influenced, Baudelaire, then Mallarmé, then Valéry—to name certain moments in the development of literary modernism. Because of these lines of development, Poe can be described as one of the great ancestors of the new criticism in France from the 1950s through the 1980s.

Poe's theoretical writings as well as his poetry and fiction have a prominent place in French literary history, particularly because of Poe's influence on the avant-garde. Patrick F. Quinn provides the fullest analysis of the influence of Poe on Baudelaire and argues that the example of Poe turned French Romanticism from a pallid academicism into a genuine literary movement. Edmund Wilson's 1926 essay, "Poe at Home and Abroad," is one of the earliest in English to argue that Poe's influence in France should be seen in terms of the development of Romanticism and the turn from Romanticism to Symbolism. Joan Dayan argues in a similar vein that Mallarmé's attempt to create "la poésie pure" was guided by Poe's alleged elimination of content, his theory of form, and his atomism and cosmology (1990). T. S. Eliot's well-known essay on Poe focuses on Valéry's attraction to Poe's idea of pure poetry, of the heightened consciousness of language turned on itself, and to Poe's doctrine of construction. Poe's "penetration of the poetic by the introspective critical activity is carried to the limit by Valéry" (218). In his 1966 essay on Valéry, "La Littérature comme telle," Gérard Genette surveys Valéry's career as a theorist, situating him in relation to the theoretical enterprise of his great precursor, Poe, and in relation to the projects of his contemporaries the Russian Formalists (cf. Vines). Valéry was inspired by the antimimetic and antiexpressive nature of Poe's theory; rejecting the "realist illusion," Valéry, much like the Formalists, valued forms that expose their artificiality and conventionality. Valéry was also inspired by the analytic, mechanistic, quasi-mathematical account of construction and of effect in "The Philosophy of Composition." We might add that Valéry surpassed Poe's mechanism. For Poe, the author calculates effects, whereas, in Valéry's conception, private consciousness and creativity do not properly exist.

Literature is a preexisting system of combinations and transformations—the author but a machine for such transformations or the site of operations. The same can be said of Valéry's appropriation of Poe's notion of pure poetry: that Valéry makes it a fully structuralist notion—a limit-case *"where the transformation of thoughts one into the other would appear more important than any thought,* where the game of figures would contain the reality of the subject" (Genette, 264–65, quoting Valéry; translation mine). Genette identifies the structuralist enterprise of midcentury as in the direct line of descent from Valéry and hence in the line of descent from Poe. Since that time in France, Poe's texts have been the pretext for structuralist, semiotic, and poststructuralist criticism, in the work of Lacan, Derrida, Todorov, Barthes, Ricardou, and others. Poe reemerges not so much as the theoretician of literature per se but as a theoretician of the sign, *écriture,* and semiosis. In the past two decades, the French structural and poststructural criticism of Poe has, in turn, been highly influential on literary theory in the United States. Poe has returned to his native country by way of his French exile.

Since Poe's lifetime, his theoretical writings as well as his poetry and fiction have occasioned very strong and discordant reactions in the United States. F. C. Prescott already remarked this phenomenon in 1909 (ix–x), and it has been surveyed recently by Shoshana Felman. This ambivalence about Poe is prominent in Eliot's essay: even when the influence of Poe's poetry and criticism seems negligible in the United States and England, Eliot claims, "one cannot be sure that one's own writing has *not* been influenced by Poe" (205). Reasons that American critics did not assimilate Poe's theoretical project until recently are that American criticism has often had a moral basis and has seldom repudiated the "realist illusion." Still, some American critics have profitably used the theoretical works as a hermeneutic tool for investigating Poe's fiction and poetry, beginning with Allen Tate's "The Angelic Imagination." This approach is elaborated in Maurice Beebe's "The Universe of Roderick Usher" and Richard Wilbur's "The House of Poe"; perhaps the most comprehensive attempt to read Poe's poetry and fiction through the lens of his theoretical writings is Joseph J. Moldenhauer's "Murder as a Fine Art: Basic Connections between Poe's Aesthetics, Psychology, and Moral Vision." Poe's theoretical writings continue to provide a tool for investigating his poetry and fiction, especially for critics working in the semiotic and poststructural field; for example, Shawn Rosenheim in "The King of 'Secret Readers' " interprets Poe's detective fiction in terms of the theory of the sign in Poe's articles on cryptography.

To discuss the key terms and structure of Poe's literary theory as well as the development of his critical and aesthetic ideas, I divide his critical writings into three groups, following a rough chronology: the early theory of poetry, the theory of the tale, and the late theory of poetry. Poe began his critical career as a theorist of poetry and continued in this vein when he himself had turned from writing poetry to writing fiction. After 1845, when his editorial career ended, Poe returned to writing poetry and also produced his best-known essays on poetic theory. In between his two periods as a poet, Poe developed a theory of the tale that, in several points, paralleled his theory of poetry. In this analysis of Poe's essays, I also refer to some literary reviews in which Poe develops important theoretical positions not contained in the essays themselves.

POE'S EARLY THEORY OF POETRY

Poe's first essay in criticism and his first statement of poetic theory, "Letter to B—" (July 1836), is a slightly revised version of his Preface to *Poems* of 1831 (Campbell). Poe's discussion of the nature of poetry in "Letter to B—" turns largely on negative criticism of Wordsworth and Coleridge, yet the very criticism Poe offers is based on an appropriation of some notions of Coleridge's. Poe mistakenly takes the Romantics' claims about the philosophic nature of poetry to mean that the aim of poetry is didactic. Poe asserts that the aim is pleasure, echoing an important passage in Chapter 14 of Coleridge's *Biographia Literaria* (Stovall 1930, 138–51). Poe presents this theory of poetry at the end of "Letter to B—," a theory from which he would never substantially deviate:

A poem, in my opinion, is opposed to a work of science by having, for its *immediate* object, pleasure, not truth; to romance, by having for its object an *indefinite* instead of a *definite* pleasure, being a poem only so far as this object is attained; romance presenting perceptible images with definite, poetry with *in*definite sensations, to which end music is an *essential,* since the comprehension of sweet sound is our most indefinite conception. Music, when combined with a pleasurable idea, is poetry; music without the idea is simply music; the idea without the music is prose from its very definitiveness. (11)

In rejecting didacticism and positing pleasure as the end of poetry, Poe was at odds with the reigning doctrine of American poetics, which had a moral and ideological basis and which was expressed in such influential journals as the *North American Review* (Charvat 1936). The antididactic and antimimetic elements of Poe's first definition of poetry point toward the language of transcendence and ideality with which Poe would subsequently describe poetry.

Criticism of the Lake school was conventional by 1831, yet in "Letter to B—" Poe cannot hide his admiration for Coleridge, "a giant in intellect and learning" (8). Early in Poe's career as critic, Coleridge was doubly important to Poe—as theoretician and as poet. Poe's criticism here of Coleridge the poet, that he wasted himself on metaphysics, Poe revised in his 1836 review of Drake and Halleck by arguing that poetry may be produced by metaphysical acumen as well as by the faculty of ideality (*T,* 511–12). In the early stage of his career as critic, Poe borrowed ideas from two of the major Romantic theoreticians, Coleridge and A. W. Schlegel; he would change what he took from them until their ideas became his own.

In his review of Euripides' plays (September 1835), Poe borrows from Schlegel the concept of ideality, which would become central to Poe's theory of poetry. Following Schlegel's analysis of the Greek tragic drama in *Lectures on Dramatic Art and Literature,* Poe uses "Ideality of conception" to designate an elevation of the character above "every day existence" and "Ideality of representation" to designate the use of mask, cothurnus, clothing, and scenic properties to elevate the action (*T,* 250). In Schlegel, two ideas are manifested by being placed in conflict in the Greek tragic drama: moral freedom, magnified by the ideality of conception, and destiny or exterior necessity, established by the ideality of representation and by the symbolism of destiny. The ideal for Schlegel is a dramatic representation of ideas, and these ideas are themselves conceptions that lie beyond the world of sense and that are comprehended by the understanding. Poe's references to ideality do not reflect the fullness of Schlegel's theoretical enterprise, which emphasizes the role of the understanding in apprehending the ideal and in apprehending the totality of the work, and, indeed, Poe's subsequent notions of ideality and of totality of effect would never incorporate Schlegel's Kantian conception of the role of the understanding. Poe's language for discussing ideality and effect would remain close to the language of sensation and sentiment so common in eighteenth-century British philosophy and literature.[3] Poe turns to the language of sentiment in the theoretical section of his review of the poetry of Drake and Halleck.

In the Drake–Halleck review (April 1836), Poe derives his notions of ideality and causality from the faculty psychology of phrenology and uses these notions to explain the nature of poetry. Poe modifies this faculty psychology to include what he calls "the sentiment of Poesy" or "the Poetic Sentiment" (*T,* 510–11). In March 1836, Poe favorably reviewed Miles's *Phrenology and the Moral Influence of Phrenology* (*T,* 329–32; Hungerford). Miles categorizes ideality as one of three imaginative faculties or sentiments and causality as one of the reflecting or philosophical faculties. In the Drake–Halleck review, Poe equates the faculty of ideality with the sentiment of poesy, which he explains by analogy with the phrenological faculty of veneration, which leads one to admiration of something higher than oneself: "Poesy is the sentiment of Intellectual Happiness here, and the Hope of higher Intellectual Happiness hereafter." In another characterization, Poe writes, "This sentiment is the sense of the beautiful, of the sublime, and of the mystical"; the three defining terms are not synonymous, but they are related, and they designate a transcendental mode (510). Poe adds that imagination is the soul of poesy, making imagination equivalent to ideality and the poetic sentiment.

Poe offers a new definition of poetry as "the practical result, expressed in language, of this Poetic Sentiment in certain individuals"; hence, "the only proper method of testing the merits of a poem is by measuring its capabilities of exciting the Poetic Sentiment in others." Swiftly interchanging cause and effect, Poe moves from defining poetry as what is produced by the poetic sentiment to poetry as what awakens the poetic sentiment: "For a poem is not the Poetic faculty, but the means of exciting it in mankind" (511). If a poem is known not by its cause (the poetic sentiment) but by its effect (awakening the poetic sentiment in the reader), then a metaphysician, who can calculate cause and effect, may be an even greater poet than the man of ideality. Poe can therefore praise both Shelley and Coleridge: Shelley is always for Poe the poet of ideality, while Coleridge is the poet of causality. Thus, with the aid of the rather primitive faculty psychology of phrenology, Poe works a startling amalgamation of the eighteenth-century mechanical philosophy with the transcendental aims of Romanticism. This remarkable combination is characteristic of Poe's imagination.

Missing from this discussion of the poetic sentiment is an indication of what in the poem is productive of ideality; in his review of Moore's *Alciphron* (January 1840), Poe identifies a feature of the text, the mystic, which produces ideality:

The term *mystic* is here employed in the sense of Augustus William Schlegel, and of most other German critics. It is applied by them to that class of composition in which there lies beneath the transparent upper current of meaning, an under or *suggestive* one. What we vaguely term the *moral* of any sentiment is its mystic or secondary expression. It has the vast force of an accompaniment in music. This vivifies the air; that spiritualizes the *fanciful* conception, and lifts it into the *ideal. (T,* 337)

Beginning with his review of de la Motte Fouqué's *Undine* (September 1839), Poe typically opposes the "mystic or under-current of meaning" and allegory, as in his late review of Hawthorne (November 1847): "[I]f allegory ever establishes a fact, it is by dint of over-turning a fiction. Where the suggested meaning runs through the obvious one in a *very* profound under-current . . . there only, for the proper purposes of fictitious narrative, is it available at all" (*T,* 256, 582–83). Allegory for Poe is fixity—a meaning to which an image or narrative is attached, whereas the mystic, being suggestive and indefinite, is transitive, carrying the reader beyond the text. Suggestiveness and indefiniteness Poe associates with music, an agency that carries apprehension beyond mere perception toward the mystic and the ideal. Unlike music, which distinguishes poetry from prose, the mystic or undercurrent of meaning may be present in either poetry or prose fiction. In a sense, Poe includes prose romance as a form of poetry. But prose romance is not Poe's own fictional form, and he shortly turns his critical attention to the tale.

POE'S THEORY OF THE TALE

Poe's only essay on the tale, his brief Preface to *Tales of the Grotesque and Arabesque* (1840), is most striking for what it omits. The key terms are not defined. Instead, Poe writes, "The epithets 'Grotesque' and 'Arabesque' will be found to indicate with sufficient precision the prevalent tenor of the tales here published." Poe does not discuss the grotesque; he notes that critics have mistakenly linked the arabesque in his serious tales with " 'Germanism' and gloom," phantasy, and terror, and he uses this occasion to defend his use of terror: "If in many of my productions terror has been the thesis, I maintain that terror is not of Germany, but of the soul,—that I have deduced this terror only from its legitimate sources, and urged it only to its legitimate results" (*M 2*, 473). Poe published *Tales of the Grotesque and Arabesque* a year before the first of his tales of ratiocination, and, with the exception of this type, the collection includes all the types of tale Poe wrote. Most critics agree that, for Poe, the grotesque and arabesque characterize different literary modes, the grotesque designating the comic, burlesque, and satiric, and the arabesque the serious, poetic, terrifying, and visionary (*AQ*, 289; Ketterer 1989, 28–29).

The concepts of the grotesque and arabesque had wide currency in Romantic art theory, literature, and criticism, and most modern discussions of Poe's grotesque and arabesque are explicitly or implicitly attempts to define Poe's Romantic aesthetics. Only a few of these discussions can be mentioned here. The best work on the art background of Poe's arabesque is Patricia C. Smith's "Novel Conceptions, Unusual Combinations: The Arabesque in Poe" and "Poe's Arabesque." In the first half of the nineteenth century, both grotesque and arabesque designated styles of intricate decoration, the arabesque deriving from Arabic design, which allowed no representation of humans and animals, and the grotesque deriving from the designs of ruins and grottoes of the Romans, which mingled heterogeneous elements. Smith concludes that Poe's literary arabesque "is an attempt to suggest something kinetic—the motion toward unity—in a static medium; symbolically, it is always moving in the direction of a form-obliterating spiral" (1974, 44–45).[4] Sources for Poe's grotesque and arabesque have also been identified in Romantic literary theory. Several critics have followed A. H. Quinn's somewhat erroneous argument that Poe took the terms from Sir Walter Scott's essay on E. T. A. Hoffmann, "On the Supernatural in Fictitious Composition" (*AQ*, 289). Poe would have known of usages in addition to Scott's, and Scott uses the terms disparagingly in his review of Hoffmann, so that his valuation of the terms cannot be precisely that of Poe. For Scott, the overstraining of Romantic imagination has produced the new form of the grotesque, the literary counterpart of the arabesque in the visual arts. Scott views the literary grotesque as an unnatural, startling, and repugnant combination of elements, the textual equivalent of madness. Burton R. Pollin points to another possible source of Poe's grotesque in Victor Hugo's Preface to *Cromwell* of 1827 (the same year as Scott's review). Hugo gives a positive valuation to the grotesque, which includes representation of the unnatural and horrible, as well as hybrid literary forms and those forms that puncture the appearance of harmony and unity, such as the comic and burlesque. The grotesque involves deformation, disillusionment, estrangement. (Both Scott's grotesque and Hugo's seem to include Poe's category of the arabesque or tale of terror.) Despite their opposite valuations of the grotesque, both Scott and Hugo posit the literary grotesque as a modern—that is, Romantic—mode. In his interesting reading of Poe's fiction in terms of German Romantic irony, G. R. Thompson idiosyncratically identifies both the arabesque and grotesque as ironic forms that yield, finally, a transcendent vision (1973; see also 1989). Even in this brief discussion of Romantic aesthetics, we can see that the grotesque and arabesque are involved in the dialectical interplay in Romanticism between the aspiration toward unity, coherence, and transcendence, on one hand, and, on the other, negation and irony.

One of Poe's major discussions of the arabesque is his essay or sketch "Philosophy of Furniture" (May 1840). Arabesque design is at the center of his philosophy of decoration. Considering interior design, like landscape architecture, one of the fine arts, Poe advises restraint and harmony. His discussion of the carpet, the soul of the room, provides one sense of the arabesque: "[D]istinct grounds, and vivid circular or cycloid figures, *of no meaning,* are here Median laws. The abomination of flowers, or representations of well-known objects of any kind, should not be endured within the limits of Christendom. Indeed . . . all upholstery . . . should be rigidly Arabesque" (*M* 2, 498). The nonrepresentational curves and spirals of the arabesque harmonize and unify the elements of the room, thereby lifting the inhabitant from the perception of the real to the apprehension of the ideal. While, in this sketch, the arabesque is capable of harmonizing elements, in some other works, the arabesque is radically disorienting, the portent either of chaos or of an apocalyptic return to unity.

Poe's explicit theory of the tale is developed in terms other than the grotesque and arabesque and takes shape primarily in his reviews of the 1840s. Poe first offers a theory of the tale in his review of Bulwer's *Night and Morning* (April 1841). (The germ of this theory is in Poe's review of Dickens's *Sketches by Boz* [June 1836].) Poe recommends a plot in which all elements are adapted to each other, thus producing unity of effect. Time both intensifies and limits effects, so Poe recommends the tale over the long narrative. Misrepresenting Schlegel, perhaps to hide his own indebtedness, Poe states that Schlegel confuses plot with mere intrigue and offers these characterizations of perfect plot: "*That in which no part can be displaced without ruin to the whole*"; "a perfect adaptation of the very numerous atoms of a very unusually involute story" (*T,* 148–49; cf. 869). Poe's description of the tale in terms of the scientific analogies of atomic structure and adaptation anticipates the cosmological argument of *Eureka,* making the tale an approximation of the structure of the universe. In the Drake–Halleck review, Poe argues that poetry can be created either by the faculty of ideality or by the faculty of causality; here he states that the creation of the tale combines these faculties: the brief tale "admits of the highest development of artistical power [i.e., artifice or calculation] in alliance with the wildest vigor of imagination" (153). Perhaps the combination of calculation and imagination produces that exquisite adaptation of parts in the tale that Poe seeks. This formal feature of unity in complexity is as important in Poe's late theory as his doctrine of effect.

In his second review of Hawthorne's *Twice-Told Tales* (May 1842), Poe's doctrine of effect links his theory of the tale to his theory of the poem. Since both forms aim at unity of effect or impression, both must be brief. Poe distinguishes the two genres, rhythm being necessary in poetry for "development of the poem's highest idea—the idea of the Beautiful," but rhythm is a bar to expression based in truth (*T,* 573). Truth as correspondence to reality is not, however, necessary to fiction, and Poe declares that, if poetry has a narrow but high field, the tale has a wider range of effects proper to it. The tale has the distinction of being capable of originality, or novelty of effect.

Paradoxically, Poe's virtual demand for originality in fiction becomes a requirement for simulation, and Poe's late writings on literary theory are haunted by the simulacra of literature. In his first review of *Twice-Told Tales* (April 1842), Poe praises Hawthorne's originality of incident and reflection and concludes in his second review that "Mr. Hawthorne is original at *all* points" (569, 574). Yet in his later review of *Twice-Told Tales* and *Mosses from an Old Manse* (November 1847), Poe claims that Hawthorne is "*not* original in any sense" and reassesses the possibility of originality with an ambiguity worthy of Hawthorne himself (579). Literary originality is to be judged by novelty, the reader's sense of the new. Thus extremes of originality may be self-defeating: a work full of originalities may "deaden in the reader all capacity for their appreciation," and originality can be best produced by avoiding "absolute novelty of combination" (580). Poe continues:

But the true originality—true in respect of its purposes—is that which, in bringing out the half-formed, the reluctant, or the unexpressed fancies of mankind, or in exciting the more delicate pulses of the heart's passion, or in giving birth to some universal sentiment or instinct in embryo, thus combines with the pleasurable effect of *apparent* novelty, a real egotistic delight. The reader, in the case first supposed, (that of the absolute novelty,) is excited, but embarrassed, disturbed, in some degree even pained at his own want of perception, at his own folly in not having himself hit upon the idea. In the second case, his pleasure is doubled. He is filled with an intrinsic and extrinsic delight. He feels and intensely enjoys the seeming novelty of the thought, enjoys it as really novel, as absolutely original with the writer—*and* himself. They two, he fancies, have, alone of all men, thought thus. . . . Henceforward there is a bond of sympathy between them, a sympathy which irradiates every subsequent page of the book. (580–81)

True originality is simulation: the production of "the seeming novelty" of a universal notion that is appreciated by the reader as if it were original with the writer and himself alone. The effect of seeming originality serves a final end: the creation of a tie of exclusive sympathy between the reader and the author. But this, too, the author has calculated, so that even sympathetic understanding is only a simulation of an original relationship.

In Poe's review of his own *Tales* (October 1845)—published anonymously— the disguised reviewer asserts the originality of Poe's tales and the novelty of their effects. The effects of the tale depend on the author's genius: "A writer must have the fullest belief in his statements, or must stimulate that belief perfectly, to produce an absorbing interest in the mind of his reader. That power of simulation can only be possessed by a man of high genius. It is the result of a peculiar combination of mental faculties. . . . It is possessed by Mr. POE, in its perfection'' (873). Genius, the source of originality for the Romantics, has become the power of projecting other identities. The effect of truth is best produced by the simulation of belief, and the tale so produced would appear to be a simulacrum, a copy with no original, as, in Poe's final review of Hawthorne, true originality can be represented only by apparent originality, another stunning instance of the simulacrum in Poe's haunted palace of literature. The idea of the simulacrum can be traced back to the Drake–Halleck review, in which Poe identifies poetry as what is produced by the poetic sentiment and what, in turn, stimulates the poetic sentiment. Given the criterion of effect, poetry can be produced as well by calculation as by sentiment—indeed, even better; thus, poetry is replaced by its better half, the simulation of poetry.

POE'S LATE THEORY OF POETRY: "THE PHILOSOPHY OF COMPOSITION," "THE RATIONALE OF VERSE," "THE POETIC PRINCIPLE"

The notion of the simulacrum previously developed throws light on the problems of reading Poe's famous late essay "The Philosophy of Composition" (April 1846).[5] Readers of the essay have often questioned Poe's intention rather than examining his method, the essay's own master concept. According to the method articulated here, both the poet's construction of the poem and the critic's reconstruction of it produce simulacra of poetry. In Poe's simulated conclusion, the simulated bird is reanimated by the spirit of poetry.

Poe's philosophy of composition follows an argument advanced in the second review of Hawthorne's tales, that the writer must work backward from a preconceived effect to construct appropriate causes. These causes are the text itself. The example of how this is done is Poe's remarkable "analysis, or reconstruction" of his own composition of "The Raven" (*T,* 14). At the beginning of the essay, Poe states: "Nothing is more clear than that every plot, worth the name, must be elaborated to its *dénouement* before anything be attempted with the pen. It is only with the *dénouement* constantly in view that we can give a plot its indispensable air of consequence, or causation, by making the incidents, and especially the tone at all points, tend to the development of the intention" (*T,* 13). This intention is synonymous with effect. Poe does not claim that the work so composed *is* a set of causes for producing a particular effect; he claims that with such a method of composition "we can give a plot its indispensable air of consequence, or causation." A well-constructed work, then, simulates causation, leading to a real effect while hiding its own emptiness. Though Poe states of "The Raven," "It is my design to render it manifest that no one point in its composition is referrable either to accident or intuition—that the work proceeded, step by step, to its completion with the precision and rigid consequence of a mathematical problem," he also calls this account "an analysis, or reconstruction'' (14). In other words, like the artist who works back from preconceived effect to create causes or an air of causation, the critic works analytically from the text as effect to reconstruct or simulate its causation or composition, thus recomposing "The Raven" (cf. Person). Like a well-made plot, this account of composition has an indispensable air of consequence. This recomposition or simulation of "The Raven" is, in a sense, more original than the original of which it is a copy, since it includes within itself its own origins in "The Raven" and in the philosophy of composition, while "The Raven," like the raven of its title, gives no account of itself.

Effect is the governing principle of Poe's tour-de-force analysis or reconstruction. Since effect or impression is his criterion, Poe desires an effect that is truly affecting, one both original and vivid. The artist may realize this aim by various combinations of incident and tone. Intense effects are transitory; thus, "through a psychal necessity," the work must be brief to achieve unity of impression and hence its strongest effect (15). Having established these literary principles, Poe shifts to consideration of poetry in particular. Beauty, "the sole legitimate province of the poem," is an effect and not a quality of the poem; as beauty causes sadness, "[m]elancholy is thus the most legitimate of all poetical tones" (16, 17). Poe then turns to "The Raven" and derives the features of the poem through apparent deduction from first principles. Beginning with the intrinsic effect of the refrain, Poe deduces the length of the refrain, the sound qualities of the refrain, the variation in the refrain, as well as the repetition in the refrain of a key word; and the choice of a particular creature, the raven, to repeat this word. Poe adds to these purely technical effects the subject the most productive of beauty and melancholy, the death of a beautiful woman. Then the necessity of combining these elements, a raven repeating the key word of the refrain and "a lover lamenting his deceased mistress," leads to the choice of setting for bringing the raven and the lover together and to the plotting of the encounter between the two. (Poe begins with the technical features of the poem. Representation or content is not primary and comes in for the sake of furthering the technical aims of the work.) With this machinery, Poe arrives at the dénouement (but not quite the end) of the poem, "the Raven's reply, 'Nevermore,' to the lover's final demand if he shall meet his mistress in another world" (23).

Arriving here, Poe can reconstruct the poem yet again, now as a narrative with an air of consequence, beginning from the beginning or even before: "A raven, having learned by rote the single word 'Nevermore,' and having escaped from the custody of its owner . . ." He ends again with the dénouement, which now has perfect psychological and narrative motivation: "The student now guesses the state of the case, but is impelled . . . by the human thirst for self-torture, and in part by superstition, to propound such queries to the bird as will bring him, the lover, the most of the luxury of sorrow, through the anticipated answer 'Nevermore.' " Through this moment in the poem, "there has been no overstepping of the limits of the real" (24).

Poe has offered a double reconstruction of the poem, as a mechanical or deductive process of composition that begins from technical considerations of effect and as a naturalistic narrative with its air of consequence and reality. But the story thus remains, perhaps, too much within the limits of the real, having "a certain hardness or nakedness, which repels the artistical eye." The poem needs "some amount of complexity, or more properly, adaptation" and "some amount of suggestiveness—some under current, however indefinite of meaning." Poe must violate his principle of beginning from the end by adding the two final stanzas that follow the dénouement, with their suggestion of the emblematical nature of the bird, a suggestiveness that pervades "all the narrative which has preceded them" (24). Poe lays bare his deductive devices, to show that he does not compose by inspiration, but we also see that his devices do not work by themselves: analysis requires the complement of synthesis, as here with the supplement that transforms all that has come before.

"The Raven" would seem to be a poor illustration of Poe's theory of poetry as transcendence, since the lover never escapes his passion and his obsession, which are represented by the monotonous cadence of the bird's "Nevermore." If the poem succeeds as an illustration of Poe's philosophy of poetry, it is not because of Poe's announced philosophy of composition, which leads the writer only to the dénouement, but because of the poetic requirement of adaptation and suggestiveness. Through this surplus, the spirit of poetry animates the simulated "Raven." This excess of form and of meaning can be appreciated by the reader but not by the lover. The poet must violate a philosophy of composition in order to fulfill a philosophy of poetry.[6]

In "The Rationale of Verse" (November 1848), the poetic requirement of complexity is developed specifically in terms of prosody. This essay has generally been read as a technical study of prosody rather than as a theoretical statement about poetry, although it announces itself as theory (the *rationale* of verse), and although it is from the same period as Poe's major theoretical statements, "The Philosophy of Composition," "The Poetic Principle," and *Eureka*. "The Rationale of Verse" has puzzled modern readers because of its peculiar statements on prosody and especially its discussion of quantity, accent, and the syllabic line. As Martin Roth notes, "Those critics and scholars who have treated 'The Rationale of Verse' in the past have either summarized it or taken Poe to task for his ignorance of prosodic or linguistic fact" (18).[7] J. Arthur Greenwood and Richard B. Eaton, Jr., instead attempt to explain Poe's prosodic theory by situating it historically, but, finally, Eaton also takes Poe to task: "He marked stresses, he confused them with quantities, and he counted syllables" (61).

Roth displaces the debate about "The Rationale of Verse" by shifting the critical perspective from Poe's various prosodic ideas to Poe's larger argument about prosody—to Poe's rationale of verse precisely. In "The Rationale of Verse," Poe offers the truth about verse for the first time, as he offers the truth about the structure of the universe in *Eureka* for the first time. "Both works tell similar stories of the unified beginning, the particularized and perverse temporal career, and the final, awful destiny of their subject matter" (14). In *Eureka* Poe argues that the poetical instinct is for symmetry. The universe begins in unity, or nothingness, is diffused into parts ever more complexly interrelated until an outer limit of development is reached, when the process is reversed, and unity is restored. Similarly, Poe roots verse in enjoyment of equality; verse originates with the spondee. Roth summarizes the poetic history: "The original beauty of simple equality is steadily obscured as a result of the poet's growing desire for complexity in beauty, which is due to the increasing perversity into which his soul has fallen. But metrics . . . continues to develop as a result of the principle of equality and monotony, insuring beauty's continued existence in and through a fallen world. The development of metrics is both angelic and perverse, as all poetic acts are in Poe" (15). Roth concludes that Poe has a double role as poet and as critic. "As a poet of the latter days, one of Poe's artistic missions is to hasten the end of creation, to vary or complicate the original, unified poetic impulse to the greatest possible extent"; similarly, as a critic, Poe recalls the beginning, "the lost spondaic basis of the ancient music," while rationalizing the "increasing complexity in verse" (17, 18).

As opposed to his rational analysis of verse and his mechanistic theory of composition, Poe's "The Poetic Principle" presents a lush description of the poetic sentiment or "sense of the Beautiful" and of the transcendental aims of poetry (*T*, 76). Poe wrote "The Poetic Principle" as a lecture, which he delivered on several occasions in 1848–1849 and which was published posthumously (October 1850). Much of the theoretical section is drawn from key passages in Poe's second review of Longfellow's *Ballads* (April 1842), and Poe stated the main ideas of "The Poetic Principle" many times in his reviews since 1840. Perhaps it is because "The Poetic Principle" has the quality of codification that critics have not given it the same kind of attention paid to "The Philosophy of Composition"—for, though "The Poetic Principle" is frequently anthologized, quoted, and summarized, it is seldom analyzed.[8]

Poe identifies three divisions of the mind—intellect, taste, and the moral sense—which have as their respective objects truth, beauty, and duty. Taste occupies the significant middle position since it also makes the objects of intellect and moral sense attractive. Taste is, indeed, the most important faculty, producing not only delight in the beauty of the world but, through the agency of poetry, glimpses of "the Beauty beyond" (*T*, 77). Poe also calls this highest faculty the poetic sentiment; it may be developed in all the arts, but in the union of poetry and music, which Poe regards as true poetry, the poetic sentiment is developed to the highest degree.

The organizing principle of the lecture is, again, a version of the doctrine of effect. The final end of poetry is the elevation of the soul; to achieve this, the poem must have unity or "totality of effect or impression," and, to attain this end, it must have a certain brevity (71). The reader's capacity for receiving impressions also sets a limit to brevity itself: "A *very* short poem . . . never produces a profound or enduring effect" (71). Poe identifies this elevation of the soul as the apprehension of beauty. Still, the representation or imitation of the beauty of the world is not poetry. Poetry "is no mere appreciation of the Beauty before us—but a wild effort to reach the Beauty above. Inspired by an ecstatic prescience of the glories beyond the grave, we struggle, by multiform combinations among the things and thoughts of Time, to attain a portion of that Loveliness whose very elements, perhaps, appertain to eternity alone" (77). Since music is necessary to achieve this transcendental end, Poe can define poetry in brief as *"The Rhythmical Creation of Beauty"* (78).

Poe argues against moral instruction ("the heresy of *The Didactic*") and the inculcation of truth as aims of poetry and against passion as a component of poetry (71). Of these three, only earthly passion seems always to interfere with "the true poetical effect." In his first review of Longfellow's *Ballads,* Poe admits a didactic aim if it does not overwhelm the proper object of the poem, and, in this essay, Poe admits truth, but not as an end in itself. "And in regard to Truth—if, to be sure, through the attainment of a truth, we are led to perceive a harmony where none was apparent before, we experience, at once, the true poetical effect—but this effect is referrable to the harmony alone, and not in the least degree to the truth which merely served to render the harmony manifest" (93). This harmony can be thought of as a dynamic symmetry. It is this that poetry approaches through both its novel combinations of existing forms and its rhythm. The novel combination and mutual adaptation of parts gives a sense of the dynamism and symmetry of the divine plot of the universe, as Poe describes it in *Eureka,* and the rhythm that surpasses the pulse of earthly passion intimates the rhythm or pulsation of Being itself (Richard 1987). Hence, in *Eureka* Poe can take the further step of equating beauty and truth, for they are two terms for a self-contained and dynamic form, and thus also of equating poetry and fiction.

"MARGINALIA"

Poe's "Marginalia" were published in seventeen installments, from November 1844 until shortly before his death in 1849. In his Introduction, which is not altogether disingenuous, Poe describes his marginalia—a term of his own invention—as thoughts occasioned by reading that, since they are addressed by the writer to himself, are bold and original. The "Marginalia" make up, in Poe's terms, a *"farrago,"* and, in fact, they are a very mixed dish of literary and nonliterary topics (*P* 2, xv, 109). Many have the brevity and wit of the epigram or Romantic fragment, while others are a few paragraphs or short articles. Baudelaire regarded Poe's "Marginalia" as "the secret chambers, as it were, of his mind" and was inspired by them, as was Valéry later, but Claude Richard claims that, by the time Poe turned to writing the "Marginalia," he was worn out by the daily practice of sensational journalism (Baudelaire, 46; Richard 1978, 50). Though Poe may have intended originality when he conceived his first installment, many of the "Marginalia" are indeed culled from Poe's earlier and contemporary writings.

Several critics have discussed the form of the "Marginalia." Michael Allen places Poe's "Marginalia," like his earlier "Pinakidia," in a late eighteenth-century tradition of learned journalism in which the author draws bits of esoteric information or curiosities of literature from his manuscripts (74). Burton R. Pollin argues that the attraction of the form "must have been the '*abandonnement*' as [Poe] terms it . . . , or the relaxed ease of the short discursive essay, so different from the neat and predetermined construction that he had always demanded for the tale and the poem" (*P* 2, xvi, quoting Intro. 108, *M Marg.,* 192). Poe's Introduction indicates other formal possibilities as well. There Poe compares his marginalic writings to the " 'brain-scattering' humor of the Germans," suggesting that they have the epigrammatic form, the wit and irony of the German Romantic fragment (108). G. R. Thompson connects the "Marginalia" to German Romantic irony, and, in one of the most interesting discussions of the "Marginalia," Joel Porte argues that much of Poe's production is marginalic writing, which functions as Romantic irony deflating Romantic imagination (Thompson 1973; Porte, 80–95).

While Poe's marginalic writing often has this ironic function, some of the "Marginalia" can be read as glosses on, or supplements to, Poe's other works. For example, *P* 2, *Marg.,* 118 on genius illuminates the discussion of analysis in the Drake–Halleck review and in "The Philosophy of Composition"; in the "Marginalia" article, Poe argues that the faculty of analysis enables "the artist to get full view of the machinery of his proposed effect, and thus work it and regulate it at will." David Ketterer cites several of the "Marginalia" to support his thesis about Poe's aesthetics of fusion, and Joan Dayan draws on *Marg.,* 197 to build an argument about Poe's prose style (Ketterer 1979; Dayan 1987). Perhaps the best-known application of one of the "Marginalia" is Richard Wilbur's "The House of Poe." Wilbur reads Poe's tales and poems as representations of the hypnagogic state. Poe explains this state by characterizing a class of delicate fancies or psychal impressions in *Marg.,* 150: "[T]hey arise in the soul (alas, how rarely!) . . . at those mere points of time where the confines of the waking world blend with those of the world of dreams. I am aware of these 'fancies' only when I am upon the very brink of sleep, with the consciousness that I am so" (258). These fancies produce an ecstasy that transcends the pleasures of both waking and dreaming. Through the power of words to convey psychal fancies, according to Wilbur, Poe seeks Romantic transcendence.

I have tried to chart the main lines as well as the complexities of Poe's literary theory and to indicate how his theory can be situated in Romantic and modernist theory. From within modernism, Valéry's apprehension of Poe's theory—the text as a system of transformations—would seem to lead to our period of post-structural inquiry. But perhaps the effects of Poe's theory on the present will become clear only in retrospect.

NOTES

1. The other significant subject of Poe's essays—his analysis of contemporary institutions of literature—lies outside the scope of this chapter. See especially Poe's "Exordium to Critical Notices," "Prospectus of *The Penn Magazine,*" and "Prospectus of *The Stylus,*" and see Michael Allen, Robert D. Jacobs, Claude Richard (1978), Lewis P. Simpson, G. R. Thompson (1988), and Burton R. Pollin (1991).

2. On the magazine trade and the literary marketplace of the antebellum period, the most important scholarship is that by Frank Luther Mott, William Charvat (1959, 1968), Perry Miller, and Michael T. Gilmore. On Poe's position in the magazine trade and the literary marketplace, see Sidney P. Moss (1963, 1970), Bruce I. Weiner, Arthur H. Quinn, Kenneth Silverman, John W. Ostrom (1982, 1987), and Michael Allen.

3. This language in Poe's fiction is discussed by Voloshin; for a counterargument about Poe's aesthetics, see Glen A. Omans.

4. Similarly, David Ketterer sees Poe's arabesque as part of his aesthetic of fusion, which might permit apprehension of an ideal reality (1979, 1–45). Rae Beth Gordon discusses Poe's grotesque and arabesque in terms of the visual arts and, particularly, representations of sexual desire.

5. Almost from the time of the essay's publication, readers have suspected that it is a hoax. Among those critics who defend "The Philosophy of Composition" as the formulation of aesthetic principles that correspond to the implicit principles or the unconscious process of Poe's composition are F. C. Prescott (1), A. H. Quinn (440), and Kenneth Burke, while Edward H. Davidson sees the essay not as an account of composition but as a statement of "what poetry should be and should do" (84). In his study of Romantic and modern theories of poetic creation, Carl Fehrman notes that Malarmé, Valéry, Pär Lagerkvist, and Gottfried Benn found Poe's "Philosophy of Composition" incredible—Mallarmé called it an intellectual game—though they "recognized their own experiences of the processes of poetic composition in Poe's philosophy of writing" (80). Mallarmé suggested that Poe transposed the craft of the dramatist and theatrical producer to the genre of poetry. Fehrman makes a number of other fertile suggestions about the relation of Poe's theory to older artistic traditions as well as to subsequent critical movements.

6. Person demonstrates how the essay undermines Poe's claim that he did not compose by inspiration but by method: "Again and again in the essay, Poe describes himself making decisions instantaneously, as if in a flash of inspiration. . . . Again and again, in other words, Poe belies his own scientific method" (5).

7. Roth cites Sidney Lanier (xiv), T. S. Omond (138–44), George Saintsbury (310), Gay Wilson Allen (57–58), Arthur Hobson Quinn (561), J. Arthur Greenwood, and Floyd Stovall (1969).

8. A. H. Quinn quotes copiously but offers few comments; Robert D. Jacobs explicitly discusses this essay in one paragraph; Joan Dayan dismisses "The Poetic Principle" as a parody of the Emersonian sublime (1987).

WORKS CITED

Abrams, M. H. *The Mirror and the Lamp: Romantic Theory and the Critical Tradition.* 1953. Rpt. in New York: Norton, 1958.

Allen, Gay Wilson. *American Poetry.* New York: American Book, 1935.

Allen, Michael. *Poe and the British Magazine Tradition.* New York: Oxford UP, 1969.

Alterton, Margaret. *Origins of Poe's Critical Theory,* 1925. Rpt. in New York: Russell and Russell, 1965.

Baudelaire, Charles. "New Notes on Edgar Poe." Trans. Lois Hyslop and Francis Hyslop. (1857). Rpt. in Carlson, *REAP,* 43–60.

Beebe, Maurice. "The Universe of Roderick Usher." *Personalist* 37 (1956): 147–60. Rpt. in *Poe: A Collection of Critical Essays.* Ed. Robert Regan. Englewood Cliffs, N.J.: Prentice-Hall, 1967, 121–33.

Burke, Kenneth. "The Principle of Composition." *Poetry* 99 (1961): 46–53.

Campbell, Killis, ed. "Letter to Mr.—." *The Poems of Edgar Allan Poe,* 1917. Rpt. in New York: Russell and Russell, 1962, 311–18.

Carlson, Eric W., ed. *Critical Essays on Edgar Allan Poe.* Boston: G. K. Hall, 1987.

———. *The Recognition of Edgar Allan Poe: Selected Criticism Since 1829.* Ann Arbor: U of Michigan P, 1966.

Charvat, William. *Literary Publishing in America, 1790–1850.* Philadelphia: U of Pennsylvania P, 1959.

———. *The Origins of American Critical Thought, 1810–1835.* 1936. Rpt. in New York: Barnes, 1961.

———. *The Profession of Authorship in America, 1800–1870.* Ed. Matthew J. Bruccoli. N.p.: Ohio State UP, 1968.

Davidson, Edward H. *Poe: A Critical Study.* Cambridge: Harvard UP, 1957.

Dayan, Joan. *Fables of Mind: An Inquiry into Poe's Fiction.* New York: Oxford UP, 1987.

———. "From Romance to Modernity: Poe and the Work of Poetry." *Studies in Romanticism* 29 (1990): 413–37.

Eaton, Richard B., Jr. "Poe's Prosody in Perspective." *PoeS* 5 (1972): 61–62.

Eliot, Thomas Stearns. "From Poe to Valéry." *Hudson Review* (1949). Rpt. in Carlson, *Recognition of Poe,* 205–19.

Fehrman, Carl. *Poetic Creation: Inspiration or Craft.* Trans. Karin Petherick. Minneapolis: U of Minnesota P, 1980.

Felman, Shoshana. "On Reading Poetry: Reflections on the Limits and Possibilities of Psychoanalytic Approaches." *The Purloined Poe: Lacan, Derrida, and Psychoanalysis.* Ed. John P. Muller and William J. Richardson. Baltimore: Johns Hopkins UP, 1988, 133–56.

Genette, Gérard. "La Littérature comme telle." *Figures.* Collection *Tel Quel.* Paris: Éditions du Seuil, 1966, 253–65.

Gilmore, Michael T. *American Romanticism and the Marketplace.* Chicago: U of Chicago P, 1985.

Gordon, Rae Beth. "Interior Decoration in Poe and Gilman." *LIT: Literature, Interpretation, Theory* 3 (1991): 85–99.

Greenwood, J. Arthur. *Edgar Allan Poe, The Rationale of Verse: A Preliminary Edition, Incorporating Cognate Documents.* Princeton: Wolfhart Book, 1968.

Hungerford, Edward. "Poe and Phrenology." *AL* 2 (1929): 209–31.

Jacobs, Robert D. *Poe: Journalist and Critic.* Baton Rouge: Louisiana State UP, 1969.

Ketterer, David. *Edgar Allan Poe: Life, Work, and Criticism.* Fredericton, N. B.: York P, 1989.

———. *The Rationale of Deception in Poe.* Baton Rouge: Louisiana State UP, 1979.

Lanier, Sidney. *The Science of English Verse.* New York: Scribner's, 1907.

Miller, Perry. *The Raven and the Whale: The War of Words and Wits in the Era of Poe and Melville.* New York: Harcourt, Brace, 1956.

Moldenhauer, Joseph J. "Murder as a Fine Art: Basic Connections between Poe's Aesthetics, Psychology, and Moral Vision." *PMLA* 83 (1968): 284–97.

Moss, Sidney P. *Poe's Literary Battles: The Critic in the Context of His Literary Milieu.* Durham, N. C.: Duke UP, 1963.

———. *Poe's Major Crisis: His Libel Suit and New York's Literati.* Durham, N. C.: Duke UP, 1970.

Mott, Frank Luther. *A History of American Magazines 1741–1850.* Cambridge: Harvard UP, 1957.

Omans, Glen A. " 'Intellect, Taste, and the Moral Sense': Poe's Debt to Immanuel Kant." *Studies in the American Renaissance 1980.* Ed. Joel Myerson. Charlottesville: UP of Virginia, 1980.

Omond, T. S. *English Metrists in the Eighteenth and Nineteenth Centuries.* London: Oxford UP, 1907.

Ostrom, John Ward. "Edgar A. Poe: His Income as Literary Entrepreneur." *PoeS* 15 (1982): 1–7.

———. "Poe's Literary Labors and Rewards." *Myths and Realities: The Mysterious Mr. Poe.* Ed. Benjamin Franklin Fisher IV. Baltimore: Poe Society, 1987, 37–47.

Person, Leland S., Jr. "Poe's Composition of Philosophy: Reading and Writing 'The Raven.' " *Arizona Quarterly* 46 (1990): 1–15.

Pollin, Burton R., ed. " 'The Living Writers of America': A Manuscript by Edgar Allan Poe." *Studies in the American Renaissance 1991.* Ed. Joel Myerson. Charlottesville: UP of Virginia, 1991, 151–211.

———. "Victor Hugo and Poe." *Revue de Littérature Comparée* 42 (1968): 494–519.

Porte, Joel. *In Respect to Egotism: Studies in American Romantic Writing.* Cambridge: Cambridge UP, 1991.

Prescott, F. C., ed. *Selections from the Critical Writings of Edgar Allan Poe.* 1909. 2d ed., with new preface by J. Lasley Dameron and new introduction by Eric W. Carlson. New York: Gordian P, 1981.

Quinn, Patrick F. *The French Face of Edgar Poe.* Carbondale: Southern Illinois UP, 1957.

Richard, Claude. *Edgar Allan Poe: journaliste et critique.* [Paris]: Klincksieck, 1978.

———. "The Heart of Poe and the Rhythmics of the Poems." Carlson, *Critical Essays* (1987): 195–206.

Rosenheim, Shawn. "The King of 'Secret Readers': Edgar Poe, Cryptography, and the Origins of the Detective Story." *English Literary History* 56 (1989): 375–400.

Roth, Martin. "Poe's Divine Spondee." *PoeS* 12 (1979): 14–18.

Saintsbury, George. *A Historical Manual of English Prosody.* London: Macmillan, 1910.

Schlegel, Augustus William. *A Course of Lectures on Dramatic Art and Literature.* Trans. John Black. Rev. ed. London: Henry G. Bohn, 1846. (Poe used the first ed., 1815.)

Scott, Walter. "On the Supernatural in Fictitious Composition; and Particularly on the Works of . . . Hoffman[n]." *Foreign Quarterly Review* 1 (1827): 60–98.

Silverman, Kenneth. *Edgar A. Poe: Mournful and Never-Ending Remembrance.* New York: HarperCollins, 1991.

Simpson, Lewis P. "Poe's Vision of His Ideal Magazine." *The Man of Letters in New*

England and the South: Essays on the History of the Literary Vocation in America. Baton Rouge: Louisiana State UP, 1973, 130–47.

Smith, Patricia C. "Novel Conceptions, Unusual Combinations: The Arabesque in Poe." Diss. Yale University, 1970.

———. "Poe's Arabesque." *PoeS* 7 (1974): 42–45.

Stovall, Floyd. *Edgar Poe the Poet: Essays New and Old on the Man and His Work*. Charlottesville: UP of Virginia, 1969.

———. "Poe's Debt to Coleridge." *Studies in English* (1930). Rpt. in Stovall, 126–74.

Tate, Allen. "The Angelic Imagination." *Kenyon Review* (Summer 1952): 455–75. Rpt. in Carlson, *Recognition of Poe*, 236–54.

Thompson, G. R. "Edgar Allan Poe and the Writers of the Old South." *Columbia Literary History of the United States*. Ed. Emory Elliott. New York: Columbia UP, 1988, 262–77.

———. *Poe's Fiction: Romantic Irony in the Gothic Tales*. Madison: U of Wisconsin P, 1973.

———. "Romantic Arabesque, Contemporary Theory, and Postmodernism: The Example of Poe's *Narrative*." *ESQ* 35 (1989): 163–271.

Vines, Lois Davis. *Valéry and Poe: A Literary Legacy*. New York: New York UP, 1992.

Voloshin, Beverly. "Transcendence Downward: An Essay on 'Usher' and 'Ligeia.' " *Modern Language Studies* 18 (1988): 18–29.

Weiner, Bruce I. *The Most Noble of Professions: Poe and the Poverty of Authorship*. Baltimore: Enoch Pratt Free Library, 1987.

Wilbur, Richard. "The House of Poe." Library of Congress Anniversary Lecture 1959. In Carlson, *Recognition of Poe*, 254–77.

Wilson, Edmund. "Poe at Home and Abroad." *New Republic* 49 (Dec. 8, 1926): 77–80. Rpt. in Carlson, *Recognition of Poe*, 142–51.

14

The Reviews: Evolution of a Critic

JAMES M. HUTCHISSON

For most of his career, Poe earned his living as a professional critic. In fact, he wrote more literary criticism than anything else: from 1835, when he became formally associated with the *Southern Literary Messenger,* until his death in 1849, when he was contributing regularly to several magazines in the Northeast, Poe wrote close to 1,000 essays, reviews, articles, columns, and critical notices. Some were no longer than a paragraph or two, and some ran to as many as a half-dozen pages, but taken as a whole, they constitute, as Edmund Wilson said in 1955, "the most remarkable body of criticism ever produced in the United States" (79). My concern here is with the reviews proper, not the critical essays, such as "The Philosophy of Composition" and "The Poetic Principle," where the criteria for evaluating literature found in the reviews are distilled into a systematic series of precepts.

The reviews are among Poe's most important legacies. Although many readers assume that, during his lifetime, Poe was most widely known for his tales or perhaps for his poetry, in fact, it was as a critic that his presence in the burgeoning literary world of the 1830s and 1840s was most deeply felt. Most important, Poe was arguably the first original literary theorist America produced. He worked in a literary climate where there was an ongoing campaign to develop a national literature that could compete with British and Continental literature. Poe often used his reviews to denounce the practice of "puffing"—lavishly praising—inferior native books simply because they were written by Americans. Because he thought the critic's task was to distinguish good literature from bad and to consign the bad to oblivion, Poe placed a strong, though not disproportionate, emphasis on negative criticism.

In writing the reviews, Poe was hammering out his aesthetic ideas in a kind of critical workshop, fitting and refitting his evaluations from book to book, making adjustments in his specific insights until he found the precise form of expression for the general principle. In these reviews, Poe looked for several specific qualities. He valued unity of design over diffuseness (and by extension, the short tale or poem over the novel); imagination over fancy; pleasure over didacticism; and technical skill over carelessness of form and structure. He applied traditional criteria to the language and metrics of a poem but sought meaning as well as beauty. Championing originality, he tried to discredit mere "imitators." Poe's criteria, however, changed over the course of his career. His early critical statements from 1831 to the time he joined the *Messenger* had elevated the imagination as the source of almost all critical and creative thought. By 1835, however, as Alterton and Craig point out in *Edgar Allan Poe: Representative Selections,* the influence of Coleridge and other British aestheticians led Poe to understand inspiration as the interplay of reason and imagination, the one as important as the other (xlv–xlviii). He then was able to distinguish between the "poetic sentiment" (variously called "poesy" and "ideality") and the poem as an artifact, or "means" to "elevate the soul" of the reader. Thus, imagination inspired the poet's "sentiment," but reason guided the poet's technical skill. According to Jacobs, Poe continued to believe that only a judicious balance of the two could produce a unified work (*Poe,* 374–75).

CRITICISM AND EDITIONS

Although Poe's importance as a critic has always been ensured by his theoretical essays, his book reviews have not attracted much extended critical commentary. Biographers A. H. Quinn and Kenneth Silverman summarize various of the better-known reviews but do not offer any extended analysis of them or examine them in the context of Poe's critical essays or his fiction. Meyers devotes approximately two and a half pages to Poe's *Messenger* reviews, but he regards them as "literary journalism" rather than as literary criticism and treats them only as one type of editorial duty that Poe assumed as a magazinist (81–84). The same is true of Meyers's selective mentions of Poe's reviews of Dickens and Hawthorne for *Graham's Magazine* (130–32); of Hazlitt, Tennyson, Barrett, and Lowell for the *New York Mirror* and the *Broadway Journal* (170–71); and of the so-called Longfellow war (171–73). Thus, like Poe's other biographers, Meyers does not address the critical importance of the reviews. Laser's and Marks's articles concern both the reviews and the essays, as do several dissertations (Kelly; Lubell; Vaughan). Among studies of Poe's criticism, important insights about the reviews can be found in Claude Richard's *Edgar Allan Poe: Journaliste et Critique* and in Eric W. Carlson's "new introduction" to the 1981 printing of Prescott's selective edition of Poe's criticism. Edd Winfield Parks's *Edgar Allan Poe as Literary Critic* concentrates on Poe's aesthetic principles and discusses a limited number of the reviews by genre and theme. Robert D. Jacobs's comprehensive study (1969) examines Poe's development as a critic chronologically and makes significant connections between Poe's criticism and his philosophy and aesthetic (especially the influence of late eighteenth-century critical theory). Jacobs further shows how some of the strictures under which Poe had to work in the magazine world shaped his critical statements (Chaps. 3, 9, 10). Jacobs also collaborated with J. Lasley Dameron on a sketch of Poe as a magazine critic for the *Dictionary of Literary Biography*; it and Carlson's introductory essay are the most worthwhile, concise overviews.

There is no single, definitive edition of all of Poe's reviews. Those quoted or referred to here are available in one of three editions. The most recent are Burton R. Pollin's *Collected Writings of Edgar Allan Poe*, Vols. 3 and 4: *Writings in The Broadway Journal (Nonfictional Prose)*, 1986; and G. R. Thompson's *Edgar Allan Poe: Essays and Reviews*, 1984. Pollin's text is a "composite facsimile edition" of the original items by Poe as they appeared in the *Broadway Journal*. Despite some reviewers' complaints about the cramped typeface of the facsimile, it is the most authoritative edition available (P. Quinn, Reilly, Thomas 1987, Walker).

It is also meticulously annotated—unlike the Thompson volume, which is intended for that elusive abstraction publishers call "the general reader." This latter edition has no introduction; its notes are sparse. Though not a complete selection of Poe's periodical criticism (see Pollin 1985), it is thus far the most comprehensive. Thompson bases his attributions on the authority of the most recent scholarship or verifies them with reference to Ostrom or to Hull's useful 1941 doctoral dissertation on the canon of Poe's critical writings. Sometimes Poe ran a notice more than once, or he wrote a brief notice, then at a later date a longer, full-dress review. Sometimes, too, he cannibalized portions of individual notices and worked them into omnibus reviews of several books. Thompson reprints the first appearance of the review, except in cases where the piece was "rewritten and expanded or reprinted as part of a later, more extensive article" (1482).

In this chapter page references are to the Thompson edition, except for the *Broadway Journal* (Pollin edition), identified as *P*. For articles that do not appear in these volumes, Harrison's is the third most reliable edition, though it also is not "complete." In volumes 8 through 13 of the seventeen-volume set, the reviews and criticism are arranged chronologically.

THE SOUTHERN LITERARY MESSENGER: 1835–1837

Poe began his career as a critic at the *Southern Literary Messenger*, though exactly when he began writing for it is not certain, and his earliest reviews show little of the stridency and trenchant analysis he came to be known for. While there is no external evidence linking Poe with the *Messenger* before March 1835, David K. Jackson determined that the review of Robert Montgomery Bird's *Calavar; or The Knight of the Conquest* in the February number was written by Poe (43–44). It is interesting for its discussion of the standards to be applied to the novel, which Poe thought was dubious as an art form, as he would later point out in reviews of Dickens, Bulwer, and others. Not a self-contained work, the novel lacked unity, the cornerstone of Poe's aesthetic. But Poe was not yet sure enough of himself to make such judgments emphatically, nor was he confident enough to dispute the prevailing critical deference to foreign literature; he praised *Calavar* as good enough to compete with "the very best European works of the same character." Very soon, he would begin to denounce this same provincialism. In reviewing his friend John Pendleton Kennedy's *Horse-Shoe Robinson* in the May issue, he was again somewhat overly generous in his praise, faulting only Kennedy's punctuation and finding the main character full of "strength, substance, and vitality" (651) and the style refreshing in its "simplicity" (652).

Not until December 1835 did Poe begin to use his reviews to make critical pronouncements. At this time, his presence as a critic quickly began to be felt: this issue of the *Messenger* established Poe's reputation as "the man with the tomahawk," an epithet (apparently coined by the *Cincinnati Mirror* [Silverman, 122]) that Poe earned for his strong negative criticism and apparent ad hominem attacks, the reports of which, as we shall see, have been greatly exaggerated. In the September number, he had ridiculed the anonymous *Mephistopheles in England; or The Confessions of a Prime Minister,* because of its "utter want of keeping" and its lack of a "just object or end" (*H* 8, 42). While Poe did not develop this point much further, it foreshadows his eventual idea of art as a teleological construct in which a preestablished design and the execution of the design were of first importance.

The *Norman Leslie* Review: A Polemical Challenge

His harsh judgment of *Mephistopheles,* however, was tame compared to his annihilation of Theodore Fay's *Norman Leslie* in the December issue, where he made his next important statement as a critic—on the business of criticism itself. Poe had been looking for a way for the *Messenger* to "kick up a dust" in the magazine world; he found the perfect target in Leslie's third-rate novel. Poe used this review to sound the first of several clarion calls for a rigorous and independent criticism in America (the other major statements appear in the "Prospectus" to his projected "Penn Magazine" [1840] and a review of Lambert Wilmer's *The Quacks of Helicon* [1841]). His ridicule of Fay touched off a skirmish with the powerful New York literary clique to which Fay belonged. The story of the battle has been engagingly told by Sidney P. Moss. *Norman Leslie* had been "puffed" to excess by the *New York Evening Mirror,* the very newspaper where Fay was an associate editor. When the novel finally came to Poe for review, he must have been lying in wait:

Well!—here we have it! This is *the* book—*the* book *par excellence*—the book bepuffed, beplastered, and be-Mirrored: the book "attributed to" Mr. Blank, and "said to be from the pen" of Mr. Asterisk: the book which has been "about to appear"—"in press"—

"in progress"—"in preparation"—and "forthcoming": the book "graphic" in anticipation—"talented" *a priori*—and God knows what *in prospectu.* For the sake of everything puff, puffing, and puffable, let us take a peep at its contents! (540)

Poe ridiculed every facet of the novel. In general terms, he criticized its unrealistic characters and convoluted plot; in more specifically analytical terms and
using abundant examples from the text, he faulted the style and diction of the
novel—an early example of Poe's eventual method of close textual analysis,
which he elaborated on in "Exordium" (1842). Poe concluded that *Norman
Leslie* was "the most inestimable piece of balderdash with which the common
sense of the good people of America was ever so openly or so villainously
insulted" (546).

The whole review imparts a strong sense of Poe's cavalier challenge to the
New York cabal with which he tilted the rest of his career. He certainly wanted
to draw more attention to himself and to the *Messenger,* knowing that controversy would increase circulation. But he also wanted to foster an honest American criticism and to gibbet amateurish writing praised only because it was a
native product. The irreverence, arrogance, and downright splenetic quality of
this, the first of several attacks on literary coteries, owe much to Poe's study of
British magazines, as Michael Allen and J. Lasley Dameron have shown, such
as the *Edinburgh Review* and the *London Quarterly Review,* and even to the
slashing reviewing styles of certain contributors, notably the infamous "Christopher North" (the pseudonym of John Wilson) and John Gibson Lockhart, two
reviewers for *Blackwood's Edinburgh Magazine,* a journal known for its ferocity
(Allen, 47–50).

After the *Norman Leslie* incident, Poe continued to develop as a literary po-
lemicist. He also began to use his reviews to develop critical principles and then
measure the work under review against them—an uncommon method in his
time. As he later said in the "Exordium," the critic should oppose the "cant
of Generality" and, instead, subject the text to "deliberate perusal." In this
practice, Poe anticipated the New Critics of the twentieth century, who held that
a work of art should be analyzed in isolation, exclusive of context (such as
history or the author's biography).

Theory of Poetry and Fiction

In the January 1836 *Messenger,* Poe led off with an omnibus review of the
three leading sentimental poets of his day: Mrs. Lydia H. Sigourney, Mrs.
H. F. Gould, and Mrs. E. F. Ellet. Nearly the entire review, however, was
devoted to Sigourney. Although, at this early stage of his career, Poe showed
only a little of his later characteristic anger at "popular" writers with undeservedly high reputations, he did seize on the fact that Sigourney was known
as "the Mrs. Hemans of America," after the British poet Dorothea Felicia Hemans. This prompted Poe to lash out at provincialism, a recurring theme in

much of his criticism. To Poe, the very fact that Sigourney had acquired that title made her "palpably convicted of that sin which in poetry is not to be forgiven" (875): Mrs. Sigourney lacked originality, and, to Poe, imitation was the deadliest of literary sins. The volume Poe found to be unoriginal in structure, versification, subject matter, and phraseology. But what most irritated Poe was Sigourney's habit of prefacing nearly every selection with a motto or quotation of some sort, which Poe thought gave the reader a predetermined "reading" of the poem; to Poe, interpretation should not depend on something outside the text.

With the possible exceptions of Robert Walsh and James Kirke Paulding, two lesser-known contemporaries,[1] Poe was also America's first literary theorist— at least he was the first to use book reviews as a means of formulating literary theories. Poe's critique of Sigourney contains the first developed explanation of what he meant by "unity." The epigraphs Poe found so damaging were one example of how outside "forces" could corrupt unity: "the *totality* of effect is annihilated." Undue length, too, may violate unity:

In poems of magnitude the mind of the reader is not, at all times, enabled to include in one comprehensive survey the proportions and proper adjustment of the whole. . . . But in pieces of less extent . . . the understanding is employed, without difficulty, in the con-templation of the picture *as a whole*—and thus its effect will depend, in a very great degree, upon the perfection of its finish, upon the nice adaptation of its constituent parts, and especially upon what is rightly termed by Schlegel "the unity of totality of interest." (876–77)

As Parks points, out, whenever Poe used the term *unity,* he always meant two things—the unity imposed by the writer on the work and the unity felt by the reader (18). This "double unity" could be achieved only in the lyric poem and the prose "tale," both forms being short and thus requiring little sustained attention by the reader. In a novel, a narrative poem, or an epic poem, it was impossible to achieve unity.

Poe drew this concept, in part, from several other theorists. First, in criticizing Sigourney's poetry for lacking "unity of impression," Poe was elaborating on the theories of organic unity put forth by Augustus Wilhelm Schlegel. For Schle-gel a work of art was the same as a living thing: all parts worked to produce a joint impression on the mind (Lubell 1953; 7). Second, Poe agreed with various of Coleridge's statements in *Biographia Literaria* that, in reading a poem, the pleasure derived from the whole is what is "compatible with a distinct gratifi-cation from each component part" (10). Coleridge emphasized structural unity. Finally, Poe was indebted to several Scottish aestheticians, among them Hugh Blair (*Lectures on Rhetoric and Belles-Lettres*), Lord Kames (*Elements of Crit-icism*), and, particularly, Archibald Alison's critical writings. In discussing length, Poe had in mind the reader's inability to grasp the design of a long poem and his therefore being denied the pleasure or "unity of emotion" that Alison said the poem should impart (Jacobs, 112).

With this theorizing, however, came constant polemics, so that, in succeeding issues of the *Messenger,* Poe was denouncing bad art through "tomahawk" reviews while at the same time developing a complex psychological or philosophical approach to criticism based on his knowledge of British aesthetics. In one extreme instance of the former, Poe showed obviously poor judgment in a January 1836 review of William Gilmore Simms's *The Partisan* that is almost as merciless as that of Fay's *Norman Leslie.*[2] Poe accused Simms of using the book's dedication to curry favor with the dedicatee (an unknown), but this was patently false. Yet, in the next issue, January 1836, Poe wrote a sophisticated analysis of *Robinson Crusoe* (it had recently been issued in a new edition), where he discussed the "faculty of imagination." What Poe here defined as the "dominion exercised by volition over imagination" was an early example of his increasing emphasis on conscious technique (202). At this stage in the development of his aesthetic, Poe tended to value the process of conscious artistic creation—reason—over the often subconscious (or unwilled) activity of the imagination.

Poe juggled aesthetic theories and journalistic polemics frequently during his *Messenger* period—though the persisting label of "tomahawk critic" is somewhat undeserved, because Poe did not denounce an unreasonably large number of books. Poe himself noted this in the September 1836 *Messenger,* where he reckoned that of the ninety-four books he had reviewed, in only five of them had censure been "greatly predominant." We must remember, too, that Poe felt it was incumbent upon the critic to discard the bad so that the good could find the audience it deserved. In the *Messenger,* he often pointed out the contrast between third-rate and first-rate books by writing reviews of each for the same issue; he therefore administered a corrective to the one by example and comparison. A case in point is the February 1836 issue, where Poe ruthlessly detailed the absurdities of plot and style in Morris Mattson's *Paul Ulric,* "despicable in every respect," as a way of indirectly praising the "artist-like eye, the originality, the fancy, and the learning" of Edward Bulwer-Lytton's *Rienzi* (142). In reviewing Bulwer's novel, Poe singled out and praised the very qualities that were lacking in Mattson's novel: clarity of purpose, artistry, technical skill, and ideation. Poe's review of Bulwer reveals another abiding component of his aesthetic: in praising Bulwer, whose novels were infamous for their "immorality," Poe was challenging the prevailing critical attitudes about the morality of art, thereby reaffirming his position as an objective critic.

The Drake–Halleck Review: Practical and Philosophical Criticism

Such theories developed as, more and more, he began to ballast his specific criticisms with general principles and therefore gradually develop a basis for praising some works and denouncing others. His maturation as a critic is visible in one of his most famous reviews, that of Joseph Rodman Drake's *The Culprit Fay, and Other Poems* and Fitz-Greene Halleck's *Alnwick Castle, with Other Poems* in the April 1836 issue. Poe began by assessing the state of American literary criticism. In the past, he said, Americans had "cringed to foreign opinion" (505) (notably that of the British quarterlies) and thereby had impeded the development of a national literature. That had produced both bad literature and bad criticism. Now, he argued, Americans were going to the opposite extreme by divorcing themselves completely from foreign opinion and finding themselves "in the gross paradox of liking a stupid book the better, because, sure enough, its stupidity is American" (506).

Poe next distinguished between the sentiment or feeling of "poesy" and the poem itself. The sentiment of poesy manifested itself in the "Faculty of Ideality" to evoke "the sense of the beautiful, of the sublime, and of the mystical," and "imagination" was its "soul" (510, 511). But Poe insisted that the poem itself was not merely "the Poetic faculty, but the *means* of exciting it in mankind" (511). An artist imbued with Ideality, the poetic sentiment, might be able to produce a great poem that stirred the imagination, but this effect would simply be adventitious. On the other hand, a careful, skillful artist, even without the poetic sentiment, could write a fine poem and arouse ideality in the reader. This theory marked a sharp break for Poe with Romantic doctrine, for he did not think that a poem should be a means of self-expression nor that a poem should be judged by what its author apparently "felt." Rather, Poe looked for how skillfully the artist communicated ideality. Poe then moved on to exhaustive analyses of several individual poems and concluded that neither poet could consistently impart ideality to the reader. Although, to illustrate this principle, Poe had picked two poets who, by today's standards, would be considered undistinguished, he had demonstrated that he could write both philosophical as well as practical criticism, and the reactions to the Drake–Halleck review were almost all favorable (Moss, 55–56, 69–70; *PoeL*, 199, 210, 215).

Authorship of the Drayton–Paulding Review

Also in the April 1836 number there appeared a review of two pro-slavery books, the anonymous *The South Vindicated from the Treason and Fanaticism of the Northern Abolitionists,* attributed to William Drayton by William Sumner Jenkins in 1935 (319), and *Slavery in the United States,* by James Kirke Paulding. The authorship of this review was traditionally ascribed to Poe (it appears in *H* 8, 265–75) until Hull rejected it from the Poe canon in his 1941 doctoral dissertation (to which I will return) and asserted that the review was the work of Nathaniel Beverley Tucker, professor of law at William and Mary College, a well-known apologist for slavery and frequent contributor to the *Messenger.* As a result, the review is absent from the G. R. Thompson volume; the *PoeL,* citing Hull's dissertation, states flatly that it is the work of Beverley Tucker

(200); and Silverman also accepts Hull's attribution (207, 484). Meyers does not mention the review. However, in 1974, Bernard Rosenthal reexamined the authorship question and concluded, in a long and intricate argument, that the review was Poe's, but his position has not been accepted by all Poe scholars. With the publication of several recent essays that assume Poe's authorship of the review, the question has again been raised. In "Romance and Race," Joan Dayan argues by analogy and by examples from Poe's fiction that, in Poe's time, both blacks and women were subjects of a white male-dominated system that reduced them to an inferior status through sentimentalization and inequality. In another essay, "Amorous Bondage: Poe, Ladies, and Slavery," Dayan sees the depiction of male–female relationships in Poe's poetry as analogous to the antebellum ideology of the "intimate relation" between master and slave. Dayan further believes that the fantasies of empowerment and revenge enacted in Poe's tales can be particularized as "the relation between a 'suffering'—alternately degraded and idealized—'servant' and an omniscient master" (258). Dana Nelson, also assuming Poe's authorship of the Drayton–Paulding review, analyzes *Pym* as a racist text through the symbolic use of *white* and *black* as "the final sanction of colonial domination" and the repression of the Other. Nelson rejects Rowe's and Thompson's postmodernist conclusion that *Pym* ends on a note of ambiguity and indeterminacy (91, 107). On the contrary, Nelson holds, the novel is "not solely about absence of meaning, but about the impulses—social, political, economic—that undergird the construction of any system of meaning" (108). John Carlos Rowe's "Poe, Antebellum Slavery, and Modern Criticism" argues by reference to the Paulding–Drayton review that Poe identified unequivocally with the southern antebellum prejudices of racism and sexism and with aristocratic pretensions (visible in *Pym*, "The Purloined Letter," and other texts). With the appearance of these recent studies, J. V. Ridgely examined the issue of attribution in the fall 1992 issue of the *PSA Newsletter.* The arguments for and against attribution offered by Rosenthal and Ridgely may be summarized as follows.

First, Rosenthal argues that the pro-slavery sentiments expressed in the Paulding–Drayton review are compatible with Poe's pro-slavery statements in four *SLM* reviews: those of Joseph H. Ingraham's *The South-West,* Anne Grant's *Memoirs,* Bird's *Sheppard Lee,* Thomas R. Dew's *Address,* and in an unpublished review by Poe of John L. Carey's *Domestic Slavery.* Ridgely points out that the sum total of these various remarks amount to "no more than a longish paragraph" (2) and thus could hardly be considered an "endorsement" of slavery. (To Ridgely, the issue at hand is not whether Poe could have written the review, but whether he did; to Rowe and other critics, even if Poe did not author the review, the fact that he published it as editor of the *Messenger* is sufficient reason for a critical reassessment of Poe's aesthetic canon.) Rosenthal next takes issue with the documentary evidence that Hull cited in attributing the review to Tucker: a May 2, 1836, letter from Poe to Tucker in which Poe evidently refers to the Paulding–Drayton review. Two passages in the letter are pertinent. First,

Poe tells Tucker that he has had to omit from the April number Tucker's verses, "To a Coquette," and leave them for the May number because "in making up the *form* containing them it was found impossible to get both the pieces in." Second, Poe apologizes to Tucker for "making a few immaterial alterations in your article on Slavery, with a view of so condensing it as to get it in the space remaining at the end of the number. One very excellent passage in relation to the experience of a sick bed has been, necessarily, omitted altogether."

Rosenthal argues that Poe's remarks about cuts in the "article on Slavery" are inconsistent with what is printed in the Paulding–Drayton review and that therefore Poe must have been referring to some other "article on Slavery" that Tucker wrote for the *SLM;* Ridgely rebuts this argument by pointing out that there are "several unelaborated allusions to sick beds" in the text and that Poe's cuts could have been made in any of these passages. Rosenthal also assumes that, in the letter, Poe is telling Tucker what he plans to do in making up the April number; to Rosenthal, it is thus impossible that Poe is referring here to the Paulding–Drayton review, since by this time the issues would have already been mailed. Ridgely, by contrast, contends that Poe was not speaking of what he intended to do, but of what he had already done.

In the rest of his essay, Rosenthal presents several pieces of internal evidence in the Paulding–Drayton review that augur Poe's authorship. He also argues against Tucker's authorship, but, as Ridgely points out, that argument is rather weak and not thorough; Ridgely, in fact, provides in outline a more detailed examination of the similarities between the Paulding–Drayton review and what essays Tucker had published to that point in the *SLM*.[3]

It is difficult to overlook what Ridgely calls "the plain sense" of the only piece of documentary evidence that bears on the authorship question: Poe's letter to Tucker. As Hull noted, in the April 1836 *SLM,* the only review is the Paulding–Drayton review. In his letter, Poe refers to "your article on Slavery," which unambiguously identifies it with the Paulding–Drayton review. It is possible that Poe was referring to Tucker's "Note to Blackstone's Commentaries . . . on the Subject of Domestic Slavery . . ." in the February 1835 *SLM* (1: 227–31) and that Poe was responding to a request by Tucker for offprints of that article. This is the only other "article" of Tucker's that Poe could have been referring to in his letter, but, as Rosenthal concedes, that "speculation has the serious weakness of postulating that an offprint would be called a 'number' " (33).

Terence Whalen, like Ridgely, believes the review to be the work of Tucker. In his forthcoming book, *Edgar Allan Poe and the Masses,* Whalen presents a meticulously detailed argument for Tucker's authorship. Whalen does not refute Rosenthal point by point; instead, he examines the ideological and stylistic similarities between the Drayton–Paulding review and other writings by Tucker. Whalen notes the strong political affinities between the review and Tucker's pro-slavery writings, as well as the existence of what are, in most cases, identical stock arguments, tropes, phrasing, and even patterns of punctuation. Beyond that, Whalen argues that the constraints of politics and of the literary marketplace put upon Poe and other antebellum writers resulted in their having to adopt a position of ''average racism'' for their white reading public, one that cut across the numerous ideological boundaries created by the multiple positions on the slavery issue. Whalen contends that Poe's ''racism'' was not a ''sociological measurement of actual beliefs, but rather a strategic construction designed to overcome political dissension in the emerging mass audience.''

In his June 1836 review of Dickens's *Watkins Tottle* (now familiarly known as *Sketches by Boz*), Poe began to develop one of his most important theories, the aesthetic of the short story or ''tale.'' The novel, Poe said, could be sustained simply by effort and perseverance; the tale, however, depended on unity of effect, a quality ''not easily appreciated or indeed comprehended by an ordinary mind.'' Tales had an advantage over novels because they could be ''taken in at one view'' (205). In commenting on ''The Pawnbroker's Shop,'' Poe drew an analogy between each sentence of a tale giving a progressively more complete view of the overall work and the component parts of a painting adding up to a total effect (206). A novel, Poe said yet again, was not, properly speaking, an art form; it could be admired ''for its detached passages, without reference to the work as a whole'' (205). The painting analogy is congruent with Poe's principle of ''totality of impression'': thematic design should be emphasized over character, setting, and plot; those elements are simply the means by which that design is fulfilled.

The July 1836 issue contains one notice worthy of comment: that of Frederick von Raumer's *England in 1835*. Poe found in this book abundant support for his belief in ''the happiness of a people . . . as practicable under a thousand forms [of government],'' the chief threat being that ''the principal social evils'' are caused by ''a love of gain'' (*H* 9, 54).

Bird's *Sheppard Lee* on ''Incredibilities''

In his September review of Bird's *Sheppard Lee,* Poe concerned himself with how ''atmosphere'' contributed to thematic design. He thought *Sheppard Lee* was original largely because of the ''incredibility'' of the central character's experiencing metempsychosis (401). But Poe criticized Bird for not treating this element more seriously, particularly at the end, when Bird explained away the presence of the supernatural by claiming that the character's experience was only a dream, whereas Poe preferred

writing as if the author were firmly impressed with the truth, yet astonished at the immensity, of the wonders he relates, and for which, professedly, he neither claims nor anticipates credence. . . . *bizzarreries* [*sic*] thus conducted, are usually far more effective than those otherwise managed. The attention of the author, who does not depend upon explaining away his incredibilities, is directed to giving them the character and the luminousness of truth, and thus are brought about, unwittingly, some of the most vivid creations of human intellect. (402–3)

Poe thought that Bird had deprived the reader of the emotional effect of identifying with the character (Parks, 27). Poe further maintained that the supernatural should not be used merely as a motif or structural tool, but rather as a device for stirring the reader's imagination. This statement provides a justification of "incredibilities" as fantasy rather than a violation of realism or verisimilitude, as some critics of *The Narrative of Arthur Gordon Pym* have assumed.

These were the most substantial pieces of criticism Poe published during 1836. In the June number, Poe also paid tribute to Coleridge, who had so strongly influenced his critical thinking, in the form of a notice of the poet's *Letters, Conversations and Recollections*. Poe praised Coleridge as "the man to whose gigantic mind the proudest intellects of Europe found it impossible not to succumb" (181).

On Bryant's Poetry

The January 1837 issue was the last for which Poe served the *Messenger* in an editorial capacity (though, in 1848 and 1849, he published several articles in that journal). His review in this issue of William Cullen Bryant's *Poems, Fourth Edition* is a high watermark in Poe's critical notices, for it shows him applying the principles used in the Drake–Halleck review to a poet who more closely approached Poe's standards. It was his first extended statement on the nature and function of poetry. Much of his analysis concerned versification. Poe was always concerned with how form followed function and particularly with how the sound of verse did or did not accomplish this task. Poe had suggested this principle in the 1831 "Letter to B——", where, as Meyers points out (53), he borrowed verbatim the key phrases in Coleridge's definition by stating that a poem should have "pleasure" for its "*immediate* object" and should impart an "indefinite" rather than a "definite" pleasure (the latter was the province of the "romance," or prose fiction) (11). Poe also made the kinship between music and poetry explicit several times in his writings, such as his observation in the December 1844 "Marginalia" that Tennyson seemed "to see with his ear." In discussing "Summer Wind," for example, he noted how Bryant attempted to make "the sound an echo to the sense" (430); in "The Forest Hymn," Bryant's greatest talent was his "delicacy of ear" (436). Poe was also concerned with the time of a poetic line. By comparing a foot to a musical measure, Poe showed Bryant's deficiencies in this regard. Poe held that the time of one foot should be the same as the others in its line, a theory he later developed in "The Rationale of Verse" (1848), where he called it "equalization." However, he praised Bryant's ability to invest a poem with a sense of "*completeness*;" again,

Poe was concerned with unity, commending "simplicity of design and execution" (437).

This review is significant for another reason. It is the first instance of Poe's using the word *didactic* in a critical context, and it is the first example of Poe's attacking the idea of historical progress in a work of literary criticism. In a landmark essay, Kenneth Alan Hovey has shown how these two issues were strongly linked in Poe's thinking by demonstrating that Poe's attack on the positive message in much of Bryant's poetry was the basis for his whole aesthetic of preferring "beauty" to "truth" or "pleasure" to "didacticism," a theory to which Poe gave fuller expression in the 1842 review of Longfellow and later in "The Poetic Principle."

Two other reviews written in 1837 are significant. In the January *Messenger,* Poe reviewed Washington Irving's *Astoria,* a chronicle of John Jacob Astor's northwest explorations and his eventual founding of the fur trade in America. Poe found the account "masterly" in its "completeness and unity" (615). Then, in October, he discussed John L. Stephen's *Incidents of Travel in Egypt, Arabia Petrae, and the Holy Land* for the *New York Review.* Both articles provide evidence of Poe's using the books he reviewed as sources for his fiction. In reviewing *Incidents of Travel,* Poe particularly recognized its "enkindling influence upon the popular imagination" (923); Richard Wilbur, in fact, demonstrates that Poe used incidents from both books as models for similar events in *The Narrative of Arthur Gordon Pym* (ix), and *Astoria* was one of several sources for *The Journal of Julius Rodman.*

BURTON'S GENTLEMAN'S MAGAZINE: 1839–1840

During the year 1838, Poe did no book reviewing but, instead, worked on *Pym* and then, at year's end, agreed to assist Thomas Wyatt in preparing *The Conchologist's First Book* and *A Synopsis of Natural History.* In May 1839, he obtained employment at *Burton's Gentleman's Magazine* in Philadelphia. Compared to the large number of reviews Poe wrote for the *Messenger,* however, he produced few critical writings during his brief tenure (one year) at *Burton's.* Many of these were perfunctory notices, and much of Poe's criticism was uninspired. Few of the *Burton's* reviews approach the major critical statements that Poe made in the *Messenger,* but he did manage to advance some new theories and further refine some "working" ones.

On Allegory

In a September 1839 notice of Baron de la Motte Fouqué's prose romance *Undine,* Poe discussed the mixed genre of the historical romance, an issue he had somewhat skirted in his earlier review of Bird's *Calavar.* He wanted to champion the romance as a legitimate genre, but, to do so, he had to demonstrate that it had utilitarian moral value, because that was what most American readers at the time looked for in fiction. Poe, however, was hostile to allegory. Therefore, he showed that, in its subtext or "under-current of meaning," *Undine* was actually a treatise on conjugal relations. Poe then said that this allegory was its only defect as romance, because allegory did not "appertain to the higher regions of ideality" (257). He was therefore able to use didacticism as a ploy to interest readers in the book, while at the same time condemning it.

But Poe was not always hostile to an "under-current" in a text. Poe's detractors, such as Norman Foerster and Yvor Winters, broadly appropriated the term to suggest that there was no moral or philosophical dimension to Poe's writings. This was untrue. In his review of Thomas Moore's narrative poem *Alciphron* in the January 1840 issue of *Burton's Gentleman's Magazine,* Poe offered a more precise definition of the term as a symbolic rather than an allegorical "meaning." Poe did not reject "undercurrents of meaning" so long as they did not constitute explicit moralizing or philosophizing: "[T]he *moral* of any sentiment is its mystic or secondary expression," Poe said. His description of poetry as music again helps to explain his concept of symbolism in poetry:

With each note of the lyre is heard a ghostly, and not always a distinct, but an august and soul-exalting *echo.* In every glimpse of beauty presented, we catch, through long and wild vistas, dim bewildering visions of a far more ethereal beauty *beyond.* But not so in poems which the world has always persisted in terming *fanciful.* Here the upper current is often exceedingly brilliant and beautiful; but then men *feel* that this upper current *is all.* No Naiad voice addresses them *from below.* (337–38)

This concern with the relationship of poetry to music, continued from the Bryant review, not only is central to Poe's own emotive and carefully crafted verse, as well as to his whole conception of sound in poetry (in his comments on Tennyson; on the song as genre in the December 1839 *Burton's Gentleman's Magazine* and the April 1849 "Marginalia" in the *Southern Literary Messenger;* and in the "Letter to B—"), but also clarifies Poe's "under-current of meaning" as a suggestiveness and a symbol-making force, not something with explicit didactic intent. Here Poe also made an important statement on fancy and imagination, contradicting Coleridge's distinction that fancy "combines" and imagination "creates." Neither one truly creates, Poe held, for "all novel conceptions are merely unusual combinations. The mind of man can *imagine* nothing which has not really existed" (334).

Early Reviews of Longfellow

Poe's other significant reviews for *Burton's* were two critiques of Longfellow, though these are relatively unimportant when compared to his more significant critique of the poet in the April 1842 *Graham's.* The first review of Longfellow, in October 1839, was a one-paragraph notice of the prose romance *Hyperion.* Poe dismissed it as lacking both "shape" and "design," but his more important basic point was that Longfellow was capable of doing better. Poe held that true artists were obliged to keep at "the great labour requisite for the stern demands of high art" and that Longfellow had let slip this responsibility. Poe's comments illustrate his belief that the critic's duty was to be an arbiter of taste and a champion of quality, protecting the public from mediocre literature. Four months later, reviewing Longfellow's *Voices of the Night* in the February 1840 issue, Poe accused Longfellow of "purloining" the central image and overall design of his "Midnight Mass for the Dying Year" from Tennyson's "The Death of the Old Year." Silverman notes that these reviews of Longfellow (like a biographical sketch of Bryant and an unpublished article on Irving from this same period), motivated by envy and sectional bias, were followed by hypocritical praising of these same authors as Poe wrote to them begging for favors and endorsements—what Silverman calls Poe's habit of "easy lies and half truths" (146). This first stage in Poe's using the reviews for personal attacks seems a prelude to the Longfellow war in 1845 and to Poe's third review of Hawthorne's tales in 1847.

GRAHAM'S LADY'S AND GENTLEMAN'S MAGAZINE: 1841–1843

Poe left Burton's employ in May 1840 but was drawn back to the periodical one year later, when its new owner, George R. Graham, merged the old *Burton's* with *The Casket* and engaged Poe as editor of the new *Graham's Lady's and Gentleman's Magazine*. In April 1841, Poe's reviews began to appear there. Poe's notice that month of Bulwer's *Night and Morning* is significant for its definition of fictional plot (i.e., design); the definition prefigures the one in his more familiar review of Hawthorne's *Twice-Told Tales,* which appeared in 1842. His statement in the Bulwer review that a good plot is one *"in which no part can be displaced without ruin to the whole"* is an advance over his earlier definitions of plot and unity in the *Messenger* reviews. He expanded on (one might say, exaggerated) Aristotle's theory that lack of unity will result in disjointedness by stating that it would be detrimental to the entire work, and he corrected Schlegel by saying that "most persons think of [plot] as simple complexity. It may be described as a building so dependently constructed, that to change the position of a single brick is to overthrow the entire fabric." "The greatest involution of incident," Poe said, would "not result in plot" (148–49).

In the May number, Poe discussed Dickens's *Old Curiosity Shop* as an example of excellence in plot. It contained none of the "involution" or complexity of incident that sometimes marred Bulwer's work. As he had in the *Messenger,* Poe again undertook to identify bad art by comparison with quality art, showing how Dickens succeeded in every instance where (this time) Bulwer missed the mark. Like most romantic critics, Poe was also interested in the psychology of genius. He saw Dickens as a true genius, Bulwer as a skilled worker who could produce novels that readers liked and could thereby be regarded as a genius. As we shall see, the distinction between reputation and getting pure art to reach the public became an important concern in Poe's criticism during the *Graham's* period.

In June 1841, he reviewed Macaulay's *Critical and Miscellaneous Essays*. In this review, Poe distinguished between "direct" and merely "analogical" proof in an argument. In an article "on Ranke's History of the Popes," Macaulay accounted "for the progress of Romanism by maintaining that divinity is not a progressive science" and that, in his day, the "enigmas" in the Bible had not been any more satisfactorily explained than in any earlier time. To Poe, this indicated the limitations of "proof direct"; by relying on only this type of proof and disregarding "analogical evidence," Macaulay put forth a "disgracefully absurd" proposition. Poe noted that "every astronomical discovery . . . throws additional light" on the subject "*by extending the range of analogy.*" Thus, to Poe, the analogies deduced from nebular cosmogony (the idea that all things in the universe exist in a state of nebular matter and are thus perpetually in a state of progress) offered compelling proof of "the soul's immortality" (323).

Like Poe, Macaulay wrote in a style characterized by "terseness and simple vigor" (322), and he, too, attacked puffery, plagiarism, and the inconsistencies of the publishing business. Macaulay also usually wrote critical notices in a manner consistent with Poe's emphasis on the text under review, not as essays on the topics under consideration. Poe's thinking about the duties of the critic was also stimulated in August, when he reviewed his friend Lambert A. Wilmer's *The Quacks of Helicon,* a satirical poem lampooning some of the "prominent *literati*" of the day. Poe agreed with Wilmer's opinions; the book may even have given Poe the initial idea for his later series, "The Literati of New York City," in which he passed sentence on the journeymen of his trade.

Several of Poe's other notices for *Graham's,* in fact, were of subliterary material—annihilations of third-rate writers who were undeservedly popular. These reviews were reminiscent of his satirical *Messenger* pieces: the collected *Writings of Charles Sprague* (May 1842), which Poe said had "negative merit" (*H* 10, 142); Frederick Marryat's *Joseph Rushbrook, or the Poacher* (September), which gave Poe occasion to bemoan the lack of intellectual content in contemporary literature (325); and William Harrison Ainsworth's *Guy Fawkes; or the Gunpowder Treason* (November), which Poe found "a somewhat ingenious admixture of pedantry, bombast, and rigmarole" (101). He attacked the epic poem *Wakondah: The Master of Life* by the ubiquitous Cornelius Mathews in the February 1842 issue as an example of puffery and found it to be "trash" "from beginning to end" (824).[4]

On the Function of Criticism

Poe had begun the year 1842 by making a developed statement on the nature and function of criticism, entitled "Exordium to Critical Notices." In this manifesto, he contradicted the assumption (held by Mathews, among others) that criticism could take any one of a number of forms—essays, sermons, history, philosophy, oratory—and he further stated that criticism should be treated as a science rather than as merely an expression of opinion. Poe criticized the vogue of the review-essay and the shallow patriotism of literary nationalism, as well as the kinds of critical standards that would allow an Ainsworth or a Mattson to be praised. Finally, Poe added a significant element to his philosophy of criticism in defining what criticism should critique: it should be employed only "upon productions which have their basis in art itself" (1032). Although Poe had always advocated a rigorous, analytical criticism, he was, by this point, becoming more predisposed toward responsible (and objective) criticism, perhaps aware of his earlier impetuousness in the *Messenger* reviews. One indication of this maturity is his somewhat negative view of John Wilson's ("Christopher North") collected *Essays* that January. Here Poe criticized Wilson for some of the very qualities that characterized Poe's own early reviews.

Poe continued to discharge his duties as a critic in accordance with the principles in his "Exordium." One of these was the pragmatic function of criticism. Poe is generally credited with inventing the detective story. In his pragmatically oriented review of *Barnaby Rudge* in *Graham's* for February, he established some aesthetic ground rules for the genre, such as not misleading the reader with "undue or inartistical means" in concealing the secret of the plot (233). He also demanded that the characters be kept sufficiently mysterious (a difficulty for the novelist, Poe pointed out, since his task was to develop characterization) and that the reader's interest be directed to particular details in order to disguise the solution to the mystery. Ultimately, Poe concluded that this could best be done with a first-person narrator rather than with an omniscient author, since the narrator could be duped—a device Poe used in his own tales of ratiocination.

Poe thought that Dickens's presentation of the raven, a bad omen, lacked "an analogical resemblance" to Barnaby (243). Perhaps Poe's own raven was, in part, inspired by Dickens's; Poe was also hoping to emulate Dickens in his own literary career, for Poe stated that critical success and popular success are not incompatible, inveighing against the "literary Titmice" who judged "solely by *result*"—that is, by popularity and sales (253). Of Dickens, whom he considered a true genius, Poe said that popularity was not in itself proof of excellence, but neither was it at cross-purposes with excellence. Poe then proceeded to show how, if a genius used "certain well-understood critical propositions" in a work of art, the "legitimate and inevitable result" would be "vast popularity," such as that which Dickens had enjoyed (226). Again and again (most notably in "The Philosophy of Composition"), Poe would circumspectly say that the writer's goal should be "to suit at once the popular and the critical taste" (15), as he himself tried to do.

On Longfellow's Poetry

The last significant review Poe wrote for *Graham's* is an April 1842 essay on Longfellow's *Ballads and Other Poems.* In its distinctions between poetry and prose and in its separation of poetry from truth, this review summarizes Poe's entire aesthetic of poetry to this time and lays the groundwork, as Hovey points out, for Poe's other criticisms of Longfellow, as well as for many of the ideas in "The Poetic Principle." Here Poe first stated that Longfellow's view of the aim of poetry was fundamentally wrong-headed: Longfellow regarded "the inculcation of *moral* as essential" to a poem (684). Of course, Poe had always objected to overt didacticism in literature. Poetry, moreover, he had said in the Drake–Halleck review, originated in the poet's state of feeling; the poem was the means by which the poet conveyed that feeling. "Beauty," he said, "has no dependence, unless incidentally, upon either Duty or Truth" (689), a position he substantially clarified and expanded upon in "The Poetic Principle":

> It by no means follows ... that the ... precepts of Duty, or even the lessons of Truth, may not be introduced into a poem, and with advantage; for they subserve, incidentally, in various ways, the general purposes of the work:—but the true artist will always contrive to tone them down in proper subjection to that *Beauty* which is the atmosphere and real essence of the poem. (78–79)

By beauty, Poe meant a "supernal" (687) or higher beauty (not merely the beauty of nature). The innate knowledge or "sense of the Beautiful," Poe said, was a basic human quality (and "an important condition of man's immortal nature"). Poe saw poetry as having a basic transcendental function; poetry went beyond "the mere *record*" of "forms and colors and sounds and sentiments" to a higher plane: "It is not the mere appreciation of the beauty before us. It is a wild effort to reach the beauty above.... and the soul thus athirst strives to allay its fever in futile efforts at *creation*" (685). Poe thus saw "poesy" as "a response ... to a natural and irrepressible demand" for an aesthetic product that comprised these (relatively "synonimous" [*sic*], as Poe put it, or at least complementary) elements: "the *novelty*, the *originality*, the *invention*, the *imagination* or lastly the *creation* of Beauty" (687).

Admitting that this type of Beauty defies precise representation, Poe stated that possibly the only way that the poet could evoke Beauty was through music; Poe reminded his audience that music was, after all, "one of the moods of poetical development," once again bringing his earlier aesthetic views (on Moore and Tennyson, e.g.) into a focused whole. In music, Poe said, "the soul most nearly attains ... the creation of supernal beauty":

> It may be, indeed, that this august aim is here even partially or imperfectly attained, *in fact*. The *elements* of that beauty which is felt in sound, *may be* the mutual or common heritage of Earth and Heaven. In the soul's struggles at combination it is thus not impossible that a harp may strike notes not unfamiliar to the angels. (688)

This link between men and angels led Poe to his ultimate definition of poetry as "the *Rhythmical Creation of Beauty*": rhythm and rhyme were simply verbal "modifications" of music (688). As Carlson points out, these statements are also "fundamental to any understanding of Poe's epistemology, his faith in intuitive insight, and the symbolism of his moral allegories, his poems and tales of psychic conflict" (xi).

Poe then analyzed how Longfellow's poetry failed because it aimed at instruction rather than beauty. Poe ended by reiterating his position on didacticism and moralizing: in his review of Fouqué and of Moore, Poe said, he had stated only that "a didactic moral might be happily made the *under-current* of a poetical theme . . . but is invariably an ill effect when obtruding beyond the upper current of the thesis itself" (691). Hovey argues that Poe's ultimate formulation of the "poem written solely for the poem's sake" was rooted in his identification with the South and with its sense of history and time as cyclical. Unlike Longfellow, who wrote poems with positive messages, Poe saw time and truth as destructive to poetry, and he resisted progressivism, because it might speed the decline of the South. Poe's criticism by the 1840s thus increasingly rejected "truth" in poetry because of the "dangerous social implications" that truth might hold. Hence, in this review and in "The Poetic Principle," as Hovey puts it, Poe advocated "a beauty no truth could invade" (349).

Poe's formal association with *Graham's* ended sometime in early April 1842. Disgusted with "the contemptible pictures, fashion-plates, love tales" and general "namby-pamby character" of the magazine (*O* 2, 197), Poe completed his editorial duties for the May number and thereafter contributed to *Graham's* only occasionally. He became increasingly concerned with how art could find an audience. For this reason, he applauded the publication of Rufus W. Griswold's *Poets and Poetry of America* in a November 1842 review for the *Boston Miscellany*. Previous anthologies, by their unrepresentative and uninformed selections, had promoted the idea that Americans were not "a poetical people" (550). Griswold's anthology satisfied the public's demand for a "compendium of . . . poetical literature . . . of our recognized poets; which, either through accident, or by dint of merit, have most been particularly the subjects of public discussion" (552).

Many of Poe's later notices, however, continue to address the issues of "popularity" and reputation, so Poe had not abandoned this part of his mission as a critic. For example, in his November 1843 review of Cooper's *Wyandotte*, Poe remarked that there were two classes of fiction writers: those who are "popular and widely circulated" but quickly forgotten—such as Cooper—and those who are "not so popular, nor so widely diffused" but who evince great "skill" and "genius" and live on in fame (480). This review is also an accurate example of Poe's typical approach in such articles: after discussing Cooper's reputation, he examined several key features—subject, originality, structure, probability in plot, and style—and then illustrated his criticisms with abundant quoted passages and long synopses of the story.

A somewhat more important statement from this period occurs in a review of James Russell Lowell's *Poems*, published in *Graham's* for March 1844, where Poe discussed the desirability of an ethical or moral dimension in poetry.

Poe rejected didacticism, as he had amply demonstrated in the 1842 review of Longfellow; but, as he had also demonstrated in his reviews of Moore and Fouqué, and as he would soon explain in "The Philosophy of Composition," he felt that an "under-current" of meaning imparted to a work of art "so much of the *richness* . . . which we are too fond of confounding with *the ideal*. It is the *excess* of the suggested meaning—it is the rendering this the upper instead of the under current of the theme" that negated the "indefinite" or associative meaning that poetry should convey and turned it into didactic discourse. In discussing Lowell's "Legend of Brittany," Poe faulted Lowell's inept handling of the moral content: "After every few words of narration, comes a page of morality," Poe said. "They are too obviously, intrusively, and artificially introduced" (812). Citing the successful handling of morality in Dickens's *Old Curiosity Shop* and Fouqué's *Undine* (which Poe emphasized was a *"poem"*), he said that ethical dimensions should be *suggested,* not stated.

THE BROADWAY JOURNAL AND ELSEWHERE: 1844–1849

The personal and professional difficulties that plagued Poe during the remainder of 1842 and throughout 1843 brought him, in April 1844, to New York in search of steady employment, and he was soon hired by Nathaniel P. Willis at the *New York Evening Mirror.* Later, he joined the staff of *The Broadway Journal* and was eventually able to borrow enough money to buy it. Much of Poe's criticism during this time, however, was inferior to his earlier writings. He often reprinted portions of earlier reviews or restated ideas from them; sometimes, too, he engaged in needless verbal duels with other writers where little of importance was at stake. The "Literati" series, as well as the "Marginalia" series for the *Democratic Review* and for *Graham's,* both comprised a good deal of his magazine work, but those articles are outside the province of this chapter.

The "Longfellow War"

However, the famous "Longfellow War" is pertinent here because, in charging that Longfellow was a plagiarist, Poe was addressing the question of originality. In reviewing *The Waif* for the *New York Evening Mirror* on January 13 and 14, 1845, Poe praised Longfellow's own "Proem" as the best in this anthology, but he also charged that Hood's "The Death-Bed" was similar to an unspecified poem in Griswold's *Poets and Poetry of America* and accused Longfellow of including only those poets whom he could "continuously *imitate* (*is* that the right word?) and yet never even incidentally commend" (702).

This article touched off a series of attacks and counterattacks between Poe and the Boston literary coterie that quickly escalated into an all-out war, lasting through the next month. Various of Longfellow's friends wrote defenses on his behalf, two of them identified by R. Baird Shuman as George Hilliard and

Charles Sumner and one an anonymous correspondent to the *Mirror* called "Outis" (Greek for "nobody").[5] That person's identity was long believed to be Poe himself, trying to fan the flames of controversy for publicity reasons,[6] but that theory has recently been challenged by Kent Ljungquist and Buford Jones, who claim that "Outis" was Leonard Labaree, editor of the *New York Rover*. Their claim has elicited almost as many rejoinders as the original "Outis" letters did.[7] In his recent biography of Poe, Silverman, basing his conclusion on stylistic evidence in the letters, concludes that Outis was indeed Poe (251); Meyers says that "Outis" was "an unknown writer" and does not review the relevant arguments (172). Whoever "Outis" actually was, Poe's original purpose in making these charges is the more important issue. In the most thorough study of Poe's obsession with "copyism," as he called it, Nelson Adkins defends Poe's "essential sincerity" and concludes: "In art, Poe stood for *genius*, and what must inevitably be the product of genius, *originality*. This high critical purpose Poe stated unequivocally" (183). If we recall that, to Poe, a work of art originated either in an idea or in the poet's feeling a particular emotion, we can see why he thought that Longfellow (and others) was guilty of plagiarism. In Poe's earlier charge that Longfellow had stolen from Tennyson, for example, it was the *idea* of Tennyson's poem that Poe saw in Longfellow's "Midnight Mass." To Poe, such a similarity constituted plagiarism.

Criticism of the Drama

The "Longfellow War" has also overshadowed, to some degree, the other serious criticism Poe wrote during this time. Much of it concerns dramatic art. In his review of Elizabeth Barrett Browning's *The Drama of Exile, and Other Poems*, published in the *Broadway Journal* in two parts, on January 4 and 11, 1845, we see Poe becoming more and more concerned with realism. As much as Poe deplored allegory, he deplored "mysticism" even more. For example, assessing the characterization of Eve in the title poem, which was based on the myth of the Fall of Man, Poe demonstrated his increasing concern with simplicity and probability in natural art:

[I]t is only in a few snatches of verbal intercommunication with Adam and Lucifer, that we behold [Eve] as a woman at all. For the rest, she is a mystical something or nothing, enwrapped in a fog of rhapsody about Transfiguration, and the Seed, and the Bruising of the Heel, and other talk of a nature that no man ever pretended to understand in plain prose. (*P* 3, 3)

Poe further reproved Browning for basing her poem on "the model of the Greek tragedies," which Poe said "solar-microscoped" it into obscurity (*P* 3, 3). In the coming months, Poe was to stringently condemn the use of ancient models in any literary form and to insist on probability in all art, such as the drama, that was mimetic in nature.[8] His concern with a literature of the here and now also anticipated by at least thirty years or more the theories of "realism" put forth by American writers in the late nineteenth century.

Observing live theater gave new dimensions to Poe's characteristic concern with the technical skill, structure, and design of a literary work. Poe wrote two notices of Anna Cora Mowatt's *Fashion; or Life in New York,* generally regarded as the first American comedy of manners. His first notice concentrated on the merits and defects of the play; the second was a more general discussion of the "prospects of the drama." In the first piece (March 29, 1845), Poe reiterated his belief that dramatic action should give an illusion of reality to the audience, and he demanded verisimilitude in all aspects of its presentation. Consequently, Poe deplored Mowatt's reliance on convention and hackneyed stage tricks such as soliloquies, reading letters in loud stage whispers, and "preposterous 'asides' " (*P* 3, 67–68). In the second notice (April 5, 1845), Poe expressed much hope for a revival of the drama in America but felt that it could be accomplished only if playwrights would stop slavishly depending on past conventions. The lack of originality remained for Poe the great enemy of progress in art. Poe was also eminently practical in his views. His concern with getting art to reach the public without sacrificing purity for popularity dates back to his earliest "tomahawk" reviews of mediocre writers with undeservedly high reputations, and it pervades the "honest and fearless opinion[s]" expressed in many of his reviews for *Graham's Magazine.* Poe was also, at this time, thinking about the ideas that would make up *Eureka*; in the June 21, 1845, *Broadway Journal,* he reviewed Tayler Lewis's critical edition of *Plato Contra Atheos,* the tenth book of the dialogue on laws. The belief that "State and Church can never properly exist apart" (*P* 3, 153) is central to *Eureka* (see *H* 15, 210–11, 310–11), as is Poe's belief that the popular acceptance of Platonic doctrine had "a strong tendency to ill—intellectually" (*P* 3, 154).

Poe amplified his comments on the theater in "The American Drama," published in the *American Whig Review* for August 1845. This article considered Nathaniel P. Willis's *Tortesa the Usurer,* which Poe had reviewed briefly in 1839 for *Burton's Gentleman's Magazine,* and Longfellow's closet drama, *The Spanish Student.* In his "new" review of Willis, Poe's criticisms were similar to those he had made of Mowatt. He again stated that the "great adversary of Invention is Imitation" (357) and that plots should be simple and unified (365). Poe dismissed Longfellow's *The Spanish Student* out of hand because it was a closet drama, a genre that Poe had earlier written off as "an anomaly—a paradox—a mere figure of speech," because to Poe a play was meant to be performed.[9]

A review of Hazlitt's *Characters of Shakespeare* in the August 16, 1845, *Broadway Journal* is significant for its comments on Hamlet as persona. Poe noted that most critics fault Shakespeare for the inconsistencies Hamlet displays, and, in so doing, critics "talk of Hamlet the man" instead of Hamlet the character. Shakespeare's "conflicting energies and indolences" were, to Poe, evidence of his "marvellous power of *identification* with humanity at large." These observations accord with Poe's concern for universal appeal and probability in art.

Reconsiderations of Bryant and Hawthorne

Except for his remarks on the drama, Poe's reviews during the remainder of his career contain little of a theoretical nature. Jacobs speculates that "the decline in the quality of Poe's criticism . . . can be blamed on circumstances rather than on a deterioration of ability" (387), but, if Poe was not advancing new theories or making judgments based on his old ones, he was reconsidering his earlier opinions of certain writers. Bryant, for one. Nine years after his 1837 review of Bryant's poems, in *Godey's Lady's Book* for April 1846, Poe repeated much of his earlier criticism but also added a few new insights that are worthy of note. He admitted that he had undervalued Bryant because he had placed too much emphasis on progressivism in art and had not given sufficient weight to Bryant's skill as a metricist who was proficient in using established conventions of verse. This was not, however, a retraction of Poe's recent remarks on the necessity of repudiating tradition. Poe simply meant that sometimes perfectly acceptable conventions were attacked in the spirit of revolt, and this should not invalidate the use of them (445). He, in fact, affirmed his view that the artist should know his craft. Poe did, however, sharpen his earlier judgment of "The Ages"; as a result of the hostility toward social progress that had been growing in him since the 1842 review of Longfellow, in the 1846 review of Bryant, Poe dismissed "The Ages" because of its didacticism and stated that "historical progression" was the one improper theme in Bryant's work (447–48).

In the November 1847 *Godey's Lady's Book,* Poe reviewed Hawthorne for a third and final time. In 1842, Poe had claimed that Hawthorne exhibited originality, but, unable to explain why Hawthorne had not reached a larger audience than he had, Poe here revised his earlier claim and distinguished between "true" or "legitimate" originality and "novelty of combination." Hawthorne's dependence on allegory, Poe now thought, was at cross-purposes with genuine originality, because that required the reader to understand the author's meaning intuitively. Poe now believed that Hawthorne's allegory was so overwhelming that it was a burden upon the reader's intellect and that it pained rather than pleased. In order to achieve true originality, Poe said, the artist had to deal with universals in thought and feeling. Poe denounced "the idea that allegory . . . can be made to enforce a truth":

[I]f allegory ever establishes a fact, it is by dint of overturning a fiction. Where the suggested meaning runs through the obvious one in a *very* profound under-current, so as never to interfere with the upper one without our own volition, so as never to show itself unless *called* to the surface, there only . . . is it available at all. (582–83)

Poe was again reinforcing his condemnation of overt moralizing while still accepting allegory when "properly handled," "judiciously subdued," and "seen only as a shadow or by suggestive glimpses.'' Poe yet again referred to his review of *Undine* as demonstrating how that novel was "the best, and undoubtedly a very remarkable specimen'' of "under-current of meaning'' (583). He also gave his definition of the tale proper as a work conceived to render "a certain *single effect,*'' and he again demonstrated how "the ordinary novel is objectionable from its length'' (586).

Silverman sees Poe's reversing his opinion of Hawthorne as part of his campaign to challenge the high critical regard bestowed upon the New England literary establishment. Indeed, in some ways, this "strange essay,'' as Silverman describes it (317), can be seen as the denouement of the series of personal attacks that began with Poe's early criticisms of Bryant and Longfellow in 1829 and 1830 and that climaxed during the Longfellow war in 1845.

Poe pioneered American literary criticism. He probably worked harder than anyone else in his time to champion the cause of belles lettres in America. Despite the harshness of some of his reviews, he made his criticisms in an intellectually honest and responsible way. Poe regarded with earnestness and sincerity the "stern demands of high art'' that he chastised Longfellow and others for ignoring. The sheer range of his reviews is itself impressive, but so is his evolution as a critic as he modified and extended his views on unity, originality, allegory, and the nature and function of poetry, fiction, drama, and criticism, testing his principles against the books he reviewed. Both a practical and a philosophical critic, Poe evaluated a wide variety of literary work and, at the same time, developed a rigorous and complex aesthetic theory to support his judgments.

NOTES

1. Walsh (1784–1859) was a Philadelphia journalist who wrote several essays defending America from British critics in the patriotic aftermath of the War of 1812. In his *American Quarterly Review,* he tilted with some of the same adversaries Poe took on. Paulding (1779–1860), better known, also answered British critics in the "paper war'' with England, and his theories of "rational fictions'' anticipated late nineteenth-century theories of realism by several decades.

2. Meyers points out that Poe "adopted this harsh critical approach because he had few literary friends and was free to speak frankly.'' Meyers also notes the irony of Poe's extreme sensitivity to criticism of his own work in the face of his "unusually cutting attacks on . . . fellow authors'' (82).

3. Kenneth Alan Hovey, who believes Tucker to be the author of the review, notes that Poe's and Tucker's critical styles were "quite similar'' (353, n. 40). Alterton (11, 46, 54–64, 89–90, 169–71) and Jacobs (*Poe,* 68–69, 72–73, 185–90) both note the wide range of views that Poe shared with Tucker.

4. Mathews was a propagandist for the passage of an international copyright law and unofficial aide-de-camp to Evert Duyckinck, leader of the Young Americans, a literary/ political group in Manhattan that pushed for a liberal, democratic literature. (Later, Poe would ally himself with this group, even though he disagreed with their principles and thought little of their work.)

5. The original review was entitled "Longfellow's *Waif*, with an Exchange" (*New York Evening Mirror*, January 13 and 14, 1845, and *New York Weekly Mirror*, January 25, 1845). Following is a list of the ensuing charges and rejoinders: "A Continuation of the Voluminous History of the Little Longfellow War" (*BJ*, March 5, 1845); "Imitation—Plagiarism—Mr. Poe's Reply to the Letter of Outis" (*BJ*, March 8, 1845); "More of the Voluminous History of the Little Longfellow War" (*BJ*, March 22, 1845); "Imitation—Plagiarism—The conclusion of Mr. Poe's reply to the letter of Outis" (*BJ*, March 29, 1845); "Plagiarism—Imitation—Postscript to Mr. Poe's Reply to the Letter of Outis" (*BJ*, April 5, 1845).

6. See Phillips 2, 955–91; A. H. Quinn, 544–55; Hovey, 341–42, 351, n. 6; Miller, 136; Pollin 1985, 242, 329; and Pollin 1987, 10–15. Campbell concluded that the stylistic qualities of the letter were so atypical of Poe that he could not have authored it (107–9). Moss (169, n. 70) does not believe Outis to have been Poe.

7. See Thomas 1988; Ljungquist; Thomas 1989a, b; Pollin 1989.

8. For more of Poe's views on this topic, see "Does the Drama of the Day Deserve Support?" *New York Evening Mirror*, Jan. 11, 1845; *New York Weekly Mirror*, Jan. 18, 1845; and "Marginalia," *Democratic Review*, July 1846.

9. See Poe's review of Robert T. Conrad in *Graham's Magazine* 24 (Jan.–June 1844): 242.

WORKS CITED

Adkins, Nelson. " 'Chapter on American Cribbage': Poe and Plagiarism." *Papers of the Bibliographical Society of America* 42 (1948): 169–210.

Allen, Michael. *Poe and the British Magazine Tradition.* London: Oxford UP, 1969.

Alterton, Margaret. *Origins of Poe's Critical Theory.* Iowa City: U of Iowa P, Humanistic Studies. Vol. 2, no. 3. 1922.

Alterton, Margaret, and Hardin Craig, eds. *Edgar Allan Poe: Representative Selections.* New York: American Book, 1935.

Campbell, Killis. "Who Was 'Outis'?" *University of Texas Studies in English,* no. 8 (1928): 107–9.

Carlson, Eric W. "New Introduction." *Selections from the Critical Writings of Edgar Allan Poe.* Ed. F. C. Prescott. New York: Gordian, 1981.

Coleridge, Samuel Taylor. *Biographia Literaria.* Vol. 2. Ed. J. Shawcross. London: Oxford UP, 1907.

Dameron, J. Lasley. "Poe and *Blackwood's* on the Art of Reviewing." *Emerson Society Quarterly* 31 (Second Quarter 1963): 29–31.

Dayan, Joan. "Romance and Race." In *The Columbia History of the American Novel.* General ed. Emory Elliott. New York: Columbia UP, 1991.

———. 1994. "Amorous Bondage: Poe, Ladies, and Slavery." *AL* 66 (1994): 239–73.

Foerster, Norman. *American Criticism from Poe to the Present.* Boston: Houghton Mifflin, 1928.

Harrison, James A. *The Complete Works of Edgar Allan Poe.* New York: John D. Morris, 1902. Rpt. in New York: AMS P, 1965. 17 vols.

Hovey, Kenneth Alan. "Critical Provincialism: Poe's Poetic Principle in Antebellum Context." *American Quarterly* 39 (1987): 341–54.

Hull, William Doyle. "A Canon of the Critical Works of Edgar Allan Poe with a Study of Poe as Editor and Reviewer." Diss. U of Virginia, 1941.

Kelly, George E. "The Aesthetic Theories of Edgar Allan Poe: An Analytical Study of His Literary Criticism." Diss. U of Iowa, 1953.

Jackson, David K. *Poe and "The Southern Literary Messenger."* Richmond: Dietz, 1934. Rpt. in New York: Haskell House, 1970.

Jacobs, Robert D. *Poe: Journalist and Critic.* Baton Rouge: Louisiana State UP, 1969.

Jacobs, Robert D., and J. Lasley Dameron. "Edgar Allan Poe." *American Literary Critics and Scholars. Dictionary of Literary Biography 59.* Detroit: Gale, 1987.

Jenkins, William Sumner. *Pro-Slavery Thought in the Old South.* Chapel Hill: U of North Carolina P, 1935.

Laser, Marvin. "Poe's Critical Theories—Sense or Nonsense?" *Emerson Society Quarterly,* no. 31 (Second Quarter 1963): 20–23.

Ljungquist, Kent. "Letter to the Editor." *PSA Newsletter* 17 (Spring 1989): 6.

Ljungquist, Kent, and Buford Jones. "The Identity of 'Outis': A Further Chapter in the Poe–Longfellow War." *AL* 60 (Oct. 1988): 402–15.

Lubell, Albert Julius. *Edgar Allan Poe: Critic and Reviewer.* Diss. New York U, 1950.

———. "Poe and A. W. Schlegel." *Journal of English and German Philology* 52 (1953): 1–12.

Marchand, Ernest. "Poe as Social Critic." *AL* 6 (1934): 28–34.

Marks, Emerson. "Poe as Literary Theorist: A Reappraisal." *AL* 33 (1961): 296–306.

Meyers, Jeffrey. *Edgar Allan Poe: Life and Legacy.* New York: Scribners, 1992.

Miller, Perry. *The Raven and the Whale.* New York: Harcourt Brace, 1956.

Moss, Sidney P. *Poe's Literary Battles.* Durham: Duke UP, 1963.

Nelson, Dana D. *The Word in Black and White: Reading "Race"* in American Literature, 1638–1867. New York: Oxford UP, 1992.

Parks, Edd Winfield. *Edgar Allan Poe as Literary Critic.* Athens: U of Georgia P, 1964.

Pollin, Burton R. "Poe as Author of the 'Outis' Letter and 'The Bird of the Dream.' " *PoeS* 20, no. 1 (June 1987): 10–15.

Pollin, Burton R., ed. *Collected Writings of Edgar Allan Poe.* Vol. 2. *The Brevities: Pinakidia, Marginalia, Fifty Suggestions, and Other Works.* New York: Gordian, 1985a.

———. *Collected Writings of Edgar Allan Poe.* Vols. 3 and 4: *Writings in The Broadway Journal.* New York: Gordian, 1986.

———. Review of "The Poe Editions of the Library of America." *PoeS* 18, no. 2 (Dec. 1985b): 29–32.

———. "Letter to the Editor." *PSA Newsletter* 17 (Fall 1989): 6–7.

Quinn, Arthur H. *Poe: A Critical Biography.* New York: Appleton-Century, 1941.

Quinn, Patrick. Review of Pollin, *Collected Writings of Edgar Allan Poe,* Vols. 3 and 4. *AL* 59 (1987): 463–64.

Reilly, John E. Review of Burton R. Pollin, ed., *Collected Writings of Edgar Allan Poe,* Vols. 3 and 4, *Writings in the Broadway Journal (Nonfictional Prose). PSA Newsletter* 15, no. 1 (Spring 1987): 3–4.

Ridgely, J. V. "The Authorship of the 'Paulding–Drayton' Review." *PSA Newsletter* 20, no. 2 (Fall 1992): 1–3, 6.

Rosenthal, Bernard. "Poe, Slavery, and the *Southern Literary Messenger*: A Reexamination." *PoeS* 7 (Dec. 1974): 29–38.

Rowe, John Carlos. "Poe, Antebellum Slavery, and Modern Criticism." In *Poe's "Pym": Critical Explorations.* Ed. Richard Kopley. Durham: Duke UP, 1993.

Shuman, R. Baird. "Longfellow, Poe, and *The Waif.*" *PMLA* 76 (1961): 155–56.

Silverman, Kenneth. *Edgar A. Poe: Mournful and Never-Ending Remembrance.* New York: HarperCollins, 1991.

Thomas, Dwight. "Poe the Magazinist: *The Broadway Journal.*" Review of Pollin, *Collected Writings of Edgar Allan Poe,* Vols. 3 and 4. *PoeS* 20, no. 2 (Dec. 1987): 51–52.

———. " 'Outis': A Gordian Knot Still Beckons." *PSA Newsletter* 16 (Fall 1988): 3–4.

———. [Reply to Letter to the Editor.] *PSA Newsletter* 17 (Spring 1989a): 6.

———. [Reply to Letter to the Editor.] *PSA Newsletter* 17 (Fall 1989b): 7–8.

Thompson, G. R., ed. 1984. *Edgar Allan Poe: Essays and Reviews.* New York: Library of America, 1984.

———. "Edgar Allan Poe and the Writers of the Old South." *Columbia Literary History of the United States.* New York: Columbia UP, 1988.

Vaughan, Joseph Lee. "The Literary Opinions of Edgar Allan Poe." Diss. U of Virginia, 1940.

Walker, I. M. "Kicking up the Dust." Review of Pollin, *Collected Writings of Edgar Allan Poe,* Vols. 3 and 4. *Times Literary Supplement,* January 8–14, 1988, 40.

Whalen, Terence. "Average Racism: Poe, Slavery, and the Wages of Literary Nationalism." In *Edgar Allan Poe and the Masses.* New York: Oxford UP, forthcoming.

Wilbur, Richard. "Introduction." *The Narrative of Arthur Gordon Pym of Nantucket,* by Edgar Allan Poe. Boston: Godine, 1973.

Wilson, Edmund. "Edgar Allan Poe." *The Shock of Recognition.* Vol. 1: 79–84. New York: Grosset and Dunlap, 1955. Rev. reprint of "Poe as a Literary Critic." *Nation* 155 (Oct. 31, 1942): 452–53. Rpt. *CE,* 109–13.

Wilson, James Southall. "Unpublished Letters of Edgar Allan Poe." *Century Magazine* 107 (Mar. 1924): 652–56.

Winters, Yvor. *In Defense of Reason.* 3d ed. Denver: Alan Swallow, 1947.

15

Eureka: Poe's "Novel Universe"

Barbara Cantalupo

FROM LECTURE TO ESSAY

Poe first presented *Eureka* as a lecture on February 3, 1848, at the Society Library in New York. According to Hervey Allen, "[T]he night of the lecture was cold and stormy. . . . Some sixty-odd persons assembled, and listened to a rapturous address of lyrical logic for about two hours and a half" (590). Arthur Quinn notes that "the lecture was favorably reviewed by the press" (539); in fact, it had a rather mixed reception, partly because of its undue length (Silverman, 337–38). In a letter written three weeks after the lecture to G. W. Eveleth, Poe expresses his dissatisfaction with the response. "All praised it—as far as I have yet seen—and all absurdly misrepresented it" (*O* 2, 361). Nevertheless, Poe maintained that his lecture demonstrated "the novelty & moment of my views. What I have propounded will (in good time) revolutionize the world of Physical & Meta-physical Science" (*O* 2, 362).

Poe hoped his presentation and the subject he had chosen—the universe[1]— would provoke enough enthusiastic interest to boost the sales of the published version of the lecture, which, in turn, would provide enough money to promote the publication of his own literary journal, *The Stylus*. It may have been for these reasons that he kept a close watch on the manuscript copy. He presented his lecture in Lowell, Providence, and Richmond[2]; yet, despite these efforts and Poe's commitment to the import of his discoveries, the lecture provided little profit or promise of future gain. In May 1848, Poe signed a contract with Putnam, who agreed to publish 500 copies of a revised text expanded to nearly 150 pages. The first edition of *Eureka* was in print by July, which, according to Kenneth Silverman, "sold poorly" (338).

Although Poe defined his subject as "*not . . . literary* at all" (*O, 359*) in a

January 22, 1848, letter to Nathanial Willis, his manner of presentation and his language moved *Eureka* far into the literary domain. In fact, in the Preface and title of *Eureka*, Poe proposes to give the reader "this Book of Truths," that he variously calls an "Art-product," a "Romance," a "Poem," a "Prose-Poem," and an "Essay." This profusion of categories has fascinated critics because it not only raises the question of genre but suggests the collapse of dichotomies posited by Poe[3] while questioning definition in language, epistemology, and vision. In his detailed analysis of the differences between the lecture and the published version, Roland Nelson concludes that "at least the beginning and the end of the text of the Putnam edition were not part of the lecture version" (163). Poe had begun his lecture by reading a letter dated A.D. 2848 that had been found in a bottle in the sea, whereas, in the Putnam edition, this letter is preceded by eleven paragraphs on his cosmic theory and a "startling conclusion" (Nelson) of sweeping pantheism.

The Main Argument

Although Susan Manning seems correct in her conclusion that "*Eureka* simply will not yield to paraphrase or summary" (237), earlier, Arthur Quinn (1941) noted that "Poe explained *Eureka* more than once in letters to his correspondents" (542). In a February 29, 1848, letter to George Isbell, Poe offered a summary, in an effort to redress "the objections of *merely* scientific men" (*O*, 363), whose notices of his lecture, Poe asserts, gave "no idea of what I said" (*O*, 363). On the same day, he wrote to George Eveleth and also provided a summary, one considered by Arthur Quinn to be "the most inclusive explanation" (Quinn, 542), but, curiously, this one, too, omits the notion of periodicity, an integral aspect of Poe's "novel" conception. Poe's summary of *Eureka* for Eveleth read as follows:

The General Proposition is this:—Because Nothing was, *therefore* All Things are.
1—An inspection of the *universality* of Gravitation—i.e., of the fact that each particle tends, *not* to any one common point, but to *every other* particle—suggests *perfect* totality, or *absolute unity*, as the source of the phaenomenon.
2—Gravity is but the mode in which is manifested the tendency of all things to return to their original unity; is but the reaction of the first Divine Act.
3—The *law* regulating the return—i.e, the *law* of Gravitation—is but a necessary result of the necessary & sole possible mode of equable *irradiation* of matter through space: —this *equable* irradiation is necessary as a basis for the Nebular Theory of Laplace.
4—The Universe of stars (contradistinguished from the Universe of Space) is limited.
5—Mind is cognizant of Matter *only* through its two properties, attraction and repulsion: therefore Matter *is* only attraction & repulsion: a finally consolidated globe of globes, being but *one* particle, would be without attraction, i e, gravitation; the existence of such a globe presupposes the expulsion of the separative ether which we know to exist between the particles as at present diffused:—thus the final globe would be matter without at-

traction & repulsion:—but these *are* matter:—then the final globe would be matter without matter: i,e, no matter at all:—it must disappear. Thus Unity is Nothingness.
6. Matter, springing from Unity, sprang from Nothingness—i, e, was *created.*
7. All will return to Nothingness, in returning to Unity. (*O* 2, 361–62)

In 1968, A. D. Van Nostrand wrote an interesting and illuminating essay comparing the attempts of Poe and Henry Adams to develop a dynamic, organic theory of being and of the cosmos (Chap. 9). "*Eureka* is enormously simple," Van Nostrand claimed. "It proposes that matter and spirit are one and the same . . . that what is commonly regarded as material is none other than God in a present and temporary state of diffusion." As mind and matter are the same, *Eureka* "finally reveals a complete and literal pantheism" (216).

The amorphous universe of Poe's tales is theorized in the three heavenly dialogues—"The Conversation of Eiros and Charmion" (1839), "The Colloquy of Monos and Una" (1841), and "The Power of Words" (1845). The fragmented nature of each of these dialogues allows ideas to remain undeveloped, while a sequence of ideas is built in the composite of the three conversations that "anticipated obvious qualities in Poe's cosmology: the existence of an ideal world; the concept of thought or will as motion; a process of the loss of self-identity in the divine merger; and the scientific language to explain it all" (224).

Whereas "Mesmeric Revelation" (1844), another colloquy, retained the mystery of God and the individuality of man, in *Eureka,* Poe, "a churchless Antinomian," eliminated the personality of God and the individuality of man. To Van Nostrand, Emerson, not Poe, represents the American vision of progress; and Poe, in *Eureka,* has displaced the mystery of God with "a vast democracy of thought, an ingenious cosmos of which the annihilated self becomes the center" (226).

To Susan Manning, however, Poe's clear outline of his cosmological principles in *Eureka* cannot be taken as a straightforward explanation of its content because of the "spurious dedication and spoof letter found in a bottle; its archly witty allusions, triumphant displays of logic and technical terms; its tantalizing compound of self-evidence and mystification" (235). But then Manning notes Poe's characterizations of his subject as " 'the most solemn—the most comprehensive—the most difficult—the most august' " and concludes that "it is indeed an appalling prospect . . . to follow his arguments, test his analogies, weigh his conclusions . . . with a similarly ponderous solemnity" (236). If appalling to Manning, to others this prospect can be envisioned; the narrator himself urges readers not to "frighten . . . our souls from that cool exercise of consciousness—from that deep tranquillity of self-inspection" that allows us to encounter the "most sublime of truths" (Poe, *Eureka* [hereafter, "Poe"], 140). But is tranquillity possible, given the insistent rhetoric of *Eureka?*

Charles Schaefer's 1971 essay, "Poe's 'Eureka': The Macrocosmic Analogue," would further the idea that *Eureka* can be clearly explicated by dividing it into three sections: the dedication and introduction, "the epistle episode," and

"the universe." The dedication, Schaefer asserts, provides a "sweeping generalization of what Poe has done in *Eureka:* he has espoused *feeling* as a more
valid approach to truth than empirically based thought and has asserted that
truth is more important for its beauty than its matter of fact" (354). The "epistle," Schaefer argues, is "almost entirely satirical" (56) and details "all those
'ways' which Poe felt frustrate the acquisition of truth by the imagination"
(357). The third section outlines Poe's cosmology, which Schaefer sees as Poe's
effort "to develop a *logos* of art" (359).

Schaefer then outlines "Poe's eight ideas in the order of their development"
(360): (1) the rejection of infinity, (2) the distinction between the universe of
stars and the universe of space, (3) "the doctrine of simplicity as the chief
property of original unity," (4) division and diffusion, (5) definitions of repulsion and attraction, (6) "explanation of how heterogeneity was achieved out of
homogeneity" (Schaefer, 363), (7) explanation of Laplace's Nebular theory, and
(8) explanation of "reunion, the final epoch" (Schaefer, 363). Schaefer concludes with the "Poean concept of the true nineteenth-century artist": one who
"saw the finished art product—but neither the artist nor the artistic impulse—
as partaking of a metaphysical quality" (360–64).

Kenneth Silverman offers "to capsulize [Poe's] treatise" (339) in two paragraphs, calling it an "ultimate theory of deathlessness" (339): "in essence, the
cosmos of *Eureka* presents a stupendous spectacle of rejuvenescence, an infinitude of pulsating universes alternately willed into orbic systems and reactively
condensed into primary particles by an infinitude of gods" (339).

CRITICAL RECEPTION

Overview

The preponderance of scientific data and the ostensible concern for methodology evident in *Eureka* have solicited readings that focus on the "validity" or
"prophetic quality" of its scientific content while the involute presentation of
this material, along with the infusion of hyperbole and fantasy, may suggest that
Poe's treatise is a hoax or, as one critic labeled it, "an encyclopedic satire"
(Holman 1969, 54). Form and content, quite obviously, are at odds in *Eureka*.
The conflation of scientific language and personification,[4] the overt promise of
"distinctness—intelligibility" (Poe, 22), alongside the convoluted accumulation
of concepts and facts, and the concern for epistemology along with the final
appeal to faith have produced a diversity of critical response. As Susan Manning
suggests in "Poe's *Eureka* and American Creative Nihilism," the real importance of *Eureka* may finally lie here, in the deliberate confounding of the categories of mind and world" (257).

Early critics[5] were either awed by the convolutions of the text or the engaging
delivery of Poe's lecture or, like Irving Stringham,[6] harshly condemned its science and method. James Campbell quotes Stringham: "*Eureka* affords one of

the most striking instances in literature of a naturally strong intellect tempted by overweening pride to an Icarian flight and betrayed, notwithstanding its merely specious knowledge, into an ignoble exposure of its own presumption and ignorance'' (Campbell, 29). The opposite extreme can be found in a review published in the July 12, 1848, *New York Evening Express:* ''A most extraordinary essay upon the Material and Spiritual Universe. . . . Mr. Poe's new theory of the Universe will certainly attract universal attention, in as much as it is demonstrated, so to speak, with a degree of logical acumen which has certainly not been equaled since the days of Sir Isaac Newton'' (Carlson 1987, 49–50). These unsigned reviews of the first edition during the summer of 1848 set the tone and the main lines of critical inquiry for the twentieth century, especially inquiry into Poe's science and theology, overlooking *Eureka* as an integrated work of literature (Nelson, 180–81). Nelson singles out Allan G. Halline's 1951 study of the theological implications of *Eureka* found in Poe's other works (e.g., ''Ligeia,'' ''Eiros and Charmion''), calling Halline's study ''another turning point in the critical history of *Eureka*'' (182). The two letters from Poe to James Russell Lowell in July 1844 are the only and the most succinct of his statements on *matter* and *spirit* and *spirituality* before *Eureka.*

Following what Edward Davidson noted in 1957 as ''more than a century'' (223) of critical denunciation of *Eureka* ''as a farrago of nonsense or the last maudlin ruminations of a diseased Romantic mind'' (223), critics have engaged the challenges of the text, finding, just as Roland Nelson does, that *Eureka* is ''not an anomaly in the Poe canon, but the natural outgrowth of some early lines of inquiry'' (Nelson, 185), as Judith Osowski demonstrated in her dissertation (1972; see Nelson, 204, n 84): ''The metaphoric construct . . . produced by Poe's cyclical theory of radiation and collapse . . . suggested that this structure is prevalent throughout Poe's fiction, as in 'Ms.,' *Pym,* 'Usher,' 'Descent,' 'Eleonora,' 'Masque' '' (183).

Generally, since the late 1950s, critics have avoided categorical approval or dismissal,[7] although some, like Kenneth Silverman, admit that ''the work abounds in digressions, obscurities, inconsistencies. . . . us[ing] for emphasis many of the same devices that create the fervid voices of [Poe's] distraught tale-tellers, but here sow confusion: double and triple negatives, involuted syntax, reiterated dashes that race across sentences'' (532). On the other hand, others like G. R. Thompson find ways to absorb these apparent disruptions: ''[T]he essay is itself an elaborate art structure, which, like the universe it describes, refers ultimately to nothing outside itself but the Nothing outside itself'' (194). *Eureka,* then, would encompass all and/or nothing or, rather, all as nothing or nothing as all so that, as Patrick Quinn concludes, *Eureka* simply might be ''unintentionally and perforce . . . a poem of death'' (7). Clearly, Poe's stated belief that ''if by any means it [*Eureka*] be now trodden down so that it die, it will 'rise again to the Life Everlasting' '' (Poe, 5) has been confirmed without a doubt.

Roland Nelson's ''Apparatus for a Definitive Edition of Poe's *Eureka*'' summarizes the critical response to *Eureka* from 1848 to the criticism of the early 1970s, documenting the "rise" that Poe predicted. The focus of the article, however, is a scholarly investigation of *Eureka*'s evolution into print and is an excellent resource for scholars interested in the version of *Eureka* that Poe last amended. Since "no holograph manuscript of *Eureka* is known to exist after that document was turned over to the Putnam firm . . . and no preliminary notes or partial drafts [are] extant" (161), Nelson takes account of Poe's corrections found in four distinct copies of the text and concludes that the Hurst–Wakeman copy indicates Poe's last and most inclusive revisions. Nelson also provides a list of these corrections and a key to inserting Poe's changes into the Benton facsimile edition of Putnam's *Eureka.*

Richard Benton's 1973 introduction to the facsimile edition of Putnam's 1848 *Eureka* suggests that Auden's praise of *Eureka*'s style and his acknowledgment of its "relevance to the bulk of Poe's earlier works—both poetry and prose" (i) initiated serious critical consideration of the text. Benton defines the 1950s as a decade of critical response that focused on *Eureka*'s ontology and epistemology, the 1960s as investigating sources and structure, and the 1970s as addressing the complications of *Eureka*'s tone, its melding of science and art, and its manifestations of ironic ambivalence. Benton concludes his introduction with some suggestions for further study and provides a helpful Bibliographic Guide to essays published before the early 1970s, divided into five categories: "The Text and Poe's Commentaries on It," "Literary Analogues," "Sources or Possible Sources," "Criticism," and "Matters Related to *Eureka*—Cosmology, Romanticism, etc." As a sequel to Benton's 1975 studies, James Campbell reviews *Eureka*'s reception and provides an extended discussion of critical response from 1974 to 1988.

The reception of *Eureka* in France that followed Baudelaire's 1859 translation has been reviewed by Reino Virtanen, who maintains that *Eureka* was especially important to the symbolists because of its "two principal themes: the value of intuition for scientific discovery, and the affinity between consciousness and the cosmos" (223). Virtanen discusses the allusions made to *Eureka* by such writers as Claudel, Mallarmé, and Valéry, among others. Valéry's "On Poe's *Eureka*" (1921, trans. 1927) praises Poe's essay into science and theology, concluding that "Poe has extended the application both of the nebular hypothesis and the law of gravity. On these mathematical foundations he has built an abstract poem, one of the rare modern examples of a . . . *cosmogony*. . . . one of the oldest of all literary forms" (*REAP,* 110).

Valéry expresses his debt to Poe for sparking a rejuvenation of his despairing intellectual enterprise:

My studies under my dull and woebegone professors had led me to believe that science is not love; that its fruits are perhaps useful, but its foliage very spiny and its bark terribly rough. . . . Literature, on the other hand, had often shocked me by its lack of discipline, connexion [*sic*] and necessity in handling ideas. Frequently its object is trifling. . . . Perhaps our feeling for the separation of literary genres—in other words, for the independence of the different movements of the mind—is such that we can suffer nothing which combines them. (*REAP*, 104)

Eureka released Valéry from this oppressive demarcation by openly embracing "different movements of mind" and showing him "the passionate interest" (*REAP*, 105) scientists had for their work. *Eureka*'s effect on Valéry was significant. Lois Vines argues that Valéry "discovered [in *Eureka*] an intellectual drama unparalleled in anything he had ever read. He was captivated by the idea that a certain truth of coherence could be discovered through poetic imagination coupled with scientific reasoning" (161).

Vines also notes that Valéry translated Einstein's work and observed that both Poe and Einstein argue for " 'the symmetrical and reciprocal relationship of matter, time, space, gravity, and light. I emphasize the word symmetrical, [continues Valéry] for the *essential characteristic of Einstein's universe is, in fact, its formal symmetry*. Therein lies its beauty' " (165). In discussing the scientific principles of *Eureka*, Valéry observes that "in matter an eternal fever rages. . . . Everything is stirred by deeper and deeper agitations, rotations, exchanges, radiations" (*REAP*, 107).

POE'S METHODOLOGY

"Infinity" and "Limited Space"

The foregoing description of matter can describe, as well, the overall design of *Eureka*. Movement informs its presentation and determines both the content and the persuasiveness of the main argument. Although the narrator asserts that "distinctness—intelligibility, at all points, is a primary feature of my general design. . . . [and that] all [subjects] are alike, in facility of comprehension, to him who approaches them by properly graduated steps" (Poe, 22), he leaves out many of these steps in his subsequent argument and begins quite contentiously with the statement: "Let us begin, then, at once, with that merest of words—'Infinity' " (Poe, 22–23).

This immediately sets up a conundrum. The narrator first questions the ability of the word *infinity* to represent the phenomena, concluding that the word "is by no means an expression of an idea—but an effort at one" (Poe, 23). He also modifies the word as "that merest of words," here playing with the definitions of *mere* as both "nothing more or other than" and "pure, unqualified, absolute"—that is, both of little consequence and of absolute consequence. He then proceeds to entangle the reader in a discussion of why this word, *infinity,* is the only one associated with the concept of "space," concluding that the trouble with entertaining the notion of limited space lies directly in man's limited ability to distinguish between "difficulty" and "impossibility": "The quibble lies concealed in the word 'difficulty' " (Poe, 23).

What Poe ultimately posits is such a ''limited space,'' but, rather than simply asserting this proposition and laying out a logical, step-by-step argument, his narrator turns the direction of his discussion around the dilemma of declaring ''a First Cause'' (Poe, 25), culminating in the assertion that ''my purpose is but to show the folly of endeavoring to prove Infinity itself, or even our conception of it, by any such blundering ratiocination as that which is ordinarily employed'' (Poe, 25). This conclusion leads to a cutting disregard for those who ''by dint of the jargon they emit . . . [have acquired] a kind of cuttle-fish reputation for profundity'' (Poe, 27).

Intuition: "Seemingly Intuitive Leaps"

A similar disregard, in this instance for Baconianism, comes directly before the dissertation on infinity and is found in the ''somewhat remarkable letter'' (Poe, 10) dated 2848, which interrupts the narrator's ''legitimate thesis'' (Poe, 21). The writer of the epistle laments the restrictions to thought imposed by the ''pompous and infatuate proscription of all *other* roads to Truth than the two narrow and crooked paths—the one of creeping and the other of crawling'' (Poe, 18) (i.e., induction and deduction), concluding that ''you can easily understand how restrictions so absurd on their very face must have operated, in those days, to retard the progress of true Science, which makes its most important advances—as all History will show—by seemingly intuitive *leaps*'' (Poe, 12). Not only does the letter confirm the narrator's disdain for ''merely scientific men,'' but it corroborates two of the narrator's beliefs: the first, in the intuition as the most valid method of understanding and the second, in consistency as the most reliable method of ascertaining truth.

The letter-writer rejoices in ''how rapid our progress since the late announcement of [the following] proposition'' (Poe, 18), namely, that ''*a perfect consistency can be nothing but an absolute truth*'' (Poe, 18). This idea is implied numerous times by the narrator of *Eureka,* who also suggests a corollary: ''Truth and Immutability are one'' (Poe, 66). An even closer connection can be found in the definitions of the intuition found in the letter and in the text. The letter-writer notes that what Kepler ''called 'intuition' was but the conviction resulting from *de*ductions or *in*ductions of which the processes were so shadowy as to have escaped his consciousness, eluded his reason, or bidden defiance to his capacity of expression'' (Poe, 20), while the narrator defines the intuition as ''*the conviction arising from those inductions or deductions of which the processes are so shadowy as to escape our consciousness, elude our reason, or defy our capacity of expression*'' (Poe, 29).

In addition, the narrator goes on to suggest that in asking *what* God created ''at some point of Space which we will take as a centre—at some period into which we do not pretend to inquire, but at all events immensely remote'' (Poe, 29), we come to ''a point where only *Intuition* can aid us'' (Poe, 29). The conclusion, ''Matter in its utmost conceivable state of—what?—of Simplicity''

(29), becomes the "primary proposition" (Poe, 29) of *Eureka,* an assumption reached by "the processes [that] lie out of the human analysis—at all events are beyond the utterance of the human tongue" (Poe, 30)—that is, by intuition.

The Semantic Problem and Poe's Art of Persuasion

"Seemingly intuitive leaps" (Poe, 12) abound in *Eureka,* manifest in the frequent convolutions, disruptions, dashes, and repetitions, making *Eureka* particularly attractive to deconstructive, structuralist, and poststructuralist critics. Such critics would argue that the inaccessibility of *Eureka*'s design is purposeful despite Poe's assertion that "abstruseness is a quality appertaining to no subject *per se*" (Poe, 22). The inadequacy of language is not only implied but openly asserted, argues Cynthia Miecznikowski—"Poe's repeated observation of the tendency of language to distort and to mystify points to the ultimate impotence of all signification" (59). She bases her comparison of *Pym* and *Eureka* on this premise, suggesting that "*Eureka* may be viewed as a kind of apologia for *Pym* to the extent that the 'poetical' treatise is an attempt to explain why language sometimes 'works' and sometimes doesn't" (56). Michael Williams also discusses the quandary of language for Poe. "*Eureka* asserts that human existence is irreducibly inscrutable, and that language both allows us what we know of the world and paradoxically displaces us from it—inaugurating a desire that it necessarily frustrates (151).

Although the effort to present the breath of the universe—"the *Physical, Metaphysical and Mathematical—of the Material and Spiritual Universe:—of its Essence, its Origin, its Creation, its Present Condition and its Destiny*" (Poe, 7)—may appear to be confined by the limits of language, the involuted and fractal-like design of *Eureka* overrides this constriction as it "rages" (to use Valéry's terms) with "deeper and deeper agitations and radiations," effectively mesmerizing the listener/reader with an involution of "facts." As the narrator openly admits: "I *prove* nothing. So be it:—I design but to suggest—and to *convince* through suggestion" (Poe, 45).

The Poe Log notes the following: a response from Maunsell Field—" 'he kept us *entranced* for two and a half hours' (720), from *The Morning Express,* February 4, 1848—'the audience had listened with *enchained* attention throughout' (721), from *The Weekly Universe,* February 6, 1848—'Mr. Poe *fastened* the attention of his audience' " (722), and from *The Morning Express,* February 9, 1848—

"I have admired the collection of tales published by Mr. Poe, some time since, ('The Gold Bug and Other Tales'), in which you may recollect, occurs a conversation with a dying man while in a state of magnetic trance. In that conversation, very much the same ideas may be found, respecting 'the universe,' which Mr. Poe has reproduced in this lecture. . . . One cannot fail to be extremely interested, in what is there said, *as well as by the manner in which it is said.*" (722; emphasis mine)

Van Nostrand makes the connection between "Mesmeric Revelation" and *Eureka:* In "Mesmeric Revelation," Poe "worked out the essentials of the ontology that *Eureka* defines." " 'Mesmeric Revelation' provides for individuality abiding; it preserves the mystery of God. But *Eureka* annihilates individuality, as it annihilates the personality of God . . . [*Eureka* is] an encyclopedic rationalization of a continuing, unseparated cosmos" (224–26).

These responses and connections to "Mesmeric Revelation" corroborate the possibility that Poe's strategy was not to convince rationally but to mesmerize an audience with an avalanche of scientific information spun circuitously through principles that overwhelm the reader into acceptance and belief. The narrator tells us early in the text that "whatever the mathematicians may assert, there is, in this world at least, *no such thing* as demonstration" (Poe, 8); nevertheless, the text appears to "demonstrate." These "demonstrations," however, accomplish obfuscation, confusion, and deliberate frenzy instead of clarity. The reader is given detail after detail regarding such problems as, for example, stellar size and distance while raising questions of whether or not parallax exists:

The fact is, that, in regard to the distance of the fixed stars—of any one of the myriads of suns glistening on the farther side of that awful chasm which separates our system from its brothers in the cluster to which it belongs . . . we [have] perceived, for example, that Alpha Lyrae cannot be nearer to us than 19 trillions, 200 billions of miles; but for all we knew, and indeed for all we now know, it may be distant from us the square, or the cube, or any other power of the number mentioned. . . . the star numbered 61 in the constellation of the Swan . . . is 670,000 times that of the Sun; which last it will be remembered, is 95 millions of miles. The star 61 Cygni, then, is nearly 64 trillions of miles from us—or more than three times the distance assigned, *as the least possible,* for Alpha Lyrae. (Poe, 115)

This example and the many others involved in this "sequence" of "proofs" are meant to convince the reader, finally, that *"Space and Duration are one"* (Poe, 117).

These calculations, like the accumulations of other detailed scientific information, lead a reader to tire of trying to apply rational synthesis; things just don't add up in *Eureka*. Given more and more input without a cumulative design, the reader is effectively dazzled into a passivity that allows suspension into a trancelike state. Poe does use "proofs," but not to demonstrate. He uses them to bring about a desired effect, that is, to whirl the reader/listener into a trancelike state with words, to cause "a mental gyration on the heel" (Poe, 9).

Argument by Analogy and Involution

Susan Welsh's 1991 essay "The Value of Analogical Evidence: Poe's *Eureka* in the Context of a Scientific Debate" offers another way to perceive textual movement—by analogy. Analogy, Welsh argues, provides Poe with the rhetorical means to demonstrate "the absolute reciprocity of nature's laws. . . . [by] narrat[ing] in a compositional form that would enact [such] reciprocity" (9).

Welsh quotes Poe: " 'The philosophical mind will easily comprehend . . . that this advance is inversely proportional with the squares of the distances of all created things from the starting-point and goal of their creation' " (12). She explains that this description of the advance of the universe readily applies not only to the design of *Eureka* but to the manner in which it can be best understood: "[A]nalogies based in the inverse-square law of gravity ripple through Poe's nebular design to unify and graduate, by repetition of a dynamic principle, our perception of larger and larger fields of spirit and matter . . . [extending] the effort to conceptualize" (12). Conceptualizing through analogical movement allows "vision into principles [that] corrects the provincialism of sense perception" (13).

Welsh's essay reviews the use of analogy in the scientific writing of the 1830s and 1840s (Alexander von Humboldt, William Wells, John Nichol, Robert Chambers, William Whewell) and places *Eureka*'s design within this context. Her focus is not on the scientific content of *Eureka* as it relates to either Poe's "anticipation" of Eddington's and Einstein's discoveries or as it synthesizes contemporary nebular theories or as it capitalizes on the growing prestige of science in American letters, although she does focus on Poe's fascination with "the absolute reciprocity of nature's laws" (9). Yet, even this focus on scientific content is applied to Poe's concern for rhetorical presentation; Welsh maintains that Poe's "somewhat impertinent" (Poe, 16) letter-writer "argues against formal rhetoric of the academy—both the old syllogistically based rhetoric and the new inductively based rhetoric" (Welsh, 10), noting that it limits perception. She argues that Poe uses an analogical method to "protect the 'impression' of absolute reciprocity from the kinds of limitation and dilution imposed by rules of thought and exposition" (10). Noting Poe's dedication to Alexander von Humboldt and his admiration of his *Cosmos,* Welsh suggests that von Humboldt's approach comes closest to providing a new prospect, a new way of perceiving the universe, even though his method "precludes 'all individuality of impression' " (11).

Cantalupo argues in " 'Of or Pertaining to a Higher Power': Involution in *Eureka*" that Poe's deference to von Humboldt comes not from admiration for his attempt to provide a "new prospect" but from the suggestion Poe derives from the excessive detail of *Cosmos.*

While [Poe] dedicates his work to von Humboldt "With Very Profound Respect" and grants him credit for producing the "nearest approach" to describing the universe in such a way "as to warrant deduction from its individuality," at the same time, he criticizes von Humboldt's work for its excessive detail. This contradiction, however, can be read as a way of deferring to von Humboldt for providing the method Poe would use to gain his desired effect of creating, in language, "a revolution of all things about a central point of sight." Precisely what he criticizes in von Humboldt's work, the "involution of idea,'' is what Poe uses to produce for his reader ''a mental gyration on the heel,'' which will enable the reader to see what has not been seen before. (82)

The movement in Poe's essay, then, could be perceived as repetitive involutions. Here the definition of involution would be understood in its mathematical sense, that is, ''of or pertaining to a higher power'' (Webster) rather than its more general definition of complexity or intricacy: ''in algebra, raising of a quantity from its root to any power assigned. Thus $2 \times 2 \times 2 = 8$. Here 8, the third power of 2, is found by involution, or by multiplying the number into itself, and the product by the same number.''

THE SCIENCE OF *EUREKA*

Clearly, *Eureka* engages scientific theories and directly refers to the ideas of von Humboldt, Laplace, Kepler, Herschel, Mädler, and Newton, among other natural philosophers and scientists. Yet, Poe's presentation of these ideas blatantly defies the principles of the scientific method again and again, as seen here:

These ideas—conceptions such as *these*—unthoughtlike thoughts—soul-reveries rather than conclusions or even considerations of the intellect:—ideas, I repeat, such as these, are such as we can alone hope profitably to entertain in any effort at grasping the great principle, *Attraction*. (Poe, 42–43)

Critics like Harriet Holman (1972) conclude that Poe's ''science'' is suspect since his method deviates dramatically from the rational, empirical model of scientific investigation. Campbell's overview of Bruce Franklin's (1978) conclusion that ''the value of *Eureka* does not reside in its scientific accuracy'' (Campbell, 257) suggests that *what Eureka* had to say is compromised by *how* Poe's narrator presents these scientific conclusions.

Nevertheless, others like George Nordstedt (1930), Frederick Conner (1949), Curtis Brooks (1975), Marshall Walker (1985) and Edward Harrison (1987) acknowledge *Eureka*'s scientific truths despite the fact that they are not expressed in the language and method used in scientific discourse. To suggest that *Eureka*'s science is merely a mask is to overlook Poe's elaborate manipulation of science and his intense engagements with its ideas. Marshall Walker, professor of physics and the history of science at the University of Connecticut, observes that Poe's text does not present a cosmological model that is ''quantitative, secular and expressed in mathematical language'' (2). But, like Harrison, Walker credits Poe for ideas that ''are similar to some of the ideas in the modern [cosmological] model'' (2), ideas that were circulating in the existing literature of physics and astronomy. But no new scientific idea evolves from Poe's text:

The literature of commentary on *Eureka* illustrates the gulf between the literary and scientific cultures. Commentators who have studied science say that *Eureka* is an interesting synthesis but contains no new ideas and in no way anticipates later scientific knowledge. Commentators without adequate scientific training tend to regard *Eureka* as highly original and a precursor of later science. One such commentator, presumably because Poe speaks of a spherical universe, says that Poe anticipated some of the ideas of Einstein's General Theory of Relativity. (Walker, 6)

Here Walker may be referring to Nordstedt's "Poe and Einstein" (1930), which makes connections between ideas held by Poe and Einstein regarding (1) "the limited extent and . . . [the] closed spherical shape" (Nordstedt, 177) of the universe, (2) the inability to perceive these other universes because "light itself must eventually return to its starting point or source" (178) so that each universe is "optically isolated" (178), and (3) the concept that " 'there is no space without matter or energy' " (178). What Walker asserts regarding *Eureka* as a collation of existing theories rather than an anticipation of twentieth-century scientific principles may be true, but Nordstedt's suggestion that the method Poe expounds in *Eureka* is equally praised by Einstein cannot be denied. "Einstein has the same view of intuition as Poe" (Nordstedt, 176). Nordstedt then quotes Einstein:

"All great achievements of science," says Einstein, "start from intuitive knowledge, namely, in axioms, from which deductions then are made. It is possible to arrive at such axioms only if we gain a true survey of thought-complexes that are not yet logically ordered; so that, in general, intuition is the necessary condition of the discovering of such axioms. And it cannot be denied that, in the great majority of minds with a mathematical tendency, this intuition exhibits itself as a characteristic of their creative power." (Nordstedt, 176)

The process of intellectual discovery validated in *Eureka* reflects the narrator's praise for Laplace's "almost miraculous mathematical instinct" (Poe, 93). "In the case of the Nebular Cosmogony, [the narrator asserts] it led him, blindfolded, through a labyrinth of Error, into one of the most luminous and stupendous temples of Truth" (Poe, 93).

Literary Critics on Science in *Eureka*

Although *Eureka* explicates Laplace's science, as it does that of Newton and others, Harriet Holman argues against engaging these explanations of science as science. She contends, rather, that Poe uses Laplace to attack the influence of the "Frogpondians" and to reinforce his overall satirical aim. "Poe's usual satiric technique would have called, therefore, for denigrating the real scientist Laplace and praising the false scientist Epicurus" (33). She comes to this conclusion by focusing on a particular point in *Eureka* when the narrator suggests that Laplace's "original idea seems to have been a compound of the true Epicurean atoms with the false nebulae of his contemporaries'' (Poe, 92). She argues that Poe's ''undercurrent'' meaning depends on the science of Epicurus, which ''taught that atoms attracted to each other in space'' (Holman, 35), rather than on Laplace's that ''asserted almost the antithesis'' (33). The tenets of Epicurean science that Holman delineates help unravel ''a complicated conceit'' (35) that Poe uses, she argues, to undermine and attack the transcendentalists, who, lost in the ''mist of delusion'' (37), thought themselves the ''beginning of a new, superior literary center'' (37).

Holman's use of Poe's ''science'' moves entirely away, engaging a literal understanding of its scientific principles,[8] and reinforces her dismissal of critics and scientists who would ''help ascertain what Poe could have been expected to know in the 1840's and, more important, to what extent he was able to foresee new concepts of twentieth-century physics'' (33). These ''findings [Holman argues] are disappointingly general, too cautious to be of specific value'' (33). Yet, cosmologist Edward Harrison points to a specific idea that was scientifically proven by Olbers twenty-five years after *Eureka*'s publication. Harrison contends that *Eureka* ''contains the first anticipation of a formally correct solution'' (148) to the ''riddle of darkness'' (148). He then quotes from *Eureka:*

Were the succession of stars endless, then the background of the sky would present us an uniform luminosity, like that displayed by the Galaxy—since there could be absolutely no point, in all that background, at which would not exist a star. The only mode, therefore, in which, under such a state of affairs, we could comprehend the voids which our telescopes find in innumerable directions, would be by supposing the distance of the invisible background so immense that no ray from it has yet been able to reach us at all. (Harrison, 148)

Susan Manning would disagree with Holman's contention that *Eureka* is, first and foremost, a satire because, Manning argues, *Eureka* ''is not sufficiently directed away from itself to be satirical, and if Poe with his usual ventriloquistic virtuosity has recreated the stance of experimental science, it is as pastiche which has absorbed the idiom rather than satire which exposes it'' (141). Ketterer, too, disagrees with Holman's assertion that *Eureka* satirizes Empedocles' cosmology. He maintains that the image of ''the figure spinning on his heel atop Mt. Aetna'' (1985, 225) does not suggest, as Holman would, ''the absurdity of this inflated image'' or its reference to ''the range of volcanic mountains to which it belongs, the Rossi Mountains'' (Holman 1972, 35), but is ''the fire and earth equivalent of Poe's maelström—it represents a unity associated with death'' (Ketterer, 225). Holman, however, held that ''through Aetna Poe the puzzlemaker and cryptographer could imply his [Rosse's] name thus first among all the men named in *Eureka*. For without Lord Rosse's telescope there would have been no belittling explanation to unriddle the nebulae, no point to his grand synthesis of erroneous science and discredited philosophy'' (Holman 1972, 35).

Rather than state the obvious—that *Eureka* is filled with scientific details and theories, that Poe's own summaries of the text emphasize its astronomical and theological principles—John Limon investigates the ways Poe's career "begins in a flight from science that puts him directly on the path to science" (Limon 1990, 96). Limon's connections between Poe's *Eureka* and the *Naturphilosophie* and chemistry of his time[9] emphasize Poe's need to challenge "the grandeur of science" (Limon 1990, 71) and its intellectual command. "To avoid science, Poe finally has to write it" (96), concludes Limon.

Limon uses "The Man of the Crowd" and "A Descent into the Maelström" to show that Poe depicts the "benefits" of the scientific method, the former proclaiming the value of aloof classification, even though "classification gives way to identification . . . [leading to] self-destruction and bewilderment," while the latter affirms "the protective power of close observation and empirical generalization" (79), although it "keeps one on surfaces, which is all to the good if one is trying not to sink"—a limited desire, at best. The culmination of this "use" of science occurs when Poe proclaims in *Eureka* that "God in Nature is himself." With this, Limon argues, Poe contends that "not only will the horror be replaced completely by the ecstasy of annihilation, but a new methodology along with a new cosmology will be allowed to defeat Bacon at long last" (81). "By the end of his career, Poe has designed as his saving disciplinary strategy the elaborate co-optation of a science more successful in turning the universe into verse than verse itself" (82).

EUREKA AS A POETIC VISION

Whether through involution or analogy, *Eureka*'s design disrupts the "rules of thought and exposition" (Welsh, 13). Welsh argues that this disruption "help[s] us to reformulate and reconceive sensory experience" (13). She quotes Poe's suggestion that "we all possess an analogical 'instinct,' says Poe, and it can either bind or free the imagination" (13). Poe sees *Eureka* as the culmination of his creative efforts, as evidence of his ultimate imaginative flight; "I could accomplish nothing more" (Ostrom, 452), he writes to Maria Clemm. *Eureka* is meant to startle us into a new sense of ourselves and our universe. As Eric Carlson argues in "Poe's Vision of Man," "a close reading of *Eureka*, the colloquies, and a few other statements of Poe's philosophic perspective will reveal . . . the quest for rebirth of mind and soul" (7). "The central theme in Poe's work, then, is not so much death and annihilation, as the spiritual rebirth or rediscovery of the lost psychal power essential to every man and artist seeking his fullest self-realization" (7, 20).

Eureka may be the manifestation of what Poe considered the writer's most challenging task: to harness the novel impressions that come during that "point of blending between wakefulness and sleep" (*H* 16, 90). 'Marginalia" # 150 continues:

[E]ven a partial record of the impressions would startle the universal intellect of mankind, by *the supremeness of the novelty* of the material employed, and of its consequent suggestions. In a word—should I ever write a paper on this topic, the world will be compelled to acknowledge that, at last, I have done an original thing. (See Introduction to this volume, p. 13.)

This stated goal is Poe's poetic charge. Richard Wilbur outlines this charge:

[I]n [the poet] alone, of all the inhabitants of Earth, the divine spark of imagination still burns brightly; his soul alone vaguely remembers, from a previous existence, a divine harmony and beauty, and yearns to return thither. Yet everything around him conspires to reduce him to its own degraded level. . . . [but] in the immaterial regions of dream, he can purge himself of all earthly taint, and deliver himself to visions of that heavenly beauty which is the thought of God. (374)

Wilbur argues that the concluding paragraphs of *Eureka* demonstrate this clearly and concludes that "all of Poe's fiction is in some measure based on this myth of the soul" (474).

Joan Dayan suggests the opposite in "*Eureka:* 'A New World of Philosophy' " when she argues that "Poe believes in the limitations of our mind, and he proves this belief [in *Eureka*] by luring us with concord and giving us chaos" (27). She goes on to suggest that "when he calls upon our 'fairy guide, Imagination,' we can be sure he is getting ready to tax us with even greater confusion, thrusting us into a place where 'Imagination' cannot help us and must become one of those *mere* words" (28). Dayan's overall assessment of *Eureka* depends on three underlying concepts: Poe's use of fiction "to question and allegorize epistemology" (28), his presentation of that fiction from "a new, and as yet unknown angle of vision. . . . that depends upon vacillation" (30), and his "search for a new kind of language (in the guise of a quest for cosmic truth)" (58). She particularizes these concepts through an analysis of Poe's use of the dash. "The dash—Poe's most aggressive device. . . . turns our attention away from words to the space in-between" (55). "Poe favors the dash whose particular and often playful application, conveys the vicissitudes of form" (56). She argues that the dash functions as a constant reminder of a position that both *Eureka*'s narrator and his "impertinent" epistle-writer hold, that is, that " 'clear and distinct' discourse" (59) does not effectively reflect or promote discovery. Earlier, Halliburton noted Poe's excessive use of the dash in *Eureka:* "The italics, the dashes, and the repetitions all suggest a mind bearing down with all the force of its volition, and, at the same time, a peculiarly insistent voice" (407). He goes on to quote Poe's conclusion that "the dash *cannot* be dispensed with" (408) because "it stands, [Poe argues] in general, for these words—'*or, to make my meaning more distinct.*' This force *it has*—and this force no other point can have" (407).

EUREKA AS ORGANIC PANTHEISM

James Campbell's survey of criticism of *Eureka*'s theology from 1973 to 1988 shows that modern critics[10] have been absorbed by "its representation of the apocalypse'' (287), while his assessment of nineteenth-century critics[11] indicates that they were concerned with *Eureka*'s pantheism and/or with comparing its spiritual implications to Emerson's transcendentalism.

Having identified numerous contradictions in Poe's logic, Frederick Conner (1949) concludes that ''a close and literal reading of *Eureka* leads us . . . [to the conclusion that] instead of sinking the world in God, like the transcendentalists, [Poe] sank God in the world'' (90). Patrick Quinn compares Emerson's *Nature* to *Eureka*, noting the various similarities to Emerson's essay but concluding that *Eureka*, unlike *Nature*, communicates ''a feeling of the incommensurate relation between man and the universe. . . . Poe was seized by . . . the thought of dissolution'' (6).

Unlike Patrick Quinn's perception of *Eureka*'s overall obsession with dissolution, Richard Wilbur had argued earlier that implicit in Poe's theory of the universe is his belief in the possibility of overcoming dissolution through the creative act.

The universe, as Poe conceived it, is a poetic or artistic creation, a ''plot of God.'' It has come about through God's breaking-up of His original unity, and His self-radiation into space. . . . Since ''the source of all motion is thought,'' it must be intellectual or spiritual in character. And since the creation is a work of art, the counter-impulse which can reunify it must be imaginative. In short, the duty of God's creatures is to think God together again by discovering, through the fusing power of poetic imagination, the primal unity in the present diversity. (Wilbur, 48)

Most recent criticism of *Eureka* has agreed with Wilbur in its emphasis on the theme of Unity in an organic conception of the universe that Poe derived from von Humboldt, Laplace, Leibniz, and Newton. In Silverman's words, these scientists pointed Poe past the cosmic thanatos of ''Ulalume'' ''to a new and ultimate theory of deathlessness,'' a theory of

an infinitude of pulsating universes. . . . After the original diffusion, every atom of every body attracts every other atom, . . . the fragments seeking reunion with each other, and with their creator. . . . Dissolved in its own embraces, the universe springs to life again, an eternal revenant eternally returning to fullness from Material Nihility. (339–340)

This complex interaction of the systemic forces of gravity and diffusion is controlled by the laws of *equality, reciprocity,* and *adaptation* within the vast rhythmic pulsations of the organic entity called the Universe moving toward its destined return to primordial Unity. This unity is clearly stated in the conclusion of *Eureka:*

Guiding our imaginations by that omniprevalent law of laws, the law of periodicity, are we not, indeed, more than justified in entertaining a belief—let us say, rather, in indulging a hope—that the processes we have here ventured to contemplate will be renewed for-

ever, and forever, and forever; *a novel Universe* swelling into existence, and then subsiding into nothingness, at every throb of the Heart Divine?
And now—this Heart Divine—what is it? *It is our own.* (Poe, 139)

This metaphor of the universe as a "Heart Divine" throbbing in and out of existence is suggestive of a comprehensive dynamic vascular system not unlike the conception of the Earth as Gaia and the Universe as a vast organismic creation similar to that conceived by Emerson, Whitman, Whitehead, Dewey, de Chardin, and modern ecologists and astrophysicists.[12]

Poe's narrator acknowledges that his conclusion could be construed as irreverent or as too fearful to contemplate, yet he insists on the truth of this proclamation: that the "Heart Divine" is "our own." His long cosmogony ends with the assertion that "the sense of individual identity will be gradually merged in the general consciousness—that Man, for example, ceasing imperceptibly to feel himself Man, will at length attain that awfully triumphant epoch when he shall recognize his existence as that of Jehovah" (Poe, 143). This conclusion allows joy: "What you call The Universe is but [the Divine Being's] present expansive existence. . . . In this view alone the existence of Evil becomes intelligible; but in this view it becomes more—it becomes endurable. . . . bear in mind that all is Life—Life—Life within Life—the less within the greater, and all within the Spirit Divine" (Poe, 143). As Manning suggests, a "ponderous solemnity" is certainly required of those who "hope to attain the presence of this, the most sublime of truths, and look it leisurely in the face" (Poe, 140).

NOTES

1. Silverman points out that, a week prior to Poe's lecture, Dr. John Nichol, an astronomy professor from the University of Glasgow and author of the popular *Views of the Architecture of the Heavens* (1837), had begun a series of lectures on astronomy at the New York Mercantile Library, which were "heavily attended and widely praised as eloquent and masterful. The *New York Tribune* carried only a brief account of Poe's talk but printed Nichol's lectures entire over several issues, on the front page" (532).

2. See pages 609–11 in Hervey Allen's *Israfel* for a description of Poe's formal and informal lectures of *Eureka*.

3. As David Ketterer reiterates, in offering "*Eureka* as a 'Book of Truths' on account of 'the Beauty that abounds in its Truth' and 'as a Romance; or if I be urging too lofty a claim, as a Poem,' the dichotomies of reason and imagination, truth and beauty thus [are] reconciled" (1975, 47). Frederick Conner (1949) notes, "In *Eureka*, however, though it was published and apparently written before 'The Poetic Principle,' this distinction [between truth and beauty] was dispensed with and the equivalence of beauty and truth proclaimed without reservation" (81).

4. Two examples: (1) "It is not to any *point* that the atoms are allied. It is not any *locality*, either in the concrete or in the abstract, to which I suppose them bound. Nothing like *location* was conceived as their origin. Their source lies in the principle, *Unity*. *This is their lost parent* [emphasis mine]. This they seek always—immediately—in all direc-

tions—wherever it is even partially to be found" (Poe 1975, 44); (2) "[B]y the time the electric influence (Repulsion) has prepared the surface for rejection, we are to understand that the gravitating influence (Attraction) is precisely ready to reject it. Here, then, as everywhere, *the Body and the Soul walk hand in hand*" (Poe, 82).

5. See Burton Pollin's "Contemporary Reviews of *Eureka:* A Checklist" and James Campbell's 1991 dissertation, *"The Heart Divine": A study of the Critical Response to Poe's "Eureka."*

6. See Campbell's dissertation for explanation of Stringham's role in the writing of George Woodberry's 1885 biography of Poe.

7. Note, for example, A. R. Wallace's response: "a remarkable work, very original, and with some beautiful and suggestive ideas, but a large part of it very prolix, laboured, and unsatisfactory. . . . his acceptance of Laplace's Nebula hypothesis, without at all seeing its difficulties or limitations is curious" (8).

8. Limon argues, similarly, in his 1983 article in *North Dakota Quarterly,* that intellectual historian Michel Serres would also remove the "science" from science when he makes "Turner honorary co-discoverer of statistical thermodynamics" (32): " 'The boiler's fire atomizes matter and gives it over to chance, which has always been its master. Boltzmann will soon understand it but Turner, in his own domain, understood it before him' " (32).

9. See Limon's analysis on pages 84–85 of *The Place of Fiction in the Time of Science.*

10. Campbell cites Perry Holberg, "Poe: Trickster-Cosmologist," *Poe as Literary Cosmologer,* ed. Richard Benton (Hartford: Transcendental, 1975); Lawrence Stahlberg, " 'And the will therein lieth, which dieth not': A Reconsideration of Ligeia's 'Gigantic Volition,' " *ATQ* 43 (Summer 1979): 199–209; Martha Banta, "American Apocalypses: Excrement and Ennui," *Studies in the Literary Imagination* 7 (Spring 1974): 1–30; David Lyttle, *Studies in Religion in Early American Literature: Edwards, Poe, Channing, Emerson, Some Minor Transcendentalists, Hawthorne, and Thoreau* (Lanham, Md.: UP of America, 1983), 33–59; Douglas Robinson, *American Apocalypses: The Image of the End of the World in American Literature* (Baltimore: Johns Hopkins UP, 1985); Edward Pitcher, "Beyond 'Gothic Flummery': A Cosmoramic View of Poe's Symbolism and Ideas," *Sphinx* 4 (1985): 241–49; Harold Bloom, *Modern Critical Views: Edgar Allan Poe* (New York: Chelsea House, 1985), 3–9; John T. Irwin, "The White Shadow," *Modern Critical Views: Edgar Allan Poe,* ed. Harold Bloom (New York: Chelsea House, 1985); and Joan Dayan, *Fables of Mind,* 19–79.

11. See Campbell, 128–54.

12. These observations come from Eric Carlson in a letter dated November 24, 1994.

WORKS CITED

Allen, Hervey. *Israfel: The Life and Times of Edgar Allan Poe.* New York: Farrar and Rinehart, 1934, 590–93, 607–9.

Beebe, Maurice. "The Universe of Roderick Usher." *Poe: A Collection of Critical Essays.* Ed. Robert Regan. Englewood Cliffs, N. J.: Prentice-Hall, 1967, 121–33.

Benton, Richard P. "Bibliographic Guide." *Poe as Literary Cosmologer: Studies on Eureka: A Symposium.* Ed. Richard P. Benton. Hartford: Transcendental Books, Drawer 1080, 1975, ii–6.

————. "Cross-Lights on Poe's *Eureka*." *Poe as Literary Cosmologer: Studies on Eureka: A Symposium*, i–ii.

Brooks, Curtis M. "The Cosmic God: Science and the Creative Imagination in *Eureka*." *Poe as Literary Cosmologer: Studies on Eureka: A Symposium*. Ed. Richard P. Benton, 60–68.

Campbell, James. " 'The Heart Divine': A Study of the Critical Response to Poe's *Eureka*." *DAI* 52 (Aug. 1991), 537A.

Cantalupo, Barbara. " 'Of or Pertaining to a Higher Power': Involution in *Eureka*." *ATQ* 4, no. 2 (June 1990): 81–90.

Carlson, Eric W., ed. *Critical Essays on Edgar Allan Poe*. Boston: G. K. Hall, 1987, 1–34.

————. "Poe's Vision of Man." *Papers on Poe*. Ed. Richard P. Veler. Springfield, Ohio: Chantry, 1972, 7–20.

————. *The Recognition of Edgar Allan Poe: Selected Criticism since 1829*. Ann Arbor: U of Michigan P, 1966, 103–10.

Conner, Frederick William. "Poe and John Nichol: Notes on a Source of *Eureka*." *All These to Teach: Essays in Honor of C. A. Robertson*. Ed. Robert A. Bryan. Gainesville: U of Florida P, 1965.

————. "Poe's *Eureka:* The Problem of Mechanism." *Cosmic Optimism: A Study of the Interpretation of Evolution by American Poets from Emerson to Robinson*. Gainesville: U of Florida P, 1949, 67–91.

Davidson, Edward H. *Poe: A Critical Study*. Cambridge: Harvard UP, 1957, 223–60.

Dayan, Joan. "*Eureka:* 'A New World of Philosophy.' " *Fables of Mind: An Inquiry into Poe's Fiction*. New York: Oxford UP, 1987, 19–79.

Dwight, Thomas, and David K. Jackson. *The Poe Log: A Documentary Life of Edgar Allan Poe, 1809–1849*. Boston: G. K. Hall, 1987.

Franklin, H. Bruce. *Future Perfect: American Science Fiction of the Nineteenth Century*. London: Oxford UP, 1978.

Golding, Alan. "Reductive and Expansive Language: Semantic Strategies in *Eureka*." *PoeS* 11, no. 1 (June 1978): 1–5.

Halliburton, David. *Edgar Allan Poe: A Phenomenological View*. Princeton: Princeton UP, 1973, 392–412.

Halline, Allan G. "Moral and Religious Concepts in Poe." *Bucknell University Studies* 2 (Jan. 1951): 126–50.

Harrison, Edward. "The Golden Walls of Edgar Allan Poe." *Darkness at Night*. Cambridge: Harvard UP, 1987, 146–50.

Hoagland, Clayton. "The Universe of *Eureka:* A Comparison of the Theories of Eddington and Poe." *SLM* 1 (May 1939): 307–13.

Holman, Harriet R. "Hog, Bacon, Ram and Other 'Savans' in *Eureka:* Notes toward Decoding Poe's Encyclopedic Satire." *Poe Newsletter* 2, no. 3 (Oct. 1969): 49–55.

————. "Splitting Poe's 'Epicurean Atoms': Further Speculation on the Literary Satire of *Eureka*." *PoeS* 5, no. 2 (1972): 33–37.

Ketterer, David. "Empedocles in *Eureka:* Addenda." *PoeS* 18, no. 2 (Dec. 1985): 24–25.

————. "Protective Irony and 'The Full Design' of *Eureka*." *Poe as Literary Cosmologer: Studies on Eureka: A Symposium*. Ed. Richard P. Benton, 46–55.

Limon, John. "How to Place Poe's *Arthur Gordon Pym* in Science-Dominated Intellectual History, and How to Extract It Again.'' *North Dakota Quarterly* 51, no. 1 (Winter 1983): 31–47.

———. *The Place of Fiction in the Time of Science: A Disciplinary History of American Writing.* Cambridge: Cambridge UP, 1990, 70–120.

McCaslin, Susan. ''Poe's Cosmogonic Poem.'' *Salzburg Studies in English Literature* 87, no. 4 (1981): 3–45.

Maddison, Carol H. ''Poe's *Eureka.''* *Texas Studies in Literature and Language* 2 (Autumn 1960): 350–67.

Manning, Susan. '' 'The plots of God are perfect': Poe's *Eureka* and American Creative Nihilism.'' *Journal of American Studies* 23 (1989): 235–51.

Meyers, Jeffrey. *Edgar Allan Poe.* New York: Scribners, 1992, 213–20.

Miecznikowski, Cynthia. ''End(ings) and Mean(ings) in *Pym* and *Eureka.''* *Studies in Short Fiction* 27, no. 1 (Winter 1990): 55–64.

Nelson, Roland W. ''Apparatus for a Definitive Edition of Poe's *Eureka.''* *Studies in the American Renaissance* (1978): 161–205.

Nordstedt, George. ''Poe and Einstein.'' *Open Court* 44 (Mar. 1930): 173–80.

Pitcher, Edward. ''Poe's *Eureka* as a Prose Poem.'' *ATQ* 29 (1976): 61–71.

Poe, Edgar Allan. ''Addenda to 'Eureka.' '' *Edgar Allan Poe's Works, Vol. 16.* Ed. James A. Harrison. New York: AMS Press, 1965, 336–54.

———. *Eureka: A Prose Poem.* In *Poe as Literary Cosmologer: Studies on Eureka: A Symposium.* Ed. Richard P. Benton. 1975. (Appendix: facsimile of 1st edition, New York: Geo. Putnam's, 1848, 143 pp.) The text cited here as ''Poe.''

———. *The Letters of Edgar Allan Poe, Volume 2.* Ed. John Ward Ostrom. Cambridge: Harvard UP, 1948.

Pollin, Burton. ''Contemporary Reviews of *Eureka:* A Checklist.'' *Poe as Literary Cosmologer: Studies on Eureka: A Symposium.* Ed. Richard P. Benton, 26–30.

Quinn, Arthur Hobson. *Edgar Allan Poe: A Critical Biography.* New York: D. Appleton-Century, 1941, 535–71.

Quinn, Patrick F. ''Poe's *Eureka* and Emerson's *Nature.''* *Emerson Society Quarterly* 31 (Second quarter 1963): 4–7.

Schaefer, Charles. ''Poe's 'Eureka:' The Macrocosmic Analogue.'' *Journal of Aesthetics and Art Criticism* 29 (1971): 353–65.

Scheick, William. ''An Intrinsic Luminosity: Poe's Use of Platonic and Newtonian Optics.'' *Southern Literary Journal* 24, no. 2 (Spring 1992): 90–105.

Silverman, Kenneth. *Edgar A. Poe: "Mournful and Never-Ending Remembrance.''* New York: HarperCollins, 1991, 338–42, 530–33.

Smithline, Arnold. ''*Eureka:* Poe as Transcendentalist.'' *Emerson Society Quarterly* 39, no. 2 (1965): 25–28.

Thompson, G. R. ''Romantic Skepticism.'' *Poe's Fiction: Romantic Irony in the Gothic Tales.* Madison: U of Wisconsin P, 1973, 187–95.

Van Nostrand, A. D. ''The Theories of Adams and Poe.'' *Everyman His Own Poet: American Romantic Gospels.* New York: McGraw-Hill, 1968, 204–27.

Vines, Lois Davis. ''On Poe's *Eureka.''* *Valéry and Poe: A Literary Legacy.* New York: New York UP, 1992, 159–77.

Virtanen, Reino. ''The Irradiations of *Eureka:* Valéry's Reflections on Poe's Cosmology.'' *Tennessee Literary Studies* 7 (1962): 17–25.

———. ''Poe's *Eureka* in France from Baudelaire to Valéry.'' *Kentucky Romance Quarterly* 29, no. 3 (1982): 223–34.

Walker, Marshall. "The *Eureka* Essay of Edgar Allan Poe." Unpublished comments prepared for Eric W. Carlson at the University of Connecticut, 1985.

Wallace, Alfred Russell. *Edgar Allan Poe: A Series of Seventeen Letters concerning Poe's Scientific Erudition in "Eureka" and His Authorship of Leonainie.* New York: Privately printed, n.d., 8–9.

Webster, Daniel. *An American Dictionary of the English Language, 1828.* New York: Johnson Reprint Corp., 1970.

Welsh, Susan. "The Value of Analogical Evidence: Poe's *Eureka* in the Context of a Scientific Debate." *Modern Language Studies* 21, no. 4 (Fall 1991): 3–15.

Wilbur, Richard. *Responses.* New York: Harcourt Brace, 1955, 39–66.

Williams, Michael. *"Eureka: 'fondle the phantom of the idea.' " A World of Words.* Durham: Duke UP, 1988, 146–51.

Part III

POE'S THOUGHT

16

Poe's Materialist Metaphysics of Man

KENNETH ALAN HOVEY

In a letter of 1844 to the poet Thomas Holley Chivers, Poe declared, "My own faith is indeed my own" (*O* 1: 259). Despite this assertion of originality, Poe suggests in the letter that his faith is closely related to two philosophies traditionally opposed to one another, transcendental idealism and materialism. At first, Poe tells Chivers, "You mistake me in supposing I dislike the transcendentalists—it is only the pretenders and sophists among them" (*O* 1, 259). Although Poe regularly attacked the New England transcendentalists and their European models, Kant, Carlyle, and Coleridge, as pretenders and sophists, he twice acclaimed what he considered authentic transcendentalism as an "ennobling philosophy" (Thompson, 119, 292), as Ottavio Casale pointed out in 1968 (94–95). Furthermore, as Robert D. Jacobs has documented, Poe never attacked idealism and frequently used "the ideal" and "ideality" as highest terms of praise (*Poe,* 140–50, 442–43). Eric W. Carlson has dubbed Poe's authentic transcendental idealism "Psychal Transcendentalism" (7–8, 14–20), and David Ketterer speaks for the majority of recent critics, whose views are collected by Casale in his chapter on Poe in *The Transcendentalists,* when he states, "On balance Poe belongs primarily with the Transcendentalists" (Ketterer, 222, cf. 44–45).

Poe went on to tell Chivers "that you will find [my faith], somewhat detailed, in . . . an article headed 'Mesmeric Revelation,' " and summarizes for Chivers some of the ideas of Vankirk, his mouthpiece in that tale: "There is no such thing as spirituality. God is material. All things are material" (*O* 1, 259–60; cf. *M* 3, 1033–37). Poe reaffirmed this materialism in "The Domain of Arnheim" (1846), the story that he said contained "more of myself and of my inherent tastes and habits of thought than anything I have written" (*M* 3, 1266), when he described Ellison, another mouthpiece character, as "tinged with what is termed materialism in all his ethical speculations'' (*M* 3, 1271; cf. 2: 706). Although Dostoevski commented in 1861, "If there is fantasy in Poe, it is a kind of materialistic fantasy" (Grossman, 32), and Woodberry declared in 1909, "Essentially Poe was a materialist" (2: 250), few recent scholars have approached Poe from the direction of materialism rather than transcendental idealism. Exceptionally, Jacobs has exposed Poe's "materialistic psychology," rooted, he says, in the Scottish "Common Sense" school and partly in Locke (*Poe*, 21, 236–37). But *Fables of Mind* by Joan Dayan is the only major work to support the overall materialism of Poe. This materialism, Dayan believes, Poe derived from Locke's speculation, once thought to be scandalous, "that God could endow matter with the power of thought" (15–16; cf. Yolton, 148–66). Poe must have known this speculation not only from the *Essay on Human Understanding* itself but also from the chapter on metaphysics in his favorite philosophical sourcebook, Bielfeld's *Universal Erudition,* where it is quoted and favorably discussed (1, 391–94).

Poe's peculiar espousal of apparently opposite philosophies led Charles Feidelson to declare quite accurately that "Poe's metaphysics . . . constitute a kind of materialistic idealism" (37). Yet, leading scholars who have emphasized Poe's idealism have frequently gone too far and denied his materialism. William Mentzel Forrest, for instance, the first scholar to examine Poe's faith in detail, equated the "spirituality" of Poe with "his anti-materialism" (19), while Richard Wilbur, probably still the most widely respected interpreter of Poe's metaphysics, claimed that Poe's "destructive transcendence" required the "negation of the real," the "symbolic destruction of the physical" or "the material fact" ("Introduction," 17, 37, 39) and the artist's "freedom from [his] material self and the material world" ("House of Poe," 267). More recently, Barton Levi St. Armand has declared Poe's metaphysic to be "a radical dualism that sees the soul trapped in the materiality of a prison-house world" (1). Dayan has not done better, since, in her deconstruction of Wilbur's and others' antimaterialist readings, she turns Poe into an anti-idealist. To her, "nearly every text [by Poe] leads to the moment when the ideal is shattered, when . . . our exaltation of revealed or transcendent wisdom" is debunked (225; cf. 136, 170, 221). Furthermore, her attempt to ground Poe's materialism in Locke alone is unconvincing. While Poe certainly admired the *Essay Concerning Human Understanding* and its "immortal author" (*T,* 1222), he regularly used Locke's masterwork simply to contradict Locke, as S. Gerald Sandler has shown.

Locke's hypothetical materialism was not the only or even the most important version of materialism known to Poe. That honor belongs to the great classical materialist Epicurus, whose basic views Bielfeld also summarized (1, 311). Although Bielfeld seems to regard all philosophers prior to the scientific revolution of the sixteenth and seventeenth centuries as sophists, his positive characterization of Epicureanism as opposing "the chicaneries and subtilties of logic" (characteristic of Aristotle), pursuing "truth by means of the senses" (in contrast to Plato), and proving "consentaneous to the nature of man" in its morality (as much as Stoicism opposed it) might well have aroused the interest of the young classically minded Poe. Poe's explicit references to Epicureanism, "the philosophy of that most noble of the sophists," as he calls it (*T,* 341), are few, but they are remarkably positive. Only the earliest reference, the devil's declaration in "Bon-Bon" (1835), "*I* am Epicurus!" (*M* 2, 109), is at all ambiguous. But in this tale, notably indebted to Bielfeld (*M* 2, 84, 114, 115; cf. Pollin, "Empedocles"), the devil is definitely the hero and victor. In his review of Moore's *Alciphron* five years later, Poe defended Epicureanism, claiming that, though it has been "habitually perverted by the moderns," "nothing could be more spiritual and less sensual than its doctrines" (*T,* 341). A year later, Poe had M. Dupin in "The Murders in the Rue Morgue" characterize the atomic "theories of Epicurus" as "the vague guesses of that noble Greek," which have "met with confirmation in the late nebular cosmogony" (*M* 2, 536). Then in *Eureka* seven years later, he declared that Laplace mixed "true Epicurean atoms with the false nebulae of his contemporaries" to produce an "absolute truth" based on "ancient imagination" and "modern inacumen" (*H* 16, 265–66). Finally, in his "Marginalia" of 1849, he quoted approvingly, " 'That is right,' says Epicurus, 'precisely because the people are displeased with it' " (*T,* 1460).

The first and last of Poe's references to Epicurus have been virtually ignored (but cf. Christie, 49–51 and *P* 2, 389–90), while a few recent critics, assuming that Poe could not have been an Epicurean, have read the positive references in the review of *Alciphron,* "Murders in the Rue Morgue," and *Eureka* as ironic (Holman; Martin, 37). What I intend to show is that these references are not ironic but perfectly serious and fit within a comprehensive metaphysics of materialism that Poe derived chiefly from Epicurus and that he did not view as opposed to idealism. To do this within the compass of a chapter, I must exclude from examination the further ramifications of Poe's metaphysics in cosmology, angelology, and theology and limit myself, instead, to his metaphysics of man. Before doing so, however, it is necessary to examine Poe's initial conception of metaphysics as a branch of knowledge that required such a reformation as that suggested to him by the antipopular and misunderstood but noble and imaginative Epicurus.

METAPHYSICS DOWNGRADED

Poe first used the term *metaphysics* significantly in the "Letter to Mr.— —" prefaced to his third volume of poems (1831). In the "Letter," he places metaphysics beside poetry and science as one of the three major fields that concern him. These fields correspond closely to the three primary mental faculties, taste, pure intellect, and the moral sense, which he was to distinguish carefully later and make an important part of his critical theory (*M* 2, 604; *T,* 76, 685; cf. Omans). Poetry, the field of taste, comprehends all the fine arts, from music, the most ethereal, to landscape gardening, the most material (*T,* 77). Science, the field of pure intellect, comprehends all the physical sciences or, as Poe sometimes termed them, "physics" (*M* 3, 989; *P* 1, 387). Metaphysics Poe considered a science as well but distinguished it from physics or science per se as the knowledge of mind and immateriality as opposed to the knowledge of body and materiality (*M* 3, 989). Thus, the human concerns of metaphysics are the soul, its faculties, and, in particular, the faculty of the moral sense or conscience (cf. *P* 2, 97). So closely does Poe identify metaphysics with the moral sense that he feels free to interchange the terms *metaphysical* and *moral* (*M* 2, 315; *H* 17, 171) and treat "metaphysician" and "moral philosopher" as equivalent (*H* 17, 185; cf. *M* 2, 96–114 passim, and 3: 1219). Although Poe ultimately brought together the fields of physics and metaphysics—and hence materialism and idealism—he initially distinguished them and poetry according to traditional (i.e., Aristotelian) notions (cf. *P* 2, 97, 146). Yet even from the beginning he ranked the fields according to his own unconventional views, as the "Letter" brings out.

The "Letter" is apparently modeled on Byron's one piece of critical prose, the *Letter to **** ****** (1821), and furthers and refines the attack Byron launched in his poetry against the "Lake school" of Coleridge, Wordsworth, and Southey. Ignoring Southey, Byron's primary target, Poe directs his attention to Coleridge and Wordsworth. In marking off poetry from science, Poe first puts Coleridge's statement in the *Biographia Literaria,* "A poem is that species of composition, which is opposed to works of science, by proposing for its *immediate* object pleasure, not truth" (Coleridge 7, 13), into his own words: "A poem, in my opinion, is opposed to a work of science by having, for its *immediate* object, pleasure, not truth" (Alterton and Craig, 248; cf. Jacobs, *Poe,* 36–37). But Poe rejects Coleridge's further claim that "truth . . . ought to be the *ultimate* end" of poetry (Coleridge 2: 12). On the contrary, Poe argues, the ultimate "end of instruction [in truth] should be pleasure" (Alterton and Craig, 243). Thus poetry, whose immediate end is pleasure, ranks higher than science, whose immediate end is truth. But metaphysics, traditionally regarded as the highest field, ranks lower than both in Poe's view and is portrayed in the "Letter" only as exercising a corrupting influence upon the higher fields. By intruding "instruction with eternity in view" into their poetry, Wordsworth and, to a lesser extent, Coleridge had become "metaphysical poets" and thereby undermined poetry's requisite pleasure (Alterton and Craig, 243–44). Similarly, by keeping his mind "buried in metaphysics," Coleridge in the *Biographia Literaria* had sought truth in "the huge abysses" of immateriality rather than in the "palpable palaces" of the physical world, where Bacon and other scientists had found her (Alterton and Craig, 244, 247).

The sharp contrast between poetry and science and the subordinate and largely negative role of metaphysics emphasized in the "Letter" form the basic groundwork of all of Poe's thinking on the three fields whenever he distinguishes them. When he wrote the "Letter," he had already sharply contrasted poetry to science in the "Sonnet—To Science," which originally prefaced his second volume of poetry (1829), and he was to continue to do so up until "The Poetic Principle," which opposes any attempt "to reconcile the obstinate oils and waters of Poetry and Truth" (*T,* 76). While he exalted poetry above science, he did not deny the considerable value of science within its own province. In fact, he idealized "the man of genius" who was both poet and scientist. Such a man, the living proof of "the old philosophy of the Bi-Part Soul, . . . the creative [i.e., poetic] and the resolvent [i.e., scientific]" (*M* 1, 533), he depicted in M. Dupin, the hero of "The Murders of the Rue Morgue" (1841) and two later tales. That Dupin had a third part to his soul was not made clear until Poe wrote the last of these tales, "The Purloined Letter" (1844). In that tale Poe created D—, the perfect opponent to Dupin, equally poetic and scientific but distinguished from him by being "an unprincipled man of genius" (*M* 3, 993). Thus, the third part of Dupin's soul is his "principle" or moral sense. But this part of the soul is not emphasized in the tale, and, in general, Poe opposed the intrusion of a moral sense and, hence, of metaphysics, as traditionally defined, into his tales. This he makes especially clear in four of his satiric tales, "The Bargain Lost" (1832), its thorough revision as "Bon-Bon" (1835), "The Psyche Zenobia" (1838), and "Never Bet Your Head. A Moral Tale" (1841).

SOCRATIC/LAKE SCHOOL VERSUS EPICUREAN/ SATANIC SCHOOL

"The Bargain Lost," the first of these satires—and even more its revision, "Bon-Bon"—is particularly important because it makes clear the sources of Poe's generally pejorative use of the term *metaphysics* and the Epicurean grounds upon which he thinks an acceptable metaphysics might be founded. The sources of false and true metaphysics appear in "Bon-Bon" on opposite sides of a classical philosophical dispute. Poe, who had distinguished himself as a classicist in his Richmond schools, at the University of Virginia, and at the *Southern Literary Messenger* (*PoeL,* 53, 73, 207), found this dispute in Diogenes Laërtius's *Lives and Opinions of Eminent Philosophers* (first translated into English in 1688; *pace* Pollin, "Empedocles"), which he cites in the tale and alludes to repeatedly elsewhere (*M* 2, 109; cf. 2, 41, 77, 169, 287, 332, 359, 633; and 3, 880, 881, 1199; cf. Page). As Pollin has shown ("Empedocles"), important parts of Diogenes are summarized in Bielfeld (and, we might add, in Moore's [*Poetical Works*] extensive philosophical notes—see, in particular, 2, 64; cf. 2, 3–9, 62–70, 122–28, 137, 167–79, 186–95, 254–58), but Poe's knowledge of him certainly goes beyond these summaries. Diogenes divided all the philosophers he described into two schools, both mentioned by Poe, the "Ionic" and the "Italic" (*M* 2, 86, 97; cf. 342). The leading Ionics are Socrates' heirs, Aristotle and Plato, the leading Italic is Epicurus, and the difference between the two schools revolves around their definitions of the chief good and their views of matter. Aristotle declared "the chief good . . . to be the exercise of virtue in a perfect life" (Diogenes, 192), and Plato regarded immaterial ideas as superior to matter, while Epicurus claimed "pleasure was the chief good" (Diogenes, 428) and considered all that was not matter mere void.

In "Bon-Bon" Poe re-creates this opposition. Pierre Bon-Bon, supposedly a great modern metaphysician, is described as not quite "a Platonist, nor strictly speaking an Aristotelian," yet many of his "notions remind [his philosophical opponent] of Aristotle" and make the opponent suggest that he "knew Plato" (*M* 2, 97, 107–8). In sharp contrast, the opponent is a green-spectacled devil who, while bargaining for Bon-Bon's soul, boldly declares himself to be Epicurus. Poe reinforces the equation of Bon-Bon's devilish opponent with Epicurus in the intended preface to the Folio Club Tales. There the presumed author of "Bon-Bon" is described as "De Rerum Naturâ, Esqr., who wore a very singular pair of green spectacles" (*M* 2, 205), *De Rerum Natura* being the title of Lucretius's renowned poetic exposition of Epicureanism. In the guise of these two fictional representatives of classical philosophical schools, Bon-Bon and the green-spectacled devil/author, Poe is evidently contrasting the opposing literary schools of his own day, the Lake School and what Southey dubbed the "Satanic School."

In the "Letter," Poe had suggested the connection between the Socratic and Lake schools when he observed that "Aristotle . . . has declared poetry the most philosophical of all writing . . . Wordsworth . . . the most metaphysical" (Alterton and Craig, 243; cf. *T,* 178). In "Bon-Bon," he furthers this transhistorical connection by claiming that "it is to Bon-Bon that Kant himself is mainly indebted for his metaphysics" (*M* 2, 97). Kant is identified in the *Biographia Literaria* as the major source of Coleridge's metaphysics, and Poe repeatedly satirized both Coleridge and Kant in later writings, often along with Coleridge's other German sources, Schelling and Fichte, and other followers of Kant— Carlyle, Emerson, the Boston transcendentalists, and, to a lesser extent, Hegel and Cousin (*M* 2, 35, 78–79, 86, 97, 297, 340–42, 495, 621–31, and 3, 1031, 1114, 1129, 1193, 1295, 1310–11). Through his character Bon-Bon, Poe is evidently caricaturing all such transcendental idealists as sophistic pretenders. While Bon-Bon is a metaphysician, he is also a restaurateur, and, as the story brings out, his real devotion is not to the soul, upon which he writes treatises, but to the body, which he gluts with food and drink.

Poe's statement in the "Letter" that "the end of our existence is happiness; . . . and happiness is another name for pleasure" echoes Bielfeld (1: 304– 5, 311) and identifies Poe himself as, at least in part, an Epicurean (Alterton and Craig, 243). His sympathies, therefore, are evidently with the devil in "Bon-Bon," as they are with Byron, the supposed leader of the Satanic School. In the "Letter" Poe never specifically parallels Byron to Epicurus, as he does Wordsworth to Aristotle, but his fictionalized portrait of Byron in "The Visionary" (1834) characterizes him as an inspired voluptuary, and Scott and other early critics justly accused Byron of Epicureanism (Redpath, 38, 94, 240). Furthermore, Thomas Moore and William Beckford, two writers associated with Byron who also served as major influences on Poe, were clearly fascinated with

Epicureanism. Moore, Byron's protégé and biographer, whose poetry served as the model for Poe's second volume, as Byron's did for Poe's first, began his literary career (1800) as a translator of Anacreon, a poet he characterized as a "voluptuary" rather than a "moralist" who "anticipated the ideas of Epicurus" (1: 25, 148, 179). The second and third poetic volumes (1801, 1806) of the "British Anacreon," as Poe and others called Moore (*T*, 1209), contain numerous allusions to Epicurus and his philosophical progenitors, Aristippus of Cyrene and Leucippus (2: 3–10, 64, 103–7, 122–29, 167–79, 253–58; cf. 3: 63, 352). In these, Moore, who even described his third volume as "a world of epicurean atoms" (2: 205), revived the lyrical tradition of Epicureanism characteristic of the Cavalier poets of seventeenth-century England (Mayo, 164–82; Kroll, 85–179). He went on to write *The Epicurean* (1827), a prose romance, which influenced a number of Poe's tales (*P*, "Light"), and its partial rendering in verse, *Alciphron* (1839), reviewed by Poe in 1840. Beckford, Byron's avowed model, whose novella, *Vathek* (1786), suggested the green spectacles and other details of "Bon-Bon" and Poe's other early works (*M* 2, 95, 116; cf. Tintner; Graham; Jacobs, *Poe*, 68), depicted in that novella an Epicurean caliph who sells his soul to a giaour for greater pleasures than those found in his palace of the five senses. Byron and his two elder compatriots clearly took a good measure of the supposed Satanism of their "school" from the hedonistic materialism traditionally identified with Epicureanism.

Poe's opposition to Aristotle and Kant and those he associates with either as "metaphysical" in the pejorative sense of the term is rooted in the notion of self-evidency. This notion, initially ascribed to Bon-Bon (*M* 2, 97), is explained in more detail in relation to both Aristotle and Kant in the "remarkable letter" found in *Eureka* (1848) and, in slightly different form, in "Mellonta Tauta" (1849). According to the letter, "Aries Tottle" was "the principle propagator, of what was termed the *de*ductive or *a priori* philosophy," which ultimately produced "one Kant . . . , the originator of that species of Transcendentalism which, with the change merely of a C for a K, now bears his peculiar name" (*M* 3, 1310–11, cf. 1295). What makes Aristotelian and Kantian metaphysics cant in Poe's view is that it relies on "self-evident truths," when it is a "now well-understood fact that *no* truths are *self*-evident (*M* 3, 1310; cf. 1295). Thus these immaterial "*noumena*" (as Poe, adapting Kant's term, calls them), unsupported by material "*phenomena*" (*M* 3, 1311, cf. 1295), become the "mere abstractions which have been so long the fashion of the moralists of England, of France, and of Germany" (*M* 3, 1031) and fail to convince Vankirk in Poe's tale, "Mesmeric Revelation" (1844), of one of the most important metaphysical doctrines, the immortality of the soul.

Poe's critique of Plato as a metaphysician aligned with Aristotle and Kant, though less developed in "Bon-Bon" and not at all in the "remarkable letter" of *Eureka*, comes to the fore in other works. In "Lionizing" (1835), Poe mocked in passing the "modern Platonist" (*M* 2, 176, 180), and ten years later he reviewed a book by just such a modern Platonist, Tayler Lewis's *Plato Con-*

tra Atheos (Plato against the Atheists). In that review, Poe declared that "if the question be put to-day, what is the value of the Platonian philosophy, the proper answer is, 'exactly nothing at all' " (*H* 12, 164). In contrast to Plato's "dreams," Poe claims to "prefer even the noise of Bacon, the laws of Combe, or the nebula star-dust of Nichols [i.e., Nichol]" (*H* 12, 165). Lewis had specifically condemned "THIS NOISY BACONIANISM ABOUT WHICH THERE IS KEPT UP SUCH AN EVERLASTING DIN," but Poe defended Bacon as a physical scientist, not a metaphysician and, with him, the two scientists of his own day that he most admired—George Combe, praised as the theorist of phrenology in "The Man of the Crowd" (*M* 2, 507; cf. *T,* 322), and John Nichol, praised as the advocate of the "nebular cosmogony" in "Murders in the Rue Morgue" (*M* 2, 535–36; cf. *H* 16, 222–23, 262–63). Yet Poe admitted the "purity of the Academy," the school of Plato, in "Bon-Bon" (*M* 2, 96) and the "purity and nobility of the Platonian soul" even in his review of *Plato contra Atheos* (*H* 12, 164). More significantly, he acclaimed the "pure contemplative spirit and majestic intuition of Plato" in "The Colloquy of Monos and Una" (1841) for advocating "the cultivation of the Taste, in contradistinction to the Pure Reason" (*M* 2, 610–11; cf. *T,* 1457). Insofar as Aristotle was also an advocate of taste, Poe approved him, too, in a review of 1842 and "The Poetic Principle" (*T,* 76, 685). Thus, though Poe primarily condemned Plato and Aristotle as metaphysicians, he admired their elevation of taste. In fact, in *Eureka* Poe makes clear that, though Plato's metaphysics may be inferior to Baconian science, Plato's poetic "guesses" are superior to the scientific "demonstrations" of Baconian scientists (*H* 16, 279).

THE MATERIAL SOUL

While one object of Poe's work from "Bon-Bon" on was to satirize the false metaphysics of the Socratic school and its modern heirs, a more important one was to develop an Epicurean metaphysics of his own. Epicureanism in itself, with its denial of an immaterial soul and reduction of mind to matter, lacked a metaphysics in the Aristotelian sense of the term. Unlike Kantian idealism and its Greek forebears, Epicureanism rests on physical phenomena, not self-evident noumena. Accepting only the evidence of the senses, Epicurus argued for a world entirely comprising atoms. Thus, he is the prototype of the scientist rather than the metaphysician, as Dupin suggests, when he says of "atomies, and thus of the theories of Epicurus" that they have "met with confirmation in the late nebular cosmogony" of Dr. Nichol (*M* 2, 536; cf. *H* 16, 266; *pace* Holman). Without a metaphysics and, hence, without an ethics based on virtue, Epicurean materialism might well lead to the kind of gross sensuality that Poe despised in his drunken gourmand, Bon-Bon. To avoid this, Poe set out to create a metaphysics that went beyond Epicurus while still carrying out his principles.

As Poe must have realized, he was not the first to try to create such an ethical materialism. The successes of Baconian science in the seventeenth century revived ancient atomism and encouraged religious thinkers, no less than Cavalier poets, to create their own unorthodox versions of materialism without denying Christian spirituality. Milton defined his own "animist materialism," as Stephen M. Fallon has dubbed it (1 and passim), in *De Doctrina Christina,* a work first published and first translated into English in 1825 and read by Poe prior to the publication of "Al Aaraaf" in 1829. Poe was clearly fascinated with Milton's heretical assimilation of body to spirit outlined in *Christian Doctrine* and depicted in the Father, the Son, and the angels of *Paradise Lost,* since he repeatedly alluded to it from 1829 on (*M* 1, 103; *T,* 120–21, 408; *H* 10, 108–9; cf. Haviland). Given the common materialism of poets so different as Milton and Moore, Poe's "two masters" in "Al Aaraaf," they were not the "incongruous pair" Mabbott considered them to be (1: 95). But, unlike Milton and unlike the title character of *The Epicurean* (who converts to Christianity), Poe was less interested in linking his materialism to traditional Christian morality and the Bible than to the metaphysical implications of various sciences or, as we now refer to them, pseudosciences of his day.

One of the most important metaphysical problems confronting Poe was the nature of the soul. Epicurus's solution to this problem was confirmed, Poe maintained after 1842, by mesmerism (cf. Lind), just as Epicurus's atoms were confirmed by the nebular cosmogony. According to Epicurus, the human soul is material, "a bodily substance composed of slight particles diffused over all the members of the body" (Diogenes, 447). In Poe, the materiality of the soul is first comically suggested by the devil in "Bon-Bon" when he characterizes souls as edible delicacies (*M* 2, 110–13). But Poe makes clear his serious adoption of Epicurean metaphysics in "Mesmeric Revelation" (1844), as John Basore pointed out in 1910. In that tale, Vankirk authoritatively declares, while in a mesmeric trance, that "there is no immateriality. . . . That which is not matter is not at all" and defines the mind or soul as an "individualized" portion of "the divine mind," which is the finest of the "*gradations* of matter," the "unparticled matter" that "permeates all things" (*M* 3, 1033, 1036). Poe's unconventional view of the soul was not unique in his day, at least among devotees of mesmerism in New York. The year before the publication of "Mesmeric Revelation," the Reverend Chauncy Hare Townshend published a book, later acclaimed by Poe (*T,* 1412), in which he suggested that mesmerism might solve "many curious questions in metaphysics," notably Locke's on the soul (133, cf. 146–48), and, two months after the publication of "Mesmeric Revelation," the Reverend George Bush, a theologian at the University of New York, published *Anastasis,* a highly controversial work that Poe later discussed in "The Literati of New York City" (*T,* 1121–22). In *Anastasis,* Bush, like Poe, seeks to "abolish the distinction, *as usually conceived,* between soul and body" by suggesting that the soul is a "*physical body* . . . pervading the whole frame," made up of "*matter . . .* [in] its more refined and subtle forms" and akin to the "active energies" with which "all nature is pervaded" (66, 71, 74, 76). Bush's views, supported, he claimed, by "the newly developed phenomena of Mesmerism'' (76), were so similar to Poe's that Poe sent him a copy of ''Mesmeric Revelation'' in 1845 and anxiously asked him if the ''thoughts [in it] which are original with myself . . . have claim to absolute originality'' (*O* 1, 273).

Having established the existence of the soul, though only as the highest gradation of matter, Poe naturally considered the further metaphysical question of whether the soul is separable from the body and hence capable of life apart from it. Epicurus left this question unanswered. Since the soul, to him, is living matter, it is as mortal as the body and dies with it, yet, since matter itself is eternal and indestructible, the matter of the soul survives. Poe frequently speculated upon the possibility of the material soul's retaining its individual existence separate from the body and continuing its existence after death. In ''Metzengerstein'' (1832) and again in ''Morella'' (1835), he identifies this speculation with the ancient Pythagorean ''doctrines of the Metempsychosis'' as revived and modified by ''Hungarian superstition'' and ''mystical . . . German literature'' respectively (*M* 2, 18–19, 229–30). In ''Ligeia'' (1838) and ''The Fall of the House of Usher'' (1839), he offers other putative sources, the seventeenth-century ''English moralist,'' Joseph Glanvill (*M* 2, 310, 314–15, 319), and the eighteenth-century British chemist Richard Watson (*M* 2, 408, 419).

But Poe, like Bush, found more authoritative support for this metaphysical speculation in two scientific concerns of the day around which he shaped a number of tales, mesmerism or ''human magnetism'' (*H* 12, 121) in ''A Tale of the Ragged Mountains,'' ''Mesmeric Revelation,'' and ''The Case of M. Valdemar'' and galvanic or voltaic shocks to the apparently dead in ''Loss of Breath,'' ''Premature Burial,'' and ''Some Words with a Mummy'' (cf. Bush, 74). A third scientific concern, not touched on by Bush, the cataleptic trances or ''suspended animation'' (*M* 3, 956) of ''Berenice,'' ''The Fall of the House of Usher,'' ''Premature Burial,'' and ''Some Words with a Mummy,'' further supported the notion of a separable soul. In all of his tales related to these scientific concerns, Poe creates his own case studies in which a vital, scientifically apprehensible energy or mind is sharply distinguished from a quiescent or apparently dead body. Such scientifically based cases, rather than the ''mere abstractions'' of metaphysicians, lead to Vankirk's ultimate affirmation of the existence of the soul apart from the body and hence of its material immortality.

THE ETHICS OF PLEASURE

While Epicurus did not concern himself with the question of the separate existence of the soul, he did concern himself with another major metaphysical question—what constitutes good and evil? As a consequence of his materialism, Epicurus replaced abstract ethical notions with a concrete ethics of pleasure and pain, and so did Poe. ''In so far as he entertained an ethical theory,'' Ernest Marchand first observed in 1934, ''Poe may be called a hedonist'' (34; cf. Jacobs, *Poe*, 155, 303–4). In 1827, Poe sought to create in ''Al Aaraaf'' a world in which ethical abstractions have been replaced by graded pleasures, a non-

Christian "medium between Heaven and Hell" where "sorrow is not excluded" but, at worst, "resembles the delirium of opium" (*M* 1, 112). But the pleasure/pain ethics of Epicurus, like the sorrow/delirium world of "Al Aaraaf," is subject to the charge of sensuality, as Poe recognized in his review of Moore's *Alciphron* (1840). In that review, Poe defends "the tenets of Epicurus, . . . habitually perverted by the moderns," by claiming that "nothing could be more spiritual and less sensual" (*T*, 341). The basis for this defense, which Epicurus himself felt called upon to provide, is that the true Epicurean, while giving some value to all pleasures, nonetheless ranks sensual pleasures, the "less holy pleasures" of "Al Aaraaf" (*M* 1, 112), below spiritual ones, since spiritual pleasures are alone productive of ultimate happiness (Diogenes, 471, 473). The devil in "Bon-Bon" ironically illustrates this view when he prefers souls to bodies, as nutmeats to their shells, and the souls of philosophers, especially metaphysicians, to those of others, especially physicians (*M* 2, 111). In contrast to the sensual Bon-Bon, who is satisfied with the coarsest matter, food, and drink, the devil is an idealistic materialist, satisfied only with the highest pleasures. Thus, Poe's Epicurean has a moral sense, but one entirely subordinate to his taste, since the job of the moral sense is only to rank pleasures. The most moral man, therefore, is the man of finest taste.

This solution to the central problem of Epicurean ethics leads, however, to a further question—what constitutes the highest or most ideal pleasure to the man of taste? In answer to this question, Poe declared in "The Philosophy of Composition" that "that pleasure which is at once the most intense, the most elevating, and the most pure is, I believe, found in the contemplation of the beautiful" (*T*, 16). Epicurus, too, had acclaimed the "contemplation of beauty" as a high, if not the highest, pleasure and associated it with women (Diogenes, 426), but Poe clearly goes beyond Epicurus when he declares that the "stain of melancholy . . . will ever be found inseparable from the perfection of the beautiful" (*M* 2, 164) and that "the death, then, of a beautiful woman is unquestionably the most poetical [and hence tasteful] topic in the world" (*T*, 17, 19). Mortality, in fact, proves the materiality of Poe's most ideal beauties. The moral implication of Poe's dead beauties is clearest, perhaps, only in the Dupin tales. In the first two of these, Dupin seeks to solve the mysterious deaths of young women—Camille L'Espanaye and Marie Roget—while, in the third, he is distinguished from his "unprincipled" opponent only by his service to an "exalted," and presumably beautiful, woman in distress (*M* 3, 977). Thus, Dupin's "principle" or moral sense seems to consist in veneration for dead or endangered women and is consequently equivalent to the highest standard of taste.

Although Poe closely linked the moral sense to the taste, he did not eliminate the distinction between them and always identified both, along with the pure intellect, as separate faculties of the mind. Since the mind to Poe was material, these faculties might well occupy distinct regions within the body. Phrenology, the supposed science that Poe first espoused in a review of 1836 and began to employ in his fiction in 1837 (*T*, 329–32; *M* 2, 298; cf. Hungerford), naturally appealed to Poe because it claimed to identify the specific locations of all mental faculties in palpable "organs" of the head. In his major piece of phrenological literary criticism, the Drake–Halleck review of 1836, and in his tales, Poe said comparatively little about most of the organs identified by Combe and others but focused instead on the three organs that corresponded most closely to his three primary faculties. The highest of these, corresponding to the taste, was the organ of "Ideality," which produced "the sense of the beautiful" (Thompson, 510) and could be seen in the "prominence of the regions above the temples" in Ligeia and Roderick Usher (*M* 2, 312, 402). Closely aligned to it and corresponding to the pure intellect was the organ of "Analysis," which Poe ascribed particularly to Dupin (*M* 2, 527, 530–31). Although akin to conventional phrenology's organs of "causality and comparison," this organ was a product of Poe's own "few farther steps in phrenological science" (*M* 2, 527; cf. *T*, 511–12).

The third organ, the one corresponding to the moral sense, raised ethical problems similar to those of classical Epicureanism. Poe defined it in the Drake–Halleck review as the organ of "Veneration," which produced "in all men a disposition to look with reverence upon superiority whether real or supposititious" and was "given to man by God as security for his own worship" (*T*, 509). The existence of such an organ, which replaces the traditional conscience much as the highest pleasure of Epicureanism replaces traditional virtue, does not, however, account for evil behavior, the refusal to yield appropriate reverence. Perhaps for this reason, Poe did not introduce the organ of veneration into his fiction but, instead, proposed in "The Black Cat" (1843) a countervenerative organ, the organ of "Perverseness" (*M* 3, 852), which the narrator then expounded at length in "The Imp of the Perverse" (1845). This organ, which produces an "overwhelming tendency to do wrong for wrong's sake," that is, simply "for the reason that we should *not*" (*M* 3, 1220–21), made more sense to Poe than the organ of veneration because it was derived by "induction, *a posteriori*" from the phenomena of human behavior rather than "concocted *a priori*" from the presumed "design of the Deity" (*M* 3, 1219–20). Furthermore, as Poe defined it, this organ not only motivated evil behavior but was "known to operate in furtherance of good" (*M* 3, 1223); while it drove the good to do evil, it drove the evil as perversely to do good not only in "The Black Cat" and "The Imp of the Perverse" but in the confessions of the guilty narrators of "William Wilson," "The Tell-Tale Heart," and "The Cask of Amontillado" and in the self-killing consciences of the mate in *Pym* and Charley Goodfellow in "Thou Art the Man."

INDIVIDUAL FREEDOM AND DISCIPLINE

While the perverseness that furthers good in Poe's murderers seems to be a product of the stimulation of their phrenological organ by guilt, the perverseness that furthers harm in his many initially good characters is a product of stimulation by their melancholy. As Pym explains, his perverse "desires" for "shipwreck and famine," "death or captivity" and his only "limited sympathy" for the "bright side of the painting" are "common . . . to the whole numerous race of the melancholy among men" (*P* 1, 65). To this race belong not only Pym but also the many protagonists in Poe's tales who have experienced the loss of idealized but still material beauty, usually personified in a woman, or the loss of wealth and station, like Dupin and Le Grand, the protagonist of "The Gold Bug." The melancholy, like the guilty, are essentially driven beings who cannot help what they do and thus seem to confirm the picture of men as "Mere puppets . . . who come and go, / At bidding of vast formless things," drawn in Ligeia's poem, "The Conqueror Worm" (*M* 2, 318). Phrenology with its implied reduction of mental propensities to physical necessity would seem, like Epicureanism, to lend credence to such a picture of human determinism.

Yet, Poe defended phrenology from this charge in his first review dealing with that pseudoscience (*T,* 331), and Ligeia rebuts her own poem and upholds, even as she is dying, the freedom of the human will (*M* 2, 319). Only if man has a will can he make choices and thus do real good or evil, instead of simply what bodily necessity and mental health drive him to. Only when he asserts his will, Ligeia argues, does his soul survive death. Though the mass of men yield themselves "unto death utterly . . . through the weakness of [their] feeble will" (*M* 2, 310, 314, 319), some individuals, the truly independent gentlemen of Poe's fiction, stand out as strongly willing their own lives. The first of these that Poe created is the hero of "The Visionary" (1834), "that Beckford of Venice" endowed with extraordinary wealth (Thomas, 173), who creates a whole environment for himself according to the highest standards of taste (*M* 2, 157–61). Yet, this "true gentleman," too, is tainted with melancholy by the loss of his beloved and yields himself to self-destruction, though in hopeful anticipation of a happy afterlife with her (*M* 2, 161–67). Poe's fullest example of an independent gentleman is Ellison, the protagonist of "The Landscape Garden" (1842) and its expansion, "The Domain of Arnheim" (1847). With a wife at once beautiful and, apparently, robust and with an enormous fortune, Ellison "refuted the dogma—that in man's physical and spiritual nature, lies some hidden principle, the antagonist of Bliss" (*M* 2, 703; 3, 1268) and thus showed what a man of taste untainted by melancholy might of his own free will attain.

The "Domain of Arnheim" 's theme, "happiness" (*M* 3, 1268), and its setting, a garden, are thoroughly Epicurean. Epicurus's chief good, pleasure, was equated with happiness in the "Letter," and Epicurus's school was known as the "school of the garden," because Epicurus retired to his garden, fully depicted in the first two chapters of Moore's *The Epicurean,* and instructed/entertained his followers there (Diogenes, 427, 430). In addition, Poe explicitly compares Arnheim to Beckford's famous estate, Fonthill (*M* 3, 1278), and the architecture of the "dwelling-house" in "Landor's Cottage, A Pendant to 'The Domain of Arnheim' " (1849) to that of the "infernal terrace seen by Vathek," both of which suggest a beauty unknown on earth (*M* 3, 1335). Poe hints that Ellison himself is an Epicurean when he states that "some peculiarities, either in his early education, or in the nature of his intellect, had tinged with what is termed materialism all his ethical speculations" (*M* 3, 1271).

Ellison, like Epicurus in his garden, makes happiness his chief end and, to attain it, lives by a discipline of "four elementary principles, or, more strictly, conditions, of bliss," which constitute the ideals of his materialism. The first and "chief" of these was "the simple and purely physical one of free exercise in the open air," which provides such pleasures, Ellison says, as "the ecstasies of the fox-hunter." The fourth, his highest ideal, was to have "an object of unceasing pursuit" that provided "happiness . . . in proportion to [its] spirituality" (*M* 3, 1268–69). In Ellison's case, this pursuit was the satisfaction of "the poetic sentiment" in a work of "physical loveliness," the making of a landscape garden (*M* 3, 1271–72). By stating that Ellison's "principles" are "more strictly, conditions," Poe underlines the difference between his materialist discipline and traditional ethics, while, in placing spiritual pleasure above physical ecstasy, he defends his materialism from the charge of sensuality. Ellison's other two conditions, "the love of woman" and "the contempt of ambition" (*M* 3, 1269), which Poe first espoused in the "Preface" to "Tamerlane" (1827; *M* 1, 22), are equally Epicurean. As fully brought out in Moore's *Epicurean* and "The Greek Girl's Dream of the Blessed Islands" (1806), Epicurus was devoted no less to "amatory pleasures" than to philosophy (Diogenes, 425–26). At the same time, he condemned worldly aspirations: "The security of men in general depends upon the tranquility of their souls, and their freedom from ambition" (Diogenes, 475).

PUBLIC DUTY AND POPULAR VIEWS RENOUNCED

"The Domain of Arnheim" further reveals the connections between Poe's Epicurean ethics and his social and political views. Upon leaving the University of Virginia, shortly after the death of its founder, Thomas Jefferson, in 1826, Poe wrote to his foster father: "Since I have been able to think on any subject, my thoughts have aspired, and they have been taught by *you* to aspire, to eminence in public life" (*O* 1, 7). This goal, typical of Virginia gentlemen raised on the model of Jefferson, seems to clash sharply with Epicurus's renunciation of public life. Rejecting ambition and pursuing private pleasure, Epicurus, unlike Jefferson, "avoided affairs of state" (Diogenes, 427, cf. 467). In the last apothegm in Diogenes' collection, Epicurus's "happiest man" hoped only "of having nothing to fear from those who surround him" (479), the mass of men who could not appreciate or attain the highest pleasure (cf. *T*, 1460). Having lost the support of his foster father and hence his position in Virginia society, Poe devoted himself increasingly to poetry from 1827 to 1831 and, following his expulsion from West Point in 1831, seems to have given up his foster father's Jeffersonian teachings for Epicurus's. In "The Domain of Arnheim," Ellison avows "little faith" in "the possibility of any improvement [through public action] being effected by man himself in the general condition of man" and admitted that "he was, therefore, thrown back, in very great measure, upon self" (*M* 3, 1271). Ellison, and Poe, did not intend, as Jacobs has off-handedly suggested, to "make epicureans of us all" ("Paradise," 413) but to please himself and only "certain classes of visiters [*sic*]," the small number of "the poetic" (*M* 3, 1277–78). Only "man, the individual" could attain perfect happiness, Poe states in the story (*M* 3, 1268), and thus, he implies, the chief job of government is to allow rich men of taste, true epicures like Ellison, the freedom to pursue their ideal pleasures unmolested.

Such a view of government is not, however, inconsistent with one side of the thinking of Jefferson. This side, reflected most clearly in Jefferson's Kentucky Resolutions of 1798, upheld state against federal authority through a strict construction of the Constitution and won wide endorsement by southerners, especially during the Jacksonian era. While Poe, like the slaveholders among whom he was raised, must have rejected the "truth" held to be "self-evident" in the Declaration of Independence that "all men are created equal," he clearly supported the individual's right to the "pursuit of happiness" and, with it, the individual state's right as well. He therefore celebrated Jefferson as a "*strict constructionist*" in words quoted from his idolized friend, Jeremiah N. Reynolds, in a review of 1837 (*T*, 1247), five years after Jackson had used federal force to coerce South Carolina to renounce its nullification of the national tariff. As Poe makes clear in his quotation of Reynolds, America's free institutions are "scarcely worth preserving" unless they encourage the "liberal pursuits" of superior individuals like Reynolds and Lewis and Clark (*T*, 1246–47), the models for the protagonists of *Pym* and "The Journal of Julius Rodman." Even greater than the explorers, Poe implies, is Jefferson himself, the "distinguished philosopher" whose "extended views and mental grasp" allowed him to envision their exploration without leaving home (*T*, 1246), and even greater than Pym and Rodman is Ellison, whose freedom from their melancholy allowed him to attain higher goals in his own ideally landscaped domain.

Jefferson in his later years might well have served as a model for Ellison himself. After an aggravating tenure in Washington, he retired in some chagrin to the privacy of his own garden estate, Monticello. Ten years after his retirement there, he declared in a letter to his adoptive son, "I too am an Epicurian [*sic*]. I consider the genuine . . . doctrine of Epicurus as containing everything rational in moral philosophy which Greece and Rome have left us." Along with the letter, he enclosed a "Syllabus of the doctrines of Epicurus," which outlined his own "creed of materialism" and his personal devotion to "Happiness [as] the aim of life," which can be procured only through "[i]n-do-lence of body, tranquillity of mind" (Peterson, 1430–33; Flower and Murphey, 301–2).

Besides Jefferson, a fictional American might also have served Poe as a model for Ellison. Charles Brockden Brown, an author that Poe placed beside Hawthorne in the first rank of American fiction writers (*T*, 480, 1342), created in the title-character of *Ormond* a democratically minded aristocrat like Jefferson who was devoted to "Epicurism" and apparently agreed with another character in the book "respecting matter and mind. He denied the impenetrability of the first, and the immateriality of the second" (132, 162). Judging things on a "scale of enjoyments," from "amorous gratifications" at the bottom to "music and landscape" at the top, Ormond delighted in his "rural retreat, in the midst of spacious and well-cultivated fields," where he could indulge his "love of the beautiful" and promote his "own happiness and not the happiness of others" (93–94, 97, 132). Thus Poe did not need to look across the Atlantic to Fonthill for a model for Arnheim. Monticello, in whose neoclassical shadow Poe studied Greek and Latin at the University of Virginia, or Ormond's fictional retreat in New Jersey or, as Jacobs has suggested, various "estates near Philadelphia and along the Hudson" ("Paradise," 412) would suffice. Indeed, as Flower and Murphey have shown in their *History of Philosophy in America,* "from New York to Charleston . . . an urbanely relaxed morality, a scientifically based materialism" established itself by the end of the eighteenth century (279), and from it Poe might easily have found support for his own Epicurean materialism.

According to Poe, even Jefferson recognized the failings of the democracy he fathered. "Jefferson's observation," Poe noted in 1846, "that in this country, which has set the world an example of physical liberty, the inquisition of popular sentiment overrules in practice the freedom asserted in theory by the laws," was all too true (*T,* 1134). Consequently, Poe satirically depicted the decline of Jeffersonian democracy into the "despotism" of the Jacksonian "Mob" in "Epimanes" (1836), "Some Words with a Mummy" (1845), and "Mellonta Tauta" (1849; *M* 2, 125–27; 3, 1194, 1300). These portraits of the mob seem to confirm the sardonic adage he ascribed to Epicurus, "That is right . . . precisely because the people are displeased with it" (*T,* 1460). At the same time that American democracy, in Poe's and many other southerners' views, was eroding state rights and leveling individual excellence, it was celebrating its triumph as proof of continuing social progress (*P* 1, 391; *M* 3, 1194, 1300). Poe characterized this belief in social progress as an assertion of "human perfectibility" and satirized it in "Lionizing" (1835), listing its leading theorists as Turgot, Price, Priestley, Condorcet, and De Stael (*M* 2, 176; cf. 2, 180). In "The Domain of Arnheim" Poe lists these "perfectionists" again and contrasts the "chimera" of their "rapt daydreams" of a perfectly happy "social condition" for mankind in general to the reality of Ellison's individual happiness, attainable only apart from general society (*M* 3, 1268).

Apart from the fiction of "The Domain of Arnheim," Poe offered what he considered factual proofs of the falsehood of egalitarian democracy and social progress. These proofs, like "The Domain of Arnheim" itself, derive largely from Epicurean teachings. While Epicurus as a materialist based his philosophy on sense perception, he maintained that philosophy could go beyond sensory data by means of "analogy founded on perception" (Diogenes, 438, cf. 456).

"We ought to judge of things which are obscure," he declared, "by their analogy to those which we perceive directly" (Diogenes, 445, 447, 451, 456, 459). While Poe condemned deductive reasoning and eventually even attacked induction, he relied heavily on analogical reasoning as fact. He used analogy in a clearly Epicurean way in 1835 when he justified Hans Pfaall's lunar journey on the "positive confirmation" of the presumed "analogy" of the moon to the earth and condemned Richard Locke's "Moon Hoax" in 1839 for failing to use "analogical reasoning on these [i.e., extraterrestrial] themes [when] . . . analogy here will often amount to conclusive demonstration" (*P* 1, 429, 438). Freely adapting Epicurean analogy, Poe claimed in a review of 1837 that "human perfectibility" flew "in the very teeth of analogy" since there was nothing in "the eternal *cycles* of physical nature, to sustain a hope of *progression* in happiness" and in "The Colloquy of Monos and Una" (1841) that the idea of "universal equality gained ground . . . in the face of analogy and of God—in despite of . . . the laws of *gradation* so visibly pervading all things in Earth and Heaven" (*T,* 412; *M* 2, 610; cf. 3, 1300). While the use of analogy here goes beyond anything in Epicurus, Poe's views are distinctly classical. All the ancients, Aristotle and Plato no less than Epicurus, believed in the cyclicality and gradation of nature and men and had no idea of general human progress or equality.

The classical social views of "The Domain of Arnheim," continued in its "Pendant," the last of Poe's tales published during his lifetime, recall the classical philosophic dispute of "Bon-Bon," whose original version, "The Bargain Lost," Mabbott considered the earliest of Poe's tales to be written (2, 17). Together, they suggest that Poe's well-known acclaim of "the glory that was Greece / And the grandeur that was Rome" (*M* 1, 167) was not a mere rhetorical flourish and that he agreed with Jefferson that Epicureanism, as defined by the Greek biographer Diogenes Laërtius and restated in part by the Roman poet Lucretius contained the best of both ancient cultures. From first to last, Poe's thought and particularly his metaphysics of man are rooted in classical materialism. Yet Poe clearly used his classical learning to establish his own position within the conflicting views of his day: the tension between Enlightenment-minded science and Romantic poetry, the battle between the Lake School and the Satanic School, the clash between strict constructionism and federalism. As a modern-day Epicurus, Poe affirmed the materialism of Baconian science yet preferred poetry to science as a higher pleasure, rejected the Socratic–Kantian subordination of pleasure to virtue, and supported the Jeffersonian insistence on the unmolested pursuit of individual happiness. Yet, going beyond Epicurus, he separated the soul from the body on the basis of contemporary scientific research; segregated the faculties of the mind into his own inductively based phrenological organs; freed ethics, at least in the ideally happy few, from pure physical and mental determinism; and extended Epicurean analogy to social and political issues. In doing so, he defined a faith that was indeed his own, a materialism that avoided sensuality and celebrated the most ideal of pleasures,

the individual's contemplation of a beauty that must die yet survive in the immortally material soul.

In the end, therefore, Woodberry is correct: Poe is "essentially . . . a materialist." But that does not mean that he does not belong, as Ketterer maintains,
"primarily with the Transcendentalists." For Poe's materialism is not the Enlightenment faith in pure mechanism derived from Hobbes and supported in part
by the rationalism of Locke and the "Common Sense" school, Baconian physical science, and modern democratic capitalism. His faith sought to transcend
such rational mechanism by linking the "ancient imagination" of one man,
Epicurus, to the non-Baconian "spiritual" sciences of the nineteenth century.
The result, while opposed to all the popular faiths of the day and especially to
that of the "pretenders and sophists" of Transcendentalism, was, in fact, transcendental. While not transcending matter, it sought to find a species of ideal
matter that transcended the five senses and mortality and was one with God.
Attuned to that matter, the sensitive individual could pass beyond ordinary materiality and attain the supreme pleasure of experiencing supernal beauty. Poe's
materialism can never be divorced from his idealism, for his metaphysics constitutes, as Feidelson has said, "a kind of materialistic idealism."

WORKS CITED

Alterton, Margaret, and Hardin Craig. *Edgar Allan Poe: Representative Selections*. New
    York: American Book, 1935.
Basore, John W. "Poe as an Epicurean." *Modern Language Notes* 25 (1910): 86–87.
Bielfeld, Jacob Friedrich, Freiherr von. *The Elements of Universal Erudition*. Trans. W.
    Hooper. 3 vols. London: G. Scott, 1770.
Brown, Charles Brockden. *Ormond*. Ed. Ernest Marchand. New York: Hafner, 1937.
Bush, George. *Anastasis: Or the Doctrine of the Resurrection of the Body*. New York:
    Wiley and Putnam, 1845.
Carlson, Eric W. "Poe's Vision of Man." *Papers on Poe*. Ed. Richard Veler. Springfield,
    Ohio: Chantry Music P, 1972, 7–20.
Casale, Ottavio. "Edgar Allan Poe." *The Transcendentalists*. Ed. Joel Myerson. New
    York: MLA, 1984, 362–71.
———. "Poe on Transcendentalism." *Emerson Society Quarterly* 50 (1968): 85–97.
Christie, James W. "Poe's 'Diabolical' Humor: Revisions in 'Bon-Bon.' " *Poe at Work:
    Seven Textual Studies*. Ed. Benjamin Franklin Fisher IV. Baltimore: Edgar Allan
    Poe Society, 1978, 44–55.
Coleridge, Samuel Taylor. *The Collected Works of Samuel Taylor Coleridge*. Ed. Kath-
    leen Coburn and Bart Winer. 16 vols. Princeton: Princeton UP, 1983.
Dayan, Joan. *Fables of Mind: An Inquiry into Poe's Fiction*. New York: Oxford UP,
    1987.
Diogenes Laërtius. *The Lives and Opinions of Eminent Philosophers*. Trans. C. D. Yonge.
    London: Bohn, 1853.
Fallon, Stephen M. *Milton among the Philosophers: Poetry and Materialism in Seven-
    teenth-Century England*. Ithaca, N. Y.: Cornell UP, 1991.

Feidelson, Charles, Jr. *Symbolism and American Literature*. Chicago: U of Chicago P, 1953.

Flower, Elizabeth, and Murray G. Murphey. *A History of Philosophy in America*. Vol. 1. New York: Capricorn, 1977. (2 vols.)

Forrest, William Mentzel. *Biblical Allusions in Poe*. New York: Macmillan, 1928.

Graham, Kenneth. " 'Inconnue dans les annales de la terre': Beckford's Benign and Demonic Influence on Poe." *Sphinx* 4 (1985): 226–40.

Grossman, Joan Delaney. *Edgar Allan Poe in Russia*. Wurzburg: Jal, 1973.

Harrison, James A., ed. *The Complete Works of Edgar Allan Poe*. 17 vols. New York: Crowell, 1902.

Haviland, Thomas P. "How Well Did Poe Know Milton?" *PMLA* 69 (1954): 841–60.

Holman, Harriet B. "Splitting Poe's 'Epicurean Atoms.' " *PoeS* 5 (1972): 33–37.

Hungerford, Edward. "Poe and Phrenology." *AL* 2 (1930): 210–31.

Jacobs, Robert D. *Poe: Journalist and Critic*. Baton Rouge: Louisiana State UP, 1969.

———. "Poe's Earthly Paradise." *American Quarterly* 12 (1960): 404–13.

Ketterer, David. *The Rationale of Deception*. Baton Rouge: Louisiana State UP, 1979.

Kroll, Richard W. F. *The Material Word*. Baltimore: Johns Hopkins UP, 1991.

Lind, Sidney E. "Poe and Mesmerism." *PMLA* 62 (1947): 1077–94.

Mabbott, Thomas Ollive. *Collected Works of Edgar Allan Poe*. 3 vols. Cambridge: Harvard UP, 1978.

Marchand, Ernest. "Poe as Social Critic." *AL* 6 (1934): 28–43.

Martin, Terry J. "Detection, Imagination, and the Introduction to 'The Murders in the Rue Morgue.' " *Modern Language Studies* 19 (1989): 31–45.

Mayo, Thomas Franklin. *Epicurus in England*. Dallas: Southwest P, 1934.

Moore, Thomas. *The Epicurean*. 1827. Chicago: McClurg, 1890.

———. *The Poetical Works of Thomas Moore*. 10 vols. London: Longman, Brown, Green, and Longmans, 1849–1853.

Omans, Glen A. " 'Intellect, Taste, and the Moral Sense': Poe's Debt to Immanuel Kant." *Studies in the American Renaissance*. Ed. Joel Myerson. Boston: Twayne, 1980, 123–68.

Ostrom, John Ward, ed. *The Letters of Edgar Allan Poe*. 2 vols. New York: Gordian, 1966.

Page, Peter C. "Poe, Empedocles, and Intuition in *Eureka*." *PoeS* 11 (1978): 21–26.

Peterson, Merrill D., ed. *Thomas Jefferson: Writings*. New York: Library of America, 1984.

Pollin, Burton R. ed. *Collected Writings of Edgar Allan Poe*. 2 vols. Boston: Twayne, 1981.

———. "Empedocles in Poe." *PoeS* 13 (1980): 89.

———. "Light on 'Shadow' and Other Pieces by Poe; Or, More on Moore." *ESQ* 18 (1972): 166–73.

Redpath, Theodore. *The Young Romantics and Critical Opinion, 1807–1824*. London: Harrap, 1973.

St. Armand, Barton Levi. "Usher Unveiled: Poe and the Metaphysic of Gnosticism." *PoeS* 5 (1972): 1–8.

Sandler, S. Gerald. "Poe's Indebtedness to Locke's *An Essay Concerning Human Understanding*." *Boston University Studies in English* 5 (1961): 107–21.

Thomas, Dwight, and David Kelly Jackson. *The Poe Log*. Boston: G. K. Hall, 1987.

Thompson, G. R., ed. *Edgar Allan Poe: Essays and Reviews*. New York: Library of America, 1984.

Tintner, Adeline. "Fire of the Heart in 'Al Aaraaf': Beckford and Byron as Source." *PoeS* 22 (1989): 47–48.

Townshend, Chauncy Hare. *Facts in Mesmerism*. New York: Harper, 1843.

Wilbur, Richard. "The House of Poe." *The Recognition of Edgar Allan Poe*. Ed. Eric W. Carlson. Ann Arbor: U of Michigan P, 1969, 255–77.

———. "Introduction." *Poe: Complete Poems*. Ed. Richard Wilbur. New York: Dell, 1959, 7–39.

Woodberry, George E. *The Life of Edgar Allan Poe*. 1909. 2 vols. New York: Biblo and Tannen, 1965.

Yolton, John W. *John Locke and the Way of Ideas*. Oxford: Oxford UP, 1968.

17

"Strange Alchemy of Brain": Poe and Alchemy

RANDALL A. CLACK

The title "Strange Alchemy of Brain" comes from the 1831 version of Poe's poem "Romance" (*M* 1, 157), and it introduces a key metaphor for Poe (as well as other nineteenth-century American writers): "The artistic imagination is . . . a creative power which disperses elements previously ordered by God and reassembles them into new unities or totalities" (Beebe, 148). D. H. Lawrence failed to see this reordering principle in Poe's work, for he maintained that Poe was concerned only with the "disintegration process" of (the American) consciousness (70). Yet Poe is concerned with more than disintegration. As Eric Carlson observes in "Poe's Vision of Man," "The central theme in Poe's work . . . is not so much death and annihilation as the spiritual rebirth or rediscovery of the lost psychal power essential to every man and artist seeking his fullest self-realization" (20). Indeed, throughout his work, Poe demonstrates his concern with the spiritual renewal that occurs after death and a philosophy that postulates a unity of the material and spiritual realms, often expressed through alchemical analogies and imagery. As Barton Levi St. Armand suggests in "The Dragon and the Uroboros," Poe's stories present the reader with the death of ordinary perceptions and with the potential for rebirth to an extraordinary state of "vision" (64).

Quite often this process operates just under the surface in what Poe referred to in his review of *Undine* (1839) as the "mystical undercurrent" of literature (*T* 256). As John P. Hussey asserts, "Poe believed in an art which would calm, strengthen, and renew its audience by creating an effect or 'undercurrent' of cosmic harmony" (37), through alchemical metaphors and tropes of spiritual rebirth.

Poe's engagement with the alchemical theme has received some previous attention in critical commentaries by Burton R. Pollin and St. Armand; acknowledging Poe's interest in esoteric lore, these studies detail the sources and background of some of Poe's more obvious uses of alchemical tropes and metaphors in works such as "Von Kempelen and His Discovery," "The Gold Bug," and "The Fall of the House of Usher."[1] In addition, Karl E. Oelke, in an ambitious unpublished dissertation, analyzed Poe's poems (especially the 1831 edition) in terms of their alchemical imagery. Both Oelke and St. Armand contend that alchemy, in its cryptographic and hieroglyphic forms, provided Poe with a central scheme of tropes to formulate and illustrate his philosophy of unity.

The use of alchemical philosophy in American literature is not solely the province of Poe, however. The Puritans brought with them a belief in hermetic science and alchemical medicine. While John Winthrop, Jr. (1606–1676), the governor of Connecticut, was known throughout New England for his alchemical abilities, the Puritan minister Edward Taylor, of Westfield, Connecticut, found in the tropes and metaphors of alchemy a unique way to illustrate (in his Meditations) his vision of God's redeeming grace upon the soul of fallen man. References to alchemy also appeared in almanacs throughout the colonial period, even finding a place in Benjamin Franklin's "The Way to Wealth" (1757).

In nineteenth-century America, in addition to Poe, Ralph Waldo Emerson, Nathaniel Hawthorne, and Margaret Fuller found in the idea of alchemical transmutation a powerful metaphor for the transformation of both the individual and society.[2] Thus, Poe's use of alchemical philosophy is not unique to early American literature, nor is it merely eccentric, for alchemy offered a ready-made framework of tropes and metaphors that pointed the way to the transformation of man.

THE NATURE OF ALCHEMY

As it was practiced in the sixteenth and seventeenth centuries, alchemy incorporated both an empirical scientific aspect—experimentation and observation—and a philosophical (or mystical) aspect. Exoteric, or scientific, alchemy was concerned with the transmutation of base metals into silver and gold through the agency of the Philosophers' Stone or tincture, or the separation of the pure seed (gold) from imperfect matter. The process of scientific alchemy also presumed the possibility of producing the elixir of life—a by-product of the Philosophers' Stone that had curative and regenerative powers.

In exoteric alchemy, the *prima materia*—the primal material of creation (often symbolized by lead)—was placed into a still that, in turn, was placed into the alchemical furnace. The alchemist, with the creative energy of the fire, combined salts, sulfur, and mercury with the *prima materia* as it moved through the chemical steps of calcination, sublimation, fusion, crystallization, distillation, and transmutation to the final product—the Philosophers' Stone.

Akin to previous schools of mysticism, philosophical alchemy presented a secret doctrine of rebirth; however, unlike the goal of exoteric alchemy—the transmutation of lead into gold—philosophical alchemy sought to produce spiritual gold through the alchemist's creative imagination, symbolized by the alchemical fire. Hence, in the emergence from the alchemical fire, a new life (and new perception) came into being. This action reflects the alchemical maxim *solve et coagula*—dissolve and make whole[3]—an alchemical variation of the death and rebirth theme.

As thousands of medieval alchemical manuscripts attest, during the alchemical process, base metal (often lead) was subjected to extreme heat while treated with chemical compounds until it crumbled into a black powder. From this stage, further chemical operations were performed on the substance as it changed in color from black to white and finally to red (gold).

After assembling his materials and chemicals, the alchemist began his work by placing the mysterious material of creation—the *prima materia*—into the still inside the furnace. At this stage, the *prima materia* was broken down—purified—by what is often described as chemical torture. This stage of the opus is called the *nigredo*—a chaotic blackness, sometimes called black death, in which the *prima materia* was metaphorically tortured, put to death, and then dismembered in an attempt to purify it for the continuation of the work. This act was seen as a return to the very source of life and creation, for an act of rebirth is usually preceded by a return to the source of life (Fabricius, 17).

Proceeding from the blackness of the *nigredo,* the next stage in the opus was the whitening of the *albedo.* This part of the alchemical process sometimes announced the formation of silver in the alchemist's retort. By the end of these first two stages, the alchemist had symbolically witnessed the material of creation (enveloped in sin since the Fall of man) tortured and put to death (*nigredo*) and then made pure and resuscitated.

The *rubedo*—the culmination of the opus—was heralded by a red light in the still. The red of the *rubedo* represented the luminous redness of pure gold, and, at this stage, the *prima materia* was said to have reached celestial, or spiritual, perfection. Symbolized by the phoenix, the sun at meridian, the Philosophers' Stone, or the creation of the homunculus (new man), this final stage in the opus represented the attainment of *Gnosis*—the freeing of divine Wisdom (*Sophia*) imprisoned in the darkness of matter and delivering it to a new life. This culminating stage was regarded as both a re-creation of the cosmos (genesis) and the creation of the New Jerusalem of Revelation—a new heaven and a new earth.

By creating the Philosophers' Stone, the alchemist was actually creating a small universe, as Thomas Norton suggests in *The Ordinall of Alchemy:*

Noble Auctors men of glorious fame,
Called our Stone Microcosmus by name:
For his composition is withouten doubt,
Like to the World in which we walke about . . .
(Ashmole, 85)

The alchemical methodology also suggests a marriage of contraries—the *conjunction apositorium*—the wedding of opposites. The alchemical marriage, imaged as the conjunction of heaven and earth, gold and silver, sun (Sol) and moon (Luna), King and Queen, or body and spirit, is effected by the alchemical mediator, philosophical mercury. With Mercurius as mediator, the chemical wedding, or conjunction, of the alchemist can be seen as a process of creating the world anew through the perceptions of the alchemist, for, in this scheme, man is the spiritual microcosm that reflects the macrocosm of God (Fabricius, 173).[4]

In the following pages, the workings of the alchemical opus are demonstrated in various works by Poe, yet one needs to remember that alchemy was only one of the many metaphors that this American writer incorporated into his work. It is useful, however, to remember, as Linday Abraham points out, that, while it is possible to illuminate a particular author's work with evidence from current texts that he could have encountered, we must keep in mind that, as an artist, the author was "adapting alchemical thought to artistic expression" (40).

POE, ALCHEMY, AND THE CRITICS

"Von Kempelen and His Discovery" (1849)

The first note of Poe's use of alchemical lore appears in Burton R. Pollin's "Poe's 'Von Kempelen and His Discovery': Sources and Significances."[5] Pollin's essay identifies the work of Sir Humphry Davy, Isaac Disraeli, and Edward Bulwer-Lytton as sources for Poe's literary hoax aimed at the California gold rush of the 1840s. In "Von Kempelen," one of Poe's last stories, Poe reveals his familiarity with the alchemical laboratory:

Opening into the garret where they caught him, was a closet, ten feet by eight, fitted up with some chemical apparatus, of which the object has not yet been ascertained. In one corner of the closet was a very small furnace, with a glowing fire in it, and on the fire a kind of duplicate crucible—two crucibles connected by a tube. One of these crucibles was nearly full of *lead* in a state of fusion, but not reaching up to the aperture of the tube, which was close to the brim. The other crucible had some liquid in it, which, as the officers entered, seemed to be furiously dissipating in vapor. (*M* 3, 1362)

The building that houses Von Kempelen's laboratory is an "old house of seven stories" (*M* 3, 1362)—an unimportant fact until we note that alchemical transmutation moved the *prima materia* through seven noble phases with seven planetary correspondences: lead and Saturn, tin and Jupiter, mercury and Mercury, iron and Mars, copper and Venus, silver and Moon, and gold and Sun. Finally, as to leave little doubt about Von Kempelen's means of producing the gold found in the scientist's quarters, Poe states:

[N]othing unusual was found about him [Von Kempelen], excepting a paper parcel, in his coat-pocket, containing what was afterward ascertained to be a mixture of antimony and some *unknown substance,* in nearly, but not quite, equal proportions. All attempts at analyzing the unknown substance have, so far, failed . . .

I need not go over the details of Von Kempelen's confession (as far as it went) and release, for these are familiar to the public. That he has actually realized, in spirit and in effect, if not to the letter, the old chimaera of the *philosopher's stone,* no sane person is at liberty to doubt. (*M* 3, 1362–63; emphasis mine)

Antimony, as Poe seems to be aware, was often considered a vital element (the *prima materia*) in the creation of the Philosophers' Stone, as in Basilius Valentinus's *The Triumphal Chariot of Antimony* (1604/1646).

Although "Von Kempelen" is a Poe hoax, Pollin draws an illuminating conclusion from Poe's gold-seeking theme that has its genesis in "The Gold Bug" (1843) and its final revelation in "Eldorado" (1849). "Von Kempelen," Pollin concludes, "serves to confirm more substantially the transmutation of Poe into the successful gold-maker [artist], Von Kempelen" (21). Yet, what we shall observe in the following sections of this chapter is that Poe understood the intricacies of hermetic philosophy and alchemy and incorporated them in his work as a way to give meaning to man's existence—through the alchemical metaphor of death and spiritual rebirth—while, at the same time, developing his own philosophy of art, the artist, and imagination.

Poe's Early Poems

Karl E. Oelke suggests in "The Rude Daughter" that, as early as the 1827 edition of *Tamerlane and Other Poems,* Poe was working with the dramatization of the conflict between the material and spiritual realms (151, 213). In *Al Aaraaf, Tamerlane and Minor Poems* (1829), notes Oelke, Poe shifts to an evocation of the transcendental world of "Al Aaraaf" (134), but, in the 1831 *Poems,* Poe first uses alchemical tropes and metaphors to provide a synthesis of the material and spiritual realms (150). Oelke presents an informed, although at times strained, analysis of the 1831 poems "Romance," "City in the Sea," "To Helen," "Israfel," "Irene," and "Fairy-Land" in terms of alchemical synthesis of the material and spiritual:

The world of the 1831 poems asserts that truth can be attained through a synthesis of the two realities. The "strange alchemy of brain" in "Introduction" ["Romance"] figures the spiritual reality of the narrator's physical maturation. The apostrophe to Helen, who is objectified in her almost empirically real (because it is so concretely realized) window-niche, at once embraces and transcends reality. Although Israfel inhabits a transcendent realm and the narrator inhabits a world of "sweets and sours," the narrator yet feels the potential to outperform Israfel. Depth and height, light and dark, movement and stasis, even death and life are captured and synthesized in "The Doomed City" (later "The City in the Sea") at the climactic moment when the waves turn a redder glow and we are left on the brink of kinesthesis. And finally, the ultimate synthesis of alchemical symbolism, that of the sun and the moon, is realized in "Irene" and the 1831 version of "Fairyland." (153)[6]

While Oelke does make an effective case for Poe's use of alchemical metaphors as a synthesis of material and spiritual reality that later developed into Poe's conception of unity, Oelke overlooks the possibility that Poe's conception of alchemy and hermetic philosophy extended beyond the 1831 *Poems* and a few of his stories and permeated the philosophy of the artist himself. For Poe, hermetic philosophy and alchemy became the *via regia* to the supernal.

Claude Richard and David Ketterer also deserve mention in this section, although they make only brief note of the alchemical images in two of Poe's stories. Richard, in "Où L'Indicibilité de Dieu," a phenomenological approach to "Ligeia," presents an often confusing alchemical analogy of an inverted alchemical process by which Poe transforms gold (Ligeia) to lead (Rowena), and, while Ligeia returns to the narrator at the end of the story, she does not communicate the divine knowledge of the unknowable divinity to the narrator. Ketterer, on the other hand, makes brief mention of the alchemical color scheme that Poe presents in "The Assignation." For Ketterer, however, the alchemical references (quoted later) in Poe's story emphasize the sexual abyss as a *mise en abîme* (9), reflecting both arabesque and grotesque reality:

Only from the embracing arabesque perspective of the stranger (and presumably of the Marchesa, and just possibly also the finally enlightened narrator) would both the genuinely bawdy, grotesque humor and the genuine arabesque seriousness of the sexual allusions be apparent. Which is to say that the ambiguous response elicited by the sexual imagery is microcosmic of the ultimately saving ambiguity of the tale as a whole. (9)

"The Gold-Bug" (1843)

The final scholar to whom we turn our attention is Barton Levi St. Armand, who offers two very informed essays concerning Poe's use of alchemy in "The Gold-Bug" and "The Fall of the House of Usher." In "Poe's 'Sober Mystification': The Uses of Alchemy in 'The Gold-Bug,'" St. Armand applies an alchemical reading to Poe's story of treasure hunting on Sullivan's Island, South Carolina, to demonstrate how Poe transmutes and domesticates the traditional symbols of the Western alchemical tradition (6) in order to fuse the " 'many divergent and sometimes conflicting elements' of his narrative into an aesthetic whole" (2).[7] St. Armand perceptively notes that alchemy "masked an incredibly complex and profound philosophy, basically Neoplatonic in content, in which the search for the 'philosopher's stone' was not just the quest for a catalytic agent which could turn base metals into gold, but a long rite of initiation which conducted the neophyte through various disciplinary types of experience toward an ideal state of soul" (1). St. Armand's analysis of "The Gold-Bug" concentrates on three aspects of Poe's story—the tulip tree as *arbor philosophorum* (2–3), the alchemical metal/color imagery (4–5), and William Legrand as alchemist (3, 5–6).

St. Armand supplies a unique interpretation of Poe's apparent misspelling of *Liriodendron Tulipifera*—*"Liriodendron Tulipiferum"* (*M* 3, 818)—the center-piece of Poe's alchemical garden in "The Gold-Bug": "Why Poe might have preferred the incorrect ending in *Tulipiferum* is, I suggest, for the sake of a pun on *ferrum*, which denotes the metal iron, a sword, or any iron implement" (2). In "The Gold-Bug" we note Poe's description of the tree with the slave Jupi-ter—the symbolic name for tin in alchemy ("Mystification," 2)—hanging from it:

> In youth, the tulip-tree, or *Liriodendron Tulipiferum*, the most magnificent of American foresters, has a trunk peculiarly smooth, and often rises to a great height without lateral branches; but, in its riper age, the bark becomes gnarled and uneven, while many short limbs make their appearance on the stem. Thus the difficulty of ascension, in the present case, lay more in semblance than in reality. Embracing the huge cylinder, as closely as possible, with his arms and knees, seizing with his hands some projections, and resting his naked toes upon others, Jupiter, after one or two narrow escapes from falling, at length wriggled himself into the first great fork, and seemed to consider the whole busi-ness as virtually accomplished. (*M* 3, 818–19)

As Legrand orders Jupiter to the seventh limb of the tree—where a human skull is secured and from where Jupiter will suspend the gold-bug attached to a cord—we are presented with a veiled alchemical analogy between the seven limbs of the tree and the seven alchemical metals and their corresponding planets, or Archons ("Mystification," 2). John Read, in *The Alchemist in Life, Literature, and Art*, offers an interesting description of the seven-rung alchemical ladder from *Splendor Solis* (1582) by which we may further glean alchemical meaning of Poe's seven-limbed tree:

> The seven-runged ladder is another common feature of alchemical symbolism, the rungs representing the seven metals and the associated heavenly bodies. One of the paintings of *Splendor Solis* (1582), for example, shows a man standing on the sixth and seventh rungs (representing silver and gold) and gathering the golden fruit of the Philosophic Tree, from the roots of which issue the Hermetic Stream. (59)[8]

The tulip tree occupies a central place not only in Poe's story but also in Poe's alchemical garden of Sullivan's Island, for, underneath the tree, Legrand and company find Captain Kidd's treasure:

> As the rays of the lanterns fell within the pit, there flashed upwards a glow and a glare, from a confused heap of gold and jewels, that absolutely dazzled our eyes. . . . There was not a particle of silver. All was gold of antique date and of great variety. . . . There were diamonds . . . eighteen rubies . . . three hundred and ten emeralds . . . sapphires . . . an

opal. . . . We estimated the entire contents of the chest, that night, at a million and a half
of dollars; and upon the subsequent disposal of the trinkets and jewels . . . it was found
that we had greatly under-valued the treasure. (*M* 3, 826–28)

Here, as St. Armand notes, we see the play of colors and light associated with
the *cauda pavonis* (4)—the peacock's tail—that signals the arrival of the Philosophers' Stone, the Stone of transmutation. It is, in fact, the gold bug itself—
the scarabæus—that the alchemist Legrand creates first by discovering Kidd's
treasure map by (al)chemical means, as Legrand recalls:

I held the vellum again to the fire, after increasing the heat, but nothing appeared. I now
thought it possible that the coating of dirt might have something to do with the failure:
so I carefully rinsed the parchment by pouring warm water over it, and, having done
this, I placed it in a tin pan, with the skull downward, and put the pan upon a furnace
of lighted charcoal. In a few minutes, the pan having become thoroughly heated, I removed the slip, and, to my inexpressible joy, found it spotted, in several places, with
what appeared to be figures arranged in lines. Again I placed it in the pan, and suffered
it to remain another minute. Upon taking it off, the whole was just as you see it now.
(*M* 3, 834–35)

Then Legrand transmutes (replaces) the lead shot with the gold bug itself. With
the equation of the gold bug with the Philosophers' Stone, the treasure becomes
a symbol for the *multiplicatio* of the alchemical phoenix. Not only has the gold
of the bug been multiplied, but the family wealth of Legrand's past is restored,
and the financial security of his future assured. As St. Armand observes:

The story of 'The Gold-Bug'' is the story of Legrand's gathering of the diverse ingre-
dients which will ensure completion of the *opus maximus,* the great work, and it records
his deciphering of the hermetic formula which details the secret of the process. . . . William Legrand is, of course, infected with the methodical ''madness'' of all alchemists in
their quest for riches, whether sacred or profane, and even his surname, which in French
means ''grand'' or ''great,'' hints at his ambition to undertake ''The Great Work'' or
''Grand Arcanum'' [of the alchemists]. (3)

Alchemically, Legrand begins with the bug and the pirate's parchment (in
code)—the elements of chaos—and as Legrand deciphers the pirate's code, the
prima materia of the alchemical work is generated. This interpretation suggests
that Legrand-the-alchemist works through the alchemical chaos and, like Poe-
the-artist, gives (creates) form and unity (treasure) from the chaos of imagination, Poe's ''strange alchemy of brain.''[9]

''The Fall of the House of Usher'' (1839)

In ''Usher Unveiled: Poe and the Metaphysics of Gnosticism,'' we find St.
Armand's second analysis of Poe's alchemy. St. Armand contends that Poe drew

on the Gnostic elements of alchemical philosophy in order to present in "Usher" "not only an aesthetic unity . . . but an intriguing and wholly respectable metaphysical unity as well" (2). According to St. Armand, when viewed in Gnostic terms, "Usher" can be seen as a tale concerning what C. G. Jung calls the "retrogressive liberation of a soul from the character imprinted by the Archons" (Jung, 23)—the seven planetary gods of classical mythology and alchemy (St. Armand, "Usher," 7).[10] As St. Armand notes:

Poe's metaphysic derives precisely from those very unorthodox and even heretical doctrines which were current at the beginnings of Christianity itself and then suppressed or driven underground by the actions of such dogmatic Church councils as that of Nicea. It was from the philosophical tree of peculiar images and mystic speculation which flourished at Alexandria in the Egypt of the first and second centuries A.D. that Poe drew much of his own imagery. In particular, he drew upon that heterogeneous school of thought known as "Hermeticism." ("Usher," 1)

After defining what he sees as the connection between Gnosticism and alchemy—the often violent liberation of the soul from matter to spirit—St. Armand presents an enlightened reading of "Usher" that concentrates on the alchemical theme presented in "The Mad Trist" and its correlation to Poe's own use of alchemical tropes in the story. Roderick Usher, Poe's alchemist, in his (Usher's) own view, "*must* perish in this deplorable folly" (*M* 2, 403); but, as St. Armand notes, alchemy—what some skeptics referred to as the "Great Folly"—requires the killing, or extinguishing, of the old (self) and a putting on of the new ("Usher," 4). Yet, in order to put on the new self, Usher and his sister Madeline (the alchemical brother–sister couple, Sol and Luna) must be separated and then united in what St. Armand identifies as an alchemical allegory that finds a unique parallel in the "Mad Trist." As St. Armand observes:

[T]he killing of the dragon by Ethelred is perfectly illustrated by the second figure of *The Book of Lambspring*. . . . In Poe's allegory, the dragon, which can be either Mercurius as "quicksilver" or as base-matter, defends neither a fortress nor the golden garden . . . but rather "a palace of gold, with a floor of silver." And Ethelred, who is suggestive of the alchemist, Mars, and "sophic sulphur" (for his name can be construed as "red ether," and we remember that Roderick Usher's "ideality" threw "a sulphureous lustre over all"), will surely be an alchemical conqueror if he wins the shield of the *lapis,* the Philosopher's Stone. ("Usher," 5)

At this point in Poe's story, Lady Madeline makes her entrance:

[T]here *did* stand the lofty and enshrouded figure of the lady Madeline of Usher. There was blood upon her white robes, and the evidence of some bitter struggle upon every portion of her emaciated frame. For a moment she remained trembling and reeling to and fro upon the threshold—then, with a low moaning cry, fell heavily inward upon the person of her brother, and in her violent and now final death-agonies, bore him to the floor a corpse. (*M* 2, 416–17)

Here, St. Armand notes, "[T]he ghastly scarlet radiance heralds a final alchemical stage known as the 'rubedo,' for the appearance of Madeline Usher [clothed in white] . . . has already signaled the materialization of the 'albedo,' the penultimate moon/silver stage of the alchemical work" ("Usher," 6).

Finally, in the last paragraph of Poe's story, St. Armand locates the alchemical stage of the *rubedo*—the culmination of the opus and the conjunction of the four elements ("Usher," 6):

Suddenly there shot along the path a *wild light,* and I turned to see whence a gleam so unusual could have issued; for the vast house and its shadows were alone behind me. The radiance was that of the full, setting, and blood-red moon, which now shone vividly through that once barely-discernible fissure, of which I have before spoken as extending from the roof of the building, in a zig-zag direction, to the base. While I gazed, this fissure rapidly widened—there came a fierce breath of the *whirlwind*—the entire orb of the satellite burst at once upon my sight—my brain reeled as I saw the mighty walls rushing asunder—there was a long tumultuous shouting sound like the voice of a thousand *waters*—and the deep and dank *tarn* at my feet closed sullenly and silently over the fragments of the *"House of Usher."* (*M* 2, 417; emphasis mine)

With the "wild light" of the moon symbolizing fire, the four elements reach an alchemical conjunction in the athanor (the house of Usher). Poe's description here finds an interesting parallel with a passage from Paracelsus's *The Tenth Book of the Archidoxies* in *The Hermetic and Alchemical Writings:*

If, then, the predestinated element has to be separated, it is necessary that the house be broken up; and this breaking up or dissolution of the house is brought about in divers ways, as is clearly said in my Metamorphosis concerning the death of things. If the house is dissolved by strong waters, by calcinations, and the like, care must be taken that what is dissolved from that which is fixed must be separated by common distillations. For then the body of the quintessence passes over like phlegm, but the fixed element remains at the bottom. (2: 84)

Previously in "Usher" (i.e., "The Haunted Palace"), Poe equates Usher's house with Roderick Usher himself (Darrel Abel, 48–50). At the climax of "Usher," the quintessence of Roderick and Madeline is produced from their conjunction as their physical bodies (the "house") are separated from their combined spirits. With the collapse of the house in the final scene, Poe presents us with the transmutation of corrupt matter into pure spirit—Usher's house, like the athanor (the alchemical furnace), becomes a bridge from the mundane world to the world of spirit, the world of perfection. The blood-red orb here is closely connected with the fifth element in alchemy—the quintessence, or the Philosophers' Stone—that is created by the union of Sol and Luna—Roderick and Madeline, the "two parts." This union is reminiscent of the alchemical hermaphrodite—a hieroglyphic for the Philosophers' Stone. The conjunction between matter and spirit—old and new Usher—mortal and divine, focuses, finally, on the image of the house as the bridge (for Usher, Poe, *and* the reader) leading to the divine.[11]

Although St. Armand presents solid evidence for the influence of alchemy on Poe as a source for his metaphysic in "Usher," we need to take these observations further in order to trace the influence of alchemical philosophy on both the writer and his work. Poe's imagery of colors and graves is highly suggestive of alchemy, and a close look at this imagery in the light of alchemical philosophy does, in fact, suggest that Poe used the hermetic science to present, as St. Armand suggests for "The Fall of the House of Usher," a unique metaphysic that draws heavily upon Renaissance hermeticism's science of alchemy.

THE ALCHEMICAL COLORS OF POE

In "The Fall of the House of Usher," we noted the blood-red moon rising at the end of Poe's story; this moon is both an odd and fantastic image (seemingly out of place in Poe's story), yet the red and white conjunction of this orb strongly suggests the creation (by both Usher *and Poe*) of the Philosophers' Stone. Furthermore, the alchemical context in which St. Armand places Poe's "Usher" suggests Poe's blood-red orb is, indeed, a bridge leading from earth to heaven—a symbolic mediator of the micro- and macrocosms. Lady Madeline herself becomes a symbol for this same conjunction as she appears newly risen from her tomb (i.e., the *nigredo*) dressed in white (the *albedo*), yet spotted with blood (*rubedo*). While the color scheme that Poe presents in "Usher" is highly suggestive of the corresponding colors associated with the opus magnum, this is not the only work in which Poe employs the colors (and metaphors) of the opus. Poe's use of colors in "The Assignation" (first published in 1834 as "The Visionary") also reveals a mystical undercurrent of alchemical color symbology. Poe, in fact, used the color scheme of alchemy in "The Assignation" to point the way toward the supernal.

"The Assignation"

Although Richard Benton and G. R. Thompson have identified "The Assignation" as a hoax, there appears to be a mystic undercurrent present in this tale that contains an alchemical theme having strong affinities with the dreamworld of the supernal. As Poe's Byronic protagonist of "The Assignation" states, "To dream has been the business of my life" (*M* 2, 165). However, the narrator of "The Assignation," like his counterpart in "Usher," sees only surface action (Pitcher, 2); he is not cognizant of the visionary, mystic world of the protagonist.

To begin, the first action in "The Assignation" that draws the reader's attention is the narrator's description of a drowning child:

A child, slipping from the arms of its own mother, had fallen from an upper window of the lofty structure into the deep and dim canal. The quiet waters had closed placidly over their victim; and, although my own gondola was the only one in sight, many a stout swimmer, already in the stream, was seeking in vain upon the surface, *the treasure which was to be found, alas! only within the abyss.* (*M* 2, 152; emphasis mine)

The next figure to appear is the child's mother, the Marchesa Aphrodite:

She stood alone. Her small, bare and silvery feet gleamed in the black mirror of marble beneath her. Her hair, not as yet more than half loosened for the night from its ball-room array, clustered, amid a shower of diamonds, round and round her classical head, in curls like those of the young hyacinth. A snowy-white and gauze-like drapery seemed to be nearly the sole covering to her delicate form. (*M* 2, 152)

Although Aphrodite correlates to the planet Venus in alchemy, the Marchesa's figure clearly shows affinities with the moon, the Luna of the *albedo*.

With all efforts to save the drowning child proving vain, a dark figure (Poe's unnamed protagonist) emerges from the shadows of the Old Republican prison to dive into the canal's waters and save the child. Yet, during all of this melodramatic action, one figure seems truly out of place—the husband of the Marchesa Aphrodite:

Many steps above the Marchesa, and within the arch or the watergate, stood, in full dress, the Satyr-like figure of Mentoni himself. He was occasionally occupied in thrumming a guitar, and seemed *ennuyé* to the very death, as at intervals he gave directions for the recovery of his child. (*M* 2, 153)

"Occasionally occupied in thrumming a guitar" while a child drowns! What nonsense, we may ask ourselves, is Poe up to now? But we should remember another one of Poe's guitar-playing characters—Roderick Usher—whom St. Armand unveiled as an alchemist par excellence.

Music and alchemy are admittedly an unusual combination, yet, according to Robert Fludd, music helped establish the harmony between microcosm and macrocosm (J. Godwin, *Fludd*, 18).[12] As Peter J. Ammann, in "The Musical Theory and Philosophy of Robert Fludd," notes, Fludd believed music to represent

an ascent from imperfection to perfection, from impurity to purity, from the depth to the summit, from crudeness to full maturity, from darkness to light, from earth to heaven, from evil to good, in fact from the devil to God. This is, according to Fludd, the secret and essential object of music. He evidently sees music in the same light as alchemy. (212)[13]

We are now afforded a new perspective from which to view the incongruous image that Poe presents in the opening of "The Assignation": Mentoni as an alchemist figure directing (and performing the music for) the alchemical drama where the divine child of the King (Sol) and Queen (Luna) is born of the dark waters of the alchemical abyss. As Edward W. Pitcher notes, "[T]he infant stands as the product and symbol of their [the protagonist and the Marchesa's] union, the offspring of a love sanctified by laws which transcend those of the marriage sacrament, sanctified by spiritual, not earthly bonds" (3).

The connection between Poe's protagonist of "The Assignation" and the King (Sol) in alchemy is further strengthened by an examination of the protagonist's apartments that Poe affords us in the second half of his story:

In the architecture and embellishments of the chamber, the evident design had been to dazzle and astound. Little attention had been paid to the *decora* of what is technically called *keeping,* or to the proprieties of nationality. The eye wandered from object to object, and rested upon none—neither the *grotesques* of the Greek painters, nor the sculptures of the best Italian days, nor the huge carvings of untutored Egypt. Rich draperies in every part of the room trembled to the vibration of low, melancholy music, whose origin was not to be discovered. The senses were oppressed by mingled and conflicting perfumes, reeking up from strange convolute censers, together with multitudinous flaring and flickering tongues of emerald and violet fire. The rays of the newly risen sun poured in upon the whole, through windows, formed each of a single pane of crimson-tinted glass. Glancing to and fro, in a thousand reflections, from curtains which rolled from their cornices like cataracts of molten silver, the beams of natural glory mingled at length fitfully with the artificial light, and lay weltering in subdued masses upon a carpet of rich, liquid-looking cloth of Chili gold. (*M* 2, 157–58)

As Ketterer points out in "The Sexual Abyss," the colors that Poe presents here are highly suggestive of alchemical transformation:

In "The Assignation," the description of the stranger's arabesque room—the agential element (according to the stranger and, I believe, to Poe) in the business of translating oneself from the realm of mundane, grotesque reality . . . —recalls a process of alchemical conversion. The movement from night to day, "the tongues of emerald and violet fire," the "crimson-tinted glass," the curtains "like cataracts of molten silver," and the "liquid-looking cloth of Chili gold" suggest the colors associated with the seven stages of the alchemical process: black (for primal matter), white (for the first transmutation into quicksilver), green, yellow, red (for sulphurous passion), silver, and finally gold. (8)

But what is the connection between the first and second parts of "The Assignation"? The common elements to both parts are the narrator, the protagonist, and the Marchesa (present in the second part of the story in both image—her painting—and spirit). I would suggest that we set the narrator aside, for he is but an unknowing witness to the events that occur, and focus on Poe's Byronic protagonist and the Marchesa—the alchemical couple of the first half of Poe's story. Both of these figures die during the first hour after sunrise, a propitious moment in the alchemical opus, for it represents dawning knowledge, the *con-*

junctio—the royal marriage of Sol and Luna—and it heralds the coming of the Philosophers' Stone.

As a "cherub with a heavy golden hammer made the apartment ring with the first hour after sunrise," Poe's protagonist states:

To dream has been the business of my life. I have framed for myself, as you see, a bower of dreams. In the heart of Venice could I have erected a better? You behold around you, it is true, a medley of architectural embellishments. The chastity of Ionia is offended by antediluvian devices, and the sphynxes of Egypt are outstretched upon carpets of gold. Yet the effect is incongruous to the timid alone. Proprieties of place, and especially of time, are the bugbears which terrify mankind from the contemplation of the magnificent. Once I was myself a decorist; but that sublimation of folly has palled upon my soul. All this is now the fitter for my purpose. Like these arabesque censers, *my spirit is writhing in fire,* and the delirium of this scene is fashioning me for the wilder visions of that land of real dreams whither I am now rapidly departing. (*M* 2, 165–66; emphasis mine)

In the protagonist's apartment, as in the *vas hermeticum,* the material elements of time and space collapse, and the spirit of Sol, awaiting conjunction with Luna, writhes in the alchemical fire. When the news of the Marchesa's death arrives, and the narrator realizes that his host is, indeed, dead, too, we are presented with the idea that through their suicide pact, the two lovers will be united—the royal marriage of alchemy—in the afterlife, a reflection of the supernal realm. This idea seems to be what Poe is foreshadowing in the first half of "The Assignation" with the image of the watery abyss, for the abyss of the *nigredo* must be overcome before the royal conjunction takes place.

The two distinct parts of "The Assignation" do, in fact, seem to carry a mystic undercurrent with them; I would suggest that the story demonstrates that Poe had in mind two distinct alchemical themes that form a golden thread by which the author weaves together the two parts of his story. The final image of the alchemical *conjunctio* in "The Assignation" suggests, as in "Usher," the attainment of the Philosophers' Stone and the synthesis of the material and spiritual realms. In fact, striking similarities between Poe's "Assignation" and "Usher" suggest that "The Assignation," written five years before "Usher," may have been an early attempt on the part of Poe to use the alchemical metaphors of hermeticism as a paradigm for his readers versed in esoteric lore.

THE CONJUNCTION AT THE GRAVE

In the works examined thus far, we observed that alchemical symbolism is a means by which Poe perceived imagination (both his own and the reader's) moving toward the divine realm—toward the supernal. In "Ligeia," Poe demonstrates a familiarity with the alchemical maxim *"Solve et coagula et habebis magisterium"*—"Dissolve and unite anew, and you will achieve mastery" (J.

Godwin, *Atalanta,* 60). As the alchemical tract *The Glory of the World* suggests, in alchemy only separate things can unite (*Hermetic Museum* 1, 238). Thus, William Bloomefield, in "Bloomefield's Blossomes," observes of the alchemical elements:

> Bring them first to Hell, and afterwards to Heaven,
> Betwixt Lyfe and death thou must then discusse,
> Therefore I councell thee that thou worke thus.
> *Dissolve and separate* them, sublime, fix, and congeale,
> Then has thou all. (Ashmole, 315; emphasis mine)

For Poe, "to dissolve" carries many connotations and images of death; for example, in "The Colloquy of Monos and Unas," there are many "corrosive hours" which the corpse of Monos spends in the grave (*M* 2, 617), yet the theme and images of alchemical death and burial are also present in "Ligeia," "The Fall of the House of Usher," and "The Assignation."

"Ligeia" (1838)

Claude Richard offers a reading of "Ligeia" exploring an alchemical sequence that moves the dark figure of Ligeia to the light (golden) figure of Rowena and then back to Ligeia as a version of the failed opus. However, a close alchemical reading of "Ligeia" reveals the mystical undercurrent of the story that Poe claimed, in his letter to E. A. Duyckinck, as "the best story I have written" (*O* 2, 309) and reveals that the opus Poe presents in "Ligeia" is, indeed, a successful transmutation!

At the beginning of "Ligeia," Poe demonstrates his familiarity with the esoteric feminine figure of wisdom:

I have spoken of the learning of Ligeia: it was immense—such as I have never known in woman. In the classical tongues was she deeply proficient, and as far as my own acquaintance extended in regard to the modern dialects of Europe, I have never known her at fault. Indeed upon any theme of the most admired because simply the most abstruse of the boasted erudition of the Academy, have I *ever* found Ligeia at fault? . . . I said her knowledge was such as I have never known in woman—but where breathes the man who has traversed, and successfully, *all* the wide areas of moral, physical, and mathematical science? I saw not then what I now clearly perceive that the acquisitions of Ligeia were gigantic, were astounding; yet I was sufficiently aware of her infinite supremacy to resign myself, with a child-like confidence, to her guidance through the chaotic world of metaphysical investigation at which I was most busily occupied during the earlier years of our marriage. With how vast a triumph—with how vivid a delight— with how much of all that is ethereal in hope did I *feel,* as she bent over me in studies but little sought—but less known—that delicious vista by slow degrees expanding before me, down whose long, gorgeous, and all untrodden path, I might at length pass onward to the goal of a wisdom too divinely precious not to be forbidden! (*M* 2, 315–16)

Clearly, Poe wants the reader to see that the figure of Ligeia possesses "forbidden" wisdom, and, by extension, she is a personification of esoteric wisdom and knowledge itself.[14] In addition, Ligeia also demonstrates her own affinity with the Philosophers' Stone: "Wanting the radiant lustre of her eyes, letters, lambent and golden, grew duller than Saturnian lead" (*M* 2, 316). Yet, at high noon on the day of her death, Ligeia hands the narrator "certain verses ["The Conqueror Worm"] composed by herself" (*M* 2, 318) and bids the narrator repeat them. In this quasi-magical context, Poe presents "The Conqueror Worm."

While the images of "The Conqueror Worm" reflect the death (*nigredo*) of "Man" (*M* 2, 319), alchemically, the poem seems to end too soon, for there is no alchemical resurrection (or transmutation), and this prompts Ligeia to state with her dying breath:

"O God! . . . O God! O Divine Father!—shall these things be undeviatingly so?—shall this Conqueror be not once conquered? Are we not part and parcel in Thee? Who—who knoweth the mysteries of the will with its vigor? Man doth not yield him to the angels, *not unto death utterly*, save only through the weakness of his feeble will." (*M* 2, 319)

It is significant that here Ligeia repeats Glanvill's words (which are also used as the epigraph to this story), for the rest of Poe's tale is the continuation and completion of the alchemical opus introduced by "The Conqueror Worm" and the death of Ligeia. As Michael Maier suggests in *Atalanta Fugiens,* from the alchemical death of the lady (Luna) comes her rebirth in the form of the Philosophers' Stone (205).

In the second half of "Ligeia" (after Ligeia's death), Poe includes a description of the chambers (in an abbey) in which the narrator resides with his new bride, the Lady Rowena Trevanion, of Tremaine. Along with his customary interior-design devices of a golden candelabra, golden carpets, and censers, Poe notes:

The room lay in a high turret of the castellated abbey, was pentagonal in shape, and of capacious size. Occupying the whole southern face of the pentagon was the sole window—an immense sheet of unbroken glass from Venice—a single pane, and tinted of a leaden hue, so that the rays of either the sun or moon passing through it, fell with a ghastly lustre on the objects within. Over the upper portion of this huge window, extended the trellis-work of an aged vine, which clambered up the massy walls of the turret. The ceiling of gloomy-looking oak, was excessively lofty, vaulted, and elaborately fretted with the wildest and most grotesque specimens of a semi-Gothic, semi-Druidical device. From the most central recess of this melancholy vaulting, depended, by a single chain of gold with long links, a huge censer of the same metals, Saracenic in pattern, and with many perforations so contrived that there writhed in and out of them, as if endued with a serpent vitality, a continual succession of parti-colored fires. (*M* 2, 321)

The pentagon shape of the room reflects the pentacle of hermetic magic (and alchemy). To emphasize the hermetic atmosphere further, the turret containing the bridal chamber is reminiscent of an alchemical furnace—the athanor—and the room an alchemical (dream) vessel. In this room Rowena is transmuted into the Lady Ligeia.

When Rowena is stricken with a sudden illness, and the narrator attempts to nurse her back to health, the narrator notes "three or four large drops of a brilliant and ruby colored fluid" (*M* 2, 325) magically falling into a goblet of wine he offers Rowena. After consuming this wine, Rowena worsens, and, on the third night after consuming the wine with the ruby liquid, she dies.

The magical appearance of the ruby liquid is, indeed, important to Poe's alchemical story of "Ligeia," for this liquid is analogous to the alchemical *elixir vitae*—the elixir of life that is a by-product of the Philosophers' Stone.[15] It seems at once ironic that the red tincture could be the cause of Rowena's death, yet from this death Ligeia is alchemically reborn.

As the narrator sits with Rowena's corpse on the fourth night (an echo of the alchemical quaternity) after she consumes the red elixir, the narrator notes (three times) signs of life returning to the corpse, and three times the narrator checks on the corpse (reminiscent of an alchemist checking on the contents of the *vas hermeticum*). Then, when the corpse stirs for the fourth time, it also rises and advances "boldly and palpably into the middle of the apartment"; the narrator notes:

Could it, indeed, be the *living* Rowena who confronted me? Could it, indeed, be Rowena *at all*—the fair-haired, the blue-eyed Lady Rowena Trevanion of Tremaine? Why, *why* should I doubt it? . . . And the cheeks—there were the roses as in her noon of life—yes, these might indeed be the fair cheeks of the living Lady of Tremaine. . . . Shrinking from my touch, she let fall from her head, unloosened, the ghastly cerements which had confined it, and there streamed forth into the rushing atmosphere of the chamber huge masses of long and dishevelled hair; *it was blacker than the raven wings of midnight!* And now slowly opened *the eyes* of the figure which stood before me. "Here then, at least," I shrieked aloud, "can I never—can I never be mistaken—these are the full, and the black, and the wild eyes—of my lost love—of the Lady—of the Lady Ligeia." (*M* 2, 330)

The rose color of Ligeia's cheeks reflects the symbolic rose of the alchemical resurrection that occurs at the end of the opus. While the image of the roses on the fair (white) cheeks of the lady with raven hair combines the primary colors of the alchemical opus, it also suggests the embodiment of the Philosophers' Stone in Ligeia herself. This final scene also reflects the royal marriage of Sol and Luna—the narrator and Ligeia—in the alchemical vessel of Poe's magical room. The narrator metaphorically has attained the supernal, for Rowena has been alchemically transmuted into Ligeia—the narrator's "lost love." Likewise, Poe has created the Philosophers' Stone in the final image of Ligeia's resurrection, for she represents a symbolic bridge to the unknown—the alchemical marriage of heaven and earth.

It is interesting to note, however, that Poe's intention concerning "Ligeia" may not have been a successful transmutation after all. In a letter to P. Pendleton Cooke on September 21, 1839, Poe writes:

Touching "Ligeia" you are right—all right—throughout. The *gradual* perception of the fact that Ligeia lives again in the person of Rowena is a far loftier and more thrilling idea than the one I have embodied. It offers, in my opinion, the widest possible scope to the imagination—it might be rendered even sublime. And this idea was mine—had I never written before I should have adopted it—but then there is "Morella." Do you remember there the *gradual* conviction on the part of the parent that the spirit of the first Morella tenants the person of the second? It was necessary, since "Morella" was written, to modify "Ligeia." I was forced to be content with a sudden half-consciousness, on the part of the narrator, that Ligeia stood before him. One point I have not fully carried out—I should have intimated that the *will* did not perfect its intention—there should have been a relapse—a final one—and Ligeia (who had only succeeded in so much as to convey an idea of truth to the narrator) should be at length entombed as Rowena—the bodily alterations having gradually faded away. (*O* 1, 118)

Yet, Poe never made the changes to "Ligeia" to which he alludes; he allowed the transmutation at the end to stand as he had written it.

In "The Fall of the House of Usher" and "The Assignation," we also find Poe working with variations of the alchemical theme *Solve et Coagula*. The endings of "Usher" and "Assignation" suggest that the male–female (Sol–Luna) couples in both stories unite in death. Yet, in these stories, death becomes a means to an end—part of *a process* that culminates with an alchemical-like conjunction in the afterlife, the supernal realm, that Poe presents in his angelic dialogues. When Madeline Usher collapses upon Roderick, and when the double suicide is accomplished in "The Assignation," the reader is afforded further examples of the alchemical *conjunctio*. Although Andrew Marvell noted, "The grave's a fine and private place, / But none, I think, do there embrace," in alchemy, Sol and Luna do embrace in the crypt. It is just such an image that Poe uses in his work to illustrate the life beyond the material realm.

I suggest that Poe viewed the artist as a mediator—at once both the alchemist-operator and the mercurial spirit (*Spiritus Mercurius,* the guide)—between the reader (the microcosm of the material world) and the supernal realm (imagination and the macrocosm). As we have noted in Poe's work, alchemical ideology becomes a symbolic paradigm for the creative imagination. The metaphors and tropes of alchemy became, for Poe, signposts that illuminated the way to the supernal. *This* was the purpose of alchemy in Poe's art and thought.

Like his images of ships, castles, and gardens, the stories and poems themselves are intended to stimulate the reader's imagination, through experience(s) of extraordinary individuals. Such experiences were (and are) capable (if understood correctly) of transmuting the mundane perceptions of the material world into the visionary perceptions of the supernal realm.

As Ernest Tuveson observes, "[T]he locus of the magical operations of the hermetist magicians is always the imagination" (160). Poe's alchemy was certainly not for the masses, as he reminds us in "Colloquy" and "Arnheim"; it was for those individuals who had the vision to perceive the possibility of spiritual transmutation. Thus, through the synthesis of the material and the spiritual—the alchemical marriage of heaven and earth—the imaginative reader creates the Philosophers' Stone of the supernal.

NOTES

1. St. Armand also examines *The Narrative of Arthur Gordon Pym* in "The Dragon and the Uroboros" in light of alchemy; yet, this study is excessively burdened by Jungian depth psychology using alchemy (via Jung). In "The Mysteries of Edgar Poe: The Quest for a Monomyth in Gothic Literature," and "Poe's Emblematic Raven: A Pictorial Approach," St. Armand also makes occasional and brief forays into Poe's alchemical themes. However, "Mysteries" concentrates on the Egyptian myth of Isis and Osiris, and "Raven" is an emblematical survey of ravens and black birds.

2. See Randall A. Clack, "The Phoenix Rising: Alchemical Imagination in the Works of Edward Taylor, Edgar Allan Poe, and Nathaniel Hawthorne."

3. See J. Godwin (Maier, 60), *The Hermetic Museum* (1: 238), and Elias Ashmole (315).

4. For the scholar who wishes further discussion of alchemy, Johannes Fabricius's *Alchemy* will prove valuable.

5. Pollin's essay is reprinted with minor revisions in *Discoveries in Poe* (166–89). All references to Pollin's essay are to "Poe's 'Von Kempelen and His Discovery': Sources and Significances."

6. In addition to Poe's *Poems* of 1831, Oelke briefly discusses the alchemical death and rebirth theme as he finds it in "MS. Found in a Bottle" and "Maelström" and the *Soror Mystica* image in "Ligeia" (177–81). Oelke also devotes a chapter to an amplification of St. Armand's discussion of alchemy in "The Gold-Bug" (discussed later).

7. Here St. Armand quotes J. Woodrow Hassell, Jr., "The Problems of Realism in 'The Gold-Bug' " (191–92).

8. St. Armand also cites this passage from Read (2).

9. This idea is also reflected in "The Purloined Letter."

10. Richard Wilbur notes a similar theme in his "Introduction" to Poe's poems (11–13, 16–17). According to Wilbur, "What he [Poe] *can* give us is an account of the process of aspiration, and a rationale of the soul's struggle to free itself of earth and move toward the supernal" (11).

11. Daniel Hoffman notes that Usher's house "collapses inward upon its inmates as inorganic matter dissolves with organic" (316).

12. Also see J. B. Craven (72).

13. Also see Debus (*Chemical Philosophy* 1: 218, 231).

14. Oelke sees Ligeia as a *scora mystica*—the alchemical figure that corresponds to the alchemist's female assistant (179–80). In a similar vein, Alice Chandler (76) and Hoffman (247, 49) see Ligeia as the personification of wisdom (76).

15. Muriel West notes this in passing in "Poe's Ligeia" (16) and "Poe's 'Ligeia' and Isaac D'Israeli" (25). Poe may have run across references to the red elixir in Rosicrucian legends found in William Godwin's *Lives of the Necromancers,* which Poe reviewed in 1835 (*T,* 259–60).

WORKS CITED

Abel, Darrel. "A Key to the House of Usher." Repr. in *Twentieth Century Interpretations of "The Fall of the House of Usher": A Collection of Critical Essays.* Ed. Thomas Woodson. Englewood Cliffs, N.J.: Prentice-Hall, 1969, 43–55. *University of Toronto Quarterly* 18 (Jan. 1949): 176–85.

Abraham, Linday. *Marvell and Alchemy.* Aldershot, England: Scolar P, 1990.

Ammann, Peter J. "The Musical Theory and Philosophy of Robert Fludd." *Journal of the Warburg and Courtauld Institutes* 30 (1967): 198–227.

Ashmole, Elias, ed. *Theatrum Chemicum Britannicum: Containing Severall Poeticall Pieces of Our Famous English Philosophers, Who Have Written the Hermetique Mysteries in Their Owne Ancient Language.* 1652. Rpt. in Kila, Mont.: Kessinger, 1991.

Beebe, Maurice. "The Universe of Roderick Usher." *Personalist* 37 (1956): 147–60.

Benton, Richard P. "Is Poe's 'The Assignation' a Hoax?" *Nineteenth-Century Fiction* 18, no. 2 (1963): 193–97.

Bloomefield, William. "Bloomefields Blossomes." *Theatrum Chemicum Britannicum: Containing Several Poeticall Pieces of Our Famous English Philosophers, Who Have Written the Hermetique Mysteries in Their Owne Ancient Language.* Ed. Elias Ashmole. 1652. Rpt. in Kila, Mont.: Kessinger, 1991, 305–22.

Chandler, Alice. " 'The Visionary Race': Poe's Attitude toward His Dreamers." *ESQ: A Journal of the American Renaissance,* Supplement Part 1, 60 (1970): 73–81.

Clack, Randall A. "The Phoenix Rising: Alchemical Imagination in the Works of Edward Taylor, Edgar Allan Poe, and Nathaniel Hawthorne." Diss. U of Connecticut, 1994.

Craven, J. B. *Doctor Robert Fludd: The English Rosicrucian—Life and Writings.* N.p.: Occult Research P, n.d.

Debus, Allen G. *The Chemical Philosophy: Paracelsian Science and Medicine in the Sixteenth and Seventeenth Centuries.* Vols. 1 and 2. New York: Science History, 1977.

Fabricius, Johannes. *Alchemy: The Medieval Alchemists and Their Royal Art.* Wellingborough, England: Aquarian P, 1989.

Fideler, David. "The Rose Garden of the Philosophers." *Gnosis: A Journal of the Western Inner Traditions* 8 (1988): 40–44.

Godwin, Joscelyn, ed. *Atalanta Fugiens: An Edition of the Emblems, Fugues and Epigrams.* Trans. Joscelyn Godwin. Grand Rapids, Mich.: Phanes, 1989.

———. *Robert Fludd: Hermetic Philosopher and Surveyor of Two Worlds.* Grand Rapids, Mich.: Phanes, 1991.

Godwin, William. *Lives of the Necromancers; or, An Account of the Most Eminent Persons in Successive Ages Who Have Claimed for Themselves, or to Whom Has Been Imputed by Others, The Exercise of Magical Power.* 1876. Rpt. in New York: Gordon P, 1976.

Hassell, J. Woodrow, Jr. "The Problems of Realism in 'The Gold-Bug.' " *AL* 25 (May 1953): 177–92.

The Hermetic Museum, Restored and Enlarged. Ed. A. E. Waite. 1678. Rpt. in York Beach, Maine: Samuel Weiser, 1991. 2 vols.

Hussey, John P. "Narrative Voice and Classical Rhetoric in *Eureka.*" *Poe as Literary Cosmologer: Studies on "Eureka": A Symposium.* Ed. Richard P. Benton. Hartford: Transcendental Books, 1975, 37–42.

Jung, C. G. *Mysterium Coniunctionis: An Inquiry into the Separation and Synthesis of Psychic Opposites in Alchemy.* Trans. R.F.C. Hull. 2d ed. Princeton: Princeton UP, 1963.

Ketterer, David. "The Sexual Abyss: Consummation in 'The Assignation.' " *PoeS* 19, no. 1 (1986): 7–10.

Maier, Michael. *Atalanta Fugiens: An Edition of the Emblems, Fugues and Epigrams.* Trans. and ed. Joscelyn Godwin. Grand Rapids, Mich.: Phanes, 1989.

Norton, Thomas. *The Ordinal of Alchemy.* Ashmole, *Theatrum Chemicum Britannicum.* 1652. Rpt. in Kila, Mont.: Kessinger, 1991, 6–106.

Oelke, Karl E. "The Rude Daughter: Alchemy in Poe's Early Poetry." Diss. Columbia U, 1972.

Paracelsus. *The Hermetic and Alchemical Writings.* Vols. 1 and 2. Ed. A. E. Waite. 1894. Rpt. in New Hyde Park, N.Y.: University Books, 1967.

Pitcher, Edward W. "Poe's 'The Assignation': A Reconsideration." *PoeS* 13, no. 1 (1980): 1–4.

Pollin, Burton R. "Poe's 'Von Kempelen and His Discovery': Sources and Significances." *Etudes Anglaises* 20 (1967): 12–23.

Read, John. *The Alchemist in Life, Literature, and Art.* London: T. Nelson, 1947.

Richard, Claude. "Où L'Indicibilité de Dieu: Une lecture de 'Ligeia.' " *Delta* 12 (1981): 11–34.

St. Armand, Barton L. "The Dragon and the Uroboros: Themes of Metamorphosis in *Arthur Gordon Pym.*" *American Transcendental Quarterly* 37 (1978): 57–71.

———. "The Mysteries of Edgar Poe: The Quest for a Monomyth in Gothic Literature." *The Gothic Imagination: Essays in Dark Romanticism.* Ed. G. R. Thompson. Pullman: Washington State UP, 1974, 65–93.

———. "Poe's Emblematic Raven: A Pictorial Approach." *ESQ: A Journal of the American Renaissance* 22, no. 4 (1976): 191–210.

———. "Poe's 'Sober Mystification': The Uses of Alchemy in 'The Gold-Bug.' " *PoeS* 4, no. 1 (1971): 1–7.

———. "Usher Unveiled: Poe and the Metaphysics of Gnosticism." *PoeS* 5, no. 1 (1972): 1–8.

Thompson, G. R. "Poe's Flawed Gothic." *New Approaches to Poe: A Symposium.* Ed. Richard Benton. Hartford: Transcendental Books, 1970, 38–58.

Trismosin, Salomon. *Splendor Solis.* Trans. Joscelyn Godwin. Grand Rapids, Mich. Phanes, 1991.

Tuveson, Ernest Lee. *The Avatars of Thrice Great Hermes: An Approach to Romanticism.* Lewisburg, Pa.: Bucknell UP, 1982.

West, Muriel. "Poe's 'Ligeia.' " *Explicator* 22, no. 2 (1963): 15–16.

———. "Poe's 'Ligeia' and Isaac D'Israeli." *Comparative Literature* 16, no. 1 (1964): 19–28.

18

Feminist "Re-Visioning" of the Tales of Women

PAULA KOT

Women often experience horrible deaths in Edgar Allan Poe's tales: premature burial, mutilation, poisoning, psychic cannibalization. Perhaps even more spine-tingling from a feminist perspective is that Poe relates these deaths to his aesthetic practice, asserting in "The Philosophy of Composition" that "the death . . . of a beautiful woman is, unquestionably, the most poetical topic in the world" (19). Though Poe's fascination with dead women is hardly unique, feminist critics, sensitive to the silencing and suppression of feminine experience, differ over what to make of Poe and his portrayal of women. Beth Ann Bassein, for example, believes that Poe should have known better than to reinscribe misogynistic attitudes toward women in his fiction. She writes that Poe's "skills as a poet and fiction writer, his theories regarding art, beauty, and pain, and the enthusiasm of his audience have all helped to perpetuate a view of woman that identifies her with the most passive state occurring, that of the dead, and thus creates negative conditioning for generation after generation of vulnerable readers" (44). More recently, critics argue that Poe did, indeed, know better, that he did not simply reinscribe conventional (repressive) attitudes toward women but that he critiqued these attitudes in his tales.[1] By pointing out that Poe's dead women refuse to stay dead, for example, critics challenge the notion that Poe's tales merely silence feminine experience. The weight of critical opinion now falls on the side of those who would exonerate Poe of the most egregious charges. In the last decade or so, Poe's once notorious reputation has undergone what J. Gerald Kennedy wryly calls a "political rehabilitation," and Poe now could be said to have joined "the vanguard of male feminists" (114).

Was Poe a misogynist, protofeminist, or, as Kennedy argues, a man whose attitude toward woman was "tortured" (114)? Critics undoubtedly will continue to interrogate Poe's attitude toward women and toward his culture's construction of gender. Of vital importance, the small but growing body of feminist criticism of Poe brings to light crucial aspects of his work that would not appear otherwise. As Joan Dayan asserts in "Poe's Women: A Feminist Poe?", "[T]here is a great deal at stake when we talk about Poe and women" (1).

This chapter, then, summarizes many of the important contributions to Poe scholarship made by critics using feminist approaches.[2] The variety of feminist perspectives represented here enables us to re-vision Poe's writings through feminist eyes. Furthermore, they allow us to decide for ourselves if, as some would have it, Poe himself was involved in a process similar to feminist re-visioning. In "When We Dead Awaken: Writing as Re-Vision," Adrienne Rich defines feminist re-vision as "the act of looking back, of seeing with fresh eyes, of entering an old text from a new critical direction" (35). Rich explains that "until we can understand the assumptions in which we are drenched we cannot know ourselves. . . . We need to know the writing of the past, and know it differently than we have ever known it; not to pass on a tradition but to break its hold over us" (35). Rich's definition captures the enterprise of feminist critics working on Poe.[3] Beth Ann Bassein's reading of Poe and of his effect on "vulnerable" readers attempts to dispel the power of a tradition that centers on dead women. But the critics represented in this chapter are more likely to find Poe himself engaged in re-vision, self-consciously working to understand the assumptions "drenching" writer and reader alike.

Critics such as Judith Fetterley examine the self-reflexivity of Poe's tales, which contain numerous artists, statues, paintings, and readers. In "Reading about Reading: 'A Jury of Her Peers,' 'The Murders in the Rue Morgue,' and 'The Yellow Wallpaper,' " Fetterley explores the relationship between reading and gender in these three tales. Engaging in feminist re-vision, Fetterley begins by exposing the assumptions behind the act of reading. Traditionally, reading has been encouraged because it opens one's mind to the experiences and perspectives of others. Fetterley argues that, in practice, however, as reading has been institutionalized through the creation of a canon of "classics," it has served to validate a masculine point of view and to protect male interests and identity. Fetterley sets Poe's "The Murders in the Rue Morgue" beside Susan Glaspell's "A Jury of Her Peers" in order to illuminate masculinist and feminist ways of reading. She points out, however, that both tales assert that "one is a competent reader only of texts that one has written or can imagine having written" (155). In Susan Glaspell's "A Jury of Her Peers," the men who search Minnie Wright's house for evidence to confirm their suspicions that Minnie murdered her husband cannot find the evidence they seek because they "can not imagine the story behind the case" (147). Indeed, because they equate "textuality with masculine subject and masculine point of view," they cannot even imagine that "women have stories" (147–48). The women in the tale are, however, competent readers of female and male texts, "having learned of necessity how to recognize and interpret male texts" (152). Glaspell's story points out that male readers could learn to read women's texts, but they are unwilling to read texts that challenge their sense of identity. In this case, the males in the story resist Minnie Wright's tale, which tells of her husband's systematic abuse of her and her culture's willingness to tolerate that abuse.

In "The Murders in the Rue Morgue" (1841), Poe also explores the gendered dynamics of reading. Except for C. Auguste Dupin, the men in the tale—who identify the orangutan's noises as foreign—cannot solve the crime because their energies are invested in dissociating themselves from the crime and the criminal. Like the men who search Minnie Wright's house but refuse to read her story, the men in Poe's tale, including the sailor who owns the orangutan, deny their own capacity for violence against women. Dupin is, on the other hand, "the master reader" in this tale of crime because he is willing "to recognize the existence of the beast in and as himself" (156). Fetterley here turns to Daniel Hoffman's argument in *Poe Poe Poe Poe Poe Poe Poe* that Dupin is able to duplicate the crime and thus solve it in "The Purloined Letter" (1845) because "he can imagine having committed it" (155). In Fetterley's words, in "The Murders in the Rue Morgue," "the beast who has done the deed becomes a metaphor for Dupin himself, and we are reading about a man who reveals his own tendency toward and capacity for violence against women, and, further, who reveals the connection between the violence and his idea of the erotic" (156). Fetterley argues that the male reader of the tale also becomes involved in this mix of violence and eroticism. Like the sailor who watches from outside the window as his beast acts out a masculine script of violence against women, the reader is positioned outside the story but derives pleasure from its reenaction as it is being resolved by Dupin. While witnessing Dupin's powerful intellect, the reader also "gets a steady supply of vignettes of violence; the mutilated bodies of the female victims remain center stage, providing the crucial though unremarked source of interest" (157). That the "criminal" is an orangutan, however, seems to corroborate the male's self-perceived innocence of violence against women. At the end of the tale, even though two women are dead, the police wonder whether a murder has actually been committed. Dupin recognizes the reality of the murders, but his resolution seems to question if a crime has taken place: "As Dupin allows the sailor his illusion of innocence, so Poe allows the reader his" (158). Fetterley concludes that Poe's tale thus "*facilitates as it exposes* the mechanisms of masculinist reading" (156).

Leland S. Person, Jr., also takes up the self-reflexive nature of Poe's writing, noting that Poe (like Melville and Hawthorne) uses women characters to explore his own relationship to art and creativity. In *Aesthetic Headaches: Women and a Masculine Poetics in Poe, Melville, and Hawthorne,* Person summarizes his argument on Poe in the following way: "My thesis is that the centrifugal tendency in Poe's imagination, which encourages the idealization and deaths of women, is matched by a centripetal tendency, a powerful if anxious attraction to the creative possibilities of relationship. This tension in Poe's imagination, moreover, accounts for the dynamic behavior of women in his tales and, because women are identified with the narrative's creative momentum, for the form that those tales assume'' (22–23). Person thus acknowledges Poe's penchant for abstracting and idealizing women and that dying women are integral to Poe's art. He argues that Poe's male characters reconceive Woman as Ideal in order to strive for a ''heightened consciousness or pure rationality'' that enables them to suppress those ''elements in her being which he fears'' (40). But this process of idealization, constructed upon repression, is inherently unstable. Far from being a murderer, then, Poe creates female characters who resist being transformed into aesthetic objects and who rise from the dead. ''For Poe, women characters become symbols of certain irrational but potentially creative forces within the male psyche'' (25). Person argues that, if Poe depicts the male imagination as attempting to objectify women, he also depicts the failure of these attempts and suggests that these projects pose a danger to female and male characters alike. For ''by transforming her into an art object and thus containing her identity, the male character robs self and art alike of their vitality'' (40). In order to account for the full complexity of Poe's ''masculine poetics,'' then, Person states that we must recognize the relationship between the male's creativity and women.

Person first examines this relationship in the love letters Poe sent to Mrs. Helen Whitman. In these letters, Poe adopts a ''persona similar to those of his narrators in his stories about women'' (21–22). Poe both idealizes Helen Whitman as ''the Helen of a thousand dreams'' and suggests that her ''poet-nature'' is important to the process whereby he creates himself as a poet. She becomes essential to Poe's creative process ''as both the source and reader of language'' (22). Person considers ''The Fall of the House of Usher'' (1839) to be ''Poe's most dramatic account of the male's self-destructive repression of women'' (35). Madeline Usher's disease and impending death serve as a reminder of materiality and ''dissolution,'' the very qualities that threaten Roderick Usher's ''imaginative self-reliance'' (36). Roderick buries her in order to free himself of the material world and to escape into art. But when she is buried in the unconscious, the narrator recognizes that the ''luminousness'' of Roderick's eye had ''utterly gone out'' (37–38, *M* 2, 411). Thus, far from freeing him from an impediment, Madeline's burial proves that she was essential to his artistic imagination. Roderick is immobilized, and Poe's narrator describes his countenance as settling into ''stony rigidity.'' Though the male imagination objectifies Madeline (and other Poe women), by the end of the tale she returns to influence the narrative of the tale itself. ''Not only do Ligeia and Madeline Usher return from the tomb,'' Person asserts, ''but their returns also interrupt the narratives, adapting them to the requirements of their own imaginations while the narrators passively observe—often petrified in the process'' (24). According to Person, Poe demonstrates that an artistic process built on robbing women of their autonomy ultimately robs men of theirs.

Person argues that ''The Oval Portrait'' (1842)—as a parable of the male artistic process—represents one of Poe's most explicit critiques of the theme he had dealt with tacitly in earlier tales: ''The male artist's penchant for objectifying a woman's character in art'' (41). The male artist, who captures his wife's image, and the male narrator, who struggles to dominate her image through the aesthetic gaze, both enable Poe to explore ''the imaginative process of male responses to women'' (42). As in earlier tales, this response proves harmful for women. The anonymous woman slowly dies as her life is transferred into the portrait. However, like other Poe women, she refuses to stay dead. Her image, which melts into the deep shadow of the background of the portrait, suggests that she ''refuses to be captured in two dimensions but inclines toward a condition of formlessness or fluidity and the suggestion of a reality beyond the reductive powers of art'' (42–43). According to Person, the tale points out that the ''male imagination can be deadly, particularly when it turns its attention to women'' (41).

In *Over Her Dead Body: Death, Femininity and the Aesthetic,* Elisabeth Bronfen analyzes the ''aesthetic coupling of Woman and death'' that appears in tales such as ''The Oval Portrait'' and in Poe's ''famous proposition''—''the death of a beautiful woman is, unquestionably, the most poetical topic in the world.''[4] She situates this coupling within the Western tradition of masking the fear of death and dissolution through images of feminine beauty (60, 59). According to Bronfen, ''This motif . . . appears as a popular though diversely utilised thematic constant in literature and painting from the age of sensibility to the modern period'' (60). This motif develops out of our fear of, and fascination with, death. At the same time that we need to repress knowledge of death because it poses a threat to our psyche, we also have a powerful desire to articulate such knowledge. Bronfen thus suggests that representations of death are peculiarly pleasing because they allow viewers to repress the ''knowledge of the reality of death precisely because . . . death occurs *at* someone else's body and *as* an image'' (v). Representations of beauty also allow viewers to repress their fears; ''[T]he idea of beauty's perfection is so compelling because it disproves the idea of disintegration, fragmentation and insufficiency, even though it actually only serves as substitution for the facticity of human existence one fears yet must accept'' (62). Furthermore, because Western culture constructs Woman as ultimate Other, images of dead women ''repress by localising death away from the self, at the body of a beautiful woman, at the same time that this representation lets the repressed return, albeit in a disguised manner'' (vi).

The conjunction of death, aesthetics, and Woman thus allows the viewer to distance himself from his own weakness and serves to protect the self from the fear of disintegration: ''The beauty of Woman and the beauty of the image both give the illusion of intactness and unity, cover the insupportable signs of lack, deficiency, transiency and promise their spectators the impossible—an obliteration of death's ubiquitous 'castrative' threat to the subject'' (64). However, Bronfen also notes the instability of representations of women and death because to represent is also to misrepresent, and slippages occur because these images are a function of repression.

Like Leland Person, Bronfen views ''The Oval Portrait'' as self-reflexive.

Bronfen argues that Poe takes up the conjunction of dead woman and art in this "metapoetic story about creation and image-making . . . in order to problematise the conventional idea of art as transformation of living matter into inanimate form" (111). According to Bronfen, the tale explores the "rivalry between a material presence of the body and its immaterial represence/representation in art" (111). For, though the male artist of the tale is married, his wife fears his first "bride, his Art" as her "rival" (*M* 2, 665). Bronfen asserts that the artist/ husband paints his wife in order to "transfer his living wife into the wife he already had" in his Art (111). She notes that here Poe inverts the Pygmalion myth by depicting the artist as transforming living material into art—and that Poe does so in order to expose the dangers associated with masculine creation. Masculine or artistic creation, in which "man is a maker and woman made," reverses and opposes natural or biological creation (112). Though traditionally artistic creation has been viewed as "analogous if not superior to natural birth," artistic creation also serves to disguise the very qualities that natural creation insists on: the materiality and thus vulnerability of the body (112).

In "The Oval Portrait," Bronfen suggests that a basic "incompatibility and rivalry between art's created image and nature's created bodies" will "prove fatal to the model" (112). For "the woman, representative of natural materiality, simultaneously figures as an aesthetic risk, as a presence endangering the art-work, so that as the portrait's double she must be removed" (112). First the artist ignores his wife and pays attention only to her painted image. Indeed, he rarely turns his eye from this image, "even to regard [her withering] counte-nance" (*M* 2, 665). The story concludes when the artist gazes at the finished product, the portrait, crying out, "This is indeed *Life* itself!" only to realize in the same moment that his wife is dead (*M* 2, 666). Person notes the uncanny quality of the woman in the portrait since she refuses objectification. Bronfen, too, argues that the woman is uncanny, but she suggests that this uncanniness develops out of the reader's inability to distinguish model from representation, reality from art. This instability of the image, this inability to define the woman wholly as art, moreover, undermines the very function of the aesthetic image: to disguise the materiality that viewers fear. Like Person, Bronfen argues for the self-destructive nature of this aesthetic. She suggests that the first title of Poe's tale, "Life in Death," describes the artist as well as his wife's image; "In an effort to deny death by denying the living mortal body, he moves into a position of 'death in life' himself" (114).

In *Second Stories: The Politics of Language, Form, and Gender in Early American Fictions*, Cynthia S. Jordan also examines the importance of stories, specifically, whose story is told and whose is suppressed. Though some critics have accused Poe of suppressing the feminine in his fiction, Jordan argues, instead, that Poe sought to recover the "second story" or "woman's story" criminally silenced by androcentric culture.[5] Jordan pinpoints three phases in Poe's career ranging from the tales that "bear women's names" to the later tales of detection through which Poe worked toward a fictional form that would allow him to "reject one-sided male-authored fictions" and to express female experience (135). These three phases demonstrate Poe's growing sensitivity to the criminal nature of silencing female experience. In his early tales about women, Poe "makes it the reader's task to see that the male narrator tells a one-sided story, that the woman's story has been criminally suppressed—and repressed—by the man's self-serving fiction" (106). In "Ligeia" (1838), for example, Jordan examines the narrator's "subconscious usurpation of [Ligeia's] authority" (136). Ligeia's "enthralling eloquence" threatens the narrator's authority over his text; therefore, she must be silenced, and the bandages that cover her mouth as she rises from the dead bear out the narrator's attempt to suppress her story. According to Jordan, the narrator quickly concludes his tale in order to retain his authority over his text by refusing Ligeia's "verbal 'revivification' " (139).

Jordan views "The Fall of the House of Usher" as the pivotal tale in Poe's development. Though critics usually remark on Roderick Usher's ambivalence, if not animosity, toward his sister, Madeline, Jordan asserts that Roderick "is but a character in the story, and his actions are at least in part the product of his narrator's construction" (140). Jordan also reminds us of the narrator's complicity in Madeline's premature burial—evidenced by Roderick's exclamation that "*We have put her living in the tomb*"—and that her interment beneath the narrator's "sleeping apartment" suggests "a consciousness plagued by its repressed underpinnings" (Jordan, 141; M 2, 416, 410). In Jordan's view, then, the narrator becomes the true "MADMAN," mad with "fear and hatred of . . . female sexuality incarnate in Madeline Usher" (141). In this reading, the narrator tries to suppress the story of Madeline's victimization. Yet, Roderick, whom Jordan defines as an androgynous being, tries to "free himself of the narrator's control" and to author "a second story that explicitly rivals the crime perpetuated against femaleness" (144).[6]

The Dupin tales—"The Murders in the Rue Morgue," "The Mystery of Marie Roget" (1842), and "The Purloined Letter"—portray startlingly grisly representations of violence against women. Jordan argues that "in the three detective tales featuring C. Auguste Dupin, [Poe] images the suppression of the woman's story as a crime perpetuated by male-dominant culture as a whole, and he assigns the task of solving the crime and recovering the lost story to a detective-storyteller with a cultural awareness that is shown to be lacking in the men around him" (106). The androgynous Dupin, whom Jordan sees as a "second draft" of Roderick Usher, is able to speak for the women victimized by patriarchal culture because he is able to imagine women's experience and, indeed, tries to teach the narrator new ways of thinking. Jordan argues that Dupin reveals his androgynous nature when he "speaks in dual modes, his normal speaking voice 'a rich tenor' that rises 'into a treble' when he delivers his analysis of a crime, that is, when he recounts the experience of a female victim" (145; M 2, 533). In "The Mystery of Marie Roget," Dupin re-creates Marie's thoughts in the first person: "We may imagine her thinking thus: 'I am to meet a certain person" (145; *M* 3, 756). The other males in these tales apply their own experience to explain the crimes against women but cannot unearth the crime and identify the criminal because they assume their experience as normative. Whereas Judith Fetterley argues that Dupin's recognition of his own criminal nature enables him to solve crimes against women, Jordan believes that his androgynous nature gives him insight into women's experience and allows him to uncover their stories.

Jordan associates Poe's concern with the excavation of women's stories with a larger attempt by nineteenth-century writers such as Cooper, Hawthorne, and Melville to give voice to "a realm of experience, values, and attitudes that has been suppressed or . . . conveniently forgotten by those who control the terms of cultural representation" (106). Poe's critique of the doubleness and suppression of meaning thus adds to a more pervasive cultural critique of paternalistic authority figures—those figures such as the Founding Fathers, who controlled discourse and representation. Jordan relates Poe's antipatriarchal stance to his lack of relationship with men early in his life. She notes that Poe's father died early, leaving Poe without "a secure social standing but also of strong, positive male role models during [his] formative years" (103). According to Jordan, this absence in his life may explain the "animosity" that Poe displays toward the early male narrators/authority figures in his early tales.

In "(Dis)Figuring Women: Edgar Allan Poe's 'Berenice,' " Jacqueline Doyle joins other feminist critics in arguing that Poe critiques patriarchal traditions, in this case patriarchal poetic traditions, rather than endorsing them. Doyle proposes that Poe's "Berenice" (1835) "dramatizes the disfiguring power of the rhetorical figures which from Petrarch to Dante to Shakespeare, from the early Church fathers to his own Romantic age and beyond, have enslaved the female body and silenced the female voice" (13). For Doyle, the silent figure of Berenice, "the earliest of [Poe's] *revenantes,*" embodies a critique of the tradition that destroys her (13). Doyle notes that Egaeus, Berenice's cousin and lover, associates himself with the ancestral library in which he himself was born and his mother died. Egaeus describes his awakening into consciousness: "Thus awaking from the long night of what seemed, but was not, nonentity, at once into the very regions of fairy land—into a palace of imagination—into the wild dominions of monastic thought and erudition—it is not singular that I gazed around me with a startled and ardent eye—that I loitered away my boyhood in books, and dissipated my youth in revery" (*M* 2, 210). Egaeus transforms Berenice into "his idealized image of herself" that has been engendered through his reading (13). He reveals the process of disfigurement and his distancing from the actual woman, for example, when he uses the definite article to describe "the forehead," "the once jetty hair," and "the eyes" of his cousin. Doyle suggests that Berenice "becomes a spectacular figure compounded of discrete bodily parts," and Egaeus "fixates on the most lifeless portion of her anatomy, her teeth" (14). Doyle concludes that Egaeus "worships a textual phantom, an inanimate feminine object which he violently imposes upon its animate feminine subject'' (16). But she also points out that Poe leaves it up to his feminine readers to ''account for Berenice's dismemberment and to articulate her silent text'' (19).

Cynthia Jordan's concern with Poe and father figures and Jacqueline Doyle's analysis of Poe and church fathers complement the critical focus on Poe and the women in his life. In ''Poe, 'Ligeia,' and the Problem of Dying Women,'' J. Gerald Kennedy ties the patterns in Poe's poetry and prose to Poe's own experience of loss and feelings of abandonment after the early deaths of his mother, Elizabeth Poe, his foster mother, Frances Allan, and his wife, Virginia Poe. Though Kennedy realizes that he risks ''autobiographical over-simplification,'' he argues that Poe's exaggerated dependency upon women (who are, after all, mortal) generated a conflicted response to women—a conflict exposed in Poe's varied treatments of women in poetry and prose. Kennedy writes that ''whenever the beloved Other becomes a figure of adoration, her very enshrinement makes her an object of fear and loathing, an embodiment of power ultimately despised because the male protagonist has surrendered that responsibility for his own well-being which would permit him to value a woman not as 'Truth, Beauty, Poetry,' but simply, humanly, as herself'' (117, 127). Thus, whereas feminist scrutiny into Poe's elimination of women in his tales leads critics such as Leland Person and Cynthia Jordan to interpret Poe's fiction as ''a deliberate, ironic critique of patriarchal attitudes toward women'' (113), Kennedy believes that says too much and too little for Poe. Kennedy suggests, instead, that critics' focus on Poe's fiction obscures Poe's ''tortured thinking about women'' (114).[7]

Kennedy argues that Poe enshrines women in his poetry, imagining them as the Ideal, the source of bliss, life, inspiration, indeed, poetry itself. For example, Poe demonstrates this adoration of Woman in ''The Poetic Principle,'' in which he writes that one feels poetry

in the beauty of woman—in the grace of her step—in the lustre of her eye—in the melody of her voice—in her soft laughter—in her sigh—in the harmony of the rustling of her robes. He deeply feels it in her winning endearments—in her burning enthusi-asms—in her gentle charities—in her meek and devotional endurances—but above all—ah, far above all—he kneels to it—he worships it in the faith, in the purity, in the strength, in the altogether divine majesty—of her *love*. (Poe, 93–94)

However, the dependence of Poe and his male characters on Woman as ''All'' in such poems as ''The Raven,'' ''Ulalume,'' and ''Annabel Lee'' exposes them to ''the terrifying threat of loss (or rejection) and the withdrawal of gratifica-tion'' (117). Furthermore, the male's impotence and passivity before the loss of the Idealized Other in the poems are transformed in the fiction into ''an urge to annihilate the Other'' because she has abandoned him (126). For Kennedy, ''Lig-eia'' ''offers the definitive projection of Poe's tortured thinking about women'' since the tale records both the narrator's devotion to Ligeia as ''mother-mentor-wife'' and his anger that she has abandoned him through her death (114). As Kennedy points out, the narrator seems most concerned with his own fate as he witnesses Ligeia's struggles with death, and her absence serves to highlight his childlike dependence upon her. In the words of Poe's narrator, "Without Ligeia I was but as a child groping benighted" (M 2, 316). Through what the narrator calls the "hideous drama of revivification"—as Rowena seems to recover, then sinks back into death, then seems to live again as Ligeia—Poe expresses the narrator's own conflicted emotions and the relationship between his poetic treatment of women and his fictional treatment: "Through the alchemy of that charged moment, the hated female has become the 'supremely beloved' Other; the beautiful, dying woman of Poe's poetry, that source of bliss and sustenance, has merged with the despised, pale lady of the tales" (125). According to Kennedy, Poe here demonstrates the relatedness of the "idolatry of the poems and the loathing of the tales"; both are generated by a relationship to Woman founded on dependency. "The very instinct to idealize Woman as 'All,' as the incarnation of 'Truth, Beauty, Poetry' and the 'only possible salvation' for man, creates the basis for inevitable bitterness by making the male's happiness and self-worth contingent on sustained female affection" (125–26).

"Eleonora" (1841), according to Kennedy, seems unique among Poe's later tales—and perhaps even a "cheerful rewriting of 'Ligeia' "—because it depicts the death of a beautiful woman "as a benign event apparently uncomplicated by antagonism, resentment, or guilt" (126). When Eleonora dies, the narrator vows never to marry and calls down a curse on himself if he fails to keep his vow. But his loneliness eventually leads him to marry Ermengarde, who inspires a "spirit-lifting ecstasy of adoration" (M 2, 642). The curse never materializes; rather, the spirit of Eleonora seems to sanction her cousin's marriage to another woman. This tale, then, seems to suggest "a tacit collaboration between two women to fill the 'void' in the narrator's heart and satisfy his longing for love" (127). However, as Kennedy argues, the tale still reproduces the pattern in which a beloved woman controls a male's happiness. Though "Eleonora" seems to have a happy ending, Kennedy asserts that it ignores the "mechanism of dependency-desolation-retribution depicted in 'Ligeia' (and elsewhere) without supplying an equally compelling rationale for its dismantling" (127). In other words, to Kennedy, the happy ending of "Eleonora" seems to mock the very idea of happy endings by its improbability.

In "Poe's Gothic Mother and the Incubation of Language," Monika Elbert takes up the *tableau vivant* that fascinates biographers who search for a context for Poe's writing: Poe's mother dying. Elbert argues the impossibility of expressing Poe's anguish at this moment and relates biographers' attempts to capture the meaning of Poe's suffering to Poe's own attempt "to express the unknowable, the unsayable, or as Julia Kristeva would have it, the language of the mother, which cannot be separated from the marginalized discourse of death/ illness, insanity, sexuality, and ultimately from silence, or nonlanguage" (23). Basing her argument on the work of French feminists, particularly the work of

Julia Kristeva, Elbert asserts that Poe's writings seek to recapture, not so much his absent mother, but the "elusive quality of non-verbal language which characterizes the mother/child experience" and which would thus enable him to "capture her essence or make sense of her absence" (24, 26). Elbert speculates that for Poe, the source of art "might just be maternal longing, or as Kristeva would say, 'an unfulfilled mourning for the maternal object' " (26).

Elbert contextualizes Poe's fascination with maternal discourse by emphasizing the central role of the mother and the cult of domesticity in nineteenth-century America. She agrees with Cynthia S. Jordan's portrayal of Poe as developing a feminist ethos that enables him to renounce "death-dealing, male-authored fictions" (Elbert, 24; Jordan, 150). But whereas Jordan focuses on father figures and Founding Fathers, Elbert believes that Poe's story—as well as his culture's—is "the (re)covery of the mother through language" (24). Elbert thus associates the suggestiveness of Poe's tales, the undercurrent of meaning that fascinates critics, with this nonpatriarchal language, the language of the mother. She argues that Poe uses suggestiveness in his tales as a way of defying "male order and structure" and retracing "his way back to the mother" (29). For example, Elbert points out that the final word uttered by the narrators in "Ligeia," "Eleonora," and "Morella" is the woman's first name. What "lingers in the reader's mind is not the narrator's madness or logic—but the essence of the dead mother" and her "incomprehensible language" (25). Here, Elbert realizes that she parts ways with Jordan, who interprets the narrator's utterance of the woman's name in "Ligeia," for example, as his attempt to name, define, and thus exert "his ultimate control over the language of the text" (Jordan, 139). Elbert reads Poe's tales of ratiocination also as championing the "mother's meaning, since intuition prevails over logic" in these tales (25). In "The Murders in the Rue Morgue," Dupin uses "feminine imagination" in order to recover the mother's story and solve the murder of the mother and daughter. Finally, Elbert argues that the many women/mothers imprisoned within Gothic mansions in Poe's Gothic tales represent his "desire to capture and appropriate the mother tongue" (25).

In "Poe's Women: A Feminist Poe?" Joan Dayan addresses the question that tantalizes many critics: Was Poe a feminist? Dayan here defines Poe as a feminist whose writings explore what Denise Riley calls "the indeterminacy of sexual positioning" (Dayan, 2; Riley, 6). Though relatively few critics have analyzed Poe and feminism because of Poe's seeming acceptance of the "brute sexualization and reification of women in the nineteenth century," Dayan argues that Poe "unsettles" constructions of both femininity and masculinity and that his writings analyze "the reversibility of all concepts," including male and female (1). As part of her project to demonstrate Poe's subversion of gender identity, Dayan takes up Poe's penchant for transforming women into superlatives and takes on the critics who have admired Poe's idealized women. Dayan argues that "most men who write about Poe too easily divinize Poe's women" (5). According to Dayan, Poe realizes that the rhetoric of praise itself becomes a tool of oppression; he thus "takes the rhetoric of praise and exaggerates it until words themselves become as stifling, as horrific and circumscribing, as any of his closed rooms, tombs, or coffins" (2). Poe critiques and separates his own voice from this rhetoric, for he understands that "the language of ideal love petrifies the lover as well as his object" (3).

Thus, what Dayan calls the most "radical" part of her argument concerns Poe's own identity in the love poems, in which he annihilates innate principles by divesting the woman, and himself, of identity. Dayan argues that, in Poe's love poems, "if his beloved is emptied of all qualities that would attach her to reality . . . , the voice of Poe as poet, its monotony and repetition—what some critics have scorned—reconstitutes himself, the male lover in nineteenth-century America, as a wholly negative consciousness" (9). Dayan demonstrates the "convertibility" of female and male in the early poem "Tamerlane" (1827), in which Poe describes the tenderness of his love: "I lov'd her as an angel might" (*M* 1, 31). Here, Poe exaggerates his appropriation of the feminine position in order to "expose and overturn all gestures of idealization" (9). According to Dayan, Poe deliberately returns to issues of "love" in order to "attack the subordination of women" and to depict women's "struggle with the ideas someone else has made of them" (8).

In the final section of her essay, Dayan turns to Poe's Gothic tales, which she asserts also function to suspend gender identity. Dayan suggests that the usual stereotypes of women as angelic or evil "become useless in interpreting Poe's fiction" (10). Like Cynthia Jordan, Dayan argues that Poe's fiction is "nothing less than an exhumation of the lived, but disavowed or suppressed experience of women in [Poe's] society" (10). Finally, then, she argues that Poe's poems and tales interact and comment upon one another: "Having understood the demonic underside of men's need to poeticize and feminize women, Poe confronts his readers again and again with scenes of terror: Morella, Ligeia, and Berenice decay, die, and are mourned, but they return to teach the oppressive idolater a lesson he will not forget" (5). Like Leland Person, Dayan emphasizes the "power and endurance" of Poe's women," who continually return from the dead (11).

In "Amorous Bondage: Poe, Ladies, and Slaves," Joan Dayan challenges the tendency in Poe criticism to ignore the relatedness in Poe's imagination between gender and race. Thus, while other critics point to the absences in Poe's life— the early loss of his mother and other surrogate mothers or, as Cynthia Jordan adds, the loss of positive male role models during Poe's formative years (Jordan, 102–3)—Dayan points to the important presence in Poe's life heretofore ignored by critics: "the black woman in the house" while Poe was growing up (264). This presence, along with the presence in his culture of African-American stories that tell "of the angry dead, sightings of teeth, the bones of charms, the power of conjuring," influenced Poe's form of Gothic (265). These stories, moreover, enabled Poe to tell a different story from the one told by white culture: "In a time when many argued for sharper categorizations and more hierarchy, when ladies, slaves, and men endured ever more difficult trials of definition, Poe managed to confound and denaturalize the so-called 'natural order' of things" (249). Dayan argues that Poe "undefines the definitions" of lady (white woman) and slave whose differentiation was the crux of slave-holding society (250). Beloved ladies, etherealized by their culture, and slaves, brutalized by theirs, though putatively distanced, are connected through their dehumanization; whether they are perceived as angel or animal, both lose their humanity. In this way, according to Dayan, love, which emphasizes *my,* like servitude, converts humans into property or possessions. The blood of mutilated women that fills Poe's tales, then, is related to the blood so important to a society that attempted to differentiate race through a "taxonomy" of blood. Dayan's conclusion, "We need to reread Poe's romantic fictions as bound to the realities of race," moves feminist readings of Poe's work in exciting new directions.

Nina Baym points out that "only a minority of [Poe's] stories and poems have women characters" (222). But Poe's treatments of women in such tales as "Ligeia," "Berenice," "The Fall of the House of Usher," and the Dupin tales continue to haunt feminists. As Joan Dayan states so eloquently, "What are we to do with Poe's bleeding, raped, decapitated, dead, and resurrected women, brutalized, buried, cemented in cellars, and stuffed up chimneys?" ("Poe's," 10). These dying and dead women, in J. Gerald Kennedy's words, raise "troubling questions about an inherent misogyny" in Poe's fiction (113). The feminist critics cited in this chapter, however, generally agree that Poe is no misogynist. Instead, most of these critics argue that Poe's preoccupation with the death of a beautiful woman in his poems and tales concerning women actually reflects his interest in recovering women's stories. Whether one agrees with this point of view—in effect, seeing Poe as involved in feminist re-visioning—feminist perspectives on Poe have contributed to disentangling the complexity of Poe's imagination.

NOTES

1. The June/December 1993 (Vol. 26) issue of *PoeS* is devoted to Poe and Women. This issue also includes an excellent review essay on "Poe and Women: Recent Perspectives" by Michael J. S. Williams. I am indebted to Alexander Hammond, the editor of *PoeS,* for allowing me to view and quote from a prepublication copy of this important addition to Poe criticism.

2. This chapter primarily examines feminist approaches to Poe's tales. Consequently, it does not include two articles that use Poe's fiction to illustrate particular issues in feminist criticism. See Naomi Schor, "Female Paranoia: The Case for Psychoanalytic Feminist Criticism," *Yale French Studies* 62 (1981): 204–19, and Gita Rajan, "A Feminist Rereading of Poe's 'The Tell-Tale Heart,' " *Papers on Language and Literature: A Journal for Scholars and Critics of Language and Literature* 24 (1988): 283–300.

3. In *Second Stories,* Cynthia S. Jordan specifically refers to Adrienne Rich's definition of feminist "re-vision" and "conclude[s] that Poe's ability to tell both stories, or

both halves of the human story, is, therefore, the sign of what we would today call feminist re-vision'' (151).

4. In Chapter 4, Elisabeth Bronfen analyzes in great detail Poe's assertion of the poetical nature of the death of a beautiful woman. She also takes up other tales such as "Ligeia." For brevity's sake, I confine my summary to her analysis of "The Oval Portrait."

5. Jordan recognizes that Poe's "now infamous" statement in "The Philosophy of Composition" that "the death . . . of a beautiful woman is, unquestionably, the most poetical topic in the world" is a "stumbling block" to accepting Poe as a feminist writer. She notes, though, that feminist critics tend to ignore the second half of Poe's statement: "—and equally is it beyond doubt that the lips best suited for such topic are those of a bereaved lover" (Jordan, 151). Though Jordan does not "intend to justify the images of death which Poe habitually chose as a vehicle for his vision," she does argue that the loss experienced by the lover is a metaphor for the pervasive sense in Poe's writings of the "need to tell not only the story of loss but the second story as well: the story of recovery and restoration, the woman's story" (151).

6. Jordan argues that Roderick Usher's androgyny is revealed through his physical resemblance to Ligeia and through his composition of a musical ballad that "is reminiscent of Morella and Ligeia, who had been characterized by their 'musical language' " (142). More important, "that he is Madeline's twin . . . implies a merging of gender identities" (142).

7. Kennedy notes that he treats in "slightly different terms" Poe's depictions of the death of a beautiful woman in his full-length study, *Poe, Death, and the Life of Writing* (New Haven, Conn.: Yale University Press, 1987), 60–88.

WORKS CITED

Bassein, Beth Ann. *Women and Death: Linkages in Western Thought and Literature.* Westport, Conn.: Greenwood, 1984.

Baym, Nina. "Portrayal of Women in American Literature, 1790–1870." *What Manner of Woman: Essays on English and American Life and Literature.* Ed. Marlene Springer. New York: New York UP, 1977, 211–34.

Bronfen, Elisabeth. *Over Her Dead Body: Death, Femininity and the Aesthetic.* New York: Routledge, 1992.

Dayan, Joan. "Amorous Bondage: Poe, Ladies, and Slaves." *AL* 66 (1994): 239–73.

———. "Poe's Women: A Feminist Poe?" *PoeS* 26, nos. 1, 2 (1993): 1–12.

Doyle, Jacqueline. "(Dis)Figuring Woman: Edgar Allan Poe's 'Berenice.' " *PoeS* 26 (1993): 13–22.

Elbert, Monika. "Poe's Gothic Mother and the Incubation of Language." *PoeS* 26 (1993): 23–34.

Fetterley, Judith. "Reading about Reading." *Gender and Reading: Essays on Readers, Texts, and Contexts.* Ed. Elizabeth A. Flynn and Patrocinio P. Schweickart. Baltimore: Johns Hopkins UP, 1986, 147–64.

Hoffman, Daniel. *Poe Poe Poe Poe Poe Poe Poe.* Garden City, N.Y.: Doubleday, 1972.

Jordan, Cynthia S. *Second Stories: The Politics of Language, Form, and Gender in Early American Fictions.* Chapel Hill: U of North Carolina P, 1989.

Kennedy, J. Gerald. "Poe, 'Ligeia,' and the Problem of Dying Women." *New Essays* on *Poe's Major Tales.* Ed. Kenneth Silverman. New York: Cambridge UP, 1993, 113–29.

Mabbott, Thomas Ollive, ed. *Collected Works of Edgar Allan Poe.* 3 vols. Cambridge: Harvard UP, 1978.

Person, Leland S., Jr. *Aesthetic Headaches: Women and a Masculine Poetics in Poe, Melville, and Hawthorne.* Athens: U of Georgia P, 1988.

Poe, Edgar Allan. "The Philosophy of Composition." *Edgar Allan Poe: Essays and Reviews.* Ed. G. R. Thompson. New York: Library of America, 1984, 13–25.

———. "The Poetic Principle." *Edgar Allan Poe: Essays and Reviews.* Ed. G. R. Thompson. New York: Library of America, 1984, 71–94.

Rich, Adrienne. "When We Dead Awaken: Writing as Re-Vision." *On Lies, Secrets, and Silence: Selected Prose, 1966–1978.* New York: Norton, 1979.

Riley, Denise. *"Am I That Name?: Feminism and the Category of 'Women' in History.* Minneapolis: U of Minnesota P, 1988.

19

Poe and Postmodernism

DAVID H. HIRSCH

This chapter on Poe and postmodernism is not intended as an exhaustive survey of contemporary Poe criticism, but rather as an attempt to assess the significance of the distinction between the "traditional" Poe of "humanist" criticism and the Poe created by those postmodernist critics who practice deconstructionist criticism, or at least use deconstructionist or postmodernist critical terminology.

First, we must distinguish between postmodernist ideology and the deconstructionist methodology of analyzing texts. The ideology is resolutely antihumanist. Richard Freadman and Seumas Miller note that, for postmodernist theorists, " 'humanism' is customarily construed as an opposing term to 'theory . . . ,' [and] is seen as requiring of its exponents at least two cardinal commitments. First, a commitment to a conception of the individual self as atomistic and unconditioned; second, a commitment to certain kinds of evaluative discourse, both moral and aesthetic" (2).[1] Freadman and Miller add that, from the perspective of postmodernist ideology, "literary texts . . . will be congenitally incapable of offering authentic representations of reality" (2). What is of interest from my own point of view is that, in terms of ideology, Poe can accurately be described as a postmodernist before the term. Writing in the milieu of nineteenth-century American individualism, Poe undermined the notion of the atomistic individual self and of traditional "evaluative discourse, both moral and aesthetic." Moreover, it has long been argued against Poe by literary historians and critics that he was a Romantic or a Gothicist whose "stories have no human interest because humanity did not in the least interest him" (Brownell, 160). Deconstructionist methodology, as the handmaiden to postmodernist ideology, concentrates on demonstrating self-contradictions in text and demonstrating that texts are nonreferential, indeterminate, and always writing about the death of writing.

What is odd is that postmodernist literary theorists and critics who write about Poe do not raise the question of Poe's own antihumanist inclinations and do not stress his anticipation of postmodernist ideology. Rather, they concentrate on attacking humanist critics of Poe and on applying deconstructionist methodology in rereading his works.

HUMANISM

Matthiessen's *American Renaissance*

Since F. O. Matthiessen has been the most influential humanist critic of American literature, it is not surprising that postmodernist criticism should find itself energized by a need to "rectify" what is perceived as Matthiessen's erasure of Poe from the canon of "classic" American literature by excluding him from *American Renaissance* (1941). Louis A. Renza, for example, announced at the 1982–1983 meeting of the English Institute that "[i]n the context of the post–World War II institutionalization of American criticism from F. O. Matthiessen to Harold Bloom, the brief quantity and 'narrow' aesthetic as well as moral range of Poe's works has consigned them to the limbo of footnotes in the *American Renaissance*" (59).

Renza's own position seems somewhat ambiguous. If, as he puts it, Poe's works can be accurately characterized as being "brief [in] quantity and 'narrow' [in] aesthetic as well as moral range," then perhaps they do not deserve to be rescued from "the limbo of footnotes in *American Renaissance.*" A similar ambivalence is reflected in Kenneth Dauber's misguided assertion that "Poe is that pervasive emptiness which American writing must neglect. Not seeing Poe constitutes the history of American literature in the nineteenth century and perhaps beyond" (657). In *American Apocalypses* (1985), Douglas Robinson continues this line, asserting: "My relative neglect of Emerson has less to do with the dynamics of historical influence than with the present state of Poe and Emerson criticism. F. O. Matthiessen's rehabilitation of Emerson in *American Renaissance* (1941) has inspired an impressive body of scholarship that has solidly established Emerson's centrality to American literature. The rehabilitation of Poe is just now, in the past decade and a half, getting under way" (xvi). Though Robinson dates the revival of Poe criticism to 1970, Eric W. Carlson has identified the years 1949 to 1959 (with the publication of essays by Richard Wilbur, Allen Tate, and others) as a more significant decade in the history of Poe criticism (*CE,* 10).

The facts seem to support neither the claims of general neglect nor the particular allegation that in leaving Poe out of *American Renaissance* Matthiessen deliberately intended to erase Poe from "the canon." Given Matthiessen's thesis, it made sense for him not to include Poe in *American Renaissance.* He explained the omission by stating that Poe "was bitterly hostile to democracy"[2] and that an honest treatment of Poe (as Matthiessen saw it, of course) would involve an examination of "the effect of [Poe's] narrow but intense theories of poetry and the short story, and the account of the first of these alone could be the subject for another book: the development from Poe to Baudelaire, through the French symbolists, to modern American and English poetry" (xii).

Concentrating on this single footnote in *American Renaissance,* Matthiessen's detractors have slighted the text the footnote was intended to elucidate. Clearly, Matthiessen's purpose was to provide an aesthetic corrective to Vernon Parrington's version of "the liberal tradition" in *Main Currents of American Thought* (1927). Matthiessen's aim was not to "rehabilitate Emerson" but to define a liberal tradition in our literature and to demonstrate the way in which that tradition, the embodiment of an egalitarian democratic humanism, had been translated into artistic works of the highest aesthetic merit. The big gainer among the writers included in *American Renaissance* was Melville. A scan of the PMLA Bibliography for the decade of the 1980s turns up 954 citations on Melville, establishing him as the uncontested front-runner among the five authors in *American Renaissance* plus Poe, who comes in third with 636 items. The *Cambridge History of American Literature* (1917, 1918) devoted separate chapters each to Emerson, Hawthorne, Thoreau, Whitman, and Poe. Only Melville failed to merit his own chapter, being given a meager five pages in a general chapter on "Fiction."

But not only quantitative evidence contradicts the persistent myth that Poe has been the most neglected and most misunderstood of our writers. To be sure, he has been disliked by some, but to be disliked is not necessarily to be neglected, or even misunderstood; some of the critics who disliked Poe had legitimate reasons for doing so (even though one may not agree with them). Poe and Emerson were among the six writers the genteel W. C. Brownell included in his *American Prose Masters* (1909), and, while he recognized the genius as well as weaknesses in both of them, he was more disturbed by Poe's weaknesses than by Emerson's and clearly preferred Emerson's particular kind of genius to Poe's. Of Emerson, he wrote that "if he is not typically, he is peculiarly, American. No other country could have produced him." In speaking of Poe, he found that "Poe's art was unalloyed" and that, "illustrated by the energy of his genius, the spirit of romantic art entered the portals of our literature" (93, 144).

The Cambridge History reinforced these assessments. In this work P. E. More expressed his reservations about Emerson as an artist but praised him "as a steady force in the transmutation of life into ideas and as an authority in the direction of life itself" (1: 349). At the same time, Killis Campbell, who wrote the Poe chapter for the *Cambridge History,* said of Poe that "there are not wanting those who account him one of the two or three writers of indisputable genius that America has produced" (2: 55). Clearly, Emerson and Poe were both highly valued, but each for different reasons: Emerson as a moralist, and Poe as a "pure" poet and short story writer.

So though Poe's work has sparked considerable controversy, and, though one may disagree with the assessments arrived at by earlier critics, by no means can

Poe be called a writer who has been ignored, or even neglected, either before or after Matthiessen's *American Renaissance.* Even after the "erasure" allegedly perpetrated by *American Renaissance,* Poe has continued to receive the kind of academic attention granted only to major writers, including societies devoted to perpetuating his reputation, a journal dedicated to documenting new discoveries in his work and life, a newsletter, and his own chapter in *American Literary Scholarship.* Anthologies of American literature continue to include Poe prominently, and even the canon-revising *Heath Anthology of American Literature,* edited by Paul Lauter et al., allows Poe nearly 100 pages.

Finally, Matthiessen compensated for excluding Poe from *American Renaissance* by including his essay on Poe in *The Literary History of the United States* (1946), which for forty years remained the unchallenged definitive history of American literature. Matthiessen concluded that "Poe's final value may hardly be judged apart from the many traditions to which his work gave rise. French Symbolism . . . began at the moment when Baudelaire recognized in Poe's logical formulas for a poem his own half-developed thoughts" (340–41). Matthiessen ended his chapter with a glowing tribute to Poe's national and international importance:

The intense investigation of the roots of Gothic horror in morbid states of mind has been part of American fiction from Brockden Brown and Poe through Ambrose Bierce and William Faulkner.

Poe wrote at a time when America was producing more real and alleged transcendental geniuses than maturely wrought poems or stories. In opposition to the romantic stress on the expression of personality, he insisted on the importance not of the artist, but of the created work of art. He stands as one of the very few great innovators in American literature. Like Henry James and T. S. Eliot, he took his place, almost from the start, in international culture as an original creative force in contrast to the more superficial international vogue of Cooper and Irving. (342)

These are hardly the words of someone who did not understand Poe or who underrated him. Nevertheless, it may be no exaggeration to say that Matthiessen set the stage for identifying a postmodernist Poe, since he excluded him from *American Renaissance* precisely because he understood that Poe represented the beginning of an antihumanist tradition antithetical to the liberal humanism Matthiessen was celebrating in his book.

Davidson's *Edgar Allan Poe*

The humanist perspective on Poe was brilliantly set forth in E. H. Davidson's *Edgar Allan Poe: A Critical Study.* Davidson advised that he was undertaking "a philosophic inquiry into the mind and writings of Edgar Allan Poe," the gist of which was to situate Poe within the context of the transition from the Enlightenment to Romanticism (5). While recognizing the importance of the irrational in human experience generally and, specifically, as an important element in Poe's art and thought, Davidson nevertheless chose to analyze the irrational within a framework of rational discourse. He asserted that "What I have attempted is an understanding of Poe according to two critical theorems: one is the general premises of what we shall, for the moment call 'Romantic idealism' ...; the other is [the belief that] art ... is a way—for Poe the primal way—of man's knowing the world" (viii). Davidson restored to primacy in the Poe canon two works that had unquestionably been slighted: *The Narrative of Arthur Gordon Pym* and *Eureka,* devoting a separate chapter to each and presenting them together as a basis for getting at the essence of Poe's thinking. Davidson took both works to be linked by the motif of the quest. "The quest in *Pym,*" he wrote, "is for ultimates, for an abstraction; it is the same quest that, nearly a dozen years later and toward the end of his life, Poe would undertake in a long exposition called *Eureka*" (171).[3] Davidson argued that Pym, in his quest, "like so many of Poe's characters, ... is possessed by the death-wish, by the passion for annihilation" (177).

The humanist point of view assumes a universe of order and moral coherence. Since Poe often undermined rationality, and since he created fictional worlds that seemed to contain neither rational order nor moral coherence, some humanist critics sought to compensate for the apparent absence of normative moral principles in Poe's poetry and fiction by emphasizing elements of apocalypticism, visionary spiritualism, and pure Romantic transcendence in the tales and poems.

HUMANISM AND POSTMODERNISM

Eureka: Davidson (1957) and Dayan (1987)

Davidson treated Poe as a writer of poetry and fiction who took an interest in philosophical problems, and he helped to resurrect the current interest in *Eureka* by devoting an entire chapter of his critical study of Poe to the proposition that *Eureka* was not, as was commonly held at the time, "a farrago of nonsense." He spent a whole section of his *Eureka* chapter discussing "the epistemological and philosophic premises which underlie the theory of 'simplicity' and the content of Poe's 'poem' " (232). Since both Davidson and Dayan analyze *Eureka* at length, a brief comparison of their discussions may help clarify differences between humanist and postmodernist approaches. Early in his discussion of the prose poem, Davidson asserts:

The book is concerned with three scientific problems relating to the physical universe: first, the concept of creation (or, how did matter become what it appears to be?); second, the nature of matter (or, what is matter and how is the observed physical universe energized?); and third, the prospect for the natural world (or, toward what end is the ever-changing universe moving?). (224)

In her deconstructionist approach, Dayan avoids such crisp categorization, which she probably considers an oversimplification of texts and a betrayal of the inherent opacity and self-reflexiveness of language. Early in her exposition, Dayan writes:

Eureka, Poe's investigation of the "Material and Spiritual Universe," clarifies the rhetorical stresses and thought puzzles of his writing. Yet it also reminds us that Poe joined the epistemological and scriptural in every one of his schemes of matter, force, identity, and thought. *Eureka* begins and ends with God's Volition or Thought. His "willing into being the primordial particle, has completed the act, or more properly the *conception* of Creation." Out of this absolute and irrelative particle, through a process of diffusion and diversity, the Universe emerges. (19–20)

Davidson's critical methodology calls for him to convert Poe's verbal turbulence into some kind of order, while Dayan's deconstructionist methodology encourages her to revel in the turbulence itself. While Davidson calls attention to parallels between Coleridge and Poe in the mediation of Locke and German transcendental philosophers, Dayan identifies some suggestive parallels between Poe and Jonathan Edwards, calling attention to the ways in which both writers attempted to reconcile Lockean empiricism and scriptural revelation. But deconstructionist ideology blinds her to differences between Edward's scriptural faith, with its moral imperatives, and Poe's non-Christian speculations on the imagistic-exploratory power of biblical cosmology.

Surely, when Dayan says that *"Eureka* begins and ends with God's Volition or Thought," she is not referring to the biblical God of Sinai or the Christian Trinity but only to a decontextualized image of a God of pure creative power, an image of God that would have struck Edwards as blasphemous. Moreover, we may ask what Dayan is claiming when she writes "that Poe joined the epistemological and scriptural in every one of his schemes of matter, force, identity, and thought." Is this just a way of saying that Poe drew on both the Bible and Locke in arriving at knowledge of the universe? It seems to me that Dayan is much more successful when she gets away from cosmology. Dayan's reading of "Berenice" is penetrating and insightful, but it does not so much reveal a new Poe as confirm Allen Tate's observation that "Poe . . . discovered our great subject, the disintegration of personality" (*REAP,* 241). Dayan's reading is impressive in its alertness and attention to detail, but she has not gone beyond Tate in her basic insight.

"The Masque of the Red Death": Roppolo (1967) and Kennedy (1987)

J. Gerald Kennedy, in *Poe, Death, and the Life of Writing* (1987), has a somewhat different, yet at the same time, similar problem. He, too, cannot quite reconcile a deconstructionist thesis with his practical criticism. As Dana Brand has pointed out in his review, "While Kennedy's work will interest those looking for new perspectives on Poe's preoccupations, it may disappoint those looking for new readings of Poe's texts" (5). Kennedy's inability to generate new readings out of his thesis is evident, to take one example, in his discussion of "The Masque of the Red Death," a story central to his thesis. Kennedy's thesis should generate a reading that supersedes Joseph Patrick Roppolo's New Critical reading, "Meaning and 'The Masque of the Red Death.'" Roppolo summarized the story and its moral:

The fear of death can kill: Prospero attempts to attack the masked figure and falls; when man's image of death is confronted directly, it is found to be nothing. The vestments are empty. The intruder in "The Masque of the Red Death" is, then, not the plague, not death itself, but man's creation, his self-aroused and self-developed fear of his own mistaken concept of death. . . . "The Masque of the Red Death" . . . can be (and has been) read as a parable of the inevitability and the universality of death. . . . What Poe has created . . . is a kind of mythic parable, brief and poetic, of the human condition, of man's fate, and of the fate of the universe. (142, 144)

Given Kennedy's thesis, we are justified, I believe, in asking how his interpretation of the story takes us beyond Roppolo and how it casts a new light on Poe's long-recognized obsession with death and dying. In his corrective to Roppolo's New Critical reading, Kennedy concludes:

But the cerements and mask are signs without a proper referent; they mark the semiotic impasse in which writing has begun to locate its own activity. The discovery of the revelers enacts the nineteenth-century perception of death as "pure negativity," a nothingness resulting from "the separation of the body and soul." Paradoxically, Poe's portrayal of pure absence signifies "the presence of the Red Death"; the revelers fall, the clock stops, and the flames of the tripods expire. Death itself has no essence; it cannot be seized, known, destroyed, or avoided. It is a presence-as-absence whose meaning is forever denied to presence and already accomplished in absence. (203)

It is almost as if Kennedy has translated Roppolo into deconstructionese. Roppolo's "[W]hen man's image of death is confronted directly, it is found to be nothing" now becomes Kennedy's "But the cerements and mask are signs without a proper referent; they mark the semiotic impasse." The gain, if there is one, is to affirm the deconstructionist view that the human dilemma is purely one of language. For Roppolo, Poe's story demonstrates that man creates his own image of terror out of his fear of death, but, for Kennedy, the message is that language is a self-referential system that renders all linguistic utterances empty. Ending the chapter titled "Revenge and Silence," which includes a discussion of "The Cask of Amontillado," Kennedy asserts that "through the act of writing by which they make known their secret deeds, Poe's narrators assume a textuality which completes the perverse self-destruction of the speaking subject'' (144). Does this really enlighten us? May we not just as easily maintain the opposite of what Kennedy says: by making known their ''secret deeds . . . through the act of writing,'' Poe's narrators redeem themselves from ''the perverse self-destruction of the speaking subject.''

POSTMODERNISM

"The Purloined Letter": Lacan, Derrida, Johnson, and Felman

Poe's constant probing of the notion of a rationally ordered and morally coherent universe and his frequent undermining of the kind of stable individual human identity envisioned by John Locke made him appear to be a postmodernist before the fact, so to speak, and, given Poe's impact on French writers and culture, it was inevitable that he should sooner or later come to the attention of the French poststructuralists. For the most part, the deconstructionist approach to Poe consists of two clusters of essays; one centered on Jacques Lacan's ''Seminar on 'The Purloined Letter' '' (1956, English version, 1972), and the other on John Irwin's deconstructionist reading of *The Narrative of Arthur Gordon Pym*. According to Lacan, ''The Purloined Letter'' provided a useful demonstration of the Freudian ''repetition automatism.''[4] Freud had discovered that the ''loosen[ing] of the [patient's] repression'' that took place in the process of psychoanalysis led the patient into a painful emotional dilemma. On one hand, the patient was now compelled to repeat the past experience that had led to the neurotic disorder; at the same time, this repetition caused the patient to relive the pain. Lacan reconstructed Poe's story into two scenes that ostensibly ''repeated'' each other: a ''primal scene'' in the chamber of the exalted personage (the ''king,'' the ''queen,'' and the Minister D. in the ''royal boudoir'') and an alleged repetition of this primal scene in ''the Minister's office,'' between Minister D. and Dupin.

Though Lacan was a psychiatrist, his seminar on the ''Letter'' seems to have had little resonance in the psychiatric community. Whereas Freud used analysis and insight to cure neurotic patients, Lacan's effort seems to have no clinical application. If there is a ''repetition automatism'' in Poe's story, it would seem to have little to do with the dilemma described by Freud, since none of the characters in Poe's story are compelled to ''repeat'' a painful past experience, and since there is no sense that ''the compulsion to repeat also recalls from the past experiences which include no possibility of pleasure'' (Freud, *Beyond the Pleasure Principle*, 21).

Jacques Derrida's 1975 response to Lacan's reading of ''The Purloined Letter'' raised five basic objections to Lacan's essay. Derrida's main points were, first, that Lacan was not as Saussurean as he pretended to be, since he permitted the ''pre-verbal'' concept of the Oedipus complex to predetermine his rhetorical analysis of the story, thus making the language system itself subservient to

Freudian ideology. Second, Derrida accused Lacan of not having taken his Freudian reading of the story much beyond the earlier Freudian readings of Marie Bonaparte, and he further charged him with having borrowed from her without acknowledgment. Third, Derrida claimed that Lacan had misread the story as a consequence of ignoring the presence and function of the narrator. Fourth, Derrida argued that Lacan could not interpret the story adequately because he failed to "frame" it properly, having neglected to place it in the context of Poe's other Dupin stories ("The Murders in the Rue Morgue" and "The Mystery of Marie Roget"). Finally, Derrida challenged Lacan's cryptic conclusion that a letter always reaches its destination, a conclusion that violates the deconstructionist claim that language is a self-enclosed system of arbitrary signs unrelated to a physical world. While all of Derrida's criticisms of Lacan may have been valid, Derrida himself did little to enhance our understanding of the story or of Poe.

The controversy between Lacan and Derrida elevated Poe to prominence among the followers of deconstruction. In 1977, *Yale French Studies* presented two essays on what had now become a controversy not over the meaning of Poe's story but over what Derrida and Lacan might have been saying about the meaning of the story: one of the essays was by Barbara Johnson, and the other was by Shoshana Felman.

Barbara Johnson's essay attempts to mediate the opposed readings of Lacan and Derrida:

A literary text that both analyzes itself and shows that it actually has neither a self nor any neutral metalanguage with which to do the analyzing, calls out irresistibly for analysis. When that call is answered by two eminent French thinkers whose readings emit their own equally paradoxical call-to-analysis, the resulting tryptich, in the context of the question of the act-of-reading (-literature), places its would-be reader in a vertiginously insecure position.[5] (110)

Two ideas emerge prominently in Johnson's analysis: (1) the texts under consideration, presumably including her own, are unstable and without boundaries (i.e., subject to infinite interpretations) and (2) meaning is always radically indeterminate. "Here," she writes, "the very fact that we are dealing with *three* texts is in no way certain" (110). She finally decides that "What is undecidable is whether a thing is decidable or not" (146). What Johnson seems to celebrate, then, is not *différance,* but what she takes to be an ultimate indeterminacy in which all distinctions are blurred, and readers can no longer distinguish between text and text, text and world, text and self, self and world, self and self.

For Felman, the main issue is Lacan's ascent to what she perceives as a new plateau of critical acumen. "Lacan's importance in my eyes," she writes, "does not . . . lie specifically in the new dogma his 'school' proposes, but lies in his outstanding demonstration that *there is more than one way* to implicate psychoanalysis in literature" (153). Felman also believes that Lacan has obliterated any "well-defined border between literature and psychoanalysis: psychoanalysis could be intraliterary just as much as literature is intrapsychoanalytic" (153). This is a puzzling claim, since the interconnectedness of literature and psychoanalysis has long been recognized. Not only did Freud himself deliberately draw on literary works for much of his insight and evidence, but it is generally agreed that Dostoevsky and Kafka probed human consciousness and the subconscious mind at least as deeply as Freud, though they never presented themselves as scientists.

As Felman sees it, Lacan departs from conventional Freudian criticism in focusing his explorations on the "signifier" rather than the "signified": "If the purloined letter can be said to be a sign of the unconscious, for Marie Bonaparte the analyst's task is to uncover the letter's *content,* which she believes—as do the police—to be *hidden* somewhere in the real, in some secret biographical *depth.* For Lacan, on the other hand, the analyst's task is not to read the letter's hidden referential content, but to situate the superficial indication of its textual movement, to analyze the paradoxically invisible symbolic evidence of its displacement, its structural insistence, in a signifying chain" (148). In other words, Lacan's advance beyond Bonaparte and other Freudians is to posit an analogy between the language and the psyche as Saussurean structures. Just as there is no "depth" to the system of sound images that refer only to each other, so there is no depth to the psyche, which is also merely a system of "signifiers" referring only to each other, rather than a facet of a human identity. In the physical and psychic worlds, as in the language system, then, there is only structure, never substance. Nevertheless, Felman herself does not seem to believe this, for she later attributes "content" to Poe's story. She writes, "If 'The Purloined Letter' is specifically the story of 'the poet's superiority in the art of concealment,' then it is not just an allegory of psychoanalysis but also, at the same time, an allegory of poetic writing" (152). But if Felman believes that Poe is writing an allegory of the "[p]oet's superiority in the art of concealment," then she seems to be acknowledging that both the "letter" and Poe's story do, after all, have not only content but a message, and she seems to be striking a very conventional note in interpreting a literary work as an allegory with a hidden meaning.[6]

Arthur Gordon Pym: Rowe (1977), Irwin (1980), Robinson (1985), and Kennedy (1994)

In his extremely useful evaluations of *Pym* criticism in the bibliographical essay written for the *Pym Explorations* volume, David Ketterer begins his listing of "Deconstructive readings" by crediting Jean Ricardou as "the first of several French critics to understand *Pym* as being about writing and a journey to the end of the page" (255). He continues with John Carlos Rowe's 1977 essay, reprinted in revised form in *Through the Custom House.* In this essay entitled "Writing and Truth in Poe's *The Narrative of Arthur Gordon Pym,*" Rowe asserts that *Pym* is, like all texts, writing about writing. "In the foregoing interpretation," Rowe says, "I have argued that writing itself is the central subject of *Pym*" (106). He asserts, further, that "[t]he 'idealistic aestheticism' that seems to control most of Poe's writings is precisely what is threatened by *The Narrative of A. Gordon Pym*. This text enacts the deconstruction of representation as the illusion of the truth and prefigures the contemporary conception of writing as the endless production of differences" (95). At another point, Rowe asserts, "The text has become a machine for the production of surplus signifiers" and "In *The Narrative of A. Gordon Pym*, Poe lingers on the verge of establishing writing itself as the constitution and facilitation (*die Bahnung*) of psychic experience" (108, 109). Consistent with deconstructionist orthodoxy, Rowe interprets *Pym* as a narrative that undermines the possibility of any notion of "representation" or "truth," since language can never be more than a self-enclosed system of signifier-signifieds trapped inside the individual mind that refer only to each other and never to a "world outside."

David Ketterer rightly describes John Irwin's analysis of *Pym* in *American Hieroglyphics* (1980) as a "tour de force" that "focuses on the relationships between writing, doubling, and an interest in hieroglyphics" (255). Irwin concludes his meticulous and highly learned analysis by summing up the significance of the equivalence (or perhaps indistinguishability) between a lived life and a narrated life:

[I]f the sense of an individual life's meaningfulness inheres precisely in its narratability, in its possessing the unified shape of a story, and if such a unified shape requires a narrative closure synonymous with death, then this precludes a person's being both the actor and the narrator of his own story, precludes at last the double role of image and mirror, so that the narrative of one's own life is always unfinished, a fragment in which meaningful closure is either a fictionalized foreshadowing or a postscript in another hand. As readers, as survivors of the textual journey to the *vor*-textual abyss . . . we see the quest for fixed certainty, that univocal sense which is the linguistic equivalent of *Eureka*'s primal Oneness, for what it is—a death wish. (235)

Despite Irwin's many insights and his deconstructionist rhetoric, the antihumanist reading arrives, with a few detours and circlings, only where the humanists have already been, discovering that *Pym* and *Eureka* constitute the same quest for oneness and meaning, which is, in essence, "the death wish," the same motif noted in both works by E. H. Davidson in his humanist reading. From the deconstructionist point of view, the inevitably unsuccessful quest for certainty in *Pym* and *Eureka* confirms the indeterminacy of meaning in all texts.

The vacillation between deconstruction and a moralistic historicism is noticeable in Douglas Robinson's *American Apocalypses* (1985). Robinson attests that Irwin's lengthy discussion of *Pym* led to "my own rediscovery of Poe as an adult, and my concomitant and growing sense of the importance of American apocalypses" (xvii).[7] But the conventional thesis of "the importance of American apocalypses'' runs counter to postmodern ideology. Robinson's conventional thesis assumes an American visionary tradition in which the poet uses language to seek a revelation of some transcendent truth. But his application of postmodern values to this thesis depends on the assumption that language is a self-enclosed, self-reflecting system of signifier-signifieds that cannot possibly lead to some transcendent truth.

While the postmodernist thesis dictates a denial of the possibility of any revelation, the traditional thesis calls for an affirmation of *Pym* precisely as a [biblical] revelation. Hence, Robinson finds that ''[w]hat Poe is concerned with is . . . the effort to plunge not into presential Being but into the abysm of *différance* that forever separates presence from absence, and there to generate an iconic dream-body that will permit a visionary habitation of the gap.'' He asserts that Poe's ''doubt of the human capacity to apprehend meaning necessarily does cast the existence of meaning into doubt'' and adds, ''[W]hat is crucial for Poe is not the meaning itself, but the interpretive act of constituting meaning through imagistic mediation'' (119, 120). In attempting to fuse a ''traditional'' American visionary Poe with a postmodernist Poe committed to arbitrary interpretive acts and the ''indeterminacy of meaning,'' Robinson manages to do a precarious bit of fence-sitting. In fact, Robinson's seemingly precise distinction between ''meaning'' and ''the interpretive act of constituting meaning'' is actually redundant, since, from the deconstructionist point of view, meaning is never anything other than interpretation.

Like some of the other deconstructive critics mentioned here, Kennedy seems to have had second thoughts about deconstruction. His ''Introduction'' to the Oxford World Classics series *Edgar Allan Poe: The Narrative of Arthur Gordon Pym of Nantucket and Related Tales* (1994) is mainly historical and biographical. While he does state that ''Pym experiences the phenomenal world as an unreadable text'' (xi), and while he does point out the ''indeterminacy'' of the novel, nevertheless, he suggests that the indeterminacy is not an end in itself but a justification for interpreting the book ''as a tale of death and transfiguration'' (xii).

"The Fall of the House of Usher"

The purest instance of a deconstructionist reading of a major Poe work aside from ''The Purloined Letter'' and *Pym* is probably Joseph N. Riddell's ''The 'Crypt' of Edgar Poe.'' Riddell tries to justify Poe as a deconstructionist *avant la lettre,* observing that ''Poe introduces . . . a self-critical or self-annihilating textual performance—the poem/story and even the critical essay (as performance that deconstructs itself). This is said to be Poe's ironic theme in 'The Philosophy of Composition' and 'The Poetic Principle' '' (124). I would like to suggest, however, that, while Poe clearly anticipates deconstructive practices in his criticism (certainly in ''The Philosophy of Composition''), the deconstructive thrust of the "poem/story" is more elusive. Citing the closing sentences of "The Fall of the House of Usher," Riddell concludes:

The fragments of the narrative collapse upon themselves, and are enclosed in a final metaphor that contains the figure of the house, the family, and the story itself—an infinitely refracted series of fictions without origin or end, without the sustaining center of the crypt. . . . The "House of Usher" is built out of old books, the fragments of legends, romances, superstitions, and quasi-scientific metaphors, all erected upon a "hollow coffin" that must be protected even as it is ultimately opened and revealed as the place of just another missing body, another simulacrum of a simulacrum. (130)

In deconstructionist thinking, with its belief that language is a system of "signs" related only to each other (i.e., signifiers-signifieds incapable of referring to either a physical or "ideal" world), metaphors are treated as commentaries on their own existence, and form is confused with content. Hence, for Riddell, the collapse of the metaphorical decaying house that also symbolizes a decaying family is equivalent to the collapse of the story. But the "story" does not "collapse" the way the house does. It remains a viable "structure" that English speakers continue to read and make sense of.

It is interesting that though "Usher" is Poe's most widely discussed tale, Riddell does not cite prior interpretations. This silence reflects the deconstructionist assumption of a rupture so total that there can be no common ground between deconstructionists and logocentrists. I cannot, of course, review all previous scholarship on "Usher" here, but I would like to provide some perspective by setting Richard Wilbur's comments on the story beside Riddell's. From Wilbur's logocentrist view, " 'The Fall of the House of Usher' is a journey into the depths of the self" (Regan, 108). In other words, both the individual metaphors and the extended metaphorical structure of the story reveal something about the ways in which human consciousness is related to a physical world. For Wilbur, the significance of the collapse at the end of the story is that it indicates that "Roderick Usher has become all soul. 'The Fall of the House of Usher,' then, is not really a horror story; it is a triumphant report by the narrator that it is possible for the poetic soul to shake off this temporal, rational, physical world and escape, if only for a moment, to a realm of unfettered vision" (Regan, 110). Riddell's refusal to engage earlier readings, such as Wilbur's, undermines the possibility of any reconciliation of humanist and deconstructionist points of view.

The American Romance

In *The Rhetoric of American Romance* (1985), Evan Carton, like Douglas Robinson, mixes a deconstructionist approach with a traditional motif in a continuing effort to reconcile traditional historicist studies of American literature with deconstructionist ideologies and methodologies of reading. Carton's vacillation between conventional ideology and deconstructionist methodology is apparent in the following discussion of Poe's concept of human identity:

Complete self-realization for Poe's isolated artists or madmen is self-annihilation; in impressing his being upon the world . . . the poet loses that being. When the self-other distinction breaks down, when [Roderick] Usher converges with "his last and only relative on earth," "proper identity" gives way to what remains, from a human perspective, the terror of integration. (75)

Though couched in deconstructionist terminology, Carton's thinking seems to be rooted in fundamental Christian mystery that is the very antithesis of deconstruction. When he says that "Usher's paradox [is] the paradox of one's loss of self through the intensity of one's effort to distinguish and preserve it," is he not echoing, in secular language, the mystery embodied in the words attributed to Jesus by both Matthew and Luke, which read, in Luke's version (17: 33): "Whosoever shall seek to save his life shall lose it; and whosoever shall lose his life shall preserve it"? Carton's focus on Roderick's fear of losing his "identity" as the motif of "Usher" was anticipated by the humanist Davidson, who considered "Usher" "an early exposition . . . of this psychic drama, a summary of Poe's ideas and method of investigating the self in disintegration," and he pointed out that "Usher represents the mind or intellectual aspect of total being," while "Madeline is the sensual or physical side of this [divided] psyche: they are identical twins" (196).

For Carton, as a deconstructionist, what is important is not so much Poe's creative thinking about the possibilities of transcendence but simply the self-other reflections in themselves. Barton Levi St. Armand has commented, rightly, I believe, that Carton "builds a hall of mirrors" in which "Hegel's Phenomenology of Spirit . . . is the true sacred text . . . , and this choice dooms Carton to the infinitely self-reflexive dialectical narcissism that must be any romantic's reading of romanticism" (4).

The Romantic Arabesque: Thompson (1989)

In his essay "Romantic Arabesque, Contemporary Theory, and Postmodernism: The Example of Poe's Narrative," G. R. Thompson finds himself in the same traditionalist versus postmodernist dilemma. He contrasts "formalist approaches" that seek to establish "a coherent, stable, and symmetrical structure of repeating elements" (263), with his own postmodernist approach, which features "indeterminacy of meaning" (265). But Thompson also finds himself stranded between postmodernist ideology and his intuitive perception that Poe does not simply render indeterminate meanings but moves from experience to writing deliberately and consciously to record his perception of an absurd universe. Poe's portrayal of an existentialist absurd universe had already been pointed out by D. H. Hirsch in his 1968 essay, "The Pit and the Apocalypse," and by E. W. Carlson in his MLA paper, "Poe's Vision of Man," without "benefit" of postmodernist ideology.

Thompson's "discovery" that Poe's vision of an "absurd" universe is also a vision of a "totally indeterminate" universe constitutes a superimposition of deconstructionist ideology onto 1950s existentialism. Thompson writes, somewhat ungrammatically:

> Embodied or inscripted in Pym's *Narrative* of a journey to the (withheld) "end" of something suggests a point made repeatedly by Paul de Man—that experience always exists simultaneously as fictional discourse and as empirical event and it is almost never possible to decide which one of the two possibilities is the right one. (265)

De Man's effort to obscure the distinction between "fictional discourse" and "empirical event" is a contrivance intended to mitigate his own personal collaborationist past.[8] But in the real world (as opposed to the fantasy world of deconstructionist theory), the inability to make such a distinction is a pathological condition. Moreover, Thompson seems not to understand that the postmodernist concept of "indeterminacy of meaning" is at the antipodes of the existential concept of an "absurd" universe. While the latter projects the image of "rational man" in conflict with a meaningless universe, the former dissolves this conflict by making human beings one with the nonhuman universe.

POSTMODERNISM INTO THE 1990s

Eureka, Pym, and Naturphilosophie: John Limon's Response (1983, 1990)

In his essay, "How to Place Poe's *Arthur Gordon Pym* in Science-Dominated Intellectual History, and How to Extract It Again," John Limon revives both *Pym* and *Eureka* not only as works that are intimately intertwined but as works that emerged from a historical-intellectual landscape and that attempt to make a statement about the human condition. Limon locates the prose poem and the sea narrative within the intellectual context of *Naturphilosophie,* and he accomplishes a brilliant interpretation of *Pym* by examining it in the light of ideas overtly expressed in *Eureka.* Although the argument is too complicated to be discussed in detail here, Limon reads *Pym* as a narrative that reflects "the basic nature-philosophic development: the subject goes over into the object . . . , into nature, as nature is humanized" (37). In the ending of *Pym,* Limon finds that "as in *Naturphilosophie,* nature falls from spirit, and builds up to humanity to regain spirit" (37).

"Poe," Limon observes, "is specifically nature-philosophic rather than Kantian. . . . At the end of *Eureka,* matter becomes . . . entirely spiritualized. It is perhaps on Coleridge's authority that Poe sees in the reduction of matter to force the implication that it may be reduced to spirit" (1983, 34–35). Limon's examination of *Pym* and *Eureka* from the perspective of *Naturphilosophie* suggests that Poe, like the great British Romantic poets, was both attracted to contemporary science and, at the same time, seeking a way to overcome the "dead" universe science seemed to be bringing into existence.

As Basil Willey has pointed out, Wordsworth was, "in a sense . . . in violent reaction against [the 'scientific tradition'], and yet it conditioned much of his poetic experience" (113). The same may be said of Poe. Wordsworth and Coleridge found their way out of the impasse, according to Willey, by way of the " 'Fancy-Imagination' distinction. . . . Owing to the bond between nature and the soul of man, this dead world may be brought to life by the modifying colours of the 'imagination' " (116). But it is difficult to find "nature . . . humanized" in Poe in the same sense that we can find it in Wordsworth and Coleridge. Rather, Poe's acquaintance with *Naturphilosophie,* which Limon describes as "an attempt to subdue empirical science with philosophical *a prioris,*" leads Poe to spiritualize, rather than humanize, Nature. If one aspect of the "naturephilosophic tradition" is the belief that "[s]ince nature is divine spirit in potential, it is all alive," then we may say that, under the influence of *Naturphilosophie,* Poe makes "matter [come] alive through the eternal that is in it" (1983, 35).

In summing up his analysis of *Pym* and *Eureka* in his book, Limon points out contradictions in Rowe's approach to *Pym.* "What," he asks, "is Rowe's loyalty to an authorial intention that the text may not manifest?" Further, "If Rowe knows that the text is trying to break loose from its period, then he must have some knowledge of the period—intellectual history is possible" (*The Place of Fiction,* 119). In other words, deconstructionists have a hard time sticking to their own radically skeptical theories. At any rate, Rowe himself would later do a complete about-face on the matter of *Pym* as a self-enclosed text whose subject was writing about writing in his paper delivered at the *Pym* conference, May 1988.

Poe and Racism: Rowe (1988), Ridgely (1992), and Dayan (1994)

Roughly a decade after the publication of his deconstructionist reading, which sealed Pym's narrative within itself, Rowe recanted. At the 1988 conference "*Arthur Gordon Pym* and Contemporary Criticism," Rowe declared that "Poe was a proslavery Southerner and should be reassessed as such in whatever approach we take to his life and writings."[9] That Poe was a "proslavery Southerner" was knowledge available to Rowe when he wrote his essay on *Pym* in the 1970s. So the question arises, What moved Rowe to transform his political oblivion of the 1970s into his now highly politicized argument that "Poe's proslavery sentiments are fundamental to his literary production and thus demand a searching reconsideration of his aesthetic canon" (117)?

We need not search long for an answer. By 1988, the ideological skeletons in the deconstructionist closet were rattling deafeningly. Roused out of their Heideggerian complacency by Victor Farias's *Heidegger et le Nazisme,* French intellectuals were once again forced to face the issue of Heidegger's Nazism. At the same time, Paul de Man's pro-Nazi collaborationist past had been exposed and was coming under scrutiny. In returning to Poe's "racism" by way of an essay on *Pym,* Rowe joined the antihumanist counterattack intended to demonstrate that liberal humanism was as deeply implicated in genocidal strategies as the antihumanist ideology underlying the writings of Heidegger, Derrida, and de Man. It had now become useful for Rowe to discuss *The Narrative of Arthur Gordon Pym of Nantucket,* not as writing about writing, but as a complex "allegory of slavery." *Pym,* he wrote, is not a *"mere* allegory of proslavery values . . .''; it is a psychological allegory, an eruption of ''"Poe's own repressed fears regarding slave rebellions in the South" (127; emphasis mine).

Reexamining Poe's pro-slavery sentiments from a deconstructionist point of view also provided Rowe one more opportunity to discredit the constructive humanism of that favorite target of antihumanists, F. O. Matthiessen. For leaving Poe out of *American Renaissance* and writing about him as an internationalist and a premodernist in the *Literary History of the United States,* Matthiessen was charged with having "repress[ed] the subtle complicity of literary Modernism with racist ideology, which now Poe may be said to represent both in his antebellum historical context and his modern 'revival' '' (Rowe, 136). Just as Paul de Man repressed his anti-Semitic writings for *Het Vlaamsche Land* and *Le Soir,* it is suggested, so Matthiessen "repressed" Poe's "racism" and its connection to the "racism" of the modernists. But this implicit comparison is misleading.

Matthiessen, however, did not "repress" his reservations about Poe's politics but stated them openly in his much-discussed footnote in *American Renaissance,* where he explained that Poe had been excluded because he "was bitterly hostile to democracy" Moreover, the shadow cast over the authenticity of de Man's mature criticism stems not so much from the fact that he did not address the evils of Nazism, as from the fact that he concealed his own Nazi collaborationist past, living a lie. All indications are that it was not feelings of guilt or shame that led de Man to cover up his nasty past, but rather the very same crass motivation that led him to write collaborationist essays in the first place—a desire to advance his career, thus diminishing his credibility.

If Poe was a "proslavery Southerner" and a "racist," however, he does not seem (at least in his stories and poems) to have been obsessed by "racism" in the way that Eliot and Pound were obsessed by Jew-hating. It is not clear that his "racism" permeates his poetry and fiction in the same way that Pound's anti-Semitism permeates the later *Cantos* and his radio speeches. Further, if Poe is a racist, we must ask whether that racism was ingested by his French admirers and imitators, like Baudelaire and Mallarmé, and whether it has infected all of French symbolist and impressionist poetry. Having raised the issue, Rowe does not tell us where he wants to go with Poe's racism. Are we to embark on a witch-hunt, looking for traces of racism in all of Poe's stories, finding racism in everything Poe wrote, as deconstructionists now find indeterminacy, aporias, and belatedness?

Joan Dayan's answer to this question seems to be an emphatic yes. In her essay "Amorous Bondage: Poe, Ladies, and Slaves," she argues vigorously and in some historical and biographical detail that Poe, indeed, was obsessed by "racism" in the way that Eliot and Pound were obsessed by Jew-hating and that his "racism" (or, at least, his consciousness of race and the institutions of slavery) does permeate his poetry and fiction in the same way that Pound's anti-Semitism permeates the later *Cantos* and his radio speeches, except that Poe's obsession with "blackness" is less explicit. She declares that "We need to reread Poe's romantic fictions as bound to the realities of race" (252). Dayan fleshes out her denunciation of Poe's racism by linking it to his alleged misogynistic attitudes toward women, both his pro-slavery position and his sexism growing out of his need to establish dominance. Although Dayan uses some historical sources, she is ahistorical in perceiving Poe within the perspective of 1990s political correctness. The fact is that Poe certainly is not politically correct by today's standards and was not even considered politically correct by many of his contemporaries.

Interestingly, Dayan, like Rowe, has, for the most part, abandoned the rhetoric of deconstructionist readings so ubiquitous in her book, in favor of feminist historicism and moralism. Her argument hinges largely on her assumption that Poe authored the now infamous "Paulding-Drayton Review" in the April 1836 *Southern Literary Messenger*. Unfortunately, she chooses to ignore J. V. Ridgely's meticulous rehearsal of the facts (*PSA Newsletter,* Fall 1992) casting considerable doubt on the contention that Poe authored the review, and she then seems to attribute to Poe the sentiments of every obnoxious statement she can find made in defense of slavery in the 1830s.

Nevertheless, she forces readers to think about the influence the institution of slavery may have had on Poe's thinking and on his fiction and poetry.

CONCLUSION

Few humanist commentators have failed to observe that Poe was obsessed with thoughts of death, nothingness, and annihilation. It is also widely recognized (by Eric Carlson, Allen Tate, Richard Wilbur, among others) that Poe sought to use his writing (as did some of the British Romantic poets) to attempt to explore that "undiscovered country from whose bourne no traveler returns." Does it add to our knowledge of Poe to convert these observations into the terminology of "sign, referent, semiotic impasse, and writing locat[ing] its own activity?" Or does it advance our understanding of the human fear of death and of Poe's attitudes toward death to cast the problem in terms such as, "It is a presence-as-absence whose meaning is forever denied to presence and already accomplished in absence"? Such language serves only to make a parody of the genuine agony expressed in Poe's fiction and experienced by most human beings.

Whatever the changes in critical fashion, clearly we cannot imagine American literature without Poe. His writings occupy a unique position not only in the history of Romanticism and French literary theory but as anticipations of modernist aesthetics and even of postmodern consciousness. One of the major innovations of nineteenth-century literature was the development of a new psychological perception, which certainly owed something to Poe (see Kahler, 176). In his probings of the human soul and the roots of moral dysfunction, Poe anticipated Nietzsche's transvaluation of values, and many Poe stories can be read as speculations on how this transvaluation would influence human behavior. Poe was one of the first thinkers to express what Erich Kahler has described as "the deep unrest, uneasiness and alarm at the effects of our modern middleclass civilization; [a sense] of the increasing hollowness and precariousness of conventional values, the derangement of human relations" (176).

As a dissident (or dark) Romantic, Poe established a new relationship between nature and consciousness that also points forward to postmodern writing and thinking. The British Romantic poets attempted, as Basil Willey notes, to "animise the 'real' world, the 'universe of death' that the 'mechanical' system of philosophy had produced." Emerson subscribed to the Wordsworthian belief "in the free relations between the mind of man and the universe to which, [Wordsworth] believes, it is 'so exquisitely fitted.' " Like Wordsworth, Emerson "constructed out of his experiences a belief in the capacity of the mind to cooperate with this 'active universe,' to contribute something of its own to it in perceiving it, and not, as sensationalism taught, merely to receive passively, impressions from without" (114–15).

Poe challenged the Wordsworthian construct and its Emersonian expansion. As Gregory Jay writes, "Poe's journeys into the disestablishment of inherited constructs are subversive versions of standard Romantic themes. For his own purposes he took up the Romantic reaction against empiricism and 'common sense' philosophy" (147). But instead of rejecting Lockean empiricism the way the transcendentalists did, by reanimizing the universe of Nature, he undermined the purely empiricist universe by pushing it to an absurd extreme.

In his psychological probing, his transvaluation of values, and his turning aside from the British Romantics by refusing to bridge what they (and he) perceived as the abyss between consciousness and nature, Poe became a harbinger of postmodernist thinking and writing. Poe's inversion of conventional middle-class values led him to create characters who are, at various times and in different stories, dehumanized, amoral, and driven by what he called "the imp of the perverse." Poe's psychological portraits anticipate Dostoevsky as well as Nietzsche in foreseeing the death of God in Western culture and its consequences. So far, deconstructionist and postmodern treatments of Poe have not met the challenge presented by Poe's innovativeness. Instead, they have concentrated too exclusively on applying to Poe such deconstructionist concepts as "indeterminacy of meaning," "writing that is always already about writing," and "the belatedness of language," so that deconstructionist readings of Poe stories have become monotonously predictable.[10] If New Critical readings of Poe had reached a dead end, deconstructionist readings, with their narrow and repetitious focus on two or three deconstructionist themes, have also reached a dead end, and in a much shorter time span.

NOTES

1. In addition to Freadman and Miller, see books by D. H. Hirsch, Merquior, Ferry and Renaut, and Ellis listed in Bibliography.

2. Matthiessen's footnote reads, in part: "I have avoided . . . the temptation to include a full-length treatment of Poe. The reason is more fundamental than that his work fell mainly in the decade of 1835–45; for it relates at very few points to the main assumptions about literature that were held by any of my group. Poe was bitterly hostile to democracy, and in that respect could serve as a revelatory contrast" (xii, fn. 3).

3. W. H. Auden (1950), Allen Tate (1952), and Patrick Quinn (1952) were also instrumental in reevaluating these works and bringing them to the attention of Poe readers, as was Sidney Kaplan in calling attention to the symbolism and racial implications of *Pym.*

4. Originally published in *Le Psychoanalyse* (1956), reprinted in *Écrits* (1966); English translation by Jeffrey Mehlman, in *Yale French Studies* 48 (1972). See John P. Muller and William Richardson, *The Purloined Poe* (Baltimore: Johns Hopkins UP, 1988), 376, for bibliographical details. Citations to Lacan, Derrida, Johnson, and Felman in this chapter are to *The Purloined Poe.*

5. I am not sure what Johnson means when she says that "a text has [no] self." When she says the text lacks a "neutral metalanguage with which to do the analyzing," I assume she is lamenting the fact that the vocabularies of Derrida and de Man were not available to Poe.

6. It is also worthwhile noting that in discussing narratives of Holocaust survivors in her recent book, coauthored with Dori Laub, *Testimony: Crises of Witnessing in Literature, Psychoanalysis, and History* (Routledge, 1992), Felman assumes the existence of content and recognizes at several points that the events being narrated must take precedence over the narrative techniques; that is, she recognizes that in real-world situations it is no error to seek to "uncover" a letter's content.

7. This intriguing confession makes one wonder why Robinson was not similarly stimulated by others who had written on *Pym,* including Auden, P. Quinn, Kaplan, and Davidson.

8. See David H. Hirsch, *The Deconstruction of Literature,* Chapters 2–6.

9. "Poe, Antebellum Slavery, and Modern Criticism," *Poe's* Pym: *Critical Explorations,* 117.

10. Jeffrey T. Nealon maintained that deconstruction is dead in American universities. In fact, in his view, deconstruction has been practiced only in a debased version that "has been and remains thematized within the North American academy precisely as 'irresponsible and irresponsible-making destruction' and as a critical movement that 'leave[s] everything as it is . . . within the university' " (1268). In other words, deconstruction in the American academy has been, for the most part, an extension of New

Criticism, and what is coming to an end, in Nealon's opinion, is "the wave of deconstruction as a method for interpreting texts" (1267). Nealon attributes this situation to Paul de Man's misunderstanding and perversion of Derrida. (see p. 16, n. 2)

WORKS CITED

Bloom, Harold. "Inescapable Poe." *New York Review of Books.* Oct. 11, 1984, 31. Rpt. as "Americanizing the Abyss" (introduction) in *Edgar Allan Poe.* Ed. Harold Bloom. New York: Chelsea House, 1985, 1–14.

Brand, Dana. Review of J. Gerald Kennedy, *Poe, Death, and the Life of Writing. PSA Newsletter* 15, no. 2 (Fall 1987).

Brownell, W. C. "Poe." *American Prose Masters* (1909). Rpt. Ed. Howard Mumford Jones. Cambridge: Belknap P of Harvard UP, 1967.

The Cambridge History of American Literature. Ed. William Peterfield Trent et al. 3 vols. New York: G. P. Putnam's Sons; Cambridge, England: Cambridge UP, Vol. 1, 1917; Vol. 2, 1918.

Casillo, Robert. "Anti-Semitism, Castration, and Usury in Ezra Pound." *Criticism* 25 (Summer 1983): 239–65.

———. *The Genealogy of Demons: Anti-Semitism, Fascism, and the Myths of Ezra Pound.* Evanston, Ill.: Northwestern UP, 1988.

Dauber, Kenneth, "The Problem of Poe." *Georgia Review* 32, no. 3 (Fall 1978)

Ferry, Luc, and Alain Renaut. *French Philosophy of the Sixties: An Essay on Antihumanism.* Trans. Mary H. S. Cattani. Amherst: U of Massachusetts P, 1990a.

———. *Heidegger and Modernity.* Trans. Franklin Philip. Chicago and London: U of Chicago P, 1990b.

Freadman, Richard, and Seumas Miller. *Re-Thinking Theory: A Critique of Contemporary Literary Theory and an Alternative Account.* Cambridge, England: Cambridge UP, 1992.

Freud, Sigmund. *Beyond the Pleasure Principle.* Trans. James Strachey. New York and London: Norton & Co., 1961.

Hirsch, David H. "The Pit and the Apocalypse." *Sewanee Review* 76 (Fall 1968): 632–52.

———. *The Deconstruction of Literature: Criticism after Auschwitz.* Hanover, N. H., and London: UP of New England, 1991.

Kahler, Erich. *The Tower and the Abyss.* New York: George Braziller, 1957.

Kennedy, J. Gerald, ed. *Edgar Allan Poe: The Narrative of Arthur Gordon Pym of Nantucket and Related Tales.* Oxford and New York: Oxford UP, 1994.

Ketterer, David. "Tracing Shadows: *Pym* Criticism, 1980–1990." In Kopley, *Poe's Pym,* 233–74.

Limon, John. "How to Place Poe's *Arthur Gordon Pym* in Science-Dominated Intellectual History, and How to Extract It Again." *North Dakota Quarterly* 51, no. 1 (Winter 1983): 31–47.

———. *The Place of Fiction in the Time of Science.* New York: Cambridge UP, 1990.

Merquior, J. G. *From Prague to Paris: A Critique of Structuralist and Post-Structuralist Thought.* London and New York: Verso, 1986.

Riddell, Joseph N. "The 'Crypt' of Edgar Poe." *boundary 2* (Spring 1979): 117–41.

Roppolo, Joseph Patrick. "Meaning and 'The Masque of the Red Death.' " *Poe: A*

Collection of Critical Essays. Ed. Robert Regan. Englewood Cliffs, N.J.: Prentice-Hall, 1967, 134–44.

St. Armand, Barton Levi. Review of Evan Carton, *The Rhetoric of American Romance.* *PSA Newsletter* 15, no. 1 (Spring 1987): 4.

Willey, Basil. "On Wordsworth and the Locke Tradition." *English Romantic Poets.* Ed. M. H. Abrams. London, Oxford, New York: Oxford UP, 1975, 112–22. Rpt. in *The Seventeenth Century Background.* New York: Columbia UP: 1950, 296–309.

Part IV

POE'S ART

20

Poe's Aesthetics

DAVID HALLIBURTON

Insofar as everything Poe writes resonates with everything else, revealing design where, at first glance, no design may appear, a study of his aesthetics could begin anywhere. So pervasive is this design that even a chance detail may disclose it: zero in on something, practically anything, and, little by little, "the full design" (*H* 5, 250) emerges; this, at any rate, is the method of Legrand in "The Gold-Bug." Although Legrand's full-blown detective counterpart employs this method as well, Dupin likes to look (as we say) at the big picture. In a game requiring contestants to spot a name on a map, beginners, he observes, send their opponents searching for something small. Experienced players, by contrast, know that the names hardest to spot are those in letters too large, as it were, to be noticed. Showing himself to be such a player, Dupin cracks the case of "The Purloined Letter" by surmising that the letter must be under the searchers' respective noses.

The central question posed by this chapter is the nature of Poe's aesthetics, a topic so broad that a treatment as brief as mine must be especially selective in choosing themes and setting priorities. I focus, accordingly, on the role of experience in Poe's aesthetics, for the intensities of which Poe is a supreme creator are *experiential* intensities. Even when the events he renders are phantasmal or fantastic, they produce in the reader the sense that, if they ever *did* happen, *this* is what it would be like to live them. In experience, all of Poe's favorite themes and motifs may be seen to intersect.

The discussion that follows takes its initial clue from Baudelaire, who was the first to insist on the essential unity of Poe's creative endeavor. The discussion further situates itself in what the editor of this volume defines as the critical "mainstream," which, for some seventy years, has favored the "transcendental-symbolic" approach to Poe (Carlson, 215).

The first of the ten sections into which the discussion is divided continues Allen Tate's exploration of the cosmic strain in Poe's aesthetic (Tate, 113–45) and deals in particular with the ways in which Poe "aestheticizes" both the earth and the cosmos. Nature being the most encompassing framework for this process, the second section inquires into the various senses of nature as term and concept and then, in the succeeding section, into matters of taste pertaining to what is deemed natural or unnatural; here the focus is on the kind of taste represented by the modes, themes, and motifs of the grotesque and the arabesque. Section four investigates the moral sense, as a corollary of the sense of nature and the natural, together with the more general functions performed by the office of taste. Poe emerges as a critical practitioner in the ensuing section, which considers the "offices" and, as Poe also says, the "provinces" of criticism. In the next four sections, the centers of interest are, respectively, the experience of the audience, specifically, histrionic experience; experience in relation to theatricality in the broad sense of the term; the phenomenon of what Poe calls "the true poetical effect" and the problem of experiencing it; and the merger of the experiential with the experimental (a venerable nexus in Western thought since the Renaissance) in what may be termed Poe's "experience experiment." Finally, attention turns to the ways in which Poe's preoccupation with the family of *re*-words and ideas may be seen to emerge as an aesthetics of revolution.

AESTHETICIZING EARTH AND COSMOS

Although cosmic contexts are made explicit in a variety of Poe's writings, including the angelic dialogues, and, above all, in *Eureka,* "The Domain of Arnheim," with its depiction of the intriguing landscape architect Roderick Ellison and its materially realized fantasies, seems more accessible than the other works named and is, in any case, the work in which the aestheticizing is most graphically portrayed. In this text, the narrator, who has evidently been pondering the relationship between landscaping and geology, surmises that the purpose of the disturbances we see in the earth's surface is to give something for art to rebel against and modify; "in the correction or allaying" of such disturbances, he says, "lies the soul of art" (*H* 6, 184). Ellison, for his part, espouses a more developmental and dialectical view and, for these reasons, a more Hegelian view. To Ellison, the disturbances foreshadow human mortality: " 'Admit the earthly immortality of man to have been the first intention. We have then the primitive arrangement of the earth's surface adapted to his blissful estate, as not existent but designed. The disturbances were the preparations for his subsequently conceived deathful condition' " (*H* 6, 184).

This rather dense account can be "unpacked" as follows. "The first intention" refers to the intention of deity, by whose design the surface of earth is originally so arranged as to be adapted to (i.e., reflect, conform with, accommodate) man's blissful estate. Here is humanity, in other words, in its Edenic condition. Adding the phrase "not existent but designed" distinguishes some-thing that is ontologically happenstance, existing only nominally, from some-thing that is divinely ordained ("designed"). According to Poe's diachronic scenario, at some later time ("subsequently"), God designed the disturbances to be symbolic of the mortality, the deathly condition, of human beings. Here, as in "Mesmeric Revelation," death is regarded as a temporary, transitional state of being. For good reason, Rieusset (46 ff.), Limon (31–47), and Muller (344 ff.) discern Hegelian overtones in conceptualizations such as these. For Poe proceeds dialectically, through negations, to a stage of metamorphosis in which the human being advances from an ontologically lower to an ontologically higher stage. If the lower is mortality, and the higher is immortality, the deathly condition is a transitional, transformative, indeed, revolutionary stage precisely analogous to the stage Hegel calls the nodal line or point (Hegel, 160); it is that through which human beings must pass in order to *become* immortal.

According to Poe's visionary dialectic, in other words, the divinely designed Edenic state is negated by the introduction of geological disturbances prefiguring the advent of mortality, only to be negated, in turn, and thereby sublated, or raised to a higher level, by God's subsequent decision to make mortality not a *terminus ad quem* but a *terminus a quo*. In this impromptu treatise, Poe presents, then, a three-phase development: (1) the blissful, Edenic state; (2) the transi-tional nodal state of the (temporary) deathful condition; (3) immortality. It is a swift passage, indeed, from such a paradise lost to such a paradise regained.

From Ellison's impromptu treatise, we learn, for the first time, of a type of being that can experience human aesthetic effects in reverse—in a reversal, moreover, that is at the same time an elevation:

"There *may* be class of beings, human once, but now invisible to humanity, to whom, from afar, our disorder may seem order—our unpicturesqueness picturesque; in a word, the earth-angels, for whose scrutiny more especially than our own, and for whose death-refined appreciation of the beautiful, may have been set in array by God the wide land-scape-gardens of the hemispheres." (*H* 6, 184–85)

Poe does not describe a human, aesthetic level of experience in contrast to a transhuman, nonaesthetic level. Both levels are aesthetic; the difference is that the second, later realm is higher: the difference at issue is, to this extent, a difference of degree and not of kind. He indicates, in other words, a *gradation* within the continuum, at the higher end of which experience is, if anything—thanks to the refining mediation of death—*more* intensely aesthetic than before. Poe points up the aesthetic character of the angels' appreciation by specifying it as an appreciation of that enduring theme in traditional aesthetics, the beau-tiful. Paralleling this dialectical ordering of experience is the progression that takes the landscape aesthetic from the realm of the earthly nature to the extra-terrestrial realm in which God arrays the wide landscape gardens of the hemi-spheres. It is at once a progression from the "natural" to "the artificial style" of gardening (*H* 6, 185) and from the *aestheticizing of earth* to the *aestheticizing of cosmos.*

THE SENSES OF NATURE

Nature is polysemous, embracing such meanings as kind, sort, or quality; *physis* in the Greek sense of that which comes into being without the aid of another kind of being; that which is not artificial or affected; the created universe as physical environment; and within the latter, the pastoral landscape that emerges in the aesthetics of the eighteenth century. The penultimate and last senses predominate when Poe praises J. F. Cooper's literary sketches of Swiss landscapes (*H* 9, 162) or "the beauty or the majesty of nature" (*H* 9, 304) rendered by William Cullen Bryant. Poe's own sketch "The Elk" (or "Morning on the Wissahiccon") employs nature in a similar way, lauding the beauty of the valley of Louisiana, one of "the real Edens of the land" (*H* 5, 157), known only to those who venture from the city. The repeated use of the term *picturesque,* the reference to a prospect, and the framing of the natural environment into scenes all place the sketch within the tradition of landscape aesthetics usefully explored by Ljungquist (27–46, 89 ff. and passim). Such aesthetics notwithstanding, Poe is rendered melancholy by "the manifest alterations for the worse, wrought upon the brook and its vicinage, even within the last few years" (*H* 5, 162).

The sketch treats sentimentally and on a small scale the kind of radical alterations wrought upon the earth in "The Colloquy of Monos and Una," where, however, they are actually of aesthetic origin. "Man, because he could not but acknowledge the majesty of nature, fell into childish exultation at his acquired and still-increasing dominion over her elements" (*H* 4, 203). It is known that the dual infection of system and abstraction combines with a political egalitarianism that violates "the laws of *gradation*" and, more surprisingly, with Art in the uppercase, Art being seen, apparently, as comparable in its consequences with the technological developments tacitly signified by the reference to acquired and still-increasing dominion. The effect of all this is that "[t]he fair face of Nature was deformed as with the ravages of some loathsome disease" (*H* 4, 203), which Monos traces directly to "the perversion of our *taste,* or rather in the blind neglect of its culture in the schools. For, in truth, it was at this crisis that taste alone . . . could have led us gently back to Beauty, to Nature, and to Life" (*H* 4, 203–4).

Poe's concept of the natural owes much to classical heritage, particularly to the idea of *mousikē* as the enabling of the educated or enlightened soul. From Plato's *Republic,* Poe would borrow "the experience of so many ages," which has demonstrated the educational value of "gymnastics for the body, and *music* for the soul," music being the cause whose effect is the assimilation into the soul of rhythm and harmony—a powerful precept for an aesthetic credo defining poetry as the rhythmical creation of beauty. A broader concept than what comes to be known as music, *mousikē* "included not only the harmonies of time and of tune, but the poetic diction, sentiment, and creation, each in its widest sense. The study of *music* was with them, in fact, the general cultivation of the taste— of that which recognizes the beautiful" (*H* 5, 204).

If the earth as an entirety could not be saved from apocalypse, a happier fate awaits the more circumscribed space of "The Landscape Garden." Like a good romantic or, for that matter, like a good eighteenth-century aesthetician, Ellison holds nature to be the supreme point of reference in all worldly things. Except, that is, in landscape, which will always prove to be, in some sort, defective (*H* 6, 182); here, the imitation of nature is a nugatory notion. But what precisely does Poe mean when he employs a selection from the family of nature words?

In the later criticism, nature tends to foreground his Addisonian preference for what is unaffected, spontaneous, and tasteful (*OED* 3, 1656). *Nature* also means natural, "[t]he condition of being natural or in accordance with nature" (*OED* 2, 1660). Poe is especially keen on this quality where theater is concerned, so that when he rejects a play for being theatrical rather than dramatic, it is because it fails to proceed "*a priori* from the infallible principles of a Natural Art" (*H* 12, 126).

The mode of representation corresponding to sense two is naturalism, a coinage attributed to D. G. Rossetti in 1850, signifying "a style or method characterized by close adherence to, and faithful representation of, nature or reality." But compare Poe's statement that "the great charm of the whole acting of Mrs. Mowatt is its naturalism" (*H* 12, 188). This is clearly Rossetti's sense, five years in advance.

Naturalism can be seen to correspond with the aesthetics of sentiment, as illustrated by, say, *A Sentimental Journey*. For Poe as for Sterne, genuineness of feeling is evidenced by display, as through gesture or weeping: "[W]e see her bosom heave—her cheek grow pale—her limbs tremble . . . and Nature's own tear rush impetuously to the eye" (*H* 12, 191). To enable the audience to experience her experience, the performance becomes an emotive exposé as the actress "lay[s] bare to the audience the movements of her passionate heart," the effect of which is that the spectators grow pale, fall silent, and weep (*H* 12, 191–92).

GROTESQUE AND ARABESQUE

To discuss nature, the natural, and naturalism is already, whether implicitly or explicitly, to enter the province of taste; it is, in Poe's case, to confront the modes, themes, and motifs variously termed grotesque and arabesque. Since so much has been written on these, they are considered briefly here in deference to matters less frequently broached.

The topic may be considered under five heads. First, the foregrounding of the terms *grotesque* and *arabesque* is a self-consciously aesthetic "statement," in which Poe shelters himself against the "bad taste" (*M* 2, 473) of those who charge him with Germanism, while at the same time suggesting that modality counts for more in his art than elements such as genre or aims such as pleasure. When Poe ordains that all carpets, curtains, tapestry, or ottoman coverings shall be "rigidly Arabesque" (*H* 14, 104), he is guided, as in "The Domain of Arnheim," by the taste for the "artificial" as against the "natural." If the latter could be seen in the organic forms of a Raphael or other Renaissance masters who depicted living creatures in their organic particularity, the former could be seen in the aesthetics of the eighteenth century, when the term applied to more stylized "surface" treatments with curvilinear floral patterns, foliage, and scrollwork. It was not that the latter were *un*natural. It was rather that the "nature" to which Pope, for example, appealed, was a divinely designed condition variously improved by the human touch that was itself not only naturally designed but designed to that specific end.

Second, the grotesque, for its part, reverses expectation, normality, the natural. Like the oddity gardeners call a "sport" of nature, it is a wild, transgressive phenomenon, gleeful in its freedom from ordinary lawfulness. The second point, following closely upon the first, is that the grotesque tends to merge with the perverse. Countering the common sense Poe respects in other contexts, wildly defining law and taste, the grotesque inverts the everyday world; it, indeed, effects a revolution in that world, a topic to which discussion will return. Third, the grotesque both diverges from, and converges with, the arabesque, which, in addition to the visual traits already noted, is suggestive of the exotic, the Oriental, and the ideal. Here Patricia C. Smith is useful, especially in suggesting how the arabesque ultimately symbolizes "dissolution into Unity" (45); G. R. Thompson, by contrast, brings out ironic, satiric, and burlesque aspects of both the grotesque and the Arabesque (138). But, in the conclusion of "The Domain of Arnheim," Ellison offers both at the same time: "semi-Gothic, semi-Saracenic architecture" (the former favoring grotesquerie, the latter arabesque), which is "the phantom handiwork, conjointly, . . . of the Genii and of the Gnomes" (*H* 6, 196), the former drawn, again, from the repertoire of the arabesque, the latter from that of the grotesque. Fourth, the grotesque, while exhibiting features of gamesmanship, is also a mode of play, an explosion of *Spieltrieb* having only such "meaning" as emerges in the playing itself. In this unusual conflation consists its experimental character. It is play in that its discourse follows no course but its own. It is game in that a certain lawfulness nonetheless inheres. For, while there may not be explicit rules for bringing it off, it nonetheless deploys certain established motifs and plays off certain known expectations and models. In "The Thousand-and-Second Tale of Scheherazade," for example, Poe's fanciful rendering of the swimming sea monster, at once hideous and humorous, bespeaks the gratuitous verve of the play instinct. At the same time, it is lawful in that it assimilates such recognized grotesque characteristics as the merger of the human and the animal, the provoking of contradictory reactions (the creatures carried by the monster are seen to be men but also vermin), the exploitation of extreme contrasts (an enormous island composed of infinitesimally tiny coral creatures), and the inversion—or, if you prefer, perversion—of cultural norms (the wives and daughters of the magi define their beauty by the size of their buttocks, to the extent that " 'the days have long since gone by since it was possible to distinguish a woman from a dromedary' ") (*H* 6, 101).

THE MORAL SENSE AND THE OFFICE OF TASTE

In Ellison's reflections of landscape, two orders of the moral and the aesthetic experience are hierarchically, rather than chronologically, arranged. Deity has designed the first of these so as to embrace both the realm of worldly things as we currently know it and the aesthetic treatment of those things. When Poe has Ellison equate the moral and the human (*H* 6, 184), he relativizes both in relation to the higher norm of the second order:

"Now," said my friend, "what we regard as exaltation of the landscape may be really such, as represents only the moral point of view. Each alternation of the natural scenery may possibly effect a blemish in the picture, if we can suppose this picture viewed at large—in mass—from some point distant from the earth's surface. . . . It is easily understood that what might improve a closely scrutinized detail, may at the same time injure a general or more distantly observed effect." (*H* 6, 184)

But this perspectival superiority enjoyed by what he reveals to be "earth-angels" (*H* 6, 185) in no way diminishes the moral dimension, the centrality of which, for Poe, is in roughly inverse proportion to its recognition by readers. Poe sees an identity between the moral or mystic signification of any sentiment, finding that identity best reflected in music, while the terms *moral, moral sense,* and *moral energy* figure prominently in other writings (Carlson, 210, 212; cf. Frushell, 43–44).

This moral dimension, far from existing separately from the aesthetic and the historical dimensions, is—to use a word Poe probably borrowed from Milton—"intervolved" with both (*H* 6, 188). It is thus that Paul Elmer More could discover a moral element even among the author's grotesques and arabesques, for which his code word is "weird":

It is this precisely that we understand by the term "weird"—not the veritable vision of unearthly things, but the peculiar half vision inherited by the soul where faith has waned and the imagination prolongs the old sensations in a shadowy involuntary life of its own; and herein too lies the field of true and effective symbolism. If Hawthorne and Poe, as we think, possess an element of force and realism such as Tieck and the German school utterly lack, it is because they write from the depths of this profound moral experience of their people. (More, 98)

Poe ends "The Philosophy of Composition" by disclosing that what he has been aiming at is no mere sensation but precisely a moral sentiment, an effect brought about by the partnership between *Nevermore* and the phrase *from out of my heart,* which together "dispose the mind to seek a moral in all that has been previously narrated" (*H* 16, 208). Moreover, in distinguishing the sovereign offices of "the world of mind," Poe names "the Pure Intellect, Taste, and the Moral Sense," pointing out that the second of these, while mediating the other two, is so close to the latter "that Aristotle has not hesitated to place some of its operations among the virtues themselves" (*H* 16, 272–73).

Prior to Kant's *Critique of Judgment,* the concept of taste was more moral than aesthetic. In the seventeenth century, as Hans-Georg Gadamer (33 ff.) points out, Baltasar Gracián grounds taste in *gusto,* the sensuous, worldly quality of which survives, at least residually, in its Anglicized sense of hearty zest and vitality; on this shared basis, all worldly things could be seen as grounded by divinity and liable, mutatis mutandis, to the critical judgment of human beings, also divinely grounded. Properly formed taste could come to represent not the type of consensus required in fashion but the type of consensus possible only in a model community in which "the ideality of good taste" would be embodied. As authentic *sensus communis,* the moral range of taste encompassed the political, for in the ideal community can be seen the ideal of a new society, a society no longer rigidly hierarchical but one whose unifying norm is "simply the shared nature of its judgments, or, rather, its capacity to rise above the narrowness of interests and private predilections to the title of judgments" (Gadamer, 34). As we will see in the section that follows, it was always Poe's aim to rise in just this way. Here it need only be said that his conception of the close proximity of taste to moral sense reverses the expectation of those who would narrow Poe's aesthetics to something purely belletristic and technical. Insofar as Poe's aesthetic precepts and practices lend themselves to aestheticism as such, they do so with the caveat that, in most of the major works, the moral dimensions of taste are rarely, if ever, overlooked.

THE OFFICES AND PROVINCES OF CRITICISM

Poe launched 1842 with an exordium on the murk and vapor of contemporary discourse touching everything aesthetic. A reviewer in Poe's period typically filled columns with extracts from the review text, ground out generic evaluations, and, depending on the clique he belonged to, loaded the author with kudos or contempt. At the other extreme, epitomized by Macaulay, the reviewer used the text to talk about anything that crossed his mind. The power of the entrenched factions was, in any case, so unreceptive to anything genuinely rigorous, high-minded, or non-Eastern that it took a brave soul, indeed, to speak out against such bias. If Poe was such a soul, the 1842 essay, in which he implicitly sees himself as a kind of revolutionary, is a declaration of independence.

In their creative writing, some fellow Americans and a few critics, in trying to do the same, had overcompensated for their prior subservience to foreign authority and taste by insisting on American cultural superiority. But such a solution was really part of the problem. Poe wanted a radical remaking of reviewing into criticism that would look beyond the magazinists' petty systems and prejudices to norms intrinsically aesthetic and natural: as Americans, we "begin to demand the use—to inquire into the offices and provinces of criticism—to regard it more as an art based immoveably in nature, less as a mere system of fluctuating and conventional dogmas" (*H* 11, 2).

To be at once properly aesthetic and properly natural, criticism needs to be recognized as a practice in its own right, but such recognition can occur only when concrete comprehension of the historical circumstances has been achieved. When another writer describes this state of affairs as normative, Poe responds that, on the contrary, it is peculiar only to the past twenty years and only to the British cultural scene. What is normative for Poe is the aesthetic mode of the Classical and Romantic Germany of Goethe, Winckelmann, Novalis, Schelling, and the Schlegels. In contrast to their current British counterparts, these writers operate—ironically—on the principles maintained in Britain in the eighteenth century, when criticism carried on sustained debates on critical aesthetic questions: the "magnificent" critiques of the Germans do not at all diverge "from those of Kames, or Johnson, and of Blair . . . (for the principles of these artists will not fail until Nature herself expires)" (*H* 11, 5).

The understanding of criticism adopted by Poe is the one adopted by Dryden, who gives us the term, at least in print form: "[t]he art of estimating the qualities and character of literary or artistic work; the function or work of a critic" (*OED* 2, 1674). Poe's aesthetic manifesto, in other words, manages, through romantic revision, to ground itself on basically Augustan precept and taste, a fact he underlies by then invoking Pope (*H* 11, 5), and elsewhere by borrowing the numinous phrase "the power of words" from the same author. Now, as in the age of the *Dunciad,* Poe avers, the critic is duty-bound to detect grammatical errors, as well as bad rhymes or wrong quantities in versification (*H* 11, 5–6), a familiar position to any reader who has borne witness to Poe's microscopic screening of grammar, syntax, versification, and punctuation—the latter two being areas in which he is especially thin-skinned (Halliburton, 406–8). His aesthetic position presupposes, then, a standard of correctness that the critic's judgment is uniquely qualified to discern, even at the expense of being didactic, which Poe sometimes is, his animadversions against that aesthetic heresy notwithstanding.

Poe's concern with identity (as in the case of Ligeia) or with identification (as in the case of Dupin) takes a different form in the case of criticism, which is self-identical, being, in no wise, anything but the judgment of aesthetic quality and performance: "Criticism . . . *can be* nothing in the world but—a criticism" (*H* 11, 6). It does not follow from this that criticism is autotelic, for it depends on the existence of the work of art, which, though similar in some respects, is finally a different sort of thing, and a relatively autonomous one at that.

Poe seems to be moving toward an aesthetics of intrinsic interpretation according to which art has no interest or significance other than the interest or significance it possesses in itself. Kantian as this may be, Poe is more usefully related to Schiller, arguably the leading aesthetician among the German writers already named, and to Philip August Boeckh, who, in the succeeding generation, influenced the development of a hermeneutics of interpretation.

Through his concept of a play drive or *Spieltrieb,* expressed supremely in art, Schiller, in a stroke, elevates the aesthetic to a higher state of being than is reachable by either the formal or the sensuous drive (*Formtrieb, Stofftrieb*). "Every other state into which we can enter refers us back to a preceding one, and requires for its termination a subsequent one; the aesthetic alone is a whole in itself, since it comprises within itself all the conditions of both its origin and its continuance" (Schiller, 428). On such a reading, a defense of art has no need to make the aesthetic a state of freedom from something else, for art is, uniquely, the very embodiment of creative autonomy and sovereignty.

When Poe distinguishes between the particular mode in which a work brings opinions to bear, or when he considers the book strictly as a book (*H* 11, 7)— which I take to mean as a provider of aesthetic experience rather than, say, a commodity or as a source of documentation—he follows the distinction Boeckh draws between hermeneutics and criticism.

Hermeneutics aims to elucidate meaning, *Sinn.* It interprets. By contrast, criticism addresses significance, *Bedeutung.* "Criticism," according to Boeckh, is "that philological performance through which an object becomes understood not by itself nor for its own sake, but for the establishment of a relation and a reference to something else" (Boeckh, 142).

Poe is right, then, in arguing that opinion falls within the purview of significance—the implications of the work for the historian, the moralist, the aesthetician, and so on. But in then defining criticism as the judgment of achieved intention or, again, design, Poe goes *against* the hermeneutic model: for Poe, criticism addresses not the significance but the meaning of the experience provided by art.

Poe looks to be moving onto different ground when he suggests that criticism "is only properly employed upon productions which have their basis in art itself" (*H* 11, 7). Given his high estimation of the aesthetic as such and his admiration for the Tennysonian manner of being artistic, it would seem to follow that art in its highest manifestation is an experience *of* the aesthetic, in which case a special value would accrue to works with art themes; certainly, Poe himself deals often with the several arts and their intricate ways. In any case, the overall effect of such tendencies is an intensification of experience that borders upon, if it does not indeed cross over into, a meta-aesthetics.

THE AUDIENCE EXPERIENCE

Poe aims at his reader through effect, which is the consequence of authorially initiated causes. So central is this concept to Poe's aesthetics that every other element of art relates to it—unity, totality, impression, interest, intensity, intention, identity, reason, process, novelty, force, power, consequence, denouement, point, and design. You name it.

In "The Philosophy of Composition," Poe, taking a cue from Milton, attempts something no other writer has attempted: he will reveal to the reader the method "by which any one of his compositions attained its ultimate point of completion" (*H* 14, 194). The statement presupposes representativeness: any composition will do. By a similar logic, it is assumed that all readers are moved by effects in the same way. When he speaks of the heart, the intellect, or the soul, Poe is speaking of a person thus idealized, a person susceptible partly through the grotesque, partly through the sublime, but primarily through the beautiful; for the beautiful, far from being a quality, is "an effect," which is to say, something experienced.

According to "an obvious rule of Art," effects eventuate from causes: "It is the business of the poet so to construct his line that the intention *must* be caught *at once*" (*H* 14, 237). Causality, never an arbitrary force, ever expresses, mediately or immediately, the lawfulness of divine design. For if the design did not immediately and eminently hold sway—in, for example, the existence of Beauty—there would be no place for the collateral mediation Poe calls Art. The same chain of reasoning binds reader to author in a crucial mutuality, the author concentrating on the production of causes, the reader on the consumption of effects. If the author claims the advantage of being the origin or, more precisely, the mediate origin of the reader's experience, the reader claims the advantage of immediately experiencing what has been authorially effectuated.

In a somewhat more sentimental mood, Poe speaks of such a relation in terms of sympathy, as in his discussion of author-excitation and reader-response in his 1847 commentary on Hawthorne's *Twice-Told Tales*. The point of departure is a distinction between a popular concept of originality, which tries to combine thoughts, incidents, and the like into something absolutely novel, and a truer originality less concerned with "content" than with purposiveness and novelty of effect. The particular effect in view is a bond of sympathy between writer and reader in relation to which true originality may be seen as "that which, in bringing out the half-formed, the reluctant, or the unexpressed fancies of mankind, or in exciting the more delicate pulses of the heart's passion, or in giving birth to some universal sentiment or instinct in embryo, thus combines with the pleasurable effect of *apparent* novelty, a real egoistic delight" (*H* 13, 146). Poe's conception of the real, a subject that interested him more than many critics have recognized, depends again on the self-evidence of experience. The delight of the reader's ego can be foreknown because the author (who is, of course, on other occasions a reader as well) has an ego, too, and human egos are essentially the same. The delight in question, Poe explains, is doubled when compared with the delight experienced by someone who reads the type of "absolutely novel" writings referred to earlier; for the latter, while it effects excitement, at the same time embarrasses and disturbs the reader who feels a fool for not having conceived of the novelty himself. But "[i]n the second case, his pleasure is doubled.

... He feels and intensely enjoys the seeming novelty of the thought, enjoys it as really novel, as absolutely original with the writer—*and himself.* ... They two have, together, created this thing. Henceforward there is a bond of sympathy between them'' (*H* 13, 146).

Poetry and drama are similarly designed with reception in mind. Poe sounds almost phenomenological when, in ''The Rationale of Verse,'' he speaks in terms of reading flow, which relates roughly to the effect of versification as scansion relates to its cause: ''Of course, then, the scansion and the reading flow should go hand in hand. The former must go hand in hand with the latter'' (*H* 14, 253), which is to say that they unite in the mutuality of their adaptation. Poe is not limiting himself, of course, to reading. In an important but little-read study of American drama, he addresses the impression that is to be made ''upon the reader, or spectator'' (*H* 13, 66).

THEATER AND EXPERIENCE

Poe's commentaries on the theatrical scene compose a more significant corpus of dramatic criticism than is usually acknowledged. The scene itself represents a major interest of this writer, this ''histrionic Mr. Poe'' (Fagin), ''who is himself the son of an actress ... and no earl was ever prouder of his earldom'' (*H* 12, 186). For acting is ''a profession which, in itself, embraces all that can elevate and ennoble, and absolutely nothing to degrade ... the theatre is ennobled by its high facilities for the development of genius—facilities not afforded elsewhere in equal degree'' (*H* 12, 185). Some of Poe's thoughts on acting will be considered later in connection with naturalism. Here, two points deserve consideration.

The first arises in connection with *Antigone,* which Poe reviewed after an 1845 performance. Sophocles' play, Poe argues, is less successful than anything of Aeschylus or Euripides by virtue of its ''baldness,'' which is ''the inevitable result of inexperience of Art'' (*H* 12, 131). Poe is not departing from the position discussed before; simplicity remains a crucial feature in all genuine art, as evidenced in Greek sculpture, which comes into being directly from a creator's working from real life, which is to say, in Poe's terms, from nature. But there is no nature in drama, Poe suggests, meaning no models to imitate directly or spontaneously, as is the case in ''the simple,'' which is to say the plastic arts. Drama belongs, on the contrary, among the complex arts, which draw upon cumulative human experience: ''In a word, the simple arts spring into perfection, at their origin. The complex as inevitably demand the long and painful progressive experience of ages'' (*H* 12, 132).

The second point arises in an essay on prospects for drama in the United States, when Poe considers theatrical corollaries to the nexus of themes we see, for example, in the revivifactions of ''Ligeia'' or the potentially fatal fall of Arthur Gordon Pym: this is the nexus of regeneration, rebirth, revival, which represent the reversal of, the rebellion against, the imperatives of decay and dissolution. Taking the affirmative reception of a new comedy as evidence that drama can't really "go down," as he puts it, Poe argues that "dramatic art is, or should be, a concentralization of all that which is entitled to the appellation of Art." Only after the other arts disappear from the face of the earth, "then and not until then, may we look for *that* to sink into insignificance, which, and which alone, affords opportunity for the conglomeration of these infinite and imperishable sources of delight" (*H* 12, 126).

EXPERIENCING THE TRUE POETICAL EFFECT

Like Shelley in particular and the Romantics in general, Poe sets a premium on the poetic, though he goes further than Shelley and most of the other Romantics in identifying the poetic principle with the beautiful, or rather with desire for Supernal Beauty. Although Poe frequently separates beauty in general from truth, in approaching the poetic effect as concrete experience, truth comes to play an intensifying, as well as a mediating, role. Thus, the Uranian love "is unquestionably the purest and truest of all poetical themes," and it is "the true Poetry" that Poe delimits in turning to the experience of the poet. Meanwhile, there is this rather dense passage on truth in both the upper- and lowercase:

And in regard to Truth—if, to be sure, through the attainment of a truth, we are led to perceive a harmony where none was apparent before, we experience, at once, the true poetical effect—but this effect is referable to the harmony alone, and not in the least degree to the truth which merely served to render the harmony manifest. (*H* 14, 290)

Since Poe then turns to the experience of the poet per se, this statement should be taken as applying to anyone and everyone and to any experience of a harmony that is not perceived *until* revealed by some attainment of a truth—though, given the context, it is the aesthetic realm that is being foregrounded here. The statement shows everyday truth, truth with a small *t*, as a mediating function that is transcended by the perception of a harmony, suggesting a hierarchy topped by Truth with a big *T,* to which the experience of the true poetical effect to this degree appertains, but without prejudice to its more essential intervolvement with Beauty and Love.

In turning explicit attention to the experience of the poet, Poe nonetheless persists in employing *true* as an intensifying modifier:

We shall reach, however, more immediately a distinct conception of what the true Poetry is, by mere reference to a few of the simple elements which induce in the Poet himself the true poetical effect. He recognizes the ambrosia which nourishes his soul, in the bright orbs that shine in Heaven—in the volutes of the flower—in the clustering of low shrubberies—in the waving of the grain-fields, in the slanting of tall, Eastern trees—in the blue distance of mountains. (*H* 14, 290–91)

Applying a criterion of truth to the poet as well as to the poetical effect enriches and arguably strengthens the predicate *induce,* which (1) underscores the process of effectuating, tracing the poetic consequence, the poem, back to its sources and (2) draws upon the more or less logical sense of induction (as Poe is wont to do), implying a parallel between the causality of (1) and the chain of inferences, each prompted by a given instance, toward a general conclusion. This distinguishes Poe's nature catalog from any catalog of Whitman, for with the latter, rhapsodic reportage wonders at worldly plenitude, in the hope that evoking a representative selection of phenomena will inspire in the reader something analogous to the experience of the poet. But if Poe also expresses a rhapsodic impulse, it is a ratiocinative one in that it tries to prove a point. The "natural" point often merges with an erotic catalog too exclusively heterosexual to be accommodated in the Whitmanian aesthetic, of the figure of the beloved woman, for the nonhuman ambrosia that nourishes his soul is equally to be found in the simplicity of Uranian *eros:* "He deeply feels it in her winning endearments . . . but above all—ah, far above all—he kneels to it—he worships it in the faith, in the purity, in the strength, in the altogether divine majesty of her *love*" (*H* 14, 291).

In the denouement of "The Poetic Principle," Poe effects a reversal that has no precise counterpart in his other writings of aesthetic interest, observing that the poem he will cite last is "very different in character from any that I have before quoted" (*H* 14, 291). "The Song of the Cavalier" is a rousing call to arms: "Then mounte! then mounte, brave gallants, all, / And don your helmes amaine." The selection, surprising as it is prima facie, is warranted, however, on several grounds. First, it may be seen as a progression from the theme of heterosexual love to fraternal sympathy, sympathy being, as noted earlier, a crucial faculty for Poe: "With our modern and altogether rational ideas of the absurdity and impiety of warfare, we are not precisely in that frame of mind best adapted to sympathise with the sentiments, and thus to appreciate the real excellence of the poem" (*H* 14, 291–92). The second ground, framed negatively here, is a desired antithesis for the rationalist inclination of the preceding argument: Poe may have felt that he had given more than their due to truth and reason and that it was time to speak of the reasons the heart has, which reason knows not of. In any case, there is a need to overcome the merely rational, which in the present passage is epochal, amounting to a prejudice that sees warfare as anachronistic when the anachronism actually *is* that prejudice. The third ground is that only by a radical reversal of expectations, only by putting aside all such predilections can the reader experience the true poetical effect, the causality of which inheres in the experience of the poet. The secret to this desired success, like the secret behind the divining that Dupin draws from a simple technique of gamesmanship, is imaginative identification: "To do this fully, we must identify ourselves, in fancy, with the soul of the old cavalier" (*H* 14, 292).

Two further points remain to be proposed regarding the necessity of another reversal, such that reason is revealed in the faculty of instinct, from which it is customarily debarred. The point of departure is the opposition of human reason and animal instinct, an opposition Poe prefers to understand as a misinterpreted liminality. Misunderstood because human beings presently exist in a limited and limiting condition; in a higher condition, they would recognize in instinct the highest reason of all: "It will appear to the true philosopher as the divine mind itself acting *immediately* upon its creatures" (*M* 2, 478).

As the sketch proceeds, Poe structures his argument, as he often does, in a rhythmical way consonant with his theory of beauty as a rhythmical creation, with his theory of versification in "The Rationale of Verse," and with the trains of ratiocination, whether inductive or deductive, in which any given point follows the preceding one in an unbroken sequence. Such a procedure represents a kind of doubling, the dialectical counterpart of which is precisely reversal or revolution. Thus, in the present text, Poe, having offered the proposition just quoted, offers it once more (the difference between the two utterances being that the later one is more fully developed). More than the similarity between human reason and animal instinct, which Poe calls "a wonderful analogy," one finds in certain creatures an instinct

referable only to the spirit of the Deity itself, acting *directly,* and through no corporal organ, upon the volition of the animal. . . . the coral-worm is not only capable of building ramparts against the sea . . . but is gifted with what humanity does not possess—with the spirit of prophecy. It will foresee . . . the pure accidents which are to happen to its dwelling, and aided by myriads of its brethren, all acting as if with one mind (and *indeed* acting with only one—with the mind of the Creator) will work diligently to counteract influences which exist alone in the future. (*M* 2, 478)

The statement largely reduplicates the thesis that concludes the preceding paragraph: the action of the creature is that of the divine mind acting immediately upon it. In respect of ulterior causality, in other words, this creatural instinct is inspired by the same supernal design wrought into aesthetic effects through the mediation of the artist.

The final reflections on these issues, for our purposes, occur in "The Imp of the Perverse," where the narrator again employs induction as a point of reference. Poe, who took phrenology seriously in his earlier days, was nonetheless willing to criticize the "science," as here, where it is rebuked for not having used induction to expose "an innate and primitive principle of human action, a paradoxical something, which we may call *perverseness,* for want of a more characteristic term" (*H* 6, 146). The irrational rationale of this something is that it causes one to reverse all normal patterns of behavior and expectation. Like instinct, it occupies a transcendental relation to traditional reason: "[W]e act, for the reason that we should *not* . . . I am not more certain that I breathe, than that the assurance of the wrong or error of any action is often the one unconquerable force which impels us, and alone impels us to its prosecution'' (*H* 6, 147).

By a strange dialectic, perverseness forces the reversal of one's attitude toward the normative condition of human experience—of ordinary well-being; this condition the perverse does not merely disregard, but absolutely negates, offering itself as absolute antithesis. The perverse is a grotesque, a thing not of gaming, which is orderly in a strictly rule-bound way, but of playing, which is not. Play's unpredictability makes it antithetical to reason, truth, prophecy; if the coral-worm is prophetic, it is not because of its *Spieltrieb,* but because it exemplifies the argument from design, because it is, to mention a subject to be developed later, fated or destined.

EXPERIENCE EXPERIMENT

From the late fourteenth to the late eighteenth centuries, *experience* meant testing, trying, experimentation, and the verb follows the same trajectory. Moreover, Bacon, a favorite of Poe's, makes much of the necessary bond between experience and experiment, a bond reflected in Poe's aesthetics, where it manifests itself, for example, as novelty or lawfulness: as discovered or as something revealing design, both of these being possible outcomes of the process of going through a kind of laboratory in life. "Mesmeric Revelation'' is a patent instance of experimental fiction, as Poe, conflating narrative and dialogue, ventures into such uncharted realms of metaphysical speculation as are usually left to philosophers. All of the hoaxes are tests of what one can get away with in experimenting with the public (and with otherwise untested technologies). In *Eureka,* Poe tries the possibilities, in an experimental blend of modes and themes, for a modern Empedoclean discourse—though deriving, in part, from Democritean impulses—in a hostile, because utilitarian, world. What is Poe's championing of originality but a recognition of the need to try new things?

These issues are woven together into the dense fabric of "Marginalia,'' 150, which was a source of both fascination and frustration to Valéry. It is about the liminality experienced when testing the power of words vis-à-vis the demands of fancies "rather psychal than intellectual'' (*P* 2, 258). Thoughts differ from fancies, which occur "at those mere points of time where the confines of the world blend with those of the world of dreams'' (*P* 2, 258). When Poe goes on to say that he is designing "experiments'' that will "prevent the lapse from the *point* . . . into the dominion of sleep,'' he reveals that the emphasized term has the same orientating function (Halliburton, 398–99) as its counterpart in the revolutions of *Eureka.*

Experimentation lies, in general, within the competence of anyone. Discussing syllabic "equality'' in "The Rationale of Verse,'' Poe says that "any one fond of mental experiment may satisfy himself, by trial, that, in listening to the lines, he does actually, (although with a seeming unconsciousness, on account of the rapid evolutions of sensation . . .) recognize . . . each and all of the equalizations detailed'' (*H* 14, 227). But the experiment with psychal fancies goes beyond evolution to revolution (as I attempt to show in the next section) because no one in the world has ever tried to do what he is doing. Anticlimactically, the discussion breaks off. The liminal state has evidently been stayed long enough to shift the fancies into memory, where they can be studied, but they have yet to be expressed as words are expressed.

In other words, Poe has reached the Hegelian nodal point, the liminal juncture at which something undergoes a revolution, the effect of which is that, even as it assimilates enough of what it was to perpetuate ontological continuity, it becomes something radically different from what it was. In ''Mesmeric Revelation,'' Vankirk provides an additional perspective on the same revolutionary phenomenon when he explains, '' 'There will be a point—there will be a degree of rarity, at which, if the atoms are sufficiently numerous, the interspaces must vanish, and the mass absolutely coalesce' '' (*M* 3, 1034). In a celebrated letter to James R. Lowell, Poe identifies such a radical transformation, in which matter becomes so ''unparticled'' as to be virtually synonymous with spirit while yet remaining material, with death itself: ''Man exists as a 'person,' by being clothed with matter (the particled matter) which individualizes him. Thus habited, his life is rudimental. What we call 'death' is the painful metamorphosis'' (*O* 1, 257).

AESTHETICS OF REVOLUTION

The revolutionary Milton took on things unattempted yet in prose or rhyme. Poe will do the same: in ''The Philosophy of Composition,'' he announces that he is giving something entirely new to the world. As if that were not enough, in the present texts, he asserts that only the lack of favorable circumstances has kept his experience experiment from achieving its designed end: ''else had I compelled the Heaven into the Earth'' (*P* 2, 259). The originality Poe thus desired was to be on a world scale, something for the ages. But, whereas Milton took part in a political revolution of epochal proportions, Poe had to settle for President Harrison and the Whig cause. But that party was sufficiently rebellious in its own eyes, opposing as it did much of the democratic and Democratic mainstream. Mutatis mutandis, so did their approximate French cousins, the Liberals, in whose cause Dupin apparently enlists in siding with the Queen in ''The Purloined Letter'' (an identification turning on the collateral identification of G. as the Prefect Gisquet). One thus leagued with the monarch who purloined the July Revolution becomes *counter*revolutionary in the very act of creating that new thing in the world, detective fiction, which some suppose to be apolitical.

Revolution can embrace modes of re-newal, re-generation, re-birth, re-vival, re-covery, re-turn, and on practically any scale—and this list is far from exhaustive. In ''The Longfellow War,'' Poe explains how a forgotten thought, originating in another's work, is re-vived: ''The frailest association will regenerate it—it springs up with all the vigor of a new birth'' (*H* 12, 106). After ''the return of animation,'' Pym declares: ''I felt a new being'' (*H* 3, 230). This large and lively family of prefixes includes the re-folding, re-sealing, and re-turn of the purloined letter, the re-crossing of ''The Man of the Crowd,'' and, climactically, the re-cognition at the conclusion of *Eureka* when ''Man . . . will at length attain that awfully triumphant epoch when he shall recognize his ex-istence as that of Jehovah'' (*H* 16, 315).

The supreme novelty in this mode, in which revolution is clearly centered in an orienting point, occurs in *Eureka,* where Poe suggests that ''only by a rapid whirling on his heel could he hope to comprehend the panorama in the sublimity of its *oneness*'' (*H* 16, 186). Here revolution is not an overturning but a revo-lution wherein one experiences the earthly-cosmic design of things. If Poe's concern for temporality here underscores speed, the requisite point of time will be stretched indefinitely, if not infinitely, as we will see, in the case of prophecy. There is, meanwhile, more than a whiff of infinity in the sublime question, ''As we find cycle within cycle without end—yet all revolving around one far-distant center which is the Godhead, may we not analogically suppose . . . life within life, the less within the greater, and all within the Spirit Divine''? (*M* 2, 601).

Turning can be poetic as well: ''[V]erse, from the Latin *vertere,* to turn, is so called on account of the turning or re-commencement of the series of feet'' (*H* 14, 223). Noticing that the purloined letter '' 'is refolded in a reversed di-rection,' '' Dupin infers that it '' 'had been turned . . . inside out, re-directed, and re-sealed' '' (*H* 6, 50). He then repeats each *re-* so he can re-turn to the Minister's home with a re-duplication, which originally signified doubling or folding (*OED* 1, 1589), then ''making or becoming double or twofold . . . also, a double or counterpart'' (*OED* 3, 1649). *Convert* combines Latin *con* + *vertere,* which suggests a transformation or revolution with possibly metaphysical over-tones, as in the tales of women. Ligeia is converted into Rowena and back again (or not, depending upon one's interpretation); Morella as mother turns into Mo-rella daughter while Eleonora turns into Ermengarde. To be thus born again may be, in some sort, to be sacrificial, to be a kind of liminal material enabling refinement or purification, as in Ellison's concept of deathly condition or death as metamorphosis—thus, the process in ''The Oval Portrait,'' by which the statuelike female turns into the spirit of romance, the one being by Poe's own admission convertible into the other (Dayan, 165, 122).

Revolutionary impulse is, in any case, a recurring feature of Poe's life and writings, whether as aggression against power or as commitment to radical in-novation. The former may be explained in a measure by the possibility that he never entirely outgrew a certain postadolescent contrariness; here his rebellion against the West Point regimen is apposite. It would take a better psychologist than I to assess the extent to which he built up rage or resentment for the tragic loss of his parents so early in his life, especially of the mother whose image he worshiped in other women, or for the fact that his surrogate father left him out of his will. More relevant for present purposes is the impulse that drives Poe to oppose the authority of the Eastern cultural establishment (Moss, 41, 82); to propose novel principles of aesthetic experience and judgment that were radical by contemporary American standards; and to embody those principles in his own poetry and prose. More perhaps than anyone but Greenough, but quite in Greenough's vein, Poe understood, as thoughtful revolutionaries do, the need to transform cultural institutions, in this case, the institution of criticism; but this could begin only if one first revealed to one's fellow citizens what they didn't even know they lacked: "I speak of art now because I think I see that it is a want—a want widely felt, deeply felt—an intellectual want, a social want, an economical want—and that to a degree which few seem to suspect" (Greenough, 5).

The author of "The Raven," as represented by the author of "The Philosophy of Composition," practices what Kenneth Burke calls prophesying after the event: the art of starting from the effect to be achieved in order then to derive the procedure that must be followed to achieve it. Like the hermeneutic circle, prophesying goes the other way around as well, as in Poe's predictions for *Barnaby Rudge.* Whichever way one proceeds, prophecy, prediction, and other proleptic acts testify to the power of design as mediated through the power of words. The greatest such power is that of deity, which, as in the figural tradition, posits the inevitable fulfillment of what has been in order, on a higher level, to be again. In this sense, dialectic, too, may legitimately be thought of as such a destining by design.

In discussing biblical prophecies, Poe insists that, again as in the figural model, whatever they foretell is destined to come true; the crux is, as in *Eureka,* to find the orienting point: "[T]he most of the predictions become intelligible only when viewed from the proper point of observation—the period of fulfillment" (*H* 10, 10). That is why, in his cosmogony, Poe situates the point around which one's perspective must revolve in order to read the design inscribed in the cosmos as its destiny.

In Poe as in Hegel, revolution begins to look like interchangeability of terms when it is not downright tautology—to look, that is, like Poe's conception of the relation of cause to effect or of destiny to design. In this respect, Lacan is not far off the mark when, as if to revolutionize the last lines of "The Purloined Letter," he transforms "*un dessein si funeste*" into "*Un destin si funeste*" (Lacan, 52). To design *is* essentially to destine, even as causing *is* essentially effecting. But Lacan's position contradicts his own experiential premise; for the analyst aims to elucidate what it is that remains inconsistent in one's experience (he is addressing an analytic audience) until the role of the symbolic is shown to tie everything together into a chain of signification. Unfortunately, when Lacan then represses one pattern of signifying in the tale, it is not just any signifier that he chooses; it is the narrator himself. But there is more to the purloined Poe—or, rather, less, since the fate is assigned to the author and the reader as well. Yet, it is surely from Poe's experience that *dessein/destin* emerges, and it is surely the reader at whom every strategy is aimed.

446 Poe's Art

To Lacan, Poe's tale is made for analysis, *as embodied in Lacan,* who bids at last to replace the ever-perceptive Dupin. This is no longer, however, a transcendental or all-seeing position. Like the novice in the map game, the analyst, squinting to detect a unique position to occupy, fails to see the words *writer* and *reader* spelled out in capital letters, as it were. But in designing effects for readers, Poe is already more, and more meaningfully, revolutionary. From start to finish, the tale is a revolving of reversals. Purloining the letter, the minister transforms the situation of the queen, which becomes the status quo until Dupin, rebelling against the authority of police forensics, transforms the minister's property (already transformed from being the queen's) into his own, whereupon he returns the letter not merely in a revised form but as facsimile or as fake, as pure negation—the most revolutionary act of all—thereby transforming the situation of the minister, and, in so doing, enabling the narrative to come, as a revolving thing should, full circle.

As a reader, I see the analyst-reader as *not* seeing, and I see further that his analysis is blind to narrator, to author, and to audience. The irony is that this same author has designed for the analyst the destiny of being less a Dupin than a dupe—one, moreover, who has purloined only others' experience but does not know, or does not care, that he has done so.

That I, in turn, have readers is a fair assurance that Poe's vertiginous game is no endgame but will keep being played into infinity, not despite the need for an aesthetics of revolution but because of it.

WORKS CITED

Boeckh, Philip August. "Theory of Criticism." In *The Hermeneutics Reader: Texts of the German Tradition from the Enlightenment to the Present.* Ed. Kurt Mueller-Vollmer. New York: Continuum, 1987.

Carlson, Eric W. *Critical Essays on Edgar Allan Poe.* Boston: G. K. Hall, 1987.

Dayan, Joan. *Fables of Mind: An Inquiry into Poe's Fiction.* New York: Oxford UP, 1987.

Fagin, N. Bryllion. *The Histrionic Mr. Poe.* Baltimore: Johns Hopkins UP, 1949.

Frushell, Richard C. "An Incarnate Night-Mare: Moral Grotesquerie in 'The Black Cat.' " *Poe Studies* 5 (1972): 43–44.

Gadamer, Hans-Georg. *Truth and Method.* Trans. Garrett Barden and John Cumming. New York: Continuum-Seabury, 1975.

Greenough, Horatio. *Form and Function: Remarks on Art, Design and Architecture.* Ed. Harold A. Small. Berkeley: U of California P, 1947.

Halliburton, David. *Edgar Allan Poe: A Phenomenological View.* Princeton: Princeton UP, 1973.

Hegel, G.W.F. *Hegel's Logic.* Trans. William Wallace. Oxford: Oxford UP, 1973.

Justin, Henri. "The Fold Is the Thing: Poe Criticism in France in the Last Five Years." *Poe Studies* 16 (1983): 25–31.

Kehler, Joel R. "New Light on the Genesis and Progress of Poe's Landscape Fiction." *AL* 47 (1975): 173–83.

Ketterer, David. *The Rationale of Deception in Poe's Fiction.* Baton Rouge: Louisiana UP, 1979.

Kennedy, J. Gerald. *Poe, Death, and the Life of Writing.* New Haven, Conn.: Yale UP, 1987.

Lacan, Jacques. "Seminar on 'The Purloined Letter.' " In Muller and Richardson, 28–54.

Limon, John. "How to Place Poe's *Arthur Gordon Pym* in a Science-Dominated Intellectual History and How to Extract It Again." *North Dakota Quarterly* 51 (1983): 31–47.

Ljungquist, Kent. *The Grand and the Fair: Poe's Landscape Aesthetics and Pictorial Techniques.* Potomac, Md.: Scripta Humanistica, 1984.

Mabbott, Thomas Ollive. *Collected Works of Edgar Allan Poe.* 3 vols. Cambridge: Harvard UP, 1978.

More, Paul Elmer. "The Origins of Poe and Hawthorne." In More, *Sherburne Essays in American Literature.* Ed. Daniel Aaron. New York: Harcourt, Brace, and World, 1963.

Moss, Sidney P. *Poe's Literary Battles: The Critic in the Context of His Literary Milieu.* 1963. Carbondale and Edwardsville: Southern Illinois UP, 1965.

Muller, John P., and William J. Richardson. *The Purloined Poe: Lacan, Dupin, and Psychoanalytic Reading.* Baltimore: Johns Hopkins UP, 1988.

Ostrom, John Ward. *The Letters of Edgar Allan Poe.* 2 v. 1948. Rpt. in New York: Gordian, 1966.

Page, Peter C. "Poe, Empedocles and Intuition in *Eureka.*" *PoeS* 11 (1978): 20–26.

Pollin, Burton R. *Collected Writings of Edgar Allan Poe.* Vol. 2: *The Brevities: Pinakidia, Marginalia, and Other Works.* New York: Gordian, 1985.

Rieusset, Isabelle, quoted in Justin, Henri.

Schiller, Friedrich von Schiller. *Letters on the Aesthetic Education of Man.* In *Critical Theory since Plato.* Ed. Hazard Adams. New York: Harcourt Brace Jovanovich, 1971.

Smith, Patricia C. "The Arabesque in Poe." *PoeS* 7 (1974): 42–45.

Tate, Allen. "The Angelic Imagination" and "Our Cousin Mr. Poe." In Tate, *The Man of Letters in the Modern World: Selected Essays, 1928–1955.* New York: World, 1964.

Thompson, G. R. *Poe's Fiction: Romantic Irony in the Gothic Tales.* Madison: U of Wisconsin P, 1973.

21

The Language and Style of the Prose

DONALD BARLOW STAUFFER

*Ces gaillards-là s'en tiennent à la vieille comparaison: La forme est un
manteau. Mais non! la forme est la chair même de la pensée, comme la
pensée est l'âme de la vie.*[1]
—*Gustave Flaubert, letter to Louise Colet, Mar. 27, 1853*

INTRODUCTION

The question of Poe's prose style has been widely debated by critics for years;
some are repelled or appalled by what they perceive as its vulgarity or meretri-
ciousness, while others view it as a powerful instrument of evocation,
characterization, and narration. In all of his prose, Poe was conscious of language, as many recent deconstructionists have been at pains to demonstrate. In
fact, language and its potential—or lack of them—are, in their view, one of the
central preoccupations of his work. On the level of what Richard Ohmann has
called epistemic choice—that is to say, the selection of the words and phrases
that embody his vision—Poe was always the conscious craftsman, fashioning
through selection and revision a many-sided, effective instrument. At times, it
is a musical style, full of the resonance of sheer sound and verbal association;
at other times, it is coldly rational. Since these qualities may be found in various
combinations in all of Poe's writing, there is no such thing as a Poe style—in
the sense that there is a Johnsonian style or an Irvingesque style. Richard Wilbur's observation that "Poe chose numerous styles for his several modes and
purposes, distinguishing between the means appropriate to criticism, fiction, and
verse, and attuning the language of his tales to the genres . . . and the natures of
his narrators" emerges as the single most important fact about Poe's prose style
(140).

CRITICS' VIEWS OF POE'S STYLE

Recently, Harold Bloom added his voice to the voices of Yvor Winters and others who have held that Poe was a bad writer, accidentally and temporarily popular. Calling attention to what he saw as the "palpable squalors" and "awful diction" of his style in "William Wilson" and other tales, Bloom writes, "Poe can only gain by a good translation and scarcely loses if each reader fully retells the stories to another. . . . The tales lose little, or even gain, when we retell them to others in our own words" (93). These views, while not unrepresentative of Poe's negative critics, are extreme in their unwillingness to acknowledge that Poe knew what he was doing and was in control of his material.

Allen Tate, one of Poe's most astute midcentury critics, was considerably more discriminating. But even he grumbled that, while Poe has several styles, "it is not possible to damn them all at once." While, in his opinion, the style of Poe's criticism is his best ("he is a lucid and dispassionate expositor"), Tate argues that the fictional style at its sustained best is in the tales of deduction: in "A Descent into the Maelström," *The Narrative of Arthur Gordon Pym,* and "perhaps one or two others in a genre which stems from the eighteenth-century 'voyage.'" These fictions demanded a Defoe-like verisimilitude which was apparently beyond his reach when he dealt with his obsessive theme [identified by Tate as unmotivated treachery and self-violence]." His one exception is "William Wilson," a tale that, in contrast to Bloom and Winters, he regards as "serious": "perspicuous in diction and on the whole credible in realistic detail." Quoting a paragraph in which Wilson describes his school, Tate says it is scarcely great prose, but "it has an eighteenth-century directness, and even elegance, of which Poe was seldom capable in his stories" (91).

Tate thus praises Poe's style, but with reservations and qualifications, at times agreeing with his detractors. Of a passage in "Ligeia" describing her appearance, he writes:

It is easy enough to agree with Aldous Huxley and Yvor Winters, and dismiss this sort of ungrammatical rubbish as too vulgar, or even too idiotic, to reward the time it takes to point it out. But if Poe is worth understanding at all . . . we might begin by asking why the writer of the lucid if not very distinguished passage from "William Wilson" repeatedly fell into the bathos of "Ligeia." I confess that Poe's serious style at its typical worst makes the reading of more than one story at a sitting an almost insuperable task . . . *unless one gets a clue to the power underlying the flummery.* (92, emphasis mine)

Notwithstanding the fact that Poe and many of his readers consider "Ligeia" his best tale, Tate is unwilling to acknowledge, as I have pointed out elsewhere, that the "bathos" of the prose in this tale is particularly suited to the effects Poe is working to achieve (Stauffer, "Two Styles"). As Daniel Hoffman puts it:

We give "Ligeia" enough credence not in spite of its stylistic grotesqueries but because of them. Poe, as we know, could write as clearly and as perspicuously as Defoe when he wanted to. But who would tolerate the plain style of Monsieur Dupin's sidekick in the mouth of Ligeia's husband? Each tells his own tale in the language, in the rhythms, in the rhetoric most appropriate to his own character. (253)

W. H. Auden also recognized the necessity to judge Poe's prose by how well it works. In his view, although Poe's prose and décor sometimes fall short, their special qualities are essential to preserving the illusion. Regarding this sentence from "William Wilson"—"Let it suffice, that among spendthrifts I out-Heroded Herod, and that, giving name to a multitude of novel follies, I added no brief appendix to the long catalogue of vices then usual in the most dissolute university of Europe"—Auden remarks: "In isolation, as a prose sentence, it is terrible, vague, verbose, the sense at the mercy of a conventional rhetorical rhythm. But dramatically, how right; how well it reveals the William Wilson who narrates the story in his real colors, as the fantastic self who hates and refuses contact with reality" (vi–vii).

But when Roger Asselineau says that Poe's style is an intellectual style and not an artist's style, it would appear he has something rather different in mind. He would agree that Poe consciously chose certain kinds of language in an effort to create certain effects. These include, in his opinion, an excess of adjectives, superlatives, false elegance, bombast, and allusions to classical and modern literature. But Asselineau claims that in his criticism and the best parts of *Pym*, Poe's desire for order and logic gives him frequent recourse to the orderliness of traditional rhetoric. "This intellectualism appeared particularly in the solid logical infrastructure that ties together all the words, phrases and paragraphs of the text. The impression is of a rigorous linking of facts and ideas. The result is great clarity." All the details have been weighed and carefully calculated; nothing has been left to chance. One senses the constant intervention of will and the refusal to allow himself any spontaneity (93). The result, Asselineau says, is a prose of conscious, though not always fortunate, choice. "In his fantastic tales, for example, when Poe ventures into still unexplored regions or seeks to describe human relations and feeling, love or hate, his rhetoric becomes empty and he falls into pomposity and false pathos" (94).

Poe [Asselineau continues] thus sought to impose an affected style and the logical forms of traditional rhetoric upon a subject matter fundamentally irrational. . . . He dared not liberate either the primitive forces that words conceal nor those that were tormenting him behind his calm mask of the "gentleman." He feared the chaos which would have resulted, the disintegration of language and his own personality which would have taken place if he had ceased to hold fast to the sober traditional modes of expression. . . . His great sin, in short, is to have felt like a romantic—or if you will, like a modern with a personality on the way to disintegration—but to have expressed himself like an English essayist of the 18th century. (97–99)

Asselineau is certainly correct in pointing out the tension that frequently exists between the undercurrent of psychological stress and the surface of stylistic orderliness in many of Poe's fictions. But it is well to keep in mind also, as James Gargano has frequently pointed out, that Poe's narrators are not Poe the writer and that the effect upon the reader is all the more intense for our sense of the fictional narrator's desperate attempts to hold on to his sanity.

In the view of Richard Fletcher, Poe used three different vocabularies singly or together: an "inspired," or evocative, vocabulary, providing a creative impetus into the tale; a related, mechanical vocabulary of stock Gothic diction; and a vocabulary full of allusions, epigrams, foreign phrases, and biblical echoes. The evocative vocabulary arouses vague and undefinable responses in the reader by clustering certain words and their synonyms together. In the opening paragraph of "Usher," for example, *windows, sedges, trees,* and the key word, *tarn,* reappear there and elsewhere in the tale, giving Poe a group of evocative words that propel him through the story. When these three types of diction worked together, as in "The Pit and the Pendulum," Fletcher says Poe was writing at his best. This study does succeed in showing how evocative or "synonymic" language works in various passages; however, he offers his analyses in a tone of grudging admiration for an artist whom he faults as a kind of literary con man working to persuade his readers into accepting a false image of him, and the monograph as a whole is seriously flawed by loose thinking and casual scholarship.

THE POWER OF WORDS: POE'S THEORY OF LANGUAGE

The subject of style inevitably raises questions about the nature and function of language itself. What is the relationship between the written word and the world it represents or evokes, between, that is, signifier and signified? Are the words themselves things, to be used as building blocks to create meaning or effect, or are they symbols, to be employed to evoke a vague and suggestive atmosphere?

Poe makes an important statement concerning the relationship between creativity and language in "The Power of Words." In this postmortem colloquy, Agathos lectures Oinos on the *"physical power of words"* and recalls the moment, three centuries earlier, when, "with a few passionate sentences," he spoke the star Aidenn into birth (*M* 3, 1215). Commenting on this tale, Maria Elisabeth Kronegger observes that, for Poe and other romantic writers, a single word may contain an incantatory magic. "The Power of Words" dramatizes the notion that words, on one hand, reveal essences, and, on the other hand, have the power to create worlds. Thus, by means of language, Agathos and Oinos are able to move from the illusion that is this sensible world to the fuller perception that is the truer reality beyond. Thus, Kronegger writes, Agathos reasserts the creative principle of the logos (131). Conducting Oinos through his realm, he explains creation and man's part in it: every word is an impulse on the air, a motion produced by thought, whereby dreams are created and a world re-created. Every act, every thought, is a creative irradiation of endless consequences into unending space. By moving his hands, Agathos says, he sets the atmosphere into a vibration that engirdles the earth. Words, too, are such creative impulsions: airy and moving incarnations of ethereal thought, as is the star that Agathos actually thought into existence.

This idealist view of the nature and function of language has been countered in recent years by a number of critics who focus on the centrality of language to Poe's thought, emphasize the self-reflexive nature of his writing, and argue against the long-prevailing view that he is an idealist or transcendentalist. One such critic is Michael Williams, who holds that language itself is the subject of Poe's texts. Poe's recognition of the arbitrary nature of language and his attempts to detach signifier from signified result, according to Williams, in writing that attempts both to realize the potential of symbolic language and to debunk the idea that language can be anything but an empty signifier: "[F]ully aware of the radical displacements inherent in the use of language, [Poe] exposes the futility and necessary failure of idealist attempts to evade them, but nevertheless struggles to develop protective strategies by which to control their consequences for his own practice" (xvi). Poe's "protective strategies" include his assertion that certain abstract ideas, such as infinity, or psychological phenomena, such as "fancies," must have words arbitrarily assigned to them, in spite of the fact that they are ultimately unknowable. Of the word *infinity*, Poe writes in *Eureka:* "This, like 'God,' 'spirit,' and some other expressions of which the equivalents exist in nearly all languages, is by no means the expression of an idea—but of an effort at one. It stands for the possible attempt at an impossible conception" (Quinn, 1272; Williams, 15).

Nevertheless, when a word refers to something concrete rather than abstract, it can become a powerful means of suggestion. When Arthur Gordon Pym, for example, reads the single word *blood* in the message he receives in the hold of the *Grampus,* he reacts strongly to it:

And "blood," too, that word of all words—so rife at all times with mystery, and suffering, and terror—how trebly full of import did it now appear—how chilly and heavily (disjointed, as it thus was, from any foregoing words to qualify or render it distinct) did its vague syllables [*sic*] fall, amid the deep gloom of my prison, into the innermost recesses of my soul!

Examples of this fusion of the world and language may be found elsewhere in Poe's works. A passage in "Al Aaraaf" suggests that the poet perceives in silent nature an ideal reality that he deciphers through the visions it reveals; yet, at the same time, he points out, as in the "Marginalia" passage quoted before, the essentially arbitrary nature of language:

Ours is a world of words: Quiet we call
"Silence"—which is the merest word of all.
All Nature speaks, and ev'n ideal things
Flap shadowy sounds from visionary wings.

The "merest word" in this passage is echoed in the "merely written words" that the narrator of "The Fall of the House of Usher" is reduced to using when attempting to describe Usher's painting: "From the painting over which his elaborate fancy brooded, and which grew, touch by touch, into vaguenesses at which I shuddered the more thrillingly, because I shuddered knowing not why; —from these paintings (vivid as their images now are before me) I would in vain endeavor to educe more than a small portion which should lie within the compass of merely written words" (*M* 405). Here once again, Poe calls attention to the inadequacy of language, as when his narrator attempts to convey the ideas and feelings embodied in Usher's paintings.

Another poststructuralist critic for whom Poe's language is a central issue is Joan Dayan, who maintains that Poe was committed to, and respected, a radically physical world. "His attachment to materiality [she writes] simultaneously deconstructs the romantic sublime and permits him to make the most fantastic fictions about mind" (15), such as "Landor's Cottage" and "The Domain of Arnheim," which she describes as "a fever of materiality" (102). In *Eureka,* Dayan writes, Poe is "obsessed with finding a mechanics of the universe that can be replicated in the forms of his writing." He plays with words, she says, "to ascertain the connection between language and thought, seeming to locate his method in the strategies of his eighteenth-century literary ancestors, who followed Locke in their demands for clarity and their satire on enthusiasm or empty speculation" (10). While this appears to be in radical opposition to the notion of Poe as an idealist, it is still consistent with the view that he seeks to capture in words what is ultimately unsayable. In many ways, Poe is actually a Platonic transcendentalist, in spite of Dayan's assertions to the contrary. Yet, he mocks the New England transcendentalists for blurring the bounds of sense and rendering language imprecise. In his review of R. H. Horne's *Orion,* he "earnestly" asks, "if *bread-and-butter* be the vast IDEA in question . . . for we have often observed that when a SEER has to speak of even so usual a thing as bread-and-butter, he can never be induced to mention it outright" (*T,* 291). Here he would seem to be calling for directness and precision in all cases.

Dayan's chapter on "The Analytic of the Dash" comes closer to the question of style by focusing on Poe's methods of imposing his language on the recalcitrant reality he confronts. "While claiming to construct a cosmology" in *Eureka,* she writes, Poe "is out to remake English prose. . . . The dash figures a language of successive approximation, graphically reenacts the stops and starts, the retakes and protracted unfinishedness so much a part of every Poe plot. . . . Through his dash, a continuous peculiarity exercised in most of his tales, Poe stamps his presence on the world of phenomena, or, more precisely, on his world of words'' (55–57).

Whether or not one agrees with her extreme position on Poe's materialism, Dayan's close stylistic analyses of his verbal and syntactical structures confirm the more general view that his self-conscious ordering of language reaches to the most minute levels, including punctuation (Poe has himself written on the importance to style of both the comma and the dash). Such attention to the material of the manuscript—the actual marks on the page—makes us realize that, in practice, words, vague or symbolic as they might be, function as things: actual objects that must be placed in certain arrangements or sequences in order to achieve the desired effect. Poe is, in fact, a literary engineer, using words as building blocks that he ''carefully, patiently combine[s]'' in order to create a functional style for a predetermined effect on the reader.

POE'S VIEWS ON STYLE

In addition to such theoretical questions as are raised indirectly by his poems and tales, Poe's critical writings contain many direct references to style. His interest in style ranges from general questions of ''tone'' and ''manner'' to quite specific questions of word choice, grammar, and syntax. In presenting his famous theories of unity of effect, he emphasizes the need for close attention to language, and his reviews frequently focus on the qualities of style he admires. However, Poe's pronouncements on the nature and importance of style are far from systematic, since many of them were hastily written under the day-to-day pressures of book reviewing. Many of his ideas about style, in fact, are derived from other sources: from his immersion in popular magazine fiction, for example, as well as from such eighteenth-century models of style as Benjamin Franklin, Edmund Burke, and Blair's *Rhetoric*.

When Poe writes about style, he is especially concerned with word choice, syntax, and grammar. Indeed, he so frequently attacked the stylistic weaknesses of the writers he reviewed that he became known as the Tomahawk man. In his reviews, he singles out for praise a number of stylistic features. Among these are brevity, precision, terseness (a favorite term), simplicity, and lucidity. Brevity, for example, is always desirable, except when it obscures rather than clarifies, as Poe notes in the case of Carlyle: ''[T]hose are mad who admire a brevity which squanders our time for the purpose of economizing our printing-ink and paper'' (*P* 2, 136, ''Marginalia'' 29). What he particularly dislikes and attacks are carelessness, awkwardness, vulgarity, and ambiguity.

Writing to Thomas W. White, the editor of the *Southern Literary Messenger*, defending his tale ''Berenice'' against accusations that it was too horrible, Poe pointed out that similar articles were appearing elsewhere, namely, in British magazines such as *Blackwood's*. ''The history of all Magazines,'' he wrote, ''shows plainly that those which have attained celebrity were indebted for it to articles *similar in nature*—to *Berenice*—although, I grant you, far superior in style and execution." His admission of the tale's stylistic weakness suggests how important he considered style to be. "Great attention must be paid to style," he wrote, "and much labor spent in . . . composition or [the tale] will degenerate into the turgid or the absurd" (*O* 1, 57–58).

His view that style should be a central concern of the writer appears in a number of other places, notably, in a review of "Peter Snook" (1836), in a letter to Judge Beverley Tucker in 1835, and in the 1842 review of Hawthorne's *Twice-Told Tales*. Unfortunately, in these various pieces, Poe is not always precise about what he meant by style; his own loose definitions, ranging from "mere language," on one hand, to "tone" and "manner," on the other, suggest that his conception of style has to do, in a general way, with conscious choice and effective use of language. In his review of Robert Montgomery Bird's *The Hawks of Hawk-Hollow* (1835), Poe commented upon that "purely mechanical portion of Dr. Bird's novel, which it would now be fashionable to denominate its *style*," adding:

But we repeat that upon the whole the style of the novel—if that may be called its style, which style is not—is at least equal to that of any American writer whatsoever. In the style properly so called—that is to say in the prevailing tone and manner which give character and individuality to the book. . . . It has no pretensions to originality of manner, or of style—for we insist upon the distinction—and very few to originality of manner [*sic*—matter?]. (*H* 8, 72–73)

Poe muddies the waters somewhat here, since he begins by equating style with "tone and manner" and ends by insisting upon the "distinction" between style and manner. Probably he means that "style" may signify either the "purely mechanical," that is, grammatical, aspects of writing, or tone/manner. This lack of precision and consistency in Poe's critical terminology—the blurring of distinctions among *style, manner,* and *tone*—should not be taken as a weakness, since his was not an age of precise definition of critical terms. He frequently relies on a reader's "taste" or powers of "reflection" to supply the meanings of the terms he employs. From his use of the term *style,* it becomes clear that he is thinking, in a general way, of the use of language to create the effects the writer desires.

Poe's view of Gibbon's style is a case in point. In his *American Museum* "Literary Small Talk" piece (1839), he mocked the popular notion of Gibbon's "splendid and stately but artificial style" and declared it to have "greatly vitiated our language" (*P* 2, 459–60). He rearranged a sentence in order to show how it "renders the idea difficult of comprehension, by subverting the natural order of a simple proposition and placing a deduction before that from which it is deduced"; he rewrote another in order to show how seventeen words could convey the full force of Gibbon's thirty-six, thereby concluding that "the most truly concise style is that which most rapidly transmits the sense" (*P* 2, "Marginalia" 29).

But Poe in his reviews also deals with more technical matters, such as grammatical errors, awkward sentence construction, and poor word choice. The "stiff and highly constrained character of the style" of Alexander Slidell MacKenzie's *Spain Revisited* derives, in part, he wrote, from the misuse of words:

The use of the word *"vomitory"* in the present instance is injudicious. Strictly speaking, a road which serves as a vomitory, or means of egress, for a population, serves also as a means of ingress. A good writer, however, will consider not only whether, in all strictness, his words will admit of the meaning he attaches to them, but whether in their implied, their original, or other collateral meanings, they may not be at variance with some of his sentence. When we hear of a *"vomitory* by which we were entering," not all the rigor of the most exact construction will reconcile us to the phrase—since we are accustomed to connect with the word vomitory, notions precisely the reverse of those allied to the subsequent word "entering." (*H* 9, 10)

As for the style of William Godwin, it "is highly artificial; but the extreme finish and proportion always observable about it render this artificiality, which in less able hands would be wearisome, in him a grace inestimable." Poe praises Godwin also for his sensitivity to language:

We are never tired of his terse, nervous and sonorous periods,—for their terseness, their energy, and even their melody are made in all cases subservient to the sense with which they are invariably fraught. No English writer . . . with the single exception of Coleridge, has a fuller appreciation of the value of *words;* and none is more nicely discriminating between closely approximating meanings (*T,* 259).

One of Poe's tales, in particular, touches upon questions of style. In "How to Write a Blackwood Article," his Mr. Blackwood lectures the would-be author, Miss Psyche Zenobia, on the techniques of writing for the magazines. In this satire is Poe's tacit admission that he employed many of these devices himself. When Mr. Blackwood offers advice on questions of "tone, or manner, of narration," he observes that several of these—the tone didactic, the tone enthusiastic, the tone sentimental, and the tone natural—are all commonplace enough. "But then there is the tone heroic, or curt, which has lately come into use. It consists in short sentences. Somehow thus. Can't be too brief. Can't be too snappish. Always a full stop. And never a paragraph." He goes on to list other "tones," or styles: the tone elevated, diffusive, and interjectional, the tone metaphysical, the tone transcendental, and finally the tone heterogeneous, "a judicious mixture, in equal proportions, of all the other tones in the world, and . . . consequently made up of everything deep, great, odd, piquant, pertinent, and pretty" (*M* 2, 341–42). Such remarks as these in his letters, reviews, and tales indicate the extent to which Poe was interested in style. In his criticism, he leaned always toward precision, purity, and simplicity, scorning writers who used vulgar expressions, long-winded or awkward sentences, and sloppy diction. As his own criticism, as well as much of his fiction, shows, he placed a high value on reason, order, and logic. His own orderly critical style was perhaps one of the ways he tried to impose order and unity upon a world that confronted him with the threat of disintegration, but he was equally at war with this world when attempting to render its own chaotic and irrational nature.

POE'S FIVE STYLES

In a letter to Philip Pendleton Cooke, Poe made these claims:

In writing these Tales one by one, at long intervals, I have kept the book-unity always in mind—that is, each has been composed with reference to its effect as part of *a whole*. In this view, one of my chief aims has been the widest diversity of subject, thought, & especially *tone* & manner of handling. Were all my tales now before me in a large volume and as the composition of another—the merit which would principally arrest my attention would be the wide *diversity* and *variety*. (*O* 2, 329)

Altogether, there are five distinct styles, which may be divided into two broad categories, the *ratiocinative* and the *intuitive*. The three ratiocinative styles are orderly styles, characterized by parallelism and antithesis, by complex sentences, by transitional elements, usually by more abstract terms, by fewer adjectives and highly charged emotional words, by normal word order, by the use of transitional devices, by a polysyllabic, latinate vocabulary, and by precise word choice. They are basically eighteenth-century, neoclassical styles, derived from his reading and his study of Blair's *Rhetoric*. This passage from ''William Wilson'' is written in a ratiocinative style:

Wilson's retaliations in kind were many; and there was one form of his practical wit that disturbed me beyond measure. How his sagacity first discovered at all that so petty a thing would vex me, is a question I never could solve; but, having discovered, he habitually practised the annoyance. I had always felt aversion to my uncourtly patronymic, and its very common, if not plebeian praenomen. (*M* 1, 433–34)

The two intuitive styles, on the other hand, are characterized by repetition, by piling on of adjectives, by loosely coordinated or short sentences, by evocative, archaic, or poetic vocabulary, by parenthetical expressions, and by emphasis upon the sound of the words themselves. Here is an example from ''The Pit and the Pendulum'':

Yet, for a while, I saw; but with how terrible an exaggeration! I saw the lips of the black-robed judges. They appeared to me white—whiter than the sheet upon which I trace these words—and thin even to grotesqueness; thin with the intensity of their expression of firmness—of immoveable resolution—of stern contempt of human torture. I saw that the decrees of what to me was Fate, were still issuing from these lips. I saw them writhe with a deadly locution. I saw them fashion the syllables of my name; and I shuddered because no sound succeeded (*M* 681).

Briefly, and at the risk of oversimplifying, the ratiocinative styles appeal primarily to the intellect, and the intuitive styles to the emotions. Altogether, there are five distinct styles: (1) the plausible or verisimilar; (2) the critical or analytical; and (3) the hyperbolic, which are ratiocinative styles, while (4) the parabolic and (5) the arabesque are intuitive styles. They can be described as follows.

The Plausible Style

Poe himself used the terms descriptive of the first of these styles in a letter to Evert Duyckinck:

> If you have looked over the Von Kempelen article which I left with your brother, you will have fully perceived its drift. I mean it as a kind of "exercise," or experiment, in the plausible or verisimilar style. . . . I thought that such a style, applied to the gold-excitement, could not fail of effect. (*O* 2, 433)

As a longtime admirer of Defoe for his ability to create an effect of verisimilitude, Poe was trying in "Von Kempelen and His Discovery" to make his "quiz" appear as real as possible by writing in a matter-of-fact style full of circumstantial detail and without any literary heightening. This style lies at the heart of any literary hoax, but Poe felt he was more successful in his own hoax than Defoe had been in *A True Relation of the Apparition of Mrs. Veal,* in which, he wrote, "we are permitted, now & then, to perceive a tone of banter" (*O* 2, 433).

The plausible style itself is more easily illustrated than described. Whenever Poe attempts a kind of realism in which the events are supposed to be true, he uses it. "The Balloon Hoax" is written entirely in this style, as are most of "Hans Pfaall" and parts of "MS. Found in a Bottle," "The Facts Concerning M. Valdemar," and the journal sections, as well as the early chapters, of *Pym.* Items purported to have appeared in newspapers, such as those in "The Murders in the Rue Morgue," are also in the plausible style.

The Analytical Style

This comes closest to being Poe's "own" style. The term *critical* might also be applied to it, as it is the ordered, reasoned prose of his essays and reviews. Gorham Munson once described its principal traits: "a high degree of abstraction in the diction—appealing to the intellect rather than to the emotions; and a syntax which embodies the technique of mathematical proof—the *quod erat demonstrandum* followed by examples supporting the principle set forth in the generalization" (36). To this, we might add that the analytical style is balanced, with parallel constructions and antitheses; it expresses causality and dependency through complex sentence structure; it uses parentheses for qualification and clarification; it contains few emotional words and many abstract ones; it uses a normal word order with transitional devices; and the words are usually chosen for precision in meaning. In its logical movement, it follows the eighteenth-century *ordonnance* characteristic of Franklin, Burke, Marshall, and the lawyers and statesmen whose works Poe studied closely in the 1830s.

The Hyperbolic Style

Although Poe claimed that "nothing . . . more vexes the true taste in general than *hyperism* of any kind" (*H* 13, 186), this term might well be applied to some of his own work. Nothing strikes us as "hyperism" more than such strained efforts at humor as "X-ing a Paragrab," "The Angel of the Odd," or "Three Sundays in a Week." The hyperbolic label is useful for describing those many tricks of rhetoric—puns, rhyming words, parody, burlesque—that Poe found irresistible. The hyperbolic style may be found in all his satires as well as those tales "conceived and executed in the purest spirit of extravaganza" to which he refers in his Preface to *Tales of the Grotesque and Arabesque*. In spite of Poe's animus against "those little critics who would endeavor to put me down by raising the hue and cry of *exaggeration* in style, or Germanism & such twaddle" (*O* 1, 121), his own fondness for verbal horseplay marks the hyperbolic style as separate and distinct from other ratiocinative styles—and characteristic of many of his satires and burlesques.

The Parabolic Style

This style appears mainly in the parables or fables. Its chief characteristics are anastrophe, or the inversion of normal word order; polysyndeton, or the use of conjunctions in close succession; archaic diction; "biblical genitive"; epizeuxis, or emphasis through repetition of a word; heavy use of dashes; and anaphora, or repetition of the same word or words at the beginning of two or more successive clauses or sentences. Poe's debt not only to the Bible but to such Bulwer-Lytton tales as "Monos and Daimonos" is clear. Whether he is satirizing Bulwer, as in "Silence," or using Bulwer's technique to create a desired effect, the parabolic style combines the biblical and the Gothic; however, it is relatively rare in Poe.

The Arabesque Style

Whereas the parabolic style has affinities with the Bible and Bulwer, the arabesque style has affinities with Benjamin Disraeli and Anne Radcliffe. Taken together, these two styles embody the characteristics most often associated with Poe's fictional prose. While the parabolic (which might be considered a special form of the arabesque) is marked by a moralizing tone, the arabesque is generally more emotional in tone and is composed of a wider range of stylistic qualities: stock Gothic epithets, bizarre and foreign words, words used for the sounds themselves; parentheses for emphasis (rather than for clarification or qualification); loose sentence construction; inversion of word order. Another aspect of Poe's arabesque style, as Wilbur has pointed out, is his mingling of rhetorics: there is the plainness of "We will say, then, that I am mad"; there is also such a phrase as "Suddenly these manifestations they ceased, and the world grew dark before mine eyes," in which we find both a French construction and an archaism; while, in the paragraph on Eleonora's death, there is a cascade of "biblical" sentences beginning with "And" (142). This style is found most frequently in the arabesque tales: "Berenice," "Eleonora," "Ligeia," "The Fall of the House of Usher," "MS. Found in a Bottle," sometimes alone, sometimes in combination with other styles. Its "intuitive" qualities make it suitable for rendering abnormal mental states or bizarre or unusual situations and settings. It lies at the opposite end of the spectrum from the analytical style: loose where the analytical is balanced; particular where the latter is abstract; emotional rather than intellectual; suggestive rather than precise.

DICTION

Poe's vocabulary has considerable variety and breadth, reflecting as it does his wide reading, partly forced upon him from a lifetime of book reviewing. Burton Pollin, in *Poe, Creator of Words,* prints three lists of over 900 words (single words, compound words, and proper nouns) that were either coined by Poe or are ascribed to him as first instances in print. Those first ascribed to him were perhaps widely used popular terms that no other writer happened to record—such as "cigar-girl," "perfumery-girl," "mail-robber," "walking advertisement," "balloon-bag" (16).

Pollin also notes that in his efforts to reduce or bar fustian, indirectness, and triviality Poe often reduced phrases to two-word compounds: "Bacon-engendered," "Willisism," "imparticularity," "punnage," "metaphysician-ism," "indignity-mist," "sea-brilliancy," "trumpet-thunder" (10). He created adjectives from common nouns: "chasmal," "cipherical," "clerky," "psy-chal," "scansional" (16). Poe was also in the habit of making comic and satirical word compounds, in the manner of the journalists of the 1830s and 1840s, who indulged in linguistic play, puns, fanciful place-names and jocular coinages, such as "come-at-able," doubt-vapors," "helter-skelteriness," "moon-hoaxy," "dunderheadism," and "carry-one's-self-in-a-basket logic" (11). He frequently indicates that he is coining a word or that one needs to be coined, as in "The Man of the Crowd," where he speaks of "deskism—for want of a better word," or in his criticism, where he uses "graphicality (why is there not such a word?)," and "literature-ism (we must coin a word)" (15).

In his early work, Poe's fascination with language led to virtuoso displays of vocabulary, such as his word lists in "Lionizing," and to mixed levels of diction, resulting in a heterogeneity of tone that looks backward to Irving and forward to Melville, Twain, Faulkner, and many other American writers. Poe was also stimulated by his knowledge of classical and modern languages as well as his own natural curiosity. One way to cast a spell of antiquity over a tale is to use archaic words and inflections. Popular nineteenth-century novels and stories (and, of course, poetry) are full of *thees* and *thou hadsts,* and the like. Romantic heroes and heroines, separated in time and distance from the reader, spoke a language peculiarly their own. Hawthorne reserved this kind of diction for his early New England settlers and, more often, for his Quakers. Poe used archaisms sparingly. "Mere *quaintness* within reasonable limit," he wrote in 1845, "is not only *not* to be regarded as affectation, but has its proper artistic uses in aiding a fantastic effect" (*T,* 130).

He is referring here to the use of both archaic and unusual words in poetry, but his views are similar in respect to prose. His most frequent use of archaisms, in fact, is in his imitations of biblical style or of the type of speech presumably used by people in biblical times. In Horatio Smith's *Tale of Zillah,* the characters all speak a kind of elevated biblical jargon. Poe's burlesque of an episode in this novel is liberally sprinkled with the same kind of jargon, but the tone is quite different: "Verily it is neither—but beware how thou lettest the rope slip too rapidly through thy fingers; for should the wicker-work chance to hang on the projection of yonder crag, there will be a woeful outpouring of the holy things of the sanctuary" ("A Tale of Jerusalem"). But, although the inhabitants of Jerusalem use this language, the Roman soldiers speak a more Latinate prose: "Is it thus you evince your gratitude to our master Pompeius, who, in his condescension, has thought fit to listen to your idolatrous importunities?" The archaic quality of Poe's more serious writing derives partly from syntactical peculiarities and partly from the diction. Such words as *erelong* appear in "Morella" and "Ligeia" to heighten the effect, even though he had earlier criticized Elizabeth Barrett Browning for using this and other "unnecessary nonsense" (*T,* 129).

One reason for the absence of the *thou didst* type of archaism is the lack of conversation or speeches in many of the tales in which this diction would ordinarily be used. In "Ligeia," for example, there is only one speech in the entire tale—spoken by Ligeia on her "bed of death"—and here, indeed, she uses this kind of diction to considerable dramatic effect. "The Assignation," with all its stylistic extravagances, is not notably marked by archaic or poetic diction. If the absence of such words from some tales can be explained by the small amount of dialogue, we must seek a different explanation for their absence from "The Colloquy of Monos and Una," "Eiros and Charmion," and "The Power of Words," all of which are entirely dialogue. Most readers in recalling these tales would probably say that the effects of otherworldliness are achieved by the diction, specifically, archaic pronouns and inflections. In actuality, none of these tales derives its effect from a consistent use of unusual diction of any sort, at least no effects that would be termed unusual out of context. We may conclude, then, that Poe scatters some poetic or archaic words, such as *yonder, ere, anon,* and the like, through many of the tales, but unless we consider them in their context their mere existence in Poe's fiction indicates little of significance about his style.

More important are the foreign words and phrases, which Poe uses in nearly every tale. Like many of his contemporaries, he exploited the humorous possibilities of pedantic references while, at the same time, satisfying his inclination to display his learning. Greek, Latin, French, Spanish, German, Italian, Hebrew, and Arabic words are therefore present in both his serious and comic works. They are often exploited for their sound quality or used for their own sake, as in this macaronic passage in "The Murders in the Rue Morgue": "Chantilly was a *quondam* cobbler of the Rue St. Denis, who, becoming stage-mad, had attempted the *rôle* of Xerxes, in Crébillon's tragedy so called, and had been notoriously Pasquinaded for his pains" (*M* 2, 534).

But, while Poe used foreign words in this way, he also used them for other reasons: he was interested in impressing his readers with his knowledge of foreign languages; the use of such words was in fashion; and, at times, perhaps no English word would work for him.

The use of detail in Poe's descriptions employing a specialized vocabulary has often been noted. He was convinced that the power of Defoe (a writer he admired) lay in his "potent magic of verisimilitude." Since an illusion of realism is created partly by means of vocabulary, Poe, in such cases, is appropriately technical and specific. His interests in such subjects as medicine and ships and sailing provided him with the technical language required, as in this passage in "The Facts in the Case of M. Valdemar":

The ossification had proceeded with very unusual rapidity; no sign of it had been discovered a month before, and the adhesion had only been observed during the three previous days. Independently of the phthisis, the patient was suspected of aneurism of the aorta; but on this point the osseous symptoms rendered an exact diagnosis impossible.

The Narrative of Arthur Gordon Pym also contains much technical jargon, in this case having to do with seamanship, a considerable amount of it drawn directly from Poe's sources.

Poe's diction in general reflects his wide and eclectic reading, as already noted. He is especially fond of such unusual words as *caprioles, simoom, coir, jaggaree, ghee, girting, crank, huggab, shawm, gemmary,* and *ortolan,* which he seems to enjoy using for the sake of their sound or their oddity. "Lionizing" is a youthful virtuoso display of learning that includes names of wines, artists, French sauces, ancient authors, theological doctrines, and geological terms in wordy profusion. This typical paragraph reflects a fascination with word sounds Poe never lost:

He informed us all about internal fires and tertiary formations; about aëriforms, fluidiforms, and solidiforms; about quartz and marl; about schist and schorl; about gypsum and trap; about talc and calc; about blende and horn-blende; about mica-slate and pudding-stone; about cyanite and lepidolite; about hæmatite and tremolite; about antimony and calcedony; about manganese and whatever you please. (M 182)

Still another type of diction is dialect and slang, found primarily in his comic tales. The most extended (and least successful) effort of this kind is "Why the Little Frenchman Wears His Hand in a Sling," told by an Irishman using Irish dialect throughout. Other dialects Poe uses are Dutch in "The Devil in the Belfry," French in "The Spectacles," and, most unusual, the Gullah dialect of the South Carolina Negro in "The Gold-Bug" (Krapp 1, 161). "The Angel of the Odd" puts into the mouth of the "angel" an outrageous mongrel accent that is a pastiche of German, French, and Southern black.

All of these taken together supply a profile of the types of diction Poe employs in his prose. It is not possible, however, to determine from this kind of analysis what is typical and what is not. Certain words and phrases may occur with regularity, but as the contexts change, so do his word choices. Therefore, word counting as part of an effort to characterize his style is of only limited usefulness, and our first impressions of those words we believe are characteristic of Poe must be modified. Pollin's *Word Index* has had a salutary effect in this respect, and much more use might be made of it. I have found, for example, that some of my own earlier, largely subjective impressions of Poe's patterns of diction are not always supported by the relentlessly objective counting of a computer.

RHETORICAL DEVICES

It is also helpful in attempting to describe Poe's prose style to observe those syntactical or rhetorical devices that occur with the most frequency in his prose. Principal among these are repetition, parallelism, parenthesis, and inversion of word order. Repetition of various kinds is a device Poe relies on heavily, ranging from a simple linear structure for the purpose of emphasis or tone (epizeuxis), to a complex arrangement with an impact upon both structure and texture. The narrator in "The Oval Portrait" says, "Long—long I read—and devoutly, devotedly I gazed." Poe achieves the incantatory quality of such passages by combining rhythmical and rhetorical patterns of repetition.

Another form of repetition is anaphora, placing the same word at the beginning of two or more successive clauses or sentences. Poe characteristically uses this device in combination with an interrupting or qualifying parenthetical expression between dashes or commas, producing the double effect of interrupting narrative flow and emphasizing the key word, as in this example from "Berenice": "In the mean time, my own disease—for I have been told that I should call it by no other appellation—my own disease, then, grew rapidly upon me." Anaphora is found in both serious and comic prose, as in "Loss of Breath": "Imagine—that is if you have a fanciful turn—imagine, I say, my wonder" or this sentence, also from "Berenice," where we also notice the repetition of a key word to help establish the mood of the narrator and the tone of the tale: "Disease—a fatal disease—fell like the simoom upon her frame." Repetition is used in a variety of ways, including its use in phrases of apposition or amplification, and in deliberately exaggerated ways for comic effect. Repetition of single words, such as the name of Ligeia in the tale of that name, or the word *shadow* in "Shadow—A Parable" (twelve times in one twenty-three-line passage in the Mabbott edition) establishes a mood as well as emphasizing the central motif or figure. An example of the repetition of a single word has been noted by Eric W. Carlson in Poe's frequent use of the word *wild* (210–11). Poe uses repetition in both the ratiocinative and intuitive styles, but his intuitive style might actually be characterized as a repetitive style, so heavily does it depend on this device.

Related to repetition are parallelism and balance. All three are, in some respects, characteristic of orderly, rational discourse and associated, for example, with the eighteenth-century *ordonnance* of Samuel Johnson and others, which includes syntactically parallel phrases, the pairing of nouns or adjectives, sometimes using alliteration, elements in series, and a few examples of what might be called antithesis.

Complaining of Poe's everyday looseness of style, E. C. Stedman once noted his habit of loading his narratives with "enough of 'however,' 'in fact,' 'it should be added,' 'to be sure,' and the like, to increase their length appreciably." "His discursive and ingenious mode of thought," Stedman added, "drove him to an absurd over-use of the parenthesis" (1: cxxiii). It is demonstrably true that Poe qualifies, amplifies, interjects, emphasizes, and exclaims in an abundance of parentheses. He uses short interjections and transitional elements, or he inserts amplifying statements, creating three different kinds of effects. One result is a tone of fussiness or overexactness or timidity of expression through the device of qualifying statements; another is to prolong and intensify the suspense of a passage by interrupting its narrative flow. In addition, he uses parenthetical expressions to amplify a word or idea through apposition or modification. Poe was quite conscious of his use of these devices, since he often used them in exaggerated forms for comic effect.

Poe also tends to use more than the usual number of inversions of normal word order, changing either the order of subject, verb, and object or the order of verbs, nouns, and their modifiers. Most of Poe's inversions produce a poetic effect or provide emphasis, and sometimes both. His most frequently used poetic inversion is the rearrangement of the verb and its negative. For example, instead of "did not move" he writes "moved not" ("Shadow"). This type of inversion often gives his style a biblical or archaic tone, which is a marked quality of his intuitive prose. In his chapter on stylistic resemblances between Poe and the Bible, Forrest links the archaic tone derived from inversion of word order specifically to the style of the King James version (84–100). Forrest finds other echoes of biblical style in Poe's use of certain types of prepositional phrases common to both the Hebrew Bible and the King James version, as well as to the Hebrew language itself, where their use was owing to a poverty of adjectives and the lack of a possessive case. This "biblical genitive," as it might be called (139–42), corresponds in other languages to the genitive of material and the possessive genitive. In Poe's prose, one can find it in such phrases as "box of wood" ("The Gold-Bug") meaning a wooden box, and "eyes of Ligeia," meaning Ligeia's eyes. The number of instances in which the *of* construction is substituted for the more commonplace possessive or material construction suggests that Poe was using it not in isolation but in connection with other devices, such as archaic inflections and words, repetition, and the frequent use of *and* as a connective between short sentences in order to give an archaic, if not necessarily biblical, texture to his style (Chap. 9 passim).

Poe can be extremely precise in his choice of words for exact meaning or effect, and he can be highly sensitive to fine distinctions in meaning, to the connotations of words, to euphony and harmony. These characteristics of his style reflect the two sides of his own nature. He is both a poet, with the poet's ear for verbal harmonies, and a clear, logical thinker with the logician's passion for precision. Repetition, parallelism, inversions of normal word order and parenthetical expressions are the chief syntactical qualities of all his styles. The diction is characterized by archaisms, stock Gothic epithets, foreign words, coinages, puns, and slang, in varying proportions.

Poe's fictional prose thus covers a wide range of stylistic possibilities, from prose poetry, at one end, through straightforward narrative and expository prose, to bantering ridicule, hyperbolism, and jeux d'esprit, at the other. These styles, especially when read out of context, have affected readers variously as admirable, tasteless, powerful, weak, original, hackneyed, polished, crude, sonorous, cacophonous, "glutinous," or "bizarre."

An examination of Poe's styles, their devices and effects, reveals by analysis what the casual reader perceives by intuition: they are deeply compelling, drawing upon the vocabulary and rhetorical resources of the language. At its best, his prose style challenges attempts to analyze it for the sources of its considerable power; at its worst, it is transparently tiresome, pompous, and annoying. These negative traits are especially noticeable in the humor, which can make present-day readers wince with pain or embarrassment at some of the puns, wordplay, and dialect jokes.

Poe's detractors, it is clear, have not always been able to get far enough beyond the surface oddities, eccentricities, or patently sensationalist devices to give Poe credit for the artistry that lies beneath them. Part of the problem takes us back to the century-old confusion between author and narrator. We may ask whether Poe the writer is to be held to account for the verbal excesses of his disturbed narrators or to be praised for creating such narrators largely by means of their self-characterization through language. Many critics have commented on the extent to which Poe's mastery of the language enabled him to convey meaning through style. Poe is, in fact, one of the great stylists of the nineteenth century. His tales survive not because of their subject matter or plots, both of which he often borrowed from *Blackwood's* magazine and other sources; they survive, to a significant extent, because of the transformative power of his language.

For Poe, language was a means to achieve both beauty and truth. Both were to be reached through the exercise of imagination and intuition, since even the act of analysis—the ratiocinative faculty itself—is intuitive at its source. "The *truly* imaginative [are] never otherwise than analytic," Poe writes of C. Auguste Dupin, summing up the tension he perceived between the poetical and the mathematical (*M* 2, 531); and, indeed, the quality of Poe's prose reflects this tension between the two aspects of a single mind.

NOTE

1. Those fellows cling to the old comparison: that form is a garment. But that's wrong! Form is the very flesh of thought, just as thought is the soul of life. (Trans. Donald B. Stauffer).

WORKS CITED

Asselineau, Roger, ed. "Introduction." *Edgar Poe, Choix de Contes.* Trans. Charles Baudelaire. Paris: Aubier, 1958, 16–104.

Auden, W. H. "Introduction." *Selected Poetry and Prose of Edgar Allan Poe.* New York: Rinehart, 1950.

Bloom, Harold. *Edgar Allan Poe.* New York: Chelsea House, 1985.

Carlson, Eric W. "Frames of Reference for Edgar Allan Poe's Symbolic Language." *Critical Essays on Edgar Allan Poe.* Ed. Eric W. Carlson. Boston: G. K. Hall, 1987, 207–17.

Dayan, Joan. *Fables of Mind: An Inquiry into Poe's Fiction.* New York: Oxford UP, 1987.

Fletcher, Richard M. *The Stylistic Development of Edgar Allan Poe.* The Hague, Netherlands: Mouton, 1973.

Forrest, William M. *Biblical Allusions in Poe.* New York: Macmillan, 1928.

Gargano, James W. "The Question of Poe's Narrators." *College English* 25 (1963): 177–81. Repr. in *REAP.*

Hoffman, Daniel. *Poe Poe Poe Poe Poe Poe Poe.* New York: Anchor, 1973.

Krapp, George Philip. *The English Language in America.* 2 vols. New York: Century, 1925.

Kronegger, Maria Elisabeth. *James Joyce and Associated Image Makers.* New Haven, Conn.: College and UP, 1968.

Munson, Gorham B. *Style and Form in American Prose.* Garden City, N.Y.: Doubleday, 1929.

Ohmann, Richard. "Prologomena to a Study of Style." *Style in Prose Fiction.* Ed. Harold C. Martin. New York: Columbia UP, 1959. English Institute Essays 1958.

Poe, Edgar Allan. *The Brevities: Pinakidia, Marginalia, Fifty Suggestions and Other Works.* Ed. Burton R. Pollin. New York: Gordian, 1985.

————. *Essays and Reviews.* Ed. G. R. Thompson. New York: Library of America, 1984.

————. *Poems and Tales.* Ed. Patrick F. Quinn. New York: Library of America, 1984.

Pollin, Burton R. *Poe, Creator of Words.* Baltimore: Enoch Pratt Free Library, Edgar Allan Poe Society, and the Library of the University of Baltimore, 1974.

————. *Word Index to Poe's Fiction.* New York: Gordian, 1982.

Stauffer, Donald Barlow. "Poe's Views on the Nature and Function of Style." *ESQ* 60 (1970): 23–50.

————. "Style and Meaning in 'Ligeia' and 'William Wilson.' " *Studies in Short Fiction* 2 (1965): 316–20.

————. "The Two Styles of Poe's 'MS. Found in a Bottle.' " *Style* 1 (1967): 107–20.

Stedman, E. C. "Introduction to the Tales." *The Works of Edgar Allan Poe.* Ed. Edmund Clarence Stedman and George Edward Woodberry. 10 vols. New York: Scribner, 1914, 1; ciii–cxxxi.

Tate, Allen. *The Forlorn Demon: Didactic and Critical Essays.* Chicago: Henry Regnery, 1953.

Wilbur, Richard. "Eleonora," from the special edition for the Print Club of Cleveland, 1979. Repr. in *CE,* 138–42.

Williams, Michael S. J. *A World of Words: Language and Displacement in the Fiction of Edgar Allan Poe.* Durham, N.C.: Duke UP, 1988.

Winters, Yvor. "Edgar Allan Poe: A Crisis in the History of American Obscurantism." *Maule's Curse.* Norfolk, Conn.: New Directions, 1938. Repr. in. *REAP.*

Part V

POE'S INFLUENCE

22

Poe in Literature and Popular Culture

JOHN E. REILLY

INTRODUCTION: THE POE LEGEND

Little more than a decade after Poe's death, Mary Gove Nichols published her "reminiscences" of several visits she had made to the Poe cottage at Fordham in 1846 and 1847. Nichols reported that, on two successive occasions, her conversation with Poe turned to the subject of "fame." " 'Fame forms no motive power with me,' " he announced imperiously when the subject first arose. " 'What can I care for the judgment of a multitude, every individual of which I despise?' " When the subject came up again during Nichols's next visit, however, Poe reversed himself entirely. It was "false," he confessed, to have said that he despised fame; on the contrary, "I love fame—dote on it—I idolize it— I would drink to the very dregs the glorious intoxication." Poe made it clear that the fame he longed for was not just appreciation by what he elsewhere called the "aristocracy . . . of intellect" with which he identified personally, those "cultivated" and "judicious" readers endowed with "minds congenial with that of the author." What he longed for was adulation by the "multitude" as well: "I would," he confided to Nichols, "have incense ascend in my honour from every hill and hamlet, from every town and city on this earth" (M. G. Nichols, 11–12).[1] It was not just fame, then, that Poe sought, but popularity as well, popularity with the "mass of mankind" of "general taste." If Nichols's "reminiscences" are accurate, then surely history has dealt generously with Poe in at least this one respect, for it has granted him far greater popularity than has been enjoyed by any other figure in American literary history.

The basis of Poe's popularity is twofold. It is, in part, our fascination with his works, especially with a core of poems and tales such as "The Raven," "Annabel Lee," "The Tell-Tale Heart," "The Black Cat," "The Pit and the

Pendulum,'' and ''The Fall of the House of Usher,'' poems and tales that fascinate us by playing upon some of our deepest fears and disturbing anxieties. Poe's popularity is based also upon our fascination with Poe himself, not so much with the historical person as with the popular image that has evolved, the image of a strange, haunted, and suffering spirit, the weird victim of both his own genius and a cruel fate, the high priest of pure beauty raging through the crass, ugly, and hostile world of nineteenth-century America. A synthesis of fact, of legend, and of the conviction that his poems and tales are, in some obscure way, autobiographical documents, this image of Poe was, in no small measure, deliberately sown by Poe himself. It took hold in his lifetime, became firmly rooted during the first half century following his death, and remains the dominant popular image of him even today. Ironically, the image was cultivated not only by admirers of Poe but by his detractors, especially by those among his enemies who, in their determination to assassinate his character, unwittingly rendered the image more fascinating and thereby assured it a long and hardy life.

Nowhere is the popularity of Poe, both the works and the image of the man, more vividly recorded than in the hundreds of poems and dozens of plays, novels, and short stories and lately in the film, radio, and television productions, dramatic readings and recordings, comic books, cartoons, posters, T-shirts, advertising copy, and much more that he has provoked and inspired. Although relegated, for the most part, to the outer fringe of traditional Poe studies, this material is increasingly recognized to deserve serious consideration as a unique and lively record of Poe in our literature and popular culture.

POE IN POETRY

The poetry is unique in several respects among the forms of literature and popular art devoted to Poe. Whereas novels, short stories, dramas, films, and the like tend to be exploitations of Poe, exploitations of the prevailing popularity of him and his work, the poetry records the impact of Poe, rather the impact of the image of Poe, upon his most responsive readers. Whereas other forms of popular art devoted to Poe are relatively recent in origin, all but a small portion dating since the 1909 centennial of his birth, the poetry constitutes a continuous record of imaginative responses to him from within his lifetime and through several distinct phases in the evolution of his reputation over the course of almost a century and a half since his death.

Some of the most tenacious features of the popular image were already emerging in poems written while Poe lived. One of the most prominent is that Poe was the victim of neglect; indeed, he was to become the very type of the neglected genius. It is to Poe in precisely this regard that his friend the editor and poet Lambert A. Wilmer sought to encourage him in an ode published in *Atkinson's Saturday Evening Post* in August 1838, when Poe was only twenty-

nine years of age. "Let the heavenly gifted mind / Not hopeless mourn,"
Wilmer counsels Poe,

> tho' fortune now
> Averts her face, and heedless crowds
> To blocks, like senseless Pagans, bow;—
> Yet time shall dissipate the clouds,
> Dissolve the mist which merit shrouds,
> And fix the laurel on *thy* brow.

Eight years later, Jane Ermina Locke of Lowell, Massachusetts, added suffering
to neglect in a poem about Poe entitled "An Invocation for Suffering Genius."
Printed in Nathaniel Parker Willis's *Home Journal* in December 1846, the poem
was written in response to published reports of the destitution of the Poe family
at their cottage at Fordham on the outskirts of New York. "Oh, Charity," Locke
complains,

> where hast thou fled with heavenly lustred wing
> While on her low and sorrowing bed genius lies suffering?
> Dost thou no cheering errand bear, to one by coldness slain,
> No blest relief from pitying souls, or coffers filled with gain? . . .
>
> Ye tempt with gold the piper's song, and speed the loitering feet
> Of harper at the festival, or minstrel in the street;
> But he who bears a nobler lyre, with strings of seraph tone,
> Ye leave to pine in actual want, unpitied and alone![2]

The most pervasive feature of the image of Poe is the assumption that his poems
and tales are somehow autobiographical documents in which we can identify
Poe himself. This assumption lies behind two poems written in 1848 and published in the *Home Journal*. One of them, carried in the *Journal* on March 18
under the title "To Edgar A. Poe," was a valentine message from Sarah Helen
Whitman, the Providence, Rhode Island, widow who was to come literally
within hours of marrying him in December 1848. Whitman wrote her valentine
six months before her first meeting with him. Playfully addressed to Poe in the
character of his "grim and ancient Raven," the valentine equates Poe with the
voice in his works and introduces still another element of the emerging image:
Poe the loner and nonconformist. To Whitman, Poe is the dissenter whose gloom
and melancholy represent his sullen denunciation of the facile optimism of his
contemporaries, those mindless celebrants of progress through technology,
through "steam" and "machinery." Whitman makes her point cleverly by
means of an appropriate bird metaphor. Poe is our solemn raven among a flock
of mere popinjays and parrots:

> While these warbling "guests of summer"
>   Prate of "Progress" evermore,
> And, by dint of *iron foundries,*
>   Would this golden age restore,
> Still, methinks, I hear thee croaking,
>   Hoarsely croaking, "Nevermore."

The other poem in the *Journal,* entitled simply "One of Our Poets" and published on May 27, is a tribute to Poe by Frances A. Fuller (subsequently Mrs. Frances Fuller Victor, prominent author and historian of the Pacific Northwest). Fuller, who may have been present when Poe recited his poetry at literary soirées in New York, "draws the picture" of the author of "The Raven"

> brooding o'er his wondrous dreams;
> Sitting motionless and weaving visions in his mighty brain—
> Visions soft, and pure, and glowing, and with scarce an earthly stain—
> Weaving into them his being, all its pleasures and its pain. . . .
>
> Talking to his love in Heaven, she who never leaves his side,
> Hovering near, a winged spirit, still his angel and his bride;
> Counting ceaselessly the hoarded treasures of his memory's store;
> Burning out his heart in incense at the shrine he loved of yore,
> Haunted by the "rare and radiant" maiden of his heart, *Lenore.*

Although some of the most prominent and persistent features of the image of Poe began to emerge while he lived, not until the event of his death did the larger outline take shape. Then, on the very day Poe was buried in Baltimore, Rufus W. Griswold launched his infamous attack upon Poe's character, portraying him as a notorious derelict whose "career is full of instruction and warning" and whose darkest works are "a reflection and an echo of his own history." Griswold's aim was to defame Poe utterly, and he succeeded famously, especially among Poe's enemies. Among those who bore no grudge against Poe, however, and who had no personal acquaintance with him, Griswold's efforts proved, unwittingly and ironically, to have quite the opposite effect. They rendered Poe not a despicable figure to be abhorred but the figure of a man, as Nathaniel Parker Willis described it, "inhabited by both a devil and an angel"; it was the fascinating figure of one man possessed of both good and evil, of both Israfel and Old Scratch.

This fascinating figure unwittingly created by Griswold was celebrated in much of the poetry devoted to Poe during the first two decades following his death. Rebecca S. Nichols of Cincinnati, whose poetry Poe had singled out for praise on several occasions, both echoed Griswold in consigning Poe to "hopeless slumber" and extolled his poetry as inspired:

> Toll the bell!—
> Let it knell for him who died,
> In his own consuming pride,
> With his scorn for man half told—
> With his errors manifold—
> How fatal was life's story!
> Yet no song-inspired mortal,
> That e'er sat at Eden's portal,
> Rapt and ravished with the singing
> Of the angels near him winging,
> Surpassed his strains in glory! (R. S. Nichols, 315–16)

In a poem entitled "On the Death of Edgar A. Poe" and published in the *Home Journal* on November 17, 1849, a poem laced with phrases from "The Raven," the Indianapolis poet Sarah Tittle Bolton (now remembered, if at all, as author of "Paddle Your Own Canoe") characterized Poe as the "lost one" whose "wild and wayward heart" is now "Safely moored from sorrow's tempest":

> If a "living human being," ever had the gift of "seeing,"
> The "grim and ghastly" countenance his "evil" Genius wore—
> It was thee, "unhappy master, whom unmerciful Disaster
> Followed fast and followed faster, 'till *thy* songs one burden bore—
> 'Till the dirges of *thy* hope one melancholy burden bore
> Of never—nevermore."

Henry Clay Preuss, the self-styled "Bard of Baltimore," was one of the first of many admirers of Poe to consider Poe the victim of his "rebel soul," his own *"traitor Genius"*:

> With bold and fearful power, thou didst tear
> The mystic veil from all life's hidden things:
> And then thy rebel soul was doomed to bear
> The penalty which too much knowledge brings;
> Life's brighter lights to thee grew dark and drear—
> The mortal drooped, though perched on angel's wings;
> And, now, with all the gifts of Genius blest,
> Thou didst but ask of Death the boon of *rest!*[3]

The young poet and editor Thomas Bailey Aldrich, whose career was just getting under way when Poe's came to an abrupt close, also associated the darkness in Poe's life and work with his suffering:

> Ah, much he suffered in his day:
> He knelt with Virtue, kissed with Sin—
> Wild Passion's child, and Sorrow's twin,
> A meteor that had lost its way!

> He walked with goblins, ghouls, and things
> Unsightly,—terrors and despairs;
> And ever in the starry airs
> A dismal raven flapped its wings! (Aldrich, 70–71)

The flurry of verse prompted by Poe's death gradually subsided through the 1850s and 1860s. During these two decades, however, the Spiritualist movement furnished a curious interlude that illustrates not only how Griswold's defamation of Poe was ultimately ironic in its outcome but also how the popular image of Poe owes much of its durability to its adaptability or, in this instance, its adoptability. Assuming Poe's strange and unearthly poems and tales to be genuine records of experiences he had undergone personally, some members of the movement were convinced that Poe was literally a kindred spirit. "He was a medium for the general inspiration that sets like a current of living fire through the universe," one prominent adherent insisted. "No special, no individual spirit wrought directly through him, but he felt the might and majesty of occult forces from the world of causes, and trembled beneath their influence" (Doten, 145). Now that he had "passed over," as the Spiritualists would have it, it was only to be expected that Poe would communicate from "the other side." Often alone but occasionally in such respectable company as Shakespeare, Shelley, Milton, Robert Burns, Sir Francis Bacon, Thomas Jefferson, Andrew Jackson, or St. Paul, Poe's "ethereo-spiritual" substance delivered posthumous messages through a number of mediums, among them Lizzie Doten, Sarah Gould, Thomas Lake Harris, R. Allston Lavender, and Lydia Tenny, posthumous messages usually in the form of pallid imitations of poetry Poe had written while on this side of the grave. Not surprisingly, what the spirit of Poe revealed of himself confirmed Griswold's picture of him as a moral derelict. The spirit of Poe, however, was pleased to report that death and subsequent purgation had cleansed him entirely. On one memorable visit in the company of Shakespeare, he delivered a sequel to "The Raven" wherein the melancholy conclusion of the original was amended to a cheerful denouement in the Spirit World: upon confronting the spirit of his raven, Poe discovered that the bird was no demon after all; in fact, it was not even a bird:

> "I'm no bird—an Angel, Brother,
>   A Bright Spirit and none other;
> I have waited—blissful—tended thee for thirty years and
>   more;
>   In thy wild illusive madness,
>   In thy blight, disease and sadness
> I have sounded, tapping, tapping, at thy spirit's Eden
>   door
>   Not a bird—an Angel more—" ("Edgar Poe in the Spirit World," 115)

By the close of the second decade after his death, Poe was no longer the vital presence to those who had known him personally or the lively issue to those who had become embroiled in the heated controversy surrounding him. A revival of interest was at hand, however, a revival led by a new generation, one anxious to reconsider the old issues surrounding Poe in the light of new facts but largely in the light of new attitudes. Poe's defamers had had their day, had had their opportunity to swathe the man in dark legend. Now the partisans, the Poe cult, as Eugene Didier was to label it, would have theirs. But the figure they venerated was, in many respects, scarcely less legendary; indeed, in many respects, it remained essentially unchanged. Denunciation gave way to atonement. Like Chatterton and Keats before him, Poe became the figure of the artist neglected and scorned. Blame for his faults rested not so much with him as with the society that had misunderstood and mistreated him. For its scorn and its neglect, that society would now atone by belatedly recognizing his genius in a series of public testimonials beginning in 1875 with the dedication of a monument at his grave in Baltimore, followed by the dedication of the Actors' Monument to Poe in New York in 1885 and by the unveiling of the George Julian Zolnay bust at the University of Virginia in 1899, marking the semicentennial of Poe's death and culminating in 1909 with numerous ceremonies celebrating the centennial of his birth, a centennial that Charles Alphonso Smith aptly called Poe's "coronation" (3–4).

The shift in Poe's public posture from villain to victim marked no decline in the feeling he was able to evoke. On the contrary, his image assumed even greater popular appeal. The fascination of his romantic figure was now enhanced by the charm of pity and the spirit of a cause célèbre. Poetry devoted to him responded accordingly. It accompanied the revival of interest and participated in each of the public testimonials, and, with the arrival of the centennial of Poe's birth, it rose to a veritable chorus of hosannas to welcome the triumph of immortal genius over defamation and neglect.[4]

The dedicatory ceremonies at Westminster Churchyard in Baltimore in 1875 were the occasion for Stéphane Mallarmé's "Le Tombeau d'Edgar Poe," the most renowned and, possibly, least understood poem about Poe. Mallarmé's sonnet was not recited at the ceremonies but was appended to the account of the proceedings published in 1877 (Rice, 93). The lines that were recited at the unveiling were the work of the poet and drama critic William Winter. A standard fixture at occasions of this nature, Winter, or "Weeping Willie," as he had come to be known, was carried beyond the edge of tears in his determination to assure the "great and injured shade" of Poe that atonement is now being made for the shabby treatment he had received in the past:

One meed of justice long delayed,
One crowning grace his virtues crave:—

> Ah, take, thou great and injured shade,
> The love that sanctifies the grave! (Rice, 48–49)

As his part in the same ceremonies, the South Carolina poet Paul Hamilton Hayne offered a picture approximating N. P. Willis's earlier characterization of Poe's psyche as "inhabited by both a devil and an angel":

> Two mighty spirits dwelt in him:
> One, a wild demon, weird and dim,
> The darkness of whose ebon wings
> Did shroud unutterable things:
> One, a fair angel, in the skies
> Of whose serene, unshadowed eyes
> Were seen the lights of Paradise.

Though it was the "wild demon" that triumphed in Hayne's scenario, the blame lay not with Poe: "sapped by want, and riven by wrong," he now stands as the "type" or symbol of the innocent victim of a "fate remorseless" (Rice, 94–95).

A number of poets expressed similar sentiments during the decades between 1875 and the centennial in 1909. Among the more prominent were John H. Hewitt ("At the Grave of Edgar A. Poe," 1877), John Henry Boner ("Poe's Cottage at Fordham," 1889), and Joel Benton ("On a Shingle [of the cottage at Fordham]," 1899). But among them all, Father John Bannister Tabb of Maryland was not only the most prolific but the most trenchant. Of the ten or so poems he devoted to Poe, none were more caustic than the quatrain he dashed off in 1905 on the occasion of Poe's failure for the second time to be elected to the Hall of Fame at New York University:

> Into the charnel hall of fame
> The dead alone should go.
> Then write not there the living name
> Of Edgar Allan Poe. (Tabb, 351)

When Poe finally gained admittance to the Hall in 1910, the announcement created scarcely a ripple of interest because it was literally anticlimactic. The climax had occurred a year earlier at the centennial of Poe's birth, an occasion marked by ceremonies throughout the world. Ceremonies in this country were held principally at the Poe cottage at Fordham, at the Johns Hopkins University, and at Poe's alma mater in Charlottesville, where exercises extended over three days. Feeling on Poe's behalf swelled to a crescendo of sorrow, sympathy, and triumph, much of it in sentiments reverberating in verse since the 1870s. There were poems by Clifford Lanier, the gifted but now forgotten brother of Sidney Lanier, and by George Sterling, Edwin Arlington Robinson, Lizette Woodworth Reese, and Edwin Markham.

One would imagine that the "emotion and commotion" of the centennial, as one wag put it, would have exhausted the urge to celebrate Poe as our neglected genius. One would imagine, too, that the subsequent success of scholars in paring away layers of legend in the interest of revealing the historical Poe would gradually have obviated the grounds for lamenting him as a pathetic and fascinating figure whose works are the painful record of a melancholy but colorful life. But such has not proved the case. Poems about Poe have continued to appear throughout the decades since the centennial, poems almost uniformly devoted to a figure that we know to be far more fiction than fact. The number of poems has risen on occasion to as many as eighteen in the 1938 *The Muse Anthology of Modern Poetry: Poe Memorial Edition* and twenty-one in the October 1984 issue of the the the offbeat magazine *Random Weirdness*. Vachel Lindsay, Hervey Allen, Hart Crane, Philip Levine, Dave Smith, and Allen Ginsberg are among prominent poets who have celebrated Poe since the centennial.

Ginsberg is typical. He was moved to express his feelings in verse after visiting Poe's grave in Westminster Churchyard in February 1977. Though the people who assembled there back in November 1875 to witness the unveiling of the monument, the people who were brought to tears by Weeping Willie Winter's old-fashioned sentimentalism, would no doubt have had serious reservations about Ginsberg's taste and manner, surely they would have recognized his image of the man they honored, an image that abides today as vigorously as ever in the popular mind:

Baltimore bones groan maliciously under sidewalk
Poe hides his hideous skeleton under church yard
Equinoctial worms peep thru his mummy ear
The slug rides his skull, black hair twisted in roots of threadbare grass
Blind mole at heart, caterpillars shudder in his rib-cage,
Intestines wound with garter snakes
midst dry dust, snake eye & gut sifting thru his pelvis
Slimed moss green on his phosphor'd toenails, sole toeing black tombstone—
O prophet Poe well writ! your catacomb cranium chambered
eyeless, secret hid to moonlight ev'n under corpse-rich ground
where thread priest, passerby, and poet
staring white-eyed thru barred spiked gates
at viaducts heavy-bound and manacled upon the city's heart. (Ginsberg, 91)

POE IN FICTION

Although Poe appeared as a minor character in several novels while he lived, in almost every instance as an object of ridicule, the practice of featuring him in fiction belongs to the decades since the centennial. This fiction is essentially of two kinds: fictionalized biography and outright fantasy.

Fictional Biographies

Poe has been the subject of a wide range of fictionalized biographies, all the way from faint imaginative tintings and fillings in of his life and character, as in Hervey Allen's *Israfel: The Life and Times of Edgar Allan Poe* (1926), to renderings so deeply colored with fiction that the historical Poe is scarcely recognizable. But whether faintly tinted or deeply colored, every fictionalized biography stands as a tacit admission that the genuine facts of Poe's life and character simply do not support the colorful legendary figure of the popular image.

The earliest and still the best-known outright fictional biography is Mary Newton Stanard's *The Dreamer* (1909, 1925). Stanard calls her book "a romantic rendering" of Poe's life story, "simply an attempt to make something like a finished picture of the shadowy sketch the biographers, hampered by the limitations of proved fact, must, at best, give us." Her "finished picture" of Poe is the uniformly sentimental portrait of a handsome, gifted, and sensitive young man into whose singularly gloomy and unsteady existence Virginia ("with a face like a Luca Della Robbia chorister") shed a ray of joy and Mrs. Clemm ("with the 'Mater Dolorosa' expression") provided timely support. Although *The Dreamer* manages to confine most of its fiction to areas beyond the reach of conventional biography, occasionally fact and fiction do collide. In an effort to endow Poe with parents as innocent as her version of him, for example, Stanard suppresses the fact that Poe's father abandoned his pregnant wife, explaining, instead, that Elizabeth Poe "had lately lost a dearly loved and loving husband whom she had tenderly nursed through a distressing illness." *The Dreamer* reduces Poe's drinking to an expression of his loneliness for Virginia or his apprehension about her health, and Stanard juggles the chronology of Poe's relationship with Frances Sargent Osgood and especially with Mrs. Whitman as a way of skirting the issue of Poe's having shown interest in other women while Virginia lived.

A number of subsequent fictionalized biographies have exploited the legendary image while keeping imaginative coloring to a minimum. Like Stanard's *The Dreamer,* Dorothy Dow's *Dark Glory* (1931) confines its fiction principally to imaginary conversations and to narrative commentary and interpolation. Although Dow describes her Poe as the "one god" among the "semigods" of nineteenth-century American writers, *Dark Glory* succeeds only in fashioning the figure of a "pitiful American poet" who, "during his whole life, wandered among realities, missing them, mixing them"; and he died "some strange figure from some uneasy nightmare of despair, . . . worn out, disillusioned, hopeless." Laura Benét's *Young Edgar Allan Poe* (1941), a book "for young readers," offers a sanitized version of Poe covering his life only up to his tenure as editor of *Graham's Magazine* in 1842. Because this was, in many respects, the apogee of his literary career and perhaps the most stable period in his personal life, Benét has the good fortune of dwelling upon a portion of Poe's biography that has an inherent structure and moves to a triumph or climax, momentary though it proved to be. Cothburn O'Neal's *The Very Young Mrs. Poe* (1956) is a love story featuring Virginia. O'Neal dwells upon Virginia's efforts to realize herself as a suitable helpmate to her husband, efforts made heroic in the face of a valiant struggle with failing health. The portrayal of Poe himself in *The Very Young Mrs. Poe* is, for the most part, free of sentimentalism, treating him as a hardworking journalist and literary artist whose relations with his contemporaries were more professional than erratic. Since the story closes with Virginia's death, it moves relentlessly to its unhappy conclusion early in 1847. Barbara Moore's *The Fever Called Living* (1976) covers only the five and a half years from Poe's arrival in New York in April 1844 to his death. Although it contains a good deal of fictive coloring and interpolation, Moore's book is, beyond a doubt, one of the most meticulously researched fictions about Poe, so carefully researched that one wonders if it were originally intended to be a legitimate biography.

At the opposite extreme from the tinting of Poe's life and character in these faintly fictionized biographies are the gross distortions in Chancellor Williams's novel *The Raven* (1943). A tasteless stew of *Uncle Tom's Cabin* and *Das Kapital,* spiced with a generous dash of *Psychopathia Sexualis,* Williams's book makes a preposterous effort to exploit Poe in the interest of socioeconomic propaganda of a decidedly left-wing variety. Utterly ignoring the fact that Poe consistently identified with Southern aristocracy, Williams casts him as a staunch abolitionist and champion of the downtrodden proletariat; and, adding a special twist to Baudelaire's old charge that Poe was the tragic victim of American philistinism, Williams has him suffer at the hands of such robber barons as Poe's foster father John Allan (a "merchant prince," "the Southern representative of the new American system of capitalism" whose slaves and "mill workers" are restless) and "the rich and powerful Ralstons" (i.e., Roysters) who deprive Poe of his "Myra." Williams's socioeconomic bent leads Poe into such extrabiographical episodes as a harrowing sojourn among the impoverished victims of industrial capitalism, a walking tour through the idyllic world of American peasant farmers, and an encounter with President Andrew Jackson (the workingman's hero) in a Baltimore tavern. We are told that one of the principal keys to Poe's personality, personal relations, and creativity is the fact that his genitals were underdeveloped, a circumstance that Poe himself interprets as evidence that "*I really belong to a higher order of life!*" *The Raven* is an incredible distortion, but it is no more incredible than the review in the *Christian Century* commending Williams for endeavoring "to give a true interpretation of the poet's character and personality and to make his narrative conform to the facts of his life so far as these are known."[5]

Fantasies

One of the principal sources of the popular image of Poe is the long-standing notion, encouraged by Poe himself, that his poems and especially his stories are

autobiographical documents in which we can identify his narrators and characters as versions of Poe himself speaking in what appears to be his authentic
voice. This notion has inspired a whole subspecies of fiction in which Poe is
featured as a character in tales based on his own works.

Until recently, fiction of this nature has confined itself to short stories. Among
the earliest is Julian Hawthorne's "My Adventure with Edgar Allan Poe"
(1891).[6] Adopting one of Poe's favorite motifs, Hawthorne has him return briefly
among the living after a premature burial forty-odd years earlier. The "adventure" consists of the narrator's interview with the resurrected author in a "small
restaurant" in Philadelphia. Although essentially unaltered in appearance, Hawthorne's resurrected Poe is radically changed in character and outlook. "His
love of fame" as well as "all traces of his weird imagination" are absent.
Absent, too, is his intemperance; indeed, he now has " 'an unconquerable aversion to all forms of liquor.' " On literary matters, Poe finds "no enduring merit"
in his own verses and dismisses both his theory and practice of fiction:

"The short story," he said, "is not a satisfactory form of fiction. To properly gauge the
quality of a genius, we must see it in longer flights. If I returned to the region of romance
at all, it would be to write a long novel, like 'Martin Chuzzlewit' or 'The Last Days of
Pompeii.' But, to tell the truth, fiction in any form has few charms for me."

Vance Thompson's short story "A Tenement of Black Fumes" is inspired by
"Ligeia," "Morella," and "Ulalume."[7] Here the widowed Poe is prevented
from remarrying when the predatory spirit of a Ligeia-like Virginia threatens to
reincarnate itself in the body of Sarah Helen Whitman. Vincent Starrett's "In
Which an Author and His Character Are Well Met" (1928) has Poe meet Legrand of "The Gold-Bug" in quest of a new treasure, a vial of water from the
fountain of youth.[8] Both John Dickson Carr's "The Gentleman from Paris"
(1950)[9] and Miriam Allen deFord's "The Mystery of the Vanished Brother"
(1950)[10] have Poe exercise the ratiocinative talents of his own Dupin. Virtually
a burlesque of "The Fall of the House of Usher," Robert Bloch's "The Man
Who Collected Poe" (1951) is the story of a mad bibliophile who has brought
Poe back to life and confined him in the basement of an Usher-like mansion in
Maryland.[11] In the manner of "Sonnet—To Science" and "Al Aaraaf," Ray
Bradbury's "The Exiles" (1951) has the spirit of Dickens, Bierce, and Poe
retreat to the planet Mars to escape the depredations of science and rationalism
upon the imagination.[12] Recently, Walter Jon Williams's "No Spot of Ground"
(1990) imagines that Poe, having averted death in Baltimore and remarried a
young woman reminiscent of Lady Rowena of "Ligeia," is now an aging and
enfeebled Confederate general whose deductive powers could lead to the lifting
of the Union siege of Richmond were his genius not ignored by the military
hierarchy much as it had been scorned by the literary establishment.[13]

The last two decades have seen the appearance of novel-length fantasies exploiting Poe as a character in little more than name only. Barry Perowne's *A*

Singular Conspiracy (1974) carries Poe to Paris early in 1844, where he meets Charles Baudelaire and conspires with him to disgrace Baudelaire's draconian stepfather in retaliation for his having humiliated both his stepson and Poe. Perowne's Poe is replete with a "face of one marked for misfortune—the haggard mask of tragedy," a "cleavage in [his] temperament which was the bane of his existence," and a "burden of guilt, growing always heavier, which rode upon his back." Set in contemporary Richmond, Anne Edwards's *Child of Night* (1975) is the story of Eddie Polk, a young man who believes he is, and indeed may be, the reincarnation of Poe and who is incestuously and fatally infatuated with his thirteen-year-old cousin, Georgina Sue Clemons—just plain "Ginny." Eddie Polk confesses: "In my former life I would not have dared to admit thoughts of sexual passion. Now they consume me." Ginny's description of Eddie's malaise recalls Roderick Usher's diseased psyche:

He is obsessed with death and the threat of death.
He is really *frightened* of death.
He is frightened *of the fear* of being frightened of death.

Taking its cue from Henry James's *The Aspern Papers,* Nancy L. Zaroulis's *The Poe Papers: A Tale of Passion* (1977) has a collector descend upon the household of Nancy Richmond of Lowell (Poe's "Annie") in search of Poeana. Both Manny Myers's *The Last Mystery of Edgar Allan Poe: The Troy Dossier* (1978) and Marc Olden's *Poe Must Die* (1978) exploit Poe's reputation for deductive brilliance. Recently (1990), *The Black Throne* by Roger Zelazny and Fred Saberhagen and *The Hollow Earth* by Rudy Rucker cast Poe as a character in tales inspired by "William Wilson," "MS. Found in a Bottle," and *The Narrative of Arthur Gordon Pym.*[14]

POE IN DRAMA AND FILM

Like the practice of featuring Poe as a character in fiction, the practice of featuring him in drama belongs principally to the decades since the centennial. One notable exception is George Cochrane Hazelton's *The Raven,* a five-act dramatization of the life of Poe enjoying the distinction of being the first to be produced in the legitimate theater.[15] *The Raven* opened at Albaugh's Lyceum Theatre in Baltimore on October 11, 1895, with Creston Clarke, who was a grandson of Junius Brutus Booth and nephew of Edwin Booth, in the lead role. Although a review in the *Baltimore Sun* the following day commended Hazelton for following "closely the life of Poe as given by his biographers," *The Raven,* in fact, makes no serious effort to do so, offering, instead, an utterly conventional melodrama replete with hapless hero (Poe), helpless heroine (Virginia), and ubiquitous villain (an entirely fictitious character named Roscoe Pelham, A.M.). Idealistic, impassioned, intractable, self-destructive, and bombastic, Hazelton's Poe is virtually a caricature fashioned from some of the best known among Poe's own creations, that is, the narrators of "Morella," "Ligeia," and "The Raven." Action in *The Raven* vaults from Richmond in the late 1820s or early 1830s to Fordham Cottage in January 1847. It does so by reducing Poe's life first to his conflict with John Allan and then to his relationship with Virginia and Sarah Helen Whitman, two women whom Hazelton links through a Morella/Ligeia-like reincarnation. Presumably, Hazelton found little he considered stageworthy in Poe's literary career and almost nothing in Poe's personal life to support his characterization. Hazelton's futile quest for material to support his characterization of Poe is a problem well worth noting because it was to haunt every subsequent effort at converting the popular image into drama.

Catherine Chisholm Cushing's *Edgar Allan Poe: A Character Study* enjoys the distinction of being the first drama about Poe to reach the New York stage.[16] It ran briefly at the Liberty Theatre early in October 1925. Just as Chancellor Williams's novel *The Raven* sought to render Poe's life in Marxist terms, so Cushing's play attempts to translate Poe into a character who would appeal specifically to an audience in the 1920s. She lays special emphasis upon Poe's life as the romance of a youth who rebels against convention (represented by the Allans and Roysters, by the "University," and by the literary establishment) and then goes down in pathetic defeat. Cushing's Poe is very much a child of the Roaring Twenties, but not the 1820s, and his literary career is represented by little more than the enmity he generated as a critic. It is, indeed, a testament to at least the minimal good taste of theatergoers in New York that, in spite of Cushing's efforts at pandering to their interests, they sent her creature to an early grave. It failed to survive opening night.

New York theatergoers eleven years later were only a little more receptive to Sophie Treadwell's *Plumes in the Dust,* another conventional dramatization of Poe's life.[17] It ran for eleven performances at the Forty-Sixth Street Theater in November 1936, with Henry Hull in the lead role. The brevity of its stage career notwithstanding, *Plumes in the Dust* comes closer than any other conventional play about Poe to achieving a successful union of dramatic essentials and biographical fact. The action is built around almost the same episodes in Poe's life that form the basis, though remote, of Cushing's melodrama. They are Poe's break with John Allan in 1826–1827, his winning of the *Baltimore Saturday Visiter* contest in the early 1830s, Virginia's decline and death at Fordham, Poe's relations with the New York literati, his last trip to Richmond, and his death in Baltimore. Both as drama and as biography, the finest moments in *Plumes in the Dust* occur in the opening scene. Tension here is created by Poe's strained relations with John Allan, whom Treadwell characterizes as a hypocrite and a tyrant. Unfortunately, the play fails to sustain anything like the emotional intensity of its opening scene in spite of Treadwell's heroic efforts to do so, especially her jockeying of events in Poe's life. In Act II, Scene 2, for example, she has an inebriated and contentious Poe in the midst of a literary soirée jolted by the news that Virginia has died in his absence. In the following scene, where Poe courts the widowed Elmira Royster Shelton in Richmond, the playwright takes the liberty of having her Poe deliver as speeches to Elmira passages from letters that Poe had, in fact, written to Sarah Helen Whitman.

Hollywood's most ambitious venture at dramatizing the life of Poe was a 1942 film released by Twentieth Century-Fox under the title *The Loves of Edgar Allan Poe*.[18] Based on a screenplay by Samuel Hoffenstein and Tom Reed, it starred John Shepperd as Poe and Linda Darnell as Virginia. Publicity described the film as "the unknown side of America's most famous literary genius, that surpasses his own startling stories of dark emotions and deep passions—[it] is the true drama of [Poe's] life, known only to the women who loved him." Though the studio insisted that there was no need of "doctoring" the facts, the film reduces "the women who loved him" to Elmira Royster ("a beautiful brunette" under the influence of whose "spell" Poe "poured out the deepest passions of his heart") and Virginia Clemm (a "Baltimore belle" whose "interesting little figure" is at one point displayed "in the pantalettes of the period"), and it reduces Poe's literary career to the simple terms of Poe as the champion of international copyright struggling against the exploitative practices of American publishers. In a vain effort to inject some life into this subplot, the film offers an entirely fictitious scene in which Thomas Jefferson counsels Poe to pursue his literary inclinations; it confronts Poe with the dilemma of choosing between editorship of the *Southern Literary Messenger* and editorship of *Graham's Magazine;* it exaggerates the significance of Poe's meeting with Dickens; and it humiliates Poe by having Rufus Griswold turn down "The Raven" for publication in the *Broadway Journal.*

The insurmountable obstacle confronting every attempt at translating the popular image of Poe into conventional drama is that the "man behind the legend," as Edward Wagenknecht has called the historical Poe, is appropriate not to tragedy or to melodrama but to documentary (Wagenknecht, 12–13; Fagin, 3–4).[19] When playwrights such as Hazelton, Cushing, Hoffenstein, and Reed and even Treadwell, playwrights beguiled by the image of the legendary Poe, have attempted to translate that popular image into something stage-worthy, their efforts invariably collide with the unyielding fact that Poe's life simply does not support the legend.

One way to avoid this collision is to write plays about Poe that steer as clearly as possible from the facts of his biography. This is precisely the direction playwrights have assumed in recent decades. They have turned from the facts of Poe's life to his mind, playing out their dramas in what they believe to be the recesses of Poe's own haunted psyche. It is a shift from conventional drama to what might be called "psychodrama" (if we can appropriate that term), and it is nicely illustrated in a work entitled *Poor Eddy.* Written by Elizabeth Dooley and produced in 1953 by the Columbia University Theatre Guild, *Poor Eddy* is what Dooley calls a "ballet-biography."[20] Its format consists of brief "realistic" scenes taken from Poe's life coupled with "arabesques," or renderings of the "otherworld" of Poe's "sleeping and waking dreams." These arabesques are ballet pieces that interpret passages recited from Poe's writings, chiefly passages from his fiction and poetry. Movement from realistic scene to accompanying arabesque is marked by distinctive "threshold" music and by the presence of a scrim behind which the actor-dancer playing Poe passes to indicate that action is moving from outward experience to imaginative or internal states of mind. Because each of its eight realistic scenes is balanced by its arabesque, *Poor Eddy* stands as a transitional work between dramatizations of Poe's life and dramatizations of his psyche, or what is believed to have been his psyche.

Nicholas Argento's opera *The Voyage of Edgar Allan Poe,* produced first in Minneapolis in 1976 and then in Baltimore the following year, goes a good deal further in shifting the balance from life to psyche.[21] Argento and his librettist, Charles Nolte, rest their version of Poe upon only one episode: his departure by boat from Richmond on his journey to Baltimore at the close of his life. In Argento's hands, this voyage becomes a recapitulatory vehicle, a complex metaphor blending Poe's life as the desperate and futile quest of a Romantic idealist with his works, principally "Annabel Lee," "Eldorado," *Pym,* and "MS. Found in a Bottle." The opera represents a hallucinatory experience in which the disturbed psyche of the dying poet is haunted by painful episodes in his past; or, as a voice informs him in the first scene of the opening act: he is "on a voyage of Discovery. A heart that hates annihilation like the tomb must gather the past into hallucination." Hovering somewhere between the simple maudlin and the traditional Byronesque, Argento's version of Poe's suffering psyche casts his wife Virginia as the Eurydice-like victim of his unquenchable and ungovernable curiosity about death and portrays his beloved mother, Elizabeth, as a "slut" and a "whore" who consorts with the merged figures of John Allan and Rufus Griswold.

The current trend in dramatizations of Poe is the "solo performance" staged by a costumed actor made up to resemble Poe. Performances of this nature are especially popular on college and university campuses and at special Poe events. Prominent among solo performers are Jerry Rockwood *(A Condition of Shadow),* Sumner Kernan *(Of Worms, Of Tombs, Of Epitaphs),* Robert Minford *(Journey to Eldorado),* Norman George *(Poe Alone),* Robert Rhode *(A Dream within a Dream),* Conrad Pomerleau *(Poe in Person),* Mel Harold *(In Search of Poe),* and Paul Clemens *(Once Upon a Midnight).* Although they vary considerably, from Pomerleau's dramatic readings of Poe's works and Rockwood's reprisal of Poe as a lecturer to Rhode's hallucinatory psychodrama in the vein of Argento's opera, all solo performances share with every other effort to dramatize Poe's life and character the assumption that his fiction and his poetry somehow constitute a window to his mind and spirit. It is an attractive and compelling assumption because it is congenial to the popular conviction that Poe's mind was a haunted palace, that he had lost a Lenore and an Annabel Lee and could find solace only in drink and drug. Although it does little to promote our understanding of the real Poe or our appreciation of his ability as an artist to distance himself from his creations, it is to this assumption that the popular image is principally indebted for its vitality and durability.

POE'S WORKS IN THE MEDIA

In light of the universally lamented decline in American reading habits, it is safe to assume that the continued widespread familiarity with Poe's work is the result not so much of firsthand knowledge of the texts of his fiction and poetry as it is with adaptations, imitations, and borrowings of one kind or another for the screen, stage, radio, and lately television, as well as voice recordings.

Poe's work has had an immense presence in films, not so much in the form of adaptations, for which feature-length films are not well suited, but in films that imitate Poe's style and tone and borrow features prominent in his fiction and poetry, especially such familiar and sensational features as scythelike pendulums, decaying mansions, the beating sounds of the human heart, ravens, black cats, and the like. Poe's presence has made itself felt from almost the outset of commercial filmmaking. *Sherlock Holmes and the Great Murder Mystery* (Crescent Film Company of New York, 1908) not only was one of the earliest but anticipated the kind of freewheeling treatment Poe's work was to receive in films over the years. Here Sherlock Holmes is substituted for C. Auguste Dupin, and Poe's orangutan becomes a gorilla in a liberal rendering of "The Murders in the Rue Morgue." Prompted, no doubt, by the lively interest in Poe accompanying the centennial of his birth, 1909 and 1910 saw films based upon "The Gold-Bug," "The Raven," "The System of Doctor Tarr and Professor Fether," "The Cask of Amontillado," "Hop-Frog," and "The Pit and the Pendulum." Among them were the first of several Poe-influenced productions directed by D. W. Griffith and made by Edison's American Mutoscope and Biograph Company. A number of films "inspired" by both poems and tales of Poe were produced throughout the era of silent films and into the age of "talkies," color, and the wide screen. According to Burton Pollin's recent "Filmography" (323–61), the poems most popular with filmmakers are "The Raven" (seventeen films) and "Annabel Lee" (ten); and the top ten among Poe's tales are "The Tell-Tale Heart" (forty-four), "The Black Cat" (twenty-two), "The Fall of the House of Usher" (twenty-one), "The Pit and the Pendulum" (eighteen), "The Mask of the Red Death" (fifteen), "The Cask of Amontillado" (fourteen), "The Murders in the Rue Morgue" (twelve), "The System of Doctor Tarr and Professor Fether" (ten), "The Premature Burial" (eight), and "William Wilson" (eight). Most have been undistinguished productions, but a few are well worth noting. Chief among them are horror films starring three masters of the genre: Lon Chaney, Sr. (*The Phantom of the Opera,* 1925), Bela Lugosi (*Murders in the Rue Morgue,* 1932), Lugosi and Boris Karloff (*The House of Doom,* 1934, and *The Raven,* 1935), and Karloff (*The Isle of the Dead,* 1945). Also worth noting is the block of thirteen Poe-related films produced by American International Pictures (AIP) in the 1960s and 1970s. Roger Corman directed eight of the thirteen, and Vincent Price starred in all but two. Price was joined along the way by Boris Karloff, Basil Rathbone, Peter Lorre, Lon Chaney, Jr., Tab Hunter, Debra Paget, and Jack Nicholson. Although "financially successful" exploitations of Poe's popularity, these AIP films were "hardly Poe" (Haydock, 138). Not unexpectedly, there is little agreement among students of film and film history about which of all the Poe-related films are the most successful as renderings of Poe's originals. Candidates include Bela Lugosi's *Murders in the Rue Morgue* (1932); Lugosi's and Boris Karloff's *The House of Doom* (1934), based upon "The Black Cat"; *The Fall of the House of Usher* (variously 1947–1952), directed by Ivan Barnett and starring Kay Tendeter, Irving Steen, and Lucy Parey; and *The Tell-Tale Heart* (variously 1960 and 1963), directed by Ernest Morris, with Laurence Payne as the murderer.

There have been attempts at adapting Poe's work for stage, radio, and television. One attempt at stage production was "a virtuoso theatrical performance" of "The Tell-Tale Heart" by Stanley Baker in 1953. Another was a production of "The Fall of the House of Usher" by the London Theatre Group in 1975. Recently (1988), the American Repertory Theatre at Harvard University produced an opera "based upon" "The Fall of the House of Usher." Owing in part to their brevity, however, Poe's tales have found themselves more appropriate to radio and, lately, to television programming than to full-length stage productions. Boris Karloff (1941) and Peter Lorre (1947) assumed the voice of Poe's deranged narrator in radio versions of "The Tell-Tale Heart," and Henry Hull (1943), Jose Ferrer (1947), and Vincent Price (1957) played the role of victim in "The Pit and the Pendulum." There have been radio adaptations of "The Fall of the House of Usher," "The Gold-Bug," and "Metzengerstein," among other tales, and, in 1947, the CBS "Mystery Theatre Show" devoted an entire week to productions of Poe tales. Lately, television has taken its turn. Among the earliest efforts at adapting Poe for television was a 1950 version of "The Tell-Tale Heart" entitled "The Heartbeat." Directed by William Cameron Menzies and starring Richard Hart, it used pantomime to depict the murder. Four years later, Tom Ewell played an office worker haunted by a double in an "Alfred Hitchcock Presents" episode obviously inspired by "William Wilson." More recently, there have been television dramatizations of "The Black Cat," "The Facts in the Case of M. Valdemar," "Murders in the Rue Morgue," and "Hop-Frog" and even a reading of "The Sphinx" by Vincent Price.

As recently as October 1994, the Arts and Entertainment (A&E) Television Network aired a made-for-television program entitled "The Mystery of Edgar Allan Poe." Produced for A&E by Greystone Communications, the program features Peter Graves as narrator, Norman George in the role of Poe reciting from his fiction, poetry, and correspondence, and a number of commentators, including J. Gerald Kennedy, John T. Irwin, Richard Kopley, Jeff Jerome, James Furqueron, Arno Karlen, and Paul Clemens. In light of the constraints of less than an hour, the program is, by and large, a well-balanced survey of Poe's life and career, a survey replete with portraits and photographs of Poe and of persons who figured prominently in his life, with drawings and photographs of places associated with him, and with some of the classic illustrations of his fiction and poetry. As its title suggests, "The Mystery of Edgar Allan Poe" leans toward the romantic image of Poe as a man "both blessed and cursed by his genius," a man for whom "there is almost no catastrophe that didn't touch his life at some point." Given its perspective that "the themes of [Poe's] stories are firmly rooted in the grim realities of his life," the program inevitably attempts to substantiate its romantic image of the man by reading his life from his works.

Voice recordings of Poe's poems and tales abound. Although some are dramatic adaptations of Poe's fiction (e.g., "Metzengerstein," "The Gold-Bug," "Murders in the Rue Morgue," and "The Purloined Letter"), the most popular and successful recordings have been readings of Poe's poems and first-person narratives, especially "The Tell-Tale Heart," "The Black Cat," and "The Pit and the Pendulum." Because these tales are, in effect, dramatic monologues and thereby avoid the problems and compromises inherent in any effort at converting narrative into drama for stage, screen, radio, and television production, voice recordings of first-person narratives have been far more in the nature of interpretations than of adaptations of Poe's work. Martin Donegan leads everyone else in the number of recordings, and among prominent actors who also have turned their talents to reading Poe are Douglas Fairbanks, Jr., James Mason, Basil Rathbone, Vincent Price, Alexander Scourby, Paul Scofield, and James Stewart.[22]

MISCELLANEOUS

Long ignored as subliterary, comic books are increasingly acknowledged to be one of the best mirrors of popular culture. There is much about Poe's work that makes it especially attractive to the publishers of comics: the recognition factor of his stories and poems is very high; their brevity minimizes the need for abridgement; horror and sensationalism abound; and the visual element is intense, for example, appalling pits, abysses, maelstroms, whirlpools, menacing pendulums, beating disembodied hearts, monstrous cats, ominous ravens, and so forth. Virgil Finlay illustrated "The Cask of Amontillado" for *Fantastic* comics back in 1956. In 1964, *Atomic* published a version of "The Gold-Bug" entitled "The Gold Hunters of '49," in which Poe himself solves the mystery. *Psycho* offered its version of "The Facts in the Case of M. Valdemar" in 1974. That same year, two of Poe's poems, "The Conqueror Worm" and "The Haunted Palace," furnished the basis for an illustrated tale in *Scream*. The following year, *Creepy* magazine published its adaptation of "The Premature Burial." *Mad Magazine* has had a go at Poe several times. Other versions of Poe have appeared in *Nightmare, Eerie,* and a series of Dell Publications comics based on the Roger Corman–Vincent Price 1960s film "adaptations." Recently (1990), Classics Illustrated published two "artistic interpretations" of Poe. One is *The Fall of the House of Usher* adapted and illustrated by P. Craig Russell and Jay Geldhof. The other, *The Raven and Other Poems,* illustrated by the well-known cartoonist Gahan Wilson, reprints nine poems, only five of which are, in fact, from among the thirty in Poe's original *The Raven and Other Poems* published in 1845. Curiously, this comic book does print ''Lines on Ale,'' an eight-line stanza never authenticated as the work of Poe. It is worth noting that Gahan Wilson's illustrations follow the widely practiced convention of peopling Poe's work with protagonists who represent Poe himself. This is yet another throwback to the very origins of the popular image of Poe sown by Poe and unwittingly promoted by people like Rufus Griswold, who suggested back in 1849 that Poe's darkest works are ''a reflection and an echo of his own history.''

Poetry, fiction, theater, film, radio, television, comics, and the like are only the traditional repositories of Poe in popular culture. Others abound. There have been cartoons of Poe, some having appeared during his own lifetime. There are Poe and Poe-related posters, T-shirts, taverns and restaurants, toys, stamps, and advertising slogans and campaigns, all testifying to the persistence and pervasiveness of Poe the man, the legend, the image, his poetry, and his fiction, in popular culture.

NOTES

1. Nichols's report of Poe's attitude toward fame is cited by Michael Allen (183–84) in his consideration of Poe's complex attitude toward his audience.

2. Entitled ''The Fate of Genius'' and printed anonymously, the poem was introduced in the *Home Journal* by a note on the plight of Poe. Locke retitled the poem as ''An Invocation for Suffering Genius'' for publication in her *The Recalled* (Boston, 1854), 93–95.

3. ''Edgar A. Poe,'' *Richmond Enquirer,* January 26, 1850, 4. Preuss enlarged the poem for republication over his own name in the *Shekinah* 2 (1853): 227–28 and in the *Washington Daily National Intelligencer,* May 19, 1853.

4. I do not mean to suggest that the attitude toward Poe in poetry during this period was uniformly favorable. Abel Reid, *Pot-Pourri* (New York, 1875), for example, contains twelve very clever parodies attacking Poe and the outpouring of feeling on his behalf. ''Abel Reid'' is said to have been the pseudonym of William J. Linton.

5. *Christian Century* 61 (January 5, 1944): 20.

6. *Lippincott's Monthly Magazine* 48 (August 1891): 240–46.

7. In Thompson's *The Carnival of Destiny* (New York: Moffit, Yard, 1916), 277–314.

8. In Starrett's *Seaports in the Moon: A Fantasy on Romantic Themes* (Garden City, N.Y.: Doubleday, Doran, 1928), 228–54.

9. In *Ellery Queen's Mystery Magazine* 15 (April 1950): 9–30. This short story was the basis of *The Man with a Cloak,* a screenplay written by Frank Fenton, directed by Fletcher Markle, and produced by Stephen Ames for Metro-Goldwyn Mayer. It was released in 1951, starring Joseph Cotten, Barbara Stanwyck, Louis Calhern, Leslie Caron, and Jim Backus.

10. In *Ellery Queen's Mystery Magazine* 16 (November 1950): 57–64.

11. In August Derleth, comp., *Night's Yawning Peal: A Ghostly Company* (New York: Arkham House, 1952), 99–113.

12. In Bradbury's *The Illustrated Man* (Garden City, N.Y.: Doubleday, 1951), 131–45.

13. In Gregory Benford and Martin H. Greenberg, eds., *What Might Have Been*, 2 vols. (New York: Bantam Books, 1990), 2: 291–354.

14. Poe has put in cameo appearances in several novels, for example, Francis Hopkinson Smith's *Kennedy Square* (1911), Anya Seton's *Dragonwyck* (1944), and Robert R. McCammon's *Usher's Passing* (1984); and he appears as a peripheral character in still others, for example, David Madsen's *Black Plume: The Suppressed Memoirs of Edgar Allan Poe* (1980) and Andrew Sinclair's *The Facts in the Case of E. A. Poe* (1980).

15. Hazelton's script was revised several times as a play and enjoyed two additional lives as a novel, *The Raven: The Love Story of Edgar Allan Poe ('Twixt Fact and Fancy)* (New York, 1909), and as a motion picture entitled *The Raven,* copyrighted in 1915 by Essaway Film Manufacturing Company.

16. I am grateful to the family of the late Miss Cushing for permission to quote from a typescript filed for copyright in 1925.

17. I am grateful to the late Miss Treadwell for permission to cite a prompt book on deposit at the New York Public Library.

18. A mimeograph of the screenplay is on deposit at the Enoch Pratt Free Library. I am grateful to the Twentieth Century–Fox Film Corporation for permission to quote from this copy.

Not to be overlooked is Sylvester Stallone's threat to star in a film biography of Poe, a threat that prompted Frank Gannon's satirical sketch ''Yo, Poe,'' published in Gannon's *Yo, Poe* (New York: Viking, 1987), 51–54.

19. This is not to say that documentaries have not been produced, especially documentaries targeted at educational audiences. A recent example is *Edgar Allan Poe: Architect of Dreams* (1991), a docudrama written, produced, and directed by Jean M. Mudge with Dave Smith as ''host,'' Jana Childers as ''narrator,'' and several actors, principally Norman George, representing Poe and reading from his fiction and poetry. Though it manages to squeeze a good deal of information about Poe and his work into its thirty minutes, this video adheres to what is essentially the popular romantic version of the man (typified by what Mrs. Whitman called ''the Ultima Thule'' daguerreotype in the opening frames) and threads a whirlpool/abyss image throughout to suggest that the man and his work are somehow convertible sources.

A Stop in Baltimore aired by the CBC radio in 1991 is another docudrama that bears noting. ''Written and presented'' by Seth Seldman of York University, it consists of two parts of approximately one hour each. The first part is structured around the last two weeks of Poe's life as a platform from which his career is surveyed, and the second part is set at the dedication of the monument at Poe's grave in 1875, where Poe's own Dupin attempts to solve the mystery of his creator's death. *A Stop in Baltimore* employs several prominent Poe authorities, including Daniel Hoffman, Joan Dayan, and Kenneth Silverman, and Norman George is called upon once again to represent and recite Poe.

Recently released is another docudrama entitled *Edgar Allan Poe: Terror of the Soul,* written by Dan Smith and produced for Film Odyssey by Karen Thomas. Several authorities on Poe and his times contributed commentary.

20. My discussion of *Poor Eddy* is based upon a prompt book on deposit at the New York Public Library. I am grateful to Mrs. Dooley for permission to quote from this text.

21. I am grateful to Boosey and Hawkes, Inc., of New York, for permission to quote from the text of the libretto that has been published in *Commemorating the World Pre-*

miere of "The Voyage of Edgar Allan Poe," ed. David J. Speer et al. (St. Paul: North Central, 1976).

22. For a recent survey of "screen, songs, and spoken word recordings" of Poe's life and works, see R. L. Smith's *Poe in the Media.*

WORKS CITED

Aldrich, Thomas Bailey. *The Ballad of Babie Bell and Other Poems.* New York: Rudd and Carleton, 1859.

Allen, Michael. *Poe and the British Magazine Tradition.* New York: Oxford UP, 1969.

Benét, Laura. *The Young Edgar Allan Poe.* New York: Dodd, Mead, 1941.

Bode, Carl. *The Anatomy of American Popular Culture, 1840–1861.* Berkeley: U of California P, 1959.

Brown, Slater. *The Heyday of Spiritualism.* New York: Hawthorn Books, 1970.

Dean, John. "Poe and the Popular Culture of His Day." *Journal of American Culture* 10 (1987): 35–40.

Doten, Lizzie. *Poems from the Inner Life.* Boston: William White & Co., 1864.

"Edgar Poe in the Spirit World." *Herald of Light* 1 (July 1857): 112–16.

Fagin, N. Bryllion. *The Histrionic Mr. Poe.* Baltimore: Johns Hopkins UP, 1949.

Gifford, Denis. "Pictures of Poe: A Survey of the Silent Film Era 1909–29." *The Edgar Allan Poe Scrapbook.* Ed. Peter Haining. New York: Schocken Books, 1978, 128–32.

Ginsberg, Allen. *Mind Breaths: Poems 1972–1977.* San Francisco: City Lights Books, 1978.

Haining, Peter. "The Poe Industry." *The Edgar Allan Poe Scrapbook.* Ed. Peter Haining. New York: Schocken Books, 1978, 141–44.

Haydock, Ron. "Poe, Corman and Price: A Tale of Terrors." *The Edgar Allan Poe Scrapbook.* Ed. Peter Haining. New York: Schocken Books, 1978a, 133–38.

———. "The Spectres of Edgar Allan Poe." *The Edgar Allan Poe Scrapbook.* Ed. Peter Haining. New York: Schocken Books, 1978b, 139–40.

Inge, Thomas M., ed. *Handbook of American Popular Culture.* 3 vols. New York: Greenwood Press, 1978–1981.

Kerr, Howard. *Mediums and Spirit-Rappers, and Roaring Radicals.* Urbana: U of Illinois P, 1972.

Moore, Barbara. *The Fever Called Living.* Garden City, N.Y.: Doubleday, 1976.

Nichols, Mary Gove. *Reminiscences of Edgar Allan Poe.* 1863. Rpt. in New York: Union Square Book Shop, 1931.

Nichols, Rebecca S. *Songs of the Heart and the Hearth-Stone.* Philadelphia: Thomas, Cowperthwait, 1851.

Pollin, Burton R. "Filmography." *Images of Poe's Works: A Comprehensive Descriptive Catalogue of Illustrations.* Bibliographies and Indexes in American Literature, Number 9. Westport, Conn.: Greenwood Press, 1989, 323–61.

Reilly, John E. "Poe in American Drama: Versions of the Man." *Poe and Our Times: Influences and Affinities.* Ed. Benjamin Franklin Fisher IV. Baltimore: Edgar Allan Poe Society, 1986, 18–31.

————. "Poe in Imaginative Literature: A Study of American Drama, Fiction, and Poetry Devoted to Edgar Allan Poe or His Works." Diss. U of Virginia, 1965.

Rice, Sara Sigourney, ed. *Edgar Allan Poe: A Memorial Volume.* Baltimore; Turnbull, 1877.

Smith, Charles Alphonso. *Edgar Allan Poe—How to Know Him.* Indianapolis: Bobbs-Merrill, 1921.

Smith, Ronald L. *Poe in the Media: Screen, Songs, and Spoken Word Recordings.* New York: Garland, 1990.

Tabb, John Bannister. *The Poetry of Father Tabb.* New York: Dodd, Mead, 1928.

Wagenknecht, Edward. *Edgar Allan Poe: The Man behind the Legend.* New York: Oxford UP, 1964.

23

Poe in Art, Music, Opera, and Dance

BURTON R. POLLIN

POE AND THE GRAPHIC ARTS

Since 1850, the year following Poe's death, his writings have attracted such world-renowned, diverse artists as Manet, Redon, Doré, Gauguin, Ensor, Cropsey, Darley, Beardsley, Whistler, and over 700 others. The many thousands of varied illustrations (easel paintings, portfolios, drawings, and plates in books), traced and recorded over eighteen years, substantiate the claim for Poe's preeminence in inspiration. His seventy tales encompass accounts of horror, the supernatural, adventure, science fiction, psychological terror and alienation, and also humorous situations; of the four dozen short poems, a few have been illustrated with astonishing frequency ("The Raven," "The Bells," "Annabel Lee," "Eldorado," "Lenore," "Dreamland").

The explanation lies possibly in a quality of style that Poe himself termed "graphicality," in alluding to passages in a work by Margaret Fuller. "[They] are unrivalled for *graphicality* . . . , for the force with which they convey the true by the novel or unexpected, by the introduction of touches which other artists would be sure to omit as irrelevant to the subject. . . . [H]er subjectiveness . . . leads her to paint a scene less by its features than by its effects" (*H* 15, 75). Poe's tales and poems have many of these memorable "touches": the hiss of the pendulum, the fainting of Pym on the brink of the precipice, the cushion in "The Raven," the sinister waving of the draperies in "Ligeia."

In reviewing illustrated books, Poe usually evaluated the quality of the cuts or plates. For an illustrated *Vicar of Wakefield,* Poe advised the sleuth-reader to puzzle out the essential narrative with clues provided by both author *and* artist (*H* 11, 8–10). Elsewhere, Poe provided a few standards for judging the merits of illustration, applicable, in turn, to those in Poe's works. A slavish adherence to the details of a scene is condemned by this man, who described the world's first abstract painting in "Usher" (Pi, 24)[1] and said: "An outline frequently stirs the spirit more pleasantly than the most elaborate picture" (*H* 11, 84). Poe approved of certain types of illustrations to accompany the letterpress. About the choice magazine that he planned to own and edit (called the *Penn,* then the *Stylus*), in 1843 he wrote to Lowell: "A part of my design is to illustrate whatever is fairly susceptible of illustration, with finely executed wood-engravings" (*O,* 233). His Prospectus noted: "Engravings, when used, will be in the highest style of Art, . . . only in obvious illustration of the text" (Pi, 219). Clearly, Poe was reacting against the current "namby-pamby" pictures—Poe's term for the sentimental, mawkish, badly drawn steel engravings illustrating tales in magazines or inserted as mere decorations.

Moreover, sometimes Poe as a contributor was required to "translate" or describe a "plate" intended as a frontispiece—a way of "stupefying our literature" (*O,* 64). For the *Columbian Magazine* (December 1844), he devised an essay on the young Byron and Mary Chaworth for an insipid sketch of two children. Other illustrations, some adapted or arranged for by Poe himself for his own works, may be noted: a reworked John Martin plate for "The Isle of the Fay" (Pk); a deer overlooking a broad river, for an elk above a creek in "Morning on the Wissahiccon"; a crude woodcut of a mounted Indian in "The Journal of Julius Rodman"; the falsified picture of a steering balloon in the newspaper hoax-account of a transatlantic crossing; two woodcuts by F.O.C. Darley for "The Gold-Bug"; and an unpublished sketch by Darley for the abortive *Stylus* (Pi, 237).

After Poe's death in 1849, the copyright for his "complete works" was assigned by Poe's aunt to Griswold as editor for the J. S. Redfield Company, and this fact oddly and adversely determined the course of American illustration of Poe's works for thirty-five years. Redfield sanctioned only the reprinting of the illustrated Sampson Low edition of the poems in America (1859, 1861) and of no British volume of the tales, wishing no competition with its own plain, four-volume set of the "works." Only a few gift-book illustrations and small pirated items slipped through the "censorship," until the copyright expired in 1884.

The first British illustrated collection, in 1852, was called *Tales of Mystery, Imagination, and Humour; and Poems,* part of the "Readable Books" series. The two small volumes, often reprinted, have forty-two woodcuts of skillful draftsmanship, every one emphasizing a scene of action or dramatic tension. The poems received the most important early Victorian treatment. Although not published during his lifetime, a half-dozen pen-and-ink wash drawings by Dante Gabriel Rossetti (1846–1848) are the earliest by a major artist. James Hannay suitably dedicated his 1853 *Poetical Works* of Poe to Rossetti. Hannay's volume, often reprinted, employed four ill-assorted illustrators in a Victorian oddity of group work: James Godwin, F. W. Hulme, the landscapist Henry Anelay, and Harrison Weir, famed for his animal pictures. Widespread are angels' wings, swirling phantom or dream forms, storm-tossed seas, clouded moons over water, melodramatic posturings, and medieval costumings. In 1857, a part of *Pym* in Beeton's *Boy's Own Magazine* with two vignette illustrations introduced the reprinting of Poe's oeuvre in cheap or juvenile magazines, often with crude pictures and adapted text.

More respectable, by far, is the Sampson Low edition of *The Poetical Works* in 1858, characteristic of sumptuous Victorian books—gilt edges, embossed and decorated cloth binding, workmanlike printing of text and plates, elaborate arabesque tailpieces, decorations, initial letters, and wide margins. To illustrate every major poem, Low engaged some of the foremost artists, including the American Jasper Cropsey, then in London. John Tenniel's four grotesque *Raven* pictures lead off, with theatrical draperies, gestures, and highlighted central focus. Cropsey contributes a pallid, featureless "Coliseum" plate. The classical porticoes and medieval motifs, the somber glens and bowers, and the posturing figures are typical of the age's bookplates.

The widespread British pictorial editions of Poe's tales and poems continue these tendencies, even in the numerous pictures for Doré's opulent folio *Raven* (1883; New York, 1884). James McNeill Whistler's two charming "portraits" of "Annabel Lee" (1867) deserve mention (Pi, 118). In 1883, William Ladd Taylor, the popular American illustrator, published *The Raven* with five plates in the rotogravure style of the magazines, in a melodramatic sequence of scenes (often reprinted, e.g., 1884 in New York, and in Spanish in 1887). The twenty-two-year-old Aubrey Beardsley was invited in 1894 to execute four pictures for a large-paper, multivolume, limited edition of Poe's works. Marvelously humorous and ingenious, they showed new possibilities for the graphic arts in the handling of black and white masses. The pedestrian Albert Sterner trade-edition illustrations were used in the Lawrence and Bullen London edition of 1896—suggesting the close connection between American and British publishers then and later.

After the 1890s, American firms were free to reprint and illustrate Poe's works; numerous mass-appeal editions employed popular illustrators in London and New York: N. H. Dole's in 1897, McCormick's *Pym* in 1899, and his *Tales* of 1905. A best-seller in one country inevitably appeared in the other, often in crude pirated form, such as the 1881 Philadelphia *Bells* by Darley and others, blurrily reprinted by R. E. King of London. Moreover, photographic processes greatly simplified the reproduction of pictures, permitting color and every type of shading. Thus, in 1898, the tales, subtitled "Mysteria Horrenda," in four volumes, had twelve "Lemerciergravures"; the process was used by Leonard Smithers in 1899 for the Chiswick Press's *The Raven / The Pit and the Pendulum,* illustrated by W. T. Horton, a friend of Beardsley and himself influenced by Blake.

In Poe's *Poems* of 1900, almost 100 woodcuts by the youthful W. Heath Robinson powerfully combine pre-Raphaelite figures and leafy, flowery patterns with art-nouveau swirls in clouds, shorelines, and draperies—without thematic insights. J. J. Guthrie composed seven ambitious but conventional pictures for a limited edition of *Some Poems* in 1901; later, Byam Shaw executed over a dozen gaudily colored, literal sketches for *Selected Tales of Mystery* (1909). Edmund Dulac, noted for his *Arabian Nights,* added exotic color in his twenty-eight plates for *The Bells* (1909 in New York, London, and Munich; 1913 in Paris).

In 1919, the Irish illustrator and stained-glass window designer Harry Clarke (1889–1931) produced a large-folio limited edition of *Tales.* The eight color plates (added to the American 1923 edition) and the twenty-six in rich black and white show cruelty and violence together with an oriental color and arabesque line that have made them well known. Clarke's spirit entered the color plates and line drawings of Arthur Rackham, which suitably start with "The Imp of the Perverse" (1935). Cheap reprints have popularized these last examples of true artistry in British Poe illustration.

The United States has been the most prolific nation for illustrated editions and also the least original and ingenious. In 1870, Widdleton, then copyright holder, apparently agreed to a reprint of the 1869 London Hyslop edition, with numerous conventional plates by Stanton, M'Whirter, Lawson, and Staniland. This, along with reprints of the Sampson Low volume, sufficed for the public until the many editions in the 1880s. The great success of the 1881 *Bells* with Darley, Riordan, King, et al. led to new graphic interpretations. But no works of the period and few commercially sponsored in the twentieth century are worth much attention, for example, in 1885, Hy Sandham's plates for "Lenore," thrice reprinted—sentimental, melodramatic, and obvious. Boston and New York publishers discovered a new source of great profit in multivolume editions of Poe's work; the same text could be printed on special paper, given a new title page, and numbered from 1 to 1,000 to be sold and resold as a limited edition. It is impossible to draw up an accurate list of the "new" editions put out by Estes or Putnam or the lessees of their plates: "Cabinet," "New Cabinet," "Eldorado," "Amontillado."

The 1894–1895 Stone and Kimball text by George Woodberry and Clarence Stedman was far better than Griswold's, but the Albert Sterner plates gave a mediocre lead to illustrators such as F. Gilbert Edge (the ten-volume "Richmond" edition of 1902) or Frederick Coburn (1902) or Arthur Becher (color rotogravures in the Collier set). Publishers imported British plates by F. C. Tilney or R. Swain Gifford. J. A. Harrison, for his seventeen-volume "definitive" edition (1902), unwisely used some of these prints and more from the 1884 Quantin edition of Paris.

A few early twentieth-century American books deserve mention. In 1903, Gates and Randall daringly dressed their "Usher" characters in modern dress. L. Blumenschein in seven tasteful color plates for seven tales gave a startling sense of Edvard Munch, probably through a common art-nouveau design and a brooding atmosphere. Woodberry's life of Poe (1909) used five imported Alberto Martini plates. Reprints of Dulac's decorative *Bells* in 1912, 1919, and 1921 disseminated his dull conventional approach. In 1930, W. A. Dwiggins's

Tales bore thirty-two decent full-page cuts and a good note on the difficulty of graphically transcending Poe's elaborate, detailed language. The same year produced the fine *Raven* of F. H. Horvath, with cubistic original designs in the John Vassos style. Also, René Clarke produced his beautifully organized, finely made black and white *Pym*, highlighting his theory of the white-black thematic opposition in the novel. The 1931 Cheshire House *Usher* contained Abner Epstein's five beautiful (and cruel) woodcuts, highly original in ideas and approach. In 1936, Paul McPharlin's *Raven* presented six colored cut-out designs, with an ingenious tinge of Matisse's late work.

In 1941, for the *Tales,* William Sharp did seventeen pictures of technical skill but vulgar and obvious conception. More successful were Hugo Steiner-Prag's lithographs for the 1943 *Poems.* Fritz Eichenberg's two dozen neat, well-organized wood engravings for the *Tales* are all rather horrifying and morbid but sometimes distinctive. However, in Knopf's 1946 two-volume *Works* are E. McKnight Kauffer's eight line drawings and twelve color plates, which are utterly disastrous, in a pointless and tasteless de Chirico style.

The 1959 Antonio Frasconi's *Face of . . . Poe* portfolio had a suite of four *Raven* woodcuts. In 1964, there appeared a charming small volume of *Tales* with twenty-four vignettes copied from the 1819–1820 *Rees's Cyclopaedia,* following Poe's own practice in his *Balloon-Hoax* (Pi 238). The Spanish-American color lithographer Federico Castellon (1915–1971), known first for his surrealism, issued a fine *Masque* with sixteen cuts in 1969. In 1976, Wilfried Sätty issued the *Illustrated . . . Poe* with eighty large pictures tastelessly imitating Max Ernst's photo-collages. Finally, Alan J. Robinson published his 1980 *Raven* with etchings and woodcuts, well presented in format, with more of ornithology than original interpretation (augmented, 1984 and 1986), and a *Black Cat* with eleven woodcuts (1984), similarly literalistic.

Without a doubt, France has been outstanding in the development of Poe illustrations, largely due to Baudelaire's devoting years to translating Poe sensitively and quite accurately into French. The resultant five volumes (1856–1865) soon became classics of French culture. Baudelaire, justly renowned for his trenchant art criticism and himself the hub of the Paris literati and artists, was to see the works of Poe illustrated. He prodded etcher Charles Méryon into doing one sketch, unpublished and unfound. Neither did the many 1861 illustrations of Alphonse Legros, whom Baudelaire encouraged and paired with Manet, achieve contemporary publication (Pi 25, 65). But Manet's 1875 *Raven* and the Quantin 1884 edition are, in part, products of Baudelaire's zeal. Also influential was the superb quality of the French graphic arts being applied to the newly developed édition de luxe. Important, too, is the adaptability of Poe's poems and tales to any size and type of unit desired by publisher or public.

In 1875, Manet's magnificent "Raven" lithographs reflected an interest in Japanese prints through the "bold simplifications, diagonal compositions, and opposition of tones" (Pi, 67). Almost all subsequent ravens in Poe images are descended from Manet's. In 1882, Odilon Redon did a most influential portfolio of lithographs freely based on Poe's themes, with a far-flung artistic progeny. No future illustrator surpassed his original and imaginative achievement (Pi, 67–68). Perhaps the Belgian René Magritte paralleled it by creating strange, discrete amalgams of hints from Poe: an orange door, a bird form with wings of Alpine rock, a volume labeled *Pym* on the mantel of a bourgeois home (Pi, 47–51). The year 1884 produced the disappointing Quantin double volume of "tales" with many commonplace plates by Hermann Vogel (wrongly printed as Wögel), deservedly obscure; the edition was slightly redeemed through the powerful "Rue Morgue" image of Daniel Vierge, Méaulle's "Silence," and Férat's "Pit and Pendulum," all taken from the 1874 *Musée Universel*.

In 1897, Louis Legrand's fine sketches for the "tales" initiated the flood of French illustrated limited editions, combining artists' interpretive intentions and publishers' awareness of potential profits. Legrand had caught some of the spirit of Belgium's early surrealistic book illustrator, Félicien Rops, obsessed by plague and death. Original, too, is Martin van Maële's volume of "ten tales" with ninety-five imaginative woodcuts, showing the effect of Redon's work. Bernard Naudin's twenty-two engravings for "tales" are somewhat less morbid, more pedestrian in their realism (1916). Daragnès's *Raven* of 1918 borrows motifs from Manet. The two dozen vignettes by Combet-Descombes for *Usher* (1919) betray the style of Ensor. Marc Roux devoted his watercolor skills to woodcuts for the *Maelström* (1920), and his *Raven* vignettes use strikingly simplified geometric forms. A pair of limited editions, *MS. Found in a Bottle* and *Pym,* illustrated by Pierre Falké, reveal his early travels to the Indies in his bright colors and peasant-style characters. The woodcuts of Daniel Wapler for *Usher* of 1922 use simplified, rather naive Fauviste forms. The almost three dozen large vignetted woodcuts by Fernand Siméon (1924) for "tales" are vigorous narrative conceptions tinged with German expressionism. In the "twenty tales" (1927) of Alméry Lobel-Riche are forty-eight superlative etchings, which have permeated the world of Poe illustration (e.g., the chronos-centered "Masque" picture and the symbolic figure of the "Man of the Crowd" looming over the city).

In 1927–1928 appeared the double-volume masterpiece, still almost unknown, by the obscure artist Carlo Farneti. The pages with 148 etchings "à la manière noire" are truly luxurious, with abstract, surrealist forms and animated landscapes determining the odd and symbolic shapes of the letterpress as well. The year 1927 also produced a splendidly ailurophiliac *Black Cat,* with woodcuts by Gyula Zilzer, in Middle European style. Less effective is the merely decorative "Usher" of "Alastair." A stylized, highly mannered treatment of Poe's texts by Alexandre Alexeïeff in *Monos and Una* and *Usher* (1929) has the touch of genius and of the stage designs of his first profession.

André Collot's *Pym* (1930) has twenty-five imaginative color etchings. The 1944 edition of *Pym* illustrated by Mario Prassinos is a work of revelation, with nine black and white drawings that finely render the varied textures of clothes, wood, and feathers and create striking compositional shapes. Another genius,

Edouard Goerg, Australian-French, produced *The Angel of the Odd* (1947), its etchings providing a wonderful sense of the dreamlike, the cloudy-whimsical, and the supernatural.

In 1966, there was an ambitious two-volume "tales" (1966) with many charcoal sketches by Van Hamme of varied conception, perhaps chiefly drawn from Redon and Goerg. In the same year, there was Léonor Fini's much-heralded six-volume set of "imaginative and poetic works," showing a succession of blank and leering women's faces devoid of charm, variety, and grace. However, Julio Pomar's splendid acrylic paintings for the large-scale *Livre des Quatre Corbeaux* (1985) show, perhaps, that France may yet retain her supremacy in Poe illustration.

Belgium, the small northern neighbor of France, has long been prominent for outstanding Poe images. Baudelaire's residence in Brussels, 1864–1865, may have been reflected in the masks and grotesques of James Ensor of 1880–1898 (five tales) and of Jan Toorop, the Dutch-Javanese artist who exhibited in Brussels in 1884 (see *The Three Brides,* Pi, 189). But these were not primarily book illustrators, as was Henri Evenepoel, whose brilliant 1893 sketches appeared only in 1944 ("four tales"). From 1956 to 1959, Lars Bo contributed to three Poe volumes thirty pictures with curious perspectives and highlighted symbolic details. (See earlier under Redon for Magritte's renowned creations, 1949 to 1962.) Finally, Anne Velghe executed an elaborate and costly *Hop-Frog* portfolio of lithographs (1986), to continue the Belgian succession.

Czechoslovakian illustrations of Poe reveal a strong, indigenous folk culture along with great sophistication. In 1929, for *Pym* and a few tales, F. Muzika's fourteen pictures of spare shapes and forms had an art-nouveau, Matisse-like line. In 1946, Josef Váchal's woodcuts for fifteen tales (without text) used one color on basic black in an expressionistic style. In 1959, Karel Soucek's over 100 plates for "poems and tales" constituted a major work, although with somewhat garish color and repetitious design. In a 1959 "tales," Ján Lebis employed a cubist style.

The illustrations in Danish Poe volumes are by two leading artists. Baron Arild Rosenkrantz, with a French and British training, issued two volumes of "weird tales" (1907–1908) with thirty-five macabre, cruel, and highly artistic black and white prints. Much later came four volumes by Povl Christensen: *Usher* (1953), *Black Cat* (1953), *Oblong Box* (1956), and *Pym* (1958). The full-page illustrations have pleasing patterns of light and dark and a blunt, folk quality. In 1969, Peter Bley drew eight humorously crude plates for Hans Pfaall's journey.

In Germany, the prolific Alfred Kubin was to become the first internationally known Poe illustrator. From the start in 1908, his "black humor" approach was individual: expressionistic, distorted, gross, somber, and morose. Bosch and Breughel, newspaper satirists, Goya, Ensor, Redon—all enter into his style, displayed in over 100 illustrations for eight groups of tales: *Valdemar* (1908), *Tell-Tale Heart* (1909), *Metzengerstein* (1910), *Gold-Bug* (1910), *Pym* (1910), *King*

Pest (1911), *Ligeia* (1920), *Hans Pfaall* (1920). In 1951, Ludwig Nawrotzky issued his own naive, simple line drawings for *Gold-Bug,* and, in 1956, a collection called *From the Depths of the Soul* showed eight imaginative plates by Vladimir Kirin (first published in 1955 in Switzerland). Deserving mention are various books of "fantastic tales" (1959–1966) illustrated by Hans Fronius, whose harsh black lines comprise the distorted, expressionistic, but surprisingly literal scenes. Also noteworthy is *Marie Rogêt* along with other tales, a handsome East Berlin book with somewhat surrealistic lurid color prints by Dieter Müller, stressing obsessive eyes and montage effects. Photomontage is used for the clever, influential "Tales" of Gottfried Helnwein (1979). On the other hand, poetic and highly decorative colors and designs grace the *Poesiealbum* of Albert Schinderhütte (1982). A German *Berenice* portfolio from Vienna (1978) has ten striking and ingenious surrealist etchings by Karl Korab. A *Pym* volume has forty-four color plates and woodcuts by Jürgen Wölbing, which engross and horrify the viewer (1980). The German interpretations now vie with the French for originality and variety.

In Italy have appeared many illustrations for Poe editions, but few of great technical merit or bookmaking artistry. Earliest was a "wonderful tales" (Milan, 1876), borrowing the fine work of Férat, Méaulle, and Daniel Vierge from the 1874 *Musée Universel.* Gaetano Previati prepared "extraordinary tales." A friend of Boccioni, he was known even in England for his Poe illustrations and his modernist influence. From 1905 to 1909, Alberto Martini ardently produced 132 ink sketches for Poe's tales, none then published. While steeped in the surrealism of Redon, art-nouveau lines, and Aubrey Beardsley black and white counterpoints, he had an original sense of fantasy. Thirty-two were reproduced in 1974 in Milan. But, finally, a complete annotated gathering has been edited by Lorandi (Milan, 1984).

A few intermediary volumes deserve mention. In 1921, Decio Cinti made imaginative lithographs for fourteen of the "extraordinary tales," and, in 1929, Luigi Servolini stressed Poe's humor in many woodcut vignettes for the "extravaganzas." In 1957, Berardino's six plates interpreted *Pym* with skill. In his "seven tales in English," Giorgio Milesi, in the Redon tradition, offers eight decorative, Picassoesque etchings with thematic titles for the mood, not the action, of the tales. In 1970, a "youth-classic" edition of *Gold-Bug* plus five more tales (Mondadori) presents the altogether captivating plates, several in color, of Ugo Fontana. The 1984 catalog raisonné of Alberto Martini's Poe works really terminates the outstanding Italian illustrated works.

In Japan, there have been published over sixty volumes since the first, 1907 illustrated Poe book, most without originality. Prints from Western books, such as Harry Clarke's, are often copied, and, until recently, most editions were for children or for readers of the detective or sensational works. In 1947, nine "tales" had delicate, fine line drawings by Susumu Nakao. In two collections (1963, 1964), Fuyuki Yamanaka ingeniously used juxtaposed paper and solid objects, all photographed in striking montages. Donge Kobayashi, in 1972, produced a sumptuous suite of ten etchings, eight with questionably seductive women. In 1977, another limited edition appeared with masterful illustrations by Yukio Fukazawa.

A few of the illustrations from the Netherlands justify mention. Alexeïeff's 1930 *Usher* (in English) curiously duplicates the 1929 French edition. The sixteen plates in "fantastic tales" by A. Hahn owe much to Harry Clarke's grim, intricate works. An English text of the *Masque* and other tales of J. Buckland Wright has ten tightly controlled, formalist woodcuts. In 1941, Jeanne Bieruma Oosting issued the first set of her arabesque-style woodcuts. Louis Favre prepared for *The Raven* (with other poems) about ten modernistic color lithographs (1951), handsome but dull. A curious "limited edition" called *The Triangle* (with no text) offers four expressionistic and surrealistic pictures by Harry Van Kruininger (1977).

In the Polish "tales" of 1912, we find six attractive art-nouveau, black and white illustrations by Witold Gordon. Alois Bilek contributes four lithographs to a limited edition of *Shadow* (Pilsen, 1926), highly stylized, with traces of Picasso's statuesque females. The rest are works for juveniles.

Of six Romanian volumes, the only one of interest is the *Scrieri Alese* of 1969 with D. Petrescu's eight photographs of sculptural objects placed against anatomically detailed figures on weird backdrops.

In Russia, Balmont early issued five volumes of translations (1901–1912), but the illustrations for Poe editions, now often numbering over 100,000, have been undistinguished. The "three tales" and *The Raven* (1923) have ten curiously woody, old-style Slavonic prints by A. Silin. A *Maelström* of 1937 in Latvian uses the style of Soviet "labor-realism." However, more sophisticated, modern interpretations infuse the drawings of Utenkov (1974), Nosikov (1977), and Kuskov (1979).

Spain published translations of Poe's works soon after Baudelaire's, their basis. Since the first thirty conventional but skillful prints for tales by Fernan Xumetra Ragull (1887), there have been more than seventy-five volumes with some illustration and over thirty picture-magazine adaptations (Pl). In 1923, the Valencian artist José Segrelles produced eight attractive color rotogravures for "tales" for children, often reprinted. In 1970, publisher Nauta, in two volumes of tales, used eighty-eight drawings by Ramón Calsina Baro—all in a peculiarly blunted, crude, and obvious style. The *Berenice* of Angel Bellido (1976), Spain's first limited edition, had eleven sensitive line etchings, resulting in an expensive and treasurable book. Even better is the 1983 *Island of the Fay,* a portfolio with twelve color etchings by Oscar Estruga that are varied, provocative, ingenious, and magnificently printed. Best of all is Norman Norotzky's *Raven* (Barcelona, 1993), nine brilliant color etchings, of keen and striking insights, sumptuously printed in a large unbound book (twenty-five copies)—the most provocative and original version since Manet's.

In Sweden, from 1881 on, the themes of horror and crime dominate the illustrated Poe volumes. Five 1935 wash drawings of Bertil Lybeck (later much augmented in reprints) are interesting, especially in the rainbow-covered "Maelström." In 1965, T. Sandberg sketches two dozen entrancing, weird scenes and personalities. Perhaps the dominance of Bertil Hedlund's work has discouraged the growth of more stimulating editions.

Various works of Poe appeared, translated into the three national tongues of Switzerland, starting in 1925, most being parallels of issues in Germany and France. A 1951 *Pym* has Gunter Böhmer's firm, clear outlines, with muscular portraitures and stances, in twenty-seven illustrations. A 1955 "tales" displays six of Vladimir Kirin's stark, powerful prints. In 1970, J.-P. Meuer offers six sharp, whimsical, surrealistic Daliesque sketches of "tales." Finally, from Albert E. Yersin, in 1974, came a costly limited edition of five color etchings for "Arnheim" and "Landor's Cottage" with delicate biological, botanic, and topographical forms.

Yugoslavia's only item of interest is *Pym* in Macedonian from Skopje (1967) with pictures in Greek-Orthodox iconic style in the faces, fingers, and proportions.

This survey enables us to note the variety of the standards that determine "interest" for all viewers of Poe illustrations: the charms of children's literature, the popular appeals in fantasy and picture magazines, the tracing of common visual source themes, and pride in national language groups or in "schools" of illustration. Surely the scope and vitality of Poe's continuing stimulus to the graphic arts will add greatly to this diverse and widely appealing repertory.

POE SET TO MUSIC

In considering the worldwide importance of Poe's works in inspiring numerous and varied musical compositions, we must note his provocative and eloquent stress on the common basis and interconnection of poetry and music, expressed in his many book reviews, his four major essays on poetry, and many short reflections.[2] For example, in his March 1842 review of Longfellow's *Ballads,* he declares: "[In] Music . . . , one of the moods of poetical development, . . . the soul most nearly attains . . . the creation of supernal beauty. . . . The highest possible development of the Poetical Sentiment is to be found in the union of song with music" (*H* 11, 74–75). In the opening installment of the seventeen sections of the "Marginalia," he adds an important element, that music affords "a suggestive and indefinite glimpse" to those longed-for "supernal ecstasies" (*P* 2, 119). In the next "Marginalia" installment, he elaborates on the desirable "suggestive indefiniteness" or "indeterminate tone" of true poetry and "true music," which should have no traffic with vocal warblings imitating birds or "bombs bursting" through orchestral kettledrums (*P* 2, 153–54). But this is no sanction for absolute freedom of form or structure, since "preconceived" and "pre-established design," intended for the goal of unified effect, is still basic to every work of art, in every genre (*H* 10, 120; 11, 108). Poe's culminating statement is in the 1846 "Philosophy of Composition," which deprecates "fine frenzy,'' ''accident,'' or ''ecstatic intuition'' in favor of ''precision and rigid'' construction for an intended effect (*H* 14, 194–95). Such passages and documents became a collective manifesto for late nineteenth-century writers, particularly of France, and for their musical associates, the composers, led by Claude Debussy.

While the aesthetic theories of the Impressionists and the Symbolists had assimilated or absorbed Poe's major tenets, the effect upon contemporary musical compositions might have been slight had not Poe himself consistently applied them to the texts of his seventy tales and fifty poems. Naturally, we should expect this corpus of creative works to be utilized for settings in the two English-speaking nations, where even the numerous straitlaced critics of Poe's intemperate and misdirected life had to grant the salient merits of his imaginative tales and his individual poetic style. Grudgingly, they admired the artfully managed elements of tone, the varied melodic and rhythmic effects, the sensitive and ingenious internal and end rhymes, the extensive use of the repetend, and the balladlike narrative themes. Yet, certain of the virtues of the lyrics for songs could be viewed as faults or weaknesses in the texts of poems when devoid of a musical frame. Since the late 1890s, critical opinions on Poe's poetic techniques have shown wide variations, from adverse to rapturously admiring— proof, perhaps, of their suitability for some types of musical settings, for example, simple, balladlike songs. In 1895, Clarence Stedman, fine editor of Poe's works and himself a poet, keenly analyzed the musicality of his poetry (10: xiii– xxxv). In 1949, after a half-century lull in popular enthusiasm for Poe's works, N. B. Fagin's brilliant analysis tried to vindicate Poe's poetical techniques as magical and effective for recitation (135–58). Charmian S. Lenhart's 1956 book on American poetry and music vigorously upheld Poe's ''musical'' artistry, as did Helen Ensley in her defense against charges of monotonous, uninventive, repetitious, identic, slant, and weak rhymes.[3] The most balanced judgment still remains that of Gay Wilson Allen in 1935 (Chap. 3). Curiously, however, both the strengths and the weaknesses of Poe's poetic approaches have attracted a large and varied group of song composers to his ''paroles,'' according to their style of writing and their aims. Indeed, Poe occasionally underscored this accessibility for twenty-two of his texts by attaching to them, in some printings, explanatory subtitles such as ''A song'' or ''A ballad'' or by calling them ''hymn'' or ''dirge'' or ''paean''—hence, the popularity of lyrics such as ''Annabel Lee,'' ''Lenore,'' ''The Bells,'' ''Hymn,'' ''To One in Paradise,'' and ''The Haunted Palace.''

In addition, Poe has provided composers with many humorous, dramatic, gripping, dreamy, and narratively simple plots for short operas, for programmatic tone poems, sometimes divided into sections or movements, and for dances of every type, ranging from formal ballets to avant-garde experimental productions (see third part). The unified moods or tones range from humor and light satire (''The Devil in the Belfry'') to the grotesque (''Valdemar'') or the morbid (''Usher'' or ''Masque''). The result has been probably a greater variety of musical forms for the works of Poe than for those of other American writers. Comparative figures for such compositions have been compiled only in recent decades. My own amassing of such data for Poe-music during a thirty-two-year period (last listed in 1994, in Pa, Pb, Pc, Pcc) leads to a figure of approximately 940 musical interpretations of Poe texts.[4] While this total does not compare impressively with the 1,223 settings of the ideally moralistic Longfellow (Hovland) and the 1,309 settings of Shelley's works (Pg), one must remember the latter's priority and the far greater quantity of his poems. Poe also suffered greatly in reputation from the damaging ''Memoir'' by Rufus W. Griswold, prefixed to Poe's works in 1850. Yet, Poe's overall total compares favorably with that for Robert Browning's (521 in 1971) and for Walt Whitman's 500 in 1963 (see Pg, xii), although many new settings for the latter are appearing (535 in Hovland). It is interesting that thirty-eight composers, several of eminence, have set both Shelley and Poe, an indication of basic similarities in their works, as Poe's numerous encomia of Shelley would suggest.[5]

The issuance in the 1850s of Poe's poems in England in well-edited, illustrated volumes, one sumptuously adorned by eight renowned American and British artists,[6] must have introduced them to composers and their potential performers and auditors. It suited both the material and the musical fashion of the period that the great majority of settings should be for solo voice with piano. These sheet-music pieces were often dedicated to a noble lady or bore a cover testimonial; for example, Sydenham's 1869 ''Eldorado'' was ''sung by Vernon Rigby,'' and Henry Leslie's ''Annabel Lee'' was ''sung by Mr. Sims Reeves.'' Frequently a song could gain wide currency by inclusion in a music magazine (Samuel Beman's 1850 ''Raven'' in *The Nightingale*) or in a collection suitable for family performance (F. Fitzwilliam's pre-1857 ''The Bells'' in his *Four Dramatic Songs*). Later in the nineteenth century, in both countries, more elaborate forms were composed, in part, for greater profit to publisher and composer and also as proof of Poe's growing stimulus: George Fox's ''The Bells,'' a cantata of 1876; Frederick Lacy's ''Annabel Lee'' of 1887 for soloist, chorus, and orchestra; and ''The Bells,'' a cantata of 1888 by D. Ezechiels in New York.

By the 1890s, the compositions showed greater variety and ingenuity, reflecting changes in public taste or personal inspiration[7] and perhaps sometimes the innovative tendencies of French and Russian musical circles (see later). The growing respect for Poe as librettist or ''parolier'' led to many ''recitations'' with background music by piano, other instruments, or orchestra. This seemingly antiquated form has strongly persisted, at least for Poe's works, into the present. In 1866, George Parker, in Cincinnati, published eight stanzas of ''The Raven'' as a ''recitative chant,'' presumably with some musical tone. In 1894, Stanley Hawley, British composer and pianist, published ''The Bells'' and ''The Raven'' and, in 1898, ''Lenore''—all as recitations with piano. Max Heinrich's 1905 ''Raven'' recitation with piano (in both German and English) came out in Cincinnati. Essentially the same was Alvin Kranich's 1908 melodrama on that poem in Dresden (with "incidental" piano music). In 1909, Arthur Bergh at the piano aided David Bisham in the "Melodrama, the Raven" and a month later conducted it for orchestra at Carnegie Hall. Bisham bore this performance to every major city of English speech (Evans). In 1910, the celebrated composer John Ireland produced a recited "Annabel Lee" with piano. In 1980, in Baltimore, Leonard Slatkin conducted his own orchestral music for "The Raven," orally delivered by Vincent Price. In May 1988, in New York, Larry Bell presented his recited "Black Cat" for cello and piano. The *Times* newspaper account of Bell's representational effects evokes for us Poe's warnings against imitative music.

Widely and favorably reviewed have been diverse Poe compositions in the last half-decade: Lowell Liebermann's chamber orchestra variations for "Domain of Arnheim" (1991); Robert Lawson's play, *Dark Cathedrals of the Heart* (1993), with a section for voice, piano, and synthesizer; Anne LeBaron's "The Devil in the Belfry" for violin and piano (1993); Augusta Thomas's chamber opera "Ligeia," given in Baltimore and Evian-les-Bains (1994); and Deborah Drattell's several Poe pieces, during a decade, including "Alone" (1983) and "Spirits of the Dead" for soprano and chamber ensemble (1981), "Tell-Tale Heart" for orchestra and chorus (1985), and "Dream within a Dream" (1984) and the "Mysterious Star" section of *Al Aaraaf* (1994), both for string quartet. Most of these have been commissioned by foundations and successfully produced.

The unusually varied forms of musical settings for Poe's works are shown in a brief survey of two foreign language groups that have been seminal in providing new types and outstanding examples. In Russia, using an unspecified early translation in 1896, M. Ostroglazov composed a one-act opera for "Masque," the second earliest Poe music drama in the world—with considerable variety and ingenuity (Pa). The first was an 1867 Spanish zarzuela or operetta version of "Tarr and Fether," set by José Rogel (the only Spanish piece yet discovered). The brilliant Russian translations by Konstantin Balmont of the poems and tales (1901 to 1912) led to trailblazing musical works. First, there was the music for a full ballet of the "Red Death" in 1909 by Nikolai Tcherepnin (see third part). In 1913 came Mikhail Gnesin's setting of "The Conqueror Worm," for tenor and orchestra, and Sergei Rachmaninoff's choral symphony "The Bells" in four movements, one for each stanza. The composer allegedly preferred to all his other compositions this one, still frequently performed throughout the world, often with the words retranslated (even into an English text necessarily different from Poe's). Moreover, it continues to evoke "arrangements," for example, for mixed chorus by Clarence Lucas, 1935, and for piano by A. Goldenweiser, 1936 (Pa). (It was surely a stimulus for Leonard Bernstein's powerful choral symphonic work *Songfest* [1977] with its "Closing Hymn: Israfel.") From 1924 to 1928, Jurgis Karnavicius (Lithuanian for George Karnovitch) produced two ambitious and effective symphonic tone poems on "Ulalume" and "The Oval Portrait," a string quartet on "Usher," and seven song-poems for voice and piano duos or trios (Evans; Pa). Finally, in 1925, Nikolai Miaskowsky published a symphonic poem on "Silence, a Fable," a tale very rarely set. Thereafter, the rest was, indeed, the "silence" enjoined by Stalin's hostility toward "decadent" American influences.

There has been great enthusiasm for Edgar Poe in France from the 1850s and 1860s, when Baudelaire (1856–1864) "naturalized" his writings in the Gallic center of European culture. Strangely, French composers were late in "setting to" the field of composition. Claude Debussy first planned an ambitious Poe work in 1889, based on "Usher" and stemming from the unifying effects of Wagnerian leitmotivs. Shelved for work on *Pelléas et Mélisande,* the idea evolved into a pair of one-act operas for joint performance, the satiric "Devil in the Belfry" to precede a morbid, impressionistic "Usher." Gatti-Casazza, manager of the Metropolitan Opera, had contracted for both. Only fragments of the aborted "Devil" survive, incorporated in the "Gigue" section of the orchestral *Images.* At least half of the hour-long "Usher" has been pieced together in different versions, first by Carolyn Abbate and R. Kyr (at Yale University), then by Juan Allende-Blin (a Chilean settled in Germany), and finally and less fully by Ian Strasfogel—all efforts dating from 1976 to 1981, with various performances in Frankfurt (radio, 1977) and later in Hartford, New Haven, and New York (Lockspeiser; Abbate).

The musical circles of Paris, for two decades, discussed Debussy's plans and progress and shared in the Poe excitement. André Caplet participated through his "Red Death" for harp and string orchestra (1908), which he modified in 1923 into its more popular form, for harp and string quartet. Florent Schmitt had already contributed in 1904 to the keen interest in Poe's hypersensitive, neurotic artist-musician protagonist Usher through his symphonic study of "The Haunted Palace"—in style entirely distinct from Debussy's. A friend and a conductor of Debussy's works, Désiré-Emile Inghelbrecht, drew inspiration from Debussy's "The Devil in the Belfry" in his 1927 ballet. The same year saw the publication of incidental music by Jacques Zoubaloff, produced in 1930 by Paris Radio for Poe's incomplete play *Politian.* Finally, Byron Schiffman's "Annabel Lee" set to Mallarmé's translation was published (Pa). A more recent continuity for French settings lies in the music created for several Poe films for television, a field more vigorously exploited by France than any other nation. In 1948, Toni Aubain composed music for "The Raven"; in 1963, Antoine Duhamel, for the "Pit and the Pendulum"; in 1967, to accompany the three tales of the film, *Spirits of the Dead,* there was music by Diego Masson, Jean Prodromides, and Nino Rota; and in 1981, for four tales, compositions by Gerard Anfasso and, for two tales, by Georges Delerue.[8]

A few remarks about the spectacular rise of Poe-inspired operas must close this short survey. A recent bibliography (Pe) presents details for thirty-nine operas, only three of which are of full length and several of which are called "ballet-operas" (see third part). Several are operas intended for production in schools of music attached to universities or as part of a special festival performance for Poe, but a few have had remarkable critical approval and widespread staying power: Dominick Argento's "Bicentenary" full-length *Voyage of Edgar Allan Poe* (1976), based on his life and several of his works, Philip Glass's "Usher" (1988), and Larry Sitsky's "Usher," commissioned in Hobart, Australia, 1965. The opera-setting figures of the most popular tales are revealing: five for "Cask of Amontillado," eight for "Usher," three for "Red Death," three for "Tarr and Fether," six for "Tell-Tale Heart," and four for stage versions of Poe's unhappy, driven, and ultimately productive and posthumously fulfilled life (Pe, Pcc). Surely, Poe would agree that his powerful influence on the music of the world might help to bring "rest" to his possibly "perturbed spirit."

POE AND THE DANCE

The influence of Poe's writings during the twentieth century has expanded beyond the field of literature into the dance. This sway stems from the striking nature of his oft-repeated symbols, the graphic quality of his imagery, and the variety of his rhythmic feats in verse and rhetorical ingenuities in prose and poetry. It may also be traced to Poe's theories about the inherent relationship of the arts and his sophisticated use of cross-currents in numerous tales and poems, ranging from passages of simple synesthesia to the ballet-drama effects of "The Masque of the Red Death." A prolegomenous treatment of these might provide significant clues to the orientation of Poe's artistic thought and practice as well as fresh new interpretations of individual works. The choreographers and dancers, in seeking to interpret or represent the poems and tales, are as qualified as are pictorial artists or literary critics to express and reveal the potent charm of Poe's works. Such a treatment demands a brief survey of the dance elements in Poe's life and social surroundings, the instances of dance in his creative works and criticisms, and the varied ways in which those works have been shown on the dance stage in the single or joint efforts of the composers or choreographers.

In his writings, Poe clearly manifests an extensive knowledge of various steps used in social dancing, all very naturally acquired at the numerous parties of the Allans and their friends in Richmond. Later, at the University of Virginia, he participated in the frequent social functions given by the townspeople for the students.[9] Another factor in Poe's sensitivity to the dance is the milieu of theatrical dancing successively available to him in New York, Philadelphia, and again in New York. Several of the famous names of imported performers were cited by Poe in his works. Marie Ronzi Vestris of a family called, in Europe, "les dieux de la danse" performed in 1829, and in 1835 Mlle. Celeste, whom Poe apparently saw, began a long series of well-patronized New York performances, often in competition with Mlle. Augusta. In 1837, when Poe moved to New York from Richmond, a ballet competition was offered by a troupe called the Ravels, and, in September, the New Olympic Theatre opened for the presentation of "Opera, Vaudeville, and Ballet." Poe, knowing about the leading European danseuse, Maria Taglioni, wrote of her preeminent "human triumph" in the "Marginalia" (no. 85) of December 1844 and in "Fifty Suggestions" of 1849 (no. 27). In 1839, her famous brother, Paul, and his wife, Amélie, made an American tour, which included Poe's city of Philadelphia; their ballet sequence in *Le Bal Masqué*, Auber's opera, may have given him a hint for his own "masked ball" tale (Ph 182).

In 1840 and 1841, to New York and elsewhere came the far-famed Fanny Elssler, whose grace was portrayed and lauded by Poe's friend Frances Osgood in a poem that he cited three times. During his last six years in New York, he could see and read about the frequent ballet performances in the National Theatre at Niblo's Gardens. As editor of the *Broadway Journal* in 1845, he served as drama critic with access to all the ballets (Fagin, 93–132). In 1846, the city press, read sedulously by Poe, lauded the dancing of Mlle. Blangy in *La Sylphide* and of several groups from abroad. He also knew well terpsichorean references in the popular fiction of that day, such as the list of dances in Disraeli's *Vivian Grey*, which he copied into "Loss of Breath" (*M* 2, 79).

Poe's growing interest in this burgeoning dance of the stage led to a stream of allusions in his creative writings that also indicated his assumption of a current common knowledge of the dance among the educated. Many of the steps, cited in French, must have been intended by Poe to suggest elegance or refinement. The earlier tales bore also a satirical thrust against the "silver-fork" novelists, such as Bulwer-Lytton and Benjamin Disraeli. In general, the references indicate Poe's constant interest in the theatrical and his own latent dramatic representations (Fagin, 165–98). Pragmatically, this theory lies in their successful dance-stage adaptation.

Let us note the significant references to, or uses of, dancing in Poe's works. His earliest complete poem (1825; published, 1868) was "Oh, Tempora! Oh, Mores!," a satire in eighteenth-century style on a young dry goods shop clerk, who may "hop o'er counters with a Vestris air, / Complete at night what he began A. M. / And having cheated ladies, dance with them;/ . . . at a ball." Clearly, Poe had seen a popular print showing Auguste Vestris in his famous leap (*M* 1, 10–12). In "Al Aaraaf," Part II (1829), are two dance references, the second implying a rich combination of synesthesia elements. Poe speaks of "night" in which "the moon danc'd with the fair stranger light," that is, the reflected rays of the sun below the horizon (*M* 1, 106, 120). Later, Poe describes the graceful, canorous nymph Ligeia, whose music is cognate with the sounds of nature: she subtends "The sound of the rain / Which leaps down to the flower, / And dances again / In the rhythm of the shower" (*M* 1, 110).

In the well-known lyric "To One in Paradise" (1834), the final couplet refers to the nightly dreams where the spirit-love's "footstep gleams—/ In what ethereal dances, / By far Italian [or "eternal"] streams" (*M* 2, 163). The dance also enters into his fine poem "The Haunted Palace" (1839), soon incorporated into "Usher." There is a large masquelike element in the narrative and setting of this allegorical poem (*M* 1, 313; *M* 2, 406–7). Through the "luminous windows" (the eyes), one first sees "spirits moving musically, / To a lute's welltunéd law," but, at the end, "Vast forms that move fantastically / to a discordant melody." The dance style here suggests the sanity or insanity of man—or specifically of Roderick Usher. Appropriately, this has led choreographers to use the whole tale as the scenario for ballet (see later). Finally, in "The Bells" (1849), the very soul of onomatopoeic appeal, Poe writes about the king of the ghouls: "And he dances and he yells; / Keeping time, time, time" (*M* 1, 438). Indeed, all four sections stimulated Darius Milhaud in 1946 to compose a score for a ballet, choreographed by Ruth Page and performed in Chicago and New York by the Ballet Russe de Monte Carlo (Ph, 181).

The dance references are more numerous in Poe's prose works. The bad baron Metzengerstein initially gazes at his ancestral tapestries, where "the voluptuous and swan-like figures of the dames of days gone by, floated away in the mazes of an unreal dance to the strains of imaginary melody" (*M* 2, 22). Typically, Poe associates immorality or sensuality with the dance. Similarly, in his tale of mock-diablerie, "The Duc de L'Omelette," also of 1832, the noble but decadent hero authors a poem called the "Mazurkiad," based on the lively Polish dance (*M* 2, 34). In "Loss of Breath" (1835), the hero pirouettes out of the room in a "Pas de Zéphyr" (an impossible exit step!). Later, Mr. Lack O'Breath deprecates a man unaware of a "pirouette" or a "pas de papillon" (*M* 2, 70–71). In "Lionizing" (1835) is a reference to Almack's Balls, held in the fashionable Assembly Rooms of London (*M* 2, 176). More significant, in "Berenice" (1835) is the mad narrator's comparison of the image of Berenice's haunting teeth with the dance steps of the celebrated Mlle. Marie Sallé (*M* 2, 216); the notion becomes the tale's motif.

In "Mystification" (1837), Poe plants a clue to his obscure satire on Theodore Fay, prominent in New York journalism, via Miss "Villanova" (possibly a name for "New York City"), the "danseuse, lecturing in the chair of National Law" (*M* 2, 294; Ph, 181). At the beginning of "A Predicament" (1838), there is stress on the dogs, who "danced," while the Psyche Zenobia's "dancing days" were unhappily "over" (*M* 2, 347–48). Toward the end, she notes the dial-plate figures on the steeple clock "dancing the mazurka," while the figure "V" or "5" does a "pirouette" in "whirling round upon her apex" (*M* 2, 354). These dizzying visions signify imminent death and hark back to the opening of the tale. "The Devil in the Belfry" (1839) is replete with terms and narrative elements evoking the dance; the interloping devil carries a ceremonial "*chapeau-de-bras*" and wears "pumps"; he shatters the strictly timed smugness of the village with his pranks and capers ("*chassez*," "*balancez*," "*pirouette*," and "*pas-de-zepher [sic]*," (*M* 2, 371). At the end, the clocks "took to dancing as if bewitched" (*M* 2, 373), while the "devil in the belfry," where he now dwells, plays Irish jigs for all the world to hear. Inevitably, the whole tale was regarded as a program for a ballet or opera, most conspicuously by Debussy.

The comic tale of "The Man That Was Used Up" (1839), about a reconstituted paraplegic soldier, "General John A. B. Smith," has a minor gossipy character named Mrs. Pirouette who twirls the narrator about in a "pas de zéphyr" (*M* 2, 385). In "The Fall of the House of Usher" of 1839, the melancholic hero Roderick is memorable for playing on his guitar "a certain singular perversion and amplification of the wild air of the last waltz of Von Weber" (Pi, 84–86). In "Why the Little Frenchman Wears His Hand in a Sling" (in late 1839), the honest "Sir Pathrick O'Grandison" is a rival for the hand of Mrs. Tracle versus "Mounseer, the Count, A . . . Maiter-di-dauns," an obviously fraudulent combination (*M* 2, 465–71). In "William Wilson," also of 1839, the fatally intemperate actions of the perverse hero take place in the seductive masquerade ambience of the Duke Di Broglio's ballroom (*M* 2, 446–48); clearly, imprudent passions, loosed by the dance, lead to the murder of the restraining double or the "conscience" of Poe's motto. The dance motif also furnishes humor to "Never Bet the Devil Your Head" (1841). Toby Dammit challenges the devil to outdo his "pigeon-wing" skill and literally loses his head as a result of his misstep (*M* 2, 629–30). In 1842 came Poe's most important dance-oriented tale, "The Masque of the Red Death" (see later). In 1843, "The Gold-Bug" began with a spurious quotation: "What ho, this fellow is dancing mad! / He hath been bitten by the Tarantula" (Pi, 181). In reality, these lines by Poe were probably rooted in the performance-sensation of Fanny Elssler—her frenzied dance in *La Tarentule*. As Jupiter views it, Poe's whole tale depends on his master's having been bitten by "dat goole-bug" (*M* 2, 812–13).

The humorous tale of "The Spectacles" (1844) hinges upon mistaken identity. The eighty-two-year-old great-great-grandmother of the nearsighted hero contrives a mock marriage with him to demonstrate his need of spectacles. In the revelation scene, she refers to the dance of "Saint Vitusse" [*sic*], "cuts" some "pigeon-wings," and dances a "fandango" of pretended rage (*M* 3, 911, 913). Also in 1844, Poe inserted a major dance note into "The System of Doctor Tarr and Professor Fether" with an implied comparison of social life to a masquerade party or banquet of asylum inmates. The opera buffa atmosphere of the whole tale led the Spanish writer Adolfo Llanos y Alcaraz in 1867 to adapt it freely with music by José Rogel for the zarzuela stage of Madrid. A major character derived from Poe's Madame Joyeuse becomes a girl afflicted with a dance mania (A. Pollin). In 1954, the tale lured composer Vieri Tossati to turn it into a two-act opera, with choreography for (1) a fandango, (2) a "passo di danza iberica," (3) three separate waltz sections, and (4) numerous marches. The most recent setting for this tale is a one-act opera by Jan Bach (1974, 1977; Pc).

The last two instances of the dance in Poe's texts are both significant. The first (January 1848) appears in the science fiction tale of the year 2848, "Mellonta Tauta" ("These things are in the future") (*M* 3, 1290). Poe expresses a Spenglerian view of the decline of the West through the custom of dancing, for in the saloon cars of the rapid trains the passengers "flirt, feast, and dance" (*M*

3, 1298). In 1849, the tale of "Hop-Frog" borrows its basic plot and masquerade situation from an 1845 *Broadway Journal* article about the death of a ballet dancer from fire. Poe calls Hop-Frog's inamorata "Trippetta," a dancelike name, probably derived from Milton (Ph, 176). More important—at the height of the ball, just after midnight, the king and his seven ministers enter in their costumes of flax and tar, to be burned to death by the vengeful court jester (*M* 3, 1352–54).

This grim use of the dance for the theme of life as a doomed masquerade for all mankind is basic to "The Masque of the Red Death," which has occasioned the most Poe ballets of any of his texts. This masterpiece, of May 1842, probably was inspired by the well-known pictorial and moralistic concept of the Dance of Death. Poe knew the relevant chapter in Disraeli's *Curiosities of Literature* and the episode in Boccaccio's *Decameron* (Ph, 181). His September 1841 review of Thomas Campbell's *Life of Petrarch* bore this thematic sentence: "This was a dance of the king of terrors over the earth, and a very rapid one" (*M* 2, 669). Poe's punning title alludes specifically to the dance nature of his plot and to costume disguises. Poe, in a sense, wrote a choreographed scenario for the playlet staged in the suite of seven varicolored rooms. He calls it a "voluptuous" scene with its "wanton" maskers "stalking" and "writhing" to the "wild music," owing something also to recent performances in Philadelphia of Hugo's *Hernani* and Auber's *Le Bal Masqué* (Ph, 177).

In turn, this tale was to become the script or scenario of many dances. The earliest was a one-act opera by M. A. Ostroglazov (Moscow, 1896) with a masquerade ballet scene. The next version was by Joseph Holbrooke of England, the most prolific composer of Poe-inspired scores. His 1914 "piano arrangement" was republished in 1936, revised as a tone poem for orchestra with a "ballet-pantomime" (Evans). The third was a setting by the eminent composer Nicholas Tcherepnin, published in "Petrograd" between 1914 and 1917. Thinking it ideally suited for the post-1917 period, choreographer Kazian Goleizovsky used "The Masque" for his new Moscow Kamerny (Chamber) Ballet Company in 1919 and in 1929 (Ph, 182).

Next, a Soviet refugee, Lazar Saminsky, in New Hampshire (1924), composed "The Galliard of a Merry Plague," described as an "opera-ballet" for performances here and abroad. In 1926 (the date indicating a widespread postwar mood), Friedrich Wilckens in Vienna used "The Masque" for a ballet named *Don Morte* or "Lord Death" and had it performed in Berlin with choreography by Max Terpis. In 1931, a short ballet by Cyril Scott was given in London, choreographed by Quentin Tod. A long tone poem by Owen Reed (unpublished) had a ballet pantomime of "The Masque." In 1957, Andrée Howard choreographed the tale as "Conte Fantastique" for the Ballet Rambert in London, to the music of André Caplet. Another medium—the cinema—has contributed an important dance passage based on "The Masque" in Roger Corman's 1964 film, produced in England with Vincent Price as "Prince Prospero"; the masked ball scene was choreographed by Jack Carter with music by David Lee. The next year, 1965, Edmond Maurat created a ''Tragédie Ballet,'' the ''poetry'' and music now available in the national music library (Paris). Save for a brief dance piece by Doris Humphrey (see later), this completes the roster of danced ''Masques,'' save for a large, experimental ''Red Death'' in Vancouver City, Canada, in 1991, presented as ''a mixed media, dramatic monologue, dance and music'' exhibition with scenes of the ''seven ballrooms.''

Other Poe narratives have served for dance compositions. In 1927, D. E. Inghelbrecht, Debussy's friend, scored ''The Devil in the Belfry'' for a one-act ballet, choreographed by Nicola Guerra for the Paris Opera. In England, Josef Holbrooke completed and published a three-movement ''dance-symphony for piano and orchestra'' (1930–1935) based on ''Bon-Bon'' and so titled. In Buenos Aires, Roberto Garcia Morillo in 1942 composed ''The Fall of the House of Usher'' for a ballet, which was successfully revived in 1955 with new choreography by Léonide Massine. ''Usher'' in 1926 had served Frederick L. Day for a play in seven scenes, the first containing a ''dance song'' (Ph, 182). Along these lines was Steven Berkoff's 1975 playscript for ''Usher,'' with an erotic dance of Roderick and his sister when produced (1978, 1985, music by A. Bolton; Pi, 130). In turn, this may have given a dance theme to Philip Glass for his ''Usher,'' widely discussed by the press for its 1988 Boston and 1989 New York performances. It incorporates a music box with figurines whose incestuous dancing is paralleled by that of the protagonists. Herbert Ross and his group used ''The Black Cat'' in 1950 in New York as one of four short ''ballets d'action'' with miming and graphic movements, set to the music of Alban Berg. Even more original and noteworthy was a 1953 ballet-drama by Elizabeth Dooley called *Poor Eddy,* with eight dramatic biographical scenes, each one followed by a danced setting of a story, poem, or narrative idea by Poe; choreographed by Doris Humphrey for Charles Weidman and his group, it included ''Masque,'' ''The Tell-Tale Heart,'' ''Ligeia,'' and ''Annabel Lee.''

This poem was the libretto for another short dance production of 1953 in Paris, choreographed by George Scibine to the music of Byron Schiffman; revived in New York, January 1990. Schiffman, more ambitiously, next wrote an ''opera ballet in 3 acts'' called *The Raven; or, Edgar Allan Poe,* in 1954. It draws upon four poems and ''The Isle of the Fay'' (Ph, 182). More recently, the eminent composer Dominick Argento produced a two-act opera based on Poe's life and writings called *The Voyage of Edgar Allan Poe.* Published in 1976 and performed in Minneapolis, Washington, and Baltimore, it makes effective use of various dance forms: a waltz sequence, a ''rag-doll'' choral dance (I, ii), a dance on shipboard (I, v), a wild tarantella solo and a group dance (I, viii). Following this prominent lead was Friday Nelson's expansion of his early *Poe* a ''play with music'' (1986) into a full musical, in fifteen scenes, eight sets, and forty roles drawn from Poe's life and works. Richard Lee Cook choreographed the rock, classical, and traditional dance pieces (Baltimore, 1988).

Returning to the subject of single-work dance settings, we find ''Annabel Lee'' being used for an eleven-minute commercial film of 1969 entitled *Seafall*;

it was danced by Michael Uthoff, its choreographer, and Lisa Bradley, with Omar Shariff intoning the poem. The tale "Four Beasts in One" was produced in 1956 in Paris under its subtitle, "The Caméléopard," using the music of Henri Sauget and danced by its choreographer Jean Babilée and his company to considerable acclaim. In 1957, "Ligeia" became a successful two-scene dance drama in Paris to a score by Mario Vittoria. More recently, in Australia, the 1986 Adelaide Festival commissioned Philip Glass to create a "dance-theatre" "Maelström" which was widely performed and praised, as was his musical "Usher" of 1988 with its important danced "music box" scene.

Poe's works have also been used by the experimental modern dance in other ways than as set narrative pieces. For example, in Dancers' Studio, New York, May 1964, John Wilson's satiric new work called "Pot-Pourri" used three lyrics distortedly recited for parodic dancing. In the summer of 1971, Jeff Duncan presented two poems in a Dance Theater Workshop production. The great teacher and choreographer Anna Sokolov persistently utilized Poe texts, first in a program of February 1972 at the New York City Forum, second, in dances in Salt Lake City in 1977, and finally, in a set of four dances for intoned poetic lines and prose excerpts, in April 1978 at the Juilliard School of Music (Ph, 182). In 1991, "The Masque of the Red Death" was presented in Vancouver City, Canada, as "a mixed media exhibition combining dramatic monologue, dance and music." Further proof of Poe's far-ranging influence was the "story-ballet" given by the company of Tetsuko Ando, drawn from several tales and called "Dancing in Poe's World," for February 1980 performance in Tokyo. Dance sequences appeared also in Friday Nelson's *Poe, a Play with Music*, first staged in 1986 near Baltimore and then altered into *Poe, a Musical* in 1988 with "rock, classical and traditional music."

Probably many modern dance programs based on Poe texts have escaped being recorded, in part, because of their somewhat ambiguous or twofold nature—dance and theater—or because productions staged in colleges and schools of music often fail to enter the indexed annals.[10] But the evidence for Poe's pervasive and perennial influence on the dance is considerable and conclusive. The dance theater has reciprocated Poe's awareness of the profuse aesthetic possibilities for grace, drama, color, ethereality, and satire in the many forms of the dance by borrowing heavily from his works. It is likely that the overlapping of fields that has been encouraged by technological advances on the stage and through television will promote even more dance settings of Poe's creative works, offering further evidence of the rich variety of his narrative and poetic conceptions.

NOTES

1. The first part of this chapter represents an adapted condensation of the Introduction to my book *Images of Poe's Works: A Comprehensive Descriptive Catalogue of Illustrations* (Westport: Greenwood, 1989). Its 414 pages contain 1,625 short-to-long entries

or articles on the Poe illustrations of 729 artists in thirty-three countries, who produced 8,000–10,000 illustrations of Poe's individual works; they are described in the articles and referenced in the four indexes. All the artists mentioned can be located in the first index. The volume is indicated in this text as "Pi," with *P* for Pollin and *i* for his ninth entry in the Works Cited. Similarly, other Pollin entries are given a letter designation.

2. These were "Letter to B—" of 1831, "Notes on English Verse" of 1843 expanded to "The Rationale of Verse" of 1848, "The Philosophy of Composition" of 1846, and the posthumously published "Poetic Principle" of 1850. The reflections lie in the 291 essays of the "Marginalia," in seventeen magazine installments (1844 to 1849), q. v. in Pollin, *Writings* of Poe, vol. 2. The parenthetical references for numerous musical compositions to Works Cited usually indicate the annotated bibliographies of Poe music, arranged alphabetically by composers. For most pre-1939 items, details may be assumed as available in the book by Evans.

3. See Lenhart, 125–60. Ensley specifically is responding to the charges of W. L. Werner, R. C. Pettigrew, and Anthony Caputi, q. v.

4. My last Supplement (Pcc) has 240 entries not yet recorded in any lists published after 1986, the date of Michael Hovland's book (q.v.), most of which came from Evans and Pollin (Pa–Pe).

5. There are thirty-five of these "double-dealers," with sixty-three compositions in all, including Beeson, Foote, Gniessin, Karnovitch, MacDowell, Mount, Myaskovsky, Rachmaninoff, Rorem, Somervell, A. Sullivan, and Tcherepnin.

6. This last was that of Sampson Low and Co., 1858 (frequently reprinted), with fifty-two illustrations, including four by Tenniel (see first part of this chapter). The 1858 and 1859 American reprints of this volume helped to provide Poe texts for musical settings.

7. For example, Josef Holbrooke composed thirty-one settings for various works, 1901–1938, for two dozen varied combinations of instruments with or without voice, all widely performed in England (Evans; Pc). See also the twenty-one settings by John Habash and Edna Lewis (lyricist) for jazz combo and voice (1963, 1967) for as many poems and tales (in versified form) published and recorded (Pa). For electronic instrumental accompaniments and "performance arts" settings, see Pc and Pcc and n. 10 here.

8. These are only a few of the forty-three separate items in Part II of Pc, which also contains a "Discography" of twelve Poe recordings with the works noted earlier by Rota and Caplet and, earlier, Rachmaninoff, plus others from America and England. Some of these appear solely on recordings, such as the rock music of *The Alan Parsons Project*. See also, in Pcc, sixty separate composers each listed for one or more works in the "Discography." The music of the Poe films of many other nations is often worthy of special study (see the 247 given in the "Filmography" section, many with music credits in Pi).

9. This third section is adapted, with considerable updating, from my study designated as Ph in Works Cited and also reprinted in Pj. Explanatory or citation pages to the former are included in my text, hereafter, as for this reference: Ph, 169–70.

10. For example, there are dance elements sometimes in the new genre of "performance art," as in Diamanda Galas's "Masque of the Red Death," announced for the "Serious Fun Festival" at Lincoln Center for July 1989 (with no discoverable review); also, the "Masque" offered as the second of two one-act plays by Director David Huffman, at the Gashouse Theatre, near the University in Austin, Texas, in April 1980, lists a choreographer on its program. Worth mentioning are two academic works: Kathleen

Yoakum's 1978 master's thesis at the Long Beach, California, State University, "Trilogy of Poe," a drama danced to modern music, with projected artwork backdrops; and Beth Mehocic's doctoral thesis (of 1980) called "Masque," using "cyclic themes" and fixed instruments for the ballet characters.

WORKS CITED

Abbate, C. "The Heart Laid Bare." *Opera News* 42 (1978): 30+.

Allen, Gay Wilson. *American Prosody.* New York: American Book, 1935.

Brunel, Pierre. "Claude Debussy, Interprète d'Edgar Poe." *Revue de Littérature Comparée* 61 (1987): 359–68.

Caputi, Anthony. "The Refrain in Poe's Poetry." *AL* 25 (1953): 160–73.

Cauthen, I. B. "Music and Edgar Allan Poe." *Notes and Queries* 194 (1949): 103. (4 entries).

Ensley, Helen. *Poe's Rhymes.* Baltimore: Baltimore Poe Society, 1981.

Evans, May Garretson. *Music and Edgar Allan Poe.* Baltimore: Johns Hopkins UP, 1939. (252 entries [80 unpub., in ms.]).

Fagin, N. B. *The Histrionic Mr. Poe.* Baltimore: Johns Hopkins UP, 1949.

Griffiths, Paul. "Poe." *New Grove Dictionary of Music and Musicians.* Vol. 15. London: Macmillan, 1980.

———. "Poe." *New Grove Dictionary of American Music.* Vol. 3. London: Macmillan, 1986.

Hovland, Michael. *Musical Settings of American Poetry.* Westport, Conn.: Greenwood, 1986. (215 Poe entries, of which 17 are "new" listings).

Idol, L. John, and S. K. Eisiminger. "Opera Performances based on Poe's Fiction" (supplementary to the previous lists). *PoeS* 15 (Dec. 1982): 42. (13 entries).

Lenhart, Charmian S. *Musical Influence on American Poetry.* Athens: Georgia UP, 1956.

Lockspeiser, Edward. *Debussy et Edgar Poe.* Monaco: Ed. du Rocher, 1961.

Pettigrew, R. C. "Poe's Rime." *AL* 4 (1932): 151–59.

Pollin, Alice M. "Edgar Allan Poe in the Works of Llanos y Alcaraz." *Hispanófila* 79 (1983): 21–37.

Pollin, Burton R. [Pa] "More Music to Poe." *Music and Letters* 54 (1973): 391–404. (203 entries, 76 unpublished).

———. (Pb) "Poe" [and music]. *Musik in Geschichte und Gegenwart.* Basel: Kassel, 1979, Supplement (Vol. 16), 1503–7. (Article and list).

———. (Pc) "Music and Edgar Allan Poe: A Second Annotated Check List." *PoeS* 15 (1982): 7–13. ("New" Poe music including 100 publications [80 since 1973], 10 recordings, 47 scores of film music [157 in all]).

———. (Pcc) "Music and Edgar Allan Poe: Supplement III." *PoeS* 26 (June–Dec. 1993): 42–46.

———. (Pd) "Music and Edgar Allan Poe: Addendum to Part I." *PoeS* 15 (1982): 42. (16 post-1976 registered but unpublished entries).

———. (Pe) "Poe" [and opera]. *New Grove Dictionary of Opera.* London: Macmillan, 1992.

———. (Pf) "Poe's 'Eldorado' Viewed as a Song." *Prairie Schooner* 46 (1973): 228–35.

———. (Pg) *Music for Shelley's Poetry: Annotated Bibliography of Musical Settings of Shelley's Poetry.* New York: Da Capo, 1974, xxxiii + 175 pp. (1,309 annotated entries).

————. (Ph) "Poe and the Dance." *Studies in the American Renaissance 1980.* Charlottesville: Virginia UP, 1980, 169–82.

————. (Pi) *Images of Poe's Works:* A *Comprehensive Descriptive Catalogue of Illustrations.* Westport, Conn.: Greenwood, 1989.

————. (Pj) *Discoveries in Poe.* Notre Dame, Ind.: Notre Dame UP, 1970.

————. (Pk) "A Hoax Detected: Poe's Illustration for 'The Island of the Fay.' " *The Mystery and Detection Annual.* Beverly Hills, Calif.: Donald Adams, 1972.

————. (Pl) "Illustrations for Poe's Works in Spanish Translation." *Círculo: Revista de Cultura* 8 (1979): 91–103.

Stedman, E. C., ed., and George Woodberry. *Works of Edgar Allan Poe.* 10 vols. Chicago: Stone and Kimball, 1894–1895.

Werner, W. L. "Poe's Theories and Practice in Poetic Technique." *AL* 2 (1930): 157–65.

24

Edgar Allan Poe: A Writer for the World

LOIS D. VINES

The French writer Paul Valéry remarked in 1924 that Poe "would today be completely forgotten if Baudelaire had not taken up the task of introducing him into European literature" (204). The two poets "exchanged values," continues Valéry, in the sense that "every aspect of Baudelaire was impregnated, inspired, deepened by Poe." In exchange for what he had taken, Baudelaire "gave Poe's thought an infinite expanse. He offered it to future generations" (204). While, in America, the debate over Poe's character raged on, one of France's greatest writers, Charles Baudelaire, was translating his stories and publishing critical essays that would launch Poe as a writer for the world.

Contrary to popular belief, Baudelaire was not the first translator of Poe's works. W. T. Bandy has identified four earlier translators, the first publishing an adaptation of a Poe tale in a French newspaper in 1844 (1973, xiii). Isabelle Meunier's translation of "The Black Cat" in 1847 captivated Baudelaire and inspired his decision to find more of the American writer's tales and translate them himself. Just a few months earlier, on October 15, 1846, the first critique of Poe's work in French had appeared in the prestigious *Revue des deux Mondes*. E.-D. Forgues's article is particularly significant because it recognized Poe "as a logician, as a pursuer of abstract truths, and as a lover of the most eccentric hypotheses and the most difficult calculations" (*CE*, 48). Although Forgues knew Poe only through twelve short stories, he initiated his renown as a serious writer by comparing Poe's ideas to those of Pascal and Laplace, thus placing emphasis on the intellectual qualities that were to have a great appeal to future generations of French writers.

The French response to Poe expressed in a selection of articles and critiques published between 1846 and 1924 is the focus of Jean Alexander's *Affidavits of Genius*, in which Poe is seen in terms of three major aspects of significance:

the Outlaw (Poe as social rebel and romantic rebel); the American (Poe's synthesis of the "scientific" and the spiritual or idealistic); and the Poet (Poe as the calculating technician and the symbolist who conceived the poetic function as the inducement of the visionary or transcendental experience). These insights and judgments remain among the most original and lasting in the history of Poe criticism.

Baudelaire's dramatic reaction to Poe's life and work has become legend in literary history. At the age of twenty-six, he discovered in Poe's family history uncanny parallels with his own life. In a letter to literary critic Armand Fraisse, Baudelaire describes the "singular shock" he experienced upon finding in Poe's poems and short stories ideas that he had thought of and that "Poe had been able to bring together to perfection" (Lloyd, 148). Baudelaire's obsession with Poe was not simply youthful enthusiasm. Between 1848 and his death in 1867, he published five volumes of Poe translations, along with articles and prefaces that were to become the source of Poe's fame in many European countries for nearly half a century.

Baudelaire's first major article on Poe appeared in the 1852 March and April issues of the *Revue de Paris*. Entitled "Edgar Allan Poe, His Life and Works," the essay is important for two reasons. First, with emotional verve, it brought details of Poe's life to the attention of French readers for the first time (Forgues's article did not include biographical information). Second, Baudelaire's analysis of Poe's literary endeavors pointed out the unique qualities in the American writer's work. He refers to Poe's tales and essays as "a totally new creation." Throughout the essay, Baudelaire emphasizes that Poe's native country had neither the desire nor the intellectual capacity to appreciate his genius. "In Paris or Germany," remarks the French poet, "he would have found friends to give him understanding and solace" (Alexander, 112, 115). Baudelaire's preface to his first collection of Poe tales, *Histories extraordinaires* (1856), is a revised version of his 1852 article (Alexander, 122).

During the period that Baudelaire devoted himself to establishing Poe as a great writer in France (1849–1867), Poe's literary reputation in the United States and England was at the mercy of the "the Griswold controversy." The infamous Rufus Wilmot Griswold (1815–1857) sent an obituary letter to the *New York Tribune*, published October 9, 1849, two days after Poe's death, in which he stated that "few will be grieved" by the poet's death. Griswold went on to describe Poe as a man who "walked the streets, in madness or melancholy, with lips moving in indistinct curses" (*REAP*, 32). Not until a year later did Griswold speak at length of Poe's writings in his "Memoir of the Author," which served as preface to *The Works of Edgar Allan Poe*. The essay attempts an objective analysis of Poe's work but concludes with a defamation of his character that had a major influence on Poe's reputation in America and abroad (*CE* 1987, 56–57).

Although Poe's friends came to his defense to counteract the damage inflicted by his literary executor, few of his well-known American contemporaries expressed great enthusiasm for him as an author. One of Poe's strongest defenders was Sarah Helen Whitman, whose moving analysis of several tales supports her view that Poe did not repudiate moral values (*CE,* 58–62). Longfellow, Lowell, and Walt Whitman appreciated specific aspects of his work, while at the same time condemning what they perceived to be a lack of moral values deemed essential in literature. Emerson's reference to Poe as "the jingle man" relegated the poems to a minor level. Henry James, who left his native America to write in England, defamed his fellow countryman with the comment that "an enthusiasm for Poe is the mark of a decidedly primitive stage of reflection" (*CE,* 82). In spite of this negative remark expressed in his article on Baudelaire (1876), James later recognized a number of outstanding qualities in Poe, a subject Burton Pollin examines in detail along with Poe's direct effect on James's own creative endeavors (189–206).

Near the turn of the century, other American writers began to acknowledge Poe's genius. In 1895, Willa Cather, while a senior at the University of Nebraska, recognized Poe as a master of "pure prose" and one of America's greatest poets, along with Lowell (*CE,* 5). Pollin traces Poe's influence into the twentieth century in his study of Thomas Mann, who praises Poe in his long novel *Buddenbrooks: The Decline of a Family* (Pollin, 226–34). Mann's American contemporary Theodore Dreiser read Poe intensively during the 1920s while noting his impressions in diaries and letters, one of which includes the remark that Poe was "our first and greatest literary genius" (Dreiser 1, 371). Joseph Conrad's *Heart of Darkness* bears similarities in theme, imagery, and structure to "The Fall of the House of Usher," as G. R. Thompson points out in his essay (*CE,* 142–43). The descriptions of hallucinations in Hemingway's novels seem to draw upon Poe's work (Tarbox). Esther Levin Rubinstein's study of the contemporary author Isaac Bashevis Singer examines significant parallels in the use of the grotesque by Poe and Singer.

The American poet who most admired Poe is Robert Frost. John Kemp quotes from Frost's letters, in which the poet recalls that, at the age of fourteen, he read all of Poe's verse and learned most of it by heart (47–48). Kemp examines numerous parallels between Frost's poems and several of Poe's, including "Dream-Land" and "Al Aaraaf" (52–58).

In a 1925 essay, William Carlos Williams argued that Poe was not simply "a fault of nature" or "a find for French eyes" but rather the first American writer to take literature seriously and bring to it a sense of originality (*REAP,* 127–28). Just a year later, Edmund Wilson's article presented Poe as the "bridge" between Romanticism and Symbolism, which took root first in France in reaction to naturalism in the late nineteenth century. In 1928, Malcolm Cowley expressed his dismay that American professors of literature did not fully understand the significance of Poe's work. Richard Wilbur, poet and Poe specialist, delivered an Anniversary Lecture ("The House of Poe") at the Library of Congress in 1959 in which he praised Poe's tales of psychic conflict as "the best things of their kind in our literature" (*REAP,* 254). Although slow to be recognized as a significant writer in his own country, Poe became a link between literary movements and continents as appreciation of his work spread throughout the world.

In Great Britain, Poe's reception was, for a long time, tainted by the "Griswold controversy," whose effects can be seen in an article published in the *Edinburgh Review* in April 1858 that begins "Edgar Allan Poe was incontestably one of the most worthless persons of whom we have any record in the world of letters" (Hutcherson, 214). The image of the American poet was rectified, thanks to the efforts of the Englishman John H. Ingram, who published Poe's collected works in 1874 and an excellent biography in 1880. Among the well-known British writers, Tennyson was the most enthusiastic in expressing his admiration for Poe. Stevenson recognized Poe's brilliance as a short story writer but became weary with "loathing and horror" in reading Poe's tales of horror (*CE*, 4). Yeats proclaimed Poe "the greatest of American poets," after earlier describing "The Raven" as "insincere and vulgar" (*REAP*, 76–77). While finding Poe's fame puzzling, Yeats admits that a writer who had so much influence on Baudelaire must have some great merit.

Kipling acknowledged a "heavy debt" to Poe, whom he greatly admired. Burton Pollin traces Poe's themes, effects, and plot devices in a succession of Kipling short stories and gives examples of the British writer's parodies of Poe's verse (207–21). Kipling's contemporary, H. G. Wells, whose science fiction bears obvious links to several Poe tales, remarked that "the fundamental principles of construction that underlie such stories as Poe's 'Murders in the Rue Morgue' . . . are precisely those that should guide a scientific writer" (Suvin and Philmus, 194). D. H. Lawrence went so far as to call Poe a "supreme scientist" rather than an artist, commenting that "a tale is a concatenation of scientific cause and effect" (*CE*, 92).

The Irishman James Joyce, who spent many years in Paris, did not escape Poe's influence, as can be seen in M. E. Kronegger's detailed examination, which concludes that Joyce was inspired by Poe's use of interior monologue, synesthesia, ratiocination, and suggestion as literary devices (254). Joyce's compatriot Samuel Beckett also spent most of his professional life in Paris publishing stories and plays in both French and English that show certain affinities with Poe in their bizarre atmosphere and concentration of the unity of effect.

After Baudelaire's death in 1867, another outstanding French poet, Stéphane Mallarmé, then twenty-five years old, was waiting in the wings to take up the banner for Poe. Mallarmé, inspired by the same boundless adoration of Poe, completed a task that Baudelaire had not had the courage to face, the translation of Poe's poems. After devoting twenty years to rendering into poetic prose thirty-six out of some sixty poems, Mallarmé published the collection in 1888 in an edition illustrated by Manet. The beautiful volume, created by two of France's greatest artists, inspired a letter from Swinburne to Mallarmé in which the British poet expressed his gratitude for "these marvelous pages in which the first American poet found himself twice so perfectly translated" (Swinburne 3, 41). Swinburne was convinced that this masterpiece, along with the excellent work of John Ingram, would "reduce to dust all the pack of lies and calumny trumped up or brought together by this infamous Griswold" (Lang, 42). Both Swinburne and Mallarmé expressed their admiration for Poe on the occasion of the erection of a monument at Poe's grave in Baltimore on November 17, 1875. Mallarmé composed his most beautiful sonnet, "Le Tombeau d'Edgar Poe," to commemorate the event (*CE,* 80–81).

Other painters since Manet have found inspiration in Poe, the most notable being James Whistler and René Magritte. Whistler's painting *Annabel Lee* is a tribute to Poe's well-known poem. The effect of Poe's tales on Magritte was extensive. The Belgian painter was captivated by Poe's theories of poetry, his melancholy, and the themes of death, terror, and mystery. Two of his works bear titles from Poe, *The Demon of Perversity,* 1928, and *The Domain of Arnheim,* 1949. Fred Miller Robinson explores the nature of contradiction in Poe, especially between the familiar and the strange, that inspired some of Magritte's comic paintings. Renée Riese Hubert examines Poe's influence on Magritte's landscapes, in particular, on *The Domain of Arnheim,* which does not portray the paradise described by Poe.

In Poe's essays, Baudelaire and Mallarmé found ideas that confirmed their own beliefs and laid the groundwork for the Symbolist movement. From Mallarmé on, the effect of Poe on French writers diverges radically. The Symbolists (Mallarmé, Kahn, de Gourmont, Moréas, Vielé-Griffin, Ghil, and Valéry) admire the Poe of ordered thought, the master of artistic calculation. In contrast, the Decadents (Huysmans and Villiers de l'Isle-Adam) and the presurrealists (Rimbaud, Lautréamont, Jarry, and Apollinaire) were inspired by the horror, mystery, dreams, and the explorations of the disordered mind, what André Breton was to call later the "convulsive beauty."

Among French prose writers, the most obvious example of Poe's influence can be seen in the stories of Villiers de l'Isle-Adam. His tale "Véra" shows many similarities to Poe's "Ligeia," especially when the main character, Véra, after a death as mysterious as Ligeia's, seems to be constantly present, not only in the memory of her lover, but in a half-human, half-spiritual form (Cambiaire, 179). Other tales from the French author's collection *Contes cruels* appear to be directly inspired by Poe's stories.

A famous writer of the pseudoscientific novel, Jules Verne, drew a great deal of inspiration from Poe. Verne's "Five Weeks in a Balloon" was directly influenced by "The Balloon Hoax." The French novelist's "The Sphinx of the Snows" reads like a continuation of *The Narrative of Arthur Gordon Pym,* and, in fact, Verne dedicates the story to "the memory of Edgar Poe, and my friends in America" (Cambiaire, 244). In "Around the World in Eighty Days," Verne uses an idea from "Three Sundays in a Week" to create suspense just at the moment when the reader thinks the story is over. While openly giving credit to Poe's work as a frequent inspiration, Verne takes his fantastic stories of adventure in a new direction, toward sunny skies, brightness, and humor.

With the publication of "The Murders in the Rue Morgue," Poe initiated the detective story, a genre that has been widely imitated, most notably by Sir Arthur Conan Doyle in England and Emile Gaboriau (1835–1873) in France. The resemblances between Gaboriau's amateur detective Tabaret and Poe's Dupin are striking. Both gentlemen have wonderful powers of deduction and induction, love books, are considered somewhat bizarre, and arouse jealousy in the heart of the Paris police chief. Like Dupin and Sherlock Holmes, Tabaret has an appreciative interlocutor, M. Lecoq, on whom to test his logic. Gaboriau's methods of using ratiocination frequently remind the reader of Poe's detective tales.

Valéry saw in Dupin a mind capable of observing its own analytical faculties, a trait developed to its extreme limits in his own creation Monsieur Teste, whose intellect is similar to Dupin's (Vines, 1977). Valéry was also influenced by Poe's essays on poetry and admired certain aspects of *Eureka,* which, for him, represented a drama of the intellect. As a young writer, he shared his enthusiasm for Poe with André Gide, whose character Michel in *The Immoralist* pursues a calculated self-destruction reminiscent of ''The Imp of the Perverse.''

During the last half of the nineteenth century, Poe's work influenced nearly every genre in France, from Symbolist poetry to the detective novel. Many of the well-known writers either acknowledged the direct effect of Poe on their own work or expressed their views on the American writer. Because of the great respect French letters, science, and philosophy enjoyed in European intellectual circles, Poe's fame spread rapidly throughout the Continent and beyond. The complicated chains of influence and affinities emanating from France showed up early in Russia, where translations of Poe's tales appeared almost simultaneously with Baudelaire's in France.

There was a mistaken belief repeated by Yarmolinsky (44) and later corrected by Bandy (1960, 479) that Poe was translated into Russian even before he made his debut in the French language. Adding to his legend in Russia was Baudelaire's account of Poe's travels to Moscow and St. Petersburg, later discounted by biographers. In spite of these misconceptions, Poe did have considerable literary impact in Russia. Grossman's research establishes 1847 as the date of the earliest Russian translation, a version of ''The Gold-Bug'' appearing in *The New Library for Education,* a journal for children and teachers. A detailed comparison of the Russian translation with the French version of the same tale published in the *Revue Britannique* of November 1945 reveals that the source was more likely French than the original English. Russian editors continued to glean Poe stories from the French press, choosing tales they considered edifying and eliminating the sensational or horrifying.

Not until 1861 did a very perceptive essay on Poe appear in Russia. In his preface to three translated Poe tales, Fyodor M. Dostoyevski describes Poe as a ''strange, though enormously talented writer'' and praises the ''vigor of his imagination'' (*CE,* 77–78). Dostoyevski does not claim Poe's influence on his own work, but a number of traits point to similarities suggesting at least an indirect connection. In *Crime and Punishment* (1866), where the central focus is the detection of a motive rather than the crime itself, the psychological ratiocination used by the examining magistrate reminds us of Poe's Dupin. In *Notes from Underground* (1864) the darker side of the mind, the irrational, and the perverse play a dominant role.

Another author of the period of the Russian realistic novel, Ivan Sergevic Turgenev, seems to have been influenced by Poe. While living in Paris, Turgenev began writing the strange tale "Phantoms," in which the female phantom's efforts to reincarnate herself suggest similarities with Poe's "Ligeia" and "Morella." The theme of postmortem love fascinated Turgenev, who described his story "After Death," the tale of a well-known actress's suicide, as being in the "vein of Edgar Poe" (Grossman, 59).

Russian interest in Poe from 1847 to the 1880s came mainly from prose writers who admired the American author but did not elevate him to the level of the cult figure found in France. In 1895, four translations of Poe's work were published, two of them by Konstantin Balmont, who became the Russian Baudelaire through his determination to make Poe's life and especially his poetry known to the budding Symbolist poets.

Poe's influence on Russian poets is more difficult to discern than in the case of the prose writers. His poetry was first introduced to the reading public in 1878, when S. A. Andreevski translated "The Raven," followed by "The Philosophy of Composition." After studying the works of Russian Symbolist poets Blok, Ivanov, and especially Bryusov, Grossman concludes that Poe's ideas about poetry and the role of the poet seem to have had a greater effect on the Russian poets than specific themes or techniques of verse. In the same way that the French Symbolists took to Poe's concept of pure poetry and the subtle effects of music and symbols, the Russian poets espoused a new direction that set them apart from their predecessors. Poe's renown in Russia reached its apogee during the Symbolist movement, which began to decline with the closing of its literary journal, *The Scales,* in 1909. A twentieth-century writer who started out as a Russian Symbolist poet is Vladimir Nabokov, known to Americans as the author of *Lolita,* an elaborate parody on Poe and his heroines written in English. Summing up Poe's impact on Russian literature, Grossman concludes that, with few exceptions, Poe's reputation in Russia exceeded his direct influence.

The last decade of the nineteenth century and the beginning of the twentieth also mark the high point of Poe's reputation and influence in Scandinavia. First translated into Danish in 1855, Poe's tales were slow to attract readers or critical attention before the Swedish poet and critic Ola Hansson took up his cause with a major essay, which appeared first in an abridged German translation in 1889. The fifty-page study of Poe's life and work came out in Danish (1890), Norwegian (1893), and Polish (1905) before the complete original Swedish version was finally published in 1921. Carl L. Anderson provides the first English translation in *Poe in Northlight,* a detailed study of Poe's influence and reputation in Norway, Sweden, and Denmark.

Hansson's opening lines, reminiscent of Baudelaire's moving evocations, describe Poe as "one of the lonely ones, one of the anointed in spirit and in sorrow, one of the prophets whom the world stones'' (Anderson, 167). Also similar to that of the French critics is Hansson's appreciation of Poe's reasoning skills and acute visionary powers. Hansson was the first critic to go to great length to attempt to find scientific corroboration for some of Poe's ideas, such as mental pathology, hypnotism, and multiple personalities. Echoing Baudelaire, Hansson concludes his study by remarking that Poe's work ''sends a shudder of pleasure through our marrow and bones'' (Anderson, 217). In Poe's tales, poetry, and essays, Hansson found confirmation of his own literary principles, the reassurance he needed to speak out against the dominance of naturalism in his country.

As Anderson points out, direct links between specific works of Poe and those of Scandinavian writers are difficult to confirm. The Swedish dramatist August Strindberg became interested in Poe through his friendship with Ola Hansson, whose correspondence with Strindberg reveals a shared enthusiasm for the American writer. Strindberg mentions in his letters several of his own works inspired by his reading of Poe, clues that scholars have investigated in hopes of discovering specific connections with Poe's work. The evidence as reported by Anderson (105–66) is scant, although a few similarities seem to be justified, such as the suggestion that the burial chamber scene in Strindberg's ''Samuum'' was inspired by ''The Black Cat'' and ''The Cask of Amontillado.''

Ola Hansson sent his Poe essay to a publisher in Berlin, aware that there was greater interest in the American writer in Germany than in his own country. Scattered publications of Poe's tales appeared in Germany in the 1850s, and, in 1860, Friedrich Spielhagen, the German Baudelaire, published a major study of Poe, whom he called ''the greatest lyric singer that America has produced'' (Smith, 7). The Romantic school in German letters had prepared the way for Poe's reception. Readers were especially familiar with the tales of E.T.A. Hoffman, with whom Poe is often compared. Although Poe has enjoyed great popularity in Germany, Bandy remarks that ''the main course of German literature was affected but little, if at all, by Poe'' (1962, 13). A notable exception is perhaps the poet Rainer Maria Rilke, whose themes of loneliness, uncertainty, and fear in modern man are reminiscent of Poe, whom he admired. Franz Kafka's use of the doppelgänger motif suggests close affinities with Poe, a subject Joseph Francavilla examines in psychoanalytic terms.

German interest in Poe has never diminished over the years, as can be seen by the constant flow of new editions and critical studies (Forclaz 1978, 49–55). A particularly important milestone in the long line of Poe publications is the four-volume, first critical edition of Poe's work in German, the result of eleven years of effort by some of Germany's best translators and scholars (Forclaz 1976, 24). Principal editor Schuhmann's goal was, according to Forclaz, to ''react against the image of Poe as a romantic genius which has always been current in Germany'' and show that ''Poe's originality does not lie in the invention of the plot, but in his treatment of the theme of a story'' (1976, 24). German speakers now have the opportunity to appreciate Poe in a new light.

During the past twenty years, scholars have documented Poe's influence and reputation in Serbo-Croatian, Hungarian, Romanian, and Czech literatures. Sonja Bašić discovered a veritable Poe cult among certain Serbo-Croatian writers, who translated "The Black Cat" as early as 1863. More than 200 translations of Poe's tales appeared in newspapers and magazines during the next century, along with nearly fifty Serbo-Croatian versions of his poems, among them "The Raven," translated fifteen times (Bašić, 305).

Serbo-Croatian literature also had its Baudelaire in the person of Antun Gustav Matoš (1873–1914), poet, critic, essayist, short story writer, and journalist, who found his double in the life and work of Edgar Allan Poe. Devoted to a purely aesthetic ideal of art that did not provide a living, Matoš had to resort to hack work and newspaper writing to survive at poverty level. Matoš's strong spiritual kinship with both Poe and Baudelaire is evident in his notebooks and in published essays, one of which states: "Read the life of E. A. Poe and you will become aware of the horrible struggle between literature and advertising, art and craft, writer and his public, between genius and the golden calf" (Bašić, 309). Like Baudelaire, Matoš discovered in Poe's work themes and techniques that inspired his own creative endeavors. Just to mention a few pointed out by Bašić, Matoš's "The Green Demon" deals with the destructive forces of alcohol and with cemeteries where people are buried alive, all recounted in the detached first-person narrative of "The Black Cat"; "Around Lobor" and "The House" include obvious similarities with "The Fall of the House of Usher"; and Matoš's sonnet "The Consoling Hair" draws its inspiration from "Lenore" (Bašić, 310–12).

While Matoš established Poe's reputation as a short story writer, the Serbian poet Svetislav Stefanović devoted his efforts to translating and commenting on Poe's poems. Stefanović and other Serbo-Croatian poets praised Poe for his attack on didactic literature, seeing his example as a liberating force opening the way for aestheticism and Symbolism. Poe's influence reached its height in Serbo-Croatian literature during the late 1800s and the beginning of the present century, led by A. G. Matoš and "The Modern School." After a forty-year decline in Yugoslavia, Poe's fame rose again in the 1950s, when new translators and critics working directly with the English brought Poe's work to public attention.

In Hungary, Poe was first introduced to readers by the 1858 translation of "The Raven," appearing in the *Budapest Review*. In 1862, a collection of eight tales launched his fame as a short story writer who would later be admired and imitated by numerous crime fiction authors. György Radó notes that Poe became popular in Hungary among readers of cheap editions of his stories and, at the same time, among the connoisseurs of fine literature (21). In 1895, the Hungarian scholar Zoltán Ferenczi edited a collection of forty Poe poems, which also included an introductory essay and copious notes. The high quality of the translations and the edition helped establish Poe's renown as a leading world poet. Hungary also had its own Poe fanatic, Arpád Pásztor, author of *How I Met Edgar A. Poe,* published during World War I. While on a sojourn to the United States to visit places where Poe had lived and worked, Pásztor claimed to have communed directly with the spirit of the dead poet (Radó, 22). On a more serious level, Poe influenced poets who contributed to the respected literary journal the *Nyugat* (The West), which published numerous translations of his poems. Hungarian writers and scholars paid their respects to Poe by commemorating the 1949 centenary of the poet's death with a new volume, *The Complete Poems by Poe,* which included poems that had been overlooked in earlier translations.

The reception of Poe in Romania has been documented by Thomas C. Carlson, whose exhaustive study adds many new sources to Aderman's earlier bibliography. T. Carlson points out that because of the long-standing cultural ties with France, Poe became known in Romania in the 1860s through French versions of his work ("Reception," 441). Poe's early reputation was based mainly on his poetry and literary essays. One of the most influential critics of the time, Titu Maiorescu, published a critical examination of Romanian poetry in 1867 in which he praised "The Raven" and "The Philosophy of Composition" as exemplary in the world of literature. Maiorescu's enthusiasm spread to other poets, including the future poet laureate Mihai Eminescu, who acknowledged an indebtedness to Poe's work. A generation of Romanian critics and Symbolist writers translated Poe's poems, the favorite being "The Raven," translated fourteen times between 1890 and 1915 (T. Carlson, "Reception," 442). The Poe cult in Romania continued into the twentieth century, when a new generation of post-Symbolist poets, including Tudor Arghezi, Lucian Blaga, George Bacovia, and Ion Barbu, recognized the American poet as the forerunner of Modernism.

The Czech mystery writer and literary researcher Josef Škvorecký claims that Poe is the most famous American author in Czechoslovakia. Škvorecký's research turned up some 200 Poe titles published in Czech between 1891 and 1954, among them twenty-five different translations of "The Raven." Poe's direct influence is evident in Karel Čapek's mystery story "The Imprint," which, according to Škvorecký, is patterned on the Dupin methods and uses motives from "The Murders in the Rue Morgue" (183). Škvorecký even goes so far as to attempt to prove that the story is a coded tribute to Poe.

A group of writers in northern Italy called the *scapigliati* (the unconventional) read Poe in Baudelaire's translations and became fervent admirers of the American author. Roberto Cagliero's research on Poe's influence on Italian literature has brought to light a number of themes from *The Narrative of Arthur Gordon Pym* found in the stories of Iginio Tarchetti (1839–1869), Emilio Salgari (1863–1911), and, most notably, Enrico Novelli (1876–1945). Publishing under the pen name Yambo, Novelli made extensive use of *Pym* in his own story "Manuscript Found in a Bottle," sold in a paper bottle when the text was first printed in 1905 (Cagliero, 8). The narrator claims to have found in a bottle the description of the protagonist's voyage in the dark hold of a ship. Saved by his dog, Lampo, the adventurer encounters a pestilence and ends up on a polar island on which all things are black and white. An escape from the hold of a vessel, again reminiscent of Poe's work, is found in a story by Luigi Motta (1881–1955), who makes frequent use of *Pym*'s motifs (Cagliero, 8). The most extensive study of Poe's influence on literary works in a foreign language is John E. Englekirk's 500-page *Edgar Allan Poe in Hispanic Literature*. The author recounts Poe's debut in Spain as rather puzzling. A revised version of "Three Sundays in a Week" appeared anonymously in a Madrid publication in February 1857, apparently translated directly from the English, since this story was not included in Baudelaire's 1856 collection, and the Spanish translation follows the original almost word for word. Although interesting from a historical perspective, this publication did not make Poe known in Spain. The following year, a Spanish translation of Baudelaire's 1856 collection of Poe tales appeared, and a major article by Pedro Antonio de Alarcón praised both Baudelaire and Poe, thus arousing readers' interest in his tales (Englekirk, 17–19). Another curious aspect of Poe's presence in Spain is the fact that for almost half a century he was little known as a poet. Englekirk's research turned up only two Spanish versions of Poe's poems, "The Conqueror Worm," translated in 1874, and "The Raven" in 1883 (19–20). The fact that the Spanish translators used Baudelaire's work as their source explains the prevailing interest in the tales, since Baudelaire translated only four of Poe's poems, including the two just mentioned.

Poe's direct influence on a Spanish writer is most evident in the works of Emilio Carrere, whose poem "El bardo maldito" (The Cursed Bard) sings of the solitary poet alone with his only friend, the raven (Englekirk, 422–23). A number of other poems show imitations of Poe's themes and poetic techniques in Carrere's collection *El caballero de la muerte* (The Knight of Death), where the Spanish poet translated Baudelaire's 1856 preface to the *Histoires extraordinaires*. Spanish poets Francisco Villaespesa, Juan Ramón Jiménez, and the Basque Pío Baroja also admired Poe's poems and were inspired by them, although to a lesser extent than Carrere (Englekirk, 442–50).

Poe's reputation on the Iberian Peninsula extended to Portugal, where Fernando Pessoa (1888–1935) found inspiration in Poe's biography and literary work. Pessoa considered himself a disciple of both Baudelaire and Poe, whom he mentions many times in his diaries (Monteiro, 136–37). Poe's influence on his poetry can be seen in the poem "Opiário," which evokes a Poe image in the concluding lines: "I'm caught in the Maelstrom, ever closer to the center./ Doing nothing at all is my perdition" (trans. Monteiro, 139). While similarities between his own sad life and Poe's inspired feelings of kinship, Pessoa also discovered views on literature that confirmed his own beliefs. Among Pessoa's papers, Monteiro found a note with the inscription "Poe. . . . A poem is a literary work in which sense is determined through rhythm" (141). The importance of music can be seen in the rejection of didactic elements in Pessoa's poetics. Like his predecessors Baudelaire and Mallarmé, whom he idolized, Pessoa paid tribute to Poe with a moving translation of "The Raven." In 1985, Pessoa's Portuguese version of Poe's most famous poem, along with translations by

Baudelaire and Mallarmé, was published in an oversized volume richly illustrated with paintings and lithographs by Júlio Pomar, one of the most important
Portuguese painters of the twentieth century (Cluny).

Poe's renown and influence in Latin America were even greater than in Spain.
Again, Poe had the good fortune of being discovered by a great poet, the Nicaraguan Rubén Darío (1867–1916), leader of the *modernista* movement. In
1893, Darío wrote a major article on Poe, "Los raros," first published in *La
Nación* in Buenos Aires and later in a collection of essays bearing the same
title. Describing the details of Poe's life, based mainly on Ingram's account
rather that Baudelaire's, Darío reveals his sympathy and spiritual kinship for the
American genius, in whom he recognized many similarities to his own life and
literary ambitions. The two poets shared a yearning for the ethereal woman of
their dreams as well as a fascination for the strange. Darío was brought up in
the ancestral home where his grandmother and the servants told stories of head-
less priests and tormented souls that made a strong impression on the young
poet (Englekirk, 171). Darío saw in Poe the supreme artist in the mysterious
regions of dreams and of death.

Darío read Poe's work in English and, in Englekirk's opinion, developed his
poetics through direct contact with the American poet rather than through the
French Symbolists. In a detailed analysis of several Darío poems, Englekirk
shows how the Nicaraguan poet imitates the repetitions, alliteration, inner
rhyme, and other effects he admired in Poe's poetry (195–210). Darío's enthusiastic adoption of the literary principles of Poe, Baudelaire, and Mallarmé had
a strong influence on his followers in the *modernista* movement.

The Colombian poet José Asunción Silva (1865–1896), by his temperament
and his art, identified with Poe, whose poems and essays helped him formulate
his own ideas on poetic technique, expressed in "Un poema." In this poem,
Silva describes the ideal poetic creation, which must be musical, evoke colors,
deal with a beautiful woman, and inspire a sense of magic in the reader. Poe
opened the way for the *modernista* poets to explore new realms of the poetic
universe, thus bringing fresh inspiration that was to produce some of the best
poetry from Latin America.

The Cuban poet Julián del Casal (1863–1893), considered a precursor of
Modernism, openly acknowledged his debt to Poe (Englekirk, 234). Many of
his poems reveal direct links to Poe or offer numerous points of resemblance
to his art, such as the poem "La Reina de la Sombra" (The Queen of Darkness)
evoking Poe's Eleonora. Fascinated by Poe's fantastic creations, his spiritual
women, and a preoccupation with death, Casal found both consolation and inspiration in a fellow poet who also suffered a tragic life that was to end prematurely.

After Darío, the Mexican poet Amado Nervo (1870–1919) is ranked among
the greatest of the *modernistas*. Nervo considered himself Poe's spiritual brother.
Like Poe, Nervo could not earn a living from his poetry and had to write prose
articles for the press early in his career. During this period, he wrote several

tales that were directly influenced by Poe. "The Sixth Sense" is told by a popular scientist who recounts in a realistic manner the human possibility of "seeing things that are beyond today" (Englekirk, 253). His most horrible of torments is foreseeing the languishing death of a beloved woman, a recurring theme in Poe's work.

Englekirk's study reveals Poe's direct effect on other Latin American *modernista* poets, including the Bolivian Ricardo Jaimes Freyre, the Argentine Leopoldo Lugones, the Uruguyan Julio Herrera y Reissig, and the Mexican Enrique González Martínez. The poet and short story writer Horacio Quiroga, claimed by both Argentina and Uruguay as their literary son, found inspiration in a number of Poe tales. The most striking example is Quiroga's story "El crimen del otro" (The Other's Crime), which was directly inspired by "The Cask of Amontillado." The narrator in Quiroga's work is so fascinated by Poe's story that he confuses his friend, whose name is Fortunato, with the characters in "The Cask of Amontillado." As Fortunato shows signs of becoming totally mad, the narrator leads him to a cellar, where he buries him in a well (Englekirk, 343–48). Quiroga's complete absorption in Poe's fiction inspired him to relive the tale in another context. Englekirk goes on to describe numerous other Quiroga tales that show direct links with Poe (348–68). As an outstanding Latin American short story writer, Quiroga and the Poesque spirit that inspired him were admired by the next generation of prose writers.

The Argentine Luis Borges (1899–1986) mentions Poe as one of the greatest inspirations for his own short stories. Maurice Bennett relates the occasions on which Borges expressed his indebtedness to Poe (1986, 107–8) and examines in detail the connections between "William Wilson" and Borges's "Deutsches Requiem." Although the opening line of the story, "My name is Otto Dietrich zur Linde," echoes Poe's "My name is Arthur Gordon Pym," the plot and narrative devices are borrowed from "William Wilson" (Bennett 1986, 108–13). In another study, Bennett examines the influence of Poe's Dupin tales on Borges's "Death and the Compass" (1983, 263–73), observing that "for both Poe and Borges, the detective story stands as a formal antithesis to the chaos of human experience" (265).

Poe was also the favorite writer of another Argentine, Julio Cortázar (1914–1984), who translated the American author's prose works into Spanish and was influenced by his essays on poetics and the novel. In two collections of Cortázar's stories, *Bestiario* (Bestiary, 1951) and *Final del juego* (End of the Game and Other Stories, 1956), Ana Hernández del Castillo examines the application of Poe's narrative technique and the use of Poesque themes, such as the monologue of the isolated madman, the fear of the returning double, and the supernatural.

The contemporary interest in Poe's short stories in Latin America can best be seen in the works of the Mexican writer Carlos Fuentes (b. 1928). Like Borges and Cortázar, Fuentes acknowledges his indebtedness to Poe and consciously incorporates elements from the tales into his own fiction. Susan and

Stuart Levine have brought to light numerous allusions to Poe in Fuentes's stories, beginning with the novelette *Aura,* in which the theme of reincarnation reminds the reader of Poe's "Ligeia" and "Morella." In *Cambio de piel* (Change of Skin), one of the main characters is nicknamed "Ligeia," and Fuentes cites the epigraph to Poe's story three times (Levine and Levine, 38). In his longest novel, *Terra Nostra,* Fuentes makes extended references to Poe's sea narratives. Fuentes's character the Peregrino describes his experience of being caught in a vortex in terms that seem to come straight from "A Descent into the Maelström" (Levine and Levine, 40). The contrast between black and white that becomes evident toward the end of *The Narrative of Arthur Gordon Pym* is also found in Part II of *Terra Nostra,* where Fuentes refers to the Poe story. The Levines conclude that Carlos Fuentes feels a spiritual and technical affinity for Poe, whose work he consciously incorporates into his own, thus making the twentieth-century reader see Poe in a new light.

Our study of Poe's influence and reputation abroad has taken us from Europe to the New World and now to the Orient, which is all the more intriguing because of the great cultural differences. In the Far East, the Japanese were the first to translate Poe and produce critical essays praising qualities in his work that would influence a generation of writers in Japan. Aeba Kōson's translations of "The Black Cat" and "The Murders in the Rue Morgue" in 1888 mark the beginning of a period of fascination with Poe as a short story writer. Through their lectures and essays, Ueda Bin and Lafcadio Hearn prepared the way for an appreciation of Poe's work among the writers and critics around the turn of the century (Lippit, "Tanizaki," 221). Hearn's lectures on Poe at the University of Tokyo in 1891 praised the American author's imaginative exploration of the mysteries of the human mind and the universe, and, most important, he emphasized Poe's rejection of didacticism and moral instruction in literature. Ueda Bin, translator and editor of a collection of Western poems, *Kaichōon,* described Poe's influence on the French Symbolists, thus inspiring interest in Poe's literary essays and poetry. By far, the major influence of Poe's work in Japan was on the short story writers who were determined to break with naturalism, which dominated the Meiji period (1868–1912).

Representing the most extreme case of Poe adoration in Japan is the mystery writer Harai Taro, who changed his name to Edogawa Rampo, an approximate Japanese pronunciation of Edgar Allan Poe. Born in 1894, Rampo arrived on the literary scene at the height of Poe's popularity in Japan. Among his many Western-style mystery stories are tales that were directly inspired by Poe, such as the crime stories "The Red Chamber," "Two Crippled Men," and "The Cliff." Although there are numerous direct imitations of Poe, James Ray King concludes from his analysis that Rampo's stories are "generally marred by a certain hollowness at the core, which is perhaps inevitable in works that are primarily the product of a clever manipulation of data" (199).

Other Japanese writers reveal more subtle effects of Poe on their work, among them Akutagawa Ryunosuke, Sato Haruo, Hagiwara Sakutaro, and Tanizaki Junichiro, all of whom recognized the important role Poe played in their writing. Noriko Lippit's in-depth study of Tanizaki and Poe brings to light many devices, techniques, and themes that the Japanese writer borrowed from Poe. Tanizaki's detective stories, "Gold and Silver," "The Criminal," and "An Incident at Yanagiyu," appear to be directly inspired by Poe's tales of ratiocination. Another Poe theme, the discovery of one's own perversity, is found in "A Story of Tomoda and Matsunaga," which deals with the double and doppelgänger. As one of Japan's major modern writers whose legacy is thirty volumes of his collected works, Tanizaki's acknowledged indebtedness to Poe has enhanced the American writer's reputation in the Far East.

Poe's influence and reputation in China came through Japan and France. During the 1920s, Poe was mentioned in Chinese literary periodicals as the "greatest 19th-century American writer," "an extraordinary genius," and the American who had the greatest influence on European literature (Ning and Stauffer, 155). Poe had the good fortune of being translated into Chinese by one of that country's most respected writers, Lu Xun, who discovered a copy of "The Gold-Bug" annotated in Japanese while studying medicine in Japan in 1903. He sent the tale to his brother Zhou Zuo-ren, who translated the story, calling it the "The Kidd Drawing," then changing the title to "The Story of a Jade-Bug" when it was published in 1905 (Ling and Stauffer, 156). The two brothers collaborated on *A Collection of Foreign Fiction,* published in Tokyo in 1909, which included Poe's "Silence." Although the two-volume edition did not sell well at the time, it was later reprinted in 1920 and 1924 in Shanghai, where it stimulated interest in Western writers and especially in Poe. Translations of Poe's tales, poems, and literary essays appeared under the signature of several Chinese writers in the 1920s, a period during which, according to Ning and Stauffer (158–59), old beliefs were being abandoned, and writers were rejecting didactic and utilitarian literary works.

As China's New Literature movement gained momentum in the 1920s, the short story became the genre par excellence. Poe's tales served as models, especially in the development of structural unity, in probing the psychological elements of the human mind and in the use of aestheticism, symbolism, and mysticism. One of the most striking examples of a prominent Chinese author who wrote under the spell of Poe is Li Jian-wu, whose story "The Last Generation of the Guan Family" (1926) appears to be a conscious imitation of "The Fall of the House of Usher." Poe's tales continued to exercise considerable influence on Li Jian-wu's fiction, in particular, "The Shadow" (1927), "The Last Dream" (1929), and "Before the Second Lover" (1930). Although Li Jian-wu's short stories show the most obvious connections with Poe, other Chinese writers of the period, especially Chen Xiang-he and Yu Da-fu, were also directly influenced by Poe's style and themes.

Chinese poetry was less affected by a knowledge of Poe, whose main influence came through his literary essays. Through contact with French literature and, to a lesser degree, with Japanese works, Chinese poets embraced basic tenets handed down through the symbolist movement, namely, that a poem is the rhythmic creation of Beauty and exists only for its own sake. Another idea that Poe emphasizes in "The Philosophy of Composition," the length of the ideal poem, which must be brief to preserve its unity, was taken very seriously by members of the Chinese New Poetry movement. When poet Wen Yi-do returned to China in 1925, after three years of study in the United States, he helped other poets initiate a new creative writing column in the *Beijing Morning Daily*. The poets were eager to experiment with new forms, syllables, and meters in an effort to break the stagnation of Chinese poetry. Wen Yi-do put his theory into practice by attempting to imitate in Chinese the musical effects of Poe's "The Bells." "The Raven," first translated in 1923, was rendered many times into Chinese by adherents of various literary groups, such as the Chinese New Poetry, the New Culture movement, and the Creation Society (Ning and Stauffer, 159–60).

When Valéry made the remark that "Baudelaire gave Poe's thought an infinite expanse" and "offered it to future generations," he probably did not realize, at the time, the extent to which Poe's work had already affected literatures as far away as Japan and China. Much of the research on Poe's influence abroad has been done in the past twenty years, and a great deal more remains to be accomplished. Pavnaskar's bibliography of Poe in India brings to light many works published in Hindi and other languages of the subcontinent, and Abdul-Hai has documented Arabic translations of Poe's poems (138). Detailed studies of Poe's reception in these major areas have not yet appeared. The "International Bibliography," published regularly in *Poe Studies,* shows evidence of scholarly activities on Poe in many foreign countries, especially in Italy and Japan, as well as in the United States. Tohru Nakamura has compiled an extensive bibliography of Poe studies published in Japan over the past eighty years. Patrick Quinn's *The French Face of Edgar Poe* was recently translated into Japanese, an indication that interest in Poe continues to be linked to France.

After Valéry's death in 1945, no other major French writer continued the Poe cult. Recently, Poe studies in France have been carried out by the late Claude Richard and other scholars, who have attempted to replace the image of Poe as Baudelaire's *poète maudit* by a more accurate portrayal of him as a lucid writer, critic, and literary theoretician. T. S. Eliot, in his famous essay "From Poe to Valéry," saw Baudelaire's translations as an improvement over the original, and Poe's literary theories as developed to maturity by Mallarmé and Valéry, whose concentration on form carried Poe's suggestions to their extreme limits. While recognizing Poe's great influence on modern poetry, especially through the Symbolist movement, Eliot believes that Poe's ideas have reached a dead end in the sense that the importance given to form over meaning in poetry can be carried no further. Eliot remarked in "From Poe to Valéry" that he was not sure whether Poe had an influence on his own work. In her essay on Eliot and Williams, Laura Jehn Menides suggests that Eliot's efforts to overcome numerous affinities with Poe are indeed manifestations of influence.

In the 1960s, Poe's tale "The Purloined Letter" became the focus of a major literary theory debate, initiated by Jacques Lacan's seminar on this story. All of the relevant texts were recently brought together in *The Purloined Poe*, edited by John P. Muller and William J. Richardson. Lacan's psychoanalytic interpretation challenged literary theorists and provoked a response from the French philosopher Jacques Derrida. Their opposing views inspired other critics to engage in a lively debate that seems less concerned with Poe and more preoccupied with the "act of analysis" and the "act of analysis of the act of analysis," as Barbara Johnson describes the exchange of views (Muller and Richardson, 213). In the same volume, Shoshana Felman argues that the contradictory judgments of Poe's poetry represent what she calls a "poetic effect," and the contradictions are "themselves indirectly significant of the nature of poetry" (134). She points out that the "impressive bulk of Poe scholarship, the very quantity of critical literature to which Poe's poetry has given rise, is itself an indication of its poetic power" (137).

Poe's worldwide importance established through years of influence is evident in the innumerable scholarly works published in many languages. Today, scholars continue to apply new critical approaches to Poe's work and to evaluate its far-reaching effects on foreign literatures. Through the Poe Studies Association, the *PSA Newsletter, Poe Studies,* and papers presented at the annual Modern Language Association and regional Modern Language Association meetings, new international scholarly activities dealing with Poe are documented each year.

For the first time, Poe's reception abroad has been treated extensively as part of his biography. In the final two chapters of *Edgar Allan Poe, His Life and Legacy,* Jeffrey Meyers describes Poe's reputation and influence in England, France, and Germany while mentioning his effect on Dostoevski and Kafka, among others. Beginning with an account of the Griswold controversy, Meyers moves on to show that Poe's literary achievements were recognized after his death by many writers and philosophers in Europe. A turning point in Poe's reputation in his own country was the 1875 memorial ceremony in Baltimore organized by Sara Sigourney Rice, who published statements about Poe's oeuvre from well-known literary figures in America and abroad. Although Meyers includes interesting anecdotes about Lincoln's and Stalin's fascination with the tales, his survey neglects Poe's pervasive influence in Eastern Europe, Latin America, and the Far East, except for a few brief references in his notes (324–34). On the other hand, his discussion of Poe's effect on British and American writers is very well presented. Meyers concludes that "though Poe has always appealed to popular taste, his originality and imagination have also had a considerable impact on the most advanced thinkers and most serious writers" (304).

The year 1995 marks the 150th anniversary of the first literal translation of Poe's work into a foreign language, "The Gold-Bug" into French in 1845. Before his death in 1849, Poe knew that a few of his tales had been translated into French. From a modest beginning, he has become the best-known American author throughout the world.

WORKS CITED

Abdul-Hai, Muhammad. "A Bibliography of Arabic Translations of English and American Poetry, 1830–1970." *Journal of Arabic Literature* 7 (1976): 120–50.

Aderman, Ralph M. "Poe in Rumania; A Bibliography." *Poe Newsletter* 3, no. 1 (1970): 19–20.

Alexander, Jean. *Affidavits of Genius, Edgar Allan Poe and the French Critics, 1847–1924.* 1971. Port Washington, N.Y.: Kennikat P, 1979.

Anderson, Carl L. *Poe in Northlight, The Scandinavian Response to His Life and Works.* Durham, N.C.: Duke UP, 1973.

Bandy, William Thomas. "New Light on Baudelaire and Poe." *Yale French Studies* 10 (1952): 65–69.

———. "Were the Russians the First to Translate Poe?" *AL* 31 (1960): 479–80.

———. *The Influence and Reputation of Edgar Allan Poe in Europe.* Baltimore: Cimino, 1962.

———. *Edgar Allan Poe.* Toronto: U of Toronto P, 1973.

Bašić, Sonja. "Edgar Allan Poe in Croatian and Serbian Literature." *Studia Romanica et Anglica Zagrabiensia* 21–22 (1966): 305–19.

Baudelaire, Charles. "Edgar Allan Poe, His Life and Works." Trans. Jean Alexander. Repr. in Alexander, *Affidavits of Genius,* 99–121.

Bennett, Maurice J. "The Detective Fiction of Poe and Borges." *Comparative Literature* 35, no. 3 (1983): 262–75.

———. "The Infamy and the Ecstasy: Crime, Art, and Metaphysics in Edgar Allan Poe's 'William Wilson' and Jorge Louis Borges's 'Deutsches Requiem.' " In Fisher, 107–23.

Bonaparte, Marie. *Edgar Poe: Sa vie, son oeuvre—Etude psychanalytique.* Paris: Demoel et Steele, 1933.

———. *The Life and Works of Edgar Allan Poe: A Psycho-Analytic Interpretation.* Trans. John Rodker. London: Hogarth P, 1949.

Bonnet, Jean-Marie, and Claude Richard. "Raising the Wind; or The French Editions of Edgar Allan Poe." *Poe Newsletter* 1, no. 1 (1968): 11–13.

Cagliero, Roberto. "*Arthur Gordon Pym*'s Influence on Italian Literature." *PSA Newsletter* 15, no. 2 (1987): 8.

Cambiaire, Célestin Pierre. *The Influence of Edgar Allan Poe in France.* 1927. New York: Stechert, 1970.

Carlson, Eric W., ed. *The Recognition of Edgar Allan Poe: Selected Criticism since 1829.* Ann Arbor: U of Michigan P, 1966.

———, ed. *Introduction to Poe, A Thematic Reader.* Glenview, Ill.: Scott, 1967.

———. *Critical Essays on Edgar Allan Poe.* Boston: Hall, 1987.

Carlson, Thomas C. "The Reception of Edgar Allan Poe in Romania." *Mississippi Quarterly* 38, no. 4 (1985): 441–46.

———. "Romanian Translations of 'The Raven.' " *PoeS* 18, no. 2 (1985): 22–24.

———. "Edgar Allan Poe in Romania, 1963–83: An Annotated Bibliography." *Bulletin of Bibliography* 44, no. 2 (1987): 75–81.

Chiari, Joseph. *Symbolisme from Poe to Mallarmé.* 1956. New York: Gordian P, 1970.
Cluny, Claude Michel, ed. *Le Livre des quatre corbeaux.* Paris: Editions de la Différence, 1985.
Cowley, Malcolm. "The Edgar Allan Poe Tradition." *Outlook* 149 (July 25, 1928): 497–99, 511.
Dameron, J. Lasley, and Irby B. Cauthen, Jr. *Edgar Allan Poe: A Bibliography of Criticism 1827–1967.* Charlottesville: UP of Virginia, 1974.
Dostoevski, Fyodor M. "Three Tales of Edgar Poe." Trans. Vladimir Astrov. Repr. in Carlson, *Critical Essays,* 77–78.
Dreiser, Theodore. *Letters of Theodore Dreiser.* Ed. Robert H. Elias. 3 vols. Philadelphia: U of Pennsylvania P, 1959.
Eliot, T. S. "From Poe to Valéry." *Hudson Review* 2 (1949): 327–42. Repr. in Carlson, *Recognition,* 205–19.
Englekirk, John E., Jr. *Edgar Allan Poe in Hispanic Literature.* 1934. New York: Russell and Russell, 1972.
Fisher, Benjamin Franklin IV, ed. *Poe and Our Times: Influences and Affinities.* Baltimore: Edgar Allan Poe Society, 1986.
Forclaz, Roger. *Le Monde d'Edgar Poe.* Berne: Herbert Lang, 1974.
———. "A German Edition of Poe." *PoeS* 9, no. 1 (1976): 24–26.
———. "Recent German Criticism." *PoeS* 11, no. 2 (1978): 49–55.
———. "Edgar Poe and France: Toward the End of a Myth?" Trans. J. Kelly Morris. Repr. in Fisher, 9–17.
Forgues, E.-D. "The Tales of Edgar A. Poe." Trans. Sidney P. Moss. Repr. in Carlson, *Critical Essays,* 41–49.
Francavilla, Joseph Vincent. "Double Voice and Double Vision: Doubling in Edgar Allan Poe and Franz Kafka." *DAI* 49 (1988): 1138A. State U of New York, Buffalo.
French, John C. *Poe in Foreign Lands and Tongues.* Baltimore: Johns Hopkins UP, 1941.
Grossman, Joan Delaney. *Edgar Allan Poe in Russia, A Study in Legend and Literary Influence.* Wurzburg: Jal-Verlag, 1973.
Hernández del Castillo, Ana. *Keats, Poe, and the Shaping of Cortázar's Mythopoesis.* Purdue University Monographs in Romance Languages 8. Amsterdam: John Benjamins B.V., 1981.
Hubert, Renée Riese. "The Other Worldly Landscapes of E. A. Poe and René Magritte." *Sub-stance* 21 (1978–1979): 69–78.
Hutcherson, Dudley R. "Poe's Reputation in England and America 1850–1909." *AL* 14, no. 1 (1942): 211–33.
Hyneman, Esther F. *Edgar Allan Poe: An Annotated Bibliography of Books and Articles in English 1827–1973.* Boston: Hall, 1974.
James, Henry. "Comments." Repr. in Carlson, *Critical Essays,* 81–82.
Karatson, André. *Edgar Allan Poe et le groupe des écrivains du "Nyugat" en Hongrie.* Paris: PUF, 1971.
Kemp, John C. *Robert Frost and New England.* Princeton: Princeton UP, 1979.
King, James Ray. "Richmond in Tokyo: The Fortunes of Edgar Allan Poe in Contemporary Japan." *Papers on Poe.* Ed. Richard P. Veler. Springfield, Ohio: Chantry Music P, 1972, 194–205.
Kronegger, M. E. "Joyce's Debt to Poe and the French Symbolists." *Revue de Littérature Comparée* 39 (1965): 243–54.

Lang, Cecil Y. See Swinburne.

Lawrence, D. H. "Edgar Allan Poe." *English Review* (Apr. 1919). Repr. in *The Symbolic Meaning: The Uncollected Versions of Studies in Classic American Literature.* Ed. Armin Arnold. Fontwell, Arundel, Sussex: Centaur P, 1962, 116–30. Repr. in Carlson, *Critical Essays,* 91–101.

Levine, Susan F., and Stuart Levine. "Poe and Fuentes: The Reader's Prerogatives." *Comparative Literature* 36, no. 1 (1984): 34–53.

Lippit, Noriko Mizuta. "Natsume Sōseki on Poe." *Comparative Literature Studies* 14, no. 1 (1977a): 30–37.

———. "Tanizaki and Poe: The Grotesque and the Quest for Supernal Beauty." *Comparative Literature* 29, no. 3 (1977b): 221–40.

Lloyd, Rosemary. *Selected Letters of Baudelaire, The Conquest of Solitude.* Chicago: U of Chicago P, 1986.

Lombardo, Patrizia. *Edgar Poe et la modernité.* Birmingham, Ala.: Summa, 1985.

Mallarmé, Stéphane. *Oeuvres complètes.* Ed. Henri Mondor and G. Jean-Aubry. 1945. Paris: Gallimard, 1961.

———. "Le Tombeau d'Edgar Poe." Trans. Doris G. Carlson. Repr. in Carlson, *Critical Essays,* 80–81.

Menides, Laura Jehn. "There, But for the Grace of God, Go I: Eliot and Williams on Poe." In Fisher, 78–89.

Meyers, Jeffrey. *Edgar Allan Poe, His Life and Legacy.* New York: Charles Scribner's Sons, 1992.

Monteiro, George. "Poe/Pessoa." *Comparative Literature* 40, no. 2 (1988): 134–49.

Muller, John P., and William J. Richardson, eds. *The Purloined Poe: Lacan, Derrida & Psychoanalytic Reading.* Baltimore: Johns Hopkins UP, 1988.

Nakamura, Tohru. "Poe in Japan—9: Bibliography 1978–1985." *Bulletin of College of General Education, Ibaraki University* 19 (1987): 159–70.

Ning, Shen, and Donald B. Stauffer. "Poe's Influence on Modern Chinese Literature." *UMSE,* new series, 3 (1982): 155–82.

Pavnaskar, Sadanand R. "Poe in India: A Bibliography, 1955–1969." *PoeS* 5, no. 2 (1972): 49–50.

Pollin, Burton R. *Insights and Outlooks, Essays on Great Writers.* New York: Gordian P, 1986.

Quinn, Patrick R. *The French Face of Edgar Poe.* Carbondale: Southern Illinois UP, 1957.

———. *Poe and France, The Last Twenty Years.* Baltimore: Enoch Pratt Free Library, 1970.

Radó, György. "The Works of Edgar Allan Poe in Hungary." *Babel* 12 (1966): 21–22.

Richard, Claude. "Poe Studies in Europe: France." *Poe Newsletter* 2, no. 1 (1969): 20–22.

———. *Cahier: Edgar Allan Poe.* Paris: Herne, 1974.

———. *Poe: Journaliste et critique.* Paris: Klincksieck, 1978.

Robinson, Fred Miller. "The Wizard Proprieties of Poe and Magritte." *Word & Image* 3, no. 2 (1987): 156–61.

Rubinstein, Esther Levin. "The Grotesque: Aesthetics of Pictorial Disorder in the Writings of Edgar Allan Poe and Isaac Bashevis Singer." *DAI* 45 (1984): 1116A. State U of New York, Albany.

Shaw, George Bernard. "Edgar Allan Poe." *Nation* (London), Jan. 16, 1909. Repr. in

Pen Portraits and Reviews. London: Constable, 1932, 231–38. Repr. in Carlson, *Critical Essays,* 86–90.

Škvorecký, Josef. "A Discovery in Čapek." *Armchair Detective* 8 (1975): 180–84.

Smith, C. Alphonso. *Edgar Allan Poe.* Indianapolis: Bobbs-Merrill, 1921.

Suvin, Darko, and Robert M. Philmus. *H. G. Wells and Modern Science Fiction.* Lewisburg, Pa.: Bucknell UP, 1977.

Swinburne, Algernon Charles. *The Letters of A. C. Swinburne.* Ed. Cecil Y. Lang. 3 vols. New Haven, Conn.: Yale UP, 1960.

Tarbox, Raymond. "Blank Hallucinations in the Fiction of Poe and Hemingway." *American Imago* 24 (1967): 312–43.

Valéry, Paul. *Leonardo, Poe, Mallarmé.* Trans. Malcolm Cowley and James R. Lawler. Ed. Jackson Mathews. Princeton: Princeton UP, 1972.

Vines, Lois. "Dupin-Teste, Poe's Direct Influence on Valéry." *French Forum* 2, no. 2 (1977): 147–59.

———. "Paul Valéry and the Poe Legacy in France." In Fisher, 1–8.

Whitman, Walt. "Edgar Poe's Significance." *The Complete Works of Walt Whitman.* Ed. Richard Bucke et al. 10 vols. New York: Putnam's, 1902, 1: 284–87. Repr. in Carlson, *Critical Essays,* 83–84.

Wilbur, Richard. "The House of Poe." Repr. in Carlson, *Recognition,* 255–77.

Wilson, Edmund. "Poe at Home and Abroad." *New Republic,* Dec. 8, 1926. Repr. in Carlson, *Recognition,* 142–51.

Woodbridge, Hensley C. "Poe in Spanish America: A Bibliographical Supplement." *Poe Newsletter* 2, no. 1 (1969): 18–19.

———. "Poe in Spanish America: Addenda and Corrigenda." *PoeS* 4, no. 2 (1971): 46.

Yarmolinsky, Abraham. "The Russian View of American Literature." *Bookman* 44, no. 1 (1916): 44–48.

25

Poe and the World of Books

GEORGE EGON HATVARY

POE'S USE OF BOOKS

Poe's fascination with books, sometimes with the mere promise of a title, is evidenced everywhere in his writings. The most notable example is the list of esoteric books in ''The Fall of the House of Usher,'' few of which Poe had probably ever seen but which he knew to be about demonic possession, fortune-telling, voyage into supernatural realms, vigil by the dead—all implying the spirituality of matter, hence of deep concern to Roderick Usher.[1] Nothing can better convey Poe's use of books primarily for the sake of his own art than this list of titles in ''Usher.''

Bookishness was in the air. As Margaret Alterton points out in her pioneering study, *The Origins of Poe's Critical Theory,* one way Poe assumed the *Blackwood's* manner in his magazine fiction was through a display of learning. It was ''not simply scholarship,'' Michael Allen explains in *Poe and the British Magazine Tradition,* ''or even an infusion of esoteric knowledge,'' but ''a combination of these with an appeal which may be comparatively sober or may approach charlatanry'' (34–35). The zest with which Poe adopted the learned manner is shown by his clinging to it even after the fashion had waned (Allen, 174–75). In ''The Purloined Letter,'' one of his last great stories, he still refers to Seneca, Rochefoucault, La Bougive (probably LaBruyère), Machiavelli, Campanella, Chamfort, Jacob Bryant, Virgil (indirectly), Crébillon, and the singer Catalani, with French and Latin phrases abounding and philosophical passages borrowed from H. B. Wallace forming parts of Dupin's discourse. Early in his career, while editor of *The Southern Literary Messenger,* Poe began his ''Pinakidia'' series—brief cullings largely about ancient lore, from such sources as Disraeli's *Curiosities of Literature,* Bielfeld's *Elements of Universal Erudition,*

Jacob Bryant's *Mythology, and Antediluvian Antiquities*—a type of writing that appealed to him strongly enough to pursue it, chiefly in his "Marginalia," to the end of his days.

What is noted here is Poe's apparent unconcern about seeing the original physical book from which he is quoting second- or thirdhand. Some of these books were unavailable to him even for consultation, and his personal library was poor. The vision we get of the narrator in "The Raven" with his "many quaint and curious volumes of forgotten lore" is not, alas, Poe's own reality. T. O. Mabbott, in an article in *Notes and Queries,* calls attention to the fact that when Poe owned a book, he was likely to want to sell it again, so he refrained from putting his name in it (much less the elaborate notations he speaks of in his "Preface to Marginalia," *M* 3, 1112–18) and that Poe's signatures Mabbott had seen in books were mainly forgeries. Mabbott can name "with some confidence" only four books owned by Poe: a Bible, Thomas Moore's *Irish Melodies,* H. B. Hirst's *The Coming of the Mammoth,* and the second volume of Ralph Hoyt's *A Chaunt of Life;* and he added six other, doubtful ones. Poe had, of course, more books than these at one time or another. Mary Gove Nichols's contemporary account of the Fordham Cottage mentions "pretty presentation copies" and the works of the Brownings "on a hanging bookshelf" (*AQ,* 509). Burton Pollin believes that for several years Poe probably owned Disraeli's *Curiosities,* Bielfeld's *Universal Erudition,* some of Bulwer-Lytton's novels, and Wallace's *Stanley,* as sources for his "Marginalia" (*P* 2, 110). To this list we may add the bound seventh volume of *Burton's Gentleman's Magazine,* containing three installments of Wallace's "Mems for Memory" series, from which he also borrowed extensively (Hatvary, 76). Poe no doubt made use of libraries wherever he could, such as those at the University of Virginia, West Point, and the Baltimore Atheneum (Campbell, "Poe's Reading: Addenda," 180); in New York, the Fordham University Library (*M* 1, 562), the Society Library, and the Mercantile Library. Professor Pollin has reminded me that the Duyckinck brothers had an extensive collection of books, which they probably invited Poe to use. There existed lending libraries as well, such as the one owned by Hocquet Caritat, but it is doubtful that Poe could afford to borrow books from them.

The first important assessment of Poe's reading was made by Killis Campbell in an article and its addenda, "Poe's Reading," which should be read in conjunction with two later essays by Campbell, "The Mind of Poe" and "The Origins of Poe," in *The Mind of Poe and Other Studies.* Campbell believes that Poe probably read "pretty carefully" some 400 books he reviewed or noted;[2] and we can be certain that he had a close acquaintance with the magazines and newspapers of his day. Among his contemporaries or near-contemporaries whom Poe read extensively, Campbell mentions Byron, Coleridge, Moore, Tennyson, Scott, Bulwer, and Dickens, together with Bryant, Longfellow, Hawthorne, Cooper, Irving, Simms and Willis on this side of the Atlantic. The list becomes sparser as it extends back in time, touching on Shakespeare, Milton, the Bible, and obvious classics in English, Continental, and ancient literature. Campbell concludes that, although Poe read widely, "much of his reading was either desultory or superficial."

Which brings us to the central point: Poe read not as a scholar, or even as a theoretical critic, but as a literary artist. He had a quick, grasping perception of essences, a keen eye for the quotable phrase. He used most of his reading toward his own creative ends—although, admittedly, he used much of it for his practical criticism—sometimes incorporating ideas, even passages, with such little change that we can speak of borrowing or, less politely, plagiarism.[3]

The investigation of Poe's sources provides a good index of his reading, although not necessarily of his firsthand or complete reading of a particular book. Campbell's conclusions about Poe's reading are based largely on a study of Poe's sources; these appear in "Origins of Poe," with an emphasis on some of the authors named earlier. It becomes evident once again how avidly Poe pored over compendia, encyclopedias, and the popular science and travel literature of his day—not to speak of the current magazine fare, always *Blackwood's*. As Campbell points out, the study of Poe's sources commenced right after his death, with the Ingram and Woodberry biographies (1880 and 1885, respectively) making the first "serious or systematic attempt" in this direction. Floyd Stovall's "Poe's Debt to Coleridge" (1930) is the first exhaustive modern study devoted to a single source; others have followed. Campbell's list of over fifty authors (or works) has been duly extended; many of them have been restudied, and new discoveries made. No one has done more in this area than Burton R. Pollin. Beyond his *Discoveries in Poe* (1970), containing a dozen of his chief source studies, his investigations have resulted in a large number of separate articles. In his edition of Poe's *Collected Writings,* sources receive major consideration, as they do in the Mabbott volumes.

POE'S RELATIONS WITH PUBLISHERS AND EDITORS

Poe is the author of eleven separate publications, counting "Valdemar" in its pirated London edition as *Mesmerism "in Articulo Mortis,"* but not counting magazine prospectuses. Three of these, namely, *Tamerlane, The Prose Romances,* and *Valdemar,* are pamphlets more than books; and *A Conchologist's First Book,* for which Poe merely sold the use of his name for fifty dollars, cannot be thought of as his. Poe's statement in a letter to Charles Anthon in 1844, "I have written no books," has caused some speculation, for by then he had published the 1831 *Poems, Arthur Gordon Pym,* and the two-volume *Tales of the Grotesque and Arabesque.* William Charvat, in *The Profession of Authorship in America, 1800–1870,* believes the statement "extraordinary" and attempts to justify it by quoting Poe's own evaluation of *Pym* as a "silly book" and by referring to Poe's original concept of the Folio Club, which was to present the tales with interspersed critical matter in order to disguise fiction in the then more respectable nonfiction form (87–90). But we need not go that far. Poe, in his long, impassioned letter, is asking Anthon to use his influence with

Harpers: Poe would like to publish his "Phantasy-Pieces" in five volumes so as to gain an appropriate reputation for starting a magazine of his own. He writes: "It has been my constant endeavour ... to ... draw attention to my exertions as Editor of a Magazine. Thus I have written no books and have been so far essentially a Magazinist" (*O* 1, 270). Making a distinction between collecting short pieces to make a book and sitting down to write one will clear up the difficulty. Even *Pym*, which, in the draft of an angry letter to William Burton, Poe calls, in fact, a "very silly book" (*O* 1, 130), began as a magazine serial.

At the same time, Charvat rightly calls attention to the dignity the word *book* connoted in the nineteenth century, the status that good paper, wide margins, unbroken type, finely tooled illustrations, and luxurious binding could bestow on an author. Poe himself speaks of the "absolute book" or "absolutely bound volumes" in his reviews; his unfulfilled desire to have a few copies of his *Tales of the Grotesque and Arabesque* printed on fine paper is a case in point.

Had Poe any money, he could have had his wish, for, in his time, authors often invested in, or even totally financed, their books—an arrangement we would consider vanity publication today. In his facsimile edition of *Tamerlane*, T. O. Mabbott doubts that Poe made any financial guarantee to his young publisher, Calvin Thomas; but the important Philadelphia firm Carey, Lea & Carey asked for $100 against possible loss before they were willing to publish Poe's *Al Aaraaf* volume (*O* 1, 20). Poe's foster father, John Allan, refused to put up the money, and *Al Aaraaf* was published by the small firm of Hatch and Dunning of Baltimore. In his facsimile edition of *Al Aaraaf*, Mabbott admits the possibility of "a guarantee of some kind" on Poe's part, but, in his edition of the *Poems*, he states flatly that *Al Aaraaf* was published "without subsidy" (98). However, it is well known that, at West Point, Poe enlisted his fellow cadets to subscribe to his 1831 *Poems*. Their disappointment in the volume Elam Bliss of New York produced for their $1.25 investment (which amounted to a total sum of $170 [Russell, 30–31; *PoeL*, 116–18]) is an interesting commentary on the author–publisher relationship of the time and on the concept of the "book" as discussed by Charvat.

Poe as a magazinist, even as a freelancer, had little trouble getting his works into print—for a pittance. Michael Allen notes that George R. Graham, who paid his contributors on a sliding scale from two to twelve dollars a page, usually paid Poe four (158). Poe, although part of him hankered after popularity, was basically an elitist who despised the masses and failed to recognize, as Allen says with insight, "the importance of an instinctive sympathy and identification with the audience in a popular writer" (165). Poe's correspondence with book publishers gives a vivid picture of his difficulties in getting a book published and his total inability to earn a living from his books.

Nineteenth-century publishers were no more hospitable to authors in whom they didn't see the promise of commercial success than their descendants are today. In fact, it is safe to say that Poe, with his magazine appearances and his name, would find a publisher more easily today—with an advance against royalties included. As Charvat sums up in his *Literary Publishing in America,* "Not a single literary work of genuine originality published in book form before 1850 had any commercial value to speak of until much later, and most of our classics were financial failures" (23; Walker, 8).

We have seen that Carey, Lea & Carey refused to publish Poe's poems without a guarantee; his stories fared no better at the firm. When, in 1834, J. P. Kennedy sent them Poe's "The Tales of the Folio Club," Henry C. Carey, although he promised Kennedy that "the book shall go to press at once" (*PoeL,* 142), ultimately declined it. Alexander Hammond has traced the intricate history of this "lost book";[4] here let us simply note that Carey's advice that Poe publish his stories first in magazines to bring his name before the public showed dubious wisdom on the part of a major publisher, for when, two years later, James K. Paulding approached Harpers with Poe's stories, they declined them because "the greater portion of them had already appeared in print." Harpers gave two further reasons for their decision: readers preferred novels to collections of stories, and Poe's writing was "too learned and mystical" (*PoeL,* 212).[5]

Two years later, Harpers published Poe's *Pym,* but the novel barely sold; and, in 1840, the Philadelphia firm now known as Lea & Blanchard, after trying unsuccessfully to withdraw from their contractual obligation, published Poe's *Tales of the Grotesque and Arabesque* in the favorite two-volume form of the period, but this work sold no better. The economic depression of 1837–1842 was, of course, a factor. Poe's one small success, with an earning of $120 from a book, came in 1845, when Evert Duyckinck selected twelve of Poe's stories, and Wiley & Putnam of New York published them as No. 2 in their "Library of American Books" series. No. 8, Poe's *The Raven and Other Poems,* had only modest sales, and, according to John W. Ostrom, Poe received only a few copies (5). For *Eureka,* Putnam paid Poe fourteen dollars and made him sign a note that, if sales did not cover expenses, he would repay this sum and that he would not ask for any more money (*O* 2, 369).

Ostrom estimates that Poe's total life earnings were $6,200, which came mostly from magazine work. From all accounts, it would appear that Poe was a good editor; his statement that, during his year at *Graham's,* the circulation of the magazine rose from 7,000 to 40,000 seems reasonable (*O* 1, 205–7). No doubt there are other factors at work, such as signs of economic recovery by the year 1841. Still, Charvat's statement that "the legend of his [Poe's] success as editor needs careful re-examination" (*Profession of Authorship,* 86) seems too harsh a judgment. Charvat, who sees Poe's lifelong hope to establish a magazine of his own as "dream work," questions "whether Poe was suited for the commercial magazine world at all" (85–86); but Poe's need to be "too learned and mystical" as a writer does not preclude an eye for commercial success when it came to evaluating the writing of others.

On the whole, Poe felt exploited by the proprietors of the magazines he worked for. Frank Luther Mott's observation that, prior to 1842, most American magazines could not afford to treat their contributors fairly (1: 504) applies to their editors as well, quite apart from the personal problems Poe encountered with T. W. White and William Burton.

There was always a personal element in Poe's relationship with his book publishers also, which, especially in light of their frequent rejections, may seem puzzling to the modern reader. In 1834, while Carey, Lea & Carey were considering Poe's tales, they sold one of them to the *Atlantic Souvenir* for fifteen dollars, a sum they sent through Kennedy to Poe. The story remained unprinted, but presumably Poe was allowed to keep the money. I. A. Walker, who, in the Introduction to his valuable collection *Edgar Allan Poe: The Critical Heritage,* gives an account of Poe's troubles with publishers, believes that, when Lea & Blanchard finally accepted Poe's tales, they perhaps "felt some responsibility towards the young author they had misled and disappointed over the past five years" (6). In 1836, Harpers, in rejecting Poe's tales, said they liked his criticism and would send him books to review; and it is possible that they accepted *Pym* two years later not only because Poe heeded the three points in their letter but also because they were favorably disposed toward him, having told Paulding that, if Poe "will lower himself a little to the ordinary comprehension of the generality of readers, and prepare a series of original Tales, or a single work, and send them to the Publishers, previous to their appearance in the 'Messenger,' they will make such arrangements with him as will be liberal and satisfactory" (*PoeL,* 193). But then in 1844, when Charles Anthon tried to interest them in Poe's "Phantasy-Pieces," they were negative because they had "complaints" against Poe (*PoeL,* 477). As we have seen, there was always the prominent interceder, with far more influence than the modern literary agent: Kennedy, Paulding, Anthon, Duyckinck—all well-wishers of Poe.

Editors and publishers figure importantly in Poe's literary quarrels, as might be expected. His lawsuit against Hiram Fuller, the editor, and Augustus W. Clason, the proprietor, of the *New York Evening Mirror* for printing an attack on him by Thomas Dunn English is a case in point. His quarrel with Cornelia M. Walter, editor of the *Boston Transcript,* over his lecture before the Boston Lyceum is another. The subject is large and intricate; the reader is referred to Sidney P. Moss's *Poe's Literary Battles* (1963) and *Poe's Major Crisis* (1970).

THE RECEPTION OF POE'S WORKS

Killis Campbell, making a study of contemporary opinion about Poe, concluded that he was best known in America as a caustic critic and story writer but not as a poet, until the appearance of "The Raven"; whereas abroad he was known almost exclusively as a poet and romancer (*Mind of Poe,* 37). Favorable reviews, which Poe often received even though his books sold poorly, contributed importantly to his growing international fame. But even sympathetic commentators often failed to understand Poe's work. L. F. Tasistro's laudatory review of *Tales of the Grotesque and Arabesque* provides a good example. Amid lengthy philosophizing about life, history, and literature, Tasistro praises Poe briefly for his ability to depict light and darkness in human nature but then comes to the curious conclusion that, if Poe is to be blamed for being "too sombre and fantastic, or [dealing] in too wild imaginings," the fault is with "the advanced state of our literature, which—the incidents of invention being somewhat exhausted—makes an author frequently turn to sentiment and metaphysics rather than description and adventure" (Walker, 126–28). Philip Pendelton Cooke's letters to Poe, written about the same time, move on a different level. In one, Cooke wants the drama of Ligeia's seizing Rowena's body to be more drawn out and suspenseful (Walker, 112), but, in his very criticism, he meets the author's mind directly—something Poe appreciated, judging by the fervent tone of his reply (*O* 1, 117–19).

Poe's stories were called trash as well, and there is something amiss in the whole reviewing establishment that encourages such wildly divergent utterances about the same work. The regional hostilities of the period that prevented Poe— not that he was blameless in this—from getting favorable reviews in the Boston area, the use of reviews as personal weapons, and Victorian squeamishness regarding certain violent subjects are well known. One wonders what nerves were touched, especially in British reviewers, who could admit Poe's technical mastery in such tales as "Murders in the Rue Morgue" or "The Black Cat" or "Usher" but needed ultimately to condemn them as hideous or revolting or juvenile (Walker, 34, 203). Across the Channel the response to Poe was more courageous and more intelligent. E. D. Forgue's long essay in *La Revue des deux mondes* (Walker, 205–19) set Poe's Continental reputation on its course of greatness.

THE COLLECTING AND RECORDING OF POE'S WORKS

Ever since book collectors became interested in American literature, Poe has been a star. In the pioneering Leon & Brother *Catalogue* of 1885, two of Poe's works, the 1831 *Poems* and the two-volume *Tales of the Grotesque and Arabesque,* were offered for twenty-five dollars each, just about the highest price asked for any book in that sale. "Our closest approach to Shakespeare, collectorwise, is Edgar Allan Poe," wrote John T. Winterich in *A Primer of Book Collecting* in 1926 (17), when prices began to soar. David A. Randall wrote in 1969, "The glamour boy of the American literary collecting scene is unquestionably Edgar Allan Poe" (*Dukedom,* 186). The reason is not hard to find. Poe's works had a compelling quality even for those who condemned them, and his life was easily the most enigmatic, the most fascinating of any American writer's, the bitter controversy set off by Rufus W. Griswold with his "Ludwig" obituary increasing the fascination and assuring its permanence. Perhaps most important, Poe's books were published in such small numbers of copies that they were always scarce, even when interest unearthed a few of them.

It is ironic—and ultimately logical—that the two publications that we can scarcely call books, *Tamerlane* and *The Prose Romances,* should be the rarest and therefore most sought-after Poeana, commanding the highest prices when-ever they have appeared. *Tamerlane* has, of course, the added glamour of a first. There is scarcely a work on book collecting that doesn't feature the story of *Tamerlane* findings. The beginnings of this pamphlet as a collectible Poe item are veiled in obscurity. Two years after its publication in 1827, it was listed in Samuel Kettell's Specimens of American Poetry; furthermore, Poe noted in *Al Aaraaf* (1829) that "Tamerlane" had been "printed for publication . . . but sup-pressed";[6] still, many doubted its existence, Richard H. Stoddard among them (Ingram list no. 692).[7] In 1874, Caleb A. Harris, a wealthy book collector, spoke to his friend Sarah Helen Whitman of having seen an allusion somewhere to a volume called *Tamerlane* (Miller, 192); six months later, Mrs. Whitman, writing to John Ingram in England, was able to ascertain *Tamerlane's* existence by citing Kettell (Miller, 242, 248). Meanwhile, Ingram discovered the first copy in a bale of pamphlets sent from America to the British Museum (Ingram list nos. 372, 692). In 1876, Mrs. Whitman wrote to Ingram: "[Mr. Harris] apparently envies you the sight of this little book" (Miller, 421). Apparently, Harris did. On learning two years previously that Mrs. Whitman had cut out the Preface and Index of her copy of Poe's *Tales and Poems* of 1846 to send to Ingram, "he opened his eyes in undisguised amazement & reproach that I recognized the infatuation of a book collector, as never before. 'This book—a gift from Poe—a presentation copy—containing his autograph—and I had cut out a leaf!!' " (Miller, 192).

   To return to *Tamerlane*. Through the following decades, a few more copies came to light: four by 1925, when Mrs. Dodd, a poor widow, saw Vincent Starrett's article, "Have You a *Tamerlane* in Your Attic?" in the *Saturday Evening Post* and produced a fifth. She sold it through the Boston bookseller Charles Goodspeed to Owen Young for $17,500 (Goodspeed, 201–7); from Young, it made its way to the Berg collection of the New York Public Library. By the time the Berg collection had its Poe Centenary Exhibit in 1949, the number of known *Tamerlane* copies had risen to eleven (Gordan). This number remained the same until 1974, when a copy at a Sotheby Park-Bernet auction was sold for $123,000 (Iacone, 25). In January 1990, the H. Bradley Martin Poe collection went up for auction at Sotheby's, and *Tamerlane* was sold to William Self for $165,000 (Omans, 3). Who doesn't think, at this point, of Poe's going hungry? Or shall we say, with Edward Newton, "No conceivable price is too high to pay for the first book of so great a genius as Edgar Allan Poe" (279)?

   The other pamphlet, less glamorous but even more rare, is *The Prose Ro-mances,* containing "Murders in the Rue Morgue" and "The Man Who Was Used Up." Published in 1843 by William H. Graham, George Rex Graham's brother, it was the first in an intended series. No more numbers appeared, and *Prose Romances,* usually referred to in works on book collecting as *Murders in the Rue Morgue,* vanished from sight. According to Winterich, it came up at an auction for the first time in 1901, when F. W. French's copy sold for $1,000. Writing in 1929, Winterich lists four known copies. One sold in the same year for $20,000 (*Books and the Man,* 264). In their *Census* (1932), Heartman and Rede list seven known copies. In the 1990 Sotheby auction, a copy was sold for $60,500. When T. O. Mabbott and I were preparing our facsimile edition in 1968, we tried to use the Owen Young copy in the Berg collection for our original, but J. D. Gordan, the curator, thought that copy too delicate to subject to photocopying; consequently, we used the one at the Library of Congress, with the added bonus that it is a presentation copy to Francis J. Grund, author of *Aristocracy in America.*

Even Poe's more common books are scarce in their first American editions— so scarce that, according to Richard Curle in *Collecting American First Editions,* "one may be thankful to find such works as *Arthur Gordon Pym, The Raven and Other Poems,* and the *Tales* of 1845 in English editions of the same dates." For, as Curle points out, *The Raven* and the *Tales* are but the American sheets with English title pages and binding; whereas *Pym* is a different book, with Pym's diary ending not on March 22, as in the American edition, but on March 21. "Therefore value is justifiable, even apart from the special magic of Poe's name" (184–85).

This magic has made presentation and other association copies especially valuable. In 1924, at the important Wakeman sale, *The Raven and Other Poems* and the *Tales* of 1845 bound in one volume, which Poe had inscribed to Elizabeth Barrett [Browning], were sold for $4,200. Newton, writing in 1928, says the book "would bring $10,000 today" (280). Two years later, Curle reported that W.T.H. Howe, the purchaser, had been offered $25,000 for it. The presentation copy of the same work to Mrs. Whitman, which she, in turn, inscribed to C. F. Harris, was sold at the Wakeman sale for $2,600; at the 1990 Sotheby auction, it was sold for $71,500. Even more spectacular is the rise in value of the first volume of *Tales of the Grotesque and Arabesque,* containing Poe's elaborate revisions and his change of the title to "Phantasy-Pieces"—intended, according to the Wakeman catalog, for Charles Dickens to give to an English publisher. The book was sold at the Wakeman sale for $3,400. In the 1990 Sotheby auction, it was sold for $130,000 (Omans, 3).

Manuscripts are not our present subject, but we may note in passing that Poe's have always commanded a high price, although they are by no means scarce. At the Jerome Kern sale in 1929, for example, a letter by Poe containing Elizabeth Barrett Browning's opinion of "The Raven" was bought by W.T.H. Howe for $19,000 (Randall, *Dukedom,* 5). In the 1990 Sotheby auction, some letters by Poe were sold for over $30,000 each. Then there is the famous story of the manuscript of "Murders in the Rue Morgue," which survived fires and discardings and was ultimately bought by Richard Gimbel for over $100,000 (Randall, *Dukedom,* 192–94).

The systematic recording of Poe's works was first undertaken by John H. Ingram. His correspondence with Mrs. Whitman, as presented by John Carl Miller in *Poe's Helen Remembers,* shows vivid glimpses of Ingram groping in the dark, working on conjectures, writing to Mrs. Whitman in November 1874,

"Mr. Neal's evidence would seem to support the idea of an 1827 edition of the poems" (230); trying desperately to see Poe's publications just to be able to write about them (200, 284); finally, after discovering the first *Tamerlane* himself (395), producing his first bibliography (442–48). It includes only Poe's four volumes of poems, and it contains some errors—Ingram readily accepted at face value Poe's statement that *Tamerlane* had been "suppressed" and that *Al Aaraaf* had been published for private circulation. Nevertheless, it is a carefully detailed work, an early fruit of the somewhat eccentric, possessive love that Ingram bore Poe.

Ingram's more extensive bibliography, included in his two-volume *Life* of Poe (1880), led the way to a series of scholarly ones forming a progression of detail and discovery. George E. Woodberry, in the last volume of the Stedman–Woodberry *Works* (1894–1895), lists only book publications, with their reprints, in America and abroad; James A. Harrison, in volume 16 of his *Complete Works* of Poe (1902), gives magazine publications also, although his list is incomplete; Woodberry in his two-volume *Life* (1909) gives the magazine publications of Poe's tales and poems only. Killis Campbell's bibliography in the second volume of *The Cambridge History of American Literature* (1919) is the most extensive one to date, locating such tales as "X-ing a Paragrab," "The Sphynx," "Von Kempelen's Discovery," and "Landor's Cottage" for the first time and providing an exhaustive list of secondary sources.

Poe has always figured prominently in checklists prepared primarily for collectors and dealers, such as Patrick Foley's *American Authors, 1795–1895* (1897; with a preface by Walter Leon Sawyer incorporating a little fantasy about seven "enraptured dreamers" finding copies of *Tamerlane* in a bookshop and buying them for five cents a piece), and its successor, Merle Johnson's *American First Editions* (1929; with later revisions by Jacob Blanck to 1942). Dealers' lists, such as the early influential Leon & Brother *Catalogue* (1885), with its jubilant preface about American collectors developing a taste for American books, and the less detailed H. S. Stone's *First Editions of American Authors* (1893), include many Poe items, but selectively. They are useful, nevertheless, for the historian of Poe collecting, as are catalogs of auctions and exhibits, for their descriptions and illustrations. Those issued for the Charles B. Foote sale at Bangs & Co. (1894), the Frank Maier sale at the Anderson Galleries (1909), the Stephen H. Wakeman sale at the American Art Association Galleries (1924), the Paul Hyde Bonner sale at Dutton's (1931), the Poe Centenary Exhibit at the Berg collection (1949), and the exhibit from the collections of Richard Gimbel and H. Bradley Martin at Yale University (1959) are especially interesting. A copy of the Wakeman auction catalog at the New York Public Library has sale prices recorded by hand; generally, prices for particular auctions are available in the *American Book-Prices Current* series.

In 1932, there appeared the first Poe bibliography in book form, Charles F. Heartman and Kenneth Rede's *A Census of First Editions,* in two thin volumes. The title alone reveals that, as T. O. Mabbott noted in his review in *American*

Literature, "our authors have used a collector's rather than a purely scholarly standard." Heartman was, in fact, a bookseller who had sought the collaboration of the young Poe scholar, Kenneth Rede—much to his later dissatisfaction (*Concerning a Poe Bibliography*). Mabbott, although raising "objections" and making "corrections," nevertheless expressed "gratitude for a great amount of really useful and often novel information."

In 1934, John W. Robertson published *A Bibliography of the Writings of Edgar A. Poe;* it, too, concentrated on first editions, and it included a psychoanalytical interpretation of Poe in the second part. "Practically useless" for collectors and dealers, as David A. Randall declared in *Publishers Weekly,* the work was attractive and printed in a large-enough edition to make its way to library reference shelves.

Meanwhile, Heartman, having discarded Kenneth Rede, was working with James R. Canny on a new Poe bibliography. T. O. Mabbott was being consulted, and he read the work in proof, although without getting Heartman always to agree with him. One instance is Heartman's refusal to accept a paper-covered *Raven* as the first issue. He believed the first issue was bound in cloth. When Heartman and Canny's *Bibliography of First Printings of the Writings of Edgar Allan Poe* appeared in 1940, limited to 350 copies and dedicated to T. O. Mabbott, Randall blasted it in *Publishers Weekly,* calling it "amateurish, inaccurate, speculative," charging that the authors "gaily build up theories . . . at absolute variance with the facts." What particularly angered Randall was Heartman and Canny's insistence that *The Raven* and *Tales* were first issued in cloth. They could not have been, Randall retorted, marshaling his evidence—convincingly, we might add.

Heartman's rebuttal, which he printed as a four-page pamphlet,[8] is illuminating. The issue of the battle was money. The booksellers whom Randall spoke for "have been selling copies in wrappers for 1,000, 1,500 bucks." But why had *Publishers Weekly* printed Randall's attack instead of providing a forum for his and Heartman's disagreement? Because they resented "my severe criticism of Merle Johnson's book"—Johnson apparently being a *Publishers Weekly* protégé. "I detested this commercial bibliographer because of his prostitution of the First Edition game, his notorious point faking, forging of errata and insert slips."

Heartman and Canny published their revised and expanded edition in 1943, again dedicating the volume to Mabbott. Many of the mechanical errors were corrected, but the authors stood by their basic convictions. Mabbott, reviewing the work in the *New York Herald Tribune,* speaks of a "great many virtues . . . and some faults. . . . The authors have but slight interest in the literary side of bibliography, but they make no pretentions to it." Mabbott, who has amplified Randall's argument about the wrappers, praises Heartman for printing "my statement of disagreement with him." Mabbott concludes, "The amount of new information is very large and the contribution to our knowledge of Poe is gratifying." Consequently, in his edition of the *Poems* and *Tales,* he makes frequent references to Heartman and Canny and notes in the third volume, "In spite of the errors that remain in the revised edition, this work is invaluable for the student of the works of Poe" (1406).

In 1983, there appeared the seventh volume of the Jacob Blanck *Bibliography of American Literature,* a project hailed by Randall at the time of its inception in the 1950s as "monumental" (*Dukedom,* 344). Compiled after Blanck's death by Virginia L. Smyers and Michael Winship, the volume includes Poe, with just the kind of meticulous and unbiased attention paid to points—variations in printings within an edition, especially—that is of value to collectors, dealers, and libraries. Scholars, too, benefit, as Kent Ljungquist has noted, in having a corrective to the errors in Heartman and Canny (*ALS* 1986, 44). Yet, the difference between the aims of bibliophiles and scholars that we have witnessed remains. Some years previously, G. Thomas Tanselle, making an otherwise judicious evaluation of the state of Poe bibliography in *Poe Studies* (1969), wrote: "Fortunately collectors and scholars are increasingly recognizing the fact that their interests and needs, far from being divergent, actually coincide. Scholars are beginning to understand the importance of bibliographical analysis in the establishment of texts, and collectors are beginning to recognize the significance of printings later than the first." No doubt. But consider Randall's own amateurishness when it comes to writing about Poe. In his *J. K. Lilly Collection of Edgar Allan Poe* (1964), he speaks of Poe's dedicating *Al Aaraaf* to the West Point cadets "much to their amusement" (3), whereas the cadets were indignant over the inferior quality of the book they had subsidized—a fact already known to Woodberry. In another place, Randall says, "Griswold's vitriolic sketch silenced most American supporters except Sarah Helen Whitman" (2), failing to mention Graham or Willis or Neal. Mrs. Whitman's defense, in fact, came later, after Griswold's death, for, as Miller suggests, she was afraid of Griswold (xxvii). But Randall's worst error in light of his bibliographical expertise is a failure to distinguish between the publisher of *Graham's Magazine,* George Rex Graham, and his brother William H. Graham, publisher of Poe's *Prose Romances* (10). In the chapter on Poe, in Randall's *Dukedom Large Enough* (1969), such errors reappear verbatim.

POSTHUMOUS EDITIONS

The posthumous editions of Poe's works begin with Rufus W. Griswold, whom Poe, according to his mother-in-law, Mrs. Clemm, had appointed as his literary executor. Griswold, putting aside the rancor that had led him to write his calumnious "Ludwig" obituary about Poe, did a quick but competent job, using whatever Mrs. Clemm could give him—magazines, books (though not the famous J. Lorimer Graham copy of the 1845 *Tales* with Poe's autograph corrections made as late as 1849), as well as manuscripts. Two volumes of the *Works* appeared early in 1850, the third in the latter part of 1850, and the fourth in 1856.

The Griswold edition underwent many reprints, and it formed the basis for future collections through the remainder of the century. But when Ingram published his four-volume *Works* of Poe in 1874–1875, he was able to add new material from various magazines, including two volumes of the *Broadway Journal* that Mrs. Whitman had sent him, which were then incorporated into future American editions. In the exhaustive bibliography in his *Edgar Allan Poe: Journaliste et Critique,* Claude Richard calls attention to the fact that, notwithstanding its shortcomings, the Ingram edition formed the basis for most subsequent English collections, as well as translations (648). It is, of course, selective, as is R. H. Stoddard's six-volume *Works* of Poe (1884), distinguished only by its attractive format; or the ten-volume Stedman–Woodberry *Works* (1894–1895), in which the poems under the aegis of Woodberry are collected independently of Griswold and supplied with variants.

In 1902, James A. Harrison published Poe's *Complete Works* in seventeen volumes, the "Virginia Edition," which was to serve as the standard scholarly edition of Poe for the next sixty years. It is not exactly complete, with two "Marginalia" installments and other pieces missing, which, however, appear in Harrison's not very precise bibliography; more important, Harrison and R. A. Stewart, who prepared the textual notes, did not have access to the manuscripts and printed versions that later editors, most notably Mabbott, were able to examine and collate. The "Virginia Edition" was a great achievement, but Poe scholarship had outgrown it.[9]

Through the first half of the twentieth century, interest in Poe's poems took precedence; scholarly editions by J. H. Whitty, Killis Campbell, and Floyd Stovall appeared in 1911, 1917, and 1965, respectively. Meanwhile, Campbell published Poe's *Short Stories* in 1927, and Arthur H. Quinn and Edward H. O'Neill published their two-volume collection of the poems, stories, and selected criticism in 1946. In 1948, there appeared John Ward Ostrom's important two-volume edition of Poe's letters; it was supplemented in 1966.

During much of this time, T. O. Mabbott was at work on his projected Poe edition, the first volume, *Poems,* appearing in 1969, shortly after his death. The work had been his life; it was as if the publication had been an anticlimax he no longer cared to see. Two more volumes appeared, *Tales and Sketches,* in 1978, completed by Mabbott's widow, Maureen C. Mabbott, and his editor at the Harvard University Press, Eleanor D. Kewer. The project had meanwhile passed on to the editorship of Burton R. Pollin, with the general title *Collected Works* becoming *Collected Writings.* Pollin has brought out four volumes thus far: *The Imaginary Voyages* (1981, 1988), *The Brevities* (1985), and *Writings in The Broadway Journal* in two volumes (1986). Since Pollin received Mabbott's papers and sought, in his work, to preserve something of the spirit of Mabbott's, it is convenient to speak of the two successive projects as a yet unfinished single edition.

No one has tried to deny the profound scholarship of the two editors. Mabbott's is legendary; and, in a review of the *Broadway Journal* in *Poe Studies,*

Patrick F. Quinn speaks of Pollin's "investigative powers" as "probably unmatched by any other Poe scholar." There are, nevertheless, differences between the commentaries of the two editors: Pollin tends to refrain from Mabbott's occasional subjectivism, and he strikes a more contemporary tone. Even Mabbott's admirers have recognized that his glosses are sometimes excessive, elementary, sometimes "verging on the absurd," as J. Albert Robbins writes in a review of the *Poems* in *American Literature.* "For the second line of 'Annabel Lee,' Robbins goes on to say, "we are told that 'Most kingdoms have seacoasts.' " Working at one time with Tom, I made my not always successful attempts to get him to eliminate some glosses; but no power on earth could have deepened his critical insights. Possibly, as Joseph J. Moldenhauer suggests in a review of the *Tales and Sketches* in *Poe Studies,* the edition "would not suffer" by the elimination of even the limited amount of criticism it contains. Claude Richard, who calls Mabbott's erudition in the poems "quelquefois inutile, et même par moments, gênant," considers the criticism "assez superficielle" (*Poe,* 694).

But Richard also writes, "Textes et notes bibliographiques sans fautes," which is worthy of note in light of the severe criticism leveled at Mabbott by textual specialists such as Moldenhauer. Before we turn to their argument, let us note that the Mabbott–Pollin editorial policy has been to select a copy-text that reflects most convincingly Poe's final intentions. This seems, in the majority of cases, to be the Griswold edition, with such notable exceptions as the Lorimer Graham copy of the 1845 *Tales,* which Griswold had not seen. Mabbott writes in a note: "I have at one time or another seen . . . every known manuscript of a poem or story" (1: xx). These, together with printed texts, whether read in proof by the author or not; printed texts showing the author's corrections; and transcripts of now lost manuscripts and printed texts, have all been collated carefully, with the variants recorded. Harrison had a deep mistrust of Griswold, which extended to his edition, and there have been some questions raised as to the primacy of Griswold's texts. It is gratifying to note that Pollin was able to demonstrate their reliability through Poe's idiosyncratic use of the diaeresis (cf. cöexist instead of coëxist), which made its way into the Griswold edition (2: xxxviii–xxxix).

All this is of secondary importance to Moldenhauer, who argues in his review of the *Tales and Sketches* that Mabbott should have used the Greg–Bowers method of critical editing, hinting strongly, if parenthetically, that the undertaking should have been a "team effort" to begin with, as exemplified by the editions of several other nineteenth-century American authors being prepared in our time. As prescribed by W. W. Greg and Fredson Bowers in their articles in *Studies in Bibliography,* the team of scholars do not look for a text reflecting the author's final intentions. They begin with the original manuscript, or as close to it as possible, and emend from later authorial corrections. Their copy-text therefore is a composite one, hence, "critical." The advantage gained is the greater preservation of the author's original accidentals (punctuation, spelling, and so on). In every volume of the Northwestern–Newberry Melville edition, the unsigned "Note on the Text" states: "The fact that he [the author] does not alter certain accidentals which were not his own but were changes made by the copyist, publisher, or compositor does not amount to an endorsement of those accidentals."

A debatable assumption, no matter how often repeated. Acceptance is not endorsement generally, but, in the creative process, it often is. Writers are sensitive to suggestion; they might conceivably prefer the copy editor's or compositor's addition or deletion of a comma. The team of posthumous editors will never know. They are committed to adhere to the author's original intentions. Fortunately, this applies mostly to accidentals—rather little.

A vast amount of money has been granted to these superprojects, scholars mobilized, the CEAA (Center for the Editions of American Authors) and its successor, the CSE (Center for Scholarly Editions), an MLA arm, magisterially bestowing "approved text" designations. In *A Companion to Melville Studies,* G. Thomas Tanselle eloquently defends the institution, protesting that it is not "oppressively monolithic" (816), but let the editions speak for themselves. They are mausoleums. After opening one of these black, austerely flat-spined Melville volumes, with the Greg–Bowers textual credo duly recited in it, one turns to the Mabbott–Pollin edition with renewed pleasure. "How different," Robbins writes in his review, "from the latter-day antiseptic, characterless editions produced by teams of scholars and carrying the official seal of editorial conformity!"

Moldenhauer wonders whether Mabbott was even aware of the new method emerging around him. He certainly was. The Hawthorne Centennial Edition was already in progress; we talked about it. But Mabbott disliked the collectivization; he chose not to conform. Donald B. Stauffer, commenting on *Tales and Sketches,* attests to the fact that "Mabbott saw and collated the revisions in over 50 more manuscripts and versions of the tales than Harrison had access to (*ALS* 1978, 30). Yet, Moldenhauer concludes that "in some fundamental respects, all turning on the copy-text philosophy, [Mabbott] makes a regression from Harrison and from Quinn and O'Neill" ("Mabbott's Poe," 46). In eight years, this textualist seems to have grown less militant. In reviewing Pollin's *Brevities,* again in *Poe Studies,* his tone is milder; he is willing to concede that the volume "has borne an abundant success" (50). Elsewhere, surprisingly, he refers the reader to Hershel Parker's *Flawed Texts and Verbal Icons* "for a vigorous questioning of whether the standardized editorial methodology should be applied to works heavily revised after the initial publication" (48). A mild retraction?

For the general reader, two recently published Poe volumes in the Library of America series have been highly recommended: *Poetry and Tales,* edited by Patrick F. Quinn, and *Essays and Reviews,* edited by G. R. Thompson. Since the innumerable single-volume selections of Poe, designed both for the general reader and for classroom use, concentrate more on the poems and tales, the *Essays and Reviews* is probably the more needed contribution.[10] The same can be said for F. C. Prescott's *Selections from the Critical Writings* of Poe, reissued recently with a New Preface by J. Lasley Dameron and a New Introduction by Eric W. Carlson.

SECONDARY STUDIES

Secondary studies, beginning with Baudelaire's "Edgar Allan Poe" in the *Revue de Paris* (1852) and Mrs. Whitman's *Edgar Poe and His Critics* (1860), have proliferated in such numbers both in America and abroad that we cannot hope to do full justice to them here. Two book-length, annotated bibliographies are useful: one prepared by J. Lasley Dameron and Irby B. Cauthen Jr., covering the years 1827 to 1967; the other by Esther F. Hyneman, listing works only in English but better categorized and extending to 1972. These are supplemented by the fully annotated bibliographies appearing annually in *Poe Studies,* the annual MLA bibliography, and the brief bibliographical and critical comments in the annual *American Literary Scholarship.* Thematic or specialized bibliographical essays appear also from time to time, such as Benjamin Franklin Fisher IV's "A Ten-Year Shelf of Poe Books" (1982) and Eric W. Carlson's two-part "Poe: New Editions" and "Poe: New Critical Studies" (1988) in *ANQ* (1988).

For fifty years—to Kenneth Silverman's *Edgar A. Poe* (1991)—the standard biography has been Arthur Hobson Quinn's *Edgar Allan Poe;* it is sentimental about Poe, weak in criticism, but factually solid. Dwight Thomas and David K. Jackson's *Poe Log* (1987) is not only a biographical supplement and corrective but an indispensable tool for any work on Poe. Similarly useful is Walker's *Critical Heritage* mentioned earlier. In the area of criticism, such older works as Patrick F. Quinn's *The French Face of Edgar Poe* (1957) and Edward H. Davidson's *Poe: A Critical Study* (1957) are still read. More recently, there have been a number of interesting studies written about Poe, but to name even a few of them would be unfair to the others. Commentary on Poe through the past 150 years is well represented by Carlson's two collections, *The Recognition of Edgar Allan Poe* (1966) and *Critical Essays on Edgar Allan Poe* (1987). The Introduction to the latter gives a concise history of Poe criticism, offering a good starting point especially for those interested in various approaches to Poe such as romantic irony, transcendentalism, Jungian psychology, and Gnosticism and in contemporary trends such as structuralism and deconstructionism as applied to Poe.

Because he was a critic, because he was a magazinist, Poe, more than any other major nineteenth-century American writer, moved in a milieu of books. In addition, as we have seen, he particularly responded to the idea of learning, both as a value and as glamor, which his age welcomed or at least tolerated in imaginative works. Learning not only embellishes but sometimes forms the texture of Poe's writings. Inevitably, Poe's interest in books, with their special aura, is reflected in much of what has been written, and will yet be written, about him.

NOTES

1. T. O. Mabbott discusses Usher's books in his edition (2: 419–21). See Barton Levi St. Armand's "The 'Mysteries' of Edgar Poe" for a reading of "Usher" as an initiation into Egyptian mysteries, with the titles of Usher's books constituting an esoteric guide.

2. Many of these were trivial, as W. H. Auden emphasizes in his Introduction to the Rinehart edition (xiii). But whether they had a limiting effect on Poe's critical powers, as Auden claims, is debatable.

3. Poe's eagerness to accuse others of plagiarism, most notably Longfellow, is well known. Was he so egocentric as not to recognize the same "sin" in himself, or was it all a game with him? The question might bear some psychological probing.

4. See also Claude Richard, "Les Contes du Folio Club," and Sybille Haage.

5. Eugene Exman, favoring the Harper brothers far more than Poe, calls this letter by Wesley Harper "skillful and sympathetic" (80).

6. T. O. Mabbott, in his facsimile edition of *Tamerlane* (1941), interprets "suppressed" as a euphemism for "had no real circulation."

7. As noted in Works Cited, John E. Reilly's revision of Miller's "Ingram List" was published in 1994 by the UP of Virginia.

8. Listed in the Library of Congress catalog as *Concerning a Poe Bibliography* . . . by C.F.H. It can be seen at the New York Public Library, tipped into a copy of Heartman and Canny's 1943 edition.

9. For a description of the early editions of Poe, see Floyd Stovall's Introduction to the 1979 AMS reprint of the Harrison edition.

10. See Pollin's review in *Poe Studies,* with its list of errors in *Essays and Reviews.*

WORKS CITED

Allen, Michael. *Poe and the British Magazine Tradition.* New York: Oxford, 1969.

Alterton, Margaret. *The Origins of Poe's Critical Theory.* 1925. Rpt. in New York: Russell, 1965.

American Book-Prices Current. New York: Dodd et al., 1895–   .

Auden, W. H. Introduction. *Edgar Allan Poe: Selected Prose and Poetry.* Ed. Auden. New York: Rinehart, 1950, v–xvii.

Baudelaire, Charles. "Edgar Allan Poe, sa vie et ses ouvrages." *Revue de Paris* (Mar.– Apr. 1852); Ed. W. T. Bandy. Toronto: U of Toronto P, 1973.

Blanck, Jacob. *Bibliography of American Literature.* 7 vols. to date (1990). Vol. 7 comp. Virginia L. Smyers and Michael Winship. New Haven, Conn.: Yale UP, 1955–   .

Bonner, Paul Hyde. *Sale Catalogue of the Private Library of Paul Hyde Bonner.* New York: Dutton, 1931.

Bowers, Fredson. "Some Principles for Scholarly Editions of Nineteenth-Century American Authors." *Studies in Bibliography* 17 (1964): 223–28.

Campbell, Killis. *The Mind of Poe and Other Studies*. 1933. Rpt. in New York: Russell, 1962.

———. "Poe's Reading." *University of Texas Studies in English*, no. 5 (1925): 1966–96.

———. "Poe's Reading: Addenda and Corrigenda." *University of Texas Studies in English*, no. 7 (1927): 175–80.

Carlson, Eric W., ed. *Critical Essays on Edgar Allan Poe*. Boston: Hall, 1987.

———. "Poe: I, New Editions." *ANQ* 1, no. 3, new series (Jan. 1988): 25–32.

———. "Poe: II, New Critical Studies." *ANQ* 1, no. 3, new series (July 1988): 105–12.

———, ed. *The Recognition of Edgar Allan Poe: Selected Criticism since 1829*. Ann Arbor: U of Michigan P, 1966.

Charvat, William. *Literary Publishing in America: 1790–1850*. Philadelphia: U of Pennsylvania P, 1959.

———. *The Profession of Authorship in America, 1800–1870. The papers of William Charvat*. Ed. Matthew J. Bruccoli. Columbus: Ohio State UP, 1968.

Curle, Richard. *Collecting American First Editions: Its Pitfalls and Its Pleasures*. Indianapolis: Bobbs, 1930.

Dameron, J. Lasley, and Irby B. Cauthen, Jr. *Edgar Allan Poe: A Bibliography of Criticism, 1827–1967*. Charlottesville: UP of Virginia, 1974.

Davidson, Edward H. *Poe: A Critical Study*. Cambridge: Harvard UP, 1957.

Exman, Eugene. *The Brothers Harper*. New York: Harper, 1965.

Fisher, Benjamin Franklin IV. "A Ten-Year Shelf of Poe Books." *UMSE*, new series, 3 (1982): 183–99.

Foley, Patrick K. *American Authors, 1795–1895: A Bibliography of First and Notable Editions . . .* Boston: Printed for subscribers, 1897.

Foote, Charles B. *Catalogue of the . . . Collection Made by Charles B. Foote . . .* New York: Bangs, 1894–1895.

Gimbel, Richard. " 'Quoth the Raven': A Catalogue of the Exhibition." *Yale University Library Gazette* 33 (Apr. 1959): 139–89.

Greg, W. W. "The Rationale of Copy-Text." *Studies in Bibliography* 3 (1950–1951): 19–36. Rpt. in *Collected Papers*. Ed. J. C. Maxwell. Oxford: Clarendon, 1966, 374–91.

Goodspeed, Charles E. *Yankee Bookseller*. New York: Houghton, 1937.

Gordan, John D. *Edgar Allan Poe: An Exhibition on the Centenary of His Death . . .* New York: New York Public Library, 1949.

Haage, Sybille. *Edgar Allan Poe's "Tales of the Folio Club": Versuch der Rekonstruktion einer Zyklischen Rahmenerzählung*. Frankfurt am Main, Bern, Las Vegas: Lang, 1978.

Hammond, Alexander. "Edgar Allan Poe's *Tales of the Folio Club*: The Evolution of a Lost Book." *Library Chronicle* (University of Pennsylvania) 41 (1976): 13–43. Rpt. in B. F. Fisher, ed. *Poe at Work*. Baltimore: E. A. Poe Society, 1978, 13–43.

Hatvary, George E. *Horace Binney Wallace*. Boston: Twayne, 1977.

Heartman, Charles F. *Concerning a Poe Bibliography . . .* n.p. [1940].

Heartman, Charles F., and James R. Canny. *A Bibliography of First Printings of the Writings of Edgar Allan Poe*. Hattiesburg: Book Farm, 1940. Rev. ed., 1943. Rpt. in New York: Kraus, 1972.

Heartman, Charles F., and Kenneth Rede. *A Census of First Editions . . . Relating to Edgar Allan Poe . . .* 2 vols. Metuchen: American Book Collector, 1932.

Hyneman, Esther F. *Edgar Allan Poe: An Annotated Bibliography of Books and Articles in English, 1827–1973.* Boston: Hall, 1974.

Iacone, Salvatore J. *The Pleasures of Book Collecting.* New York: Harper, 1976.

Ingram, John H. *Edgar Allan Poe: His Life, Letters and Opinions.* 2 vols. London: Hogg, 1880. Rpt. in New York: AMS, 1965.

Johnson, Merle, ed. *American First Editions: Bibliographic Check Lists . . .* New York: Bowker, 1929. 2d ed.: 1932. 3d ed.: Jacob Blanck, 1936. 4th ed.: Jacob Blanck, 1942.

Leon & Brother. *Catalogue of First Editions of American Authors.* New York: Leon, 1885.

Mabbott, Thomas Ollive. Bibliographical Note. *Al Aaraaf, Tamerlane and Minor Poems.* By E. A. Poe. Fac. ed. Mabbott. New York: Facsimile Text Society, 1933, [v–x].

————. Introduction. *Tamerlane and Other Poems.* By E. A. Poe. Fac. ed. Mabbott. New York: Facsimile Text Society, 1941, v–xlvi.

————. "A List of Books from Poe's Library." *Notes and Queries* 200 (May 1955): 222–23.

————. Rev. of *A Bibliography of First Printings of the Writings of Edgar Allan Poe,* by Charles F. Heartman and James R. Canny. *New York Herald Tribune,* Apr. 2, 1944, sec. 6:23.

————. Rev. of *A Census of First Editions . . . Relating to Edgar Allan Poe . . . ,* by Charles F. Heartman and Kenneth Rede. *AL* 6 (1934): 92–94.

Maier, Frank. *First Editions of American Authors, the Library of Frank Maier to be Sold . . .* 3 vols. New York: Anderson Auction, 1909.

Miller, John Carl. *John Henry Ingram's Poe Collection at the University of Virginia.* Charlottesville: U of Virginia P, 1960. 2d ed. by John E. Reilly. UP of Virginia, 1994, vii–xii. 220 pp.

————, ed. *Poe's Helen Remembers.* Charlottesville: UP of Virginia, 1979.

Moldenhauer, Joseph J. "Mabbott's Poe and the Question of Copy-Text." Rev. of *Collected Works of Edgar Allan Poe: Vols. II and III, Tales and Sketches.* Ed. T. O. Mabbott. *PoeS* 11 (Dec. 1978): 41–46.

————. "Miniatures under the Magnifying-Glass." Rev. of *Collected Writings of Edgar Allan Poe: Vol. 2, The Brevities.* Ed. Burton R. Pollin. *PoeS* 19 (Dec. 1986): 44–50.

Moss, Sidney P. *Poe's Literary Battles: The Critic in the Context of His Literary Milieu.* Durham: Duke UP, 1963.

————. *Poe's Major Crisis: His Libel Suit and New York's Literary World.* Durham, N.C.: Duke UP, 1970.

Mott, Frank Luther. *A History of American Magazines.* 5 vols. Cambridge: Harvard UP, 1938–1968.

Newton, A. Edward. *This Book-Collecting Game.* Boston: Little, 1928.

Omans, Glen A. "Poe at Auction." *PSA Newsletter* 18 (Spring 1990): 3–4.

Ostrom, John Ward. "Edgar A. Poe: His Income as Literary Entrepreneur." *PoeS* 15 (June 1982): 1–7.

Parker, Hershel. *Flawed Texts and Verbal Icons: Literary Authority in American Fiction.* Evanston, Ill.: Northwestern UP, 1984.

Poe, E. A. *Prose Romances.* Fac. ed. George E. Hatvary and Thomas O. Mabbott. New York: St. John's UP, 1968.

Pollin, Burton R. *Discoveries in Poe.* Notre Dame: U of Notre Dame P, 1970.

———. "The Poe Editions of the Library of America." Rev. of *Edgar Allan Poe: Poetry and Tales.* Ed. Patrick Quinn. New York: Library of America, 1984; and *Edgar Allan Poe: Essays and Reviews.* Ed. G. R. Thompson. New York: Library of America, 1984. *PoeS* 18 (Dec. 1985): 29–32.

Quinn, Patrick F. *The French Face of Edgar Poe.* Carbondale: Southern Illinois UP, 1957.

———. "The Poe Edition: Annotating *Pym.*" Rev. of *Collected Writings of Edgar Allan Poe: Vol. 1, The Imaginary Voyages.* Ed. Burton R. Pollin. *PoeS* 16 (June 1983): 14–16.

Randall, David A. *Dukedom Large Enough.* New York: Random, 1969.

———. *The J. K. Lilly Collection of Edgar Allan Poe: An Account of Its Formation.* Bloomington: Lilly Library of the U of Indiana, 1964.

———. Rev. of *A Bibliography of the Writings of Edgar A. Poe,* by John W. Robertson. *Publishers Weekly,* Apr. 21, 1934, 1540–43.

———. Rev. of *A Bibliography of First Printings of the Writings of Edgar Allan Poe,* by Charles F. Heartman and James R. Canny. *Publishers Weekly,* Nov. 30, 1940, 2033–38.

Richard, Claude. "Les Contes du Folio Club et la Vocation Humoristique d'Edgar Allan Poe." *Configuration Critique d'Edgar Allan Poe.* Ed. Richard. Paris: Minard, 1969.

———. *Edgar Allan Poe: Journaliste et Critique.* Paris: Klincksieck, 1974.

Robbins, J. Albert. Rev. of *Collected Works of Edgar Allan Poe: Vol. I, Poems.* Ed. T. O. Mabbott. *AL* 42 (1970): 246–47.

Robertson, John W. *A Bibliography of the Writings of Edgar A. Poe.* 2 vols. San Francisco: Russian Hill Private P, 1934.

Russell, J. Thomas. *Edgar Allan Poe: The Army Years. USMA Library Bulletin,* no. 10. West Point: U.S. Military Academy, 1972.

St. Armand, Barton Levi. "The 'Mysteries' of Edgar Poe: The Quest for a Monomyth in Gothic Literature." *The Gothic Imagination: Essays in Dark Romanticism.* Ed. G. R. Thompson. Pullman: Washington State UP, 1974, 65–93.

Silverman, Kenneth. *Edgar A. Poe.* New York: Harper/Collins, 1991.

Stone, Herbert Stuart. *First Editions of American Authors: A Manual for Book-Lovers.* Cambridge: Stone and Kimball, 1893.

Stovall, Floyd. Introduction. *The Complete Works of Edgar Allan Poe.* Ed. James A. Harrison. 17 vols. 1902. Rpt. in New York: AMS, 1979, 1: 1–23.

———. "Poe's Debt to Coleridge." *University of Texas Studies in English,* no. 10 (1930): 70–127.

Tanselle, G. Thomas. "Melville and the World of Books." *A Companion to Melville Studies.* Ed. John Bryant. Westport: Greenwood, 1986, 781–835.

———. "The State of Poe Bibliography." *PoeS* 2 (Jan. 1969): 1–3.

Trent, William P. et al. *The Cambridge History of American Literature.* 4 vols. New York: Putnam, 1917–1921.

Wakeman, Stephen H. *The Stephen H. Wakeman Collection of Books of Nineteenth Century American Writers . . .* New York: American Art Association, 1924.

Walker, I. M., ed. *Edgar Allan Poe: The Critical Heritage*. London and New York: Routledge, 1986.
Whitman, Sarah Helen. *Edgar Poe and His Critics*. New York: Rudd, 1860. Rpt. in New York: Gordian, 1981.
Winterich, John T. *Books and the Man*. New York: Greenberg, 1929.
———. *A Primer of Book Collecting*. New York: Greenberg, 1926. Rev. ed., 1935.
Woodberry, George Edward. *The Life of Edgar Allan Poe, Personal and Literary*. 2 vols. Boston: Houghton, 1909.

WORKS BY POE

Collected Sets

The Works of the Late Edgar Allan Poe. With a Memoir by Rufus Wilmot Griswold and Notices of His Life and Genius by N. P. Willis and J. R. Lowell. 4 vols. New York: Redfield, 1850–56.
The Works of Edgar Allan Poe. Ed. John H. Ingram. 4 vols. Edinburgh: Black, 1874–1875.
The Works of Edgar Allan Poe. Ed. Richard H. Stoddard. 6 vols. New York: Armstrong, 1884.
The Works of Edgar Allan Poe. Ed. Edmund C. Stedman and George E. Woodberry. 10 vols. Chicago: Stone, 1894–1895.
The Complete Works of Edgar Allan Poe. Ed. James A. Harrison. 17 vols. New York: Crowell, 1902.
The Complete Poems and Stories of Edgar Allan Poe, with Selections from His Critical Writings. Ed. Arthur H. Quinn and Edward H. O'Neill. 2 vols. New York: Knopf, 1946.
Collected Works of Edgar Allan Poe. Ed. Thomas Ollive Mabbott with the assistance of Eleanor D. Kewer and Maureen C. Mabbott. 3 vols. Cambridge: Harvard, 1969–1978.
Collected Writings of Edgar Allan Poe. Ed. Burton R. Pollin. 4 vols. to date (1990). Boston: Twayne; New York: Gordian, 1981– .
Edgar Allan Poe: Poetry and Tales and *Essays and Reviews*. Ed. Patrick Quinn and G. R. Thompson. 2 vols. New York: Library of America, 1984.

Composite Volumes

Selections from the Critical Writings of Edgar Allan Poe. Ed. Frederick C. Prescott. 1909. New Pref. J. Lasley Dameron; New Introd. Eric W. Carlson. New York: Gordian, 1981.
The Complete Poems. Ed. James R. Whitty. Boston: Houghton, 1911.
Poems of Edgar Allan Poe. Ed. Killis Campbell. New York: Glen, 1917.
Poe's Short Stories. Ed. Killis Campbell. New York: Harcourt, 1927.
Edgar Allan Poe: Representative Selections. Ed. Margaret Alterton and Hardin Craig. 1935. Rev. ed. New York: Hill, 1962.
The Portable Poe. Ed. Philip Van Doren Stern. New York: Viking, 1945.
Edgar Allan Poe: Selected Prose and Poetry. Introduction by W. H. Auden. New York: Rinehart, 1950.

Selected Poetry and Prose. Ed. T. O. Mabbott. New York: Modern, 1951.

Selected Writings. Ed. Edward H. Davidson. Boston: Houghton, 1956.

Literary Criticism of Edgar Allan Poe. Ed. Robert L. Hough. Lincoln: U of Nebraska P, 1965.

The Poems of Edgar Allan Poe. Ed. Floyd Stovall. Charlottesville: UP of Virginia, 1965.

Edgar Allan Poe: Selected Tales. Ed. Kenneth Graham. London: Oxford, 1967.

Introduction to Poe: A Thematic Reader. Ed. Eric W. Carlson. Glenview: Scott, 1967.

Selected Writings. Ed. David Galloway. Baltimore: Penguin, 1967.

Great Short Works. Ed. G. R. Thompson. New York: Harper, 1970.

The Short Fiction. Ed. Stuart Levine and Susan Levine. Indianapolis: Bobbs, 1976. Rpt. in Champaign: U of Illinois P, 1990.

Selected Bibliography

Each chapter ends with a list of Works Cited, as in *PMLA*. Basic texts (Harrison, Mabbott, Pollin, Thompson) appear mainly in the list of Abbreviations. At the end of his chapter on "Poe and the World of Books," George Hatvary has added lists of Collected Sets and of Composite Volumes of the works of Poe. For the history of Poe criticism, the earlier annotated bibliographies by Hutcherson and Dameron are useful, and the more recent book-length bibliographies by Dameron and Cauthen (1827–1967) and Hyneman (1827–1973) are indispensable. For a concise survey of Poe as person and author during the nineteenth and twentieth centuries through World War II, my Preface to *The Recognition of Edgar Allan Poe* (1966) may be consulted. The Introduction (1–34) to my *Critical Essays on Edgar Allan Poe* (1987) extends the earlier survey of major critical studies to 1985 in greater detail. The most comprehensive bibliographies are those in *Poe Studies* (1971–1993) and the annual *MLA International Bibliography* that is now available on the MLA FirstSearch database with downloading capacity for the years 1963 to the present. Each computer entry runs to eight or ten lines, and as of spring 1995 about 900 entries on "Poe and Criticism" alone had accumulated for the past fifteen years. Prospects are bleak for the addition of Poe's works to the "Wordcruncher" CDROM, as the Library of America has refused permission to Johnston & Co. (Indiana), successor to the Electronic Text Co. But the Internet will undoubtedly make all texts available eventually.

Abrams, M. H. "How to Do Things with Texts." *Partisan Review* 46 (1979): 566–88.
Adams, Robert M. *NIL: Episodes in the Literary Conquest of the Void during the Nineteenth Century.* New York: Oxford UP, 1966.
Alexander, Jean. *Affidavits of Genius: Edgar Allan Poe and the French Critics, 1847–1924.* Port Washington, N.Y.: Kennikat P, 1971.
Allen, Hervey. *Israfel: The Life and Times of Edgar Allan Poe.* 2 vols. New York: George H. Doran, 1926.
Allen, Michael. *Poe and the Magazine Tradition.* New York: Oxford UP, 1969.

Alterton, Margaret. *Origins of Poe's Critical Theory.* Iowa City: U of Iowa P, 1925. Rev. ed. New York: Russell & Russell, 1965.

Alterton, Margaret, and Hardin Craig. *Edgar Allan Poe: Representative Selections.* Rev. ed. New York: Hill and Wang, 1962.

The American Face of Edgar Allan Poe. Ed. Shawn Rosenheim and Stephen Rachman. Baltimore: Johns Hopkins UP, 1995.

American Renaissance Literary Report. Ed. Kenneth Cameron. Transcendental Books, Box Sta A, Hartford, CT 06106. Annually since 1987.

Anderson, Carl L. *Poe in Northlight: The Scandinavian Response to His Life and Work.* Durham, N.C.: Duke UP, 1973.

Andriano, Joseph. *Our Ladies of Darkness: Feminizing Daemonology in Male Gothic Fiction.* University Park: Penn State UP, 1993.

Annotated Tales of Edgar Allan Poe. Ed. Stephen Peithman with introduction, notes, and bibliography. New York: Doubleday, 1981.

Armistead, J. M. "Poe and Lyric Conventions: The Example of 'For Annie.' " *PoeS* 8, no. 1 (June 1975): 1–5.

Asselineau, Roger, ed. "Introduction." *Edgar Poe, Choix de Contes.* Trans. Charles Baudelaire. Paris: Aubier, 1958, 16–104.

Auden, W. H. "Introduction." *Edgar Allan Poe: Selected Prose and Poetry.* New York: Rinehart, 1950. Repr. in Carlson, *REAP.*

Auerbach, Jonathan. *The Romance of Failure: First-Person Fictions of Poe, Hawthorne, and James.* New York: Oxford UP, 1989.

Barth, John. " 'Still Farther South': Some Notes on Poe's Pym." In *Poe's Pym: Critical Explorations.* Ed. Richard Kopley. Durham, N.C.: Duke UP, 1992, 217–30.

Barthes, Roland. "Textual Analysis of a Tale by Edgar Poe." *PoeS* 10 (June 1977): 1–12. Repr. in *Untying the Text: A Post-Structuralist Reader.* Boston: Routledge, 1981, 133–61.

Bassein, Beth Ann. *Women and Death: Linkages in Western Thought and Literature.* Westport, Conn.: Greenwood, 1984.

Baudelaire, Charles. *Baudelaire on Poe.* Trans. and ed. Lois and Francis E. Hyslop, Jr. State College, Pa.: Bald Eagle P, 1952.

Baym, Nina. *Feminism and American Literary History: Essays.* New Brunswick: Rutgers UP, 1992.

Beaver, Harold. "Introduction." *The Narrative of Arthur Gordon Pym.* New York: Penguin, 1975.

———. "Introduction." *The Science Fiction of Edgar Allan Poe.* New York: Penguin Books, 1976.

Bennett, Maurice J. "The Detective Fiction of Poe and Borges." *Comparative Literature* 35, no. 3 (Summer 1983): 262–75.

———. " 'The Madness of Art': Poe's 'Ligeia' as Metafiction." *PoeS* 14, no. 1 (June 1981): 1–6.

———. " 'Visionary Wings': Art and Metaphysics in Edgar Allan Poe's 'Hans Pfaall.' " Fisher, *Poe and His Times,* 76–87.

Benton, Richard P. *"Bedlam Patterns": Love and the Idea of Madness in Poe's Fiction.* Baltimore: Poe Society of Baltimore, 1979.

———. "The Mystery of Marie Roget." *Studies in Short Fiction* 6 (Winter 1969): 144–51.

————. "Platonic Allegory in Poe's 'Eleonora.' " *Nineteenth-Century Fiction* (Dec. 1967): 293–97.

————. "Poe's 'The Cask' and the 'White Webwork Which Gleams.' " *Studies in Short Fiction* 28, no. 2 (Spring 1991): 283–97.

Berressem, Hanjo. "Godolphin, Goodolphin, Goodol'phin, Goodol'Pyn, Good ol'Pym: A Question of Integration." *Pynchon Notes* 10 (Oct. 1982): 3–17.

Bickman, Martin. "Animatopoeia: Morella as a Siren of the Self." *PoeS* 8 (Dec. 1975): 29–32.

————. *The Unsounded Centre: Jungian Studies in American Romanticism.* Chapel Hill: U of North Carolina P, 1980.

Bieganowski, Ronald. "The Self-Consuming Narrator in Poe's 'Ligeia' and 'Usher.' " *AL* 60, no. 2 (May 1988): 175–87.

Bielfeld, Jacob Friedrich, Freiherr von. *The Elements of Universal Erudition.* Trans. W. Hooper. 3 vols. London: G. Scott, 1770.

Bloom, Harold. "Introduction: Americanizing the Abyss." *Edgar Allan Poe* (Modern Critical Views). New York: Chelsea House, 1985, 1–14. Repr. of "The Inescapable Poe," *New York Review of Books* 31, no. 15 (Oct. 11, 1984).

Bonaparte, Marie. *Edgar Poe: Sa vie, son oeuvre—Étude psychanalytique.* Paris: Denoel et Steele, 1933. Trans. John Rodker. *The Life and Works of Edgar Poe: A Psychoanalytical Interpretation.* London: Imago, 1949.

Bradfield, Scott. *Dreaming Revolution: Transgression in the Development of American Romance.* Iowa City: U of Iowa P, 1993.

Brand, Dana. " 'Reconstructing the Flaneur': Poe's Invention of the Detective Story." *Genre* 18 (Spring 1985): 35–56.

————. *The Spectator and the City in Nineteenth-Century American Literature.* Cambridge: Cambridge UP, 1991.

Bronfen, Elisabeth. *Over Her Dead Body: Death, Feminity and the Aesthetic.* New York: Routledge, 1992.

Broussard, Louis. *The Measure of Poe.* Norman: U of Oklahoma P, 1969.

Bryant, Jacob. *A New System, or, an Analysis of Antient Mythology* 6 vols. London, 1807.

Budd, Louis J. (ed. and series introd.); Cady, Edwin H. (ed. series introd.). *On Poe: The Best from American Literature.* Durham, N.C.: Duke UP, 1993.

Buranelli, Vincent. *Edgar Allan Poe.* New York: Twayne, 1961.

Butler, David W. "Usher's Hypochondriasis: Mental Alienation and Romantic Idealism in Poe's Gothic Tales." *AL* 48 (1976): 1–12.

Campbell, Killis, ed. "Introduction." *Poems of Edgar Allan Poe.* New York: Ginn, 1917.

————. *The Mind of Poe and Other Studies.* Cambridge: Harvard UP, 1933.

Caputi, Anthony. "The Refrain in Poe's Poetry." *AL* 25 (1953): 160–73. Repr. in *On Poe: The Best from AL,* 1993.

Carlson, Eric W., ed. *Critical Essays on Edgar Allan Poe.* Boston: G. K. Hall, 1987.

————. *Edgar Allan Poe: The Fall of the House of Usher.* Ed. Eric W. Carlson. The Merrill Literary Casebook Series. Columbus, Ohio: Charles E. Merrill, 1971.

————. "Edgar Allan Poe." *Dictionary of Literary Biography.* Vol. 74. Detroit: Gale, 1980, 303–22.

————. "Edgar Allan Poe." *Fifty Southern Writers before 1900.* Ed. Robert Bain and Joseph M. Flora. Westport, Conn.: Greenwood Press, 1987, 365–88.

————. "Frames of Reference for Poe's Symbolic Language." *Critical Essays on Edgar Allan Poe.* Boston: Hall, 1987, 207–17.

————, ed. *Introduction to Poe: A Thematic Reader* with introduction, notes, and bibliography. Glenview, Ill.: Scott, Foresman, 1967.

————. "New Introduction." *Selections from the Critical Writings of Edgar Allan Poe.* Ed. F. C. Prescott. New York: Gordian, 1981.

————. "Poe on the Soul of Man." Baltimore: Edgar Allan Poe Society of Baltimore, 1973.

————. "Poe's Vision of Man." In *Papers on Poe.* Ed. Veler, 7–20.

————, ed. *The Recognition of Edgar Allan Poe: Selected Criticism since 1829.* Ann Arbor: U of Michigan P, 1966.

————. "Symbol and Sense in Poe's 'Ulalume.' " *AL* 35 (Mar. 1963): 22–37.

————. " 'William Wilson': The Double as Primal Self." *Topic: 30* 16 (Fall 1976): 35–40.

Casale, Ottavio M. "The Battle of Boston: A Revaluation of Poe's Lyceum Appearance." *AL* 45, no. 3 (Nov. 1973): 423–28.

————. "Edgar Allan Poe." *The Transcendentalists.* Ed. Joel Myerson. New York: MLA, 1984, 362–71.

————. "Poe on Transcendentalism." *Emerson Society Quarterly* 50 (First quarter 1968): 85–97.

Cather, Willa. Untitled speech on Poe in "The Passing Show" column of the Lincoln *Courier,* Oct. 12, 1895, 6–7. Repr. in *The World and the Parish: Willa Cather's Articles and Reviews 1893–1902.* Ed. William M. Curtin. Lincoln: U of Nebraska P, 1970, 157–63.

Chandler, Alice. "The Visionary Race": Poe's Attitude toward His Dreamers." *New Approaches to Poe.* Ed. Richard P. Benton. Hartford: Transcendental Books, 1970, 73–81.

Charvat, William. "Poe: Journalism and the Theory of Poetry." In *The Profession of Authorship in America, 1800–1870: The Papers of William Charvat.* Ed. Matthew J. Bruccoli. Columbus: Ohio State UP, 1968, 84–99.

Clarke, Graham, ed. *Edgar Allan Poe: Critical Assessments.* 4 vols. University of Kent, East Sussex, England: Helm Information, 1991. (U.S.: Routledge, Chapman Hall).

Conron, John Joseph. "Poe and the Theory of the Short Story." Diss. U. of Michigan, 1970.

Cowley, Malcolm. "The Edgar Allan Poe Tradition." *Outlook* 149 (1928): 497–99, 511.

Crews, Frederick. *The Critics Bear It Away: American Fiction and the Academy.* New York: Random House, 1992.

Croce, Benedetto. "Poe's Essays on Poetry." In *Benedetto Croce: Essays on Literature and Literary Criticism.* Trans. M.E. Moss. Albany: SUNY P, 1990, 151–55.

Culler, Jonathan. *On Deconstruction: Theory and Criticism after Structuralism.* Ithaca, N.Y.: Cornell UP, 1982.

Dameron, J. Lasley. "More Analogues and Resources for Poe's Fiction and Poems." *UMSE* 9 (1991): 154–66.

————. "Poe's Concept of Truth." *Mississippi Quarterly* 43, no. 1 (Winter 1989–1990): 11–21.

————. "Popular Literature: Poe's Not So Soon Forgotten Lore." Baltimore: Edgar Allan Poe Society, 1979.

———. "Pym's Polar Episode: Conclusion or Beginning." Kopley, *Poe's Pym: Critical Explorations,* 33–43.

Dameron, J. Lasley, and Irby B. Cauthen, Jr. *Edgar Allan Poe: A Bibliography of Criticism: 1827–1967.* Charlottesville: UP of Virginia, 1974.

Dameron, J. Lasley, and Pamela Parker. *An Index to the Critical Vocabulary of Blackwood's Edinburgh Magazine, 1830–1840.* Introduction by Kenneth J. Curry. West Cornwall, CT: Locust Hill P, 1993.

Davidson, Edward H. *Poe: A Critical Study.* Cambridge: Harvard UP, 1957.

Dayan, Joan. "Amorous Bondage: Poe, Ladies, and Slaves." *AL* 66 (1994): 239–73.

———. *Fables of Mind: An Inquiry into Poe's Fiction.* New York: Oxford UP, 1987.

———. "Poe, Locke and Kant." Fisher, *Poe and His Times,* 30–44.

———. "Poe's Women: A Feminist Poe?" *PoeS* 26, nos. 1, 2 (1993): 1–12.

———. "Romance and Race." *The Columbia History of the American Novel.* Ed. Emory Elliott. New York: Columbia UP, 1991, 89–109.

Deas, Michael J. *The Portraits and Daguerreotypes of Edgar Allan Poe.* Charlottesville: UP of Virginia, 1989.

Deconstruction and Criticism. Essays by Harold Bloom, Paul de Man, Derrida, et al. New York: Seabury P, 1979.

de Man, Paul. *Insights and Blindness: Essays in the Rhetoric of Contemporary Criticism.* New York: Oxford UP, 1971. 2d, rev. ed., Minneapolis: U of Minnesota P, 1983.

De Prospo, R. C. "Deconstructive Poe(tics)." *Diacritics* 18, no. 3 (Fall 1988): 43–64.

Doyle, Jacqueline. "(Dis)Figuring Women: Edgar Allan Poe's 'Berenice.' " *PoeS* 26, nos. 1, 2 (June–Dec. 1993): 13–21.

Eakin, Paul John. "Poe's Sense of an Ending." *AL* 45 (Mar. 1973): 1–22. Repr. in *On Poe.* Ed. Budd and Cady, 1993.

Eaves, Morris, and Michael Fischer, eds. *Romanticism and Contemporary Criticism.* Ithaca, N.Y.: Cornell UP, 1986. (Essays by M. H. Abrams, Stanley Cavell, et al. on postmodernism.)

Eddings, Dennis W., ed. *The Naiad Voice: Essays on Poe's Satiric Hoaxing.* Port Washington, N.Y.: Associated Faculty P, 1983.

Eliot, T. S. "American Literature and the American Language." *To Criticize the Critic.* New York: Farrar, Straus, and Giroux, 1965, 43–60.

———. "From Poe to Valéry." *Hudson Review* 2 (Autumn 1949): 327–42. Repr. in *REAP.*

Ellis, John M. *Against Deconstruction.* Princeton: Princeton UP, 1989.

Engel, Leonard W. "Claustrophobia, the Gothic Enclosure and Poe." *Clues: A Journal of Detection* 10, no. 2 (Fall–Winter 1989): 107–17.

Englekirk, John H. *Edgar Allan Poe in Hispanic Literature.* New York: Instituto de las Españas en los Estados Unidos, 1934.

Fagin, Nathan B. *The Histrionic Mr. Poe.* Baltimore: Johns Hopkins UP, 1949.

Falk, Doris V. "Poe and the Power of Animal Magnetism." *PMLA* 84, no. 3 (May 1969): 536–46.

Fehrman, Carl. *Poetic Creation: Inspiration or Craft.* Trans. Karin Petherick. Minneapolis: U of Minnesota P, 1980.

Finholt, Richard. "The Vision at the Brink of the Abyss: 'A Descent into the Maelström' in the Light of Poe's Cosmology." *Georgia Review* 27 (Fall 1973): 356–66.

Fisher, Benjamin F., ed. *Myths and Realities: The Mysterious Mr. Poe.* Baltimore: Edgar Allan Poe Society, 1987.

————, ed. *Poe and His Times: The Artist and His Milieu.* Baltimore: Edgar Allan Poe Society, 1990.

————, ed. *Poe at Work: Seven Textual Studies.* Baltimore: Edgar Allan Poe Society, 1978.

————, ed. *Poe in Our Times: Influences and Affinities.* Baltimore: Edgar Allan Poe Society, 1986.

————. "Poe's 'Metzengerstein': Not a Hoax." 1971. Repr. in *On Poe.* Ed. Budd and Cady.

————. *The Very Spirit of Cordiality: The Literary Uses of Alcohol and Alcoholism in the Tales of Edgar Allan Poe.* Baltimore: Edgar Allan Poe Society, 1978.

Forclaz, Roger. *Le Monde d'Edgar Allan Poe.* Berne: Herbert Lang; Frankfurt: Peter Lang, 1974.

————. "Psychoanalysis and Edgar Allan Poe: A Critique of the Bonaparte Thesis." In Carlson, *Critical Essays.*

Forrest, William M. *Biblical Allusions in Poe.* New York: Macmillan, 1928.

Fox-Genovese, Elizabeth. *Within the Plantation Household: Black and White Women of the Old South.* Chapel Hill: U. of North Carolina P, 1988.

Friedman, William F. "Edgar Allan Poe, Cryptography." 1936. Repr. in Budd and Cady, *On Poe.*

Fuller, Margaret. *Women in the Nineteenth Century.* New York: Norton, 1971.

————. Review of *Tales* (1845) and *The Raven and Other Poems* (1845). Repr. *CE,* 36–41.

Fuller, Robert C. *Mesmerism and the American Cure of Souls.* Philadelphia: U of Pennsylvania P, 1982.

Furst, Lilian R. "Romantic Irony and Narrative Stance." *Romantic Irony.* Ed. Frederick Garber. Budapest: Chademai Kiado, 1988, 293–309.

Fussell, Edwin. "Edgar Allan Poe." In *Frontier: American Literature and the American West.* Princeton: Princeton UP, 1965, 132–74.

Galloway, David, ed. *The Other Poe: Comedies and Satires.* New York: Penguin Books, 1983.

Gargano, James W. "The Distorted Perception of Poe's Comic Narrators." *Topic 30* (Fall 1976): 23–34.

————. " 'The Fall of the House of Usher': An Apocalyptic Vision." *UMSE,* new series, 3 (June 1982): 53–63.

————. "Poe's 'Ligeia': Dream and Destruction." *College English* 23 (1962): 337–42.

————. "The Question of Poe's Narrators." *College English* 25 (Feb. 1963): 177–81. Repr. in *REAP.*

Garrison, Joseph M., Jr. "The Function of Terror in the Work of Edgar Allan Poe." *American Quarterly* 18 (1966): 136–50.

Gibaldi, Joseph, ed. *Introduction to Scholarship in Modern Languages and Literatures.* New York: MLA, 1992. Chapters on textual, historical, interpretive, feminist studies, and literary theory, among others.

Ginsberg, Allen. *Mind Breaths: Poems 1972–1977.* San Francisco: City Lights Books, 1978.

Girgus, Sam B. "Poe and R. D. Laing: The Transcendent Self." *Studies in Short Fiction* 13 (1976): 299–309.

Gordon, Rae Beth. "Interior Decoration in Poe and Gilman." *LIT: Literature Interpretation Theory* 3, no. 2 (1991): 85–99.

Graff, Gerald. *Literature against Itself.* Chicago: U of Chicago P, 1979.

Griffith, Clark. "Poe and the Gothic." In Veler, *Papers on Poe,* 21–27.

———. "Poe's 'Ligeia' and the English Romantics." *University of Toronto Quarterly* 14 (Oct. 1954): 8–25.

Griswold, Rufus Wilmot. "Ludwig" obituary. *New York Daily Tribune,* October 9, 1849. Repr. *REAP,* 28–35.

———. "Memoir of the Author." In *The Works of the Late Edgar Allan Poe.* New York: J. S. Redfield, 1850, vol. 3: vii–xxxix. For excerpts, see *CE,* 52–57.

Grubb, Gerald G. "The Personal and Literary Relationship of Dickens and Poe." *Nineteenth-Century Fiction* 5, no. 3: 209–21.

Hallberg, Robert von. "Edgar Allan Poe, Poet-Critic." *Nineteenth-Century American Poetry.* Ed. A. Robert Lee. London: Vision and Totowa: Barnes and Noble, 1985.

Halliburton, David. *Edgar Allan Poe: A Phenomenological View.* Princeton: Princeton UP, 1973.

Hammond, Alexander. "Edgar Allan Poe's *Tales of the Folio Club*: The Evolution of a Lost Book" *Library Chronicle* 41 (1976):13–43.

———."A Reconstruction of Poe's *Tales of the Folio Club*: Preliminary Notes." *PoeS* 5 (June 1972): 25–32.

Hansen, Thomas S. "Arno Schmidt's Reception of Edgar Allan Poe; Or, The Domain of Arn(o)heim." *Review of Contemporary Fiction* 8, no. 1 (Spring 1988): 166–81.

Hansen, Thomas, with Burton R. Pollin. *The German Face of Edgar Allan Poe: A Study of Literary References on His Works.* Columbia, S.C.: Camden House, 1995.

Heckman, Susan J. *Gender and Knowledge: Elements of a Postmodern Feminism.* Boston: Northeastern UP, 1990.

Heller, Terry. *The Delights of Terror: An Aesthetics of the Tale of Terror.* Urbana: U of Illinois P, 1987.

Higonnet, Margaret, and Carolyn G. Heilbrun, eds. *The Representation of Women in Fiction.* Baltimore: Johns Hopkins UP, 1983. Papers from the English Institute.

Higonnet, Margaret, and Maria de Valdes, eds. *Voices Spring to Life.* New York: Feminist P, 1993.

Hirsch, David H. *The Deconstruction of Literature: Criticism after Auschwitz.* Hanover, N.H., and London: UP of New England, 1991.

———. "The Pit and the Apocalypse." *Sewanee Review* 76 (Autumn 1968): 632–52.

———. "Poe's 'Metzengerstein' as a Tale of the Subconscious." *UMSE* 3 (1982): 40–52.

Hodgson, John A. "Decoding Poe? Poe, W. B. Tyler, and Cryptography." *Journal of English and Germanic Philology* 92, no. 4 (Oct. 1993): 523–34.

Hoffman, Daniel. *Poe Poe Poe Poe Poe Poe Poe.* Garden City, N.Y.: Doubleday, 1972.

Hofrichter, Laura. "From Poe to Kafka." *University of Toronto Quarterly* 29 (July 1960): 405–19.

Hollander, John. "The Music of Silence." *Prose* 7 (Fall 1973): 79–91.

Howarth, William L., comp. *Twentieth Century Interpretations of Poe's Tales.* Englewood Cliffs, N.J.: Prentice-Hall, 1971.

Hubbell, Jay B. "Edgar Allan Poe." *Eight American Authors: A Review of Research and Criticism.* Rev. ed., James Woodress et al. New York: Norton, 1981, 3–36.

———. "Poe and the Southern Literary Tradition." *Texas Studies in Literature and Language* 2 (1960): 151–71.

Hull, William Doyle. "A Canon of the Critical Works of Edgar Allan Poe with a Study of Poe as Editor and Reviewer." Diss. U of Virginia, 1941.

Hungerford, Edward. "Poe and Phrenology." *AL* 2 (Nov. 1930): 209–31. Repr. in Budd and Cady, *On Poe.*

Hyneman, Esther. *Edgar Allan Poe: An Annotated Bibliography of Books and Articles in English: 1827–1973.* Boston: G. K. Hall, 1974.

Irwin, John T. *American Hieroglyphics: The Symbol of the Egyptian Hieroglyphics in the American Renaissance.* New Haven, Conn.: Yale UP, 1980.

———. "Knight's Gambit: Poe, Faulkner, and the Tradition of the Detective Story." *Arizona Quarterly* 46, no. 4 (Winter 1990): 95–116.

———. *The Mystery to a Solution: Poe, Borges, and the Analytic Detective Story.* Baltimore: Johns Hopkins UP, 1994.

———. "The Quincuncial Network in Poe's *Pym.*" *Arizona Quarterly* 44, no. 3 (Autumn 1988): 1–14.

———. "Reading Poe's Mind: Politics, Mathematics, and the Association of Ideas in 'The Murders in the Rue Morgue.' " *American Literary History* 4, no. 2 (Summer 1992): 187–206.

Iser, Wolfgang. *The Act of Reading: A Theory of Aesthetic Response.* Baltimore: Johns Hopkins UP, 1978.

Jacobs, Robert D. *Poe: Journalist & Critic.* Baton Rouge: Louisiana State UP, 1969.

———. "Poe and the Agrarian Critics." *Hopkins Review* 5 (1952): 43–54.

———. "Poe's Earthly Paradise." *American Quarterly* 12 (1960): 404–13.

Johansen, Ib. "The Madness of the Text: Deconstruction of Narrative Logic in 'Usher,' 'Berenice,' and 'Doctor Tarr and Professor Fether.' " *PoeS* 22 (June 1989): 1–9.

Johnson, Barbara. "The Frame of Reference: Poe, Lacan, Derrida." In *Psychology and the Question of the Text: Selected Papers from the English Institute, 1976–1977.* New series, no. 2. Ed. Geoffrey Hartman. Baltimore: Johns Hopkins UP, 1978, 149–71. Repr. in *The Critical Difference.* Baltimore: Johns Hopkins UP, 1985.

———. *The Wake of Deconstruction.* Blackwell; Cambridge, Mass.: Oxford UP, 1994.

Jones, Howard M. "Poe, 'The Raven,' and the Anonymous Young Man." *Western Humanities Review* 9 (1955): 127–38.

Jordan, Cynthia S. *Second Stories: The Politics of Language, Form and Gender in Early American Fictions.* Chapel Hill: U of North Carolina P, 1989.

Kaplan, Sidney, ed., with introduction. *The Narrative of Arthur Gordon Pym.* New York: Hill and Wang, 1960.

Kennedy, J. Gerald. ed. *Edgar Allan Poe: The Narrative of Arthur Gordon Pym of Nantucket and Related Tales.* Oxford World Classics Series. Oxford and New York: Oxford UP, 1994.

———. "The Invisible Message: The Problem of Truth in *Pym.*" *The Naiad Voice.* Ed. Dennis W. Eddings. Port Washington, N.Y.: Associated Faculty P, 1983, 124–35.

———. *The Narrative of Arthur Gordon Pym and the Abyss of Interpretation.* New York: Twayne, 1995.

———. *Poe, Death, and the Life of Writing.* New Haven, Conn.: Yale UP, 1987.

———. "Poe, 'Ligeia,' and the Problem of Dying Women." *New Essays on Poe's Major Tales.* Ed. Kenneth Silverman. New York: Cambridge UP, 1993, 112–29.

———. "*Pym* Pourri: Decomposing the Textual Body." Kopley, *Poe's Pym,* 167–74.

Kesterson, David B., ed. *Critics on Poe.* Coral Gables, Fla.: U of Miami P, 1973.

Ketterer, David. *Edgar Allan Poe: Life, Work, Criticism.* Fredericton, N.B.: York, 1989.

———. *The Rationale of Deception in Poe.* Baton Rouge: Louisiana State UP, 1979.

———. "Tracing Shadows: *Pym* Criticism, 1980–1990." In Kopley, *Poe's Pym,* 233–74.

Kopley, Richard, ed. *Poe's Pym: Critical Explorations.* Durham, N.C.: Duke UP, 1992.

———. "The '*Very* Profound Under-Current' of *Arthur Gordon Pym.*" *Studies in the American Renaissance: 1987.* Ed. Joel Myerson. Charlottesville: UP of Virginia, 1988.

Krutch, Joseph Wood. *Edgar Allan Poe: A Study in Genius.* New York: Knopf, 1926.

Lawrence, D. H. "Edgar Allan Poe." *English Review* (Apr. 1919). Repr. in *The Symbolic Meaning: The Uncollected Versions of Studies in Classic American Literature.* Ed. Armin Arnold. Fontwell, Arundel, Sussex; Centaur P, 1962; Viking P, 1964. Repr. in *CE.*

———. "Edgar Allan Poe." Rev. ed. In *Studies in Classic American Literature.* New York: Viking Press, 1923, 1951, 1961.

Lee, A. Robert, ed. *Edgar Allan Poe: The Design of Order.* Totowa, N.J.: Barnes and Noble, 1987.

Legacy: A Journal of American Women Writers. University Park, Pa.: Penn State P, 1984–current.

Leitch, Vincent B. *American Literary Criticism from the Thirties to the Eighties.* New York: Columbia UP, 1988.

Lenz, William E. "Poe's *Arthur Gordon Pym* and the Narrative Techniques of Antarctic Gothic." *CEA Critic* 53, no. 3 (Spring–Summer 1991): 30–38.

Levin, Harry. *The Power of Blackness.* New York: Knopf, 1964.

Levine, Stuart C. *Edgar Poe: Seer and Craftsman.* Deland, Fla.: Everett/Edwards, 1972.

———. "Poe and American Society." *Canadian Review of American Studies* 9, no. 1 (Spring 1978): 16–33.

Levine, Stuart, and Susan F. Levine. *The Short Fiction of Edgar Allan Poe.* Indianapolis: Bobbs-Merrill, 1976. Repr. U of Illinois P, 1990.

Lewis, Paul. "Poe's Humor: A Psychological Analysis." *Studies in Short Fiction* 26, no. 4 (Fall 1989): 531–46.

Liebman, Sheldon W. "Poe's Tales and His Theory of the Poetic Experience." *Studies in Short Fiction* 7 (1970): 582–96.

Limon, John. "How to Place Poe's *Arthur Gordon Pym* in Science-Dominated Intellectual History, and How to Extract It Again." *North Dakota Quarterly* 51, no. 1 (Winter 1983): 31–47.

———. *The Place of Fiction in the Time of Science.* New York: Cambridge UP, 1990.

Lind, S. E. "Poe and Mesmerism." *PMLA* 62 (1947): 1077–94.

Ljungquist, Kent. *The Grand and the Fair: Poe's Landscape Aesthetics and Pictorial Techniques.* Potomac, Md.: Scripta Humanistica, 1984.

———. "The Growth of Poe Texts." *Review* 5 (1983):49–57.

———. "Howitt's 'Byronian Rambles' and the Picturesque Setting of 'The Fall of the House of Usher.'" *ESQ* 33 (4th Quarter 1987): 224–36.

———. "Poe and the Sublime: His Two Short Sea Tales in the Context of an Aesthetic Tradition." *Criticism* 17, no. 2 (Spring 1975): 131–51.

———. "Prospects for the Study of Edgar Allan Poe." *Resources for American Literary Study* 21, no. 2 (Fall 1995): 173–88.

———. "The Short Fiction of Poe." *Survey of Modern Fantasy Literature.* Vol. 4. Englewood Cliffs, N.J.: Salem P, 1983, 1665–78.

London, Rose. *Cinema of Mystery.* N.p.: Crown, 1975.

Long, David A. "Poe's Political Identity: A Mummy Unswathed." *PoeS* 23 (June 1990): 1–22.

Lowell, James Russell. "Edgar Allan Poe." *Graham's Magazine* 27 (February 1845): 44–53. Repr. in *REAP*, 5–16.

Lynen, John F. "The Death of the Present: Edgar Allan Poe." In *The Design of the Present: Essays on Time and Form in American Literature.* New Haven, Conn.: Yale UP, 1969, 205–71.

McCaslin, Susan. "*Eureka:* Poe's Cosmogonic Poem." In *Romantic Assessment.* Ed. James Hogg. Salzburg Studies in English Literature 87: 4. Institute für Anglistik und Amerikanistik, Universität Salzburg, 1981.

McCormick, Kathleen, Gary Waller, and Linda Flower. *Reading Texts: Reading, Responding, Writing.* Lexington, Mass.: D. C. Heath, 1987.

Mabbott, Thomas O. "The Astrological Symbolism of Poe's 'Ulalume.'" *N&Q* 161 (1931): 26–27.

———, ed. *Collected Works of Edgar Allan Poe.* 3 vols. Cambridge: Harvard UP, 1969–1978.

Mailloux, Steven. "Reader-Response Criticism?" *Genre* 10 (Fall 1977): 413–31.

Malloy, Jeanne M. "Apocalyptic Imagery and the Fragmentation of the Psyche: 'The Pit and the Pendulum.'" *Nineteenth Century Literature* 46, no. 1 (June 1991): 82–95.

Manning, Susan. "'The Plots of God Are Perfect': Poe's *Eureka* and American Creative Nihilism." *Journal of American Studies* 23, no. 2 (Aug. 1989): 235–51.

Marchand, Ernest. "Poe as Social Critic." *AL* 6 (Mar. 1934): 28–43. Repr. in *On Poe*, ed. Budd and Cady.

Marry, Robert T. "'The Fall of the House of Usher': A Checklist of Criticism Since 1960." *Poe Studies* 5, no. 1 (June 1972): 23–24.

Marshall, Donald G. *Contemporary Critical Theory: A Selective Bibliography.* New York: Modern Language Association, 1993. (A bibliographic overview of major theories.)

Matthews, J. Brander. "Poe and the Detective Story." *REAP*, 81–93.

Matthiessen, F. O. "Poe." *Sewanee Review* 54 (April–June 1946): 175–205. Repr. in "Edgar Allan Poe." *Literary History of the United States.* New York: Macmillan, 1946, vol. 1, 321–42.

Meyers, Jeffrey "Edgar Allan Poe." *The Columbia History of American Poetry.* Ed. Jay Parini. New York: Columbia UP, 1993, 172–202.

———. *Edgar Allan Poe: His Life and Legacy.* New York: Scribner's, 1992.

Michelson, Bruce F. "Richard Wilbur: The Quarrel with Poe." *Southern Review* 14, no. 2 (1978): 245–61.

Miller, James E., Jr. "'Ulalume' Resurrected." *Philological Quarterly* 34 (Apr. 1955): 197–205.

Miller, John C., ed. *Building Poe Biography.* Baton Rouge: Louisiana State UP, 1977.

———. *John Henry's Poe Collection at the University of Virginia.* 2d ed. by John E. Reilly. Charlottesville: UP of Virginia, 1994.

———, ed. *Poe's Helen Remembers.* Charlottesville: UP of Virginia, 1979.

Miller, Perry. *The Raven and the Whale: The War of Words and Wits in the Era of Poe and Melville.* New York: Harcourt, Brace, 1956.

Mitchell, W.J.T., ed. *Against Theory: Literary Studies and the New Pragmatism.* Chicago and London: U of Chicago P, 1985.

Moldenhauer, Joseph J. "Murder as a Fine Art: Basic Connections between Poe's Aesthetics, Psychology, and Moral Vision." *PMLA* 83 (May 1968): 284–97.

Moon, Michael, and Cathy Davidson. *Subjects and Citizens: Nation, Race, and Gender from Oroonoko to Anita Hill.* Durham, N.C.: Duke UP, 1995.

Mooney, Stephen L. "Comic Intent in Poe's Tales: Five Criteria." *Modern Language Notes* 76 (May 1961): 432–34.

———. "The Comic in Poe's Fiction." *AL* 33 (Jan. 1962): 433–41.

———. "Poe's Gothic Waste Land." *Sewanee Review* 70 (Jan.–Mar. 1962): 261–83. Repr. in *REAP.*

Moss, Sidney. *Poe's Literary Battles.* Durham, N.C.: Duke UP, 1963.

Muller, John P., and William J. Richardson, eds. *The Purloined Poe: Lacan, Derrida, and Psychoanalytic Reading.* Baltimore: Johns Hopkins UP, 1988.

Nelson, Dana D. *The Word in Black and White: Reading "Race" in American Literature, 1638–1867.* New York: Oxford UP, 1992, 90–108.

Omans, Glen A. " 'Intellect, Taste, and the Moral Sense': Poe's Debt to Immanuel Kant." *Studies in the American Renaissance 1980,* ed. Joel Myerson. Boston: G. K. Hall, 1980:123–168.

———. "Passion in Poe: The Development of a Critical Term." Baltimore: Edgar Allan Poe Society, 1986.

———. "Poe's 'Ulalume': Drama of the Solipsistic Self." *Papers on Poe: Essays in Honor of John Ward Ostrom.* Ed. Richard P. Veler. Springfield, Ohio: Chantry Music P, 1972, 62–73.

Parks, Edd Winfield. *Edgar Allan Poe as a Literary Critic.* Athens: U of Georgia P, 1964.

Peirce, Carol, and Alexander G. Rose, III. "Poe's Reading of Myth: The White Vision of Arthur Gordon Pym." In Kopley, *Poe's Pym,* 57–74.

Person, Leland S., Jr. *Aesthetic Headaches: Women and a Masculine Poetics in Poe, Melville, and Hawthorne.* Athens: U of Georgia P, 1988.

———. "Poe's Composition of Philosophy: Reading and Writing 'The Raven.' " *Arizona Quarterly* 46, no. 3 (Autumn 1990): 1–15.

Phillips, Elizabeth. *Edgar Allan Poe: An American Imagination—Three Essays.* Port Washington, N.Y.: Kennikat P, 1979.

Pollin, Burton R., ed. *Collected Writings of Edgar Allan Poe.* 4 vols. Vol. 1, Boston: Twayne, 1981; vols. 2–4, New York: Gordian P, 1985–1986.

———. *Dictionary of Names and Titles in Poe's Collected Works.* New York: Da Capo P, 1968.

———. *Discoveries in Poe.* Notre Dame: U of Notre Dame P, 1970.

———. *Images of Poe's Works: A Comprehensive Descriptive Catalogue of Illustrations.* Westport, Conn.: Greenwood, 1989. Includes "Filmography," 323–61.

———. *The Living Writers of America:* A Manuscript by Edgar Allan Poe." *Studies in the American Renaissance 1991,* ed. Joel Myerson. Boston: G.K. Hall, 1991: 151–212.

———. "Marie Clemm, Poe's Aunt: His Boon or His Bane?" *The Mississippi Quarterly* 48, no. 2 (Spring 1995): 211–24.

———. "More Music in Poe" *Music and Letters,* 54, 1973, 391–404.

———. "Music and Edgar Allan Poe: A Second Annotated Checklist." *PoeS* 15, (1982): 7–9.

———. "Music and Edgar Allan Poe: A Third Annotated Check List." *PoeS* 26, nos. 1, 2 (1993): 41–58.

———. "A New Englander's Obituary of Poe." *American Periodicals* 4 (1994):1–11.

———. "On Shakespeare in the Works of Edgar Allen Poe" *Studies in the American Renaissancce 1985*, ed. Joel Myerson. Boston: G.K. Hall, 1985: 157–86.

———. *Poe, Creator of Words*. Baltimore: Enoch Pratt Free Library, Edgar Allan Poe Society, and the Library of the University of Baltimore, 1974; rev. 1980.

———. "Poe and Opera." In *Groves' Dictionary of Opera*. New York and London: Macmillan, 1992, 1093.

———. "Poe's Word Coinages: Supplement II." *PoeS* 22, no. 2 (Dec. 1989): 40–42.

———. *Word Index to Poe's Fiction*. New York: Gordian, 1982.

Porte, Joel. "Poe: Romantic Center, Critical Margin." In *In Respect to Egotism: Studies in American Romantic Writing*. Cambridge: Cambridge UP, 1991.

Prescott, F. C., ed. *Selections from the Critical Writings of Edgar Allan Poe,* with new preface by J. Lasley Dameron and new introduction by Eric W. Carlson. New York: Gordian P, 1981.

Pritchard, John Paul. *Criticism in America*. Norman: U of Oklahoma P, 1956.

Quinn, Arthur Hobson. *Edgar Allan Poe: A Critical Biography*. New York: Appleton-Century, 1941.

Quinn, Patrick P. "Emerson's *Nature* and Poe's *Eureka.*" *Emerson Society Quarterly* 31, no. 2 (1963): 4–7.

———. *The French Face of Edgar Poe*. Carbondale: Southern Illinois UP, 1957.

———. "A Misreading of Poe's 'The Fall of the House of Usher.' " In *CE*.

———. "Poe: Between Being and Nothingness." *Southern Literary Journal* 6 (Spring 1974): 81–100.

———. "The Poe Edition: Annotating *Pym,*" *PoeS* 16, no. 1 (June 1983) 14–16.

———. ed. *Poetry and Tales*. New York: Library of America, 1984.

Rainwater, Catherine. "Poe's Landscape Tales and the 'Picturesque' Tradition." *Southern Literary Journal* 16, no. 2 (Spring 1984): 30–43.

Rajan, Gita. "A Feminist Rereading of Poe's 'The Tell-Tale Heart.' " *Papers on Language and Literature* 24, no. 3 (Summer 1988): 283–300.

Rans, Geoffrey. *Edgar Allan Poe*. Edinburgh: Oliver and Boyd, 1965.

Rayan, Krishna. "Edgar Allan Poe and 'Suggestiveness.' " *British Journal of Aesthetics* 9 (1969): 73–79.

Reilly, John E. *The Image of Poe in American Poetry*. Baltimore: Enoch Pratt Free Library, Edgar Allan Poe Society, and University of Baltimore, 1976.

———., ed. *John Henry Ingram's Poe Collection at the University of Virginia*. 2d ed. Charlottesville: UP of Virginia, 1994.

———. "The Lesser Death-Watch and 'The Tell-Tale Heart.' " *ATQ* 2 (Second quarter 1969): 3–9.

———. "Sarah Helen Whitman as a Critic of Poe." *UMSE,* new series, 3 (1982): 120–27.

———. "A Source for the Immuration in 'The Black Cat.' " *Nineteenth Century Literature* 48, no. 1 (June 1993): 93–95.

Reynolds, David S. *Beneath the American Renaissance: The Subversive Imagination in the Age of Emerson and Melville*. New York: Knopf, 1988.

———. "Poe's Art of Transformation: 'The Cask of Amontillado' in Its Cultural Context." In *New Essays on Poe's Major Tales*. Ed. Silverman, 93–112.

Richard, Claude. "Destin, Design, Dasein: Lacan, Derrida and 'The Purloined Letter.' " *Iowa Review* 12, no. 4 (Fall 1981): 1–11.

———. ed. *Edgar Allan Poe: Journaliste et Critique*. Paris: Klincksieck P, 1978.

———. "The Heart of Poe and the Rhythmics of the Poems." In *CE*.

———. "The Tales of the Folio Club and the Vocation of Edgar Allan Poe as Humorist." Trans. Mark L. Mitchell. *UMSE* 8 (1990): 185–99.

Ridgely, J. V. "The Authorship of the 'Paulding–Drayton' Review." *PSA Newsletter* 20, no. 2 (Fall 1992): 1–3, 6.

Riggio, Thomas P. "American Gothic: Poe and *An American Tragedy*." *AL* 49, no. 4 (Jan. 1978): 515–32.

Robinson, Douglas. *American Apocalypses: The Image of the End of the World in American Literature*. Baltimore; Johns Hopkins UP, 1985.

———. "Reading Poe's Novel: A Speculative Review of *Pym* Criticism, 1950–1980." *Poe Studies* 15, no. 2 (Dec. 1982): 47–54.

Robinson, E. Arthur. "Cosmic Vision in Poe's 'Eleonora.' " *PoeS* 9, no. 2 (December 1976): 44–46.

———. "Order and Sentience in 'The Fall of the House of Usher.' " *PMLA* 76 (Mar. 1961): 68–81.

Rosenheim, Shawn. " 'The King of Secret Readers': Edgar Poe, Cryptography, and the Origins of the Detective Story." *English Literary History* 56 (Summer 1989): 375–400.

Rosenthal, Bernard. "Poe, Slavery, and the *Southern Literary Messenger:* A Reexamination." *PoeS* 7 (Dec. 1974): 29–38.

Rountree, Thomas J. "Poe's Universe: The House of Usher and the Narrator." *Tulane Studies in English* 20 (1972): 123–34.

Rourke, Constance M. *American Humor: A Study of the National Character*. New York: Harcourt Brace, 1931.

Rowe, John Carlos. "Poe, Antebellum Slavery, and Modern Criticism." In Kopley, *Poe's Pym*, 177–38.

———. *Through the Custom House: Nineteenth-Century American Fiction and Modern Theory*. Baltimore: Johns Hopkins UP, 1982.

St. Armand, Barton Levi. "The Dragon and the Uroboros: Themes of Metamorphosis in *Arthur Gordon Pym*." *ATQ* 37 (1978): 57–71.

———. "The Mysteries of Edgar Poe: The Quest for a Monomyth in Gothic Literature." *The Gothic Imagination: Essays in Dark Romanticism*. Ed. G. R. Thompson. Pullman: Washington State UP, 1974, 65–93.

———. "Poe's Landscape of the Soul: Association Theory and the 'The Fall of the House of Usher.' " *Modern Language Studies* 7, no. 2 (Fall 1977): 32–41.

———. "Usher Unveiled: Poe and the Metaphysic of Gnosticism." *PoeS* 5 (June 1972): 1–8.

Sanford, Charles L. "Edgar Allan Poe." *Rives* 18 (Paris) (Spring 1962). Repr. in *REAP*, 297–307; *American Quarterly* 20 (1967): 54–66.

Scheick, William J. "An Intrinsic Luminosity: Poe's Use of Platonic and Newtonian Optics." In *American Literature and Science*. Ed. Robert J. Scholnick. Lexington: UP of Kentucky, 1992, 77–93.

Schulman, Robert. "Poe and the Powers of Mind." *English Literary History* 37 (1970): 245–62.

Scientific American. Special issue on "Life in the Universe" (Oct. 1994). (Articles by Carl Sagan, S. J. Gould, Stephen Weinberg, and others.)

Silverman, Kenneth. *Edgar A. Poe: Mournful and Never-Ending Remembrance.* New York: HarperCollins, 1991.

———. "Introduction." *New Essays on Poe's Major Tales.* Ed. Kenneth Silverman. New York and Cambridge: Cambridge UP, 1993, 1–26.

Sippel, Erich W. "Bolting the Whole Shebang Together: Poe's Predicament." *Criticism* 15 (Fall 1973): 289–308.

Sloane, David E. E. "Usher's Nervous Fever: The Meaning of Medicine in Poe's 'The Fall of the House of Usher.' " In Fisher, *Poe and His Times,* 146–53.

Smith, Grover. "Eliot and the Ghost of Poe." In *T. S. Eliot: A Voice Descanting: Centenary Essays.* Ed. Bagchee Shyamal. London: Macmillan, 1990, 149–63.

Smith, Patricia. "Poe's Arabesque." *PoeS* 7 (1974): 42–45.

Smith, Ronald L. *Poe in the Media: Screen, Songs, and Spoken Word Recordings.* New York: Garland, 1990.

Smithline, Arnold. "*Eureka:* Poe as Transcendentalist." *Emerson Society Quarterly* 31 (1965): 25–28.

Snell, George. "First of the New Critics." *Quarterly Review of Literature* 2 (1945): 330–40.

Spitzer, Leo. "A Reinterpretation of 'The Fall of the House of Usher.' " *Comparative Literature* 4 (Fall 1952): 351–63.

Stauffer, Donald Barlow. "Poe's Views on the Nature and Function of Style." *ESQ* 60 (1970): 23–50.

———. "Style and Meaning in 'Ligeia' and 'William Wilson.' " *Studies in Short Fiction* 2 (1965): 316–20. Repr. in *CE.*

Stedman, E. C., and G. E. Woodberry, eds. *The Works of Edgar Allan Poe.* 10 vols. Chicago: Stone and Kimball, 1894–1895 (Definitive Edition); New York: Scribner's, 1914. Vol. 1: "Introduction to the Tales" by Stedman, ciii–cxxxi. "Memoir" by Woodberry, xix–xcix.

Stovall, Floyd. *Edgar Poe the Poet.* Charlottesville: UP of Virginia, 1969.

———. "Introduction." *The Complete Works of Edgar Allan Poe.* Ed. James A. Harrison. 17 vols. 1902. Repr. in New York: AMS, 1979, 1: 1–23.

———. "Poe as a Poet of Ideas." *University of Texas Studies in English* 11 (1931): 56–62.

———, ed. with introduction. *The Poems of Edgar Allan Poe.* Charlottesville: UP of Virginia, 1965.

Tate, Allen. "The Angelic Imagination." *Kenyon Review* 14 (Summer 1952): 455–75. Repr. in *REAP.*

———. "Our Cousin, Mr. Poe." *Partisan Review* 16 (Dec. 1949): 1207–19. Repr. in *Collected Essays.* Denver: Alan Swallow, 1959, 455–71.

———. "The Poetry of Edgar Allan Poe." *Sewanee Review* 76 (Apr.–June 1968): 214–25.

Thomas, Dwight R., and David R. Jackson. *The Poe Log: A Documentary Life of Edgar Allan Poe, 1809–1849.* Boston: G.K. Hall, 1987.

Thompson, G. R. "Circumscribed Eden of Dreams: Dreamvision and Nightmare in Poe's Early Poetry." Baltimore: Poe Society and Enoch Pratt Library, 1984.

————. "Edgar Allan Poe." *Antebellum Writers in New York and the South. Dictionary of Literary Biography* 3. Detroit: Gale Research, 1979, 249–97.

————. "Edgar Allan Poe and the Writers of the Old South." *Columbia Literary History of the United States.* Ed. Emory Elliot. New York: Columbia UP, 1988, 262–77.

————. "Literary Politics and the 'Legitimate Sphere': Poe, Hawthorne, and the 'Tale Proper.' " *Nineteenth-Century Literature* 49, no. 2 (Sept. 1994): 167–95.

————. "Locke, Kant, and Gothic Fiction: A Further Word on the Indeterminism of Poe's 'Usher.' " *Studies in Short Fiction* 26, no. 4 (Fall 1989): 547–60.

————. *Poe's Fiction: Romantic Irony in the Gothic Tales.* Madison: U of Wisconsin P, 1973.

————. "Romantic Arabesque, Contemporary Theory, and Postmodernism: The Example of Poe's *Narrative.*" *ESQ* 35 (1989): 163–271.

Tompkins, Jane P., ed. *Reader-Response Criticism: From Formalism to Post-Structuralism.* Baltimore: Johns Hopkins UP, 1980.

Townshend, Chauncy Hare. *Facts in Mesmerism.* New York: Harper, 1841 (London, 1840). (Lind believes Poe used the London, 1844, reprinting.)

Van Leer, David. "Detecting Truth: The World of the Dupin Tales." In Silverman, *New Essays on Poe's Major Tales,* 65–91.

Van Nostrand, A. D. "Theories of Adams and Poe." In *Everyman His Own Poet: American Romantic Gospels.* New York: McGraw-Hill, 1968, 204–27.

Veler, Richard P., ed. *Papers on Poe: Essays in Honor of John Ward Ostrom.* Springfield, Ohio: Chantry Music P, 1972.

Vines, Lois, ed. *Poe Abroad: Influences and Affinities.* Iowa City: U of Iowa P, forthcoming.

————. *Valéry and Poe: A Literary Legacy.* New York: New York UP, 1992.

Wagenknecht, Edward C. *Edgar Allan Poe: The Man behind the Legend.* New York: Oxford UP, 1966.

Walker, I. M., ed. *Edgar Allan Poe: The Critical Heritage.* New York: Routledge and Kegan Paul, 1986.

Walsh, John. *Poe the Detective: The Curious Circumstances behind "The Mystery of Marie Roget."* New Brunswick, N.J.: Rutgers UP, 1968.

Warhol, Robyn R., and Diane Price Herndl, eds. *Feminisms: An Anthology of Literary Theory and Criticism.* New Brunswick, N.J.: Rutgers UP, 1991.

Watkins, G. K. *God and Circumstances: A Lineal Study of Intent in Edgar Allan Poe's "The Narrative of Arthur Gordon Pym" and Mark Twain's "The Great Dark."* New York: Peter Lang, 1989, 254 pp.

Whalen, Terence. "Average Racism: Poe, Slavery, and the Wages of Literary Nationalism." In *Edgar Allan Poe and the Masses.* New York: Oxford UP, forthcoming.

————. "Edgar Allan Poe and the Horrid Laws of Political Economy." *American Quarterly* 44, no. 3 (Sept. 1992): 381–417.

Whitman, Sarah Helen. *Edgar Poe and His Critics.* New York: Rudd, 1860. Repr. in New York: Gordian P, 1981.

Wilbur, Richard. "Eleonora." In *CE.*

————. "The House of Poe." In *Anniversary Lectures 1959.* Washington, D.C.: Library of Congress, 1959. Repr. in *REAP.*

————. "Introduction" and "Notes" to *Poe.* The Laurel Poetry Series. New York: Dell, 1959.

————. "Poe and the Art of Suggestion." *UMSE* (1982). Repr. in *CE.*

———. *Responses; Prose Pieces, 1953–1976.* New York: Harcourt Brace Jovanovich, 1976. Repr. of "Edgar Allan Poe" from *Major Writers in America, 1962;* "The Poe Mystery Case," 1967; and *"The Narrative of Arthur Gordon Pym,"* Introduction to the Godine edition, 1973.

Williams, William Carlos. "Edgar Allan Poe." *In the American Grain.* New York: New Directions, 1956, 216–34.

Wilson, Edmund. "Poe as a Literary Critic [1955]." In *The Shock of Recognition.* New York: Grosset & Dunlop, 1955, vol. 1, 79–84; revision of original in *Nation* 155 (1942): 452–53.

———. "Poe at Home and Abroad." *New Republic* 49 (Dec. 8, 1926): 77–80. Repr. in *The Shores of Light.* New York: Farrar, Straus, and Young, 1952, 179–90, and in *REAP,* 142–51.

Winters, Yvor. "Edgar Allan Poe: A Crisis in the History of American Obscurantism." *Maule's Curse.* Norfolk, Conn: New Directions, 1938, 93–122. Repr. in *REAP.*

Woodberry, George E. *The Life of Edgar Allan Poe, Personal and Literary.* 2 vols. Boston: Houghton, 1909.

Woodward, Servanne. "Lacan and Derrida on 'The Purloined Letter.' " *Comparative Literature Studies* 26, no. 1 (1989): 39–49.

Zanger, Jules. "Poe's 'Berenice': Philosophical Fantasy and Its Pitfalls." In *The Scope of the Fantastic—Theory, Technique, Major Authors.* Ed. Robert A. Collins and Howard D. Pearce. Westport, Conn., and London: Greenwood P, 1985, 135–42.

Zapf, Hubert. "Entropic Imagination in Poe's 'The Masque of the Red Death.' " *College Literature* 16, no. 3 (Fall 1989): 211–18.

Ziolkowski, Theodore. "The Tell-Tale Teeth: Psychodontia to Sociodontia." *PMLA* 91 (1976): 9–22.

Index

About the Editor and Contributors

RICHARD P. BENTON is Associate Professor Emeritus of English and Comparative Literature, Trinity College, Hartford, Connecticut. He is a member of the editorial boards of *Poe Studies* and the University of Mississippi *Studies in English*, as well as editor of *New Approaches to Poe*; *Poe as Literary Cosmologer*; *Journey into the Center—Studies in Poe's Pym*, and other symposia. He is the author of articles on American, English, French, Japanese, and Chinese literature, and a translator in English of Chinese poetry and prose. He has Contributed to the *Reference Guide to Short Fiction* (1993) and to the Salem Press Magill's reference books.

BARBARA CANTALUPO is Associate Professor of English at Penn State, Allentown; she has published articles on Poe, Melville, Chivers, Tillie Olsen, Emma Wolf, and Yvonne Rainer. She is Associate Editor of *Bestia*.

ERIC W. CARLSON is Professor Emeritus at the University of Connecticut. He was a founding member and first president of the Poe Studies Association, whose newsletter he co-founded and co-edited with John E. Reilly for a decade or more. He is the author of Poe lectures, reviews, introductions, and lecture-essays including "Poe's Vision of Man," "Poe on the Soul of Man," and "Frames of Reference for Poe's Symbolic Language." He has also edited, with introductions and notes, *The Recognition of Edgar Allan Poe*, *Introduction to Poe: A Thematic Reader*, *Poe: The Fall of the House of Usher* (casebook), as well as a new introduction to *Selections from the Critical Writings of Edgar Allan Poe*, ed. F. C. Prescott, and chapters on Poe in *Fifty Southern Writers before 1900*, the *Dictionary of Literary Biography 74*, and his edition of *Critical Essays on Edgar Allan Poe*.

RANDALL A. CLACK is a Visiting Assistant Professor of American Literature at the University of Connecticut. He is working on a book-length manuscript, *The Phoenix Rising: Alchemical Imagination in the Work of Edward Taylor, Edgar Allan Poe, and Nathaniel Hawthorne*, and an essay on alchemical metaphor in Margaret Fuller's gender theory.

GRACE FARRELL, Rebecca Clifton Reade Professor of English at Butler University, has written numerous essays on nineteenth- and twentieth-century fiction including a series on mythic subtexts in *The Narrative of Arthur Gordon Pym* and *Moby-Dick*. Winner of four National Endowment for the Humanities awards, her books include *From Exile to Redemption: The Fiction of Isaac Bashevis Singer, Isaac Bashevis Singer: Conversations*, and *Critical Essays on Isaac Bashevis Singer*. Books in progress include editions of Lillie Blake's *Fettered for Life* and *The War Press Stories* and a study of late nineteenth-century American women's fiction, *Beyond Silence: Concealed Voices of War, Revolution, and Realism.*

WILLIAM GOLDHURST is Professor Emeritus of American Literature at the University of Florida. In 1969 he was Fulbright Professor of American Literature to the University of Buenos Aires, Argentina. He has published articles on John Steinbeck, J. D. Salinger, Poe, and other authors, as well as a book length study of F. Scott Fitzgerald (1963). He has delivered papers on a variety of subjects to the MLA and its branches, as well as lectures to art groups on American art. He has recently finished his book, *The Eagle and the Raven: Poe's America*, which interprets Poe's tales and poems against the cultural background of his period.

DAVID HALLIBURTON is Professor of English, Comparative Literature, and Modern Thought and Literature at Stanford University. He is the author of *Edgar Allan Poe: A Phenomenological View, Poetic Thinking: An Approach to Heidegger*, and *The Color of the Sky: A Study of Stephen Crane.*

ALEXANDER HAMMOND is Associate Professor of English at Washington State University. He is Editor of *Poe Studies / Dark Romanticism* and author of articles on American cultural responses to the nuclear arms race, on Poe's Folio Club tales, on *Pym*, and on Poe biography. His current work on Poe deals with the fiction in relation to issues of gender, authorship, and the literary marketplace.

GEORGE EGON HATVARY is Professor Emeritus at St. John's University, New York. He assisted T. O. Mabbott in his *Collected Works* of Poe, and edited (with T. O. Mabbott) Poe's *Prose Romances*. His scholarly works include "Poe's Borrowing from H. B. Wallace" (*American Literature*), *Horace Binney Wallace*, and an edition of Wallace's *Henry Pulteney*. He has contributed articles to *Poe Studies, Bibliography of American Fiction,* and other publications. He also writes fiction.

DAVID H. HIRSCH is Professor of English and Judaic Studies at Brown University. His recent publications include *The Deconstruction of Literature: Criticism after Auschwitz.* He has written on a number of Poe's stories and poems, including "Metzengerstein," "The Pit and the Pendulum," "The Duc De L'Omelette," and "The Raven." He has also published essays on various aspects of American Literature, as well as the literature of the Holocaust. He is now working on several projects on Poe and the Holocaust.

KENNETH ALAN HOVEY is an Associate Professor of English at the University of Texas at San Antonio. He has published in American literature on Poe, Longfellow, Melville, and Bradford and in European literature on Montaigne, Bacon, and Herbert. His articles have appeared in *PMLA, American Quarterly, ATQ,* and various other journals as well as in several separately published collections of essays and the *Heath Anthology of American Literature.*

JAMES M. HUTCHISSON is Associate Professor of English at The Citadel, where he teaches nineteenth- and twentieth-century American literature. He has published on Poe, Melville, Simms, Dreiser, and Sinclair Lewis in such journals as *Studies in the Novel, Studies in the American Renaissance, Journal of Modern Literature,* and *PBSA.*

THOMAS JOSWICK is a Professor of English at Western Illinois University, where he teaches a wide range of courses in American literature. He is also editor of *Essays in Literature.*

PAULA KOT's dissertation, "Thrice-Told Tales: Nineteenth-Century American Women's Romances," was a study on women's contributions to the romance genre. She delivered a paper on Poe, "Excising the Wild Eye from 'The Oval Portrait,' " at the MLA conference in San Diego. As visiting Assistant Professor of English, she has recently taught at St. Andrews Presbyterian College and Colorado College.

STUART LEVINE wrote *Edgar Poe / Seer and Craftsman,* (1972) and a number of articles on Poe and U.S. society, Poe scholarship, and *Julius Rodman.* With Susan F. Levine he has published on Poe's relationships to other authors. Today he is a professional musician and fiction author (his *The Monday-Wednesday-Friday Girl and Other Stories* won the 1994 Gross Award). Prior to 1992 he taught in the departments of English, American Studies, History of Music, History of Art, and other areas for the University of Kansas. He founded, then for thirty years edited, *American Studies,* and published books and articles on U.S. art, Native Americans, U.S. literature, the arts in society and other subjects. He holds the Naples Chair, a Fulbright Distinguished Lectureship.

SUSAN F. LEVINE has a Ph.D. in Spanish from the University of Kansas, where she was Assistant Dean of the Graduate School until 1992. She has published on both American and Latin American literature, and on the relationships between them. She is co-editor with Stuart Levine of *The Short Fiction of Edgar Allan Poe: An Annotated Edition* and *Eureka and Essays on Literature and Prosody* in *The Collected Writings of EAP.*

MICHAEL J. PETTENGELL is an Instructor in Humanities at Kansas City Kansas Community College. His publications include articles on American Humor, Film, and Detective Fiction, as well as interviews with popular fiction writers and blues musicians. He is currently involved in writing fiction and working in radio broadcasting. His Ph.D. is in American Culture Studies from Bowling Green State University.

ELIZABETH PHILLIPS, Professor emerita of English, Wake Forest University, Winston-Salem, N.C., is the author of *Edgar Allan Poe: An American Imagination, Marianne Moore,* and *Emily Dickinson: Personae and Performance.* She contributed the entries on Marianne Moore to the *Dictionary of Literary Biography: American Poets, 1880–1945,* First Series, and the *Concise Dictionary of American Literary Biography: The Age of Maturity, 1929–1941* as well as essays on Elizabeth Fries Lummis Ellet, Jean Garrigue, Annie Somers Gilchrist, Estelle Anna Robinson Lewis, Frances Sargent Locke Osgood, Caroline Ticknor, Mabel Loomis Todd, and Sarah Helen Power Whitman to *American Women Writers: A Critical Reference Guide,* vols. 1–4 (Frederick Ungar, 1979, 1980, 1981, and 1982). She has also published articles on Walt Whitman, Vladimir Nabokov, John Steinbeck, the new American poetry of the sixties, and North Carolina writers in the seventies. In 1992, she received the Medallion of Merit, Wake Forest University's highest award for service.

BURTON R. POLLIN is Professor of English Emeritus at City University of New York. After writing and editing six books on William Godwin, one on Shelley, and forty-one articles on both and on other writers of England and America, he published *Discoveries in Poe; Dictionary of Names and Titles*; *Poe, Creator of Words*; *Images of Poe's Works*; *The German Face of Poe* (in collaboration); and the first four volumes of the critical edition of *Poe's Writings,* plus 120 articles on Poe's life, works, and varied, world-wide influence. He is now at work on Poe and Bulwer Lytton, Poe and Walter de la Mare, and the next three volumes of the edition of *Poe's Writings.*

JOHN E. REILLY is Professor Emeritus at the College of the Holy Cross. He is co-founder of the Poe Studies Association, founding co-editor of its newsletter, and member of the editorial board of *Poe Studies/Dark Romanticism*, as well as the author of numerous essays on Poe and his circle including, most recently, "Poe's 'Diddling': Another Possible Source and Date of Composition" (*Poe Studies/Dark Romanticism*, June/December, 1992), "Robert D'Unger and His Reminiscences of Edgar Allan Poe in Baltimore" (*Maryland History Magazine*, Spring 1993), and "A Source for the Immuration in 'The Black Cat' " (*Nineteenth-Century Literature*, June 1993). Professor Reilly is the editor of the second edition of *John Henry Ingram's Poe Collection at the University of Virginia* (Alderman Library, University of Virginia, 1994). Currently he is preparing a critical biography of Sarah Helen Whitman.

DAVID E. E. SLOANE has published articles on Poe in *American Transcendental Quarterly* and *Poe and His Times* (ed., Fisher). A professor of English at the University of New Haven, Connecticut, he is the past president of the American Humor Studies Association and the Mark Twain Circle. His books include *Mark Twain as a Literary Comedian* (1979), *The Literary Humor of the Urban Northeast* (1983), *American Humor Magazines and Comic Periodicals* (1987), *Adventures of Huckleberry Finn: American Comic Vision* (1988), *Sister Carrie: Theodore Dreiser's Sociological Tragedy* (1992), and *Mark Twain's Humor: Critical Essays* (1993).

DONALD BARLOW STAUFFER is Professor Emeritus of English at the University at Albany, State University of New York. He is the author of *A Short History of American Poetry* (1974) and essays on Poe and Whitman; he surveyed Poe scholarship for *American Literary Scholarship* from 1975 to 1982. He has taught in Beijing, Würzburg, and Seoul, in the last as a Fulbright lecturer.

DWAYNE THORPE has published several articles on Poe's poetry and poetic theory. He teaches at Washington and Jefferson College, where he frequently conducts seminars on Poe.

LOIS D. VINES is Distinguished Professor of French at Ohio University, where she teaches courses in language and literature. Named "Chevalier dans l'Ordre des Palmes Académiques" by the French government, she is the author of *Valéry and Poe: A Literary Legacy* and numerous articles on literature, the French media, and teaching.

BEVERLY R. VOLOSHIN is Associate Professor of English at San Francisco State University, where she teaches courses in English and American literature and literary theory. She has edited *American Literature, Culture, and Ideology: Essays in Memory of Henry Nash Smith* and has published essays on American fiction in *Early American Literature, The New England Quarterly, Modern Language Studies, Studies in Short Fiction*, and other journals. Her essay on the post-structural critical field is forthcoming in *Pacific Coast Philology*.

IAN WALKER is Senior Lecturer in American Literature at the University of Manchester, England. He has written on a variety of American authors from the Colonial period onwards, and is the author of *Edgar Allan Poe: The Critical Heritage* (1986).

ISBN 0-313-26506-2

90000>

EAN

9 780313 265068

HARDCOVER BAR CODE